Nicaragua

Northern Highlands
p167

Caribbean Coast
p203

León & Northwestern Nicaragua
p135

Managua
p42

Granada
p80

Masaya & Los Pueblos Blancos
p65

Southwestern Nicaragua
p102

San Carlos, Islas Solentiname & the Río San Juan
p240

Bridget Gleeson, Anna Kaminski, Tom Masters

IGLESIA DE LA
RECOLECCIÓN P139, LEÓN

PHILIP LEE HARVEY / LONELY PLANET ©

GREAT CORN ISLANDS P228

R.J.LERICH / GETTY IMAGES ©

ON THE ROAD

Contents

VOLCANO MOMBACHO P96
& LAGUNA DE APOYO P98

UNDERSTAND

SURVIVAL
GUIDE

SPECIAL
FEATURES

Welcome to Nicaragua

An affable all-rounder, Nicaragua embraces travelers with diverse offerings of volcanic landscapes, colonial architecture, sensational beaches, remote, idyllic islands, wave-battered Pacific beaches and pristine forests.

Beaches

Whether it's dipping your toes into the crystalline Caribbean or paddling out to the crashing waves of the pounding Pacific, Nicaragua's beaches always deliver the goods. The big barrels of the Pacific coast are revered in surfing circles while the clear waters of the Corn Islands are superb for snorkeling. More sedentary beach bums can choose between accessible slices of sand lined with fine restaurants and happening bars, and natural affairs backed by a wall of rainforest. Even the best beaches in the country are refreshingly free of development.

Outdoor Adventures

Looking for the ultimate rush? Nicaragua's diverse geography, intense energy and anything-goes attitude is perfect for exhilarating outdoor adventures. Get ready to check off lots of new experiences from your list including surfing down an active volcano, diving into underwater caves, canoeing through alligator-infested wetlands, swimming across sea channels between tiny white-sand islands and landing a 90-plus-kilogram tarpon beneath a Spanish fortress in the middle of the jungle. Nicaragua's great outdoors are relatively untamed making this so-called 'land of lakes and volcanoes' a fantastic place for an independent adventure.

Colonial Architecture

Nicaragua's colonial architecture comes in two distinct flavors. The elegant streetscapes of Granada, Nicaragua's best-preserved colonial town, have been entrancing travelers for centuries with their architectural grace. The town boasts a meticulously restored cathedral, well-groomed plaza and perfectly maintained mansions that shelter lush internal courtyards. Far less polished, working-class and vibrant León offers a different colonial experience where crumbling 300-year-old houses and churches are interspersed with revolutionary murals, and architectural masterpieces house corner stores.

Getting Off the Beaten Track

Few destinations have such beauty as Nicaragua, yet remain undeveloped. Before you know it, you've dropped off the tourist trail and into a world of majestic mountains, cooperative farms, wetlands thronged with wildlife and empty jungle-clad beaches. Rent a 4WD vehicle, if you're up for it – it's the best way to access some of the less-traveled corners of the country, or hop abroad an east-coast-bound boat – and discover remote indigenous communities, overgrown pre-Columbian ruins and untouched rainforests. No matter how far you go, you'll always find friendly locals willing to share their culture with strangers.

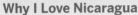

Why I Love Nicaragua

By Anna Kaminski, Writer

I first got to know Nicaragua many years ago, when backpacking across Central America. I learned of the proxy war played out on Nicaraguan soil, courtesy of the USSR and the USA, and witnessed the still-healing scars from the conflict. Even then, Nicaragua struck me as an incredibly resilient country and Central America's ultimate all-rounder. It has a rich and fascinating history, and beautiful and varied landscapes – from barely explored jungle to arid volcanoes and windswept Pacific beaches. But what draws me back, above all, is the warmth and tenacity of its people.

For more about our writers, see p320

At the time of writing Nicaragua had been experiencing political unrest since April 2018, see p290.

Above: Iglesia El Calvario (p141), León

Nicaragua

Cerro Negro
Surf an active
volcano (p157)

**Reserva Natural
Estero Padre Ramos**
Wild mangroves (p165)

León
Heart of Nicaraguan
literature and politics (p138)

Volcán Masaya
Hike up an active
volcano (p71)

Playa Popoyo
An empty shoreline in a
surfer's paradise (p121)

Around San Juan del Sur
Ride Nicaragua's legendary
waves (p123)

**Refugio de Vida
Silvestre La Flor**
Coastal turtle haven (p134)

Isla de Ometepe
Mystical island of twin
volcanoes (p107)

ELEVATION

	2000m
	1500m
	1000m
	500m
	200m
	0

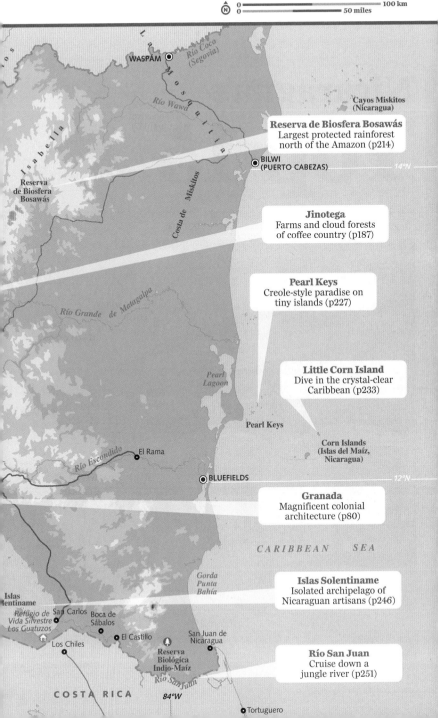

N

| 0 | | 100 km |
| 0 | | 50 miles |

WASPÁM

Río Coco (Segovia)

La Mosquitia

Río Wawa

Cayos Miskitos (Nicaragua)

Reserva de Biosfera Bosawás
Largest protected rainforest
north of the Amazon (p214)

BILWI
(PUERTO CABEZAS) ———————— 14°N

Isabella

Reserva de Biosfera Bosawás

Costa de Miskitos

Jinotega
Farms and cloud forests
of coffee country (p187)

Río Grande de Matagalpa

Pearl Keys
Creole-style paradise on
tiny islands (p227)

Pearl Lagoon

Little Corn Island
Dive in the crystal-clear
Caribbean (p233)

Pearl Keys

**Corn Islands
(Islas del Maíz,
Nicaragua)**

Río Escondido   El Rama

BLUEFIELDS ———————— 12°N

Granada
Magnificent colonial
architecture (p80)

CARIBBEAN   SEA

*Gorda
Punta
Bahía*

Islas Solentiname
Isolated archipelago of
Nicaraguan artisans (p246)

Islas
olentiname   San Carlos   Boca de
Sábalos
Refúgio de
Vida Silvestre
Los Guatuzos
Los Chiles   El Castillo   San Juan de
Nicaragua

**Reserva
Biológica
Indio-Maíz**

Río San Juan

Río San Juan
Cruise down a
jungle river (p251)

COSTA RICA   84°W

Tortuguero

Nicaragua's
Top 15

Granada

1 Granada (p80) is a town of immense and palpable magnetism. At the heart of the city's charms are the picture-perfect cobblestone streets, polychromatic colonial homes and churches, and a lilting air that brings the city's spirited past into present-day focus. Most trips here begin and end on foot, and simply dawdling from gallery to restaurant to colonial church can take up the better part of a day. From there, it's off to explore the myriad wild areas, islands, volcanoes and artisan villages nearby.

Little Corn Island

2 With no cars and no noise, just white-sand beaches and secluded coves mixing with the crystal-clear Caribbean, Little Corn Island (p233) is the paramount place to take a break from the big city. There is plenty to keep you occupied during the day, including diving with hammerhead sharks or through underground caves, kitesurfing the stiff breeze or scrambling over jungle-covered headlands, and there's just enough to do at night. Add some great food to the mix and it's no surprise that many find it so hard to leave. Sea fan on coral reef

FOTOS593 / SHUTTERSTOCK ©

PETE NIESEN / SHUTTERSTOCK ©

Isla de Ometepe

3 Lago de Nicaragua's beloved centerpiece, Isla de Ometepe (p107) has it all. Twin volcanoes, lush hillsides cut by walking tracks, archaeological remains, ziplines, monkeys and birdlife, waterfalls, lapping waves at your doorstep, and a laid-back island air that keeps travelers in the now as they step, kayak, bike and climb their way through this once-lost paradise. At the heart of the island's charms are the cool hostels, camping areas and peaceful traveler scenes. From high-end luxury lodges to groovy-groupie hippie huts, Ometepe is big enough for all kinds. Volcán Maderas (p116)

León

4 A royal city with revolutionary undercurrents, León (p138) both enchants and baffles the legions of backpackers and adventure seekers who gravitate here. Within the city, you'll find an artsy, slightly edgy vibe originally fueled by the Sandinista revolution and now by the university and a 120-horsepower party scene. Come sunrise, you can spend a good day exploring the cathedral, museums and downtown area, before heading further afield to honey-blonde beaches, volcanoes and brokeback cowboy towns with some of the friendliest people you'll find anywhere on earth. Catedral de León (p139)

Pearl Keys

5 As you approach the dozen tiny islands ringed by snow-white sand and brilliant Caribbean waters that make up the Pearl Keys (p227), you will enter the realms of the ultimate shipwreck fantasy. Fortunately, you'll be marooned with a capable Creole guide who will cook a spectacular seafood meal and source ice-cold beers from a mysterious supply, leaving you heaps of time to swim, snorkel, spot sea turtles, or just lie back in your hammock and take in the idyllic panoramic views.

Río San Juan

6 Once favored by both pirates and prospectors as a sure path to riches, today the Río San Juan (p251) is exalted by nature lovers. All along the river, scores of birds nest on branches overhanging its slow surging waters while its lower reaches are dominated by the Reserva Biológica Indio-Maíz, an impenetrable jungle that shelters jaguars and troupes of noisy monkeys. The only human-made attraction along the river's entire length is the grand Spanish fort over the rapids at El Castillo.

Plumed basilisk lizard

Coffee Country

7 A visit to Nicaragua's coffee zone is about more than just sipping plenty of joe, it's about getting out and seeing where it all comes from. Hike among the bushes shaded by ethereal cloud forest around Jinotega (p190) and pick ripe cherries alongside your hosts in a community farming cooperative near Matagalpa. And why stop there when you can follow the beans to the roasting plant and then learn to identify flavors in a cupping session. After this, you'll savor your morning cup in a whole new way.

7

Surfing Near San Juan del Sur

8 Nicaragua sparked into international stardom on the wake of tanned-and-toned surfer dudes and dudettes. And the surfing scene north and south of regional hub San Juan del Sur (p123) remains cool, reefed-out, soulful and downright brilliant. The stars of the scene are the long rideable waves that fit the bill for surfers of all abilities, but the relaxed surf camps, beach parties and cool breezes add to the vibe, ensuring a great beach vacation for everybody in your crew (even the boogie boarders). Playa Hermosa (p132)

8

9

10

Volcán Masaya & Laguna de Apoyo

9 Hovering above the artisan villages of Nicaragua's Central Plateau, the smoldering Volcán Masaya (p71) and its surrounding national park are a highlight not to be missed. This is one of the region's most active volcanoes, and it's pretty exciting just to see the sulfurous columns of gas billow toward the sky as you relish the million-dollar views. Gaze into the maw of hell at night, when lava bubbles restlessly in the crater. Nearby, cool off with a dip in gorgeous crater lake Laguna de Apoyo.

Turtles at La Flor

10 Head to Nicaragua's southern Pacific coast between July and January to witness sea turtles by the thousands come to shore to lay their eggs at Refugio de Vida Silvestre La Flor (p134). There's a decent beach here, as well, but the highlight is a night tour (generally from nearby San Juan del Sur), where, if you're lucky, you'll see a leatherback or olive ridley mama come to shore to lay her eggs at the end of one of nature's most inspiring and remarkable journeys. Olive Ridley turtle

Islas Solentiname

11 The Islas Solentiname (p246) are straight out of a fairy tale. You simply must visit in order to experience the magic of this remote jungle-covered archipelago where a community of exceptionally talented artists live and work among the wild animals that are their inspiration. It's a place where an enlightened priest inspired a village to construct a handsome church alive with the sounds of nature, and shooting stars illuminate the speckled night sky. Even after having been there, you will still find it hard to believe it's real.
Isla San Fernando p247

Volcano Boarding on Cerro Negro

12 What goes up must come down. But why walk when you can strap on a custom-built volcano board and rip-roar your way down a slope of fine volcanic ash? And one of the best spots on the planet to dig the new adrenaline sport of volcano surfing is atop 700-plus-meter Volcán Cerro Negro (p157) in northwestern Nicaragua's Reserva Natural Pilas-El Hoyo. Tour operators in León (p147) will even provide you with cool jumpsuits before you begin your dusty-bottomed descent.

Reserva Natural Estero Padre Ramos

13 The Reserva Natural Estero Padre Ramos (p165) is a vast nature reserve located in the far northwestern corner of Nicaragua. The largest remaining mangrove forest in Central America, the reserve is home to ocelots, alligators and a universe worth of birds that call the forest home. While this is a wild corner of Nicaragua, boats and kayaks will get you into the spider-webbing mangrove forest, to the beaches where sea turtles lay their eggs and good surf dominates, and into local communities.

The Remote Beaches of Popoyo

14 It's a bumpy ride from Rivas to the remote beaches of Popoyo (p121), famous for their surf breaks. The reward: huge, hollow breaks, laid-back surf lodges, sandy shores strewn with vibrant pink shells, looming rock formations and miles of empty shoreline where you can walk for an hour without seeing another person. While new surf lodges and guesthouses have popped up in recent years, the village communities are down-to-earth and friendly and these beaches still feel wild. Bring your board, or a good book.

Wildlife-Watching

15 From the colorful parakeets flying over busy Managua to ubiquitous iguanas scratching across your hotel roof, exotic wildlife is everywhere in Nicaragua. Dedicate some energy to the pursuit and you'll discover some truly phenomenal natural spectacles. Head into the rugged rainforest-covered mountains of the Bosawás (p214) to spot three types of monkeys, toucans and tapirs, while reptile fans will not want to miss the alligators of Los Guatuzos. Wherever you go, keep your binoculars handy – a wild encounter is never far away. Geoffroy's spider monkey

Need to Know

For more information, see Survival Guide (p289)

Currency
Córdoba (C$),
US dollar (US$)

Language
Spanish

Visas
Generally not required
for stays up to three
months.

Money
ATMs are widespread
in most midsize towns.
Credit cards are widely
accepted in larger
towns. US dollars are
widely accepted; keep
córdobas for small
purchases.

Cell Phones
Local phone costs start
at around US$15. You
can also buy a SIM
card (around US$3.50)
for any unlocked GSM
phone. Numerous
cell-phone networks
offer free roaming in
Nicaragua. The two
phone companies are
Claro and Movistar.

Time
Central Standard Time
(GMT/UTC minus six
hours)

When to Go

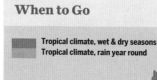

■ Tropical climate, wet & dry seasons
■ Tropical climate, rain year round

Matagalpa ●
GO Nov–Apr

● **Managua**
GO Nov–Dec

Corn Islands ●
GO Feb–Apr

San Juan del Sur ●
GO Nov–Apr

● **San Carlos**
GO Feb–Apr

High Season
(Dec–Apr)

➡ Prices increase by
up to 25% in popular
tourist spots.

➡ Make reservations
in advance
for beachside
accommodations.

➡ Hot, sunny and
dry conditions
throughout the
country.

Shoulder (Nov)

➡ Rains ease
throughout the
Pacific but the
Caribbean is still wet.

➡ Cool weather and
green countryside
make for the best
trekking.

➡ Coffee harvesting
energizes the
northern region.

Low Season
(May–Oct)

➡ Heavy rains make
some roads in rural
areas difficult to pass
and mountain hiking
trails slippery.

➡ The biggest swell
on the Pacific side
pulls a crowd to the
best breaks.

➡ Advanced
reservations are
generally not
necessary.

Useful Websites

Lonely Planet (www.lonely-planet.com/nicaragua) Destination information, hotel bookings, traveller forum and more.

Vianica.com (www.vianica.com/traveling) Log on to this interactive map and click on your route to find Nicaraguan road conditions, travel-time estimates and more.

Intur (www.intur.gob.ni) The official government website is in English and Spanish, with lots of cheerful, vague information and an awesome photo gallery.

Important Numbers

Nicaragua country code	✆505
International access code	✆00
Fire	✆115, from cell phones ✆911
Police	✆118
Ambulance	✆128

Exchange Rates

Australia	A$1	C$23.42
Canada	C$1	C$24.92
Costa Rica	₡100	C$5.38
Europe	€1	C$37.30
Japan	¥100	C$29.87
New Zealand	NZ$1	C$22.52
UK	UK£1	C$42.44
US	US$1	C$32.81

For current exchange rates see www.xe.com.

Political Unrest

At the time of writing, Nicaragua had been experiencing political unrest since April 2018. For more information see p290.

Daily Costs

Budget: Less than US$35

➡ Dorm bed: US$9–15

➡ Typical meal: US$4

➡ Museum admission: US$2

➡ Local bus: US$0.15–1

Midrange: US$35–80

➡ Double bed in a midrange hotel: US$20–45

➡ Restaurant meal: US$10–12

➡ Adventure tour: US$25–30

➡ Short taxi ride: US$2–3

Top end: More than US$80

➡ Double bed in a luxury hotel: US$80–120

➡ Gourmet meal: US$18–22

➡ Car hire: US$40–60

➡ Internal flight: US$100–120

Opening Hours

Opening hours vary wildly in Nicaragua as there are many informal and family-run establishments. General office hours are from 9am to 5pm.

Comedores (cheap eateries) usually open for breakfast and lunch while more formal restaurants serve lunch and dinner.

Banks 8:30am to 4:30pm Monday to Friday, to noon Saturday

Comedores 6am to 4pm

Government Offices 8am to to noon & 1 to 4pm Monday to Friday, 8am to noon Saturday

Museums 9am to noon & 2 to 5pm

Restaurants noon to 10pm

Bars noon to midnight

Clubs 9pm to 3am

Shops 9am to 6pm Monday to Saturday

Arriving in Managua

Managua International Airport (Managua) Official taxis inside the airport meet all incoming flights and charge around US$20 to US$25 to most local destinations. During the day, more-economical licensed collective taxis wait outside the domestic terminal.

If you're heading out of Managua, it's possible to book a pickup with a private shuttle service.

Urban buses head into town from the highway across the road from the terminal, but are rife with pickpockets and are not a good option if you have baggage.

Getting Around

Transport in Nicaragua is functional rather than comfortable.

Air Moderately priced and the fastest way to travel; however, they only serve more remote destinations. Often slightly delayed, but rarely canceled.

Car Renting a car enables travel at your own pace and access to off-the-beaten-track destinations. There is not much traffic on the roads outside Managua and driving in Nicaragua is fairly stress-free.

Bus Nicaragua's old-school buses are slow and uncomfortable but will get you anywhere you want to go for next to nothing. There are more comfortable, but far from luxurious, coach services to some long-distance destinations.

Shuttle Tourist-oriented and air-conditioned, these minivans are the fastest and most comfortable way of traveling between popular destinations.

For much more on **getting around**, see p301

First Time Nicaragua

For more information, see Survival Guide (p289)

Checklist

➡ Make sure your passport is valid for at least six months

➡ Check latest visa requirements online

➡ Arrange travel insurance with medical evacuation cover

➡ Inform your debit/credit-card issuer that you are traveling to Central America

➡ Organize vaccinations against hepatitis A and typhoid, and consult your doctor about malaria prophylactics

What to Pack

➡ Sturdy walking shoes

➡ Comfortable sports sandals

➡ Insect repellent containing DEET

➡ An emergency supply of US dollars in small bills

➡ A two-pronged electrical adapter

➡ A lightweight raincoat capable of resisting tropical downpours

➡ Contact lens solution and other personal toiletries

Top Tips for Your Trip

➡ Always go for a window seat in public transport: the landscapes are absolutely breathtaking.

➡ Take some Spanish classes. Nicaraguans are outgoing and friendly but few have foreign-language skills.

➡ Hire local guides wherever possible; they're cheap and you'll learn about the attraction you're visiting and about the culture.

➡ Forget about keeping a tight schedule in Nicaragua. Allow extra days in your trip, especially if you're traveling by public transport.

➡ When in doubt about getting into a taxi, just ask your hostel or hotel to call you one – and agree on a price before getting in.

What to Wear

The heat in Nicaragua can be oppressive, so you'll probably spend most of your time in lightweight T-shirts and shorts or cotton trousers. If you're heading to the northern highlands, you may need a medium pullover for the cool evenings.

Note that in general, men in Nicaragua don't wear shorts unless practicing sports. Go for a jeans and short-sleeved shirt or polo shirt if you are going out with locals and be prepared to dress up for a night on the town in Granada or Managua.

On the beach women going topless is almost never acceptable and in rural areas bikinis may draw unwanted attention; consider swimming in shorts and a T-shirt like the locals.

Sleeping

Hospedajes These cheap guesthouses are often family-run and are sometimes the only option in smaller towns.

Hotels Larger and more polished; boutique hotels can be intimate and characterful.

Hostels Traveler's hostels with dormitories and common areas are only found in the main tourist areas.

Ecolodges Usually at the higher end of the market, these offer comfortable rooms surrounded by nature.

Surfing lodges Offer all-inclusive surfing packages, and often shared accommodations and great food.

Safe Travel

At the time of writing, political unrest in Nicaragua had led to street protests, road blocks and outbreaks of violence. For more information see p290.

Despite the fact that Nicaragua has one of the lowest crime rates in Central America, as a 'wealthy' foreigner you will at least be considered a potential target by scam artists and thieves.

➡ Pay extra attention to personal safety in Managua, the Caribbean region, around remote southern beaches and in undeveloped nature reserves.

➡ In larger cities, ask your hotel to call a trusted taxi.

➡ Backcountry hikers should note there may be unexploded ordnance in very remote areas, especially around the Honduran border. If in doubt, take a local guide.

Bargaining

All-out haggling is not really part of Nicaraguan culture. However, a bit of bargaining over a hotel room is considered acceptable, and negotiating the price in markets or with roadside vendors is the norm.

Tipping

Tipping is not widespread in Nicaragua except with guides and at restaurants.

Guides Tipping guides is recommended as this often makes up the lion's share of their salary.

Restaurants A tip of around 10% is expected for table service. Some high-end restaurants automatically add this to the bill. Small and/or rural eateries may not include the tip, so leave behind a few coins.

Local bus in Granada

Language

In major tourist destinations such as Granada, San Juan del Sur and León, you'll find a number of people who speak at least some English. Elsewhere, very little English is spoken. Learning some basic Spanish phrases will make your travels much more rewarding, especially if you're traveling to remote destinations. Hiring a translator to accompany you around town or on longer trips is affordable – ask at your hotel.

On the Caribbean coast English speakers will have no problem communicating with Creole residents, once you're used to the accent and grammar.

See the Language chapter on p304.

Etiquette

Greetings A firm handshake for men and a peck on the cheek for women.

Titles When addressing Nicaraguans add *don* (for men) or *doña* (for women) before their given name.

Drinking If you are sharing a bottle of rum, use the supplied shot glass to measure your drink; don't pour freely from the bottle.

If You Like...

Beaches

The Pacific has the waves, the Caribbean has the reefs.

Little Corn Island Brilliant turquoise waters meet snow-white sand in secluded coves on this enchanted isle. (p233)

Playa El Coco A spectacular stretch of sparkling sand framed by imposing forest-covered headlands. (p133)

Pearl Keys Live out shipwreck fantasies beneath the coconut palms on this group of idyllic Caribbean islands. (p227)

El Ostional Charming fishing village with a sweeping brown-sand beach. (p134)

Playa Aserradores Long, smooth stretch of sand with a powerful, hollow beach break. (p163)

Great Corn Island Often overlooked, Great Corn has several gorgeous expanses of beautiful golden sand beach. (p228)

Popoyo Famous surf breaks and miles of practically untouched shoreline make Popoyo a hot spot. (p121)

Volcanoes

Volcán Masaya Watch lava bubble restlessly in the crater of one of the country's most active volcanoes. (p71)

Volcán Maderas Hike up through cloud forest to reach a chilly jade-green crater lake. (p116)

Volcán Momotombo Perched regally at the top of Lake Managua, its perfect cone is a symbol of Nicaragua. (p157)

Volcán San Cristóbal Nicaragua's tallest volcano and toughest trek, with epic summit views. (p157)

Volcán Cosigüina Climb the remnants of what was Central America's biggest volcano to look out over three countries. (p166)

Volcán Mombacho Accessible cloud forest with great hiking and even better birdwatching. (p96)

Colonial Architecture

Granada Nicaragua's colonial showpiece lays on the charm from the moment you get off the bus. (p83)

León Energetic and unpretentious, this gregarious city has stunning colonial streetscapes, awe-inspiring churches and cosmopolitan eateries. (p139)

Ciudad Antigua Boasting a remarkable Moorish-influenced 17th-century church, this is one of Nicaragua's oldest towns. (p183)

San Rafael del Norte Surrounded by peaks, this charming town is centered around the light-filled Templo Parroquial San Rafael Arcángel. (p186)

Coffee

Matagalpa and Jinotega departments have the pedigree but Estelí and little-visited Nueva Segovia also produce some outstanding beans.

La Bastilla Ecolodge Hike through immense shade-grown coffee plantations before improving your cupping skills at the laboratory. (p191)

San Ramón Try your hand picking coffee beans at local farms then visit a community roasting plant. (p198)

Eco-Albergue La Fundadora Stay at this epically located hilltop *finca*, surrounded by cloud forest and coffee plantations (p191)

Área Protegida Miraflor Combine your coffee tour with birdwatching or a visit to waterfalls surrounded by cloud forest. (p175)

DeLaFinca Cafe If you can't make it out to coffee country, sample Nicaragua's finest beans in the capital. (p56)

Wildlife

Refugio de Vida Silvestre La Flor Watching turtles laying their eggs on this beach is one of Latin America's superlative experiences. (p134)

Refugio Bartola Head into the jungle to spot monkeys, fluo-

rescent frogs and maybe even a tapir. (p257)

Volcán Mombacho Accessible cloud forest with great hiking and even better birdwatching. (p96)

Refugio de Vida Silvestre Los Guatuzos Perfectly preserved wetlands with fantastic bird-watching during the day and action-packed crocodile spotting at night. (p250)

Islas Solentiname Bring binoculars to spot some of the thousands of migratory birds nesting in this remote archipelago. (p246)

Reserva Natural Macizos de Peñas Blancas Clinging to magnificent mountain peaks, this jungle is home to pumas, jaguars and ocelots. (p200)

Reserva Natural Isla Juan Venado Take a nighttime turtle tour during laying season – July through January – at this barrier island. (p155)

Artisan Crafts

San Juan de Oriente Head to the homes of ceramics masters to pick up Central America's most exquisite pottery. (p74)

Artesanias La Esquina Pick up a sculpted wooden bowl or ceramic cup at this artisan co-op in Estelí. (p175)

The Garden Shop This fair-trade boutique stocks clothing, crafts, shoes, paper goods and gourmet products produced at women's co-ops. (p94)

Paseo Salvador Allende On weekends, artisans sell their wares on Managua's newly revamped waterfront promenade. (p44)

Mercado de Artesanía You might not take one home, but Masatepe is famous for cane-woven rocking chairs. (p77)

Top: Colonial-era building in León (p138)

Bottom: Ceramic pots for sale in San Juan de Oriente (p74)

Month by Month

January

Perfect beach weather in the Pacific region with almost nonstop sunshine, but it's the peak of high season so expect bigger crowds and more expensive accommodations.

🎖 Baseball Finals

Stadiums get packed for the finals of Liga Nacional de Beisbol Nicaraguense (Nicaraguan National Baseball League). Catch games at the Estadio Denis Martínez in Managua. (p58)

February

Crowds thin out but it's still all sunshine, making this one of the best times to plan a beach break. It can be uncomfortably hot in cities.

📅 International Poetry Festival

Top Spanish-language wordsmiths from around the globe gather for this festival in Granada that celebrates the spoken word, with regular readings and well-attended fringe events. (p89)

March

The heat wave continues with soaring temperatures and dry conditions. Whether it falls in March or April, Easter is big business: prices spike, accommodations sell out and beaches are packed.

🎖 Semana Santa

Easter is a huge deal all over the country, but nowhere does it quite like León, where the traditional fireworks and parades are accompanied by sawdust mosaics and a sandcastle competition. (p147)

April

More sunshine, this time accompanied by big, consistent surf in the Pacific and calm seas throughout the Caribbean, ideal for diving and snorkelling. After Easter, crowds drop dramatically.

🏃 Surf's up!

The combination of big swells along the Pacific and bright sunshine brings optimal conditions (and big crowds) to many of Nicaragua's best surf breaks, including the acclaimed Popoyo. (p121)

May

Low season is underway with sunshine still sticking around, but by the end of the month the skies open, marking the beginning of the wet season.

🎖 Maypole

Bluefields' fertility celebrations culminate in a boisterous carnival on the last Saturday of the month. During the closing Tululu, the entire town takes a midnight romp through the streets, accompanied by a brass band. (p221)

June

Heavy rains drench the entire country. This brings significantly cooler

temperatures, but turns some rural roads into pools of mud that are difficult to negotiate.

🎎 San Juan de Bautista

The normally serene flower-growing town of Catarina is transformed by this wild festival in honor of San Juan Bautista, featuring dancing, ceremonial fights and music. (p74)

July

Rains continue throughout the country, though rain showers rarely last more than several hours. Most hiking trails are now muddy but many waterfalls are at their spectacular best.

📅 Aniversario de la Revolución

Dress in red and black, and head to the plaza in Managua to celebrate the revolution alongside hard-drinking Sandinista supporters from across Nicaragua. The bohemian fringe event in nearby San Antonio means more music.

August

Rains generally ease a little in the Pacific with most days enjoying long stretches of sunshine. Meanwhile, the Caribbean experiences one of its wettest months.

🎎 Fiesta del Cangrejo

Corn Island celebrates the end of slavery with a parade, concerts, plenty of

Top: Colorful sawdust 'carpets' created for Semana Santa (p147), León

Bottom: Parade at the International Poetry Festival (p89), Granada

beer, and free bowls of crab soup and ginger bread for all in attendance.

⭐ Fiestas de Agosto

Halfway through August, Granada honors the Assumption of Mary. Expect religious processions – the most important one on August 15 – equestrian parades, food stands, fireworks and live music in the parks, and revelry by the lakefront. (p89)

September

The height of hurricane season in the Caribbean may disrupt travel plans, although when there are no storms the weather is generally bright and there are great deals on accommodations.

⭐ Feria de Maíz

The farmers of Nueva Segovia descend on the northern town of Jalapa for a celebration of everything corn. There are corn clothes, corn altars and corn dances, not to mention *chicha* (fermented corn drink).

October

Rains return with a vengeance throughout the Pacific with frequent heavy downpours in the afternoons. Traveler numbers reach their lowest point, with accommodation prices being the most competitive.

📅 Turtle-Watching

Refugio de Vida Silvestre La Flor is the backdrop for one of nature's most amazing spectacles when olive ridley turtles arrive (sometimes up to 3000 in one night) to lay their eggs in the sand. (p134)

⭐ Noche de Agüizotes

This spooky festival in Masaya brings to life characters from horror stories of the colonial period with locals in elaborate creepy costume dancing in the street. Keep an eye out for the headless priest.

November

Things get moving again following the easing of the rain. Travelers spread out around the country and the festival season warms up with a number of important events.

⭐ Garifuna Week

Nicaragua's Garifuna community celebrates their rich cultural heritage with drums, dancing and gastronomy in the remote community of Orinoco on the shores of Laguna de Perlas. The concert features Garifuna artists from throughout Central America. (p227)

December

The end of the rains in the Pacific region sees the high season begin in earnest and beaches becoming busy, particularly north and south of San Juan del Sur.

⭐ La Purísima

Celebrated on the eve of the Immaculate Concepcíon, La Purísima (and La Griteria) sees hordes of children going door-to-door singing songs to the Virgin Mary and receiving candies. León gets into it with unrivaled vigor. (p147)

Itineraries

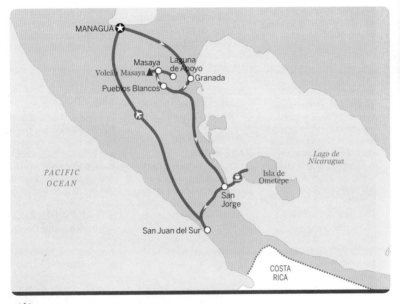

West Coast Highlights

Pack several heavyweight highlights into a week, making the most of the country's history, nature and culture.

From **Managua**, make a beeline for **Granada**, and spend a day exploring the rich historic offerings of its colonial architecture and vibrant dining scene. The following day, spend the morning shopping for excellent quality handicrafts in the **Pueblos Blancos** and **Masaya**, then make a beeline for the **Laguna de Apoyo** for an afternoon's relaxation beside the crater lake. In the evening, head for the **Volcán Masaya** to watch lava bubble in its crater. The following morning, head to the San Jorge dock and take a boat to **Isla de Ometepe**. Spend two days exploring the island, trekking up one of its volcanoes, kayaking through mangroves, hiking to the waterfall and staying on a tranquil *finca* (farm).

Return to the mainland, and head for **San Juan del Sur** for a couple of days of sea, surf and partying. Explore the beaches north and south of town in search of the best place to hit the waves.

On the final day, return to **Managua** and devote your time to visiting historic landmarks, and finish off the day bar-hopping in Los Robles and Altamira.

MLENNY / GETTY IMAGES ©

Top: Volcán
Concepción (p112), Isla
de Ometepe
Left: San Juan del Sur
(p123)

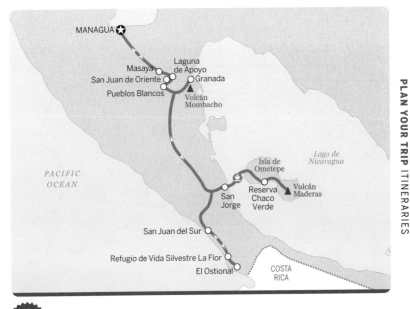

10 DAYS Stunning Southwest

If you have limited time in Nicaragua, a trip through the southwest is big on awesome and small on hours in the bus. The region is a condensed wonderland of barreling surf, volcanoes, crater lakes, colonial towns and artisan villages that includes many of Nicaragua's must-see highlights.

Fly into **Managua** and take in the view across town from Sandino's silhouette on the Loma de Tiscapa before heading south and descending into the lush crater at **Laguna de Apoyo** for the night. Spend the next day swimming in the rich sulfuric waters or spotting birds and howler monkeys in the forest, before enjoying the spectacular night sky.

The following morning, visit the artisan workshops of the nearby **Pueblos Blancos**, including the pottery cooperative at **San Juan de Oriente**. Then head 30 minutes down the road for some colonial splendor in charismatic **Granada**. Spend three nights taking in the wonderful streetscapes, visiting the museums and churches, and dining in the fine restaurants. While you're here take a kayaking day trip through the islets just offshore, and hike among the cloud forest atop Volcán Mombacho.

Next head down the highway to **San Jorge**. From here take the ferry to the out-of-this world **Isla de Ometepe** with its twin volcanoes and endless outdoor activities. Spend a night among the howler monkeys at **Reserva Charco Verde** and another at the base of Volcán Maderas, from where you can hike to the emerald-green crater lake.

Proceed across the isthmus to the surfing capital of **San Juan del Sur**, where you'll spend three days lazing on the splendid surrounding beaches or surfing some of the excellent breaks in the area. If you can drag yourself off the beach, take a day trip to the charming fishing village of **El Ostional** or, if you're lucky, watch sea turtles arrive en masse at **Refugio de Vida Silvestre La Flor**. In the evenings, work your way though the happening beachfront bars and restaurants.

On your way back to Managua, stop at **Masaya** to shop for souvenirs and gifts in the excellent Mercado Artesanías (National Artisans Market) and visit the hammock workshops.

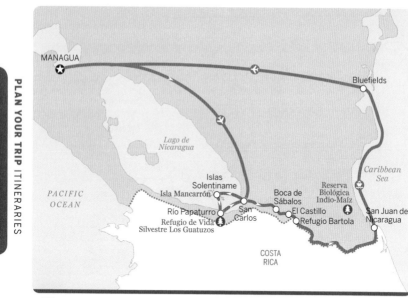

2 WEEKS Cruising the Río San Juan

The southeast corner of Nicaragua is an unparalleled playground for nature lovers of all dispositions. It boasts both comfortable eco-retreats and more strenuous adventures among lush wetlands and towering rainforests filled with fascinating ruins, reptiles and birdlife.

From **Managua** fly or bus it to. Spend a morning checking out the old Spanish fort and waterfront before taking the afternoon boat to the enchanted archipelago of the **Islas Solentiname**. Spend a night on both Isla San Fernando and Isla Mancarrón, following jungle trails to in situ petroglyphs, swimming in the clear waters and visiting local artist workshops.

From Mancarrón, charter a boat to the **Río Papaturro** in the Refugio de Vida Silvestre Los Guatuzos, stopping to spot the amazing birdlife at some of the smaller islands on the way. Hike through the thick monkey-inhabited forest or kayak in the wetlands before heading out on an alligator safari in the evening.

Next take the public boat back to San Carlos. Pick up a riverboat down the Río San Juan to **Boca de Sábalos**, a small river town surrounded by steamy jungle. Among the many excursions on offer here is a tour to a local cacao plantation and chocolate factory. Or simply relax on your hotel balcony and spot aquatic birds on the banks of the majestic river.

After two nights in Sábalos, continue downstream to **El Castillo**, where an imposing Spanish fort looms over the rapids. Spend two days here riding horses through the rolling green hills and and enjoying the charms of this delightful little jungle-bound town.

If you have a day to spare, detour north on a day trip to **Refugio Bartola** biological station, with a network of trails through towering old-growth forest and kayaks to paddle up the narrow jungle-clad Río Bartola to crystal-clear swimming holes. Otherwise, continue the journey by picking up a riverboat heading downriver to **San Juan de Nicaragua**, where the Río San Juan pours into the Caribbean Sea. Give yourself three days to explore the ruins of Greytown, spot manatees in hidden lagoons and head up the Río Indio into the heart of the Reserva Biológica Indio-Maíz. From San Juan fly directly back to Managua or take a *panga* (motorboat) on to **Bluefields** and return from there.

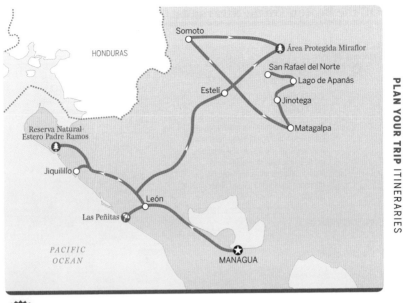

Northern Loop

3 WEEKS

Rich in nature and revolutionary culture, northern Nicaragua is equally rugged and refined. In one trip you'll go from sipping organic coffee at the source to surfing an active volcano. Charge your batteries: you'll want to take plenty of pictures or no one will believe you when you get home.

Upon arrival skip through **Managua** and head for the crumbling colonial beauty of **León** to give Nicaragua the fantastic introduction it deserves. Spend three days exploring this endearing city on foot, visiting fascinating museums, spacious mansions and glorious churches. If you're feeling energetic, hike one of the nearby volcanoes or surf the slopes of Cerro Negro.

From León head west to the beach at **Las Peñitas** and find a spot in a sand-floor beachside bar for the spectacular sunset. In the morning make an early start to travel north to **Jiquilillo**. Spend a couple of days soaking up the ambience in this pretty fishing village and paddling through the mangroves of the nearby Reserva Natural Estero Padre Ramos.

Then travel across the Maribios volcanic chain and into the mountains to **Estelí**, where you can visit cigar factories and check out revolutionary murals. After a couple of days head into the mountains in the **Área Protegida Miraflor** for two days of horseback riding, wildlife spotting and farm-culture immersion.

Move on to **Somoto** and to Monumento Nacional Cañon de Somoto to swim, jump and rappel your way through the canyon. Next morning travel to **Matagalpa** for a few caffeine-fueled days picking coffee beans and hiking on local plantations. Continue climbing higher into the mountains, stopping at the gorgeous Selva Negra coffee estate, before arriving in **Jinotega**, gateway to the cloud forests of Reserva Natural Cerro Datanlí–El Diablo. Spend a day in town to climb Cerro la Cruz and then spend a couple of days hiking in the reserve.

Give your muscles a break with a boat cruise on **Lago de Apanás** before continuing on to **San Rafael del Norte**. Here you can visit one of Nicaragua's most magnificent churches or fly through the pine forest on a zipline.

Off the Beaten Track: Nicaragua

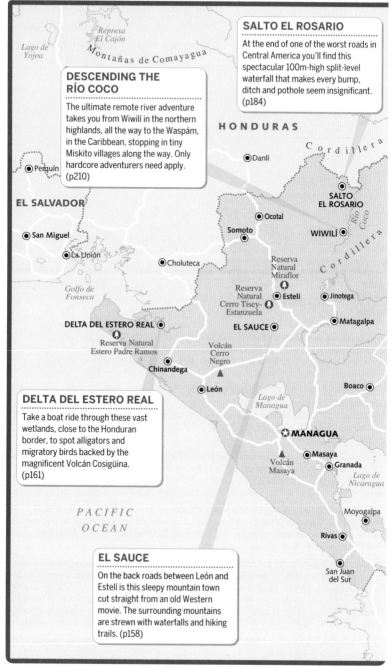

SALTO EL ROSARIO

At the end of one of the worst roads in Central America you'll find this spectacular 100m-high split-level waterfall that makes every bump, ditch and pothole seem insignificant. (p184)

DESCENDING THE RÍO COCO

The ultimate remote river adventure takes you from Wiwilí in the northern highlands, all the way to the Waspám, in the Caribbean, stopping in tiny Miskito villages along the way. Only hardcore adventurers need apply. (p210)

DELTA DEL ESTERO REAL

Take a boat ride through these vast wetlands, close to the Honduran border, to spot alligators and migratory birds backed by the magnificent Volcán Cosigüina. (p161)

EL SAUCE

On the back roads between León and Estelí is this sleepy mountain town cut straight from an old Western movie. The surrounding mountains are strewn with waterfalls and hiking trails. (p158)

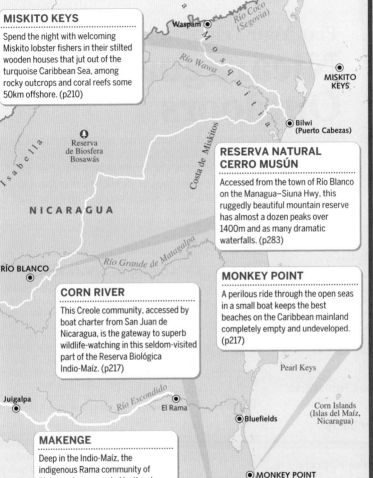

MISKITO KEYS

Spend the night with welcoming Miskito lobster fishers in their stilted wooden houses that jut out of the turquoise Caribbean Sea, among rocky outcrops and coral reefs some 50km offshore. (p210)

RESERVA NATURAL CERRO MUSÚN

Accessed from the town of Río Blanco on the Managua–Siuna Hwy, this ruggedly beautiful mountain reserve has almost a dozen peaks over 1400m and as many dramatic waterfalls. (p283)

MONKEY POINT

A perilous ride through the open seas in a small boat keeps the best beaches on the Caribbean mainland completely empty and undeveloped. (p217)

CORN RIVER

This Creole community, accessed by boat charter from San Juan de Nicaragua, is the gateway to superb wildlife-watching in this seldom-visited part of the Reserva Biológica Indio-Maíz. (p217)

MAKENGE

Deep in the Indio-Maíz, the indigenous Rama community of Makenge is surrounded by the class of jungle you've probably only seen in wildlife documentaries. (p257)

Plan Your Trip
Nicaragua Outdoors

Pristine, largely unpopulated and with an increasing degree of environmental protection, Nicaragua is wide open for authentic wilderness adventure without the corporate sheen. Whether it's sand-boarding down active volcanoes or a leisurely hike through orchid-scented cloud forests, in Nicaragua you are never far from a spectacular nature experience.

Best...

Wildlife-Watching

Reserva Biológica Indio-Maíz, Refugio de Vida Silvestre La Flor, Reserva de Biosfera Bosawás and Refugio de Vida Silvestre Los Guatuzos

Volcano Climbs

Volcán San Cristóbal, Volcán Maderas and Volcán Telica

Cloud-Forest Trek

Reserva Natural Macizos de Peñas Blancas

Surf Spots

Playas Popoyo, Gigante and Aserradores

Extreme Sports

Volcano boarding Cerro Negro, abseiling in Monumento Nacional Cañon de Somoto

Diving & Snorkeling

Great Corn Island, Little Corn Island and Pearl Keys

Fishing

Río San Juan, San Juan del Sur and Río Escondido

Diving & Snorkeling

It's no wonder that people are interested in getting all wet in Nicaragua, with its 1040km of coastline, most of it untainted and underdeveloped.

You can dive Nicaragua's Laguna de Apoyo, cruising past underwater fumaroles and saying hello to fish not found elsewhere in the world. But the best place in the country to dive – especially if you like cave dives – is the Corn Islands, where hammerhead sharks and 40 species of coral await.

The reefs surrounding the islands are also great for snorkeling, especially around Sally Peachie on the big island, and Otto Beach on the *islita*. For more outstanding snorkeling, head to the spectacular Pearl Keys, where you can swim among marine turtles and then rest on wonderful white-sand beaches.

Need to Know

Serious snorkeling enthusiasts will want to bring their own mask, snorkel and fins as rental jobs vary greatly in quality and are not widely available apart from on the Corn Islands.

The following dive shops are PADI certified and offer both courses and leisure dives: Dive Little Corn (p236) and Dolphin Dive (p235). For the novel experience of diving into an extinct volcanic crater, hook up with Volcano Divers (p98).

Hiking

Thanks to an unlikely environmental consciousness (the Nicaraguan government found time to protect dozens of wilderness areas during the turbulent 1980s) and the war, which probably did more to save the rainforests than Unesco did in most countries, there's a lot of fairly pristine forest out there to see.

Some of the most interesting and easily accessible are at Área Protegida Miraflor, Reserva Natural Macizos de Peñas Blancas and Reserva Natural Cerro Datanlí–El Diablo.

The climbs with the real cachet, however, are any of the dozens of volcanoes, including the Maribios chain, Volcán Cosigüina and the volcanoes of Isla Ometepe. And if you're into dominating nature, consider the full-day climb to the peak of Cerro Mogotón (2106m), Nicaragua's highest mountain.

Need to Know

Guides are usually recommended (and sometimes compulsory) for hikes in all but the best developed natural parks and reserves, particularly for the volcanoes. Even on easy hikes, guides can almost always find things you never would. In smaller towns, ask about guides at the *alcaldía* (mayor's office), usually right on the Parque Central (central park).

Base yourself in the hiking havens of Estelí, Matagalpa or Jinotega to explore the mountains of the north. For volcanoes, the best access is from León.

There are a number of companies offering organized hikes. We recommend Quetzaltrekkers (p146), Tree Huggers (p171) and Matagalpa Tours (p194).

Surfing

For beginners, the center of Nicaraguan surfing remains San Juan del Sur, with Las Peñitas being another popular hotspot. Expert wave-shredders tend to head to the surf camps spreading northwards around Popoyo, past flawless beach breaks, scary-fun lava point breaks and lots of barrels, when conditions are right. Playa Gigante has a few surf camps, where all-inclusive means room, meals and boat rides out to the best waves in the area every day; Popoyo has even more to offer, and there are clusters of surf camps around Playa Aserradores, Miramar and El Tránsito, closer to León and fronting some world-class waves.

The best breaks often require boats to get to, not just because they're offshore, but because housing developments along the coast block land access. To make up for it, southern Nicaragua is caressed by an almost constant offshore wind, perhaps caused by the presence of Lago de Nicaragua and Lago de Managua.

HIKING GEAR CHECKLIST

Trekking for leisure is not particularly popular among Nicaraguans and quality gear is hard to find on the ground. If you plan on getting off the beaten track, make sure you bring the following:

Comfortable footwear Consider both leather hiking boots for long days in the mountains and comfortable, sturdy sports sandals for treks involving river crossings.

Water purification tablets

Lightweight sleeping bag Believe it or not it does actually get cold in mountainous regions of Nicaragua.

Hammock Indispensable for long boat rides or taking a break in the jungle high above the creepy crawlies of the forest floor.

Tent If you find one in Nicaragua, it's likely to be bulky and barely waterproof, bring a lightweight hiking model from home.

Surfer at Miramar (p155)

Need to Know

Nicaragua has great waves year-round. March to November is considered the best time to surf, with the biggest waves usually in March, April and October (consistently 1m to 2m, frequently 3m to 4m). November to March is the dry season, with smaller waves (averaging under 2m) but better weather – this is the best time for beginners.

Water temperatures average around mid-20°C (mid-70°F) year-round, but from December to April an upwelling offshore means that the water's temperature can drop; consider bringing a long-sleeve wetsuit top.

You can buy, sell and rent boards in San Juan del Sur and Popoyo, but it's generally better to bring your own board (consider selling it when you leave).

Numerous surfing outfits offer everything from one-on-one instruction to week-long all-inclusive surf packages. Listings are provided in the closest city to the waves.

Best Breaks

Here are some favorite waves, which we've listed northeast to southwest. All of these beaches are on the Pacific coast. For recommendations of the best breaks, check out www.giantsfootsurf.com, https://surfnicaragua.wordpress.com and https://matadornetwork.com/trips/6-best-surf-spots-in-nicaragua.

Playa Aserradores Just northeast of Chinandega, the beach is also called Boom for the powerful, hollow beach break making all that noise. There's another left five minutes offshore and plenty more waves around.

El Corinto This is one of the best waves in the country, beyond Playa Paso Caballos, but it goes almost unsurfed because it's only accessible by boat. Easier to get to is the river-mouth break with left-breaking peaks.

Poneloya & Las Peñitas Only decent surfing for beginners and intermediates, but the easiest access on Nicaragua's north Pacific, just 20km from León.

Miramar The stretch from Puerto Sandino to El Velero has half a dozen reef and rocky-bottomed beach breaks, including one spectacular left.

Playa Huehuete Now is that golden time between when the road is paved and when the gated communities go up: check out the point, beach and river-mouth break now!

Playa Popoyo This collection of sandy-floored surf lodges may be Nicaragua's next bona fide surf town, with at least four named waves: Popoyo, a right and left point break; aggressive Bus Stop; fast and rocky-floored Cobra; and the best wave in the region, Emergencias, with a left for longboards and hollow right for short boards.

Playa Gigante With access to another handful of named waves, most of them a boat ride away, it's no wonder that surf lodges are springing up all over this beautiful beach.

Playa Maderas Sometimes called Los Playones, this excellent surf spot, with easy access from San Juan del Sur, has a slow wave with two rights and two lefts that's perfect for beginners.

Playa Yankee Powerful, fast point break that's for expert surfers only.

Swimming

From sunny Pacific beaches to cool crater lakes, and lots of rivers and waterfalls, you'll always find places to put your bathing suit to work.

There are eight major crater lakes, with excellent swimming at Laguna de Apoyo, surrounded by lodging options, or undeveloped Laguna de Asososca, near León.

Isla de Ometepe has some excellent swimming opportunities, including the remarkable natural sand jetty at Punta Jesús María and the mineral-rich waters of La Presa Ojo de Agua.

The best beach swims are at some of the stunning coves around San Juan del Sur and in the crystal-clear waters of the Caribbean around the Pearl Keys and the Corn Islands.

Wildlife-Watching

Nicaragua is home to an impressive array of tropical ecosystems, each offering their own outstanding wildlife-spotting opportunities.

BEST BIRDWATCHING

Islas Solentiname Tiny islands with Nicaragua's highest concentration of birdlife including tiger herons and flocks of roseate spoonbills.

Boca de Sábalos Pick your spot along the river and observe a fantastic array of waterfowl and rainforest species without moving a muscle.

Área Protegida Miraflor Accessible cloud forest boasting quetzals and toucans.

Refugio de Vida Silvestre Los Guatuzos Immense wetlands home to around 400 bird species.

Volcán Mombacho Hike the cloud forest trails and try to spot the 100-plus bird species that call it home.

The best spots to try and see big animals are in the tropical rainforests of the Reserva Bíologica Indio-Maíz and the Reserva de Biosfera Bosawás. One of the rarest ecosystems in the world is the cloud forest, a cool, misty tropical rainforest above 1200m, offering opportunities for seeing wildlife and flora, most famously colorful quetzals and orchids. The most accessible is at Volcán Mombacho, easily reached from Granada.

Nicaragua's Pacific coast is a haven for literally hundreds of thousands of nesting turtles each year, and some of their nesting sites are surprisingly accessible. In the San Juan del Sur area, you're within easy reach of Refugio de Vida Silvestre La Flor and Refugio de Vida Silvestre Río Escalante Chacocente. There's more turtle action further north at Reserva Natural Volcán Cosigüina.

Birders will also be drawn to Nicaragua's sweet-water wetlands and jungle-lined rivers, which offer outstanding birding opportunities.

Regions at a Glance

Stretching from the sizzling Pacific with its colonial treasures, smoking volcanoes and superb surf beaches to the crystalline Caribbean with its indigenous communities and islands that groove to an altogether different tune, Nicaragua's geographical diversity is topped only by the range of cultures living within its boundaries.

The country is crowned in the north by spectacular mountain ranges covered in a patchwork of small farms, coffee plantations and cloud forest that offer great hiking and birdwatching opportunities. In the south you'll find the largest freshwater lake in Central America, with more outdoor activities than you could dream of cramming into your itinerary, wetlands brimming with birdlife and the virgin rainforests of the magnificent Río San Juan.

Managua

History
Nightlife
Culture

Revolutionary Roads

Key moments in Nicaragua's tumultuous modern history continue to play out here. Take a stroll down the National Assembly Pedestrian Walk for an overview, ending up at the eerie abandoned cathedral, a reminder of the devastating 1978 earthquake.

Up All Night

This town knows how to party. From the craft beer and cocktail bars of Los Robles and Altamira to the discos of Belo Horizonte, painting Managua red is an unforgettable experience.

Culture Capital

This is the cultural fulcrum of a nation, home to the country's best history museum, numerous art galleries, theaters and venues for catching traditional music, poetry and more.

p41

Masaya & Los Pueblos Blancos

Shopping
Culture
Outdoors

Artisan Headquarters

San Juan de Oriente village produces the most exquisite pottery in Central America, while Masaya has a lively crafts market and artisan workshops.

Local Encounters

This is a great place for encounters with locals, particularly if you visit the villages during their exuberant religious festivals or seek out a local *curandero* (medicine man).

Volcanoes & Craters

Volcán Masaya offers never-ending vistas and the chance to look into the fiery maw of a very active volcano. Southward, you'll come across the unrelenting beauty of Laguna de Apoyo, a volcanic crater lake you can dive into.

p65

Granada

History
Eating
Islands

A Storied Past

Granada's centuries-long history is as complex as it gets. You'll see it in the city's architecture, its festivals, art and living culture.

Culinary Variety

The city's vibrant restaurant scene will keep foodies busy for several hours each day. There's fusion, superlative examples of Nicaraguan cuisine, and experimental spots that cater to travelers of all palates.

Archipelago Exploration

From the shores of Lake Nicaragua you can head out by launch or kayak to explore an archipelago of tiny islands, stay overnight in a tranquil ecolodge or go in search of petroglyphs on remote Isla Zapatera.

p80

Southwestern Nicaragua

Surf
Island Escape
Party Time

Famous Breaks

Not many places have surf as good as this. Hit dawn patrol at legendary spots such as Playas Hermosa and Maderas, or ride the huge hollow breaks around Popoyo and Playa Aserradores.

Enchanted Island

Isla de Ometepe is a paradise found. Discover petroglyphs, climb volcanoes, hike to a waterfall, kayak to lost coves, gallop through remote villages on horseback and chill out in cool travelers' enclaves on the edge of the wild.

Party Central

For many travelers, San Juan del Sur is synonymous with hedonism, with numerous bars and beach clubs. It's also home to Sunday Funday, a legendary pool-bar crawl that attracts hundreds.

p102

León & North Western Nicaragua

History
Volcanoes
Outdoors

Liberal Hotbed

León is where the revolution was televised from and where current protests take place. You can feel the palpable and intense strands of fiery rhetoric flowing from this intellectual powerhouse. The partying isn't bad either.

Dramatic Geography

The fire theme continues in the nature preserves that encircle massive volcanoes, forgotten islets and wide-open spaces of the interior. You can trek to their peaks and greet the sunrise.

Uncharted Territory

Head north to get further from the tourist track and closer to the wild. There are volcanoes, waves and mangrove estuaries who only see a human once in a blue moon.

p135

Northern Highlands

Nature
Adventure
Ecotourism

Birdwatching

Nature lovers will have no shortage of opportunities to spot toucans, motmots and even quetzals among the region's swaths of precious cloud forest.

Treks & Hikes

Whether it's a mountainous trek to a hidden waterfall or tubing through an ancient canyon, the northern region offers unlimited opportunity for off-the-beaten-path adventure.

Finca Life

For a real taste of Nicaraguan life, stay on a working farm in one of the nothern highlands' protected reserves, where collectives cultivate coffee against a stunning background of soaring peaks.

p167

Caribbean Coast

Beaches
Diving & Snorkeling
Culture

Island Paradise

Romantic tropical islands with turquoise-fringed white-sand beaches shaded by coconut palms anyone? While you may find such idyllic beauty elsewhere, it won't be as empty or undeveloped.

On the Reef

Get underwater at all costs on the Corn Islands, where superb snorkeling and sublime diving awaits; you may even see hammerhead sharks.

Vibrant Music Scene

An ethnic melting pot overflowing with culture, the Caribbean coast has maypole rhythms and Miskito pop providing the soundtrack for performances by Nicaragua's best dancers, while Garifuna drummers punctuate the night.

p203

San Carlos, Islas Solentiname & the Río San Juan

Boating
Nature
Art

Boater's Delight

Río San Juan is the ultimate boating playground, with epic *panga* journeys, kayak and canoe adventures, and alligator-spotting safaris all on offer.

Through the Binoculars

Southeastern Nicaragua offers outstanding birdwatching, including at the remote Islas Solentiname, and along the Río San Juan, home to a grand variety of aquatic and rainforest species.

Indigenous Art Forms

A visit to the workshops and studios of Islas Solentiname offers fascinating insights into the Primitivist paintings and bright balsa carvings of the island.

p240

On the Road

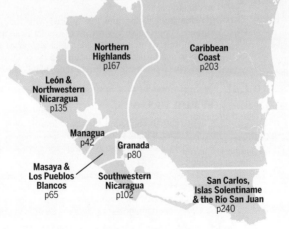

Northern Highlands p167

Caribbean Coast p203

León & Northwestern Nicaragua p135

Managua p42

Granada p80

Masaya & Los Pueblos Blancos p65

Southwestern Nicaragua p102

San Carlos, Islas Solentiname & the Río San Juan p240

Managua

POP 1,033,622 / ELEV 83M

Best Places to Eat

➡ Terraza Peruana (p54)

➡ Don Cándido (p55)

➡ Asados Doña Tania (p54)

➡ Cafe Las Marias (p54)

➡ Ola Verde (p54)

Best Places to Stay

➡ Casa Lucia (p52)

➡ Elements Boutique Hotel (p52)

➡ La Posada del Arcangel (p51)

➡ Hotel Casa Colonial (p52)

➡ La Bicicleta Hostal (p52)

Why Go?

Managua is not the easiest place to get your head around. It has no discernible center; its attractions are scattered around its many neighborhoods and the trick is to know when to go where.

Stay a day or two and you will see that big, bad Managua ain't so bad after all, and that this truly is the heartstring that holds the nation's culture and commerce together. Skip it altogether, and you miss out on the revolutionary landmarks, vibrant dining and nightlife scenes and a slice of down-to-earth urban life that you're unlikely to see anywhere else.

Aside from diving into the spirited whirl of sprawling markets, improbable electric trees, remarkable street art and impressive monuments, Managua also gives you easy access to nearby lagoons, the nature reserve of Chocoyero-El Brujo, plus a smattering of fun beaches like Pochomil.

When to Go

➡ September through April is the best time of year for birdwatching. It's also good for turtle tours at nearby beaches and wildlife encounters in the lagoons and natural attractions just outside the city.

➡ December through April are the dry months. Visiting at this time makes plying the city's streets easier, market days drier and chance encounters just a little more pleasant. Hotels can be a bit pricey now and during Semana Santa, so book ahead.

➡ The best festivals happen around the Day of the Revolution on July 19 or the Festival of Santo Domingo, the first 10 days in August.

History

A fishing encampment as early as 6000 years ago, Managua has been an important trading center for at least two millennia. When Spanish chronicler Fernández de Oviedo arrived in 1528, he estimated Managua's population at around 40,000; most of these original inhabitants fled to the Sierritas, the small mountains just south, shortly after the Spanish arrived. The small town, without even a hospital or school until the 1750s, didn't really achieve any prominence until 1852, when the seemingly endless civil war between Granada and León was resolved by placing the capital here.

The clever compromise might have worked out better had a geologist been at hand: Managua sits atop a network of fault lines that have shaped its history ever since. The late 1800s were rocked by quakes that destroyed the new capital's infrastructure, with churches and banks crumbling as the ground flowed beneath their feet. In 1931 the epicenter was the stadium – dozens were killed during a big game. In 1968 a single powerful jolt right beneath what's now Metrocentro mall destroyed an entire neighborhood.

And on the evening of December 23, 1972, a series of powerful tremors rocked the city, culminating in a 6.2 magnitude quake that killed 11,000 people and destroyed 53,000 homes. The blatant siphoning of international relief funds by President Somoza touched off the Sandinista-led revolution, which was followed by the Contra War, and the city center, including the beautiful old cathedral, was never rebuilt. Rather, it was replaced by a crazy maze of unnamed streets, shacks that turned into shanties that turned into homes and later buildings. There have been some efforts to resurrect the old city center – the restoration of the

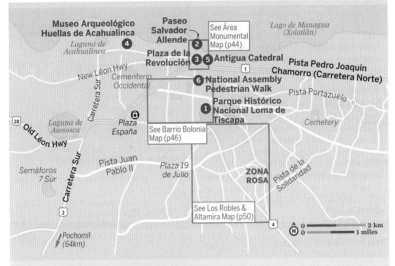

Managua Highlights

1 **Parque Histórico Nacional Loma de Tiscapa** (p45) Taking in views over the city while standing in Sandino's shadow on a volcano's rim.

2 **Paseo Salvador Allende** (p44) Exploring the newly revamped waterfront and eating, drinking and dancing with the locals at sunset.

3 **Plaza de la Revolución** (p44) Marveling at the crumbling colonial grandeur and enjoying the sight of promenading Managuans, particularly on weekends.

4 **Museo Arqueológico Huellas de Acahualinca** (p48) Following in the footsteps of Managua's early inhabitants.

5 **Antigua Catedral** (p44) Taking in the eerie sight of the once grand, hollowed-out shell of a cathedral.

6 **National Assembly Pedestrian Walk** (p45) Brushing up on modern Nicaraguan history while you stroll.

Malecón (waterfront) was certainly a promising development – but new construction had come to a standstill at research time due to the outbreak of violence in April 2018.

◉ Sights

Many of Managua's historic sights are concentrated in the Área Monumental. There are also a number of art galleries scattered across Managua's various neighborhoods. Since Managua is spread out and much of it is not pedestrian-friendly, taxis are a cheap and worthwhile investment in Managua's muggy climate.

◉ Área Monumental & El Malecón

★ **Antigua Catedral**   CATHEDRAL
(Catedral de Santiago; Map p44; 14 Av Sureste, Área Monumental) The hollow shell of Managua's Old Cathedral remains Managua's most poignant metaphor, shattered by the 1972 earthquake – and slowly undergoing restoration. Though its neoclassical facade is beautiful and serene, attended by stone angels and dappled in golden light, its interior is empty and off-limits: the cathedral without a heart, in the city without a center.

Plaza de la Revolución   PARK
(Map p44; Av Bolívar, Área Monumental) Inaugurated in 1899 by national hero and original anti-American General José Santos Zelaya, this open plaza has been the scene of countless protests, parades, romances and more. On the northeast of the plaza rests the tomb of Sandinista commander Carlos Fonseca. It's particularly atmospheric on afternoons and weekends, when it fills with promenading Managuans.

Paseo Salvador Allende   WATERFRONT
(Map p44; Paseo Xolotán, Área Monumental; per person/car US$0.10/0.70; ☺ 2-9pm Mon-Fri, 9am-9pm Sat & Sun; 🖪) The *malecón* (pier) has been perked up by the Puerto Salvador Allende tourist complex at its base, and comes alive in the evenings (particularly on weekends), with several restaurants, bar and food stalls, lit up 'trees of life' (courtesy of first lady Rosario Murillo) and promenading families. There's a scale replica of Av Bolívar before the 1972 earthquake, a water park (US$1), a Boeing 737 for kids to explore, replicas of Nicaragua's most famous churches and two bland museums.

Área Monumental

Área Monumental

Parque Luis Velásquez   PARK
(Av Bolívar; 🖪) This park is a prime spot for observing local life. It really comes alive on weekends and in the evenings, when it seems like all of Managua's families pour out onto its footpaths, with kids splashing in the fountains or playing baseball at the stadium, teenagers breakdancing and young couples canoodling.

Museo Nacional   MUSEUM
(Map p44; 4 Calle Noreste, Palacio de la Cultura y Biblioteca Nacional; US$5; ☺10am-4:30pm Mon & Wed-Fri, 9am-3:30pm Tue, 10am-noon Sat) Inside the Palacio de la Cultura y Biblioteca Nacional, the beautiful national museum is an enjoyable romp through the country's history – from Nicaragua's prehistory and the formation of the lakes and volcanoes – not to mention gold mines – to pre-Columbian statuary and one of the best pottery collections in the country, all well signed and explained.

Palacio de la Cultura y
Biblioteca Nacional   HISTORIC BUILDING
(Map p44; 4 Calle Noreste, Área Monumental; ☺10am-4:30pm Mon & Wed-Fri, 9am-3:30pm Tue, 10am-noon Sat) The 1930s-era Palacio de la Cultura (Palace of Culture) housed the National Congress until 1994. The historic building now houses the national museum and library.

Monumento a Rubén Darío   MONUMENT
(Map p44; Av Bolívar, Área Monumnetal) On the lake side of Plaza de la Revolución, this monument was refurbished after the original 1933 statue fell into graffitied disrepair. A group of artists did a guerrilla installation, veiling the city's shame from public view and demanding poetic justice. In 1998 the cash-strapped government bowed to public opinion and, with Texaco Oil's help, restored the likeness of Nicaragua's favorite son.

Tomb of Carlos Fonseca   MONUMENT
(Map p44; Plaza de la Revolución, Área Monumental) The tomb of Carlos Fonseca, founder of the Sandinista National Liberation Front (FSLN). He was killed fighting Nicaraguan National Guard forces loyal to dictator Anastasio Somoza.

Monumento al Trabajador
Nicaragüense   MONUMENT
(Map p44; Parque Central, 2c S, 1c E, Área Monumental) A monument to Nicaraguan workers – a man and a woman, taking part in manual labour.

Estatua de Montoya   STATUE
(Map p46; 17 Av Suroeste) A statue dedicated to national hero Ramón Montoya, a Nicaraguan soldier who died (at the age of 14) in 1907.

Casa del Pueblo   NOTABLE BUILDING
(Map p44; Plaza de la Revolución, 1c N, 1c E, Área Monumental) This was rebuilt during the Alemán years with the help of the Taiwanese government, and is now home to the controversial Consejos de Poder Ciudadano (CPCs), an organization created by the Nicaraguan government in 2007 allegedly to incentivize people to take part in decision-making that affects their communities. Many Nicaraguans argue today that the CPC's primary function is to attack opponents of Ortega.

Estatua al Soldado   MONUMENT
(Map p44; Carretera Norte (Dupla Norte), Área Monumental) The monument to Nicaraguan soldiers dates from 1909.

Casa del Obrero   LANDMARK
(Map p46; 11 Av Suroeste & Calle Colón) A downtown landmark originally dedicated to the Nicaraguan worker.

◎ Barrio Bolonia & Around

National Assembly
Pedestrian Walk   PUBLIC ART
(Map p46; Av Central) East of the National Assembly along Av Central is a pedestrian walk with open-air exhibits on Nicaragua's history, featuring everything from historic photos of Sandino to evocative pictures of pre-earthquake Managua. It's a great path to take if you're walking from Barrio Bolonia to the lakefront, especially if you're interested in Nicaragua's political and literary histories.

Epikentro Gallery   GALLERY
(Map p46; www.facebook.com/epikentrocentrovisual.nic; del Canal 2 TV, 1c N, 2½c E, Barrio Bolonia; ☺10am-4pm Mon-Sat) FREE Straddling the divide between fine and contemporary art.

Parque Histórico Nacional
Loma de Tiscapa   PARK
(Map p46; 12 Calle Sureste, Barrio Bolonia) Home to what's easily Managua's most recognizable landmark, Sandino's somber silhouette, this national historic park was once the site of the Casa Presidencial, where Sandino and his men were executed in 1934; what looks like a dilapidated parking structure was for decades one of Nicaragua's most notorious prisons.

You can see Sandino, hastily erected by the departing Frente Sandinista de Liberación Nacional (FSLN; Sandinista National Liberation Front) government after its electoral loss in 1990, from almost anywhere in town; begin your ascent at the Crowne Plaza. You'll pass Monumento Roosevelt (p46), constructed in 1939, with lovely lake views (today it's a memorial to those killed in the revolution).

Barrio Bolonia

The top of Loma de Tiscapa is actually the lip of Volcán Tiscapa's beautiful little crater lake, with incredible views of the city, both cathedrals and Volcán Momotombo. Keep in mind that, despite a vigorous clean-up campaign, the lake is polluted with untreated sewage.

Monumento Roosevelt
MONUMENT

(Map p46; 12 Calle Sureste) Acsending Loma de Tiscapa from Crowne Plaza, you'll pass Monumento Roosevelt, constructed in 1939 and offering lovely lake views over the Laguna de Tiscapa. Today it's a memorial to those killed in the revolution.

Parque El Carmén
PARK

(Map p46; antiguo Cine Dorado, 2c O; ⊙dawn-dusk) A couple of blocks from Barrio Bolonia's concrete jungle, this surprisingly pretty park is a little slice of suburbia, with kids' riding bikes, a playground, and a kiosk selling snacks and cold drinks. The park is surrounded by some fairly opulent homes, including that of President Ortega – if your taxi driver doesn't know it, tell him 'donde vive Daniel' (where Daniel lives).

Códice Espacio Cultural
GALLERY

(Map p50; ☑2253-8390; 32 Calle Sureste, Hotel Colón, 1c S, 2½c E; ⊙11am-1pm Mon-Fri) **FREE** The best place to catch really cutting-edge contemporary art in Managua.

Arboretum Nacional Juan Batista Salas
GARDENS

(National Arboretum; Map p46; Av Bolívar; US$0.30; ⊙8am-5pm Mon-Fri) These modest gardens, inconveniently located halfway between Barrio Bolonia and the Plaza Monumental on Av Bolívar (well, it's convenient if you're making the hot 40-minute walk between them), features more than 200 species of plants, divided into Nicaragua's five major life zones. Of these only the dry tropical forest and central lowlands look happy.

Barrio Bolonia

Your fee includes a guided tour, where you'll see a *madriño,* the national tree, and *sacuanjoche,* the national flower.

Parque Las Palmas   PARK
(Estatua de Montoya, 3c O, 50m N; ☺ dawn-dusk)
A cute and shady little neighborhood park with the requisite benches, snack kiosks and even a laid-back bar in the middle.

UCA   UNIVERSITY
(Universidad Centro America; Map p50; www.uca.edu.ni; Rotonda Rubén Darío, 500m O) Founded in 1960 as a Jesuit school, this is one of Nicaragua's premier universities, with a curriculum heavy on science and alternative technologies, Che Guevara sculptures, and vegetarian eateries out front. It's worth a wander – in particular the **Centro Historia Militar** (free admission), with relics from Sandino to the Sandinistas.

UNAN   UNIVERSITY
(Universidad Nacional Autónoma de Nicaragua; Map p50; www.unan.edu.ni; Enitel Villa Fontana, 500m O) The Managua branch of Nicaragua's oldest university (the original is in León, the

former capital) was founded in 1958 and has more than 24,000 students.

Carretera a Masaya

Catedral Metropolitana   CATHEDRAL
(Map p50; www.catedralmga.blogspot.com; 14 Av Sureste; ⊙10am-noon & 4-6pm Tue-Sun) Just north of the Metrocentro mall is an unforgettable Managua landmark that's practically new (the doors opened in 1993). It's an architectural marvel that leaves most visitors, well, scratching their heads. It's not a mosque, really: the 63 cupolas (or breasts, or eggs; speculation continues) symbolize Nicaragua's 63 Catholic churches, and also provide structural support during earthquakes – a good thing, since it sits astride a fault line.

The interior is cool, heartfelt and unspectacular, although the shrine on the northwest side is nice. Of the US$45 million used to construct the cathedral, US$3.5 million was donated by avid pro-lifer Tom Monaghan, former owner of Domino's Pizza.

Parque Japon   PARK
(Map p50; Av Miguel Obando y Bravo, Star City, 2c E; ⊙dawn-dusk) FREE This not-particularly Japanese park, nestled in the back blocks of the Metrocentro area, is a great place for a bit of time out. There are plenty of trees, some walking tracks and a couple of kids' playgrounds.

Casino Pharaoh   LANDMARK
(Map p50; Carretera a Masaya Km 4.5) A landmark locals use to give directions in the neighborhood.

La Vicky   LANDMARK
(Map p50) The grocery store called 'La Vicky' doesn't stand here anymore, but locals still use it as a point of reference for navigating the town.

Star City   LANDMARK
(Map p50; cnr Av Miguel Obando y Bravo & Paseo de la Unión Europea, Altamira) A former casino (now closed) and current landmark that locals use to give directions in the area.

Northwest of the Center

★**Museo Arqueológico Huellas de Acahualinca**   ARCHAEOLOGICAL SITE
(☑2266-5774; Calle Museo de Acahualinca, Barrio Acahualinca; US$3; ⊙8am-4pm Mon-Fri) Discovered by miners in 1874, these fossilized tracks record the passage of perhaps 10 people – men, women and children – as well as birds, raccoons, deer and possum across the muddy shores of Lago de Managua some 6000 to 8000 years ago. Despite early speculation that they were running from a volcanic eruption, forensics specialists have determined that these folks were in no hurry – and, interestingly, were fairly tall at between 145cm and 160cm. Come here by taxi (US$2 to US$4).

The excavation was undertaken by the Carnegie Foundation in 1941 and 1942, and unearthed 14 layers, or 4m, of earth. They found some later Chorotega ceramics (about 2m down) and other intriguing artifacts, though there's no money to take it further. The nifty on-site museum, with human skulls, a fossilized bison track and lots of ceramics, was closed for renovation at research time, but there's a detailed bilingual exhibition on the excavations and different theories surrounding the footprints. Don't skip this one; it's an international treasure.

🏃 Activities

Nica on Pedals   MOUNTAIN BIKING
(Map p50; ☑8281-1512; www.nicaonpedals.com; Monte de los Olivos, 1c N, 1c O, ½c N, Casa No 55, Colonial Los Robles) Based at Managua Backpackers Inn (p52), these guys offer an active, adrenalin-packed way of exploring Nicaragua's great outdoors. They take you downhill biking on Ventarron Hill, just outside Managua, with great views of Volcán Masaya (US$63 per person), where there are several trails of varying difficulty.

🐊 Courses

Viva Spanish School   LANGUAGE
(Map p50; ☑2270-2339; www.vivaspanishschool.com; Metrocentro, 5c E, del Edificio Banco Produzcamos, 2c S; lessons per hour US$10; ⊙8am-5pm Mon-Fri) Highly recommended by long-term volunteers and NGO workers, classes here start at US$175 for a 20-hour week. Homestays can be arranged for an additional US$140 per week.

La Academia Nicaragüense de la Danza   COURSE
(Map p50; ☑2277-5557; http://asodanza.com; Av Universitaria, UCA, 50m N) Offers a huge range of dance classes (salsa, merengue, reggaetón, folk, ballet, flamenco and bellydancing, to name a few).

Alianza Francesa COURSE

(Map p50; ☑ 2267-2811; www.alianzafrancesa. org.ni; de la Embajada de México, ½c N, Planes de Altamira) Offers classes in painting, drawing, French, German and Portuguese, along with occasional art exhibits and poetry readings.

🖝 Tours

★ **Claudio Perez Cruz** OUTDOORS

(☑ 5889-89105; https://casaluciamanagua.com) Based at Casa Lucia (p52), young, knowledgeable, bilingual Claudio is extremely passionate about Nicaragua and all it has to offer. He has contacts all over the country and can either travel with you or make arrangements for you, depending on your interests and the amount of time you have. Exploring Managua with him is a blast.

Green Pathways ADVENTURE

(☑ 7877-2940; www.greenpathways.com; del semáforos de Club Terraza, 1c E, ½c N) 🏄 Socially conscientious operator with a focus on nature tourism, offering tailor-made tours according to your interests.

🎋 Festivals & Events

Carnaval Alegría por la Vida STREET CARNIVAL

(www.facebook.com/carnavalnicaragua; ⊙ early Mar) The 'Joy for Life' festival is Managua's version of Carnaval, featuring a lively parade of costumed performers, live music, food, dancing and the crowning of a festival queen. There's a different theme each year.

Día de la Revolución CULTURAL

(⊙ Jul 19) Thousands of red-and-black-flag-waving faithful pour into the streets during the Día de la Revolución (Day of the Revolution) to celebrate the Sandinista revolution that overthrew the dictator Somoza in 1979.

Festival de Santo Domingo de Guzman RELIGIOUS

(⊙ Aug 1-10) Managua's *fiestas patronales* (patron saint parties) feature a carnival, sporting events, *hípicos* (horse parades) and a procession of *diablitos,* which takes Santo Domingo to his country shrine at the Sierritas de Managua, followed by music and fireworks.

La Purísima RELIGIOUS

(⊙ end Nov–mid-Dec) The Feast of the Immaculate Conception is celebrated throughout Nicaragua, with festivities culminating on December 8. In Managua, the celebration is particularly colorful, with massive altars to the Virgin Mary set up along the blocks of Av Bolívar leading to the lake. After dark, the avenue turns into a huge street party with food stands and live music.

🛏 Sleeping

Most budget travelers stay in Barrio Bolonia, the grid of streets immediately east of Laguna Tiscapa – due to easy access to the Tica bus station. There's a cluster of luxury hotels near the Metrocentro mall, and a number of appealing budget and midrange options in the suburban-feeling Los Robles and Planes de Altamira, further south, off the Carretera a Masaya.

Barrio Bolonia & Around

Better known to *taxistas* as 'Tica Bus,' the international bus terminal upon which the barrio (district) is centered, Bolonia's been hosting shoestringers for a generation. Much of it is sketchy after dark, but there are several boutique hotels on its leafy southern fringes. Directions here are usually given from Canal Dos (Canal 2 TV Building).

Pandora Hostel HOSTEL $

(Map p46; ☑ 7524-5303; www.pandorahostel.com; 10 Calle Suroeste, Tica Bus, 1c S, 1c E, Barrio Bolonia; dm US$12, r with/without bathroom US$30/40; ❋🛜) Clean, friendly and around the corner from the Tica Bus terminal, ominously named Pandora surprises you with pleasant offerings from her box: Moorish-style arches and hookahs alongside comfy couches, vast dorms and rooms, and an onsite bar. Lili the dog usually mills underfoot and these are by far the most popular budget digs in Barrio Bolonia. Smoking allowed in lounge, though.

Casa Luna HOSTEL $

(Map p46; ☑ 2266-3982; www.facebook.com/casalunabnb; de la clinica sumédico 2c O, ½c S, Barrio Bolonia; dm US$10, r with/without bathroom US$25/20; ❋🛜) Guests tend to congregate on the cheery patio at one of Barrio Bolonia's nicest options. Owner Bernardo is quick to give advice if you want to go forth and explore, and while the walls are a little on the thin side, that's easy to overlook in favor of the friendly vibe, guest kitchen and other backpacker boons.

Hostal Dulce Sueño HOTEL $

(Map p46; ☑ 2228-4125; www.facebook.com/hostaldulcesueno; Tica Bus, 70m E, Barrio Bolonia; s/d from US$14/19; 🛜) This optimistically named

Los Robles & Altamira

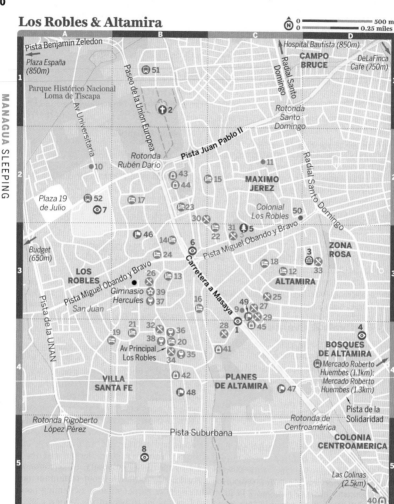

guesthouse has spotless, no-frills rooms, and a central patio with a TV and a shared kitchen. It's a few steps from the Tica Bus terminal, in a fairly sketchy neighborhood; convenient for overnighting but not lingering.

Hotel y Apartamento Los Cisneros HOTEL **$$**
(Map p46; ☑ 2222-3235; www.hotelloscisneros. com; 8 Calle Suroeste, Tica Bus, 1c N, 1½c O, Barrio Bolonia; s/d from US$27/30, 2-/4-person apt US$45/60; 🅿 ❋ 🛜) A great deal with colorful rooms, and a hammock-strung courtyard overflowing with artwork and plants. The apartments are basically just big rooms with

a kitchenette, but they're upstairs and you get your own balcony and hammock. Convenient for Tica Bus departures.

Casa Vanegas HOTEL **$$**
(Map p46; ☑ 2222-4043; 9 Calle Suroeste, Tica Bus, 1c O, Barrio Bolonia; s/d from US$17/25; 🛜) Clean and secure, this friendly spot, run by Giovanni and Maria Elena, just steps from Tica Bus, is convenient if you have an early bus to catch. Casa Vanegas offers decent-sized, fairly unremarkable rooms around a small patio plus hammocks, a spacious lounge area, and laundry facilities.

Los Robles & Altamira

★ **La Posada del Arcangel**   GUESTHOUSE $$$
(Map p46; ☑ 2254-5212; www.hotellaposada
delarcangel.com; Calle Los Pinos, Canal 2 TV, 100m
O, 150m S, Barrio Bolonia; r from US$60; ✻ 🛜)
There's much to love about colonial-style
Posada de Arcangel, from the quirky art col-
lection and leafy garden to the guest rooms
with crimson accents, bold splashes of con-
temporary art, and hand-carved wooden
furnishings, including four-poster beds.
The included breakfast is excellent, too, and
owners go above and beyond the call of duty
to be helpful.

Hotel Europeo   BUSINESS HOTEL $$$
(Map p46; ☑ 2268-2130; www.hoteleuropeo.com.
ni; Canal 2 TV, 75m O, Barrio Bolonia; s/d incl breakfast from US$69/82; 🅿✻🛜♨) 🍃 A business
favorite in central Managua, the Europeo
combines instantly forgettable beige rooms

with punchy contemporary art in common
areas with a thatched-roof restaurant out
back, large gardens and a swimming pool.
All profits go to benefit the Dianova Nicaragua Foundation (www.dianovanicaragua.
org.ni), funding education in vulnerable
communities. It's off busy Av Monumental,
making it relatively safe to walk to at night.

Hotel El Conquistador   HOTEL $$$
(Map p46; ☑ 2222-4789; www.elconquistador
nicaragua.com; del Banco BDF de Plaza Inter, 1c E;
s/d from US$50/60; 🅿✻🛜) One of the few
hotels with any real style in the area, this gat-
ed mansion masks itself as a business hotel,
but the granny quilts and wrought-iron bed-
stands reveal a homespun bed-and-breakfast
at heart. Rooms are big and comfortable and
Nica breakfast spreads are generous.

Hotel Crowne Plaza HOTEL $$$
(Map p46; ☑ 2228-3530; www.ihg.com/crowne-plaza; Plaza Inter, 1c S; r from US$100; ✳🛜🏊) The latest upscale franchise to inhabit the landmark neo-Aztec pyramid by the mall, the Crowne Plaza offers what you'd expect: comfortable and somewhat bland modern rooms, plus an outdoor pool, big buffet breakfast and tepid showers. Book a room with a view of the lake – the higher the floor, the better.

Los Robles & Planes de Altamira

Although this cluster of upscale neighborhoods includes Metrocentro mall and Managua's busiest intersection, walking around these shady side streets is rather nice, plus it's convenient to some of the country's best hotels, bars, restaurants and clubs.

★**La Bicicleta Hostal** HOSTEL $
(Map p50; ☑ 2225-2557; www.labicicletahostal.com; Calle San Juan, Restaurante La Marsellaise, 2½ c E, Villa Santa Fe; dm US$13; r with/without bathroom US$32/40; ✳🛜) 🌱 At this sustainably built hostel in a stellar location, dorms and guest rooms are named after bicycles – try the Tandem for two people, or the Penny Farthing if there's four of you; all are individually styled with inspirational quotes on walls and good beds. There's a lovely hammock-strung garden, guest kitchen, but the biggest shout-out goes to the super-helpful staff.

Managua Backpackers Inn HOSTEL $
(Map p50; ☑ 2267-0006; www.managuahostel.com; 15 Av Sureste, Monte de los Olivos, 1c N, 1c O, ½c N, Casa No 56, Los Robles; dm/s/d from

BOUTIQUE BEAUTY

The modern boutique **Hotel Contempo** (☑ 2264-9160; Carretera a Masaya Km 11, 400m O, Residencial las Praderas; r US$99-151; 🅿✳🛜🏊) is one of the finest in all of Managua. We wish it were a little more centrally located, but the large, individually styled, ultramodern rooms with flat-screens, MP3 docks, funky architecture and cool attention to detail are delightful. The gardens and pool area are equally impressive, as are the French dishes at Restaurante Azul and top-notch service.

US$10/22/30; 🅿✳🛜🏊) In the quiet suburb of Los Robles, this shoestring hostel is minutes away from the Metrocentro mall and endless nightlife and restaurant options. Rooms are basic but popular with a friendly, boisterous crowd that doesn't mind the clammy embrace of an inadequate shower curtain or a little dirt. Perks include a good-sized pool, well-stocked kitchen and plenty of tourist assistance.

★**Casa Lucia** B&B $$
(Map p50; ☑ 8898 9105; https://casaluciamanagua.com; 33 Calle Sureste, frente Parque Los Robles, Planes de Altamira No 1; s/d US$35/45; ✳🛜) In a quiet, walkable neighborhood, this cheery, peach-colored family-run B&B stands out not just for its warm hospitality, but for the its wonderful host, Claudio. A young, bilingual Managuan, he's very passionate about his city and can show you places you're unlikely to discover by yourself. Your morning coffee is likely to be among the best in the country, too.

Elements Boutique Hotel BOUTIQUE HOTEL $$$
(Map p50; ☑ 2270-0052; https://elements-hb.com; Colonial Los Robles, frente Plaza Cuba, Planes de Altamira No 1; s/d US$165/195; 🅿✳🛜🏊) Walk beneath the showpiece chandelier in the lobby, and you find yourself in a tranquil walled space where you can sip a cocktail or woo your sweetie over a fusion dinner, overlooking the vertical garden and infinity pool. The rooms are individually styled after different elements, with bold contemporary art and slate walls. Numerous restaurants are just around the corner.

Hotel Casa Colonial BOUTIQUE HOTEL $$$
(Map p50; ☑ 7967-4883; http://casa-colonial-boutique.hotelsinmanagua.com; Carretera a Masaya Km 4.5, del Restaurante Tip Top 75m O, No 10, Planes de Altamira; s/d from US$55/65; 🅿✳🛜🏊) This intimate, hacienda-style hotel has an attractive arched breakfast patio centered on a babbling fountain. Dark-wood furniture, high ceilings, and heavy wooden beams are the rooms' defining features, along with subtle illumination. Head into the surrounding streets for dining and nightlife.

Real Intercontinental Metrocentro Managua LUXURY HOTEL $$$
(Map p50; www.ihg.com; Carretera a Massaya, frente a Metrocentro; r/ste from US$106/342; 🅿✳🛜🏊) If you have some money to spend and wish to hole up in a place with good

dining on your doorstep, you could do a lot worse than this luxurious behemoth. Perks include four restaurants, a vast swimming pool, sleek, carpeted rooms and polished service.

Hilton Princess Managua Hotel   HOTEL **$$$**
(Map p50; ☎ 2255-5777; www.hilton.com; Carretera a Masaya Km 4.5; s/d/ste from US$157/169/278; P ✸ ☎ ☎) An outdoor swimming pool and 24-hour fitness center are welcome perks at this Hilton branch across the busy highway from the Metrocentro shopping mall.

Hotel Los Robles   HOTEL **$$$**
(Map p50; ☎ 2267-3008; www.hotellosrobles. com; Av Los Robles, Restaurante La Marseillaise, 30m S, Planes de Altamira No 3; r from US$81; ✸ ☎ ☎) This Spanish-colonial-style hotel is an effortless marriage of chintzy bed covers and antique-style wooden furnishings with an attractively landscaped courtyard, centered on a burbling marble fountain. Each guest gets two free drinks and a 15-minute massage, and there are numerous bars nearby.

Hotel Los Pinos   HOTEL **$$$**
(Map p50; ☎ 2270-0761; www.hotellospinos. com.ni; Calle San Juan 314, Gimnasio Hercules, 1c S, ½c E, Reparto San Juan; s/d from US$80/95; P ✸ ☎ ☎) This friendly, family-run hotel is located in a good neighborhood, with numerous restaurants an easy walk away. Rooms are modern and spacious with minimalist decoration, facing a cheerful garden and patio area dominated by a large swimming pool.

Hotel Casa Real   HOTEL **$$$**
(Map p50; ☎ 2278-3838; 26 Calle Sureste, Seminole Plaza Hotel, 3c N, ½c O; s/d from US$65/80; ✸ ☎) On a residential street a short walk from the busy UCA bus terminal, this hotel is lauded by travelers for its personalised service and spacious and modern guest rooms. It's within easy walking distance of Metrocentro, too.

Hotel Brandt's   HOTEL **$$$**
(Map p50; ☎ 2277-1884; www.hotelbrandt.com; Zona Hippos, 1c S, 1c O, Los Robles de San Juan; r from US$75; ✸ ☎) Beyond the vaguely hacienda-meets-Hooters exterior, this hotel in the relatively upscale Los Robles neighborhood has modern, unexciting rooms that sleep up to three people. It's a reliable favorite for business travelers passing through, and the buffet breakfast is above par. It's tucked

away a few blocks behind the Metrocentro shopping mall.

Seminole Plaza Hotel   BUSINESS HOTEL **$$$**
(Map p50; ☎ 2270-0061; www.seminoleplaza.com; Bancentro, Carretera a Masaya, 1c O, 1c S; s/d from US$90/105; P ✸ ☎ ☎) Business class with a quirky baroque touch: gilded accents, flawless concierge service, surprisingly modern rooms (with '70s-style bathrooms), within walking distance from the Metrocentro mall. There's a free airport shuttle service (arguably half the reason to stay here) and a swimming pool.

Hotel Colón   HOTEL **$$$**
(Map p50; ☎ 2278-2490; Edificio BAC, 2c E, Altamira; s/d US$60/70; P ✸ @ ☎) This intimate neocolonial, family-run hotel offers easy access to nearby nightlife in the Zona Rosa. Some English is spoken, the sparsely decorated rooms are comfortable enough and the Nica breakfast is ample.

✖ Eating

Go budget in Barrio Bolonia or upscale in Los Robles, Planes de Altamira or Las Colinas off Carretera a Masaya. Managua has a great dining scene, with everything from cheap and cheerful *fritangas* (grills) to sophisticated fusion. All the upscale shopping malls have a decent food court.

✖ Barrio Bolonia & Around

This neighborhood caters to both business-people and backpackers, so expect a number of *fritangas* and family-run eateries. For a bit of variety, try the food court at Plaza Inter (p59).

Doña Pilar   NICARAGUAN **$**
(Map p46; Tica Bus, 1c O, ½c N, Barrio Bolonia; dishes US$3-5; ☉ 6-9pm Mon-Sat) Doña Pilar's been here for years, and this popular evening *fritanga* is a neighborhood institution, both for its juicy, crispy BBQ chicken and the range of ever-so-slightly greasy tacos and enchiladas. It's a good introduction to typical Nicaraguan cuisine, with huge side servings of *gallo pinto* (rice and beans), chopped pickled cabbage and plantain chips.

Licuados Ananda   VEGETARIAN **$**
(Map p46; ☎ 2228-4140; Paseo Salvador Allende, frente Estatua de Montoya, El Carmen; mains US$2-5; ☉ 8am-3pm Mon-Sat; ☑) Enjoy freshly prepared vegetarian plates and a wide range

of *licuados* (fruit and veggie juices and smoothies) on this spacious patio overlooking lush gardens. There's a lunch buffet from 11am to 3pm.

Cafetín Mirna
NICARAGUAN **$**

(Map p46; Tica Bus, 1c O, 1c S, Barrio Bolonia; mains US$2-5; ⊙8am-5pm Mon-Sat) Come here for a big breakfast with fluffy pancakes, fabulous fresh juices and a good lunch buffet, too – it's a local tradition.

Panadería Cafetín Tonalli
BAKERY **$**

(Map p46; Tica Bus, 2c E, ½c S, Barrio Bolonia; dishes US$2-5; ⊙8am-2pm Mon-Sat) If you're jonesing for some *pan integral* (wholewheat bread), this simple bakery and cafe, run by a women's co-op, is the place to be. The fresh-baked treats are also good to grab for a long bus ride out of town (it's near the Tica Bus terminal).

Los Robles, Planes de Altamira & Carretera a Masaya

Metrocentro (p59) and Galerias Santo Domingo (p59) malls both have large food courts. There is a good mix of family-run *fritangas* and international offerings in Los Robles and Planes de Altamira, as well as hip upscale offerings in Las Colinas, further south along the Carretera a Masaya. It helps to have your own car (or a good taxi driver) to navigate between the neighborhoods.

★ Asados Doña Tania
NICARAGUAN **$**

(Map p50; ☑2270-0747; www.facebook.com/asadosdonatania; Hotel Colón, 1c S, ½c O, Los Robles; mains US$3-5; ⊙4:30-10:30pm Sun-Fri) Come evening, Managuans make their way to this *fritanga* temple where Doña Tania has perfected her craft over 20 years. There is only one thing worth ordering: strips of marinated meat, smoky and seared and bursting with flavor, plus sides of *gallo pinto, ensalada criolla* (salad of onions, peppers and tomatoes), fried plantain, and fried cheese. Portions are large enough to get you through a siege.

★ De Muerte Lenta
ICE CREAM **$**

(Map p50; ☑8272-9877; www.facebook.com/demuertelenta.ni; frente Parque Altamira, Planes de Altamira; ⊙11:30am-7:30pm) This diminutive ice-cream stall kills you softly with its 12 flavors of ice-cream on a stick. It's some of the best ice cream you'll ever have; we're particularly partial to mint with brownie chunks.

La Ventecita
NICARAGUAN **$**

(Map p50; ☑2278-3307; 32 Calle Sureste, Códice Espacio Cultural, 1c E, Planes de Altamira; nacatamal US$1; ⊙7am-9pm Thu-Sat, 7am-1pm Sun) During the week this is a mom-and-pop grocery store, but from Thursday to Sunday, this is where Managua's student population comes for one thing: the city's superlative *nacatamal:* a moreish mix of corn dough, annatto-flavored chicken, congo chillies, tomatoes, onions and olives, steamed in a plantain leaf.

★ Terraza Peruana
PERUVIAN **$$**

(Map p50; ☑2278 0013; de la Pasteleria Sampson, 100m N; mains US$5-12; ⊙noon-11pm Tue-Sun) Set on a cool front balcony overlooking a leafy side street, refined Terraza's authentic Peruvian menu takes you from coastal *ceviches* (marinated seafood) and *tiraditos* (Japanese-Peruvian raw fish), to high Andean cuisine. Classics such as *anticuchos de corazón* (ox-heart skewers) and *suspiro limeño* (dulce de leche and merengue-based dessert) are present and correct. Don't miss a cocktail from the pisco list.

Ola Verde
INTERNATIONAL **$$**

(☑2276-2652; www.facebook.com/olaverdenicaragua; Carretera a Masaya Km 8, primera entrada a Las Colinas, 1c E; mains US$5-10; ⊙8am-10:30pm Mon-Sat, 11am-9pm Sun; ❋ 🛜 🖈) In affluent Las Colinas, Ola Verde falls squarely into the 'hipster eatery' category but without flogging you with the concept of wellness in a tiresome fashion. Dishes such as gazpacho verde, quesadillas and beef carpaccio are executed with flair and attention to appearance and flavor, and there's a lovely garden area for sipping your organic fruit juice or smoothie.

Cafe Las Marias
CAFE **$$**

(☑2231-2524; www.facebook.com/lasmariascafe; Uniplaza Las Colinas, primera entrada, 3c E; sandwiches US$6-8; ⊙7am-8pm Mon-Fri, 8am-8pm Sat, 8am-6pm Sun; ❋ 🛜 🖈) At this bang-on-trend cafe you can peruse the map of Nicaragua's coffee-growing regions while deciding which way you want your superlative brew: chemex, V60, aeropress, cold press... There's a decent supporting cast of zucchini muffins, imaginative sandwiches and salads, too.

Cocina Doña Haydee
NICARAGUAN **$$**

(Map p50; ☑2270-0426; www.lacocina.com.ni; Carretera a Masaya Km 4.5, Casino Pharaoh, ½c S, 1c O; mains US$5-10; ⊙7am-10pm) This traditional Nicaraguan eatery does classic dishes, well presented and carefully prepared, from *gallo pinto* (rice and beans) and *guiso de chilote* (cheese soup with baby corn) to steak with all the trimmings. There are takeaway locations in the food court at Plaza Inter and Metrocentro shopping malls, too.

Predio Food Park
FOOD TRUCK **$$**

(www.elprediofoodpark.com; primera entrada a Las Colinas, de las gasolineras, 300m E; dishes US$4-7; ⊙3-10pm Wed-Fri, noon-10pm Sat & Sun; 🖨) Las Colinas' latest hip hangout is this outdoor space decked out with fairy lights, where food trucks entice passersby with gourmet burgers, shawarma, falafel, tacos, *ceviche* and artisanal ice-cream. The stage hosts anything from live music to puppet shows for kids.

Casa del Café
CAFE **$$**

(Map p50; www.casadelcafe.com.ni; Lacmiel, 1c E, ½c S, Altamira; mains US$5-10; ⊙8am-7pm; 🌐🤍) One of the main locations of Nicaragua's popular coffee chain. Grab a table on the spacious and airy upstairs balcony and you'll find it hard to leave. All the standard and gourmet coffee options are available (including a very satisfying frozen *mochaccino),* plus pastries, sandwiches, salads and a couple of breakfast options.

La Hora del Taco
MEXICAN **$$**

(Map p50; ☑2270-6712; www.facebook.com/restaurantelahoradeltaco; Monte de los Olivos, 1c N; mains US$4.50-9; ⊙noon-midnight Mon-Sat) This sprawling Mexican bar and restaurant has a wide-ranging menu that includes standards like nachos and fajitas, plus a few southern Mexican favorites like *cochinita pibil* (suckling pig).

★ Don Cándido
STEAK **$$$**

(Map p50; ☑2277-2485; https://restaurantedoncandido.com; de donde fue el Chaman 75 vrs al Sur, 15 Av Sureste, Los Robles; steaks US$18-35; ⊙noon-10pm Mon-Fri, 2pm-midnight Sat & Sun; 🌐🤍) All heavy wooden beams, exposed brick walls and contemporary art, this smart steakhouse means business. Choose from a sizable list of cuts of meat – from the beautifully grilled sirloin with crisped ribbons of fat, the T-bone and New York steak to short ribs and baby back ribs. The wine list spans the world but is particularly strong on Spanish tipples.

TRAVELING WITH CHILDREN IN MANAGUA

Parts of Managua are kid-friendly. Área Monumental, in particular, has wide footpaths, squares popular with families, plus several parks with play areas. Parque Luis Velásquez has fountains for kids to splash in and there's a bona fide waterpark along the Paseo Salvador Allende on the *malecón*. There's a good number of highchair-equipped restaurants in Altamira and Las Colinas, and some high-end hotels even have portable cribs.

Marea Alta
SEAFOOD **$$$**

(Map p50; ☑2278-2459; www.mareaalta.net; del Hotel Los Robles, 1c S, Planes de Altamira; mains US$10-30; ⊙11am-midnight) One of the more highly respected seafood restaurants in town, with white linen service and a chance to hobnob with well-heeled Managuans. Some of the dishes work better than others: the live *conchas negras* (black clams) wrestle your tongue into submission and the lobster thermidor sauce is somewhat gloopy, but we like the seared tuna tataki and steamed garlicky clams.

La Marseillaise
FRENCH **$$$**

(Map p50; ☑2277-0224; www.facebook.com/lamarseillaise.restaurante; Calle Principal Residencial Los Robles, 3 Etapa, Casa No 5, Seminole Hotel, 4c S, Planes de Altamira; mains US$12-20; ⊙noon-3pm & 6-11pm Mon-Sat) The gold standard in Nicaraguan fine dining has tastefully art-bedecked walls, outstanding wine pairings and authentic French cuisine. Dress nicely and make reservations.

Intermezzo del Bosque
INTERNATIONAL **$$$**

(☑2271-1428; www.intermezzodelbosque.com; del Colegio Centroamérica, 5km S, Urbanización Intermezzo del Bosque; mains US$15-25; ⊙5-11pm Tue-Sat, 1-6pm Sun) Light years away from the bustle of downtown Managua, this verdant hillside terrace, strung with gently twinkling lights, seems to recall a mythologized age of gentlemen in open-top carriages, romancing ladies by candlelight. Your fellow diners at this converted hacienda with an international menu are likely to be well-heeled Managuans out on dates, or families enjoying Sunday brunch.

BELLO HORIZONTE DISCOS

Dubbed 'the heart of Nicaribeña,' Bello Horizonte is home to the largest concentration of Caribbean-descended Nicaraguans in Managua. Clubs out here have a predictably Caribbean-coast flavor, with a heavier reggae, soca and *punta* (a traditional Garifuna dance involving much hip movement) influence than their counterparts down south. This is a sketchy area and you will be patted down before being allowed to enter a club; it's a really good idea for visitors to go with locals rather than by themselves.

Casa de Los Nogueras   EUROPEAN $$$

(Map p50; ☑ 2278-2506; www.lacasadelosnogueras.com; Av Principal Los Robles 17; mains US$14-25; ☉ noon-3pm & 7pm-late Mon-Sat) One of the most elegant restaurants in town, this cozy European bistro has delightful art, a wonderful garden out back for alfresco eating and top-notch but overly formal service. This is where you can rub shoulders with Managua's movers and shakers as they tuck into escargots and steak. Reserve ahead and dress smartly.

🍷 Drinking & Nightlife

Managua has several nightlife clusters, from the cheaper dive bars in Barrio Bolonia, to the upmarket bars around the Metrocentro mall and inside nearby hotels. There's a good mix of craft beer and cocktail bars along Av Principal Los Robles in the Los Robles/Planes de Altamira neighborhoods, and a few more options in upmarket Las Colinas.

There's some terrific coffee in Las Colinas and further east in Barrio San Cristóbal.

★ DeLaFinca Cafe   COFFEE

(☑ 2252-8974; www.delafincanicaragua.com; Parque El Dorado, costado Sureste; ☉ 7am-8pm Mon-Fri, 8am-7pm Sat & Sun; 🐾) No self-respecting coffee connoisseur should miss out on visiting this altar to the coffee bean, whose owner comes from generations of coffee farmers and who has perfected *viñedo* – a novel coffee bean fermentation method. Come here to buy beans and to sample the best of Nicaragua's single origin coffees, each prepared using a method that best suits each one.

★ Estación Central   CRAFT BEER

(Map p50; ☑ 2225-3274; Av Gabriel Cardinal, ado Hospital Monte España, 2½c N, Planes de Altamira; ☉ 4-10pm Mon & Tue, 4pm-midnight Wed-Fri, noon-1am Sat, noon-10pm Sun) The pick of the neighborhood bars, hip and relaxed Estación Central is your first port of call for the best range of Nicaraguan craft beers, from the original Moropotente brews to Erdmann's, Pinolera, Campo and La Porteña. There are quite a few Belgian beers also, plus decent bar food, served to the tune of some ambient beats.

Art Factory   COCKTAIL BAR

(Map p50; ☑ 8126-3428; Marea Alta, ½c E, Planes de Altamira; ☉ 4pm-late; 🐾) The brainchild of a young French entrepreneur, Art Factory wears many hats and we like all of them. It's a swanky yet chilled-out space for an intimate tête-à-tête over a cocktail overlooking the greenery-filled patio, it hosts changing art and photography exhibitions, and it lures foodies with its Nicaragua-meets-Mediterranean fusion.

Garabato   CLUB

(Map p50; ☑ 2278-2944; www.facebook.com/elgarabatoo; Seminole Plaza Hotel, 2½c S, Los Robles; ☉ noon-11pm Mon-Sat) Fairy lights are strung around this popular club, where local students take to the alfresco stage to the *cumbia* beats or the interesting salsa-Macarena fusion. The kitchen serves carefully prepared versions of traditional Nica dishes like *vigorón* (steamed yucca and pork rinds), *nacatamales* (banana-leaf-wrapped bundles of cornmeal, meat, vegetables and herbs) and *repocheta* (cheese-stuffed tortillas).

Spanglish Craft Cocktail Bar   COCKTAIL BAR

(Map p50; ☑ 8191-2615; www.facebook.com/barspanglish; Av Gabriel Cardenal, Restaurante La Marseillaise, ½c S, 30m O, Los Robles; ☉ 5pm-late) Let's start with what's important: the cocktails here are seriously good and served by expert mixologists. The 'Rum Old Fashioned' arrives in a smoked dome and the lemongrass daiquiri is delicate and moreish. However, at US$4 to US$7 apiece, they're also out of reach of most Managuans, and as a result, the clientele either comprises travelers or is largely absent.

Reef   BAR

(☑ 8913-5787; Galerias Santo Domingo; ☉ 6pm-3am Wed-Sat) This popular bar and lounge in the emerging *zona viva,* the nightlife zone behind the Santo Domingo mall, is a favorite pre-dance spot for scenesters.

El Grillo   BAR

(Map p46; Intur, ½c N, Barrio Bolonia; ⊙noon-late)
There are a few little outdoor bars like this
in the area, but this one consistently gets
a good crowd. A range of snacks and more
substantial meals (mains US$3 to US$6) are
on the menu and the music volume is con-
versation-friendly.

Tabú   GAY

(Map p46; ☑8580-8052; Intur, 100m S, Barrio
Bolonia; ⊙9pm-late Wed-Sat) One of the few
gay bars with any longevity in town, Tabú's
dance floor gets going on weekends (cover
charge varies by night).

☆ Entertainment

There are dozens of venues around town that
occasionally have live music, folkloric dance,
alternative theater, poetry readings and other cultural offerings. Your best bet for Managua event listings is Facebook. You can also
check Thursday editions of *La Prensa* and *El
Nuevo Diario* and take a walk through the
UCA (p47) to see what's on.

Cinema

Alhambra Cine VIP   CINEMA

(www.cinemas.com.ni; Camino Oriente; tickets
US$8) An upscale movie theater showing
Hollywood blockbusters.

Cinema Plaza Inter   CINEMA

(Map p46; Plaza Inter; tickets US$3-4) Close to
Barrio Bolonia. Mostly mainstream Hollywood films are screened with subtitles.

Metrocentro Cinemark   CINEMA

(Map p50; www.cinemarkca.com; Carretera a
Masaya, Metrocentro Mall; tickets US$3) This big-
ger-is-better mall has six screens and shows
blockbuster movies with English subtitles.

Live Music

Art Café   LIVE MUSIC

(☑8880-7705; www.facebook.com/artcafeni; Parque Las Palmas, contiguo universidad UDO; ⊙hours
vary) Always worth a look, this bohemian little space in front of Parque Las Palmas hosts
poetry and open-mic nights on Wednesday,
electronica DJs on Thursday and other un-
derground-type events the rest of the week.

Ruta Maya   LIVE MUSIC

(Map p46; ☑2268-0698; www.facebook.com/ruta.
maya; Estadio Denis Martínez, 1½c O; cover US$1-5;
⊙9am-5pm Mon-Thu, 9am-5pm & 6-11pm Fri & Sat)
Look around for flyers (or check their Facebook page) for happenings at this thatch-
roofed cultural center. You get everything
from Bee Gees cover bands to Caribbean *palo de mayo* (Afro-Caribbean dance
music) to *son nicaragüense* (traditional
Nicaraguan folk music). Barbecued meat is
the specialty on the menu, and dinner shows
are worth booking ahead for.

Ron Kon Rolas   LIVE MUSIC

(Map p50; ☑2299-0996; www.facebook.com/ron.
kon.rolas.oficial; de Seminole Plaza Hotel, 2½c S,
Planes de Altamira; ⊙5pm-1am Sun & Mon, 2pm-
1am Tue-Thu, to 3am Fri & Sat) This dark, cave-
like hangout of local metalheads regularly
hosts local live bands. Expect classic rock as

MANAGUA ENTERTAINMENT

SAFE TAXI TRAVEL

Express kidnappings – where a taxi driver holds the passenger hostage by knifepoint
and then takes them to ATMs around town until their bank is depleted – are occasionally
reported in Managua, as well as in Granada, Masaya and San Jorge. Here are a few tips
to stay safe.

Take radio taxis with a bubble on top. There are thousands of illegal cabs in Managua. The ones with the bubble on the roof and/or red plates are considered safer. There
should be a name tag with the driver's information on the dashboard. These are registered with a company, and can be ordered by phone.

Ask your hotel to call you a cab. There are reports of people being kidnapped after a
friendly stranger on the street helped them hail a cab.

Take cabs after dark. As a general rule, if you see women and kids walking around, you
are probably safe to walk there. Don't risk even a short two-block walk at night.

Agree to a price before getting in. Also be sure to ask if you will be going as a *colectivo*
(collective that stops to pick up other passengers) or *privado* (private).

Make sure the cab takes you where you want to go. Often cabbies will say a certain
hotel is closed just to take you to a spot where they get a commission.

well, especially during the Wednesday jams. DJs take the stage some nights, with the enthusiastic audience lubricated with plenty of beer.

Sports

Estadio Denis Martínez SPECTATOR SPORT
(Map p46; Av Monumental) The national baseball stadium is absolutely packed between mid-November and early April, when Nicaragua's four professional teams, including the Managua Bóers, compete in the national championships. Get stats, schedules and more at the Liga de Beisbol Profesional (www.lnbp.com.ni) website.

Theater

Teatro Nacional Rubén Darío THEATER
(Map p44; ☑ 2266-3630; www.tnrubendario.gob.ni; Av Bolívar, Área Monumental; ⊙ hours vary) One of the few Managua buildings to survive the 1972 earthquake, this 'temple to Nicaraguan art and culture' often has big-name international offerings on the main stage. It's worth trying to catch some experimental jazz or performance art in the smaller Sala Experimental Pilar Aguirre. Prices vary.

INCH PERFORMING ARTS
(Instituto Nicaragüense de Cultura Hispanica; ☑ 2276-0733; www.facebook.com/INCHNICA; Av del Campo 40-42, Las Colinas; ⊙ 8am-5pm Mon-Fri) In the very ritzy hill suburb of Las Colinas to the south of town, this center hosts some of the city's best cultural events, including cinema, theater, art and photography exhibitions, concerts and art-themed workshops.

La Sala de Teatro Justo Rufino Garay THEATER
(☑ 2266-3714; www.rufinos.org; Estatua de Montoya, 3c O, 20m N; tickets US$5-8; ⊙ hours vary) Fans of alternative theater should check out the program at this small, not-for-profit theater space, which specializes in experimental, contemporary works – often with a political bent. Plays are generally staged on Friday and Saturday nights.

🛈 Shopping

There are some excellent places to shop, mostly dotted around Altamira, Los Robles and Las Colinas, from Nicaraguan designer wear and gourmet chocolate to cigars, fairtrade gifts and bespoke wooden furniture. Some of the art galleries sell some of their works.

★**Nostalgia de Nicaragua Cigar** CIGARS
(Map p50; ☑ 2270-1450; Carretera a Masaya, frente Casino Pharaoh; ⊙ 10am-10pm Mon-Sat, 10am-4pm Sun) Step inside the humedor to choose from Nicaragua's finest cigars, handrolled in Mombacho and Estelí. Look out for Joya de Nicaragua, Padrón, AJ Fernández, Don Pepín García and other top brands. You can sample the wares in the attached lounge.

Crafted for Connaisseurs GIFTS & SOUVENIRS
(Map p50; ☑ 2278-1478; www.facebook.com/craftednica; Carretera a Masaya Km 6.5, contiguo a Café las Flores; ⊙ 11am-9pm Mon-Sat) Mostly a gourmet food store, Crafted for Connaisseurs sells boxes of handmade Nicaraguan Momotombo chocolates, superb Cielo Isla coffee, plus other single origin coffees, and has an excellent wine selection. There are also some premium cigars for sale and some evenings (Thursday to Saturday) there's a short and sweet tapas menu to go with wine tastings.

Esperanza En Acción ARTS & CRAFTS
(☑ 8388-2844; www.esperanzaenaccion.org; Casa de Ben Linder, de la Estatua Monseñor Lezcano, 3c S, ½c E, Barrio Monseñor Lezcano; ⊙ 9am-5pm Mon-Fri) 🖉 An excellent selection of fair trade crafts from all over Nicaragua, made by 31 groups of local artisans. There is exquisite pottery, woven bags, jewelry, single origin coffee, toys and weavings. Proceeds go to the artisans themselves and help some of the most economically disadvantaged corners of the country.

Simplemente Madera ARTS & CRAFTS
(☑ 8884-8146; de los semáforos del Club Terraza, 4c O, Villa Fontana Sur; ⊙ 9am-5pm Mon-Sat) Simplemente Madera ('Simply Wood') makes gorgeous bespoke furniture out of sustainable Nicaraguan wood. It can help you with shipping your acquisitions home.

Fabrica de Chocolate Momotombo CHOCOLATE
(Map p50; ☑ 2270-2094; www.momotombochocolatefactory.com; Plaza Altamira, de la Pastelería Sampson, 1c al Sur, Planes de Altamira; ⊙ 7:30am-7pm Mon-Fri, 9am-7pm Sat) These artisanal bean-to-bar chocolate makers create sweet concoctions using Nicaragua's finest cacao. Chocolate beverages, hand-crafted chocolates and gift boxes for sale.

Frontera Books BOOKS

(Map p50; ☑ 2270-2345; www.facebook.com/
fronterabooks; Av Principal Los Robles, Enitel Villa
Fontana, 200m N; ☺ 9am-6pm Mon-Sat) This
bookstore has the best bilingual selection of
books by local and international authors, as
well as maps and magazines.

Niní Fashion Style FASHION & ACCESSORIES

(Map p50; ☑ 8872-3000; www.facebook.com/nini
fashionstyleni; Av de las Naciones Unidas, Metrocentro; ☺ 9am-6pm Mon-Sat) Women's high-end
fashion by Nicaraguan designer and fashion
blogger Norma López.

Jincho FASHION & ACCESSORIES

(☑ 2276-1285; www.soyjincho.com; Carretera a
Masaya Km 4.5, contiguo al Casino Pharaoh, Las Colinas; ☺ 10am-7pm Mon-Fri, 9am-5pm Sat) Modern, urban Nica design for men and women.

Mercado Roberto Huembes MARKET

(Pista de la Solidaridad; ☺ 7:30am-5pm) Next to
the southbound bus terminal, this sprawling
beast of a market offers an authentic slice of
Managuan life. There are labyrinthine rows
of stalls heaped with fresh produce and *curandero* (healer) herbal wares, a pungent
meat and fish section, slippery with discard-
ed scales and entrails, plus a selection of less-
than-amazing Nicaraguan souvenirs – decent
enough coffee, masks, pottery, cheap cigars.

Librería Hispamer BOOKS

(www.hispamer.com.ni; Contiguo Pista de la UNAN;
☺ 8am-6pm Mon-Fri, 9am-noon Sat) This bookstore on the premises of UNAN campus has
a good selection of Nicaraguan and Latin
American literature, history and poetry.

Plaza España MALL

(Pista Benjamin Zeledon; ☺ 8am-7pm Mon-Fri, to
6pm Sat) A shopping mall with high-street
fashion, a decent supermarket and a food
court.

Plaza Inter MALL

(Map p46; www.plazaintermall.com.ni; Av Bolívar;
☺ 11am-9pm) Adjacent to Barrio Bolonia, it's
convenient, with a cinema (with subtitled
movies), lots of discount shops, Colonia supermarket, a couple of department stores
and a solid food court that's bustling with
Nicaraguan families at mealtimes.

Galerías Santo Domingo MALL

(www.galerias.com.ni; Carretera a Masaya Km 8;
☺ 10am-8pm) See and be seen at the discos,
eateries and shops of Managua's most upscale mall.

Metrocentro MALL

(Map p50; www.metrocentro.com; Carretera a
Masaya; ☺ 8am-9pm) Upscale mall with restaurants, high street fashion and a good
food court.

ℹ Information

DANGERS & ANNOYANCES

Managua has a reputation for being a dangerous
city, and with fairly good reason. But by using
common sense and general caution, you can
avoid problems.
- Don't flash expensive items.
- Look at the map before venturing out on a
walk.
- Make ATM transactions during daylight
hours.
- Ask your hotel or hostel to call you a taxi
instead of hailing one in the street.
- Carry only as much money as you'll need for
the day.

EMERGENCY

Ambulance (Cruz Roja)	☑ 128
Fire	☑ 115 (emergency), ☑ 2222-6406
Police	☑ 118 (emergency), ☑ 2249-5714

INTERNET ACCESS

Free wi-fi can be found in the vast majority of
accommodations and, increasingly, at cafes and
restaurants.

MEDICAL SERVICES

Managua has scores of pharmacies – some open
24 hours (just knock) – and the nation's best
hospitals.
Hospital Alemán-Nicaragüense (☑ 2249-
3368; Carretera Norte Km 6) Modern equipment and German-speaking staff.
Hospital Bautista (☑ 2264-9020; www.
hospital-bautista.com; Casa Ricardo Morales
Avilés, 2c S, 1½c E, Barrio Largaespada) Some
English-speaking staff and modern facilities.
Hospital Metropolitano Vivian Pellas
(☑ 2255-6900; www.hospitalvivianpellas.com;
Carretera a Masaya Km 9.75) Best hospital in
the country, with English-speaking staff.

MONEY

Managua has scores of banks and ATMs, most
on the Visa/Plus system. BAC, with machines at
Metrocentro mall, Managua International Airport
and Plaza España, accepts MasterCard/Cirrus
debit cards and gives US dollars and córdobas.

Any bank can change US dollars and many businesses accept them.

TELEPHONE

You can purchase a chip to make your cell-phone function on local networks, or make phone calls from your hotel. There's a handy **Claro** (⊙8am-7pm) outlet inside the Managua Airport building.

TOURIST INFORMATION

Intur Central (Nicaraguan Institute of Tourism; Map p46; ☑2254-5191; www.visitanicaragua. com; Hotel Crowne Plaza, 1c S, 1c O; ⊙8am-5pm Mon-Fri) Flagship tourism office with heaps of flyers. There's another office in the international terminal at the airport.

Marena Central (Ministry of the Environment & Natural Resources; ☑2263-2830; Carretera Norte Km 12.5) Bring ID to the inconveniently located headquarters if you want to get info on most of Nicaragua's 82 protected areas.

ℹ Getting There & Away

AIR

Managua International Airport (MGA; www. eaai.com.ni; Carretera Norte Km 11) is a small, manageable airport located about 30 to 45 minutes from most hotels. **Intur** (☑2263-3174; www.intur.gob.ni; ⊙8am-10pm) has an office inside the international terminal, next to the luggage belt in the arrivals area, where English-speaking staff can recommend hotels, confirm flights and share flyers.

The smaller, more chaotic domestic terminal is adjacent to the main building.

Departures to the USA include flights to Houston with United Airlines (www.united.com), Miami and Dallas with American Airlines (www. americanairlines.com) and Fort Lauderdale with Spirit Airlines (www.spirit.com). Copa Airlines (www.copaair.com) serves San José, Costa Rica, Panama City and Guatemala City, while Avianca (www.avianca.com) flies to San Salvador.

Domestic carrier La Costeña (www.lacostena. com.ni) has regular service to Bluefields, the Corn Islands, Siuna, Isla Ometepe, San Carlos, Río San Juan, Bonanza, Puerto Cabezas and Waspán.

BUS

Managua is the main transportation hub for the country, with several major national bus and van terminals, plus a handful of international bus lines (most grouped in Barrio Martha Quezada).

Tica Bus (Map p46; ☑8739-5505; www. ticabus.com; 9 Calle Suroeste, Barrio Bolonia) is located in a terminal in the heart of Barrio Martha Quezada and has a number of services (see box International Tica Bus Services).

NATIONAL BUS SERVICES FROM MANAGUA

DESTINATION	COST (US$)	DURATION (HR)	DEPARTURES	FREQUENCY	LEAVES FROM
Boaco	2.20	3	4am-6:30pm	every 15min	Mayoreo
Carazo (serving Diriamba & Jinotepe)	1.40	1	4:30am-6:20pm	every 20min	Lewites
Chinandega/El Viejo	2.70	3	5am-6pm	every 30min	Lewites
Chinandega minibus	3	2	4am-6pm	when full	Lewites
El Astillero	3	3	3pm	daily	Huembes
El Tránsito	1.20	1½	11:15am, 12:40pm, 2pm	3 daily	Lewites
Estelí	3	2	5:45am-5:45pm	hourly	Mayoreo
Granada	0.75	1	4am-6pm	every 15min	Huembes
Granada minibus	1.25	1	6am-8pm	when full	UCA
Jinotega	3.50	4	4am-5:30pm	hourly	Mayoreo
Jinotepe minibus	1.15	1	5am-8pm	when full	UCA
Juigalpa	2	4	3:15am-10pm	every 20min	Mayoreo
La Paz Centro	1.60	1½	6:15am-8pm	every 30min	Lewites
León expreso (via New Hwy & La Paz Centro)	1.85	1½	10am-6:30pm	every 2hr	Lewites
León ordinario (via Old Hwy)	1.50	2	5am-7pm	every 20min	Lewites

INTERNATIONAL TICA BUS SERVICES

DESTINATION	COST (US$)	DURATION (HR)	FREQUENCY
Antigua, Guatemala	77-89	33	5am, 11am
Guatemala City, Guatemala	63-74	30	5am, 11am
Panama City, Panama	75-107	34	6am, 7am, noon, 1pm
San José, Costa Rica	29-44	10	6am, 7am, noon, 1pm
San Pedro Sula, Honduras	46	12	5am
San Salvador, El Salvador	40-52	11	5am, 11am
Tegucigalpa, Honduras	30	7	5am

International Buses

In addition to the Tica Bus services there is the following:

Transnica (Map p50; ☑ 2270-3133; www.transnica.com; Metrocentro, 300m N, 50m E) Serves Costa Rica and Honduras, and has offices over on the other side of the laguna.

Costa Rica (US$29, nine hours, four daily at 5am, 7am, 10am & noon) To San José. There's also a luxury bus (US$38) that leaves daily at 1pm.

Honduras (US$30, 10 hours, one daily at 11:30am) For Tegucigalpa.

Transporte del Sol (Map p46; ☑ 2422-5000; frente Tica Bus, Barrio Bolonia) Daily buses leaving for San Salvador (US$50, 13 hours, two daily at 3am & 10am), Guatemala City (US$70, six hours, one daily at 3am) and San José (US$35, 9½ hours, daily at noon).

Central Line (Map p46; ☑ 2254-5431; www.transportescentralline.com; Rotonda Hugo Chávez Frías, 1c S, 1½c O) Offers one daily bus to San José, Costa Rica (US$29, eight hours), with stops in Granada and Rivas.

National Buses & Minivans

Buses leave from three main places: **Mercado Roberto Huembes** (Pista de la Solidaridad) for Granada, Masaya and southwest Nicaragua; **Mercado Israel Lewites** (semáforos de Mercado Israel Lewites, 1c N) for León and the northern Pacific; and **Mercado Mayoreo** (frente Aduana Managua) for the Caribbean coast and the

DESTINATION	COST (US$)	DURATION (HR)	DEPARTURES	FREQUENCY	LEAVES FROM
León minibus	2.75	1½	4am-6pm	when full	Lewites
León minibus	2.75	1½	5am-9:15pm	when full	UCA
Masatepe minibus	1.10	1	6:30am-6:30pm	every 20min	Huembes
Masaya	0.50	1	5:30am-9pm	every 30min	Huembes
Masaya minibus	0.90	½	6am-9pm	when full	UCA
Matagalpa	2.25	2¾	3am-6pm	hourly	Mayoreo
Mateare	0.30	40min	5:50am-6:30pm	every 2hr	Lewites
Naindame	1	1½	11am-3:30pm	every 20min	Huembes
Ocotal	4.25	3½	5am-5pm	hourly	Mayoreo
Pochomil/Masachapa	1.30-1.60	2	6am-7pm	every 20min	Lewites
Río Blanco	5	4	9:15am-12:15pm	hourly	Mayoreo
Rivas expreso	3.25	1½	8:30am-1pm	6 daily	Huembes
Rivas ordinario	2	2	4am-6pm	every 30min	Huembes
San Carlos	7.50	9	5am-6pm	6 daily	Mayoreo
San Juan del Sur expreso	3.25	2½	9:30am-5:30pm	6 daily	Huembes
San Marcos minibus	1	1	4am-6pm	when full	Huembes
Somoto	4	4	5am-6pm	8 daily	Mayoreo
Ticuantepe minibus	0.40	40min	4am-6pm	when full	Huembes

northern highlands. Some also leave from the Mercado Oriental, mainly to rural destinations not covered here.

It's faster, more comfortable and a bit more expensive to take **minivans from UCA** (Map p50; frente UCA), pronounced 'ooka', or *expreso* (express) versus *ordinario* (regular) services.

Shuttle Buses

There are established shuttle pickups from Managua Airport with the likes of Adelante Express (p129), Casa Oro (p129) and Bigfoot Hostel (p152) that whisk travelers straight off to Granada (US$25), León (US$15), San Juan del Sur (US$25) and other popular destinations along the west coast. Hostels in Managua also offer direct shuttle services to all of these destinations. All remote hotels and surfing lodges offer pickup from Managua Airport.

CAR

Driving in Managua presents the usual challenges of driving in a big city, but it's perfectly manageable as long as you have a good GPS (Maps. me app is very useful) and you know where you're going. Parking is not usually a problem, either. International car rental companies have offices at Managua airport and around the city.

Alamo (☑2298-0030; www.alamonicaragua. com; Managua Airport; ⊗6am-9pm)

Avis (☑2233-3011; www.avis.com; Managua Airport; ⊗6am-9pm)

Budget (☑2278-9504; www.budget.com.ni; Managua Airport)

Easy Rent-a-car (Map p50; ☑2270-0654; www.easyrentacar.com.ni; Rotonda Santo Domingo, 700m S; ⊗8am-7pm)

Hertz (☑2233-1237; www.hertz.com.ni; Managua Airport; ⊗6am-9pm)

Lugo (Map p46; ☑2266-4477; www.lugorenta car.com.ni; de la Estatua Montoya, 300m S; ⊗8am-7pm)

🔂 Getting Around

BUS

Local buses are frequent and crowded and unless you actually live in Managua or are a serious penny-pincher, these convoluted local bus routes with unmarked bus shelters are not

> ### ⓘ PACK A PICNIC
>
> There are casual eateries on or near the beach in Pochomil and Masachapa, most specializing in seafood. If staying anywhere other than the ecolodge in San Diego, it's worth bringing cooking ingredients/snacks from the city, as eating options are limited.

useful to travelers. Backpackers prefer to spend a bit more on a taxi to travel around the city.

CAR & MOTORCYCLE

Take care and stay vigilant if driving in Managua at night – even if you have a rental car, consider getting a taxi, and make sure your car is in a guarded lot. At research time, navigating Managua after dark by car was highly inadvisable due to road blocks.

TAXI

➡ Most taxis in Managua are *colectivos*, which pick up passengers as they go. There are also more expensive private taxis based at the airport, shopping malls, Mercado Roberto Huembes and other places. These are safer, but regular taxis also always congregate close by.

➡ Licensed taxis have red plates and the driver's ID above the dash; if yours doesn't, you're in a pirate taxi. This is probably OK, but don't go to the ATM, and beware of scams no matter what kind of taxi you're in.

➡ At night, take only licensed taxis – there has been an increase in reports of taxi drivers robbing passengers after dark.

AROUND MANAGUA

Managua might not be a city you'd like to linger in for long, but there are a few more attractive destinations within easy reach of the capital. The beach towns of Masachapa and Pochomil are laid-back getaways on the Pacific coast, San Diego is a surfers' village with world-class waves, while Montelimar has a resort that brings a steady stream of beachgoers on a well-beaten path from the airport. Elsewhere, just south of the city, Reserva Natural Chocoyero-El Brujo is a green mini paradise famed for its waterfalls and lively parakeet population.

Masachapa & Pochomil

An easy day trip from Managua, the twin villages of Masachapa and Pochomil are so close together that they might as well be one. They tend to attract weekenders from the capital and a contingent of surfer visitors. A handful of bars, hotels and restaurants are dotted along the sleepy, unpaved streets. Some will rent surfboards.

⊙ Sights

Centro Turistico Pochomil   BEACH
(car/pedestrian US$1/free; 🅿) This is where you find ample visitor parking and access

Around Managua

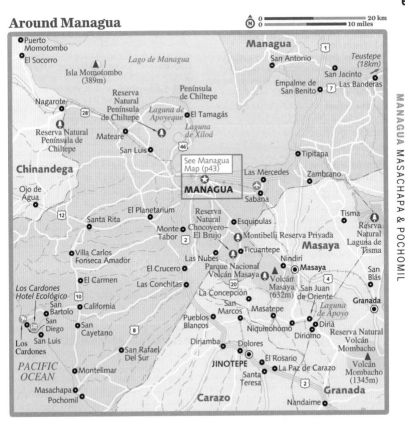

to Pochomil's dense cluster of beach restaurants and bars.

🛏 Sleeping

Hotel Alta Mar   HOTEL $$
(☑ 8692-7971; Centro Turístico Pochomil, Terminal de buses, 1c E; d US$45; 🅿❄) Right near the clutch of restaurants at Centro Turistico Pochomil, Alta Mar has good ocean views and small, spotless rooms.

Casa del Titito   HOTEL $$$
(☑ 8484-7724; www.casadeltitito.com; San Rafael del Sur, Pochomil; r US$70; 🛜❄) Right on the beach and featuring an outdoor pool, this easygoing hotel with a breezy hammock area overlooking the waves is a good budget pick with a complimentary Nicaraguan breakfast. French, English and Spanish are spoken.

Hotel Vistamar Resort   RESORT $$$
(☑ 2265-8099; www.vistamarhotel.com; Playa de Pochomil; s/d incl all meals from US$145/216; 🅿❄🛜❄) A favorite with well-heeled Managuans, this is one of the prettiest hotels on this stretch of coast. Accommodations are in two-story wooden bungalows and upstairs rooms catch the sea breeze. Three swimming pools, an on-site day spa and a gorgeous stretch of white-sand beach seal the deal. Check here for turtle tours or volunteer opportunities with its turtle-release program.

Casa Larocque Villa   VILLA $$$
(☑ 8995-5970; Vistamar, 100m E, Pochomil; villa $475; 🛜❄) If you're traveling with family or a group of friends, this seven bedroom villa is well-equipped for an extended stay. There's an excellent kitchen, a thatched bar area next to the small pool and breezy, tiled rooms. The English- and French-speaking owner rents surfing equipment and arranges horseback rides. Bring supplies for cooking, or dine out at the attached restaurant.

❶ Getting There & Away

For Masachapa, get off at the *empalme* (T intersection).

Buses run from Pochomil and Masachapa to Managua's Mercado Israel Lewites (p61) (US$1.30 to US$1.60, two hours) roughly every 30 minutes from 8am to 5pm.

The two villages are a straightforward drive along the paved NIC-2 and NIC-8. NIC-10 is a shortcut towards León.

Reserva Natural Chocoyero-El Brujo

This deep, Y-shaped valley 30km south of Managua has a small, 184-hectare natural reserve (✆8864-8652; de la vuelta de Telcor, 75m E; US$5; ⊙8am-5pm) that was originally created to safeguard almost one-third of Managua's water supply. El Brujo (The Warlock) is a waterfall that seems to disappear underground, separated by a 400m cliff from El Chocoyero (Place of Parakeets), the high but less immediately impressive cascade. Show up at around 3pm and you'll see bands of parakeets come screaming home for their evening gossip.

Start at the interpretive center, with displays about the park's five parakeet species, then follow the trails leading to the waterfalls. Ask the staff about hiking guides or special tours, like the nighttime bat tour or a birdwatching hike.

❶ Getting There & Away

The Managua–La Concepción bus can drop you off at the turnoff to the reserve, but it's much easier to get a cab (about US$10) or *tuk-tuk* (about US$5) in Ticuantepe. If you're driving from Managua, after going 14km on the main road, turn west to Ticuantepe and La Concepción; at Km 21.5 a partially paved, but otherwise seriously bumpy, 7km dirt road goes to the entrance. In dry weather, a city car can make it.

San Diego

As you drive through cane fields when you turn off Hwy 10, the tarmac gives way to packed dirt, and you can smell the salty tang of the sea. Then you're in San Diego, a one-street village with an uncrowded beach and some world-class waves for surfers of all abilities.

🛏 Sleeping

Mind The Gap Nica HOSTEL $
(✆5859-7050; http://mindthegapnica.com; Playa San Diego; dm/s/d US$15/25/30, camping per person $5; ⑤) This beachfront hostel attracts steady local traffic; they come for the fish tacos and beer and the live music on weekends; surfing guests get all of the above, plus breezy, basic rooms a stone's throw from the surf. There are boards for rent and even an on-site spa with massages for sore muscles and a Mexican-style temescal sweat lodge.

Los Cardones Hotel Ecológico LODGE $$$
(✆8364-5925; www.loscardones.com; Carretera Montelimar Km 49, 15km O, Finca Del Mar Beach Community; 2-person bungalows/cabañas without bathroom incl all meals US$214/146; ⑤) ✦ Just south of San Diego village, this rustic ecolodge has great food and some of the best surfing in Nicaragua, steps from your hammock. Owners offer fishing, snorkeling and horseback riding, and sea turtles lay their eggs on the beach. The whole operation is low-impact (solar energy, composting toilets) and also family friendly, with surf breaks for kids under 12 years.

The hotel arranges transportation from the airport: US$70 one-way for one or two people.

❶ Getting There & Away

Buses run from Managua's Mercado Israel Lewites (p61) to San Cayetano (US$2, 1½-2 hours, every 45 minutes from 5am to 5pm); get off at the California crossroads, 1.5km from San Cayetano, and then either hitch a ride for the remaining 13km to San Diego, or pay a *tuk-tuk* to drive you. If driving, take NIC-12 north from Managua, then NIC-10, and turn off at California; the last 8km to the beach are unpaved and bumpy. You can also arrange to be picked up directly from Managua airport.

Masaya &
Los Pueblos Blancos

Best Places to Eat

➜ La Mestiza (p70)

➜ Mi Viejo Ranchito (p74)

➜ Mondongo Veracruz (p77)

➜ Pizzeria Colisseo (p78)

➜ Cafe La Nani (p70)

Best Places to Stay

➜ Centro Ecoturístico Flor de Pochote (p76)

➜ La Mariposa Spanish School & Eco Hotel (p72)

➜ Hotel El Casino (p79)

➜ MyrinaMar B&B Hotel (p79)

Why Go?

Nicaragua's Meseta Central (Central Valley) offers a picturesque patchwork of lagoons, volcanic peaks and sleepy colonial villages. Few visitors head here for more than a short day-trip from nearby Granada, leaving plenty of room for exploration and singular encounters with the region's remarkable natural, cultural and artistic imprint.

Head out to the Pueblos Blancos, where each village has its own specialty, from exquisite pottery to handcrafted wooden furniture. The villages also hold exuberant religious festivals.

Towering over all of this is cantankerous Volcán Masaya whose recent activity briefly pelted the surrounding countryside with rocks, and whose crater bubbles restlessly with molten magma.

Sloping down from the *meseta* are the Carazo towns – home to some of Nicaragua's oldest coffee farms and pleasant stopovers on the way to a stretch of coast with several low-key fishing villages.

At the time of writing, political unrest in the country had turned Masaya, a popular destination known for its artisan market and aficionados of traditional craftsmanship, into the center of political strife and violence.

When to Go

➜ Thursday evenings rock in Masaya with the Jueves de Verbena (p69). Stay the evening to sample local food, watch folkloric dances, and stroll through the large crafts market and museum.

➜ December through August is the dry season – ideal for hiking around Volcán Masaya or skinny dipping in Laguna de Apoyo.

➜ In late October, Masaya parties with the creepy figures from local legend; come and join the festivities of the Noche de Agüizotes (p69).

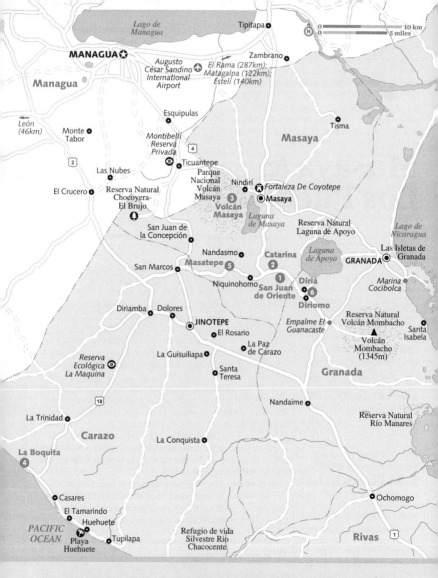

Masaya & Los Pueblos Blancos Highlights

1 San Juan de Oriente (p74) Watching history in action as the local artists continue the centuries-old craft of ceramics production (with a contemporary twist).

2 Catarina (p74) Peering into the magnificent Laguna de Apoyo from this spectacular lookout.

3 Volcán Masaya (p71) Driving to the 'gates of hell,' and watching the bubbling lava in the Santiago crater.

4 La Boquita (p79) Eating fresh seafood in thatch-roofed restaurants overlooking the waves.

5 Masatepe (p76) Sampling *mondongo* (tripe stew), and watching the *hipica* (horse parade) in May.

6 Diriá & Diriomo (p75) Whacking other participants with dried bulls' penises during the Fiestas Patronales de San Pedro.

History

A thriving population center long before the arrival of the Spanish, Masaya and the network of small towns that surround it show signs of Chorotega habitation for at least the last 3000 years. While Masaya is without doubt the modern-day regional center, in pre-Colombian times the tiny town of Diriá was the Chorotega capital, a place where 28 chieftains would meet every seven years to elect a new leader.

Artesanías (handicrafts), the region's claim to fame, has a long tradition, too – as far back as 1548 the Spanish required Masaya to provide hammocks and shoes for the colonizers as a tribute.

Masaya gained official status as a town in 1819, pre-dating Nicaraguan independence by only two years. The delay was most likely due to the fierce fighting spirit of the locals – their opposition to the Spanish in 1529, to William Walker in 1856, to US Marines in 1912 and to the Guardia Nacional throughout the revolution is legendary.

These last skirmishes took a particular toll on the region, none more so than in 1977, when the Masaya suburb of Monimbó rose up against Somoza's forces. During the struggle much of the town's colonial architecture was destroyed. As if that weren't enough, a massive earthquake in 2000 badly damaged the majority of the remaining historical buildings, many of which today still await funding in order to be properly restored.

🛈 Getting There & Around

Masaya is the regional transportation hub, with regular buses to Managua and Granada, as well as throughout the Pueblos Blancos and Carazo towns. Jinotepe is the western transportation center. Minivans run regularly between villages.

Main roads are paved throughout the region, whereas minor roads through the coutryside tend to be of the unpaved, bumpy variety (though generally passable by a regular car).

The fastest way to travel between the villages is to ride in a *moto* (tuk tuk), a tiny, three-wheeled taxi that uses a motorcycle engine. They're everywhere.

MASAYA

🎵 / POP 125,800 / ELEV 248M

If you're coming from Granada, Masaya may seem a bit down at heel. This is a very workaday little town, unexceptional but for a few things: a proliferation of excellent peo-ple and a picturesque, crumbling *malecón* (water-front walkway). Nicaraguan tourists, by the way, always make sure their visit coincides with one of Masaya's many spectacular festivals, and there are cultural exhibitions and dances every Thursday evening.

Masaya is 29km southeast of Managua and 16km northwest of Granada. The city sits at the edge of Laguna de Masaya, beyond which rises Volcán Masaya, which can be visited on day trips from here or Granada.

At the time of writing, Masaya had been the worst affected by political violence of Nicaragua's towns (from April 2018 onwards). Neighborhoods barricaded themselves off from the riot police and a number of residents had been killed.

🔘 Sights

Museo del Folclore MUSEUM
(Folklore Museum; Mercado Artesanías; US$2; ⊘8am-5pm Fri-Wed, to 7pm Thu) Inside the Mercado Artesanías complex, this small museum focuses on dance, local myths and the cultural traditions of Masaya. Apart from excellent photos taken at various festivals, it showcases outlandish costumes from the *fiestas patronales* (saints days). Look out for the black devil, the red devil and macabre figures from Nicaragua's folklore: the ghostly cart, drawn by skeletal bullocks, the Padre Sin Cabeza, La Llorona and the Chancha Bruja.

Fortaleza De Coyotepe FORT
(Carretera al Coyotepe; US$2; ⊘8am-5pm) Built in 1893 atop Cerro de los Coyotes, this fortress saw the last stand of Benjamín Zeledón, the 1912 hero of resistance to US intervention. The marines managed to take the fortress – as witnessed by a young man named Sandino, who vowed his revenge. Later, it was Somoza's worst prison and the Guardia Nacional's last stronghold, overrun during the Sandinistas' 1979 offensive. Entrance includes a dungeon tour. Hop in a Managua-bound bus (US$0.40) or taxi (US$1) to get here.

It's worth the climb just for the view: Laguna de Masaya, Lago de Managua, Volcán Mombacho and, if it's clear, Volcán Momotombo, rising red and black above Managua.

Taxis may charge extra to take you up the steep hill. Otherwise it's a sweaty half-hour hike.

Iglesia de San Jerónimo CHURCH
(www.facebook.com/parroquiasan.jeronimomasaya.5; cnr Av San Jerónimo & Calle Palo Blanco; ⊘hours vary) Among the major buildings

worst hit by the earthquake of 2000 (which also destroyed about 80 homes) was Iglesia de San Jerónimo, built in 1928, the spiritual heart of Masaya and one of the most recognizable silhouettes on the skyline. But that hasn't stopped anyone from celebrating the longest *fiestas patronales* (saints days) in Nicaragua, with their epicenter, as always, right here. Seek permission to climb the bell tower for impressive views of the city.

Antigua Estación del Ferrocarril de Masaya   MONUMENT

(Av Zelaya) Masaya's elegant former train station, built in 1926 on the north side of the city, is a local landmark. In 2013, the city announced plans to convert it into a cultural center, but at the time of writing the project was still underway.

Malecón & Laguna de Masaya   WATERFRONT

(Malecón de Masaya) Seven blocks west of the Parque Central is an inspiring view in a region famed for them: across Laguna de Masaya to the smoking Santiago crater. The attractive, if crumbling, *malecón* (waterfront promenade) was constructed in 1944, when you could still swim, drink or fish in the impressive (but now very polluted) lagoon. Watch your valuables here.

Museo y Galería de y Mártires   MUSEUM

(Av San Jerónimo, Parque Central, 1½c N; by donation; ⊙8am-noon & 1-5pm Mon-Fri) FREE Inside the *alcaldía* (mayor's office), this museum honors Masayans who gave their lives during the revolution. There are walls of photos and interesting displays of bomb-building materials and weapons, as well as personal effects including musical instruments and a few Chorotegan funeral urns. An unexploded bomb that Somoza dropped on Managua in 1977 has the place of honor.

Iglesia San Sebastián   CHURCH

(cnr Av Real de Monimbó & Calle Las Cuatro Esquinas; ⊙hours vary) The original church at this location, also called Iglesia San Sebastián, was built around 1700; it was burned down by William Walker in 1856. The current version, built in 1925, sits at the ancient center of Monimbó, which is (from a historical point of view) Masaya's most important neighborhood.

Parroquia El Calvario   CHURCH

(Calle El Calvario, Parque Central, 7c E; ⊙hours vary) Parroquia El Calvario is a squat colonial structure with no spire, it's most remarkable for the extra-gory statues of Jesus and the thieves being crucified found right at the en-

---

MASAYA'S CHURCHES & PLAZAS

There are 12 major barrios (neighborhoods) in Masaya, all of which were once separate communities with their own churches, plazas and identities: Monimbó, San Jerónimo, Santa Teresa, Villa Bosco Monge, Aserrío, Santa Susana, Las Malvinas, El Palomar, La Ceibita, Cerro Fortaleza de Coyotepe, Sylvio Renazco and Cerro la Barranca.

At the center of it all is the 1750 Parroquia de la Asunción, an attractive but scarred late-baroque beauty that the Spanish government has offered to help repair. It watches over the Parque Central, formally known as Parque 17 de Octubre, in honor of the 1977 fire fight that pitted local residents against Somoza's Guardia Nacional.

Monimbó is Masaya's most famous neighborhood, its ancient center now marked by the 1935 Iglesia San Sebastián. Perhaps more important, Iglesia María Magdalena, sort of the sister church to San Sebastián, is where many of Monimbó's most important festivals begin or end.

Although Iglesia San Juan is usually closed to the public, check out the surrounding neighborhood strung between La Asunción and the lake, with more than a dozen hammock workshops. Other churches worth seeing include the more modern Iglesia San Miguel de Masaya, whose resident San Miguel Arcángel makes the rounds during the procession of St Jerome.

Parroquia El Calvario is a squat colonial structure with no spire, most remarkable for the extra-gory statues of Jesus and the thieves being crucified, right at the entrance. Those are original – the rest had to be remodeled after the earthquake of 2000.

Among the major buildings worst hit by the earthquake, which also destroyed about 80 homes, was 1928 Iglesia de San Jerónimo (p67), the spiritual heart of Masaya and one of the most recognizable silhouettes on the skyline.

trance. Those are original – the rest had to be remodeled after the earthquake of 2000.

Parroquia de La Asunción CHURCH
(Parque Central; ☺hours vary) At the center the town is the 1750 Parroquia de La Asunción, an attractive but scarred late-baroque beauty that the Spanish government has offered to help repair.

Iglesia San Miguel de Masaya CHURCH
(Calle San Miguel, Mercado Nuevo, 1c E; ☺hours vary) The modern Iglesia de San Miguel, whose resident San Miguel Arcángel makes the rounds during the procession of St Jerome, is worth a peek.

Iglesia María Magdalena CHURCH
(Av Magdalena; ☺hours vary) Iglesia María Magdalena, sort of the sister church to San Sebastián, is where many of Monimbó's most important festivals begin or end.

🏃 Activities

Casa de las Artesanías MAKING HANDICRAFTS
(📱8995-0206; www.facebook.com/Casa-De-Las-Artesanias-Masaya-280412258984030; Calle Simpson, Antiguo Edificio CECAPI; ☺hours vary) If you want to try your hand at producing traditional Nicaraguan handicrafts, such as pottery and making masks used in various celebrations, contact these artisans in advance.

🎭 Festivals & Events

Festival de San Sebastián CULTURAL
(☺mid-Jan) The saint is celebrated in an exuberant fashion in Barrio Monimbó, the highlight being the Baile de Chinegro de Mozote y Verga. It involves a mock battle between the participants, who hit each other with big sticks before making peace.

La Virgen de la Asunción RELIGIOUS
(☺Mar 16) Better known as the Virgin of the Burning Finger or the Festival of the Cross. The town's top Virgin is taken to the lake for a blessing of the waters and a good look at the slender protrusion of lava that threatened the town during the 1772 eruption – which she stopped.

Jesús del Rescate RELIGIOUS
(☺Apr 3) Scores of *carretas* (ox carts) begin their journey from Masaya to San Jorge.

San Lázaro RELIGIOUS
(☺week before Palm Sunday) One of Nicaragua's more unusual religious festivals pays homage to San Lázaro, a folk saint who

bestows blessings upon dogs. Locals dress their pets to the nines; festivities include a procession of costumed canines.

Día de la Virgen de la Asunción RELIGIOUS
(☺Aug 15) The patron saint María Magdelena is hoisted atop the shoulders of revelers for her annual tour of Monimbó; fireworks are involved, as usual.

★Noche de Agüizotes CULTURAL
(last Fri in Oct) Not to be confused with the Day of the Dead, this spooky festival features legends such as the *mocuana* (the spirit that haunts La Mocuana hill), the *chancha bruja* (pig witch) and La Cegua, a monstrous woman who appears to womanisers on deserted roads, as well as ghosts of the dead, plus the costumed living, parading through the streets.

El Toro Venado CULTURAL
(☺last Sun of Oct, 3rd Sun of Nov) This dance involves a mythical creature that is half bull, half deer (read: half Spanish, half indigenous), whose mission is to make fun of the rest of the fair.

Baile de los Diablitos CULTURAL
(☺last Sun of Nov) Little devils dance in honor of Mephistopheles and San Jerónimo.

Procesión de San Jerónimo RELIGIOUS
(☺1st Sun in Dec) At the culmination of patron saint celebrations that start in September, the patron saint (in the guise of a bearded *campesino* named 'Tata Chombó,' or 'Doctor of the Poor') is taken from the Iglesia de San Jerónimo (p67) altar and carried around Masaya amid bouquets of flowers. A mock battle ends with peacemaking ceremonies to commemorate the September peace treaties of 1856, 1912 and 1979. Fireworks, marimbas, parades, drag queens and more make this a fiesta to remember.

Jueves de Verbena CULTURAL
(Av Mártires y Héroes; US$0.50; ☺5-11pm Thu) Once a week this festival has food, music and ballet *folklorico* (folk music) at the Mercado Artesanías; most Granada tour outfits offer this as a weekly add-on to their regular Masaya trips. It's not as good as it used to be, according to locals.

🛏 Sleeping

There are several decent hotels and guesthouses here, mostly in the budget and midrange categories. Most lodgings are dotted around the center along Calle Central and

Avenida el Progreso. Nearby Granada has a much better selection.

Hotel Masaya HOTEL $$

(☑ 2522-1030; www.hotelmasaya.com; Parque Rubén Darío, ½c N; s/d US$35/40; ❀ ⬤) On the northern approach into Masaya, this budget hotel wears its love for Harley Davidson motorcycles and the Beatles prominently on its sleeve. Have a look at a few rooms, since some have no natural light, but all are spotless and fan-cooled, with canary-yellow walls.

Hostal Ruta del Cacique GUESTHOUSE $$

(☑ 2522-3410; www.hostalrutadelcacique.com; Parque Central, ½c N; s/d from US$15/25; ⬤) About as central as it gets, this friendly little guesthouse accommodates visitors in snug, spotless rooms, and there's a guest kitchen. The owner is happy to share local knowledge.

Hotel Maderas Inn HOTEL $$

(☑ 2522-5825; www.hotelmaderasinn.com; Calle Central, Cuerpo de Bomberos, 2c S; dm US$10, d with fan/air-con US$25/45; ❀ ⬤) This family-run inn is simple and homely: there are firm mattresses, splashes of tropical art, and service is friendly. Some rooms share facilities. Ask for a room upstairs.

Hotel Monimbó HOTEL $$

(☑ 2522-6867; www.hotelmonimbo.com; Iglesia San Sebastián, 1c al E, 1½ c al N; s/d US$25/35; ℗ ❀ ⬤) At this friendly, family-run six-room hotel in Barrio Monimbó, south of the center, the rooms are surprisingly nice and spacious, if not terribly exciting.

✗ Eating

Inexpensive *comedores* (basic eating places) cling to the outside of the Mercado Municipal Ernesto Fernández. Granada speciality *vigorón* (mashed yucca topped with coleslaw and pork rinds) and *gallo pinto* (blended rice and beans) can be had for around US$1;

MASAYA ARTS & CRAFTS

Masaya itself has been famous since the days before the arrival of the Spanish for its excellent crafts. **Intur** (☑ 5501-9312; www.facebook.com/InturMasaya; Calle El Calvario, semáforos del Colonel Bautista, 1/2c E; ⊙ 8am-5pm Mon-Fri) has an excellent map of the town showing where the various workshops are – you're welcome to drop in, have a look around and, of course, buy something.

a sit-down meal with a drink costs around US$2 to US$3. There are several excellent places to eat near the Mercado de Artesanías.

Cafe La Nani CAFE $

(☑ 2522-3909; www.lananicafe.com; Calle San Miguel, frente Mercado de Artesanías; mains US$2-6; ⊙ 8am-6pm; ❀) Whoever said that Masaya wasn't sophisticated enough for latte art? Join the local yuppies here for iced (and regular) coffee in pleasant, air-conditioned surroundings, as well as Nica and American breakfasts, wraps, Caesar salad and more.

★ La Mestiza MEXICAN $$

(☑ 2522-2186; Parque Central, ½c N; mains US$3-10; ⊙ 11:30am-9pm; ❀ ⬤ ✐) An unexpected surprise, La Mestiza serves some of the best and most authentic Mexican food in Nicaragua. We love their *tacos de chicharrón en salsa verde* (pork scratchings with salsa verde) and *cochinita pibil* (Yucatan-style pork), their hearty *sopa de tortilla* (tortilla soup) and their moreish enchiladas and burritos.

🍷 Drinking & Nightlife

La Ronda BAR

(Frente Parque Central; ⊙ noon-midnight) Masaya's most popular bar gets packed with locals in the evenings. Join them for a beer.

El Toro Loco CLUB

(Calle Simpson; cover US$3; ⊙ 9pm-3am Thu-Sun) A local favourite on Thursdays for reggae night, and pumps out Latin pop, reggaeton and *bacchata* (romantic Dominican dance music) the rest of the week.

Coco Jambo CLUB

(Malecón de Masaya; ⊙ 9pm-3am Fri-Sun) Local danceheads opt for this big club at the southern end of the *malecón*, where a cheesy good time can usually be had.

🔒 Shopping

Masaya's artisans make Nicaragua's finest hammocks, with hammock factories and workshops congregating in Barrio San Juan, between Parque Central and the lagoon. There are excellent shoemakers in Barrio Monimbó who specialise in custom-made leather shoes (allow a week after the initial fitting); ask the tourist office or locals for specific recommendations. Savvy shoppers head directly to the source, rather than the overpriced and increasingly mediocre craft market.

BUS SERVICES FROM MASAYA

DESTINATION	COST (US$)	DURATION	DEPARTURES (DAILY)
Carazo (Diriamba & Jinotepe)	0.30-0.50	1¼hr	5am-6pm, every 30min
Catarina, Diriomo & Diriá	0.30-0.50	40min	6am-5pm, every 20min
Catarina, San Juan de Oriente, Niquinohomo & Masatepe	0.50	1¼hr	5am-6pm, every 30min
Granada	0.50	40min	5am-6pm, every 30min
Laguna de Apoyo entrance	0.40	20min	5am-5pm, at least hourly
Managua	0.50	1hr	5am-5pm, every 20min
Matagalpa	3	3hr	5:30am & 6am

Fábricas de Hamacas　　　　　HOMEWARES
(Hammock Factories; Parque San Juan, 2½c O; ☺hours vary) One of several places where you can not only watch traditional hammocks being handmade by local families, but you can buy them for a fairer price than at the Mercado de Artesanías. Each one takes two to three days to produce, and they make wonderfully durable gifts.

Mercado Municipal Ernesto Fernández　　　　　MARKET
(Mercado Nuevo; Calle San Miguel; ☺6am-6pm) This is the 'regular' marketplace – ie not the Mercado de Artesanías, which brings many travelers to town – though the *mercado municipal* also has a small section dedicated to artisanal goods. Colorful and chaotic, it's a transport hub, and a pungent place where locals go to buy their household goods.

ⓘ Information

DANGERS & ANNOYANCES
At the time of writing, Masaya had become both an epicenter of violence and a symbol of resistance against the Ortega government, with entire neighborhoods barricading themselves against riot police and pro-government gangs, fighting them off with rocks and homemade mortars. Masaya was a ghost town, and the situation on the ground remained very volatile.

A unit of 600 riot police began forcibly clearing the barricades after Masaya announced that it no longer recognized Nicaragua's government and that the city would govern itself. On June 22, 2018 the police were due to storm Barrio Monimbo, which was a massacre waiting to happen. But the Catholic Church sent a van-load of bishops to Masaya with the sole aim of preventing bloodshed; the bishops bodily put themselves between the protesters and the riot police and the police didn't dare open fire.

MEDICAL SERVICES
Hospital Hilario Sanchez Vásquez (☏2522-2778; Calle San Miguel) Public hospital with emergency services, but it's better to head to Managua if possible.

MONEY
BAC (cnr Calle La Reforma & Av El Progreso)
Bancentro (Av Nindirí; ☺9am-5pm Mon-Fri)
BanPro (cnr Calle San Miguel & Av El Progreso)

ⓘ Getting There & Away
Minivans (Parque San Miguel) to Managua's Universidad Centro America (US$0.90, 30 minutes) leave the park in front of Iglesia de San Miguel (when full); services peter out late afternoon. Other buses (US$0.50) and minivans arrive and depart from the **bus station** (Blvd Doctor Manuel Maldonado) at the eastern side of the Mercado Municipal.

ⓘ Getting Around
Central Masaya is perfectly walkable. Taxis charge around US$0.80 for a ride across town.

Parque Nacional Volcán Masaya
Nicaragua's largest national park is built around Volcán Masaya and its system of calderas and craters – including the enormous and ancient crater called El Ventarrón, with a barely perceptible rim that runs from Ticuantepe to Masatepe – and around the Laguna de Masaya.

The Spaniards said this was the gate to hell, and put the Bobadilla cross (named for the priest who planted it) atop a now inaccessible cliff. **Volcán Masaya** (☏2528-1444; Carretera a Masaya Km 23; day/evening US$4/10; ☺9am-4:30pm & 5:30-7:30pm) is the most heavily venting volcano in Nicaragua, and in a more litigious nation there is no way you'd be allowed to drive up to the lip of a volcanic cone as volatile as the Santiago crater. In 2012, there was an explosion of gas and rocks, and the crater continues to bubble with red-hot lava – a particularly dramatic sight during evening visits. In 2016, National Geographic shot a drone video of the lava, with explorer and cinematographer Sam Cossman descending right to the edge of the bubbling magma.

From the entrance, a paved 5km road leads to the Plaza de Oviedo, which honors the intrepid priest who descended into the volcano to find out whether the lava was pure gold.

At the time of writing, visitors were only allowed to access the Plaza de Oviedo, a clearing by the Santiago crater's rim named after the 16th-century Spanish monk who, suspecting that the bubbling lava was gold, descended to the crater with a bag and small shovel – and came back alive. Here, the smell of sulfur is strong, and you only get 15 minutes at the viewpoint – enough to watch the molten magma play – before you're ushered back into your vehicle.

The park has several marked hiking trails, many of which require a guide (prices vary). These include the lava tunnels of Tzinancanostoc and El Comalito, a small, steam-emitting volcanic cone. They were closed at the time of writing, but may reopen in future.

From the summit of Volcán Masaya (632m), the easternmost volcano, you get a wonderful view of the surrounding countryside, including the Laguna de Masaya and town of Masaya.

LA MARIPOSA SPANISH SCHOOL & ECO HOTEL

Just out of San Marcos, on the road to Ticuantepe, **La Mariposa Spanish School & Eco Hotel** (☑ 8669-9455; www.mariposaspanishschool.com; El Cruce, 50m E, Carretera a La Concepción, San Juan de la Concepción; per week per person incl classes, accommodations & activities US$520; ☎) ✐ is one of Nicaragua's prettiest Spanish schools. Set out in the rolling hillside at the base of Volcán Masaya, this wonderful school-hotel minimizes impact through the use of solar electricity, water recycling and reforestation. The setting is lush; afternoon activities include hikes and horseback rides.

ℹ Information

Pay your park entry fee (US$4 by day, US$10 at night) and any guides' fees at the entrance to the park.

The **visitor information center** (Volcán Masaya; ⊙ 9am-4.30pm & 5.30-7.30pm) has a good natural history museum (Spanish only) that introduces you to the mysteries of volcanoes.

ℹ Getting There & Away

The park entrance is signposted off NIC-4 7km north of Masaya. Travelers who come here on organized tours have transportation included in the price.

Any Managua-bound bus from Masaya or Granada can drop you at the entrance, but it's a steep, hot climb to the crater; hitchhiking is definitely possible, if you're up for it. Alternatively, consider taking a round-trip taxi from Masaya (around US$10) or Granada (around US$15 to US$20), including an hour's wait at the top.

Nindirí

POP 25,866

Only 3km north of Masaya, the much more adorable town of Nindirí may have been even more important than Monimbó during the Chorotega era – at least if you're judging by the wealth of archaeological treasures that have been found here. Pre-Columbian artifacts, from urns to masks, tell the story of an ancient indigenous culture that once lived here: you can see them at the tiny Museo Arqueológico Tendirí. If the museum is closed, check out the 1529 Catholic church, which has been left in adobe simplicity by subsequent renovations. It's home to the statue of Cristo del Volcán, credited with stopping a lava flow from destroying the town during the 1772 eruption that opened the Santiago crater.

◉ Sights

Museo Arqueológico Tendirí   MUSEUM
(☑ 8954-0570; www.manfut.org/museos/nindiri. html; Parque Central, 1c O; US$0.50; ⊙ 8:30am-noon & 2-5pm Mon-Fri, by reservation only Sat & Sun) Started in 1910, this private collection consists of a wealth of objects - mostly from the Chorotega culture that flourished between AD 1250–1500. The curator is happy to lead you around and explain to you the purpose of the incense burners, various ceremonial objects, jaguar-headed metates and funereal urns. Also look out for the collec-

'MONIMBÓ IS NICARAGUA!'

Masaya may have been declared the 'Cradle of National Folklore,' but the folklore of Masaya is the folklore of Monimbó. Once the region's most important indigenous city, this famous Masaya neighborhood, centered on Iglesia San Sebastián, is still populated mainly by people of Chorotegan descent.

In many ways Monimbó remains a world apart: indigenous government structures such as the Council of Elders are still in place, even if largely relegated to ceremonial status.

One reason for Monimbó's cultural autonomy is its celebrated history of almost continuous rebellion against the Spaniards and other occupiers. Most recently, in 1977, the people of Monimbó famously attacked Somoza's feared Guardia Nacional using homemade weapons – contact bombs, machetes and lances – produced by their own artisans and craftspeople. They held the barrio for a week.

After the battle, the Monimboseños donned traditional Spanish masks, borrowed from folkloric dances that ridiculed those occupiers, and denounced to the newspapers the abuses and atrocities of the Guardia Nacional. The country was inspired by the barrio's spectacular resistance, and streets across the nation echoed with the battle cry 'Monimbó is Nicaragua!' Ernesto Cardenal wrote that the masked Monimboseños had declared their barrio 'Free Nicaragua.' And in the end, Masaya and Monimbó were among the first cities to see a complete withdrawal of Somoza's troops.

MASAYA & LOS PUEBLOS BLANCOS LOS PUEBLOS BLANCO

tion of wooden masks (c 1936) from the regional *fiestas patronales* (saints days).

Fun fact: the Chorotega didn't actually bury their dead in the funereal urns - those were the repositories for the bones of the already buried dead who would then be dug up three of four years after their demise, and re-interred in the urns.

✕ Eating

La Llamarada NICARAGUAN $$
(☑ 8138-6824; Parque Central, 1c N; dishes US$4-7; ⊘ 8am-10pm) A more formal option than most of Nindirí's *fritanga* (home-style Nicaraguan food) joints, this is a beloved local restaurant that serves the likes of chicken in wine sauce, as well as mixed grill and other local staples.

❶ Getting There & Away

Frequent local buses and *colectivos* (shared taxis) ply the 3km route between Nindirí and Masaya, from where you can catch a bus to Granada, Managua, and a range of other destinations.

LOS PUEBLOS BLANCOS

Originally built from the chalky, pale volcanic tuff upon which this pastoral scene is spread, this series of rural communities, often called the White Villages or Pueblos Blancos, once shimmered a blinding white amid the pale-green patchwork of pasture and jungle.

Today the centuries-old buildings have been painted and the shady roads are paved. Most days the roads between the villages are lined with stands selling vividly painted *artesanías* (handicrafts). Each town has its specialty: handcrafted ceramics, homemade sweets, wooden furniture or freshly cut flowers. The region is also famous for its *curanderos* (folk healers). The villages are most often visited as a day trip from Granada, but take the time to explore and the inner workings of life in rural Nicaragua may reveal itself.

🛏 Sleeping & Eating

Though most visitors pass through Los Pueblos Blancos on road trips, sleeping in nearby Granada or Masaya, there are a few good places to stay in the region – mostly in the ecolodge category, tucked away in rural areas outside the towns.

There are traditional Nicaraguan restaurants, basic food kiosks and *fritangas* (grills) scattered throughout the towns. Catarina and Masatepe have a better range of dining options than the other villages.

❶ Getting There & Away

It's relatively easy to visit some of the more popular villages – Catarina, Diriomo, Masatepe – by boarding public buses and minibuses from Masaya, Granada or Managua. A faster and more convenient way of getting around involves either taking *tuk-tuks* between the villages, or even commandeering one to take you around for an entire day. Various tour operators run day trips to the Pueblos Blancos from Granada; these typically involve stops in Catarina, San Juan de Oriente, Diriá and Diriomo.

Catarina

POP 8500

At the crossroads of Los Pueblos Blancos, Catarina is known for its spectacular *mirador* (viewpoint) over Lago de Nicaragua and Laguna de Apoyo, and for its *viveros* (nurseries) that supply ornamental plants for households across Nicaragua.

◎ Sights

Mirador   VIEWPOINT

(Viewpoint; 300m Oeste del centro) Catarina's main claim to fame offers views across the startling blue waters of Laguna de Apoyo to Granada and Lago de Nicaragua all the way to Ometepe. This spot is rumored to have been the favourite place to meditate of a youthful Augusto C Sandino (Nicaraguan revolutionary who rebelled again the US), though don't come with expectations of peace and quiet, since the *mirador* comes with its own attendant circus of marimba players, street-food sellers and pony rides.

There's a half-hour trail to the water, with excellent views.

✹ Festivals & Events

San Juan Bautista   RELIGIOUS

(☉ Jun 21) Coincidentally falling on the summer solstice, this lively festival features dances, ceremonial fights and music.

Santa Catalina de Alejandría   RELIGIOUS

(☉ Nov 25-26) This religious festival features ballet *folklorico* (folk music) and a parade.

San Silvestre Papa   RELIGIOUS

(Dec 31-Jan 1) This New Year's parade is famous for its bouquets of flowers.

✗ Eating

Mi Viejo Ranchito   NICARAGUAN $$

(☑ 2558-0473; www.miviejoranchito.com; Carretera Masaya-Catarina, Km 39.5; mains US$5-8; ☉ 7am-7pm Mon-Fri, to 10pm Sat & Sun) Slightly out of town, towards Masaya, this thatch-roofed restaurant is locally famous for its *quesillos* (tortillas stuffed with fresh quesillo cheese, topped with pickled onions and sour cream), and also serves an array of grilled meats and ample Nicaraguan breakfasts.

La Casona   NICARAGUAN $$

(☑ 2558-0292; Del parque, 1c E, 1½c S; mains US$7-11; ☉ 7am-8pm Sun-Thu, to 10pm Fri & Sat) Popular with both locals and tour groups, and justifiably so, this family-run restaurant serves up filling breakfasts as well as BBQ chicken, *tostones con queso* (fried green plantains with cheese), grilled fish and more.

❶ Getting There & Away

Catarina is a popular stop on Granada–Masaya tours. There are also microbuses for destinations throughout the *meseta*, and tuk tuks that you can hire, while buses run regularly between the *mirador* and destinations including the following:

Granada (US$0.50, 30 minutes, 6am to 6pm, at least hourly)

Managua (US$0.60, 50 minutes, 6am to 6pm, half-hourly) Arrives/departs Mercado Roberto Huembes.

Masaya (US$0.40, 30 minutes, 6am to 6pm, half-hourly)

If driving, avoid the insanely busy parking lot by the *mirador*.

San Juan de Oriente

POP 2800

This attractive colonial village – known to some as the sister 'bewitched village' of Catarina – is renowned for its artisan traditions. San Juan de Oriente, indeed, has been in the pottery business since before the Spanish conquest, and 95% of the residents are artisans. While production of inexpensive and functional pottery for local consumption is still important, the recent generations of craftspeople have upped their game. A number of the local masters are international award winners who exhibit abroad, and their vases, plates, pots and other creations are exquisitely decorated and very fairly priced.

At the time of writing, this town had experienced a big drop off in tourism as a result of the political unrest which began in 2018, for further information see p290.

⛒ Shopping

★ **Galería de Helio Gutiérrez**   ART

(☑ 8230-9892; ☉ 8am-5pm) The recipient of more international awards than any other master in the village, Helio combines geometric, traditional and contemporary design elements in his unique ceramics and is known as the father of the contemporary potter movement in San Juan de Oriente. Pieces start from US$130.

Red Clay
ART

(☏ 8687-0484; ⊘ 9am-5pm) This stellar shop mostly stocks high-end pieces by Miguel Maldonado, winner of national and international awards, which blend traditional, geometric and contemporary design. There are also a number of excellent pieces by Gregorio Bracamonte, a master of pre-Columbian design who excels at making intricate jaguar vessels, decorated with natural dyes.

Galería de Arte Ortíz
ART

(☏ 8296-2616; ortizartenic@hotmail.com; ⊘ 7am-8pm) Internationally renowned José Ortiz produces very distinctive contemporary pottery known for its cubistic forms reminiscent of Picasso and its use of bold colors (particularly blue). His style is unmistakable and he works on canvas, glass and wood; come here for a great selection of his work.

Artesanías Jacobo
ART

(☏ 8750-1100; ⊘ 9am-6pm) Young artist Jacobo Potosme specializes in traditional pottery styles, combined with fine geometric detail. Some of his pieces combine several patterns in one, making them intricate works of art. His mother, wife and sisters make finely decorated bowls and cups, also sold here.

Cerámica Miguel Ángel
ART

(☏ 8164-0611; ⊘ 7am-8pm) Miguel Ángel Calero, known locally as Michelangelo, is well-known for his finely detailed geometric pieces, as well as pottery influenced by pre-Columbian designs. There's something for every budget here, including plenty of geometric, utilitarian and modern pieces.

Centro de Artesanía Cooperativa Quetzalcóatl
ARTS & CRAFTS

(☏ 2558-0337; ⊘ 9am-5:30pm) Stocking the work of a number of artists from around the village, this cooperative has a wide selection of inexpensive vases, plates, bowls, cups and platters, as well as exhibition pieces. There's plenty of utilitarian, traditional and geometric design here, as well as numerous works of pre-Columbian design.

ⓘ Getting There & Away

Buses leave more or less hourly for Granada (US$0.50, one hour) from the **bus stop** (Parque Central) on San Juan de Oriente's Parque Central. Alternatively, flag down any passing bus making the Granada–Rivas run on the highway. A more convenient option is a tuk tuk (US$0.50 to Catarina, $2 to Granada).

Diriá & Diriomo

POP 12,300

Diriomo, home to a number of so-called 'witch doctors,' has long been known as the Witch Capital of the Meseta and it is here that people come if they're looking to curse an enemy, cure an ailment or bewitch a paramour. Most healers work out of their homes, which are unsigned. Ask at the *alcadía* (mayor's office). It's also famous for its *cajetas* (rich, fruit-flavored sweets), *chicha bruja* (an alcoholic corn beverage) and even stiffer *calavera del gato* ('skull of the cat' – drink at your own risk).

Diriá, a twin town across the road, boasts Mirador el Boquete, the mellower, less-touristed overlook of Laguna de Apoyo, where the viewpoint features a few eating places that get packed with families on weekends. From the lookout, there's a steep, half-hour trail to the bottom, where a muddy little beach offers access to the bright-blue water for swimming.

◉ Sights

Mirador el Boquete
VIEWPOINT

(Calle Laguna de Apoyo, Diriá) From the village of Diriá, a road leads up to the Mirador el Boquete, a peaceful viewpoint overlooking Laguna de Apoyo, without the crowds that the similar viewpoint in Catarina attracts. Ignore the lackluster places to eat and, if you're feeling energetic, take the steep trail down to a little beach (30 to 40 minutes) from where you can swim in the lagoon.

Iglesia Nuestra Señora de Candelaria
CHURCH

(Frente plaza, Diriomo; ⊘ hours vary) This canary-yellow church – the perfect centerpiece for this witchy town – has rather Gothic stone walls and an extra-interesting collection of saints. It marks the spot where Cacique Diriangén, chief of the Dirian peoples at the time of the Spanish conquest, first met conquistador Gil González Dávila on April 17, 1523. Unlike Nicarao, Diriangén didn't trust the newcomers and opted to ignore their three-day deadline to become a Christian. Diriangén attacked, which in retrospect was the best course of action.

Today, both Diriá and Diriomo – as well as Diriamba in Carazo – are named for the indomitable *cacique* (chief).

✹ Festivals & Events

Virgen de la Candelaria RELIGIOUS
(Diriomo; ☺ Feb 2-8) Wake up early – the fireworks will help – to see the Virgin off on her annual trip to nearby Los Jirones.

Fiestas Patronales de San Pedro RELIGIOUS
(Diriá; Jun 17–mid-Jul) Diría celebrates its patron saint, San Pedro Apóstol (Peter the Apostle). The festivities include the crowning of a festival queen and 'dicking' – when participants go around whacking each other with dried bulls' penises.

❶ Getting There & Away

Buses leave almost hourly from Diriomo for Mercado Huembes in Managua (US$0.80) and every 40 minutes for Masaya (US$0.50). If you're in a rush (or heading south), make your way out onto the highway and flag down any passing bus.

To get to the *mirador*, take any Niquinohomo-bound bus (US$0.50, every 30 minutes) from Diriá, which will stop in the city center. It's a 2km walk or a quick taxi ride to the lookout.

Niquinohomo
POP 16,400

This quiet, 16th-century Spanish-colonial village is the birthplace of General Augusto César Sandino, the Nicaraguan revolutionary who fought against US military occupation of Nicaragua between 1927 and 1933, and who did indeed appreciate the fact that its name is Náhuatl for 'Valley of the Warriors.' Sandino's childhood home, located just steps away from the quiet Parque Central, has been turned into a basic museum. Anyone in town can point you toward the building. Nearby, the town's church, **Parroquia Santa Ana**, is over 320 years old and allegedly Nicaragua's oldest.

◉ Sights

Biblioteca Augusto C Sandino MUSEUM
(Esquina Parque Central; by donation; ☺ 9am-noon & 2-5pm Mon-Fri) This simple corner building was the childhood home of revolutionary leader Augusto C Sandino. Now it's a library and small museum devoted to Sandino memorabilia, but opening hours are erratic.

✹ Festivals & Events

Santa Ana RELIGIOUS
(☺ Jul 26) Ballet *folklorico*, fireworks and parades make this one of the country's biggest celebrations for this popular saint.

❶ Getting There & Away

Niquinohomo is located 10km south of Masaya via highways NIC-118 and NIC-18.

Frequent buses make the trip to Granada (US$0.60, 40 minutes) via Catarina.

Masatepe
POP 20,600

This photogenic colonial town has well-kept plazas and churches, and is renowned for two things: the exuberant horse parade in June that's part of its *fiestas patronales*, and its carpenters, who make Nicaragua's finest furniture, showcased at Masatepe's old train station which has been reincarnated as one of the better artisan markets in the country.

Towering over Masatepe's attractive central plaza, **Iglesia San Juan Bautista** is home to El Cristo Negro de La Santísima Trinidad, whose feast days mean a month of parties between mid-May and mid-June, and features nationally famous folkloric dances like La Nueva Milpa, Racimo de Sacuanjoche and Masatepetl. The sweeping adobe makes a fine colonial centerpiece, but it's the views from its gates, of fuming Volcán Masaya, that add depth to your prayers.

✹ Festivals & Events

Domingo de Trinidad CULTURAL
(☺ mid-May–mid-Jun) Forty days after Semana Santa, this is the biggest *hipica* (horse parade) in Nicaragua; festivities honour El Cristo Negro de La Santísima Trinidad and peak on May 23, but keep going for another month.

⮕ Sleeping

Centro Ecoturístico Flor de Pochote ECOLODGE $$
(☎ 8885-7576; www.flordepochote.com; Iglesia Católica de Masatepe, 4km N, El Pochote; cabins US$35; ⓟ ⓢ ⌘) This beautiful ecolodge lies within the Reserva Natural Laguna de Apoyo, perched right on the crater rim. The cabins (which sleep two) scattered around the 10-hectare *finca* (farm) are made from natural materials. There are lots of activities on-site, from birdwatching to biking; the owners also make wine. It's a 4km downhill walk or taxi ride from Masatepe. Reservations required.

Walking trails crisscross the property, where you can see scores of bird species, including falcons, vultures and hummingbirds.

✗ Eating

Mondongo Veracruz NICARAGUAN **$$**
(Parque de Veracruz, 2c E; dishes US$3-6; ◔10am-8pm) Masatepe is perhaps best known for delicious, steaming bowls of *mondongo* (tripe soup marinated with bitter oranges and fresh herbs, then simmered with garden vegetables for hours). This is one of the best places in town to sample the stew (with a traditional side of Flor de Caña Rum), though several other eating houses serve good versions, too.

🛍 Shopping

Mercado de Artesanía ARTS & CRAFTS
(Artisan Market; Carretera Masatepe-Masaya; ◔9am-6pm) While Masatepe's famous furniture market features beautiful hardwood and rattan furniture items that probably won't make it home in your backpack, the town's hallmark cane-woven rocking chairs can be disassembled and are well worth buying.

ℹ Getting There & Away

Buses leave the Parque Central **bus stop** (Parque Central) half-hourly for Masaya (US$0.40) and Mercado Roberto Huembes in Managua (US$1.30, one hour), while minivans make the run to Jinotepe (US$0.50, 15 minutes) when full. Alternatively, take a tuk tuk between the villages.

CARAZO TOWNS

Consisting of several coffee-growing highland towns with a refreshingly cool climate (bring a sweater) and a couple of wide, sandy beaches along the coast (bring your swimsuit), Carazo is central in Nicaraguan history and myth. It's not only where the first Nicaraguan coffee was sown but also where the nation's most famous burlesque, *El Güegüense,* was anonymously penned in the late 17th century. The comedy, which pits Nicaraguan ingenuity against Spanish power, always gets a laugh. It was written (and is still performed) in Náhuatl, Spanish and Mayangna.

Diriamba

POP 42,000 / ELEV 532M
Diriamba is considered the birthplace of coffee production in Nicaragua; it was already a bustling settlement when the Spanish arrived. Today, it has a pleasant central plaza and interesting European-style architecture that dates back to the coffee boom in the late 19th and early 20th centuries, but the only real reason to stay here is for the exuberant Fiesta de San Sebastián in January.

◉ Sights

Gaia Estate NATURE CENTRE
(Bosques de Gaia; ☏8681-5356; www.facebook.com/GaiaEstate; Comarca San Carlos, Del Colegio Ideas, 4 Km al Sur Oeste; ◔9am-5pm) Bird-watching and coffee tours are conveniently rolled into one at Gaia Estate, a lush, 90-acre organic coffee farm. Over 150 species of birds live here, and forested trails lead past 60 species of trees. From Diriamba's Puma gas station turn right towards Diriamba Stadium, then right again in front of the stadium and drive 4.5km to the village of San Carlos. The road curves left and the entrance to Bosques de Gaia (known locally as 'Miramar') is past the curve.

Museo Ecológico Trópico Seco MUSEUM
(☏8422-2129; Frente Hotel Mi Bohio; US$2; ◔8am-noon & 2-4pm Mon-Fri) Nicaragua's first natural history museum (sort of) offers informative, if low-budget, displays that focus primarily on the ecosystem of the Río Grande de Corazo and turtles of the Refugio de Vida Silvestre Río Escalante Chacocente. It's sometimes inexplicably closed.

✦ Festivals & Events

★ Fiesta de San Sebastián RELIGIOUS
(◔Jan 11-19) The most remarkable of the *fiestas patronales* (saints days) celebrated in the Pueblos Blancos, this week-long folklore celebration blends pagan and Catholic elements with exuberant costumes and dance. Look out for the Güegüense dance that satirizes the indigenous people's first meeting with the Spanish conquistadors, plus the Toro Huaco dance, with its peacock feather hats and pre-Columbian roots.

🛏 Sleeping

Ecolodge Carazo LODGE **$$**
(☏2534-2948; www.ecolodgecarazo.com; Frente Parque Regina, NIC-2, Km 40; s/d US$25/50; ☏) 🌿 This lodge located on a former coffee farm about 1km outside of town, on the way to Managua, has beautiful gardens with centuries-old trees and plenty of birdlife and wildlife, simple cabin-style rooms, and a laid-back atmosphere.

MASAYA & LOS PUEBLOS BLANCOS DIRIAMBA

FIESTA DE TORO GUACO

Carazo's four major towns celebrate the interesting, ancient ritual of **Fiesta de Toro Guaco** (☉ Jan). La Concepción brings out her patron saint, the Black Virgin of Montserrat, to meet Santiago, patron of Jinotepe, the old Nicarao capital; San Sebastián emerges from Diriamba, Jinotepe's ancient Chorotegan rival; and San Marcos appears from the university town of the same name.

Four times throughout the year – the saints' feast days – the saints pay ceremonial visits to each other, the processions livened up with striking costumes and masks displayed in dances, mock battles and plays that satirize their Spanish invaders. The biggest bash is from April 24 to 25, in San Marcos.

Hotel Mi Bohio HOTEL **$$**
(☏ 2534-3300; www.hotelmibohio.com; Costado este Policía Nacional; s with/without air-con US$45/35, d US$55/45; ❄ 🖥) Your best bet in town, this colonial-style hotel has a pretty, central garden and a **restaurant** (open to the public) serving good food and cocktails. There's a spa and fitness center on-site, and the rooms are clean and cheery. (And in case you were wondering, *bohio* is Cuban slang for a small house.)

❶ Getting There & Away

Jinotepe is the main transportation hub, and you can get a Jinotepe microbus (US$0.40, 15 minutes) any time at the market in front of the clock tower. A few other buses and microbuses do leave from this station, including the following services.

La Boquita (microbus; US$0.70, 45 minutes, 6am to 6pm, half-hourly)
Casares (microbus; US$0.70, 1½ hours, 5am to 5pm, hourly)
Managua (minibus; US$1.30, 1¼ hours, 5am to 6pm, roughly every 30 minutes)

Jinotepe

POP 38,800 / ELEV 569M

Historically separated from its eternal rival by the Río Grande de Carazo, proud Jinotepe is the capital of Carazo. It's famous in Nicaragua for its neoclassical architecture and local-ly produced ice cream, and has a lively, youthful vibe due to its large student population.

🛏 Sleeping

La Residencia Inn B&B **$$**
(☏ 2532-1204; www.laresidenciainn.com; Esquina sureste Parroquia Santiago, 1c E, ½c S; r from US$40; ❄ 🖥) A pocket of tranquility in the bustling heart of Jinotepe, this delightful B&B has several snug rooms on offer, arranged around a greenery-filled courtyard. The English-speaking local proprietress makes you feel welcome and breakfast includes an omelet, excellent local coffee, and fruit.

🍴 Eating

Cafe Paris CAFE **$**
(Costado sur de BanPro; snacks US$1.50-5; ☉ 11am-9:30pm Mon & Wed-Fri, from 9:30am Sat, from 8:15am Sun) Half a block southwest of the main square, this Parisian-inspired cafe specializes in coffee drinks and freshly baked pastries. Breakfast and light meals are also served.

Buen Provecho INTERNATIONAL **$**
(Del BAC, 1½c N; dishes US$3.5-5; ☉ 7am-10pm Mon-Fri) A block and a half north of Parque Central's northwest corner, this basic place serves up typical Nicaraguan dishes.

MamaYamna El Chante INTERNATIONAL **$$**
(☏ 8662-9890; www.facebook.com/mamayamna elchante; De Policía Nacional, ½c O, ½c S; mains US$5-7; ☉ Wed-Sun 3:30-8pm; 🖥) MamaYamna defies pigeon-holing. But if you imagine an art gallery with a wall-high psychedelic mural of Che Guevara, a gangsta Marilyn Monroe wearing a bandanna, framed photos of Gandhi, jazz and funk music playing in the background, and a youthful clientele polishing off pulled pork sandwiches, jalapeno poppers and bottles of Carreta Nagua and Tabu craft beer, you're in the ballpark.

Pizzeria Colisseo PIZZA **$$**
(☏ 2532-2150; De BanPro, ½c S; pizzas US$7-9; ☉ noon-2:30pm & 6-10pm Tue-Fri, noon-10pm Sat & Sun) The locals call the authentic brick-oven-baked pizza here the best in Nicaragua: the owner's originally from Rome and has been serving them for a quarter of a century. It also serves beer and wine, and doubles as an excellent B&B (singles/doubles $35/50), so if you've had a raucous evening you only have to stagger to your spotless room upstairs.

ⓘ Getting There & Away

Jinotepe is a transportation hub, and the big, confusing **bus station** (Carretera Panamericana) is six blocks east of the Parque Central, across the Panamericana (Pan-American Hwy). Microbuses to Managua line up directly on the highway.

Reserva Ecológica La Maquina

Take a break from dodging potholes at this excellent, respected private reserve about halfway between Diriamba and the beaches. It's a fine place for a swim and a picnic.

◎ Sights

Reserva Ecológica
La Maquina   NATURE RESERVE
(☑ 8887-9141; www.manfut.org/carazo/maquina.html; Carretera a La Boquita Km 58.5; US$3; ☉ daylight hours Tue-Sun) Take a dip in the pools beneath spectacular waterfalls at this lovely nature reserve, then explore the short hiking trails that traverse the 154-hectare property – mainly primary dry tropical forest with a few bonus waterfalls and big trees, including huge strangler figs.

ⓘ Getting There & Away

The entrance to the reserve is just off the paved road from Diriamba to the beaches. You can also catch one of the buses running between the beaches and Diriamba (US$0.30, 20 minutes), which pass near the entrance every 40 minutes or so during daylight hours.

La Boquita

POP UNDER 2000

At this low-key fishing village, most tourists are day-trippers from the *meseta* towns. At the very end of the road, a big, concrete archway marks the entrance to the Centro Turistico La Boquita, with beach-friendly services and numerous thatch-roofed restaurants serving fresh fish and seafood.

La Boquita is more a swimming than a surfing beach, but when swells are big, restaurants sometimes rent boards.

◎ Sights

Centro Turistico La Boquita   AREA
(car entry US$1) This waterfront complex offers amenities for beachgoers, from bars and restaurants to public restrooms. Just follow the only road west to the end.

⌸ Sleeping

MyrinaMar B&B Hotel   HOTEL $$$
(☑ 8421-8306; Del empalme Casares–La Boquita, 1km hacia La Boquita; d/5-person apt US$82/105; ☞) A refreshing standout in a coastal area with very few good hotels, the French-owned MyrinaMar perches on a cliff above the beach; there's a private walkway leading down to the sand. The hotel has airy guest rooms with sea views; the suites have loft beds – and an excellent breakfast is served outside. There's also a cocktail bar and bicycle rental.

ⓘ Getting There & Away

Many travelers drive here along the paved road (40 minutes), but you can also catch a bus (US$0.70, 1½ hours, 5am to 5pm, hourly) or taxi (expect to pay from US$10 one-way) from nearby Diriamba.

Casares

POP UNDER 2000

Casares is a fishing village that sits on a rocky beach and attracts mostly Nicaraguan day-trippers, as well as the odd foreigner. There's not much to do here except relax, swim in the surf and watch the local fishers carrying in their daily catch from colorfully painted wooden boats.

⌸ Sleeping

Hotel El Casino   HOTEL $$$
(☑ 2532-8002; www.hotelcasinocasares.com; Playa Casares; s/d US$30/40; ❋ ☞) Given this hotel's isolated location in a small fishing village, the sophisticated lobby and dining area, full of abstract soapstone sculpture and contemporary art, takes you by surprise. You can hear waves crashing from your bed and it's worth spending the extra $5 on sea views from the top-front rooms. Excellent seafood is served here, too.

ⓘ Getting There & Away

Buses from Diriamba (US$0.70, 1½ hours, 5am to 5pm, hourly) stop at the *empalme* (junction) above the beach. For Hotel El Casino, head straight downhill toward the water. It takes 40 minutes to drive here along the beautifully paved road from Diriamba.

MASAYA & LOS PUEBLOS BLANCOS RESERVA ECÓLOGICA LA MAQUINA

Granada

POP 100,496 / ELEV 62M

Best Places to Eat

➡ Bocadillos Tapas Kitchen & Bar (p92)

➡ Miss Dell's Kitchen (p93)

➡ Espressonista (p93)

➡ Pita Pita (p93)

➡ El Garaje (p92)

Best Places to Stay

➡ Hotel Gran Francia (p90)

➡ Isleta El Espino (p101)

➡ Hotel Patio del Malinche (p90)

➡ Jicaro Island Lodge (p101)

➡ Hotel Bahía Zapatera (p100)

➡ Casa Marimba (p99)

Why Go?

Nicaragua's oldest town is also its most beguiling and photogenic. It's no wonder many travelers use the city as a base, spending at least a day bopping along cobblestone roads from church to church in the city center, then venturing out into the countryside for trips to nearby attractions.

Just out of town, adventures take you to an evocative archipelago waterworld at Las Isletas and fun beaches at the Peninsula de Asese. Volcán Mombacho has walking trails, not to mention a few hot springs dotted around its foothills. The Laguna de Apoyo is another must-see: its clear turquoise waters and laid-back waterfront lodges offer a splendid natural respite.

Culturally curious travelers might consider a trip to community-tourism operations in nearby villages such as Nicaragua Libre, or out to Parque Nacional Archipiélago Zapatera, home to one of the most impressive collections of petroglyphs and statues in the country.

When to Go

➡ November 28 to December 7 is the celebration of La Inmaculada Concepción, or La Purísima as it is known in Nicaragua. It is celebrated throughout the country, but is especially vibrant in Granada, with parades, dances and, yes, plenty of fireworks.

➡ During February the International Poetry Festival brings bards and wannabes from across Latin America to celebrate the word and wax poetic. Expect a city of magic surrealism with just a touch of pretension.

➡ The December to May high season brings more people, higher prices and better weather. Book at least a week in advance during these times, especially Christmas and Easter weeks and during the mid-August festivals.

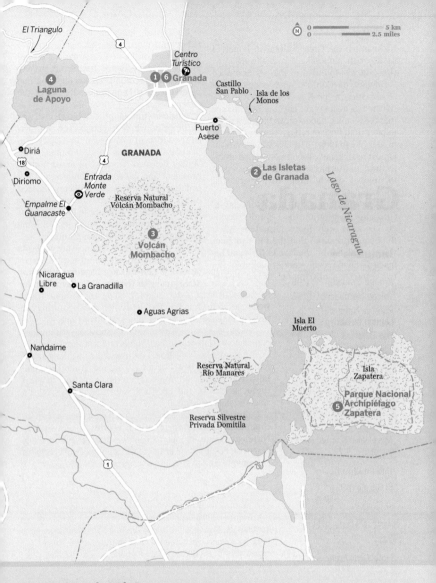

Granada Highlights

1 Granada (p80) Checking out gorgeous, centuries-old churches and feasting on some of Nicaragua's most innovative cuisine.

2 Las Isletas de Granada (p100) Paddling your kayak at dawn among the fishermen and ample birdlife, and relaxing on a private island.

3 Volcán Mombacho (p96) Hiking below the imposing summit and tasting locally produced coffee.

4 Laguna de Apoyo (p98) Taking a dip in this gorgeous volcanic lake, said to be the cleanest water in all of Nicaragua.

5 Parque Nacional Archipiélago Zapatera (p99) Checking out ancient petroglyphs and interacting with one of Nicaragua's most unique island communities.

6 Iglesia La Merced (p84) Catching a stunning sunset over the lake from the bell tower of this church in Granada.

History

Nicknamed 'the Great Sultan,' in honor of its Moorish namesake across the Atlantic, Granada was founded in 1524 by Francisco Fernández de Córdoba, and is one of the oldest cities in the New World. It was constructed as a showcase city, the first chance that the Spanish had to prove they had more to offer than bizarre religions and advanced military technology. The city still retains an almost regal beauty, each thick-walled architectural masterpiece faithfully resurrected to original specifications after every trial and tribulation.

A trade center almost from its inception, Granada's position on the Lago de Nicaragua became even more important when the Spanish realized that the Río San Juan was navigable from the lake to the sea. This made Granada rich – and vulnerable. Between 1665 and 1670, pirates sacked the city three times.

Undaunted, Granada rebuilt and grew richer and more powerful, a conservative cornerstone of the Central American economy. After independence from Spain, the city challenged the colonial capital and longtime Liberal bastion León for leadership of the new nation.

Tensions erupted into full-blown civil war in the 1850s, when desperate León contracted the services of American mercenary William Walker and his band of 'filibusterers.' Walker defeated Granada, declared himself president and launched a conquest of Central America – and failed. Walker was forced into a retreat after a series of embarrassing defeats, and as he fell back to his old capital city, he set it afire and left in its ashes the infamous placard: 'Here was Granada.'

The city rebuilt – again. And while its power has waned, its importance as a tourist center and quick escape from bustling Managua keeps the city of Granada vibrant.

Granada

Sights

There's plenty to see in pretty Granada to keep you occupied for a day or two, though you'll likely feel the pull of attractions in the immediate surroundings: Las Isletas, Laguna de Apoyo and Volcán Mombacho.

★Convento y Museo San Francisco — CHURCH

(Map p86; ☎2552-5535; Plaza de los Leones 1c N, 1c E; US$5; ⏲8am-4pm Mon-Fri, 9am-4pm Sat & Sun) One of the oldest churches in Central America, Convento San Francisco boasts a robin's egg-blue birthday-cake facade and houses both an important convent and one of the best museums in the region. The highlight is the museum that focuses on Nicaragua's pre-Columbian people. Don't miss the Zapatera statuary, two solemn regiments of black-basalt statues, carved between AD 800 and 1200, then left behind on the ritual island of Zapatera.

0
500 m
0
0.25 miles
E
F
1
2
3
4
Calle El Almendro
Lago de Nicaragua
4
6
34
Calle El Caimito
Parque
Río Sacuanatoya
Calle El Caimito
Las Isletas (5km);
Marina Cocibolca (5km)
11

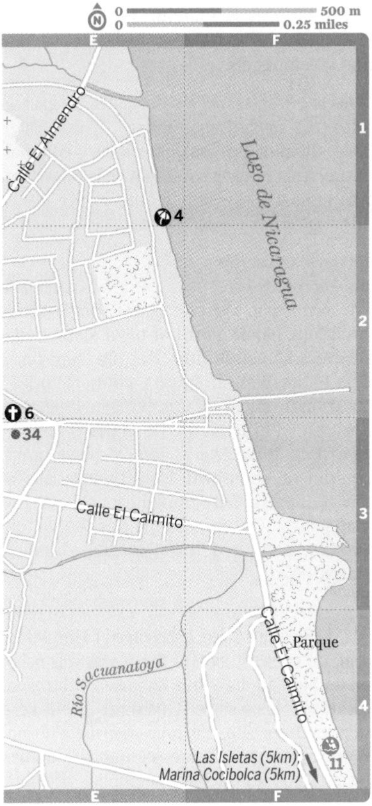

The museum is through the small door on the left, where guides (some of whom speak English) are available for tours; tips are appreciated. Other museum highlights include top-notch primitivist art, a scale model of the city and a group of papier-mâché indigenous people cooking, relaxing in hammocks

Granada

Sights

- 1 Antigua Estación del Ferrocarril C1
- 2 Antiguo Hospital A2
- 3 Cementerio de Granada A4
- 4 Centro Turístico E1
- 5 Fortaleza La Polvora A3
- 6 Iglesia de Guadelupe E2
- 7 Iglesia de Xalteva B3
- 8 La Capilla María Auxiliadora A3
- 9 Mercado Municipal C3

Activities, Courses & Tours

- 10 Casa Xalteva B3
- Corazón Trips .... (see 17)
- 11 Inuit Kayaks F4
- 12 Nicaragua Mia Spanish School D3
- 13 Pure D2
- 14 Xpress Spanish School C2

Sleeping

- 15 Hotel Boutique Adela D2
- 16 Hotel Casa San Francisco C2
- 17 Hotel Con Corazón C2
- 18 Hotel La Polvora A3
- 19 Hotel Los Patios D2

Eating

- Bocadillos Tapas Kitchen & Bar .... (see 16)
- 20 Cafe de los Sueños D3
- 21 Curry House D2
- 22 El Garaje D2
- 23 Espressonista B3
- 24 La Frontera B2
- 25 Palí C3
- 26 Supermercado Colonia B1

Drinking & Nightlife

- 27 Hog's Breath Saloon D2
- Inuit Bar .... (see 11)

Shopping

- 28 Doña Elba Cigars B3
- 29 Soy Nica D3

Transport

- 30 Budget B1
- 31 Buses to Destinations South C4
- 32 Buses to Managua A2
- 33 Buses to Masaya C3
- 34 Colonial Travel Granada E3
- 35 Tica Bus A2
- 36 TransNica A3

and swinging on *comelazatoaztegams,* a sort of 360-degree see-saw.

Most of the Isla Zapatera statues were discovered in the late 1880s and gathered in Granada in the 1920s.

The convent itself was originally constructed in 1585, subsequently burned to the ground by pirates and later William Walker, rebuilt in 1868 and restored in 1989.

★Museo de Chocolate   MUSEUM
(Map p86; ☎2552-4678; www.chocomuseo.com; Calle Atravesada, frente Bancentro; chocolate workshop adult/child US$21/12; ⊙7am-6:30pm; 🖌) **FREE** Granada's new chocolate museum is excellent if you're traveling with children: the 'beans to bar' chocolate workshop, where participants learn to roast and grind cocoa beans, and mold their very own Nicaraguan chocolate bar, is hands-on fun for all ages. Cigar-making workshops are also held here. The museum is located at the Mansión de Chocolate hotel (p90), which also has a chocolate-oriented spa and a popular buffet breakfast (US$7), plus a great swimming pool you can use for an extra US$6.

Iglesia La Merced   CHURCH
(Map p86; cnr Calle Real Xalteva & Av 14 de Septiembre; bell tower US$1; ⊙11am-6pm) Perhaps the most beautiful church in the city, this landmark was built in 1534. Most come here for the spectacular views from the bell tower – especially picturesque at sunset. Originally completed in 1539, it was razed by pirates in 1655 and rebuilt with its current baroque facade between 1781 and 1783. Damaged by William Walker's forces in 1854, it was restored with the current elaborate interior in 1862. Today Catholics come here to see the Virgen de Fatima.

Cementerio de Granada   CEMETERY
(Map p82; Nandame s/n; ⊙7am-6pm) Used between 1876 and 1922, this beautiful cemetery on Granada's outskirts has lots of picturesque mausoleums and tombs, including those of six Nicaraguan presidents. Most people come to see the 1880 neoclassical stone Capilla de Animas (Chapel of Spirits), a scale model of the French chapel of the same name. Close by is another scale model, this time of Notre Dame cathedral.

Casa de los Leones & Fundación Casa de los Tres Mundos   NOTABLE BUILDING
(Map p86; ☎2552-4176; http://c3mundos.org/es/inicio; Parque Central, 50m N; ⊙8am-6pm) Founded in 1986 by Ernesto Cardenal, the Fundación Casa de los Tres Mundos moved to elegant Casa de los Leones in 1992. Casa Los Leones was built in 1720, but what you see now is a reconstruction, since William Walker burned down the original. At the entrance, a board lists special events: poetry readings, classical ballet, folkloric dance and free movies. During regular business hours, you can enjoy the beautiful mansion, historical archive, cafe and art displays.

Mi Museo   MUSEUM
(Map p86; ☎2552-7614; Calle Atravesada, Cine Karawala, ½c N; US$5; ⊙8am-5pm) This museum displays a private collection of ceramics dating from at least 2000 BC to the present. Hundreds of beautifully crafted pieces were chosen with as much an eye for their artistic merit as their archaeological significance.

La Capilla María Auxiliadora   CHURCH
(Map p82; Calle Real Xalteva; ⊙hours vary) This gorgeous 1918 Gothic church with white-and-blue trim is worth a look for its interior – arguably the most beautiful of all of Granada's churches – all neo-Gothic arches and blue-and green-pastels.

Iglesia de Xalteva   CHURCH
(Map p82; frente Parque Xalteva; ⊙hours vary) The dilapidated but attractive colonial church that houses La Virgen de la Asunción was almost completely rebuilt in the 1890s after suffering serious earthquake damage.

Antigua Estación del Ferrocarril   LANDMARK
(Old Train Station; Map p82; frente Parque Sandino) Nine long blocks north of town along Calle Atravesada you'll find **Parque Sandino**, next to the old train station, now a technical vocational school. It was built in 1882 and operational in 1886; the US Marines remodeled it in 1912. There's lots of playground equipment, some with train themes, and a few well-preserved railroad cars are on display nearby. Out front is the **Parque de los Poetas**, dedicated to Nicaragua's literary giants.

Catedral de Granada   CATHEDRAL
(Map p86; Parque Colón; ⊙hours vary) The cathedral, on the east side of the plaza, was originally built in 1583 but has been destroyed countless times since. This most recent version, built in 1915, has four chapels; a dozen stained-glass panels are set into the dome. It's occasionally open to the public.

Fortaleza La Polvora
FORT

(Map p82; Calle Real Xalteva; by donation; ⊙8am-5pm) Originally called the Fortaleza de Armas when it was constructed in 1748, this lavishly turreted Spanish fortress still has the best views in town, over ancient, water-stained church domes all the way to Lago de Nicaragua. There's a small museum inside.

Mercado Municipal
MARKET

(Map p82; Calle Atravesada; ⊙7am-5pm Mon-Sat) Head to the overflowing and lively Mercado Municipal, a neoclassical building constructed in 1892, for a chance to observe locals haggling over fresh produce.

Iglesia de Guadalupe
CHURCH

(Map p82; cnr Calle La Calzada & El Ganado; ⊙hours vary) The imposing, twin towered Iglesia de Guadalupe was originally built as a fort in 1626 and refurbished in 1945.

Antiguo Hospital
RUINS

(Map p82; Av Arellano, Iglesia Xalteva 1c O, 1½c N) The city's old hospital ruins are a landmark locals often use when giving directions.

Plaza de la Independencia
SQUARE

(Plaza de los Leones; Map p86; frente Parque Central) North of Parque Central is Plaza de la Independencia, also known as the 'Plaza de los Leones.' The obelisk is dedicated to the heroes of the 1821 struggle for independence, while the Cruz de Siglo was erected in 1900 to mark the new century.

Centro Turístico
BEACH

(Map p82; frente Lago de Nicaragua; ⊙8am-late) **FREE** This lakefront tourist center has restaurants, discos, sandy beaches, kids' play areas, and picnic spots, though the location is no good for swimming and the place is often plagued by *chayules* (tiny biting flies). Take cabs to and from here after dark.

🏃 Activities

Las Tortilla Cooking School
COOKING

(Map p86; ☏5503-2805; Calle El Martirio 305, entre Calle La Libertad y El Arsenal; basic class US$45 per person; ⊙cooking classes daily 10:30am & 4:30pm) A really fun, hands-on experience that teaches you all about the origins and methods of Nicaraguan cuisine. Spend two

---

PIRATES OF LAKE NICARAGUA!

The sacking of Central America's crown jewel, Granada, was one of the most daring exploits in pirate history, a career coup for dashing up-and-coming buccaneer Henry Morgan and his band of rum-soaked merry men.

It couldn't have been done in a full-sized sailing vessel – if you follow Morgan's path up the Río San Juan you'll see how those rapids would tear a regular ship apart. But this crafty band of quick thinkers appropriated six 12m wooden canoes (after their regular pirate ships were impounded by Spanish authorities) following an equally spectacular sacking of Villahermosa, Mexico. The atypical craft proved more than adequate for further pillaging along the Caribbean coast, which gave the 30-year-old Morgan an idea.

The crew battled the currents of the Río San Juan at night, hiding their canoes during the day. They then made their way across the great lake. The June 1665 attack caught complacent *granadinos* completely off guard: the pirates occupied the city for 16 hours – just like the Disney ride, but more violent – then stole all the ammunition, sank all the boats and sailed off to a warm welcome, as heroes and legends in Port Royal, Jamaica. Eat your heart out Jack Sparrow.

Between 1665 and 1670, Granada was sacked three times, even as Morgan took more pirate canoes up the Río Coco, where he made powerful allies of the Miskitos. With their help, pirates sacked Ciudad Antigua and Estelí, where Morgan himself stayed for a while, and founded several of the surrounding towns.

Pirates actually founded more cities in Nicaragua than they ever sacked, including Pueblo Viejo and several surrounding towns in the Segovias, Bilwi, on the Caribbean coast, and most famously Bluefields, named for founder Abraham Blewfeldt, a Dutch pirate who worked the waters from Rhode Island to Panama.

Although the 1697 Treaty of Ryswick guaranteed that England, Spain, France and Holland would respect each other's property in the New World, the pirates continued to try for Granada. In 1769, 17-year-old Rafaela Herrera commanded Spanish forces at El Castillo against pirates trying to sack Granada yet again. She won, signalling the beginning of the end for the pirates of the Caribbean.

Central Granada

or three hours learning to make five typical dishes and throw in a market tour (US$15 to learn about the ingredients).

Massiel Torres POTTERY CLASS
(Map p86; ☑ 8672-7465; Calle Calzada, el catedral, 1½c E; pottery classes from US$15; ⊗ noon-9pm) Near Wok & Roll, this ceramics artist from San Juan de Oriente offers pottery-making classes to visitors.

Erick Tours TOUR
(Map p86; ☑ 8974-5575; www.ericktoursnicaragua. com; Parque Central, 3c E; tour prices vary) All the standard tours (Las Isletas, Mombacho, a one-day trip to Ometepe) plus airport transfers for US$15 per person. The reliability of Erick's shuttle services has been called into question, though.

Pure SPA
(Map p82; ☑ 8481-3264; www.purenica.com; Calle Corrales, Convento San Francisco, 1½c E; day/weekly/monthly pass US$5/15/29, class & treatment prices vary; ⊗ 7am-9pm, class times vary) Sign up for yoga classes (US$5), daily, weekly or monthly gym memberships, or massages (US$26) at this peaceful day spa and gym.

Inuit Kayaks KAYAKING
(Map p82; ☑ 7876-9030; Centro Turístico, frente del lago; per person US$25-35) Inuit Kayaks runs

several recommended guided tours around Las Isletas.

🎓 Courses

Nicaragua Mia Spanish School LANGUAGE
(Map p82; ☑ 7779-0209; www.facebook.com/nicaraguamiaschool; Calle El Caimito, alcaldía, 3½ c E; 1 week all-inclusive per person US$280) Run by a women's co-op, with a range of teaching methods and years of experience.

Xpress Spanish School LANGUAGE
(Map p82; ☑ 2552-8577; Calle Cervantes, Parque Central, 2½c N; class prices vary) Centrally located, with a young and dynamic staff.

Casa Xalteva LANGUAGE
(Map p82; ☑ 2552-2993; www.casaxalteva.org; Calle Real Xalteva, Iglesia Xalteva, 25m N; 1-week language course from US$160; ⊗ 8am-5pm Mon-Fri) 🖋 Next to the church of the same name, Casa Xalteva also runs a program providing breakfast and education for street kids, as well as language classes and homestays.

Alianza Francesa de Granada LANGUAGE
(Map p86; www.alianzafrancesagranada.org; Calle El Arsenal s/n, el catedral, 1½c N, ½c E; prices vary; ⊗ 9am-9:30pm Mon-Fri) French and Spanish language courses, plus French-inspired cultural events.

Central Granada

La Calzada Centro de Arte   ART

(Map p86; ☑8616-7322; www.facebook.com/
nicaragua.art; Calle La Calzada, Parque Central, 1c
E; classes from US$6; ⊙class times vary) This
friendly art center offers painting and
drawing classes courtesy of Amy from the
Carolinas.

Spanish Dale! Language School   LANGUAGE

(Map p86; ☑8866-4581; http://spanishdale.com;
Calle Atravesada, frente Bancentro; 1 week per person from US$150; ⊙8am-5pm Mon-Fri) A Span-
ish-language school inside the Mansión de
Chocolate (p90).

☞ Tours

Numerous operators offer worthwhile city
tours of Granada, that take in the best of the
colonial architecture, as well as the *malecón*
(waterfront esplanade). Half-day boat or
kayak tours of Las Isletas are also on offer,
though it's worth staying out on the islands
overnight, if you can afford it.

Adventour Nicaragua   OUTDOORS

(Map p86; ☑5760-6733; www.adventournicaragua.
com; Calle Calzada, el catedral, ½c E; ⊙8am-9pm)
Ramiro and his passionate, professional
team run highly recommended tours of Las
Isletas, Isla Zapatero, Volcán Mombacho
(from US$25) and Granada itself, with small
groups accompanied by bilingual guides.
Shuttles available to destinations across the
country, too.

Livit Water   WATER SPORTS

(☑8580-7014; www.livitwater.com; Marina Cocibolca; SUP tours per person from US$40) Scott
and Gea run professional SUP tours on the
water, both here and in Laguna Apoyo, with
pickup from Granada. Combine your SUP
experience with yoga or half-day tours up
Volcán Mombacho.

Nicaragua Escapade   OUTDOORS

(☑8963-8162; www.facebook.com/nicaraguaesca
pade) The popularity of this local operator

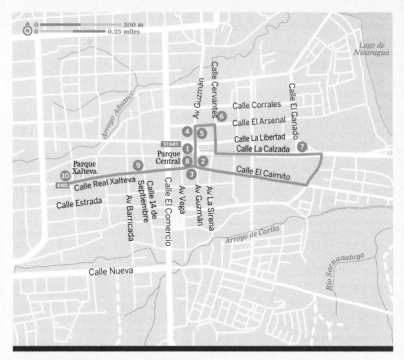

City Walk
Colonial Explorer

START PARQUE CENTRAL
END IGLESIA DE XALTEVA
LENGTH 2.5KM; THREE HOURS

Begin at the fine ❶ **Parque Central**, pleasantly shaded by mango and malinche trees. The ❷ **Catedral de Granada** (p84), on the eastern side of the plaza, was originally built in 1583 but has been destroyed countless times since. This version was built in 1915.

On the park's southeastern corner, the beautifully restored ❸ **Hotel Gran Francia** (p90) was formerly the home of William Walker. Head north to ❹ **Plaza de la Independencia** (p85). The obelisk is dedicated to the heroes of the 1821 struggle for independence, while the Cruz de Siglo was erected in 1900 to mark the new century.

On the eastern side of this plaza is the Casa de los Leones, named for the carved lions on the stone portal, the only part of the original structure that survived Walker's 1856 retreat. Rebuilt as a stately private home in 1920, it's currently home to ❺ **Fundación Casa de los**

Tres Mundos (p84), hosting art exhibitions, poetry readings and other cultural events.

Head one block east on Calle El Arsenal to check out the awesome facade of ❻ **Convento y Museo San Francisco** (p83), best photographed close to sunset. Don't miss out on seeing the priceless statuary in the cloisters. From here, head south on Calle Cervantes until you get to Calle La Calzada. Heading towards the lake, you'll pass ❼ **Capilla del Sagrado Corazón** (p85), originally built as a fort.

Head back to ❽ **Parque Central**, where you can stop for a snack and a spot of people watching on a shady park bench. From here, proceed west along Calle Real Xalteva, which once connected the Spanish town of Granada to its much older indigenous neighbor, Xalteva. Four blocks west of Parque Central, you'll pass ❾ **Iglesia La Merced** (p84), one of Granada's most beautiful churches.

The old indigenous neighborhood, now wholly assimilated, is marked by ❿ **Iglesia de Xalteva** (p84), the attractive 19th-century church that houses La Virgen de la Asunción.

has increased through word of mouth. Rodolfo (Rudy) and his team are highly regarded for their kayak tours (from US$25 per person), Granada city tours and transfers to different parts of the country.

Corazón Trips　　　　　　　　　　TOURS
(Map p82; ☑ 2552-8852; www.hotelconcorazon. com; Calle Santa Lucia 141) Located inside the Hotel Con Corazón (p91), this nonprofit tour operator offers well-organized trips including bike tours, cooking classes and trips to Mombacho.

Leo Tours Comunitarios　　　　　TOURS
(Map p86; ☑ 8422-7905; www.facebook.com/ leotourscomunitarios; Calla la Calzada, Parque Central, 1½c E; ⊙8am-9pm) Enthusiastic locally owned business that offers all the usual options – Las Isletas boat tours (US$15), Mombacho (US$30), and a full-day trip to Masaya (US$40) – as well as some interesting visits to local communities.

Tierra Tour　　　　　　　　　　TOURS
(Map p86; ☑ 2552-8723; www.tierratour.com; Calle La Calzada, catedral, 2c E) A recommended company that offers kayaking on Lago de Nicaragua, Volcán Mombacho tours, volcano boarding and other standard trips, plus camping and day trips to Finca La Calera.

★ Festivals & Events

International Poetry Festival　PERFORMING ARTS
(www.festivalpoesianicaragua.com; ⊙2nd week in Feb) This festival brings together scores of wordsmiths, artists and musicians – not just Nicaragua's finest, but also poets from all over Latin America and around the world as well. Events are held in open spaces in front of major landmarks.

Fiestas de Agosto　　　　　　RELIGIOUS
(⊙3rd week Aug) Granada celebrates the Assumption of Mary with fireworks, concerts in the park, horse parades and major revelry by the lakefront.

Inmaculada Concepción　　　　RELIGIOUS
(Purísimas; ⊙Nov 28–Dec 7) Neighborhoods bear elaborate floats through the streets in honor of Granada's patron saint, the Virgen Concepción de María. They signal their arrival by blowing on conch shells to drive the demons away.

🛏 Sleeping

There's a huge range of sleeping options in Granada, from budget-friendly hostels and guesthouses to some of the country's loveliest and most characterful boutique and historic hotels, inside former colonial buildings.

Oasis Hostel　　　　　　　　HOSTEL $
(Map p86; ☑ 2552-8005; www.nicaraguahostel. com; Calle Estrada 109, Mercado Municipal, 1c N, ½c O; dm/s/d US$8/15/20; ❄ 🛜 🏊) A five-minute walk from the main square, this hostel is a Granada institution. It's extremely well-run, with numerous daily shuttles and activities, and the owners are really clued-up about backpacker needs: there is generous locker space, free international phone calls, kitchen, ample breakfast and more. Rooms are basic, but then, they're not the main attraction here.

Lemon Tree Hostel　　　　　　HOSTEL $
(Map p86; ☑ 8912-8764; www.lemontreehostels. com; Calle La Libertad, Parque Central, 2c O; dm/r US$10/35; ❄ 🛜 🏊) A boutique hotel in its previous incarnation, this is the grandest hostel in Granada – all vast ceilings, graceful courtyard, spa and hammocks strung around the pool. The huge doubles share facilities, though, as do the dorms. Staff are happy to arrange excursions and shuttles.

Hostel de Boca en Boca　　　　HOSTEL $
(Map p86; ☑ 2552-3386; Calle 14 de Septiembre, Iglesia La Merced, 1c N; dm/r US$8/23; ❄ 🛜) With a leafy, hammock-hung garden a block from the main square, this hostel is extremely well-run, with lots of thoughtful touches, such as individual reading lights and large lockers for bunk beds. Friendly, approachable staff organize all manner of excursions.

Hostal El Momento　　　　　　HOSTEL $
(Map p86; ☑ 2552-7811; www.hostelgranadanicaragua.com; Calle El Arsenal, Mi Museo, ½c E; dm/d US$10/40; ❄ 🛜) Catering to the non-partying backpacker set, this hip hostel has cool common spaces, iPads in the lobby, a book exchange and a shared kitchen. Private rooms are a good bet, some maintaining the historic character of the building, while others are smallish and hot, in spite of the fan.

Glifoos Hotel　　　　　BOUTIQUE HOTEL $$
(Map p86; ☑ 7542-9835; http://glifoos-ni.book.direct; Real Xalteva 205, Iglesia La Merced, ½c E; r from US$38; ❄ 🛜) Carnival masks and giant wooden crocodiles line the corridors at this quirky boutique-on-a-budget hotel. High ceilings, high beds and hand-carved wooden furnishings define the sparsely decorated yet comfortable rooms, and there's a good cafe on-site.

Casa del Agua
HOTEL $$

(Map p86; ☑ 8872-4627; www.casadelaguagranada. com; Av Guzmán, Parque Central, ½c S; d/tr from US$40/50; ❋🤖💺) Spacious rooms surround a small pool (with a suspended swing) in a prize location just off Parque Central. Furnishings inside this beautiful colonial building are all new and tastefully selected, and owner Gerry is a treasure trove of local knowledge. There's a fully stocked kitchen for guest use, on-site bike rentals and a pancake breakfast.

Hotel La Pérgola
HOTEL $$

(Map p86; ☑ 2552-4221; www.lapergola.com.ni; Calle El Caimito, alcaldía, 3c E; s/d from US$43/56; 🅿❋🤖) This cozy hotel with its little center courtyard, spacious rooms and big, firm beds is a decent bet. Note: there's no hot water.

★Hotel Gran Francia
HISTORIC HOTEL $$$

(Map p86; ☑ 2552-6000; www.lagranfrancia.com; Av Guzmán, Parque Central, ½c S; r from US$110; 🅿❋🤖💺) Just off the main plaza, this elegant hotel is set in an opulent historic building, with hardwood floors, hand-painted sinks, wrought iron detail and heavy wooden beams in its characterful rooms. Across the street, the Gran Francia's restaurant, bar and lounge (set in William Walker's former home) are equally impressive.

Hotel Patio del Malinche
HISTORIC HOTEL $$$

(Map p86; ☑ 2552-2235; www.patiodelmalinche. com; Calle El Caimito, alcaldía, 2½c E; s/d incl breakfast US$75/94; ❋🤖💺) This lovely house has been thoughtfully restored and outfitted with authentic features such as cane-inlaid ceilings. There are actually two patios, both comfortably appointed with wicker furniture, the back one featuring a pool and bar area. Rooms are moderately sized and stylish in a minimalist way.

Hotel La Polvora
BOUTIQUE HOTEL $$$

(Map p82; ☑ 2552-1227; www.hotellapolvora.com; Calle El Consulado, Fortaleza La Polvora, ½c E, 1c N, 1c E; r from US$75; ❋🤖💺) Barring the sound of church bells, nothing is likely to disturb your rest at this intimate boutique hotel on a quiet residential street, near the namesake fort. Beyond the beautifully tiled lobby there are just 10 comfortable rooms, most with rocking chairs on the terrace or balcony. Liam and his staff go above and beyond the call of duty.

Casa Xanadu
BOUTIQUE HOTEL $$$

(Map p86; ☑ 8380-9035; http://casaxanadu.com; Calle Arsenal, contiguo al Convento San Francisco; ste US$72-120; ❋🤖💺) From the polished, hand-carved wooden pillars in its courtyard to the six colorful, individually styled suites in the beautifully restored colonial mansion, this boutique hotel aims to impress. Vaulted ceilings and spa baths are just some of the rooms' features, and you can ask the chef for a barbecue dinner if you don't feel like dining out.

Hotel Boutique Adela
BOUTIQUE HOTEL $$$

(Map p82; ☑ 2552-2040; https://hotelboutique adela.com; Calle El Arsenal, Convento San Francisco, 2c E; ste US$100; ❋🤖💺) This exquisite 1840s colonial property is decorated with abstract wooden sculpture and antique pottery, and there are just four airy suites, each individually decorated and with doors opening out onto the greenery-filled courtyard. You can hire out the entire mansion and make use of the fully equipped kitchen, too.

Mansión de Chocolate
BOUTIQUE HOTEL $$$

(Map p86; ☑ 2552-4678; www.mansiondechocolate. com; Calle Atravesada, frente Bancocentro; r/tr from US$77/101; ❋🤖💺) This elegant and expansive Spanish colonial mansion – once a hospital – is now a chocolate-themed hotel with a lovely pool (available for day use, US$6) and a hands-on chocolate museum, the Museo de Chocolate (p84), perfect for families. Guest rooms are spread out; some face courtyards, others are located up quaint wooden staircases. The all-you-can-eat breakfast is open to the public (US$7).

Hotel Casa del Consulado
HISTORIC HOTEL $$$

(Map p86; ☑ 2552-2709; www.hotelcasaconsulado. com; Calle Consulado 105, Parque Central, 1½c O; d from US$89; 🅿❋🤖💺) This elegant boutique hotel, in an immaculately preserved *casona* (historic home), is one of the nicer options in town. The large pool in the central garden is the focus of the cane-roofed patio areas. Guest rooms have high ceilings and massive bathrooms with river-rock showers.

Hotel Los Patios
BOUTIQUE HOTEL $$$

(Map p82; ☑ 2552-0641; www.lospatiosgranada. com; Calle Corrales 525, Iglesia de Guadelupe, 3c N, ½c O; s/d US$120/150; 🅿❋🤖💺) Contemporary style and colonial charm come together at this five-room boutique hotel. Scandinavian design sensibilities, including low-slung beds, modern fixtures, light-filled common spaces, a lovely pool and space-age Zen gardens add to the allure.

Hotel Casa San Francisco
HISTORIC HOTEL $$$

(Map p82; ☑2552-8235; www.hotelcasasanfrancisco.com; Calle Corrales 207, Convento San Francisco, ½c O; d from US$87; P※☎☀) ❋ There's plenty of charm in the ivy-covered walls, mosaic tiles, Turkish lamps, cute little balcony sitting areas and stylish decorations in this lovely colonial house turned boutique hotel: it's the passion project of a pair of sisters from California who each served in the Peace Corps before falling in love with Granada.

Hotel Con Corazón
HOTEL $$$

(Map p82; ☑2552-8852; www.hotelconcorazon.com; Calle Cervantes, Parque Central, 3c N; s/d/tr/f US$75/91/117/139; ※@☎☀) ❋ Spreading goodwill one country at a time, this is one of 10 nonprofit hotels worldwide that direct earnings to the development of local educational programs. The rooms are simple and spacious without being luxurious. The building blends modern and traditional styles, with much of the decoration coming from recycled materials made by local craftspeople.

On Monday nights it has salsa classes that are open to the public and there's a good attached cafe.

Hotel Plaza Colón
HISTORIC HOTEL $$$

(Map p86; ☑2552-8489; www.hotelplazacolon.com; costado oeste Parque Central; r from US$139; P※☎☀) The last word in plaza-side luxury, this chart-topper contends for the best high-end spot in town. Rooms are large and airy, with serious dark-wood and wrought-iron trimmings, and come equipped with all the modern conveniences. It's worth splashing out the extra US$20 to get a room with a deep, wide balcony overlooking the plaza.

✗ Eating

Granada caters to international tastes with a wide variety of cuisines, and new options are opening all the time. The city has excellent street food too. Look for it around Parque Central and Mercado Municipal (p85) in the morning, and just before sunset, at *fritangas* (grills) set up around town.

Café de las Sonrisas
NICARAGUAN $

(Map p86; www.tioantonio.org/cafe-de-las-sonrisas; Iglesia La Merced, ½c E; dishes US$2.50-4; ⊙7am-4pm Mon-Fri, to 3pm Sat) ❋ Practice your in-

ternational communication at this nonprofit cafe run by staff who are hearing-impaired. It has a picture-gram menu, sign charts and basic, hearty and wholesome Nicaraguan fare.

Comidas Tipicas y Más
NICARAGUAN $

(Map p86; Calle La Calzada, el catedral, 1c E; dishes US$3-5; ⊙6pm-late Thu-Tue) Typical Nicaraguan dishes here cost more than at your local *comedor* (basic eatery), but it has a sweet patio setting and the portions are huge. Try the *indio viejo* (beef stew; US$2.50), *nacatamales* (banana-leaf-wrapped bundles of cornmeal, meat, vegetables and herbs; US$2) or quesadillas (US$2.50).

Pizzeria Don Luca
PIZZA $

(Map p86; ☑2552-7822; https://pizzeriadonluca.com; Calle La Calzada, Parque Central, 3c E; pizza US$3-5, mains US$6-10; ⊙noon-2pm & 6-10pm Tue-Thu & Sun, to 11pm Fri & Sat) This friendly pizzeria offers outdoor seating – a great vantage for people watching – and a wide selection of Italian faves.

Supermercado Colonia
SUPERMARKET $

(Map p82; Calle La Inmaculada, Esso, 3c E; ⊙8am-8:30pm) An upscale supermarket.

Cafetín El Volcán
NICARAGUAN **$**

(Map p86; ☑ 8889-2345; Calle 14 de Septiembre, Iglesia La Merced, 1c S; quesillos US$0.50-2) You could come to this family-run place for the good-value set lunches (US$3), but most people agree that the real draw here are the *quesillos* (grilled corn tortillas stuffed with cheese and topped with pickled onions and cream), and the passionfruit drinks.

Café Blue
CAFE **$**

(Map p86; Calle Vega, Parque Central, 1c S; dishes US$2.50-5) A refreshingly simple little cafe serving up good American and Nica breakfasts, some spicy *huevos rancheros,* pancakes, burgers and sandwiches, under a cane ceiling.

Palí
SUPERMARKET **$**

(Map p82; Calle Atravesada; ☺ 9am-8pm) A grocery store with basic stock, good prices and a tiny bakery, in front of Mercado Municipal.

★ Bocadillos Tapas Kitchen & Bar
INTERNATIONAL **$$**

(Map p82; ☑ 2552-5089; www.bocadillosgranada. com; frente Convento San Francisco; dishes US$4-8; ☺ noon-9pm; ☎) The interior leafy courtyard of this stylish yet casual restaurant is an ideal setting for a cocktail (including some original ones!), a local craft beer or two or three, and imaginative tapas that span the globe, from spicy samosas and pulled pork sliders to Thai noodle salad and roasted garlic hummus. There's a handful of substantial dishes, too.

El Garaje
VEGETARIAN **$$**

(Map p82; ☑ 8651-7412; Calle Corrales, Convento San Francisco, 2c E; mains US$5-8; ☺ 11:30am-3:30pm Mon-Fri; ☑) Hands down, the best place for vegetarians in Granada, El Garaje serves imaginative fare such as curry chickpea pita, vegan 'pulled pork', sloppy joes, and salads, all in a bright setting, surrounded by contemporary art. Outstanding lime cheesecake, too.

Cafe del Arte
NICARAGUAN **$$**

(Map p86; ☑ 2552-6461; Calle Cervantes, el catedral, 1c E, ½c N; mains US$4-7; ☺ 7:30am-9pm) Sit in the courtyard, filled with greenery and paintings by local artists, and savour an excellent coffee and an ample Nica breakfast.

La Frontera
BURGERS **$$**

(Map p82; ☑ 2558-2120; www.facebook.com/ comedorlafrontera; Iglesia de Xalteva, 1½c N; mains US$5-7; ☺ noon-9pm Wed-Sun; ☑) Some of

Granada's best 'fast good' treats are served in this grungy courtyard, surrounded by posters of Nirvana and The Police and to a Guns N' Roses and Queen soundtrack. We particularly like the Heavy Metal Burger and the Pig Metal Sandwich, though there are veggie quesadillas and burritos for non-carnivorous customers.

Kathy's Waffle House
BREAKFAST **$$**

(Map p86; ☑ 2552-7583; www.kathyswafflehouse. com; Calle El Arsenal; dishes US$5-10; ☺ 7am-9pm; ☎☑) Drop into Kathy's, a long-time breakfast institution for tourists and locals alike, for pecan waffles, pancakes, bottomless coffee and great views of Convento San Francisco from the front porch. Dinner mains include pastas and chicken soup.

Cafe de los Sueños
INTERNATIONAL **$$**

(Map p82; ☑ 2552-7272; Calle La Calzada, frente Centro Escolar Carlos A Bravo; dishes US$4-8; ☺ 11am-10:30pm) A few steps from the loudest stretch of Calle La Calzada, this adorable cafe does good salads, freshly grilled fish, and a few international dishes such as Mexican-style tacos and jalapeño chicken.

Taco Stop
TEX-MEX **$$**

(Map p86; www.tacostopnicaragua.com; Calle Atravesada, Parque Central, 1c O, ½c N; mains US$3-8; ☺ 10:30am-midnight Sun-Tue, to 3am Wed & Thu, to 5am Fri & Sat; ☎) Inside the shell of a vintage movie theater, this is a fast-food-style *taquería* (taco stall) chain. Grab a burrito to go, or sit down for a spicy Mexican stew and cold beer. The tortillas are made in-house; there's even a small salsa bar. Be warned – the salsa verde is made with locally grown jalapeños and has a real kick.

El Camello BBQ
MEDITERRANEAN **$$**

(Map p86; ☑ 8811-2655; www.granadarestaurant. wordpress.com; Calle El Caimito, Hotel Gran Francia, 2c E; mains US$6-8; ☺ noon-10pm Wed-Mon) This expat favorite takes you on a tour of the Mediterranean and the Middle East, featuring lamb stews, falafel and hummus.

El Zaguán
STEAK **$$**

(Map p86; ☑ 2552-2522; Av La Sirena, Parque Central, 1c E, ½c S; meals US$7-13; ☺ noon-11pm) Scoring consistent props for the best steak in town, this large yet somehow cozy restaurant just behind the cathedral specializes in locally sourced steaks, flame-grilled before your eyes. Some solid chicken and fish dishes and a good wine list round out the menu.

Make reservations in high season; it's popular with tourists.

★ Miss Dell's Kitchen
FUSION $$$

(Map p86; ☑2552-2815; cnr Calle Cervantes & Calle El Arsenal; mains US$10-14; ☺5:30pm-midnight) Mellow jazz plays in the background at this candlelit spot, with a mural of a rooster, Mr Beautiful, gracing the back wall. The rooster belonged to Miss Dell, a Haitian cook, whose recipes have been adapted by the chef for the short and sweet menu. The *piri piri pescado* (fish in a chilli sauce) is one of the best things we've ever tried, anywhere.

Espressonista
FUSION $$$

(Map p82; ☑2552-4325; www.facebook.com/ espressonistacoffee; Calle Real Xalteva, frente Iglesia de Xalteva; mains US$10-18; ☺noon-8pm Wed-Sun; 🛜) Tall ceilings, hand-carved furniture and gilded mirrors give this place a certain old-world grandeur, but the succinct menu is as contemporary as it gets, with French influences. Feast on the likes of mackerel and passionfruit *ceviche* (marinated seafood), rabbit confit and ox cheek à la bourguignonne, along with some of Granada's best gourmet coffee.

Pita Pita
MIDDLE EASTERN $$$

(Map p86; ☑2552-4117; www.facebook.com/ ThePitaPita; Calle La Libertad, Parque Central, 1c E; mains US$10-12; ☺noon-10pm; 🛜🍴) A long-time favorite Italian trattoria has expanded and morphed into a Middle Eastern restaurant, though the wood-fired thin-crust pizza remains the best in town. Roasted, garlicky eggplant with yogurt hits the spot, as does the Palestinian kebab and the Israeli shakshuka.

Curry House
NORTH INDIAN $$$

(Map p82; ☑2552-6772; Calle La Calzada, Parque Central, 3½c E; mains US$7-12; ☺6-10pm Tue-Sun; 🍴) Authentic Indian dishes served in a greenery-filled courtyard. The eggplant and cauliflower curry is a triumph and the supporting cast of samosas, naan bread, saag paneer and chana masalas isn't bad either.

🍺 Drinking & Nightlife

Granada hops most nights, but Thursday to Saturday is when the real action takes place. Most people start or end the night off at one of the numerous bars along or just off Calle La Calzada, known for outdoor drinking and prime people watching.

Hog's Breath Saloon
LOUNGE

(Map p82; ☑8337-6225; www.hogsbreathgranada.com; Calle La Calzada, frente Iglesia de Guadelupe; ☺noon-11pm) Modeled on the original Hog's Breath Saloon in Florida and run by a friendly Minnesotan couple, this safari-themed lounge bar is the antithesis of the backpacker haunts up the street – a place to sip a whisky, gin or a cocktail and munch on some delicious tapas while checking out the stuffed animal heads and guitars that deck the walls.

Nectar
BAR

(Map p86; www.facebook.com/NectarNicaragua; Calle La Calzada, Parque Central, 1½c E; dishes US$5-8; ☺11am-11pm) This place wears many hats and we like all of them. It's a small lounge-bar with a good list of cocktails and local craft beers (come for happy hour). In high season it often gets visiting DJs and live rock bands to liven the place up. Internationally inspired light dishes and snacks make up the creative menu.

O'Sheas
IRISH PUB

(Map p86; Calle La Calzada s/n; ☺8:30am-2am) One of the most popular pubs with tourists along the Calzada, O'Sheas has friendly service, cold beer and hit-and-miss pub grub. Attracts its share of local hustlers, though.

Inuit Bar
BAR

(Map p82; ☑8661-7655; Centro Turístico; ☺24hr) This lakeside bar is a spot for a cold beer by the water, with young locals dancing to loud reggaeton into the wee hours on weekends.

☆ Entertainment

For a city of this size and popularity, there aren't as many cultural offerings as you'd expect in Granada, though live music and film screenings happen on and around Calle La Calzada on weekends.

La Hacienda
LIVE MUSIC

(Map p86; ☑8473-5194; www.facebook.com/ lahaciendaengranada; Calle Cervantes, Parque Central, 2c N, 1c E; ☺noon-midnight Tue-Sun) The Tex-Mex dishes here are seriously hit and miss, so we suggest you come here for sunset cocktails, a great view of Convento San Francisco and live music most evenings, including a Guns N' Roses tribute band.

GRANADA DRINKING & NIGHTLIFE

🛍 Shopping

There are several excellent shops where you can buy high-quality crafts handmade in Nicaragua, as well as gourmet coffee. Granada is also the best place in Nicaragua to find English-language books (including Lonely Planet guidebooks).

★ The Garden Shop
ARTS & CRAFTS

(Map p86; www.gardencafegranada.com; Calle La Libertad, Parque Central, 1c E; ☺9am-6pm; 🛜) 🏄 A fantastic addition to the popular Garden Café, this sustainably minded boutique offers crafts, jewelry, clothing and artwork produced through NGOs and fair-trade organizations throughout Nicaragua. Artisans from Chinandega, Diriamba, Granada, Masatepe, Managua and Masaya are all represented here; you can also buy coffee beans and postcards, and there's a good-sized book exchange at the entrance.

Soy Nica
FASHION & ACCESSORIES

(Map p82; ☑2552-0234; www.facebook.com/soynica.dk; Calle La Calzada, Iglesia de Guadelupe, 100m O; ☺9am-6pm Mon-Thu, to 8pm Fri & Sat, to 2pm Sun) Come here for stylish purses, shoulder bags, belts and other accessories made of Nicaraguan leather. You can see them being made at the workshop next to the store.

Cooperativa El Parche
ARTS & CRAFTS

(Map p86; ☑8473-7700; Calle 14 de Septiembre, Hostal Entre Amigos) 🏄 Inside the Hostal Entre Amigos, this excellent gift shop sells crafts made by local artisans. What makes it special are the items made of recycled products and local materials, and your purchase helps to support recyclable art in rural communities.

Lucho Libro Books
BOOKS

(Map p86; www.luchalibrobooks.com; Calle Cervantes, Parque Central, 1c E, ½c N; ☺8am-6pm Wed-Mon) Swing in to this friendly store with a good selection of English-language books and maps, including numerous Lonely Planet guidebooks!

Doña Elba Cigars
GIFTS & SOUVENIRS

(Map p82; ☑2552-3217; Iglesia Xalteva, 1c S; ☺8am-5pm) If you aren't heading to Estelí this trip, stop here for a cognac-cured taste of Nicaragua and a peek at the cigar-manufacturing process. You can even practice rolling a cigar.

Olé
ARTS & CRAFTS

(Map p86; ☑8895-4287; www.facebook.com/olegranadanic; Calle La Calzada, Parque Central, 1c E; ☺9am-7pm Tue-Sun) 🏄 A clothing boutique and handicrafts store specializing in produce from local cooperatives. Expect jewelry, purses, and gifts made out of bamboo, aluminum and wood.

ℹ Information

DANGERS & ANNOYANCES

➡ Always take a cab after dark between the lake and the Centro Turístico.

➡ Avoid cycling to Peninsula de Asese due to occasional robberies.

➡ The anti-government protests that erupted in mid-April 2018 did not spare Granada. In early June, the city hall was set on fire and there was violent clashes between government-funded Sandinista mobs and protesters. There was also some looting of businesses.

EMERGENCY

| Ambulance (Cruz Roja) | ☑2552-2711 |
| Police | ☑2552-2929 |

INTERNET ACCESS

The vast majority of accommodations, and many restaurants and cafes, have free wi-fi.

MEDICAL SERVICES

For serious medical emergencies, it's best to go to Managua.

Hospital Amistad Japonés (☑2552-2022; Carretera a Masaya–Granada Km 45; ☺24hr) The most frequently recommended private hospital is out of town, on the road to Managua. Basic emergency care.

Cruz Roja (Ambulance; ☑2565-2081) Ambulance.

MONEY

Several banks are within a block of Parque Central.

BAC (Map p86; Calle La Libertad, Parque Central, 1c O)

BanPro (Map p86; Calle Consulado, Parque Central, 1c O)

Western Union (Map p82; Calle Real Xalteva; ☺9am-5pm Mon-Fri) International money transfers.

TOURIST INFORMATION

Check at hostels and tour operators for the latest tourist info.

Intur (Map p82; ☑2552-6858; www.visita nicaragua.com; Calle Corrales; ☺8am-5pm

Mon–Fri) The Granada branch of the national tourist office has up-to-date transportation schedules, a reasonable city map, and lots of information and flyers.

VOLUNTEERING

Hotel Con Corazón (p91) Hotel with a heart is a good place to learn more about volunteer ops.

❶ Getting There & Away

BOAT

Marina Cocibolca (☑ 2552-2269; desvio a Posintepe), about 2km southeast of town, has boats for Las Isletas and Parque Nacional Archipiélago Zapatera.

BUS

Granada doesn't have one central bus terminal. **Buses to Managua** (Map p82; Calle El Tamarindo; US$0.75, 1½ hours, 5am to 7pm, every 20 to 30 minutes)Arriving at Managua's Mercado Roberto Huembes, buses depart from the lot just north of the old hospital on the western edge of town. **Microbuses to Managua** (Map p86; Calle Vega; US$1, one hour, 5am to 7pm, every 20 minutes), arriving at UCA in Managua, leave from the convenient lot just south of the Parque Central on Calle Vega; change at UCA for microbuses and chicken buses to León.

Buses to Masaya (Map p82; Calle 14 de Septiembre; US$0.50, 30 minutes, 4:30am to 4:30pm, every 20 to 30 minutes) Buses leave from two blocks west of the Mercado Municipal, around the corner from Palí. Change in Masaya for buses to Tipitapa (US$0.25, one hour, every 45 minutes from 3:30am and 5:50pm), and in Tipitapa for buses to Estelí (US$1, every 45 minutes, three hours) or Matagalpa (US$1, three hours, every 30 minutes from 4am to 7pm).

Buses to destinations south (Map p82; Mercado Municipal, 1c S) Leave from a block south of the market, across from the Shell petrol station.

Carazo (US$0.75, 45 minutes, 6am to 5:05pm, every 20 minutes) For San Marcos, Diriamba (with connections to the Carazo beaches) and Jinotepe.

Catarina & San Juan de Oriente (US$0.60, 30 minutes, 6am to 6pm, every 30 to 60 minutes)

Rivas (US$1.10, 2½ hours, 6:30am to 3pm, seven daily) Early afternoon buses will allow you to make the last boat to Isla de Ometepe. Change in Rivas for chicken buses to San Juan del Sur and San Jorge.

International Buses

For most international services to Honduras, El Salvador and Guatemala, you'll need to go to nearby Managua. If you're headed south to

Costa Rica, though, you can get on a passing **TransNica** (Map p82; ☑ 8287-1188; Av Arellano, del Antiguo Hospital, ½c S; ⊙ 8am-6pm) or **Tica Bus** (Map p82; ☑ 2298-5500; www.ticabus. com; Av Arellano, del Antigua Hospital, ½c S; ⊙ 8am-6pm); purchase tickets a couple of days in advance at their respective offices. Tickets cost around US$29 for San José, Costa Rica, and US$75 for Panama City.

Shuttle Buses

For most travelers, daily scheduled door-to-door shuttles are the fastest and most convenient way of getting to Managua Airport, San Juan del Sur, San Jorge (for Isla Ometepe) and León; there are numerous shuttle operators and your accommodations can book one for you. Most accommodations offer shuttles to Laguna del Apoyo (US$5/10 one way/return). Private shuttles to more remote destinations, such as the Tola beaches, can also be arranged, though most shuttle operators require a minimum of four people.

Shuttle operators include the following:

Oasis Shuttles (Map p86; ☑ 2552-8005; Calle Estrada 109, Oasis Hostel) Daily shuttles to Rivas, San Jorge and San Juan del Sur (US$12, 10am & 12:30pm); León via Managua Airport (US$12-US$25, three hours, 9:30am, noon & 5pm); Popoyo (US$35, 10am & 12:30pm, two people minimum) and Peñas Blancas (US$25, 10am & 12:30pm, two people minimum).

Adelante Express (p129) Shuttles to San Juan del Sur (US$25, two hours, 10:50am, 2pm & 5:30pm) via San Jorge, Managua Airport (US$25, 1½ hours, 1pm, 2pm & 4pm).

Erick Tours (p86) Airport transfers (US$15).

❶ Getting Around

BICYCLE

While cycling in town might require nerves of steel, there are several mellow rides around town; many tour operators and some hostels rent bikes for around US$7 to $10 per day.

CAR & MOTORCYCLE

Nicaragua is (relatively) traffic-free, and decent roads around Granada make motorbiking an enjoyable way of getting around, particularly if you're planning a day trip to the Laguna de Apoyo or a tour of the Pueblos Blancos. Ask at tour operators around town. Several accommodations rent scooters for around US$20 per day, as do **Colonial Travel Granada** (Map p82; ☑ 8980-3966; Calle Calzada, frente Iglesia de Guadelupe; ⊙ 8:30am-5pm Mon-Sat).

It's generally cheaper to rent cars in Managua, where your rental is probably parked right now – so be sure to allow a couple of hours for it to arrive. This region has good roads, and many

GRANADA GETTING THERE & AWAY

attractions. Parking in Granada's narrow streets can be a nightmare.

Budget (Map p82; ☑ 2552-2323; www.budget.com.ni; Calle Inmaculada, Plaza Inmaculada) At the Shell station.

Dollar (Map p86; ☑ 2552-8515; www.dollar.com.ni; Calle Vega) At Hotel Plaza Colón.

TAXI

Taxis are plentiful. Always agree on a fare before getting into the taxi, which should be less than US$1 per person if you're getting into a shared taxi anywhere in the city.

It's inexpensive and convenient to take taxis to other destinations, including Masaya and Laguna de Apoyo, keeping in mind that fares vary according to gas prices and your bargaining skills. You can always ask your hotel or hostel to call you a taxi and settle on a price before you're picked up.

AROUND GRANADA

Even on the shortest trip through Granada, you'll understand why Nicaragua's nickname is the 'land of lakes and volcanoes.' Volcán Mombacho and the gorgeous crater lake of Laguna de Apoyo are both within easy proximity of the city, accessible on day trips – either DIY or organized by tour outfitters – from town. Mombacho, active and often shrouded with clouds, is a great destination for quiet hiking and birdwatching. If you have time to spare, spend the night at one of the hotels or hostels on the shores of the lake: an early morning dip in these clean, clear waters is a rare pleasure. Also in this region you'll find the dormant volcano on the little-visited island of Zapatera on Lago de Nicaragua, as well as dozens of tiny islands and islets that make up the Isletas de Granada – a tranquil archipelago that seems a world away from bustling Granada.

Volcán Mombacho

This looming 1345m volcano is the defining feature of the Granada skyline. It has thriving rural communities, coffee farms and cooperatives along its foothills, and the volcano's slopes, covered in ferns and cloud forest, are home to howler monkeys, dozens of bird species, and many of Nicaragua's shy mammals, including the jaguarundi.

Managed by the Fundación Cocibolca, Reserva Natural Volcán Mombacho does the crucial work of maintaining this important ecosystem, and visitors are welcome to explore the volcano's three hiking trails, or else go horseback riding through its picturesque rural communities. It's particularly rewarding to overnight on the volcano's misty slopes and be welcomed in the morning by the incomparable chorus of howler moneys and birds.

☉ Sights

★**Reserva Natural
Volcán Mombacho**   NATURE RESERVE
(☑ 2552-5858; www.mombacho.org; Empalme de Guanacaste, Carretera Granada–Nandaime Km 50; park entrance per car/pedestrian US$20/5, mariposario US$2; ☉ 8am-5pm) It's been a few decades since this 1345m volcano, the defining feature of the Granada skyline, has acted up, but it is still most certainly active and sends up the periodic puff of smoke. It's easy to get to the crown of cloud forest, steaming with fumaroles and other bubbling volcanic activity beneath the misty vines and orchids. Attractions include three hiking trails of varying difficulty, an organic coffee farm and more. Take a tour from Granada or drive yourself.

Reserva Natural Volcán Mombacho is managed by the Fundación Cocibolca, which since 1999 has been building trails and running an eco-mobile (think refurbished military jeeps seating 25) on the 40% grade up to 1100m. Get there early to take the short trail through the **organic coffee farm**, or check out the **mariposario** (butterfly garden) and **orchid garden** (free with entrance), close to the parking lot.

At the top you can find three species of monkey, 168 species of bird and more than 100 types of orchids as part of the jungle canopy that this park is intent on preserving. There is a choice of several trails, including **Sendero del Cráter**, a 1.5km jaunt to the fumaroles, plus great views of Granada and Las Isletas, and **Sendero la Puma**, a steeper 4km trek around the lip of the crater, with even better views. Guides, many of whom speak English, are available at the entrance and cost US$12 to US$22 per group of up to seven. Guides are required for a trek up **Sendero el Tigrillo**, a heart-pumping two-hour tromp up to two overlooks.

The park is open to the public with regular hours on Friday, Saturday and Sunday. However, groups of 10 or more can make arrangements to visit on other days. Time your arrival to coincide with an eco-mobile departure, at 8:30am, 10am and 1pm.

If you have a 4WD, you can drive up the volcano for an extra US$22 – plus US$5 for every adult and US$3 for every child in the vehicle.

Aguas Agrias –
La Nanda Community   NATURE RESERVE
(✍2552-0238;   www.ucatierrayagua.org/
aguas-agrias; Entrada de Monte Verde, Carretera Granada–Nandaime, 12km E; guided tours US$3-5; ☺tours by reservation) This rural community, just south of Mombacho volcano, is an off-the-beaten-path destination where local guides lead hikes through a traditional plantation. The volcanic landscape, dotted with a series of lagoons – some of which you can swim in – makes for an interesting excursion. If driving from Granada, turn left at the Monte Verde entrance; follow the first road for 12km.

Lunch is available on-site for US$5.

The community is run by the UCA Tierra y Agua (Union of Cooperative Agriculturalists). Transport here is tricky – contact UCA for details.

Nicaragua Libre   NATURE RESERVE
(✍2552-0238; www.ucatierrayagua.org; Entrada de Monte Verde, 500m SE; per person guided tour US$5; ☺tours by reservation) This small rural community at the base of Volcán Mombacho is part of the UCA community-tourism project. It offers guided trips through organic coffee farms, horseback rides to San Juan de Oriente and walks to Mombacho. It's a 1km walk from where the bus drops you on the Granada–Nandaime road; contact UCA's Granada office by phone for more details.

A concerted effort has been made to preserve the art of traditional handicrafts here; look for young artisans selling their work.

🏃 Activities

Aguas Termales de Calera   HOT SPRINGS
(✍2222-4208; Carretera Granada–Nandaime Km 55.5, 14km E) FREE Tucked away on Finca Calera, inside the reserve and right by the lake, these 45°C (113°F) hot springs are rich with sulfur, calcium and other beautifying minerals. Due to their location, it's best to visit on a day trip from Granada. Outfitters offer the excursion for around US$25 per person, including round-trip transportation.

🛏 Sleeping

Treehouse Nicaragua   HOSTEL $
(✍8569-0191;   www.treehousenicaragua.com;
Carretera Granada–Nandaime Km 57.5; hammock/

dm/d/tr US$8/10/25/40; ☎) After the effort of the uphill hike, you find yourself in the canopy on the slopes of Volcán Mombacho, amid troupes of howler monkeys. At night, beers are cracked open, guests and staff jam on musical instruments and revelry continues into the wee hours at this 'treehouse for adults' before you fall asleep in your hammock. Day visits are available.

La Granadilla   LODGE $
(✍2552-0238; www.ucatierrayagua.org/la-grana dilla; Entrada de Monte Verde, 1½km S, 1km E; lodging per person US$10, meals US$3-5) A bit further down the road from Nicaragua Libre, La Granadilla (a member of the UCA project) offers rustic accommodations and meals. Electricity is iffy, but you're only 20 minutes from the entrance to Volcán Mombacho. You can arrange guided hikes up the mountain, visits to farms in the area, horseback excursions, ox-cart rides and bicycle tours.

Albergue Rural
Nicaragua Libre   GUESTHOUSE $$
(✍8965-7017; www.ucatierrayagua.org; Entrada de Monte Verde, 500m SE, El Coyolar; r US$25) The rustic guesthouse at Nicaragua Libre is a good place to base yourself for excursions in the area. Hosts Donald and Rene are happy to show guests around the rural cooperative and take you horseback riding to a nearby swimming hole. Simple guest rooms have beds with mosquito nets.

El Respiro Ecolodge   LODGE $$$
(✍8951-9573; www.elrespiroecolodge.com; Carretera Granada–Nandaime Km 55, Camino El Momón; r US$100-150; ☎❄) Living up to its name ('breath' or 'break'), El Respiro offers the opportunity to connect with nature, and go hiking and horse riding along the volcano slopes, but without roughing it or having your room invaded by tiny jungle denizens. The three rooms and the *casita* (cottage) come with four-poster beds and open-air showers; join hosts Romain and Emi for dinner.

Mombacho Lodge   LODGE $$$
(✍8499-1029; www.mombacholodge.com; Camino Volcán Mombacho; 2-person cabin US$95; ❂) Imagine waking up in the cloud forest high up on the slope of Volcán Mombacho, and taking your morning coffee on your cabin porch to the sound of howler monkeys. During the day you can trek the volcano's three trails, or go horseback riding or ziplining, courtesy of friendly lodge owner Cynthia. Bring a torch and prepare to disconnect.

GRANADA VOLCÁN MOMBACHO

✕ Eating

Cafe Las Flores
CAFE $$

(☑8768-9678; Empalme de Guanacaste, 4km E; mains US$5-7; ☺9am-5pm) Halfway up Volcán Mombacho, around 4km from the turnoff, this branch of a popular chain offers salads, Nicaraguan standards and good coffee, paired with expansive views.

❶ Getting There & Away

You can take any Nandaime bus from Granada and ask to be let off at the entrance. From here, you'll walk two steep kilometers (stay left where the road splits) to the spot where the eco-mobiles pick up passengers for the uphill drive.

Some visitors come by organized tour from Granada. If you drive yourself, bear in mind that you need a 4WD to drive to the viewpoint near the summit; a city car will only get you halfway up the volcano, up to Cafe Las Flores.

Reserva Natural Laguna de Apoyo

A vision in sapphire set into a lush forest crater, this 200m-deep, 200-centuries-old crater lake is said to be the country's cleanest and deepest. The warm undersea fumaroles feed the healing and slightly salty waters, howler monkeys bark overhead every morning, and there's a cool air that makes this a favorite respite for travelers.

While technically a natural reserve, this wild area has plenty of hotels dotting the lake's shore and limited environmental protection from the various agencies that claim jurisdiction. Tread lightly.

Some visitors are content with just taking in the view from the crater's edge in Catarina or Diriá. But it's well worth making your way to the bottom for one of the finest swims you'll ever enjoy. A tiny village lies at the bottom of the paved road into the crater, accessible via an often unsigned turnoff about 15km north of Granada, along the Carretera a Masaya.

✖ Activities

SelvAzul
WATER SPORTS

(☑8631-1890; www.hotelselvazul.com; El Triangulo, 250m N; per tank dive US$40, introductory course US$60) Located in the Hotel SelvAzul, this PADI operation offers dives in the unique underwater world of a volcano crater. Plus, there are SUPs and kayaks for hire.

Volcano Divers Nicaragua
DIVING

(☑8266-8404; www.facebook.com/volcanodiver-snicaragua; de los Ranchos, 100m N; dives US$50) Ever enjoyed the novel feeling of diving inside a volcano crater? This sustainably minded outfitter and community organization offers introductory courses and excursions for certified divers, plus lodging and volunteer opportunities.

Apoyo Spanish School
LANGUAGE

(☑8882-3992; www.gaianicaragua.org; El Triangulo, 900m N; classes from US$125/week) Located at the **Estación Biológica** (☑8882-3992; www.gaianicaragua.org), this language school claims to be the longest-running in Nicaragua. Certainly the location is tough to beat.

🛏 Sleeping

Monkey Hut
HOSTEL $

(☑2520-3030; www.themonkeyhut.net; El Triangulo, 200m N; dm/s/d/cabins US$16/48/52/90; ❄🕸) This popular waterfront hostel (US$7 day use for nonguests) features a small beach on the edge of the lake, terraced lounge and picnic areas, plus a floating dock with plenty of kayaks, inner tubes and other flotation devices. Overnight guests have kitchen and grill access; choose between dorms, private rooms or a freestanding cabin. The restaurant food is hit-and-miss.

Hostel Paradiso
HOSTEL $$

(☑2520-3571; www.hostelparadiso.com; El Triangulo, 500m N; dm/r without bathroom US$12/30, tr/f US$50/60; ❄🕸) A great pick for budget travelers, this lakefront hostel has a large terrace, private dock, kayaks and shared kitchen, plus a good restaurant and bar. A cut above other budget lodgings, Paradiso offers massages and other opportunities to pamper yourself. Day passes cost US$7 per person. The hostel runs a shuttle to and from Granada for US$3.50 each way.

La Orquidea
GUESTHOUSE $$

(☑8872-1866; www.laorquideanicaragua.com; El Triangulo, 1.5km NE; r with/without air-con US$60/45; ❄🕸) If you need to rent a whole house for up to six people, this place has a certain unkempt charm to it. You get your own living room, gorgeous, spacious rooms – there are just two bedrooms – with big windows leading out onto balconies with excellent lagoon views. The water's a short walk down the hill.

Posada Ecologica la Abuela   CABIN $$

(☑ 2520-1634; www.posadaecologicalaabuela.com.
ni; El Triangulo, 2.2km NE; 2/4 person bungalow
US$75/120; ☀☎) On a steep hillside leading
down to the water, Granny's House consists
of comfortable, cute little cabins that are not
entirely bug-proof, so a passion for tiny wild-
life is a must. The restaurant and dock offer
spectacular lake views, but the food fails to
wow. No English is spoken.

★ Casa Marimba   B&B $$$

(☑ 2520-2837; www.casamarimba.com; El Triangulo, 1.6km NE; r US$55-75, f US$120; ☀☎) ✐ Run
by three friends, this sweet five-room B&B
offers the best lakeside accommodations –
individually styled rooms, meals involving
lovingly grown organic veggies and herbs
from their own garden, and lake access. Ideal for romancing your sweetie or just getting
away from it all for a few tranquil days.

San Simian Eco Lodge   LODGE $$$

(☑ 8850-8101; www.sansimian.com; El Triangu-
lo, 2km S; s/d from US$58/70; ☀☎) ✐ This
Swiss-owned lodge has beautiful little cab-
ins that blend into the hillside. Most have
stone-walled, alfresco bathrooms, all have
plenty of air and light, and there's mosquito
nets over the beds. You can access the beach
and kayaks if you come for the day (US$5
per person). A daily shuttle from Granada
(US$12 including day pass) is available on
request.

Apoyo Resort   RESORT $$$

(☑ 2520-2085; www.apoyoresort.com; El Triangulo,
1.5km S; r US$110, 1-bedroom villa US$145; ☀☎☲)
Running up the hill from the lakeside road,
this revamped resort has spacious apart-
ments and villas – many with kitchens –
that are ideal for families. There's also a
swimming pool and a good restaurant, the
Grill.

✗ Eating

Vista Restaurant   INTERNATIONAL $$

(☑ 2220-3287; El Triangulo, 1.5km S; mains US$5-
10; ☺9am-9pm) Let's face it: you're not here
for the food, which is average at best. What
you're here for is the spring-break vibe, for
a chance to horse around on the floating
dock or sun yourself on the beach below, or
to sip a beer while staring at the lagoon in a
dreamy haze.

❶ Getting There & Away

Many hotels and hostels on the lake offer daily
shuttle transportation to and from Laguna de
Apoyo from Granada (from US$3.50 one way),
including options for day visitors and overnight
guests.

Outside the posted shuttle times, you could
also arrange a taxi from Granada (US$12 to
US$15), Masaya (US$10 to US$12) or Managua
(US$30 to US$40) to the door of your hotel or
destination in Laguna de Apoyo.

Public 'La Laguna' buses run all the way down
to Laguna Apoyo from the market in Masaya at
10:30am and 3:30pm (US$0.90, 45 minutes);
the last bus departs Laguna Apoyo at 4:30pm.
Hourly buses from Masaya (US$0.70) run rough-
ly between 6am and 6pm, dropping passengers
off near the crater rim, from where it's a half-
hour, 2km descent.

If driving, you have to take the unsigned minor
road towards the Laguna; the turnoff is 15km
north of Granada, along the Carretera a Masaya
(Hwy 4).

Isla Zapatera

Isla Zapatera, a dormant volcano rising to
629m from the shallow waters of Lago de
Nicaragua, is an ancient ceremonial island
of the Chorotega and male counterpart to
more buxom Isla de Ometepe, whose smok-
ing cone can be seen after you take the
three-hour hike to the top. The island and
surrounding archipelago of 13 islets com-
prise the 45-km-sq Parque Nacional Archip-
iélago Zapatera, designated to protect not
only the wildlife-rich remaining swaths of
virgin tropical dry and wet forest, but also
the unparalleled collection of **petroglyphs**
and **statues** left here between 500 and 1500
years ago by the Nahuatl, to whom the is-
lands were an important sacrifice spot and
burial ground.

About 500 people live here quasi-legally,
fishing and subsistence farming and hop-
ing that no one puts pressure on Marena
(Ministry of the Environment and Natural
Resources) to do anything about it. Visitors
get a glimpse of their unique life.

◉ Sights

Isla El Muerto   ISLAND

This crescent-shaped islet off the north coast
of Isla Zapatera has perhaps the most im-
pressive expanse of petroglyphs carved into
a 95m-by-25m expanse of bedrock at its

ISLAND HISTORY

A handful of archaeologists have worked the sites on the islands, including Ephraim Squier, who shipped several of the 15 statues he discovered here in 1849 to the US, where they are displayed at the Smithsonian Museum. Swedish scientist Carl Bollivius discovered more statues, many of which are displayed at Granada's Convento y Museo San Francisco (p83).

center, where archaeologists have found numerous stone statues (now displayed in the Convento San Francisco (p83) in Granada). Several of the other islands also have petroglyphs and potential archaeological sites.

🛏 Sleeping

★ **Hotel Bahía Zapatera**   HOTEL $$$
(☑ 8864-0521, 8884-0606; www.hotelzapatera. com; Bahia Zapatera; d US$297, incl all meals & tours; ☎) Overlooking Isla el Muerto across the water, Isla Zapatera's wonderful hotel is run by knowledgeable Rafael. It consists of four comfortable bungalows with hammocks, and meals include fresh grilled fish and fruit juices. Also included are extensive tours of Isla Zapatera and the archipelago, nature walks for the whole family, birdwatching and more.

❶ Getting There & Away

The island is located about 20 to 90 minutes by boat (depending on weather and the boat) from the Asese port of Granada. Catch a ride with locals in a shared boat (US$8) or organize transportation with the Isla Zapatera Community (www.zapatera.blogspot.com). The most reliable option involves going with Zapatera Tours, whose tours include travel to and from the island by speedboat.

Isletas de Granada

With an islet for every day of the year (there are 365 in total), this spectacular archipelago, within easy reach of Granada, was created during a spectacular eruption by Volcán Mombacho some 20,000 years ago. Several hundred fishing folk make the islets their home; if you're out on the water after daybreak, you can see them casting their nets among the herons and other birdlife,

as their kids paddle their dugout canoes to school. Many visitors come by day trip from Granada, but it's much more rewarding to spend the night on one of the islands.

🏃 Activities

Boat Trips
Half-day trips from Granada (around US$20 per person) typically involve a boat ride, though morning tours get to the lake too late to catch the early morning birdlife. Most tours also pass Isla de los Monos (Monkey Island). The spider- and capuchin-monkey residents are friendly (they were brought here by a veterinarian living on a nearby island), but may run off with your picnic lunch. If you drive yourself to the dock, you have more flexibility, and a sunset boat ride is spectacular.

An easy morning or afternoon trip from Granada takes you by boat to this miniature archipelago of 365 tiny tropical islands. Along the way you'll spot rare birds, colorful flowers and some interesting indigenous fauna – keep an eye out for osprey, kingfishers, caimans and howler monkeys (along the mainland). The privately owned islands that would make a tremendous evil lair are highlights, as well as lunch at the handful of island hotels and restaurants.

There's even a Spanish fortress. Castillo San Pablo was built in 1784 and has great views of Granada and Volcán Mombacho, plus a fine swimming hole nearby.

Formed some 20,000 years ago when very visible Volcán Mombacho exploded into its current ragged silhouette, these islands were once one of the poorest neighborhoods in Granada, and some are still home to impoverished families, who in general have no official property rights. They are being gradually supplanted by the beautiful homes of folks such as the Pellas family (Flor de Caña owners), former president Chamorro, and lots of expats in paradise.

Most tour companies run trips to Las Isletas, or do it yourself with Inuit Kayaks, about 1km from the Centro Turístico entrance, an outfitter that runs several guided kayak tours. Touts will offer to hook you up with a boat tour as soon as you enter the Centro Turístico. If you're on your own or in a small group, wait around until a larger group forms (unless you want to pay for the whole boat yourself – around US$20 for a one-hour tour); the boat operators will offer discount seats just to fill their boat up. For the best birdwatching, arrange your trip the day before to leave at dawn. Sunset is also quite nice, but the tour is quicker, with less exploration of the further-afield corners of the island group.

A turnoff to the right, just after Inuit Kayaks (look for the sign saying 'Marina Cocibolca'), takes you to the other side of the Peninsula de Asese to Puerto Asese, where you can hire boats to tour the isletas on this side. This is a less popular option, so chances of forming an impromptu group are slimmer. The advantage of a tour here is that there are fewer power lines and other boats, so it's a more tranquil experience, but it does involve a fair bit of time in open water.

There are numerous restaurants in the island chain. Ask your boat operator to include a stop at one, where a large meal of locally caught fish will cost around US$7.50.

Kayaking

Ecolodges on several of the islets have kayaks for guest use – fantastic for wildlife watching. Some Granada operators give you the option of renting a kayak (around US$25 per person) rather than taking a boat tour.

🛏 Sleeping & Eating

★**Isleta El Espino**   BOUTIQUE HOTEL **$$$**
(☑ 7636-0060; www.isletaelespino.com; r US$135-210; 🕿🖃) 🍃 Kayaking at dawn among the reeds and the herons, delicious meals, yoga, massages and a chance to disconnect from it all are on offer at this island ecolodge. Isleta El Espino is a study in luxurious tranquility, and whether you stay in a lakefront *casita* or the jungly Treetop Rancho, you're guar-

anteed seclusion and stellar views of Volcán Mombacho.

The five rooms/*casitas* and their furnishings are all made of sustainable local materials and the ecolodge is run by a staff of islanders.

Jicaro Island Lodge   BOUTIQUE HOTEL **$$$**
(☑ 2558-7702; https://jicarolodge.com; r from US$450; 🕿🖃) 🍃 Close to the northern end of the peninsula, this Londoner-owned boutique hotel takes its eco-credentials very seriously, with its use of solar power, water filtration, hiring of locals and investment in local community education. Expect spacious, breezy two-story *casitas* with hammocks, local ingredients turned into gourmet meals, and plenty of activities, from kayaking and SUP, to yoga and local tours.

Isleta El Recedo   VILLA **$$$**
(☑ 2552-1227; www.hotellapolvora.com/isleta-el-recedo; ste US$220; 🕿🖃) 🍃 A 10-minute ride by speedboat from Marina Cocibolca, this solar-powered ecolodge is run by La Pólvora Hotel in Granada. Sustainable local materials have gone into the construction of its two spacious suites, and you can choose to kayak with the birds at dawn, relax in the infinity pool, go fishing with a local and come back to home-cooked meals.

❶ Getting There & Away

From the Cocibolca marina (p95) in Granada, set-price tours include a 30-minute boat jaunt (US$2 per person or US$40 per yacht), a nature tour (US$16 per person), a thorough tour of the islets (US$40 to US$80) and a full day on Isla Zapatera (US$180). Don't expect to haggle over the prices.

Southwestern Nicaragua

Best Places to Eat

➡ Café Campestre (p117)

➡ La Vaca Loca (p122)

➡ Barrio Café (p128)

➡ King Curry (p128)

➡ Mama Lin's (p120)

Best Places to Stay

➡ Finca Mystica (p118)

➡ Sirena Surf Lodge (p123)

➡ Casitas Pacific Hotel (p121)

➡ Morgan's Rock (p131)

➡ Buena Vista Surf Club (p131)

➡ Playa Hermosa Ecolodge (p132)

Why Go?

Packed with attractions, the southwest offers up some of Nicaragua's hallmark vistas and adventures. Surfers have been hitting this coastline for years, drawn by perfect, uncrowded waves and laid-back surfing encampments. Beginner surfers and partygoers head for San Juan del Sur, where there are better accommodations, high-octane parties and a solid selection of restaurants catering to international appetites. Beyond this are quiet fishing villages, sea-turtle nesting grounds and beaches rocked by world-class waves.

No trip to the southwest would be complete without a few days on Isla de Ometepe. The island itself is shaped like an infinity symbol, with bookend volcanoes dominating either side of a secluded universe where you'll discover waterfalls, wildlife, lost coves and enchanted forests. There's kayaking, swimming, hiking and biking, and many travelers extend their stay as they dive into paradise, lost in the quiet spots and friendly traveler encampments that define this island escape.

When to Go

➡ November through May is the dry season. It means less verdant foliage, slightly longer days, plenty of adventure opportunities and remarkable sunsets over the curving Pacific Ocean.

➡ March to November is surf season, when you get big barrels and double-overhead exposure. Book ahead for surf camps during this time. Beginners may want to consider other times of the year to avoid the wave traffic.

➡ September to October is the peak season for sea-turtle arrivals at Refugio de Vida Silvestre La Flor. If your timing is right, you could see more than 3000 turtles arrive on the same day.

History

Although first inhabited by the little-known Kiribisis peoples, it's the Chorotega who really left their mark on this region, most famously with the stone monoliths that are today on display beside the church in Altagracia. The Chorotega were soon overrun by the Nicarao, however, and it was Cacique Nicarao who met Spanish conquistador Gil González on the shores of Lago de Nicaragua in 1523. The Cruz de España marks the spot where the chief famously traded over 18,000 gold pesos for a few items of the Spaniard's clothing – a trade that some say set the tone for Nica–Euro commerce for centuries to come.

With time, this narrow strip of earth became the only land crossing for the gold-rushers traveling from New York to California. Talk continues today of a 'dry canal' railroad that would carry goods between the Pacific and Lago de Nicaragua to continue on by boat.

Rivas was the site of some stunning defeats for filibuster William Walker, whose later plans to attack San Juan del Sur were thwarted by the British in 1858. Once the railroads connected the USA's East and West Coasts, gold prospectors gave up on this route and the region slipped back into its former torpor. This was briefly disturbed in the 1979 revolution, as spirited resistance to Somoza troops turned the hills behind San Juan del Sur into bloody battlegrounds. The Isla de Ometepe was spared from such scenes and the horrors of the Contra War – possibly one reason that the island's nickname, 'the oasis of peace,' has stuck.

ℹ Getting There & Away

Rivas is the regional travel hub, and its enormous, chaotic bus lot connects the region to Granada, Masaya and the rest of the country. Frequent ferries run from San Jorge to Isla de Ometepe; Ometepe is also connected by twice-weekly flights to Managua.

Handy tourist shuttles connect Granada with San Juan del Sur, San Jorge and even some of the Tola beaches. Daily shuttles connect San Juan del Sur with Playa Popoyo; there are shuttles to Playa Gigante on request.

Regular buses and shuttles serve the beaches around San Juan del Sur, though for the more remote ones you'll need your own wheels. Public buses run from Rivas to El Astillero, passing the turnoffs to other Tola beaches. Outside dry season, it's a good idea to rent a 4WD to access Tola's beaches.

Rivas

POP 34,357

Rivas has a few fans – some say it's authentic and lively, with some wonderful buildings downtown. However, little remains of the old colonial charm that gold seekers would have seen in the mid-19th century on their way to California. The commonly held view is that Rivas is a busy urban sprawl – a necessary evil that you whizz through on your way to more exciting coastal and island destinations.

Rivas' strategic position on the only sliver of land between the Pacific and Atlantic oceans made it an essential stop along the arduous overland crossing to San Juan del Sur during the gold rush. Now, with all the development on the southwestern beaches and Ometepe, it is once again an important trading and transport hub.

🛏 Sleeping & Eating

Hospedaje Lidia GUESTHOUSE **$**

(☑ 2563-3477; Texaco, ½c O; s without/with bathroom US$10/18, d US$25; ☎) The location is within easy walking distance from several restaurants and this no-frills, family-run operation offers decent budget lodging, with well-scrubbed rooms and a better-than-average room-to-bathroom ratio.

La Parilla NICARAGUAN **$$**

(☑ 2563-1700; Museo de Rivas, 1c O; mains US$5-8; ⊙10am-11pm) Come here for excellent Nicaraguan dishes, including grilled seafood and *tostones con queso* (fried plantains with cheese). Locals perch outside to watch baseball on the big screen.

ℹ Getting There & Away

BUS

Rivas is a transportation hub. The main **Terminal de Buses** (☑ 8669-0330; Frente mercado) is adjacent to the *mercado* (market). You can catch more luxurious long-distance buses (most headed to and from Managua, not Granada) at the **long-distance bus stop** (Carretera Panamericana) just north of the exit to San Jorge. If you're headed south to Costa Rica, catch a **Transnica** (☑ 2563-5397; www.transnica. com; Carretera Panamericana) bus or **Tica Bus** (☑ 8877-1407; www.ticabus.com; Frente Estadio Yamil Rios) on its way to San José (US$35 to US$45) from Managua.

Several express buses to Managua's Mercado Roberto Huembes start in San Jorge and pass through Rivas, stopping at the Puma gas station by the traffic circle, a 10-minute walk from the Terminal de Buses. Four express buses from

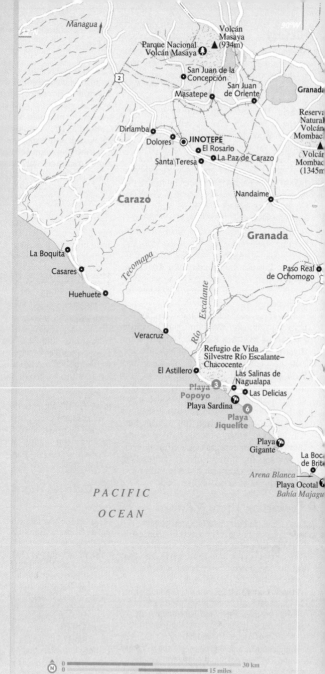

South-western Nicaragua Highlights

1 **Isla de Ometepe**
(p107) Climbing a volcano, kayaking the wetlands or swimming in a lagoon...or all three.

2 **San Juan del Sur** (p123) Hitting the excellent restaurants, bars, pool parties and clubs at Nicaragua's premier party town.

3 **Playa Popoyo**
(p121) Enjoying the waves, sand and solitude on this wild and far-flung beach before grabbing a sunset pizza and beer.

4 **Refugio de Vida Silvestre La Flor**
(p134) Welcoming the thousands of endangered olive ridley and leatherback turtles that lay their eggs at this wildlife refuge.

5 **Playa Maderas**
(p130) Riding big waves and working on your tan at this world-class beach enclave.

6 **Playa Jiquelite**
(p123) Surfing by day and retreating to your boutique digs at night.

7 **Playa Hermosa**
(p132) Sunning yourself on one of Nicaragua's prettiest beaches or learning to ride the waves.

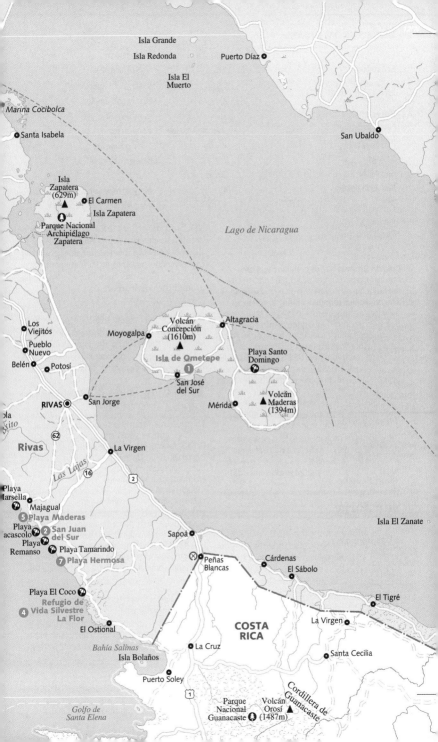

BUSES FROM RIVAS

DESTINATION	COST (US$)	DURATION	FREQUENCY
El Astillero	2	3 hr	5:30am & 4:50pm
Granada	1.20	1¾ hr	9 daily, 6am-6pm
Jinotepe	2	2hr	8 daily, 5:50am-5pm
Managua	2	3hr	every 30 min
Peñas Blancas	0.70	40 min	every 30 min
Playa Gigante	1.50	1½-2hr	1:30pm Mon-Sat
Salinas	1.70	2hr	6 daily, 5:30am-4:50pm
San Jorge	0.30	20 min	hourly
San Juan del Sur	1	45 min	every 45 min, 5am-5pm
Tola	0.80	40 min	every 45 min, 5:30am-5:45pm

Managua to Peñas Blancas also stop at the Puma gas station; check times locally.

TAXI

Colectivos (shared taxis or minibuses) run regularly to San Jorge (US$0.70) and San Juan del Sur (US$2). Private taxi drivers also hang around the bus terminal, waiting to scoop up travelers who need a ride to the Tola beaches or San Juan del Sur. They'll quote a wide range of prices, depending on exactly where you're going (and whether you're toting a surfboard,) but it shouldn't cost more than US$20 to San Juan del Sur, or more than US$35 per carload to the Tola beaches. It's best to hook up with other travelers here to share the cost.

Around Rivas itself, pedicabs are cheap and fun for shorter trips; the usual cost is US$1 to US$2 to any destination in town.

Regular taxis (holding up to four passengers) charge locals about US$1 for a ride between the Rivas bus terminal and the San Jorge ferry terminal, but may try to charge you around US$5.

San Jorge

POP 8849

Just 15 minutes from the bustle of Rivas is the port town of San Jorge, lined with inexpensive seafood restaurants and casual bars, and with excellent views of Isla de Ometepe. It gets packed during Semana Santa, and on sunny weekends, with day-trippers from all over the region.

For international visitors there is very little reason to linger here, given the frequency of boats and ferries to Ometepe.

🛏 Sleeping & Eating

Hotel Hamacas   HOTEL $$
(📞8810-4144; www.hotelhamacas.com; El muelle; 1½c O, 1c S; s/d with fan US$25/30, with air-con

US$35/40; P ❄ 🛜 🏊) Cute little brick rooms painted in cheerful colors make this hacienda-style hotel the most atmospheric offering in town. Rooms surround a leafy courtyard, with the requisite hammocks strung up around the porch areas.

Fritanga   NICARAGUAN $
(Parque Central; dishes US$2-3; ⊙5-9pm) In town, there's a great *fritanga* (grill) that sets up in the kiosk in the Parque Central – satisfying your barbecued-chicken and people-watching cravings at the same time.

ⓘ Getting There & Away

BOAT

The paved road from Rivas to San Jorge ends at the ferry terminal, where there's guarded parking (US$3) for your car and a regular boat service to Isla de Ometepe. Up to 18 boats make the trip from San Jorge to Isla de Ometepe (US$1.50 to US$3, one hour) each day between 7am and 5:45pm, though not all sail reliably. Most are ferries headed to Moyogalpa, though some are smaller boats that go to San José del Sur – these are best avoided on windy days if you're prone to seasickness. There's no need to reserve ahead. Passengers simply board and pay on the boat. However, if you're trying to put your car onto a ferry you might have to kill some time: there's often a short waiting list.

BUS

Buses leave for Rivas (US$0.25) almost hourly from the ferry terminal.

Alternatively, *colectivo* taxis between the Rivas bus terminal and the San Jorge ferry terminal should cost around US$1, though some will try to charge at least US$5.

SHUTTLES

Several shuttle operators in Granada (US$20) and San Juan del Sur (US$18) offer direct, convenient drop-offs at the ferry terminal. If

BORDER CROSSING TO COSTA RICA

Whether you've booked an international bus from Rivas or Managua or are taking a local bus and crossing on your own, the busy border crossing between Sapoá (Nicaragua) and Peñas Blancas (Costa Rica) is fairly easy to navigate. If you're on a Tica Bus (p103) or Transnica (p103) bus, the process will be largely managed for you. Two Tica Buses pass through Rivas en route from Managua in the morning, and two midafternoon. Three Transnica buses pass through Rivas midmorning and a couple midafternoon.

The 1km-long, enclosed border is relatively simple, although the sudden (and strategic) crush of 'helpers' can be intimidating. Pedicabs (US$1 to US$3) not only roll you through, they also protect you from the masses. Banks on either side exchange local currency for US dollars, while money changers (called *coyotes* for a reason) exchange all three currencies freely. It's a really good idea to have your entrance and exit money in small bills or local currency.

On the Nicaraguan side, get your passport stamped at a window in the large, poorly marked cement building just east of the main road. It costs US$12 to US$13 to enter Nicaragua and US$1.50 to leave. It's free to enter Costa Rica, but note that there's a US$10 exit fee when you leave. Costa Rica's immigration building has a restaurant, clean restrooms and a bank with an ATM. Everyone entering Costa Rica technically needs a ticket for leaving the country, and many travelers get asked for it. If it's your unlucky day, Transportes Deldu and Transnica, both located right outside, sell tickets from San José to Managua.

Don't plan on spending the night on either side: Sapoá has no real lodgings, other than a few dodgy, unsigned guesthouses, and Peñas Blancas has none at all. Although the border is open 6am to 10pm Monday to Friday, and until 8pm Saturday and Sunday, buses run only between 6am and 6pm – after which taxis triple their fares.

Buses from the border run at least hourly to Rivas (US$1, 45 minutes) between 6am and 5:30pm, where you can make connections throughout Nicaragua. *Taxistas* (taxi drivers) may tell you that Nicaraguan buses aren't running, or are unsafe, but pay no attention to them.

Transportes Deldu buses leave from Peñas Blancas to San José (US$10, six hours) about eight times per day; the last bus leaves at 5.30pm. There are also regular departures to Liberia in Costa Rica (US$3, two hours, every 45 minutes).

It's always, of course, faster and easier to take a taxi, which may be prohibitively expensive on the Costa Rican side (US$50 to Liberia), but much more reasonable from Sapoá to Rivas (from US$12), San Jorge (from US$15), San Juan del Sur (from US$20) and Granada (around US$50). Find other tourists to share your taxi while you are still inside the border zone, and bargain hard.

you want to be picked up at the San Jorge ferry terminal and taken to either destination, that can be arranged through lodgings in both towns or on Ometepe; most accommodations can recommend a trusted driver who'll be waiting for you on the dock.

ISLA DE OMETEPE

POP 29,800

Ometepe never fails to impress. Its twin volcanic peaks ('fire' and 'water'), rising up out of Lago de Nicaragua, have captured the imagination of everyone from precolonial Aztecs (who thought they'd found the promised land) to Mark Twain (who waxed lyrical about it in his book *Travels with Mr Brown*) – not to mention the relatively few travelers who make it out here. The island's fertile volcanic soil, clean waters, wide beaches, wildlife population, off-the-beaten track farmstays, archaeological sites and dramatic profile are quickly propelling it up traveler must-see lists.

More than 1700 petroglyphs have been found on Ometepe, making this a DIY archeologists' fantasy island.

🏃 Activities

Hiking

The island's two volcanoes can be ascended from Moyogalpa or Altagracia for Volcán Concepción (p112), and Fincas Magdelena, El Porvenir and Hacienda Mérida for Volcán Maderas (p116). Guided ascents of Concepción cost around US$40 per person; Maderas is less expensive. The uphill slog to Cascada

Isla de Ometepe

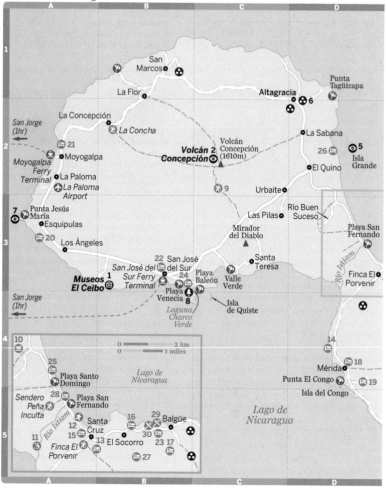

San Ramón (p118), more a walk than a hike, makes for an excellent half-day trip.

Relatively less challenging hikes abound, including to the halfway point up Maderas on the Finca Magdalena trail, and **El Floral**, a five- to seven-hour round-trip to a viewpoint about 1000m up Concepción (around US$30 per person).

Swimming

Swimming off Ometepe's beaches is excellent. Keep in mind that Lago de Nicaragua rises dramatically in the rainy season (and, if the rains are particularly heavy, the couple of months afterwards), shrinking the beaches to thin strands. By the end of the dry season in April, however, some 20m of gray volcanic sand may stretch out to the water.

The most popular beaches are Playa Santo Domingo, Playa Balcón and the other beaches around Charco Verde and Punta Jesús María. If you're just looking for a dip, the mineral-rich rock pools at Ojo de Agua (p115) make a fine day trip.

Kayaking

Kayaking is also big on the island, with Isla del Congo, Isla de Quiste and the Río Istiam (p115) being the most popular destinations. Most hotels near these places rent kayaks.

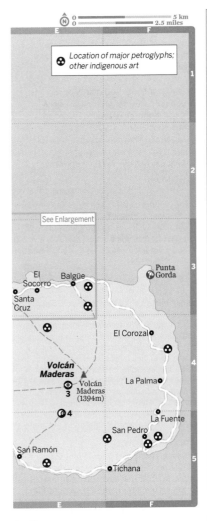

0 — 5 km
0 — 2.5 miles

Location of major petroglyphs; other indigenous art

See Enlargement

Punta Gorda

El Socorro   Balgüe

Santa Cruz

El Corozal

Volcán Maderas   Volcán Maderas (1394m)

La Palma

La Fuente

San Pedro

San Ramón

Tichana

Isla de Ometepe

SOUTHWESTERN NICARAGUA ISLA DE OMETEPE

☞ Tours

Many tour operators are based in Moyogalpa. However, just about any lodging on the island can organize horseback riding and tours. Guides are not really necessary for San Ramón waterfall or Reserva Charco Verde, although it's always easier to have someone else arrange transportation.

After various tourists got lost and died climbing volcanoes solo, it's now illegal to climb the volcanoes without a guide. Guides are available at or near the major trailheads in Altagracia, Moyogalpa, Balgüe and Mérida. Another place where it's worth having a guide along is a kayak cruise of the Río Istiam – they know where all the animals are.

Cycling

Cycling is a fun way to get around and mountain bikes can be rented in Moyogalpa, Altagracia, Playa Santo Domingo and at many lodgings.

Horseback Riding

Horseback riding is another popular local transportation choice here. Any tour operator or hotel can set you up with a ride. Prices are generally US$5 to US$7 per hour, with guides US$10 to US$20 per group. Hari's Horses (p118) offers the most challenging day rides.

THE ISLAND'S LAYOUT

Isla de Ometepe's 78km main road runs in a rough barbell shape, circling each volcano and running along the northern shore of the isthmus between them. The Concepción side of the island is more developed, and the major towns of Moyogalpa and Altagracia are connected by a paved road.

Moyogalpa is the island's largest and busiest town: you'll find the majority of services for tourists here. Altagracia is the only other real population center and is a smaller, much more laid-back and less-touristed place. That said, there's not much reason to come here, except to check out the statues and museum.

Playa Santo Domingo is the most popular lodging spot on the isthmus; the road splits upon arriving on the less-developed Volcán Maderas side of the island, going right to Mérida and the San Ramón waterfall, and left to Balgüe, a backpacker hot spot where new accommodations keep popping up.

❶ Getting There & Away

AIR

On Thursdays and Sundays at noon, La Costeña Airlines flies 12-seater aircraft from Managua to La Paloma Airport (around US$80, 20 minutes) – an airstrip some 2km south of Moyogalpa. From Ometepe, the flights continue to San Carlos and San Juan del Norte.

BOAT

Up to 15 boats and ferries ply the 17km route daily between San Jorge on the mainland and the Moyogalpa ferry terminal (p112), Ometepe's main port. Departures are between 7am and 5:45pm (US$1.50 to US$3, one hour); some are more reliable than others. There are three departures from San Jorge to the San José del Sur ferry terminal (p113) at 9:30am, 2pm and 5pm. Between November and February, winds can make the sea rough, particularly in the afternoon; consider taking a car ferry instead of a smaller boat. The Ferry Schedules page on www.ometepenicaragua.com has up-to-date departure information.

Most boats can transport bikes and other equipment without a problem. If you're loading your car onto the ferry, you might have to wait, depending on availability; otherwise, no reservations are required. Passengers pay on the boat.

❶ Getting Around

Half of the southern loop between Moyogalpa and Altagracia (the island's two major towns), that passes through San José del Sur, is a beautifully paved road. The paved road continues along Playa Santo Domingo all the way to Balgüe. The other half of the loop between Moyogalpa and Altagracia is unpaved, rough and bumpy, and best tackled on an ATV or motorcycle; the same goes for much of the loop around Volcán Maderas. The unpaved roads actually get better during the rainy season, when the jutting rocks sink into the softer ground.

The island is bigger than it looks and very few destinations are really walkable. The lack of traffic makes hitchhiking a problem (although any passing pickup will almost certainly give you a ride) – but you'll also be happy if you have your own wheels.

BUS

There's only one main road on the island; this simplifies things. Take a good look at a map before boarding any buses, consult the latest bus schedules at www.ometepenicaragua.com and check locally whether the scheduled bus is running (some departures are more reliable than others). Bus fares range from US$0.25 to US$1.50, depending on how far you're going. There are direct services from Moyogalpa to Altagracia, Santo Domingo, Balgüe, Mérida and San Ramón, with fewer services on Sunday. There is no public transport along the southeastern part of the island, between Balgüe and San Ramón.

CAR & MOTORCYCLE

Moyogalpa is the best place to rent scooters (US$15 per day), ATVs (US$60 per day) and motorbikes (US$25 per day); you'll also find places to rent scooters and motorbikes around Playa Santo Domingo, as well as in Balgüe and Mérida. There are no car rental places on Ometepe, so you're better off bringing one from the mainland.

TAXI

Taxis are rare and expensive, and they're all minivans, jeeps or pickups with 4WD. They meet all ferries, but otherwise you should have your hotel make arrangements with a driver at least a few hours in advance.

From Moyogalpa, expect to pay at least US$25 to Altagracia, US$25 to Playa Santo Domingo, US$35 to Balgüe, US$35 to Mérida and US$40 to San Ramón, though your drivers might quote you higher prices – and on an island as remote as this, you won't have a lot of options other than to pay what they request.

Moyogalpa

POP 10,422

Moyogalpa is home to the ferry terminal for hourly boats from the mainland, and, as such, the nerve center for Ometepe's nascent tourist industry. There are numerous guesthouses, budget hotels and restaurants here, and many of the island's tour companies; it's also base camp for the climb up Volcán Concepción. However, it's not exactly an island paradise you'll want to linger in.

🏃 Activities

Fundación Entre Volcánes VOLUNTEERING
(☑2569-4118; www.fundacionentrevolcanes.org; Frente a BanPro) 🖉 A locally founded grassroots NGO involved in education, health, nutrition and environmental projects on the island. It accepts volunteers with an intermediate level of Spanish and a minimum two-month commitment.

☞ Tours

Cultu Natural OUTDOORS
(☑8364-7211; NIC-64, al lado de supermercado; Volcán Concepción ascents US$30, waterfall hike US$15; ☺9am-5pm) Friendly Danilo and his team get great feedback from travelers for their combination of local knowledge and bilingual tours to Ometepe's biggest attractions. Ascents of Volcán Concepción, kayaking at dawn, the waterfall hike, horseback riding and more can be organized here.

Green Expeditions Ometepe OUTDOORS
(☑8421-1439; www.facebook.com/greenometepe; Frente a Hospedaje Central; Volcán Concepción trek per person US$25; ☺9am-5pm) This highly regarded operator runs trekking tours up Volcán Concepción with bilingual guides and transport included. The motorbikes for rent are in excellent condition.

🌟 Festivals & Events

Fiestas Patronales RELIGIOUS
(☺Jul 23-26) Moyogalpa's *fiestas patronales* (saints days), honoring the patron saint Santa Ana, are famous for the Baile de las Inditas, a celebration of both Spanish and indigenous culture. The festival includes a procession to Punta Jesús María, where there are fireworks and drinking by the lake.

🛏 Sleeping

Hostel Coco's GUESTHOUSE $
(☑8843-1246; El muelle, 2c E, 3c S; d/tr/q US$15/20/28; ❄️🛜) Rooms here may be very simple, but the friendly owner goes out of her way to make you feel like part of the family. Nothing is too much trouble, from organizing excursions and cooking meals to making onward travel plans.

Hospedaje Soma GUESTHOUSE $$
(☑2569-4310; www.hospedajesoma.com; Frente del Instituto J.R. Smith; dm US$12, r with/without bathroom US$40/30, 2-person cabins with aircon/fan US$70/60; ❄️🛜) Book ahead at this relaxed but professionally run guesthouse, set a 10-minute walk from the ferry dock. Choose between a dorm, private room or cabin, all scattered around a large and beautiful tropical garden. The German owners are helpful with planning excursions around the island and have folders full of useful info about the island.

Hotel Nicaraus HOTEL $$
(☑2569-4233; NIC-64, 100m al S del hospital; dm/d/tr US$12/45/60; ❄️🛜🏊) Excellent, wallet-friendly hotel, where you can combine frugality (staying in a dorm) with ample creature comforts (air-con, splashing in the swimming pool after a volcano hike). Ample breakfasts are served and staff are very helpful.

🍴 Eating

Moyogalpa has a few good places to eat, particularly along the street leading up from the ferry dock, or immediately off it.

ℹ️ GETTING YOUR WHEELS ONTO OMETEPE

Taking a car to Ometepe involves a bit of forward planning, some runaround and cash. Four-wheel drives are best for the spiky volcanic roads.

To do it, get an early start on one of the early ferries from San Jorge to Moyogalpa (or call ahead – it doesn't hurt to try to get on a waiting list the day before.) Otherwise, be prepared to wait your turn if it's busy – only a small number of cars fit on each ferry – and come with cash to pay the port tax, 'car tax' and ferry transit fee, around US$20 to US$25 each way. Passengers buy separate tickets.

Viky's BBQ NICARAGUAN $

(El muelle, 3½c E; mains US$3-5; ⊙6-9pm Wed-Mon) Viky cooks up nightly portions of chicken, pork and beef on the grill, accompanied by generous helpings of fried plantains, *gallo pinto* and cabbage salad. Look for the unmarked red place next to the grocery store.

★**Cornerhouse** CAFE $$

(☑2569-4177; www.thecornerhouseometepe.com; Muelle 1c E; mains US$4-7; ⊙7am-5pm Mon-Fri, to 3pm Sat; ☎☑) Easily the most stylish eating venue on this corner of the island. All-day breakfast is served at this rustic-chic cafe just uphill from the port; the menu features eggs Benedict with roasted tomatoes and fresh basil. There are also gourmet sandwiches and salads, including a great one with papaya and toasted almonds, and wi-fi. It's part of the **Cornerhouse B&B** (s/d/tr US$25/35/45; ☎). Locally grown coffee and honey for sale here.

ⓘ Information

MEDICAL SERVICES

Hospital (☑2569-4247; Parque Central, 3c S) Offers basic emergency services. For anything serious it's best to get off the island, to Rivas at least.

MONEY

Banco Lafise (El muelle, 200m E)

BanPro Credit (El muelle, 3c E) Accepts Visa. Not always operational.

ⓘ Getting There & Away

BOAT

Boats (www.ometepenicaragua.com) leave San Jorge for Moyogalpa's **ferry terminal** (El muelle; Calle Santa Ana) up to 15 times each day between 7am and 5:45pm, but not all ferries sail when they're supposed to. Fares are around US$2 to US$3 per person, depending on the boat. Consult reliable locals regarding the most reliable departures.

BUSES

Bus departures are more frequent here than anywhere else on the island. Bus timetables are subject to change, so if you're going out for the day, ask your driver what time the last bus returns.

TAXI

If you don't want to wait around for a bus, ask your lodgings about getting a taxi or go down to the port when ferries are pulling in and talk to other travelers and taxi drivers about sharing a ride.

ⓘ Getting Around

Moyogalpa has the greatest choice of motorbike, ATV and scooter hire places on the island. It typically costs US$15/day for a scooter, US$25/day for a motorbike and US$60/day for an ATV. Vehicle condition varies, so shop around before you commit to renting.

Volcán Concepción

The massive (and active) Volcán Concepción is an Ometepe landmark. The seven- to 10-hour hike up loose volcanic stone to the summit of this looming peak can be tough, so be in good physical condition and bring water, snacks and real hiking shoes. Most hikes leave from either Moyogalpa or Altagracia. Remember that there's no shade above the tree line, it's even steeper than it looks, and it can get windy and cold at the top, particularly if it's cloudy out.

There are three main trails to the top: La Concha and La Flor (the most popular trail), both close to Moyogalpa, and La Sabana, a short distance from Altagracia. It's almost always cloudy at the top, which means your chances of seeing the fuming craters and awesome views over the lake and across Central America's volcanic spine are slim, even during the dry season.

Guided treks up the volcano cost around US$25 to US$40 per person and can be organized by most outfitters on the island.

BUSES FROM MOYOGALPA

Following is the official timetable, but bear in mind that the 8:20am bus to Balgüe is not always reliable.

DESTINATIONS	COST (US$)	DURATION	FREQUENCY
Altagracia	0.80	45min	6 daily from 8:20am to 4:40pm
Balgüe	1.20	2¼hr	8:20am, 10:15am, 3:45pm
Mérida	1.40	2½hr	9:30am, 2:20pm, 4:40pm
San Ramón	1.50	3hr	daily at 9:30am

Around Volcán Concepción

This has been the more populous side of the island (despite the looming, active volcano overhead) since the Chorotega arrived, and remains so today. You can see its main attraction, Volcán Concepción, at 1610m, Nicaragua's second-highest volcano, from a great distance away, and climbing it is Ometepe's toughest hiking challenge.

Esquipulas

This small village, south of Moyogalpa on the road that circumvents the island, is unremarkable except for a few attractions nearby. There's the turnoff for **Punta Jesús María**, a naturally formed sand spit and lookout point on the lake. A little further along the road, on the other side of town, is the turnoff to the farmstay and restaurant at Finca Samaria. And beyond that, about halfway between Esquipulas and San José del Sur, there's the turnoff to the island's best museums, Museos El Ceibo.

◉ Sights

★ **Museos El Ceibo**   MUSEUM
(☑8874-8706; www.museoselceibo.com; Camino Moyogalpa a Altagracia; one/both museums US$5/8; ☺8am-5pm) The excellent **Museo Numismástico** (Money Museum) documents the troubled history of the Nicaraguan economy through its coins and banknotes. Across the road, **Museo Precolombino** (Pre-Columbian Museum) displays an excellent collection of more than 1500 pieces of ceramics, metates, funeral urns and jewelry, spanning the different civilizations from all around the island, and some over 5000 years old. The museums are located 2km down a shady lane off the main road, about halfway between Esquipulas and San José del Sur.

In the Money Museum, look for cacao – the edible currency of the Nahuatl people – and the notes showcasing the hyperinflation during the Contra War.

⌂ Sleeping & Eating

Finca Samaria   LODGE $
(☑8824-2210; Cementerio Esquipulas, 30m al lago; dm/d US$10/25; 🐾) 🌱 A beautiful and ecofriendly farmstay option not far from Moyogalpa. Rooms are fairly basic, but the farm is lovely, with hammocks galore in the

shady garden, which backs onto a tree-lined beach with some of the best sunset views on the island. There's a great vegan-friendly restaurant on-site that's open to the public; the family also rents bikes and horses.

❶ Getting There & Away

Buses from Moyogalpa pass through Esquipulas (10 minutes, US$0.40) many times each day.

San José del Sur

This sizable workaday village is an arrival point for boats from San Jorge. There are several places to stay, a couple located on the gray-sand beach near the ferry dock, but little reason to linger, unless you are catching the ferry from here.

⌂ Sleeping

Hostal La Casona   GUESTHOUSE $
(☑8139-1021; Calle el Madroño; r/f US$15/25; 🅿🛜🐾) This family-run guesthouse is your best bet in San José: the friendly hosts help to arrange excursions around the island, there's good home-cooked food, a tranquil garden and some very funky rocking chairs to chill in, with chickens, dogs and pigs running around underfoot. Rooms are simple and fan-cooled.

❶ Getting There & Away

Ferries and boats for the 40-minute trip to San Jorge depart from the **ferry terminal** (El muelle), just off the main road in the center of the village, at 5:40am, 7:30am and 3pm, returning from San Jorge at 9:30am, 2pm and 5pm. Buses meet the *lanchas* (small motorboats) at the dock.

Buses between Moyogalpa and Altagracia pass through six times daily.

Charco Verde & Isla de Quiste

On the southern side of Concepción lies a lush, less windblown clutch of beaches, centered on Reserva Charco Verde (p114). The fine green Laguna Charco Verde is accessible from a short hiking trail that begins at Hotel Charco Verde.

Not only is this a lovely spot for swimming, hiking and wildlife-watching, it's also the home of Chico Largo, a tall, thin and ancient witch who often appears swimming or fishing in the lagoon. His primary duty is to protect the tomb and solid-gold throne of Cacique Nicarao, buried nearby.

Just offshore, Isla de Quiste is within swimming distance of the beach. Any of the area's hotels can arrange boat service and perhaps rental tents, as it's a prime camping, fishing and birding spot.

⊙ Sights

Reserva Charco Verde NATURE RESERVE
(US$2; ☉7am-5pm) Rich with wildlife and fringed with black-sand beaches, this wooded ecological reserve is a quiet spot for hiking, birdwatching and taking a dip in the lake. There are three trails, totalling 4km in length; a flat one suitable for wheelchairs and two more strenuous ones. You're likely to have them mostly to yourself and are likely to spot monkeys and a plethora of birds. The enchanted city of Chico Largo is said to lie beneath the Laguna Charco Verde.

🛏 Sleeping

Hotel Finca Venecia HOTEL $$
(☎8887-0191; d US$30, cabins with fan/air-con from US$40/60; P❋☎) With terracotta walls and ancient funereal urns dotted around the lush property, this *finca* (farm) dates back to 1915. Guests are housed in an assortment of cabins and rooms (all with hot water and air-con); nab a lakefront cabin if you can. The restaurant is good for Nica standards and the owners can organise volcano ascents with bilingual guides.

Hotel Charco Verde CABIN $$$
(☎2560-1271; www.charcoverde.com.ni; Charco Verde, San José del Sur; 2-/3-person cabins from US$55/93; ❋☎☀) Next to the entrance to Reserva Charco Verde, this hotel occupies a fabulous beach, and has a growing collection of cabins, all with private patios and some with beach views. There are kayaks and laundry facilities, and a decent on-site restaurant. The pool is open to non-guests (US$5).

❶ Getting There & Away

Charco Verde is close to the ferry terminal at San José del Sur, convenient if you're arriving here by boat from Moyogalpa. Otherwise, it's about a 10-minute walk from the main road if you're catching a bus to Moyogalpa (US$0.50, 20 minutes, 6 daily between 5:30am and 5:20pm) or Altagracia (same price, 25 minutes, 6 daily from 9am to 5pm).

El Quino

Just south of Altagracia, El Quino is an intersection that's used as a point of reference for hotels and natural attractions on this side of the island. From here, you can access many of Ometepe's loveliest stretches of coastline, and access public transportation to either side of the island.

🛏 Sleeping & Eating

★**San Juan de la Isla** LODGE $$$
(☎8210-6957; www.sanjuandelaisla.com; El Quino, 500m N; r from US$75, cabañas US$125; ❋☎) ♠ This top-end choice is located just north of the village of El Quino. Set on a working farm right on the beach, the hacienda-style hotel has a private beach, remarkable volcano views from the well-tended grounds, and a good restaurant. It's worth splurging on one of the eight *cabañas* on stilts that overlook the sea.

❶ Getting There & Away

All buses from Moyogalpa that are headed to Playa Santo Domingo and Volcán Maderas stop in Altagracia, just north of El Quino.

Altagracia

POP 7000
With more natural protection from Concepción's occasional lava flow than Moyogalpa, this soporific little town was the original indigenous capital of Ometepe, and now lags behind Moyogalpa in importance since it's no longer an active port. For travelers, there's not much to see here, but it can be a convenient base for climbing Volcán Concepción.

⊙ Sights

Isla Grande ISLAND
Close to Altagracia, this island, basically a plantain *finca* gone feral, is rarely visited despite being a fantastic place for birdwatching. If you're interested, you could certainly arrange a custom trip – ask at your hotel.

Monoliths ARCHAEOLOGICAL SITE
(Frente Iglesia Católica; by donation; ☉24hr) A place to see some of the finest remaining ancient excavated statues on Ometepe is beside the Altagracia church, close to the Parque Central, where a handful of softly eroding monoliths still stand sentry.

🏃 Activities

This is base camp for the other trailhead to Concepción, called La Sabana, which begins about 2km from town. Hotels can arrange guides.

🛏 Sleeping & Eating

Hotel Kencho
HOTEL $

(☎ 8944-4087; www.facebook.com/Hotel-Kencho-Ometepe-252495888158233; iglesia, 1½c S; r from US$12; ❀ 🖥) This three-story hotel is the newest and best option on Altagracia's otherwise paltry accommodation scene. Rooms are simple, but clean and comfortable, and owner Manual is super helpful. The restaurant and bar serves some of the best food in town, including ample Nicaraguan breakfasts.

Hotel Central
HOTEL $

(☎ 2569-4420; www.hotelcentralometepe.blogspot.co.uk/; iglesia, 2c S; s/d US$10/19, cabins from US$25; ❀ 🖥) This central hotel is a simple affair but a good deal. Rooms at the front are arranged around a garden, with hammocks strung outfront; the cabins out the back (sleeping two) are basic but cute, and the hotel restaurant serves good, cheap Nicaraguan food and cold beer.

Playa Santo Domingo & Santa Cruz

Windswept sandy beaches and several good hotels lie southeast of Altagracia, on the long and lovely lava isthmus that cradles Playas Santo Domingo, San Fernando and Santa Cruz, which flow seamlessly from north to south.

Heading south to Santa Cruz along the island's main road, the beach gets progressively less crowded and the waves are popular with kiteboarders.

🏃 Activities

The main attraction is the **beach**, a 30m to 70m (depending on lake levels) expanse of gray volcanic sand that retreats almost to the sea wall during the rainy season.

Kiteboarding instruction can be found at Sun Kite School.

Río Istiam
KAYAKING

🖊 On the south side of the isthmus, this river shimmers as it snakes through the island's lava valley. The best way to explore the river (which is really a swamp) is by kayak – you're pretty much guaranteed to see turtles, caimans and howler monkeys. Inquire at nearby hotels, like **Caballito's Mar** (☎ 8842-6120; www.caballitosmar.com; dm/r/cabins US$8/25/35), which offers the trip for US$25 per person.

Ojo de Agua
SWIMMING

(btwn El Quino and Santo Domingo; US$5; ☺ 7am-6pm) Take a pleasant stroll through banana plantations to the well-signed, shady swimming hole about 1.5km north of Playa Santo Domingo. The mineral-infused water in the pool here bubbles up from 35 small underground springs; with an average temperature of 22°C to 28°C (71°F to 82°F), it makes for a refreshing dip.

Sun Kite School
KITESURFING

(☎ 8287-5023; www.kiteboardingnicaragua.com; Santa Cruz, 700m del Norte; 3hr advanced course US$150, intermediate refresher US$260) Towards the south end of Playa Santa Cruz, Ometepe's only kitesurfing operator offers instruction for all abilities. If you want to ride Lago Nicaragua's waves, choose from the half-day introduction or three-hour advanced course that teaches you to land jumps, the two-day beginner package or intermediate refresher.

🛏 Sleeping & Eating

Xalli Beach Hotel
HOTEL $$

(☎ 2569-4876; www.xallihotel.com; Playa San Fernando; r with/without bathroom from US$45/85; ❀ 🖥 🏊) It's hard to imagine a more tranquil location along this stretch of the island: listen to the waves while swaying in a hammock or go out onto the windswept beach. The standard rooms are comfortable but nothing special, so it's worth splurging on a lake view *cabaña*. Good

---

BUSES FROM ALTAGRACIA

Buses heading south from Moyogalpa all pass by here one hour after leaving before continuing south. Services include the following:

DESTINATION	COST (US$)	DURATION	FREQUENCY
Balgüe	1.10	1hr	4:30am, 9:30am, 11:30pm, 1:30pm & 4:30pm
Mérida	1.25	1½hr	7:30am, 10:30am, 2pm, 4pm & 5:30pm
Moyogalpa	0.75	45min	12 daily from 5:15am to 7pm
San Ramón	1.50	2hr	10:30am & 2pm

BULL SHARKS: A TALE OF OVERFISHING

There was a time when the people of Lago de Nicaragua, then called Cocibolca ('Sweet Sea' in Náhuatl), did not learn how to swim. From the gulf of the Río San Juan to Granada's shores, the bull shark ruled these waters, and had a taste for human flesh.

Carcharhinus leucus is among the Caribbean's most ferocious sharks, not enormous but strong, with an appetite for anything terrestrial that might fall into its realm. Its small eyes, adapted to the silty water of the river mouth, are useless, but it can smell blood from 100m away. Its flattened tail fin is perfect for the punishingly shallow rapids of rivers, which it – unlike any other shark – can penetrate well inland.

Though always hunted, the bull shark became a major cash earner as the 20th century began. By the 1930s Chinese buyers were paying as much as US$70 a kilogram for the fins, a legendary 'restorative.' As the market grew, Nicaraguans found buyers for the shark's liver, rich in vitamin A, and the skin, which can be prepared as fine leather. The bull shark's meat, however, rotted too quickly to export – the bulk of this brutal catch was ground into fertilizer or dog food, or simply thrown away.

In 1969 the Somoza family decided to take full advantage of this 'renewable' natural resource, and built a shark-processing plant in Granada. By some estimates, 20,000 sharks flowed through it during its decade of operation. More than 100 boats fed the facilities, even as the sharks became rarer, perhaps endangered, and ever more difficult to catch. The revolution coincided with this unprofitable decline, and the entire operation was shut down in 1979. It has never recovered.

These days, bull-shark sightings are a very rare occurrence. Some locals say that they lurk out in the deep waters, far from the shoreline, others say that the only colonies left are around the entrance to the Río San Juan. Now that the shark has no natural predators, it's possible that the population will make a comeback.

A great book about Nicaraguan bull sharks is the page-turner *Savage Shore: Life and Death with Nicaragua's Last Shark Hunters*, by Edward Marriot.

cocktails, Nica and international dishes at the restaurant.

El Encanto HOTEL $$
(☑ 8867-7128; www.goelencanto.com; Santa Cruz; d/cabin from US$33/50) Set on a banana farm, rooms here are simply but pleasantly decorated, with big, screened windows and clean, modern bathrooms. Hammocks out the front of your room have great lake views. The restaurant gets mixed reviews for its mix of Nica classics and international food, including curries, wholemeal bread and several vegetarian options.

Hotel Villa Paraíso HOTEL $$
(☑ 2569-4859; www.villaparaiso.com.ni; Playa Santo Domingo; d/cabin/apt from US$35/80/70; ℙ ❄ 🛜) Lodgings at this friendly beachfront hotel range from tidy rooms and elegant *cabañas* (with air-con, TV and private terraces) to compact apartments drowning in orchids and bougainvillea. Helpful staff can arrange tours and taxi transfers, and the on-site restaurant reliably serves a mix of Nicaraguan and international dishes. Backup generator precludes power cuts.

🛈 Getting There & Away

From Santo Domingo there are 10 buses daily to Altagracia (US$0.50, 30 minutes) and six buses to Moyogalpa (US$1, 1¼ hours). Buses run to Balgüe at 5am, 10am, noon, 2pm and 5pm (US$0.50, 30 minutes) and pass through from Altagracia on the way to Mérida five times daily (US$0.90, one hour) and at 11am and 2:30pm for San Ramón (US$1.20, 1½ hours). A taxi will cost US$20 to US$30 from the Moyogalpa ferry dock.

🛈 Getting Around

You can hire bikes (US$10 per day) and motorbikes (US$25 per day) along this stretch of road.

Volcán Maderas

★ **Volcán Maderas** VOLCANO
Climbing this 1394m volcano is challenging but worthwhile. Guides are required for the seven- to eight-hour round-trip trek (with four to five hours of climbing); at the top, you'll reach cloud forest ending with a steep crater descent to a chilly jade-green lake. There are three trails to the top: the most popular at **Finca Magdelena** and two

slightly longer trails beginning at **Hacienda Mérida** and **Finca El Porvenir**. The Finca Magdalena trail offers the money shot of Volcán Concepción (p112).

Prices depend on where you start, whether you need transportation, and how many are in your group: you'll pay anywhere between US$15 and US$30 per person. Your lodgings can help you arrange the excursion.

If climbing is not your thing, consider horseback riding or cycling around the circumference of Maderas (35km) on the rough dirt road; you'll be passing through one of the remotest parts of Nicaragua. Both can be arranged through local accommodations.

Around Volcán Maderas

This is the lusher, wilder side of the island. It's even less developed than Concepción's side, and petroglyphs are much more common. The star attraction, of course, is the towering, dormant Volcán Maderas (1394m), covered with coffee plantations at the bottom and cloud forest at the top, and with a lake in its crater.

Santa Cruz to Balgüe

The northern side of Volcán Maderas has become one of the island's hot spots: apart from being an excellent base for volcano ascents, spread-out little Balgüe has an organic chocolate farm for you to explore, an increasing number of excellent budget accommodations and a burgeoning dining scene.

🛏 Sleeping

There's an ever-increasing number of eco-farms, good hostels, and guesthouses in the area, many with a sustainable ethic.

El Pital Chocolate Paradise   HOSTEL $
(📞2560-3249; www.elpitalometepe.com; Santa Cruz, 1.4km del Este; camping per person US$5, dm US$10-12; 🌐) 🌱 Reached via an atrociously bumpy road leading to the water, this hippy-esque place wears many hats. It's an organic cacao farm, a place to learn to make artisanal chocolate (US$15 per person), a hostel consisting of wonderfully breezy bamboo dorms, a venue hosting fire shows, guided meditation and aerial silks, and a chilled-out cafe.

Hostal La Urraca Loca   HOSTEL $
(📞5766-0128; Carretera Finca Magdalena, 80m S, 50m E; dm US$8, r with/without bathroom

US$27/20; 🌐) Hand-carved furniture and private balconies are not the first things you expect in a hostel, but here we are. This Edenic little place has been lovingly put together by its Spanish owners, who work with local guides to provide an excellent Volcán Maderas experience for their guests. Rooms are spotless and the hammock-strung garden is great for chilling.

Finca Magdalena   FARMSTAY $
(📞8418-5636; www.fincamagdalena.com; hammock/camping per person US$4/6, dm/d US$8/18, cabins US$70) 🌱 This Ometepe mainstay next to the Volcán Maderas trailhead is a classic backpacking spot. Rooms and dorms on this working coffee *finca* are set in a rickety old wooden farmhouse and are overdue for a revamp, but really – for the sweeping views of the lake and Volcán Concepción, lush surroundings and good food – you can rough it for a few days.

Note that it's a 1.5km climb to the *finca* from the bus stop.

Totoco Ecolodge   LODGE $$$
(📞8358-7718; www.totoco.com.ni; Callejon de la Palmera, 800m arriba, Balgüe; budget casita US$45, lodge US$102; 🅿🌐🍽) 🌱 This gorgeous ecolodge features *cabañas* perched high above the beach on a large organic farm that runs on solar power and recycles grey water. It's not on the beach, but there's a beautiful pool with views from here to eternity. The romantic rooms are the best on the island, and the **restaurant**, open to the public, is excellent.

🍴 Eating

Some of the best dining options on the island are found in and around Balgüe, offering increasingly sophisticated cuisine. There's also a cluster of casual, locally run cafes near the main road, just to the north of town.

Café Comedor Isabel   NICARAGUAN $
(Hospedaje Así Es Mi Tierra, 50m O; mains US$4-6; ⏰8am-9pm) Run by a friendly woman, this no-frills cafe is the place to come for hearty portions of traditional Nicaraguan food.

★Café Campestre   INTERNATIONAL $$
(📞8571-5930; www.campestreometepe.com; Hospedaje Así es Mi Tierra, 50m O; mains US$5-10; ⏰11:30am-9pm; 🌐) 🌱 This popular cafe using local ingredients from the adjacent organic farm has something for everyone: excellent coffee, freshly baked breads, huge

salads and international dishes from hummus platters to Thai curries. They do wonderful things with eggplant and you can buy local coffee and honey here.

Bamboo INTERNATIONAL $$
(📞8716-7640; Lazy Crab Hostel, 30m S; mains US$7-12; ⊘noon-10pm; 🍴) Che and friends cook up delicious homemade pasta, whole grilled fish from the lake with *gallo pinto* (rice and beans) and fried plantain, and more, at this Argentinian-run place. Eat it under the giant palapa-style thatched roof and then swing in a hammock with a beer.

❶ Getting There & Away

Buses leave Balgüe for Altagracia (US$1.10, one hour) six times per day between 5:30am and 4:30pm, with four of the buses continuing to Moyogalpa. Altagracia-Balgüe buses run between 4:30am and 4:30pm. To catch a bus to Mérida or San Ramón, change in Santo Domingo.

Santa Cruz to Mérida & San Ramón

This lush part of the island feels progressively wilder and more untamed the further south you travel. Here, lush *fincas* dot the foothills of Volcán Maderas and, if you travel past San Ramón, beyond the reach of public transportation, you'll find yourself in one of the remotest parts of Nicaragua, amid indigenous villages where visitors are seldom encountered.

❍ Sights

Some of Ometepe's must-see attractions are accessed from this part of the island, including the **petroglyphs** at Albergue Ecológico El Porvenir, where a well-marked trail meanders past approximately 20 of these rock carvings. Other heavyweight attractions include the Cascada San Ramón, and of course Volcán Ometepe.

Cascada San Ramón WATERFALL
(US$5; ⊘8am-5:30pm) This stunning 40m waterfall is one of the jewels of the island. The 3.7km trail begins at the Estación Biológica de Ometepe. You can drive 2.2km up to the parking area, from where it's a 30- to 40-minute hike up to the waterfall, with a steep scramble near the end. At the top, the cascade tumbles down a sheer, mossy rock face into a cold pool that's fabulous for a dip on a hot day.

🏃 Activities

Hari's Horses HORSEBACK RIDING
(📞8383-8499; www.harishorsesnicaragua.com; Finca Montania Sagrada, Mérida) Located at the Finca Montania Sagrada, this reliable operator offers several different horseback riding outings in the vicinity of Volcán Maderas. These include rides to the San Ramón waterfall (US$50), trail rides with swimming in the lake (US$25) and, for expert riders only, a five to six-hour endurance gallop all the way around the volcano (US$100).

🛏 Sleeping & Eating

★**Finca Mystica** FARMSTAY $$
(📞8751-9653; www.fincamystica.com; Punta El Congo, 500m S, 300m E; dm/d/f US$15/42/46; ▦🛜) Travelers looking for ecofriendly accommodation in the midst of lush jungle hit the mother lode with Finca Mystrica. A labor of love by US expats Ryan and Angela, this eco-farm receives its guests in round cob (soil, rice straw, sand and horse manure) cabins, with a chorus of howler monkeys at dawn and nights filled with fireflies. Exceptional restaurant, too.

Finca Montania Sagrada FARMSTAY $$
(📞8383-8499; www.fincamontaniasagrada.com; r/f US$45/75; ▦🛜) At the southern end of Mérida, a bumpy road leads uphill to this Edenic property where cabins peek out from between the fruit trees. Swing in a hammock at sunset, play with the resident dogs and cats, or join owners Hari and Mirca for a cup of coffee. The restaurant serves authentic Italian food. English, Italian and German are spoken.

Albergue Ecológico El Porvenir LODGE $$
(📞2560-0496; www.porvenirometepe.blogspot.gr/p/ometepe.html; 1km SE de Santa Cruz; s/d from US$13/23; 🛜) At the foot of Volcán Maderas, this sunny lodge and restaurant has it all – great volcano views and petroglyphs amid attractive gardens, a restaurant serving good-value meals, and simple but spacious guest rooms. You can arrange everything here, from horseback riding to guided hikes.

❶ Getting There & Away

Buses leave Mérida for Altagracia (US$1.20, 1½ hours) at 4am, 5:45am, 8:30am, 10:15am and 3:30pm, with the 4am, 8:30am and 3:30pm buses continuing to Moyogalpa (US$2, 2½ hours), though only the 8:30am bus in considered reliable. Buses from Mérida to San Ramón depart at noon and 3:30pm (US$0.30, 30 minutes), and return at 5:15am, 9:45am and 3pm. The San Ramón-Altagracia buses (US$1.50, 1¼–2 hours) depart at 5:15am, 9:45am and 3pm, with the 3pm bus continuing to Moyogalpa (US$1.50, three hours).

If you're headed to a specific *finca* or guesthouse, consult with them first – they can help you come up with the best plan for the time of day you're arriving so you can avoid getting stranded.

PACIFIC BEACHES

Southwestern Nicaragua's Pacific beaches offer amazing surf, sand and sun. The beaches around San Juan del Sur attract more beginners and intermediate surfers, while the waves further north are where the serious surfers head. To get to the Tola beaches – El Astillero down to Playa Gigante – most travelers pass through Rivas and Tola and follow the unpaved roads to the remote strips of sand. The party town of San Juan del Sur serves as the access point for the beaches between Playa Majagual in the north downward to El Ostional.

ⓘ Getting There & Away

To access the region from elsewhere in Nicaragua, you'll most likely need to pass through the transport hub of Rivas. El Astillero can also be accessed by a rough, more direct road if you're coming from Managua or Granada; one bus daily makes the trip from Managua during dry season.

For beaches north and south of San Juan del Sur, you can catch beach shuttles from San Juan del Sur. Buses run south from San Juan del Sur to Playa El Ostional (US$1.50, 20 minutes to one hour, three to four times daily) via Playa El Coco, which can also drop you by the turnoffs to Playa Remanso, Playa Yanqui, Playa Hermosa, Playa Tamarindo, and Refugio de Vida Silvestre La Flor.

Tola & the Tola Beaches

Tola ('the land of the Toltecs') is an unassuming agricultural town, famous in Nicaragua for the common expression: *Te dejó esperando come la novia de Tola* ('He left you waiting like the bride of Tola'), after a young local woman was left at the altar by her groom, who went on to marry his ex-lover.

Pass through Tola, and you hit the rugged and gorgeous nearby coastline. Once almost inaccessible and totally wild, these 30km of beaches are slowly coming into their own. They still retain some of that lost-paradise feel, with top-notch surf, uncrowded sand and good vibes.

The fishing villages here attract serious surfers, though some travelers come for the time-warp vibe. There are no banks or real grocery stores, and internet and cell-phone coverage is patchy at best, so enjoy getting away from it all.

ⓘ Getting There & Away

There are eight buses daily from Rivas to Las Salinas, but while they'll get you to Playa Guasacate (Playa Popoyo), they can't be called convenient – they can drop you at the turnoffs to the other beach villages and you have to walk (or hope to hitch a ride) several kilometers to your destination. Let your driver know where you're going. There's a single direct plantation pickup truck (with benches for passengers) between Tola and Playa Gigante (Monday to Saturday).

Surf camps and hotels offer transportation to and from Managua Airport. Several taxi drivers in Playa Popoyo offer airport pickup from Managua airport (US$70). A tourist shuttle runs at least once daily between San Juan del Sur and Playa Popoyo (US$15) with a roof rack for surfboards (US$3); ask at Casa Oro (p129) about departure times.

A taxi to Playa Gigante from Rivas costs around US$30, and around US$60 from San Juan del Sur, depending on your bargaining prowess.

BUSES TO THE PACIFIC BEACHES

Bus services from Rivas (p103) include the following:

DESTINATION	COST (US$)	DURATION	FREQUENCY
El Astillero	2	3hr	5:30am & 4:50pm
Playa Gigante	1.50	1½-2hr	1:30pm Mon-Sat
Salinas	1.70	2hr	6 daily, 5:30am-4:50pm
Tola	0.80	40 min	every 45 min, 5:30am-5:45pm

THE FIVE BEACHES

The only way to enjoy some of the prettiest beaches on this stretch of coastline – Las Cinco Playas (the Five Beaches), also known as Playa Escondida, Playa Santana, Playa Duna, Playa Rosada and Playa Los Perros – is if you're a guest or resident of the plush **Rancho Santana** (☑8882-2885; www.ranchosantana.com; Playa Santana; casitas from US$250, ste from US$500; ❊☎☁) resort. Spread over 2700 acres, this thriving resort village has it all, almost – clubhouses, ocean view homes, pools, horses, tennis courts, and a helipad, to name a few.

The most famous of these beaches is probably Playa Rosada, with pretty pink sand, great surfing and an odd hydro-geological formation that shoots ocean water several meters into the waves.

Most travelers coming here arrange shuttle transportation with the resort itself. If taking NIC-62 from Rivas, it's a straightforward 35km drive via Tola.

Driving from Rivas, the road is unpaved once you pass through Tola, but perfectly passable in a city car in the dry season. Coming from Managua or Granada in dry season, it's possible to take the minor road from the NIC-2 highway directly to Las Salinas, though there's a minor river crossing involved.

Playa Gigante

POP UNDER 2000

This glorious crescent sweep of white sand, tucked into forested hills, was once a traditional fishing village. Today, though fishing still takes place, the popular sandy beach break right in front of the one-street Playa Gigante gets hollow and fun when conditions are perfect, attracting a steady stream of surfers and sun-seekers.

🏃 Activities

Salty's Beach Rentals SURFING
(www.facebook.com/pg/saltysbeach; surfboard rental half/full day US$10/15, SUP rental per day US$10, boogie board rental per day US$5, surf lessons US$55; ☺8am-6pm) This recommended outfit rents surfboards, SUPs and boogie boards, and offers beginner surf lessons.

🛏 Sleeping

Camino del Gigante HOSTEL $$
(☑8743-5899; www.gigantebay.com; Playa Gigante; dm US$10, d with/without bathroom US$39/30; ☎☁) The location's the draw at this beachfront hostel: the dorms, rooms and five-person bungalow are bare-bones, but who cares? You're here for the ocean views, the mellow communal areas decked out in psychedelia, and access to great surf spots. There's a bar and restaurant, and, more importantly, the hostel runs a sunset booze cruise (US$10).

Aqua Wellness Resort RESORT $$$
(☑8739-2426; www.aquanicaragua.com; Redonda Bay; r/ste from US$216/378; ❊☎☁) Overlooking a private beach cove, the elegant jungle treehouses at this excellent spa and resort have tremendous ocean views and all the high-end amenities you could wish for. The suites come with plunge pools and there's a private beach, plus lush forest on all sides. Meditation and yoga are a focus, though you can also arrange surfing, fishing and more.

Giant's Foot Surf Camp LODGE $$$
(☑8384-2331; www.giantsfootsurf.com; Playa Gigante; per week per person from US$1300; ❊) Set on the southern end of the beach, this laid-back surf camp offers guided boat trips to 14 breaks along the coast. The camp accommodates 10 surfers at a time. Packages include surfing, boat, transfers, three daily meals – even local beer and rum – plus a daily wake-up call with coffee and cereal.

🍴 Eating & Drinking

There are a handful of simple restaurants on the beach and on the road leading to it, and a small *pulpería* (general store) on the main drag.

★Mama Lin's SEAFOOD $
(☑8652-7502; Punta del Arco; mains US$3-6; ☺8am-8pm) By the rocks at the north end of the beach, local matriarch Mama Lin feeds you fantastic lobster, grilled snapper, *sopa de mariscos* (seafood stew) and chicken dishes, as well as hearty Nica breakfasts.

Juntos Beach Bar & Grill INTERNATIONAL $$
(☑5749-8756; mains US$4-8; ☺8am-10pm Sun-Thu, to midnight Fri & Sat) This Canadian-Nicaraguan cafe in the middle of the village turns into the local nightspot on weekends, sometimes with DJs. Come for pizza night, the poutine, the generous breakfasts involv-

ing Bloody Marys, or to watch the game on their big-screen while shooting some pool.

El Mirador Margarita
SEAFOOD **$$**

(☑ 8948-2042; Playa Gigante; dishes US$3-9; ☺ 8am-10pm) In a prime sunset-viewing spot in the center of the village, Margarita's is the place to come to for cold beers and heaped portions of grilled fish. Solid Nica breakfasts, too.

❶ Getting There & Away

Those attending surf camps often have their transportation pre-arranged. Chicken buses between Las Salinas and Rivas stop at the turnoff for Playa Gigante eight times daily between 6:30am and 3:40pm (US$1, 1½ hours); from there it's a 4km walk to the beach. There's also one large pickup truck that departs Playa Gigante directly at 6am Monday to Saturday and returns from Tola at 1pm.

It's possible to arrange shuttles from San Juan del Sur or Playa Popoyo, if there are enough people (ask at your accommodation). A taxi from Rivas or Tola costs approximately US$20 to US$30 for up to four people, depending on your bargaining skills.

Playa Popoyo & Around
POP UNDER 1000

Home to one of the most storied waves in Nicaragua, Playa Popoyo (Playa Guasacate; www.popoyo.com) is a long stretch of remote coastline several kilometres northwest of the little town of **Las Salinas de Nagualapa**, named for the salt evaporation ponds you'll pass on the way in. Apart from a few surfers and fishers, this stretch of sand is almost empty, ideal for a long walk at sunset. The large, dramatic rock formations on the beach are fun to explore at low tide.

Playa Guasacate is often called Playa Popoyo in honor of its famed beach break near the southern end, where a shallow lagoon and slow river shift through the long, sandy beach. Don't confuse it with the community of Popoyo that was moved south of Playa Sardinas following the 1992 tsunami.

🏃 Activities

Popoyo Surf Shop
SURFING

(☑ 8464-9563; www.facebook.com/popoyosurfshop; La Bocana, 200m N; board hire per day US$10; ☺ 8am-5pm) Friendly French guy Cristobal rents all manner of boards and repairs any dings your favorite board might have suffered during a wipeout.

🛏 Sleeping

Wild Waves Surf House
GUESTHOUSE **$**

(☑ 8578-6102; www.wildwavesnicaragua.com; De la Bocana, 250m N, Playa Guasacate; dm/r US$14/40; ❋ ☎) Run by friendly Italian surfer Gianni, this three-room guesthouse is the perfect retreat for serious wave-riders. The doubles have king-sized beds, there's a guest kitchen and Gianni arranges boat trips to catch waves further up and down the coast. Week-long surf packages are US$699 for beginners and from US$399 for experienced surfers.

Club Surf Popoyo
HOTEL **$$**

(☑ 8237-7417; www.clubdelsurf.com; De la Bocana, 200m del Oeste, Playa Popoyo; s/d from US$40/50; ❋ ☎) Owned by a friendly Italian family, this popular hotel has six spotless and spacious rooms, as well as an excellent, authentic pizzeria that's open to the public. You're not quite on the beach – that's about 100m away – but there's good access to the Popoyo break right away, and guests rave about the helpful staff and hearty breakfast.

Popoyo Beach Hostel
HOSTEL **$$**

(☑ 8106-8017; www.popoyobeachhostel.com; De la Bocana, 350m N, Playa Popoyo; dm/d/tr US$10/25/35; ❋ ☎) This friendly beachfront hostel is all soaring ceilings and heavy timber. The en-suite rooms and four-bed dorms are dark, but with powerful ceiling fans and large lockers. When not surfing, its residents can be found cooking, playing table tennis or hanging out in hammocks on the beachfront patio. It's roughly in the center of Playa Popoyo.

Red Pepper
GUESTHOUSE **$$$**

(☑ 8860-2750; www.facebook.com/RedPepper-Popoyo; De la Bocana, 150m N, Playa Guasacate; r US$87; ❋ ☎) This guesthouse is run by friendly Dutch couple Marc and Marieke and has just four quirkily decorated, snug rooms. It's a simple setup, with a private, hammock-strung terrace for each room and lots of thoughtful little touches, and the warmth and helpfulness of the owners makes for a wonderful experience.

Casitas Pacific Hotel
BOUTIQUE HOTEL **$$$**

(☑ 7841-4533; www.casitaspacific.com; De la Bocana, 300m N; d/q from US$72/81; ❋ ☎) With eight individually decorated rooms, gorgeous native-wood furniture, hammocks and swings on private terraces and thatched roofs, this two-story boutique hotel is Playa Popoyo's most stylish accommodation. The quads, with their two sets of bunk beds, are

CATCH OF THE DAY

The region is known for seafood and there are several good restaurants in Playa Popoyo, Playa Gigante and Playa Jiquelite, with fewer options elsewhere. San Juan del Sur has an extensive dining scene that caters to the gringo palate – everything from vegan wraps and burgers to curry and sushi.

excellent value for groups of surfer friends, and Popoyo's famous beach break is a 300m-walk down the beach.

Hotel Popoyo HOTEL $$$

(✉ 8885-3334; www.hotelpopoyo.com; Calle del Toro 29, Playa Popoyo; r from US$50, 2-person apt US$100; ❧ ☒) This hotel, popular with Managuans, hits all the marks: a lovely swimming pool, stylish and spacious guest rooms, a fantastic on-site restaurant and bar (El Toro, open to the public) and easy access to a near-empty beach that's a one-minute walk from the front gate. There's also an independent apartment with a fully equipped kitchen and a private ocean-view balcony.

✖ Eating

★ **La Vaca Loca** CAFE $$

(✉ 8584-9110; www.lavacalocaguasacate.com; De la Bocana, 180m N, Playa Guasacate; mains US$5-7; ☉ Wed-Sun 8am-1pm; ❋ ❧) La Vaca Loca wears several hats and we love them all: it's an art house with beautifully carved furnishings; a tranquil cafe in a flowering garden, serving American breakfasts and artisanal coffee; and a B&B with just two beautiful, breezy rooms (singles/doubles US$40/50).

Viento Este PIZZA $$

(✉ 8783-0493; Al lado de Casitas Pacific, Playa Guasacate; pizzas from US$6; ☉ 6-10pm Tue-Sat; ✐) Perch at one of candlelit driftwood tables, dig your toes in the sand and order a wood-fired pizza, while watching the white crests of the crashing surf in the darkness beyond. Strung with fairy lights, this Uruguayan joint is great for whiling away an evening.

❶ Getting There & Away

Buses leave Rivas for Las Salinas about eight times daily (US$2.50 to US$4, two to three hours.) Tell the driver you're going to Guasacate to be dropped off closer to most hotels and services. You can also arrange a private taxi for about US$35 per carload.

From Popoyo, a 7:30am shuttle (reserve ahead) departs from Cafe Con Leche for San Juan del Sur (US$15) via Rivas (US$10), returning from San Juan del Sur's Remax office at 10:30am. There is also sometimes a 2pm shuttle from Popoyo.

Several local taxi drivers, including **Pancho's Transportation** (✉ 8425-8693), do Managua Airport runs for US$70.

El Astillero

POP 5815

This picture-perfect fishing village fronts a gently scalloped white-sand beach. Apart from an excellent beach break with consistent barrels, there's surf north of here (accessible when turtles aren't arriving) and, if you're serious about hitting the more elusive waves, it's possible to talk a local fisherman into helping you explore the coastline.

⌂ Sleeping

Hostal Las Hamacas HOSTEL $$

(✉ 8810-4144; www.hostalhamacas.com; Escuela, 50m S; s/d with fan US$25/30, with air-con US$40/45; ❋ ❧ ☒) Set on a grassy lot with wide beachfront access, this laid-back guesthouse has peaceful, marine-blue rooms with comfy beds, TV and spacious bathrooms, plus a small swimming pool and – as the name suggests – plenty of hammocks to relax in.

Las Plumerias Lodge LODGE $$$

(✉ 8979-7782; www.lasplumerias.com; Playa Gavilan, El Astillero; surfer/non-surfer package per week from US$750/500, incl all meals; ❧ ☒) Run by French surfing instructors Etienne and Emeline, this wonderful surfers lodge is uphill from the road to El Astillero. Breezy traditional, thatch-roofed bungalows come with composting toilets and you can watch the sunset from your hammock or the pool after a day of surfing. Packages include expert surfing instruction and access to waves either by 4WD or boat.

❶ Getting There & Away

From Rivas there's a single bus to El Astillero at 5am (US$4.50, three hours), and a couple of buses daily from Nandaime (US$4; 9am and 2pm). From Rivas, you can also take a bus to Las Salinas (US$2.50 to US$4, two to three hours, eight daily), then connect to El Astillero. From Astillero, there are usually two buses daily to Rivas, at 5.45am and 10am, but only the 10am is reliable.

Playa Jiquelite

POP UNDER 1000

With Las Cinco Playas (five beaches area) to the south and separated from Playa Popoyo to the north by the Río de Nagualapa estuary, the Jiquelite area comprises two long beaches buffeted by Pacific waves: Playa Sardina and Playa Jiquelite, separated by a tall cliff. The former attracts novice and intermediate surfers, while Playa Jiquelite, accessed via the village of Limón Dos, is the playground for expert wave riders.

🛏 Sleeping

Hotel Magnific Rock　　　　　HOTEL $$

(📞 8916-6916;　www.magnificrockpopoyo.com; Punta Sardinas; 2-person cabins US$40, 2-person studios from US$70, 4-person apt from US$100; ✳️🛜) Built on a magnificent rock outcropping, this friendly surfer's hotel has amazing views overlooking Playa Sardina and Playa Jiquelite. The cabins are simple, but good enough, and the studio doubles have incredible beach views. The excellent restaurant serves fish tacos, garlic shrimp, French toast and jumbo smoothies. It's located 2km off the road to Las Salinas; look for the signs.

★ Sirena Surf Lodge　　　GUESTHOUSE $$$

(📞 8556-5392;　www.facebook.com/sirenasurfhouse; Playa Jiquelite; r US$70; 🛜) The moment you step out of your room, you can bury your toes in the sand. These two beautiful rooms with king-sized beds are all individually designed by owner and surfing instructor Bella, who feeds her guests a phenomenal breakfast and is happy to organize surfing lessons, boat trips and other local excursions.

SoLost　　　　　　　BOUTIQUE HOTEL $$$

(📞 2224-9246; www.solostinnica.com; Playa Jiquelite; bungalows US$185; 🛜✖️) ♦ Comprising eight spacious, fan-cooled bungalows with thatched roofs, made of sustainable local materials, this eco-hotel invests heavily in the community of Limón Dos, so not only do you get to stay in comfort, but you're also helping local kids get an education. Yoga classes, spa services, and a bistro catering to vegetarians and vegans are some of the perks.

❶ Getting There & Away

Buses from Rivas to Las Salinas (US$2.50 to US$4, two to three hours, eight daily) can drop you either by the access road to Hotel Magnific Rock, or the one to Playa Jiquelite; it's a 2km walk to the beach from both.

Refugio de Vida Silvestre Río Escalante-Chacocente

Much less visited than Refugio de Vida Silvestre La Flor, this wildlife refuge (📞 8603-3742, 2532-3293; www.marena.gob.ni; US$5) also gets *arribadas* (flotillas) of more than 3000 nesting olive ridley turtles at one time, as well as hawksbill, green and leatherback turtles, all of which make their nests here between July and December (peaking in August and September). The refuge protects 48 sq km of dry tropical forests and mangrove swamps, also home to such endangered birds as the great green macaw and the quetzal.

Marena (Nicaragua's Ministry of the Environment and Natural Resources) runs a helpful biological station here where you can camp, grab a meal or sleep in hostel-style accommodations. A community tourism group, Cosetuchaco, organizes all manner of wildlife watching tours, from turtle viewing to looking for birds and monkeys by the Río Escalante hot springs.

❶ Getting There & Away

There's currently no public transportation or regularly offered organized tours to the refuge, but if you have a 4WD you can take a signed, rough track 7km north of El Astillero. Alternatively, you could walk the 7km along the shore from El Astillero.

San Juan Del Sur

POP 15,762

Easygoing San Juan del Sur is the hub for exploration of Nicaragua's toned-and-tanned southern Pacific beaches. The town itself, with its clapboard Victorian houses, a towering statue of Christ on a neighboring hillside and a steady influx of young and beautiful international travelers and surfers, is Nicaragua's beach party central – Matthew McConaughey used to hang out here before the place got too popular.

And while the once-sleepy fishing village doesn't sit on an amazing stretch of coastline – you need to head just north or south for that – its half-moon, brown-sugar beach is pretty for a sunset stroll. Top it all off with a string of world-class surfing enclaves located within easy distance of town, and you have all the workings to kick off an amazing adventure on the waves.

◉ Sights

Cristo de la Misericordia MONUMENT
(Christ of Mercy statue; US$2; ⊙8am-5pm) This 25m statue of Jesus – one of the tallest in the world – overlooks the town from its perch 2km to the north. Take the one-hour hike up from the north end of Playa San Juan del Sur to catch a great bird's-eye (or son-of-God's eye) view of the harbor and ocean.

Petroglyph ARCHAEOLOGICAL SITE
(off Carretera San Juan del Sur) There's a spectacular petroglyph not far from town, depicting an enormous and elaborate hunting scene carved perhaps 1500 years ago. To find it, walk toward Rivas, passing the Texaco station, and make a left after the bridge. Pass a school and then a gate on your right. Continue to the old farmhouse; if anyone's around, you should ask permission to cross the land. Otherwise, follow the irrigation pipes to the river.

⚡ Activities

Surfing & Sailing
The best surfing is generally from April to December. There's a beach break for beginners on bigger swells at the northern end of the beach, but most surfers get taken to breaks north and south of town by 4WD or boat (or stay at the respective beaches). There are numerous surf shops and surfing instructors. Casa Oro Hostel runs daily shuttles out to Playa Maderas, Playa Hermosa and Playa Remanso.

Barefoot Surf Travel (www.barefootsurftravel.com) organises surf camps in the San Juan del Sur area (and in other parts of Central America).

One Love Surf School & Shop SURFING
(☑8251-5525; www.facebook.com/onelovenicaragua; Av Vanderbuilt; surfing lessons from US$20; ⊙8am-7pm) Gianni from One Love gets much love from rookie surfers for his patient surfing instruction. He also rents quality boards and sells surfing gear.

Arena Caliente SURFING
(☑8815-3247; www.facebook.com/ArenaCalienteSurf; Mercado, ½c N; surfing lessons from US$25) Everyone loves this locally owned and operated shop, which rents boards and arranges group transportation to the best breaks.

Nica Sail and Surf BOATING
(☑8980-1213; www.nicasailandsurf.com; Calle del Paseo del Rey; half-/full-day sailing excursion US$80/120) Runs popular catamaran sailing cruises that depart at 11am and 1pm and involve a stop either on Playa Blanca or Playa Brasilito. Freshly made *ceviche* (marinated seafood) is served, and rum cocktails and Mai-Tais keep flowing.

Horseback Riding

★Rancho Chilamate HORSEBACK RIDING
(☑8849-3470; www.ranchochilamate.com; Escamequita; daytime/sunset ride US$79/85) Excellent horseback-riding tours at a beautiful ranch located a 20-minute drive south of San Juan del Sur (round-trip transportation provided). Daily rides last around three hours and take place at low tide. Riders must be at least 18 years old. It's well worth staying out at the ranch, too (rooms US$99-US$129); guests rave about the lodgings and food.

Fishing
If you look south, you'll see an enormous peninsula jutting out into the sea, a wall of rock that hems in currents – and the critters that ride them, including sailfish and dorado (best June through October), yellow-fin tuna (April and May) and marlin (August and September). In addition to the pricier professional operations at the surf and dive shops in town, such as San Juan Surf & Sport, you can always book a trip with local fishers more cheaply.

Cycling
Several outfitters in town rent mountain bikes if you want to pedal the dirt roads heading to the northern and southern beaches (bear in mind that not all access roads south of San Juan are safe; ask locals before setting off). You can also take your bike on buses that run between San Juan del Sur and El Ostional.

Yoga
Zen Yoga HEALTH & WELLBEING
(☑8465-1846; www.zenyoganicaragua.com; Frente Parque Central; drop-in class US$10) Get in touch with your inner Zen at this friendly yoga retreat.

☞ Tours

San Juan Surf & Sport BOATING
(☑8984-2464; www.sanjuandelsursurf.com; Av Gaspar García Laviana, above Arena Caliente; booze cruises US$24) Though these guys also organize surfing lessons and deep-sea fishing excursions, they're particularly well-known for their boozy sunset cruises, where drinks flow freely during the two-hour spin around the bay.

Da Flying Frog
ADVENTURE

(☎ 8613-4460; www.daflyingfrog.com; off NIC-16; from US$30; ⏰ 8am-4pm Mon-Sat; 🚗) With 17 platforms and 2.5km of cables, it's one of the biggest ziplines in Nicaragua. Getting to and from the rural site, outside of town on the road to Playa Maderas (transportation provided, if you need it) is a great opportunity for monkey- and birdwatching, too. Rappelling and a Tarzan swing can be thrown in for good measure.

⭐ Festivals & Events

⭐ **Sunday Funday**
POOL CRAWL

(☎ 2568-2043; www.facebook.com/SundayFunday PoolCrawl; US$35; ⏰ from 2:30pm) Infamous on the Nica party scene, Sunday Funday is known to have involved more than 800 participants on one occasion. It's a highly organised pool/bar crawl with DJ sets, involving Hostel Pachamama, Naked Tiger and other hostels and bars (though the lineup can change). Minibuses shuttle revelers between venues as part of San Juan's most epic party.

Semana Santa
RELIGIOUS

(⏰ Mar or Apr) Holy Week (the week before Easter) is one of the busiest times of the year in San Juan del Sur and the surrounding area. In addition to a full range of religious pageants and processions, the beaches explode with parties and celebrations.

🛏 Sleeping

Choose between boutique hotels, sedate guesthouses, surf camps and party hostels. Prices rise dramatically during the high season (December to March) and double for Semana Santa and Christmas.

Casa de Olas
HOSTEL $

(☎ 8326-7818; www.casa-de-olas.com; Lot 6, Las Escaleras; dm/d US$16/45; ❄🛜🏊) Run by a friendly Aussie couple, this is a party hostel – unashamedly so, but very well-run and with epic hilltop views. There's a large pool, a bar, two rescued spider monkeys out back (don't give them beer!), simple dorms with thatched roofs, and communal meals. It's 3km east of San Juan del Sur, with several daily shuttles into town.

Hostel PachaMama
HOSTEL $

(☎ 2568-2043; www.facebook.com/hostelpachamama; Easy Rent a Car, 1c E; dm US$13, r with/without bathroom US$36/26; ❄🛜🏊) This party circuit stalwart is a very sociable place, with

TAKE A HIKE

A popular daytime expedition from San Juan Del Sur starts at the north of town, heading for the spectacular lookout at the Cristo de la Misericordia statue. There are also worthwhile hikes up the Antennas Trail to a nearby petroglyph. Ask the driver of any Rivas-bound bus to let you off at 'Bocas de las Montañas.' Follow the dirt road past the Chez Nous guesthouse, through jungle and pasture up to the radio antennas, from where you have stunning views of the countryside and sea. This is a serious, two-hour hike – take plenty of water, a sun hat and snacks.

staff organizing nightly activities – from pub crawls to beer pong. There's a bar by the little pool out back, a rack for your surfboard, and a relaxed vibe. Don't expect much sleep on Sundays, since PachaMama is an active participant in Sunday Funday.

Buena Onda Backpackers Hostel
HOSTEL $$

(☎ 8743-2769; www.sanjuandelsurbackpackers. com; Casa de Dragon, 50m a mano izquierda, Barrio Frente Sur; d with/without view US$27/22; ❄🛜) A few minutes' climb from the center of San Juan del Sur, in the hilltop neighborhood known as Barrio Frente Sur, this quiet hostel with a mellow atmosphere has beautiful views – especially from the rooftop terrace (and the vantage point of a hammock). The two deluxe rooms have ocean views, too; there's a communal kitchen and owner Baba is super-helpful.

El Coco Azul
HOTEL $$

(☎ 2568-2697; www.elcocoazul.com; Av del Parque (Calle Iglesia); d with/without bathroom US$60/50; 🛜) This petite, boutique-style hotel, cheerfully painted in blue and white, is youthful and affordable. The place has plenty to offer: a location just a stone's throw from the beach, inviting common areas and clean, airy guest rooms, each with a private balcony.

Casa Oro Hostel
HOSTEL $$

(☎ 2568-2415; www.casaeloro.com; Av Vanderbuilt, Parque Central, 1c O, 50m N; dm/d from US$10/48; ❄@🛜) This rambling backpacker favorite has all the amenities – a great information center, free breakfast, communal kitchen, lounge space, rooftop bar with ocean views – and good vibes 24/7. Dorm beds and rooms are only available by walk-in: first-come,

San Juan del Sur

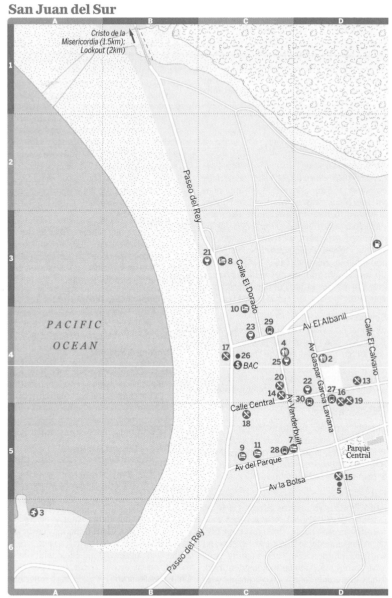

first-served. Casa Oro also runs the most popular and reliable beach shuttles; check the website for the latest schedules.

★ **La Posada Azul**   HISTORIC HOTEL **$$$**
(☎ 2568-2524; www.laposadaazul.com; Av del Parque/Calle Iglesia; d from US$100; ❋ 🖥 🏊)

This classy converted Victorian boutique is located just a half-block from the beach. Rooms have a blue color scheme, vaulted ceilings, tasteful decorations and whimsical artwork, while the gardens and pool area provide a lush retreat, complete with a *palapa* (open-sided thatched shelter) and

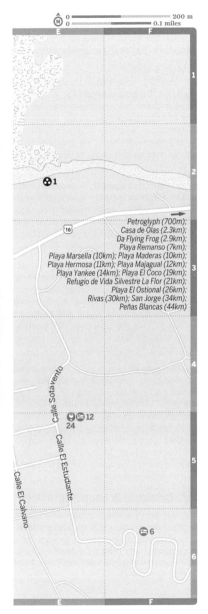

learn to surf, but didn't want to share the waves with dudes, Chica Brava may be the answer. This women-only surfing retreat is right in the heart of San Juan del Sur, with breezy rooms, beach access across the street and 4WDs whisking you off to the best surf spots.

Pelican Eyes Resort RESORT **$$$**
(☑ 2563-7000; www.pelicaneyesresort.com; De la Parroquia 1½ c E; r from US$257, villa for 4 US$586; ✳ ⬆ ☒) With sweeping bay views and fairly fabulous villas featuring hacienda-style furnishings, kitchens, terraces and satellite TV, this resort is the best in town. It has three pools, bookstores, a spa and two

honor bar. The breakfast, served on a pretty porch, is legendary in San Juan del Sur.

Chica Brava Surf House LODGE **$$$**
(☑ in US 713-893-5261; www.chicabrava.com; El Timón, 2c N; 7-day surfing package per person from US$1290; ✳ ⬆) If you've always wanted to

restaurants; the beach is a short stroll away. Even if you're not staying here, you'll want to come up to Pelican Eyes for sunset drinks at La Cascada.

✖ Eating

Dining out in San Juan del Sur is a pleasure: you'll find everything from taco shops and traditional Nicaraguan places to higher-end seafood restaurants, sushi, Indian food and pubs.

Asados Juanita NICARAGUAN **$**
(Av Central; mains US$3-5; ⊙6-10pm Mon-Sat) Follow the plumes of smoke to this hugely popular outdoor *fritanga* (grill) where you'll choose between pork or chicken, sweet or savory plantains, and *gallo pinto* (blended rice and beans). Eat in, or take away – it's delicious and inexpensive.

Super Frutto ICE CREAM **$**
(Hotel Estrella, ½c E; ice cream US$2-3; ⊙10am-9pm) Arguably the best frozen treat in San Juan del Sur, Super Frutto does terrific Italian-style ice cream, all made in-house.

★Barrio Café INTERNATIONAL **$$**
(☑2568-2294; www.barriocafesanjuan.com; cnr Av Vanderbuilt & Calle Central; dishes US$5-9; ⊙6:30am-10pm) Excellent coffee, gourmet breakfasts, killer *ceviche*, imaginative fusion dishes, an all-Nica staff, and potent, fruity rum cocktails – what's not to like? This breezy cafe is on a centrally located corner just a block from the beach. There's a nice little boutique hotel attached (r US$40).

Buddha's Garden VEGETARIAN **$$**
(www.facebook.com/buddhasgardenSJDS; cnr Av Mercado & Av La Bolsa; mains US$7-10; ⊙7:30am-9pm; ☎🍴) 🌿 Kitty-corner to Parque Central, this vegetarian and vegan restaurant serves excellent curries, salads and an assortment of fresh fruit and vegetable juices in a whitewashed, minimalist setting. Most ingredients are locally sourced and organic.

Surfing Buddha SUSHI **$$**
(☑7632-0099; www.facebook.com/thesurfingbuddhaSUSHI/; C Central; mains US$7-12; ⊙7am-10pm Mon-Sat) Decorated with cherry blossom murals and Christmas baubles, this diminutive restaurant is owned by a friendly Canadian from Toronto who turns out imaginative sushi roll combos and excellent breakfasts.

Taco Stop TEX-MEX **$$**
(www.tacostopnicaragua.com; Av Vanderbuilt; mains US$3-7; ⊙8:30am-5:30am) This centrally located branch of Nicaragua's modern taco chain offers tacos, quesadillas, burritos, salads and soups – you can eat in-house or take it to go. Note the hours: it's almost never closed.

King Curry FUSION **$$$**
(☑8375-7618; www.facebook.com/pages/King-Curry/176871972510703; cnr C Central & Av Mercado; mains US$8-10; ⊙5-11:30pm) Perch at one of several communal tables and go for an Indian or Thai-style curry at this thimble-sized, candle-lit place. We love both the ambience and the authentic flavors.

Restaurante El Timón SEAFOOD **$$$**
(☑2568-2243; www.eltimonsanjuandelsur.com; Beachfront, Av del Mar; dishes US$8-25; ⊙8am-late; ☎) This classic beachfront restaurant, the best of the offerings along this stretch of sand, is the place to go to for an upmarket seafood dinner or sunset cocktails. There's folkloric music on Thursday evenings, and good happy-hour specials on food and drink many nights of the week.

🍷 Drinking & Nightlife

Most of the beachfront restaurants double as bars and lounges. There's also an excellent craft-beer brewery and cocktail bars. Nicaragua's party central holds an infamous pool-party crawl on Sundays, often involving hundreds of revellers.

★Parlour COCKTAIL BAR
(☑8255-2501; www.facebook.com/parloursanjuandelsur; Av Vanderbuilt; ⊙noon-late) A great addition to 'gringo street', this small tiki-style bar serves really good cocktails – the passionfruit mojitos and the watermelon margaritas, in particular. As the evening progresses, the tequila and coco rum shots flow freely, but the music is always chilled beats.

FESTIVAL DE CERVEZA ARTESANAL

Gaining in popularity over the last couple of years, Nicaragua's first craft beer festival (www.facebook.com/Beerfest SJDS) attracts brews from Moropotente (Carazo), La Porteña (San Juan del Sur), Erdmanns (Ticuantepe), Campo (Tola), Pinolera (Managua) and San Juan del Sur Cervecería – the festival's organizers. Expect plenty of beer, live music and more. Location changes from year to year; check locally.

Arribas
CLUB

(☑8882-1616; www.facebook.com/arribasbar; Paseo del Rey; ☺11am-4am) A sedate place for a beer during the day, this place heaves to DJ sets by night. Arribas is an active participator in Sunday Funday and attracts a fun and rowdy crowd of backpackers and young locals.

Bar Republika
BAR

(☑8292-8421; www.facebook.com/RepublikaSJDS; Calle Central; ☺8:30am-midnight) When you're tired of Toña and rum, this cool French-style bar should be your first stop: it does martinis, White Russians, and gin and tonics – to name just a few – and offers food specials from tacos and burgers to salads and pitas with hummus. Laptop-toting gringos haunt it during the day.

La Cascada
BAR

(www.pelicaneyesresort.com; De la Parroquia, 1½c E, Pelican Eyes Resort; ☺noon-10pm) The hilltop bar and restaurant at Pelican Eyes (p127) is a lovely spot for canoodling with your sweetie over sunset cocktails by candlelight – happyhour specials often include access to the small but scenic swimming pool. There's live music and entertainment on Wednesday nights and at other times, too.

ⓘ Information

DANGERS & ANNOYANCES
➡ Don't walk alone on the beach at night.
➡ When heading home from the bars, walk in a large group or jump in a cab.

MONEY
BAC (Hotel Casa Blanca, Av del Mar) One of several banks and ATMs in town.

POLITICAL UNREST
At the time of writing, San Juan del Sur had avoided the violent protests that have afflicted Managua, Masaya, Granada and León, but the drop in tourism numbers meant that a number of businesses had closed.

ⓘ Getting There & Away

Public buses are the best option for those on a budget. For speed and convenience, it's hard to beat the shuttles run by various operators to nearby beaches and other popular destinations in Nicaragua. Note that there is no public transport to beaches north of San Juan del Sur.

BUS
There is regular **bus service** (Av Central, Mercado Central) from the bus stop in front of the market to destinations including the following:

Managua (US$2, two hours, daily at 5am, 5:40am, 7am and 3:30pm)

Rivas (US$1, 45 minutes, 6am to 6pm, roughly every 30 to 60 minutes) Ask to be dropped at the bus stop in front of the Puma gas station to catch a Managua-bound bus (look for *expreso* to catch a faster bus).

Peñas Blancas/ Costa Rica To get to the Costa Rican border, take any Rivas- or Managua-bound bus, get off at the Empalme La Vírgen turnoff on the Panamericana and flag down south-bound buses. You can purchase international **Tica Bus** (☑2568-2427; www.ticabus.com; Calle Central s/n; ☺8am-7pm) tickets at their San Juan office.

Southern beaches (US$1.50, 20 minutes to one hour, three daily) Service to Playa El Coco, Refugio de Vida Silvestre La Flor and Playa El Ostional. Departure times change occasionally; call into a hostel in San Juan del Sur to see or ask about the latest posted times.

Shuttle Bus
Several outfitters in San Juan del Sur offer shuttle service to the beaches north and south of town, as well as to destinations across the country. **Casa Oro** (☑2568-2415; www.casaeloro.com; cnr Av Ral & Calle Vandervilt) has the lion's share of the shuttle business, with shuttles to Playa Maderas (round-trip US$5, five daily), Playa Hermosa (9am & 11am, US$10 roundtrip) and Playa Remanso (round-trip US$5, 10:30am & 11am); there's also a 9:30am shuttle to León (US$25) via Rivas (US$8), San Jorge (US$15), Granada (US$15) and Managua Airport (US$25) and a 3pm shuttle to Managua Airport via Granada. In addition, there's a daily shuttle to Playa Popoyo from in front of the Remax office at 10:30am (US$15). **Adelante Express** (☑2568-2083; www.adelanteexpress.com) and **Iskra Travel** (☑2568-2054; www.iskratravel.com; UNO Station, 2½c O; shuttle to San Jorge or Granada US$30, shuttle to Managua US$40; ☺9am-6pm) run shuttles to Managua Airport, Granada and San Jorge. Private shuttles to other Nicaraguan destinations can be negotiated, as long as you have enough people.

CAR
Alamo (☑2277-1117; www.alamonicaragua.com; Av del Mar) rents sedans and 4WD vehicles. You'll probably want the latter, especially if you're heading to the beaches south of town. **UNO station** (NIC-16) is the only place to get gas.

TAXI
Taxis congregate close to the market. In theory, each driver has a list of set rates for destinations outside of town, but you'll hear a small range of prices. Get together with other travelers for the best deal. Casa Oro organizes four-person taxis to Playa Gigante (US$50), Laguna Apoyo

(US$70), Playa Popoyo (US$60), the Costa Rican border (US$25) and more.

ℹ Getting Around

Numerous outlets around town rent dirt bikes (US$25 per day), quad bikes (US$65 per day) and other rugged wheeled transport that's ideal for the bumpy roads to the beaches. **Big Wave Dave's** (☑ 2568-2151; www.facebook.com/Big-WaveDavesSJDS; UNO Station, 2½c O; ⊘ 8am-late Tue-Sun) has the best motorbikes.

Beaches North of San Juan del Sur

The gorgeous beaches north of San Juan del Sur each have their own unique character. Playa Maderas is a surfers' beach, Playa Marsella is a place to chill out and watch the sunset, Playa Magajual is good for swimming and Playa Ocotal is a private sheltered cove. All can be easily visited on a day trip from San Juan del Sur.

Playa Marsella

This beautiful beach lies some 10km north of San Juan del Sur. The water is calm and makes for a good swimming spot, though don't do it near the river estuary, where a sign warns about crocodiles. Separated by a headland from the surfers' haunt of Playa Maderas, this beach is perfect for sunbathers and sunset-watchers.

🛏 Sleeping

Li'l Aussie Hut HOSTEL $$
(☑ 8385-6644; www.aussiehut.com; Playa Marsella; dm/d US$25/50, campsites US$15, hammock US$20; 🛜) By day, hang out with Paul, Charlie and their kids, go fishing with the locals or sip a beer while putting some freshly caught fish on the barbecue. By night, be lulled to sleep by the sound of the waves from your spacious, bamboo-walled room. Nothing fancy; just great atmosphere. Take the southern access road to the beach.

You can also camp (tents available for rent) or sleep in a hammock.

Hotel Villa Mar HOTEL $$
(☑ 8663-0666; www.hostalvillamar.com; Playa Marsella; s/d/q from US$43/49/102; ❄🛜) Across the road from the estuary, but close enough to the beach to be rocked to sleep by the sound of crashing waves (ask for a room out front). Rooms are plain but comfortable, with tile floors and colorful bedspreads.

There's a good on-site restaurant and a breezy common area strung with hammocks.

🍴 Eating

Rancho Marsella NICARAGUAN $
(☑ 8687-8764; Playa Marsella; dishes US$3-6; ⊘ 9am-8pm) Rancho Marsella serves simple meals and cool drinks on the beachfront, next to the estuary. Try the *sopa de mariscos* (seafood stew).

ℹ Getting There & Away

There are two access road to Playa Marsella; the signposted southern turnoff is around 6km north of San Juan del Sur, while the northern access road is 8km north, with the signposted left fork leading to Playa Marsella. Some outfitters offer a direct shuttle (US$5), while others, like the Casa Oro (p125) shuttle to Playa Maderas (US$5, four daily) will drop you off at the fork in the road, from where it's a 2km walk to the beach.

Playa Maderas

A good-time-vibe backpacker and surfer hangout, this stunning beach – with a shark's fin rock at the northern end and wonderful, wide sandy stretches for sunbathing – is famed for having one of the best beach breaks in the country.

🏊 Activities

The consistent surf break here, sometimes called **Los Playones**, is a medium-speed wave in fairly deep (2m) water with a sandy bottom, good for beginners, with two right and two left breaks that get hollow on a rising tide.

If the swell is really big on a low-to-medium tide, there's a faster, intermediate-level reef break between Madera and Majagual called **Panga Drops** – accessible by boat only – that offers an awesome ride before dumping you onto the rocky shallows. It gets choppy and you can be caught in the shore break, so watch the wind. Waves get big, as do the crowds.

Rebelde Surf School SURFING
(Playa Maderas, 100m del Este; lessons US$30, surfboard rental per hr US$10) Around 100m from the Playa Maderas parking lot, this surf shack rents surfboards and offers instruction.

🛏 Sleeping & Eating

Hostel Clandestino HOSTEL $
(☑ 8258-0687; www.hostel-clandestino.com; Playa Maderas; dm/s/d US$15/25/40; 🛜) 🌿 A steep 10-minute walk up from Playa Maderas,

the airy, thatch-roofed cabins and hammock-strung bar area of this delightful hostel catch the Pacific breeze. The Chilean-German owners put a lot of love into the hostel, from using sustainable materials in its construction to the easygoing vibe that prevails. Take the steep right by Big Drop Surf House.

The Big Drop Surf House
GUESTHOUSE $$

(☑8833-2799; www.facebook.com/Thebigdropsurfhouse; Playa Maderas, 300m del Este; r $40; ⊖❄🍵) An excellent addition to the surfers' lodging scene, this bright and breezy Aussie-run guesthouse offers a handful of spotless, spacious rooms with river-rock showers, smatterings of colorful art and shady terraces in front of every room with deck chairs to sink into. The kitchen is a boon for self-caterers and the on-site cafe serves filling breakfasts (US$3 to US$5).

Tacos Locos
INTERNATIONAL $$

(Playa Maderas; dishes US$7-14) A breezy, shady taco restaurant overlooking the beach, serving passable tacos and a smattering of decent fish dishes.

★Buena Vista Surf Club
LODGE $$$

(☑8863-4180; www.buenavistasurfclub.com; Playa Maderas; s/d US$115/140; 🍵) 🍴 Take a right where the road dips after Parque Maderas to get to this lovely getaway with spectacular views over the bay. Six treehouse-style cabañas, all tucked into the forest, are outfitted with beautiful natural wood, huge mirrors and comfortable beds. Traditional Nicaraguan food is served family-style; yoga and surf lessons are also on the menu.

Arte-Sano Hotel Cafe
BOUTIQUE HOTEL $$$

(☑8872-9672; www.artesano-hotelcafe.com; Playa Maderas; r US$90, adults only; ❄🍵🍴) Arte-Sano's infinity pool overlooks Playa Marsella from its lofty hilltop location. Bold contemporary artworks, painted cattle skulls and exquisite pottery from San Juan de Oriente decorate the vast lounge and cafe-bar area where a succinct mix of international dishes is served. Take the left turnoff steeply uphill just before reaching Playa Maderas.

❶ Getting There & Away

Many surf shops and hostels in San Juan del Sur – including Casa Oro (p125), which goes four times daily – offer shuttles here (US$5). Coming by car, Playa Maderas is 11km north of San Juan del Sur via a decent (though sometimes narrow) dirt road.

Playa Majagual

With its white-sand beach framed by two jutting cliffs, this beautiful bay is good for swimming – watch the rip current, though. There's no surfing off this beach, though Playa Los Playones, a two-minute walk to the south, has a strong shore break.

🛏 Sleeping & Eating

Hostal Matilda's
HOSTEL $

(☑8456-3461; www.hostalmatilda.com; Playa Los Playones; dm/s/d from US$7/15/30) A psychedelic maze of sultry mermaids, shoals of tropical fish, Poseidons brandishing their tridents and giant frogs carrying mushroom umbrellas, this basic, family-run guesthouse consists of somewhat musty but serviceable rooms with high beds and bug netting – all just metres away from the surf.

Bar El Ranchito
INTERNATIONAL $$

(Playa Majagual; mains from US$7; ⊙noon-9pm) Enjoy your grilled fish with garlic sauce, ceviche, sopa de mariscos (seafood soup) and grilled chicken at this basic beachfront joint that overlooks the southern end of Playa Majagual.

❶ Getting There & Away

Majagual is 12km north of San Juan del Sur via an unpaved road that's good enough for regular cars (though getting here on an ATV or dirt bike is more fun). Several shuttle companies in San Juan offer drop-off services to Majagual (US$5); it's also possible to take one of the more frequent shuttles to nearby Playa Maderas and walk to Majagual (10 minutes).

Playa Ocotal

The only way to visit this shady cove beach is by booking a cabin at what may be the very best hotel in all of Nicaragua, the fantastic ecolodge Morgan's Rock.

Beyond Ocotal, on the north side, is the beach called **Arena Blanca**, with some of the clearest water and whitest sand on the Pacific coast. This little inlet is accessible only by rented boat or along a very rough dirt road that runs across very private property – ask permission to cross, or ask around in San Juan del Sur to see about renting a boat.

🛏 Sleeping

★Morgan's Rock
LODGE $$$

(☑2254-7989; www.morgansrock.com; Playa Ocotal; r from US$379; 🍵🍴) 🍴 With its own idyllic tropical beach and 4000 acres of jungle, this fabulous ecolodge offers a superlative experience. Swim in the infinity pool and cross a suspension bridge to reach your dream treehouse cabin – gleaming with precious woods and dappled with the forest light – which filters through the parrot- and monkey-filled jungle canopy right into your screened-in porch.

Activities on offer include tours of the on-site sugar mill where Morgan's Rum is brewed, plus kayaking in the estuary, and meals include vegetables and herbs grown on the property.

ⓘ Getting There & Away

Nearly all travelers here arrange transportation with Morgan's Rock or drive here themselves; it's 13km north of San Juan del Sur on a mostly unpaved but good road. Follow the signs to Majagual and turn right after passing a black-and-yellow gate; continue until you get to the beach.

Beaches South of San Juan del Sur

Heading south from San Juan del Sur toward the border of Costa Rica, a string of low-key beach villages offer surf breaks and sea-turtle-watching opportunities. There's an interesting wildlife refuge, but you'll also see plenty of monkeys in the trees if you just keep your eyes open while traveling along the hilly forested road. Playa Hermosa is one of the better beaches for surfing, along with Playa Yankee and Playa Remanso.

PLAYA TAMARINDO

Playa Tamarindo is located about a half-hour walk down the beach from Playa Remanso. It's generally less crowded; surfers come with the rising tide to try for a long wave with right and left breaks, which can get hollow coming off the rock wall when swells are under 1m.

You'll want to bring your own snacks from town. Buses roll past the Tamarindo turnoff on their way from San Juan del Sur to Playa El Ostional (US$1, 25 minutes, three daily). But the beach is a 3km hike from the bus stop and robberies have taken place along the access road in the past; if driving, come with friends and leave well before sunset.

Playa Remanso

The most accessible in a cluster of pretty beaches, this crescent of white sand has decent surfing, interesting caves and good opportunities for swimming and lounging around in tide pools. The smallish, slow beach break is good for beginners and intermediates, so expect a crowded lineup. When there's a big swell, it's a playground for advanced surfers.

🛏 Sleeping

Bella Vista Surf House GUESTHOUSE $$
(☑5724-6801; Playa Remanso; r US$50; ❈ 🤶)
Just a couple of minutes from the beach, this surfers' retreat is presided over by friendly owner José. The four tiled rooms are spotless and comfortable and there's a guest kitchen. At sunset, you can watch the fire in the sky from the sun loungers on the terrace.

ⓘ Getting There & Away

Buses stop by the Remanso turnoff on their way from San Juan del Sur to Playa El Ostional (US$1, 20 minutes, three daily). Outfitters in San Juan del Sur also offer shuttle service (US$5). At the time of writing, Casa Oro (p125) was going daily at 10:30am and 11am and returning at 4pm and 6pm. If driving, go as part of a group, as robberies have taken place along the access road in the past.

Playa Hermosa

This long, wide, strikingly beautiful beach was the setting for two seasons of the US television series *Survivor*. Playa Hermosa is famous for great surfing – there are five breaks on this beach alone – and a cool, lost-in-paradise vibe. The left and right beach breaks are fun for intermediate and advanced surfers alike; sometimes the conditions are right for beginners, too. It's a privately owned beach; pay an entrance fee of US$3 at Playa Hermosa Ecolodge.

🛏 Sleeping

Playa Hermosa Ecolodge LODGE $$$
(☑8671-3327; www.playahermosabeachhotel.com; Playa Hermosa; dm US$25, d US$90-100; 🤶) Considered by many to be one of the best beach hostels on Nicaragua's south Pacific coast. The open-air, six-bed dorm rooms in this rustic paradise catch the breeze to stay cool at night. Private rooms upstairs have giant mosquito nets. There's a great vibe and surf scene

here, with a chilled-out, open-air restaurant. Transfers from San Juan del Sur are included.

ⓘ Getting There & Away

Playa Hermosa Ecolodge includes transfers to and from San Juan del Sur in the room prices and day-use passes (US$10.)

Otherwise, buses stop in Playa Hermosa on their way from San Juan del Sur to Playa El Ostional (US$1.25, 35 minutes, four daily); the beach is a 3km walk from the turnoff. Casa Oro (p125) offers daily shuttles (US$10, at 9:30am and 11am, returning at 4pm and 6pm).

There are several shallow stream crossings along the access road; fine for city cars during dry season and for quad bikes and high clearance vehicles the rest of the time.

Playa Yankee

Some 15km south of San Juan del Sur, Playa Yankee is renowned in surfer circles for its powerful point break, which is best at mid- to high-tide.

🛏 Sleeping

Orquidea del Sur   VILLA **$$$**
(☑ 8984-2150;   www.hotelorquideadelsur.com; Calle Playa Yankee; apt US$525; ❄🛜🏊) Consisting of several luxurious oceanview apartments with shared access to an infinity jacuzzi and large swimming pool, plus beach access, this villa is an excellent retreat for families or groups of friends. Ample Nicaraguan breakfasts and other meals are prepared on request.

ⓘ Getting There & Away

Buses from San Juan del Sur to El Ostional can drop you at the turnoff for the beach; it's another 2km to the beach along a decent unpaved road.

Playa El Coco

POP UNDER 500

This is a world-class beach – a spectacular stretch of sparkling sand punctuated by cliffs so pretty that they grace about half of the country's tourist literature. Playa El Coco makes a great day trip from San Juan, or a handy base for visiting the nearby Refugio de Vida Silvestre La Flor.

🛏 Sleeping

There are half a dozen places to stay on or around Playa El Coco. The beach is the closest place to sleep near Refugio de Vida Silvestre La Flor.

ⓘ PACK A PICNIC

Unless you're staying at the villa on Playa Yankee, bring all food and drink with you. San Juan del Sur is your best bet for dining.

⭐ **Tortugas Hostel**   HOSTEL **$$**
(☑ 7894-7139; Playa El Coco; dm/d US$20/100; 🛜🏊) Who needs a fancy seaside villa when you can get exceptional views of the Pacific from the infinity pool at this hilltop hostel? The location is second to none, the thatched-roofed dorms catch the breeze and the on-site restaurant serves great pasta (the owner's Italian), plus Nica breakfasts. The double is very spacious, but overpriced – but that's our only complaint.

Parque Maritimo El Coco   CABIN **$$**
(☑ 8999-8069; www.playaelcoco.com.ni; Beachfront, Playa El Coco; d from US$30, bungalows from US$120, houses for up to 8 people US$180; 🅿❄@🛜) Location, location, location: gorgeous Playa El Coco is the reason to stay in this forested beachfront complex. Accommodations range from spartan doubles with shared baths (best avoided, according to traveler reports) to private bungalows with superb views. The on-site restaurant, Puesta del Sol, is your only choice on the beach.

La Veranera   GUESTHOUSE **$$$**
(☑ 8328-6260; www.laveranera.net; Playa el Coco; d with/without bathroom US$120/90; ❄🛜🏊) This sweet beachfront B&B has just four fan-cooled guest rooms, all with access to a pretty swimming pool. There's a simple on-site bar and restaurant. Though relatively pricey, the one quad room that sleeps four (with shared bathroom) is a good budget pick. Air-con costs US$10 extra per night.

🍴 Eating

Puesta del Sol   SEAFOOD **$$$**
(☑ 8999-8069;   www.playaelcoco.com.ni/restaurante; Parque Maritimo El Coco, beachfront; mains US$9-18; ⏱7am-late; 🛜🍽) A beachfront restaurant serving breakfast as well as lunchtime specials like *ceviche,* grilled seafood and Austrian dishes such as *Wienerschnitzel.* There's also a children's menu. The cuisine and service can be hit or miss, but the sunset views are sublime. There's also a small pool for the use of restaurant guests.

SOUTHWESTERN NICARAGUA BEACHES SOUTH OF SAN JUAN DEL SUR

WILDLIFE WATCHING

Turtles lay their eggs in Refugio de Vida Silvestre La Flor, usually between 9pm and 2am, from July to January, peaking in September and October. Leatherbacks usually arrive solo, but olive ridleys generally come in flotillas or *arribadas*, when more than 3000 of them pack the beaches at a time. Some people time these arrivals by moon cycles, but no one really knows for sure until the ladies arrive; call the ranger station if you want to be sure.

Rangers can do guided walks on request along the short nature trails, pointing out the local flora and fauna (US$10).

ℹ Getting There & Away

Buses stop in Playa El Coco on their way between San Juan del Sur and Playa El Ostional (US$1.30, 40 minutes), departing San Juan at 7am, 11am, 1pm and 5pm. Some outfitters in San Juan del Sur also offer shuttle service (US$10), usually with a minimum of five passengers required.

Refugio de Vida Silvestre La Flor

One of the principal laying grounds for endangered olive ridley and leatherback turtles, this wildlife refuge (☑ranger station 8419-1014; US$8, campsites per tent US$15) 🏊, locally known as 'La Flor', is 20km south of San Juan del Sur. It's easy to visit on a guided tour from San Juan del Sur or from Playa Hermosa Ecolodge in Playa Hermosa.

When there aren't any turtles around, the park still has an attractive, undeveloped beach, a couple of monkeys on-site and a few short trails; there's a decent beach break (right and left) at the northern end. (But during turtle season there's no surfing as the beach is off-limits.)

You can camp at the reserve (US$15 per tent). The closest hotels are in Playa El Coco. There aren't many services here; bring your food and water from town.

Playa El Ostional

POP UNDER 1000

This fishing village, practically a stone's throw from the Costa Rican border, has an attractive brown-sugar beach that's often totally empty. These calm waters can be full of seaweed, but are otherwise good for swimming. It's a scenic, peaceful spot for watching pelicans dive-bombing into the sea and fisherfolk pushing their colorful wooden boats out into the surf.

🏃 Activities

Manglar de Ostional   WALKING
(Playa El Ostional) 🚶 Branching off the road leading towards the beach, this short boardwalk showcases the mangrove environment. There are handy explanations at the start of the boardwalk, telling you which native birds to look out for, and several plants are labeled along the way, including the poisonous machineel tree.

🛏 Sleeping & Eating

Most travelers spend the night elsewhere and come here during the day, though there are a couple of basic lodging options on the beach. There are a couple of small beach bars between the bus stop and the beach but head for Playa El Coco or San Juan del Sur for better offerings.

Manta Raya Hospedaje   GUESTHOUSE $$
(☑8353-7091; www.facebook.com/mantaraya.hospedaje; north end of beach; r US$40; 🖥) Friendly host Salvador runs a breezy four-room guesthouse at the north end of Playa Ostional. The rooms here are quite basic – a bed, fan and lamp – but some come with ocean views (and a slight breeze).

ℹ Getting There & Away

Buses (Carretera Costanera) depart Ostional for San Juan del Sur three times daily at 5am, 7.30am and 4pm, returning from San Juan at 7am, 11am and 5pm (US$1.50, one hour); double-check departure times locally. The bus stop is located in the center of the village, about 600m inland from the beach.

León & Northwestern Nicaragua

Best Places to Eat

➡ Imbir (p150)

➡ La Bombora (p155)

➡ Al Cielo Hotel & Restaurante (p164)

➡ Pan y Paz (p149)

Best Places to Stay

➡ Mano a Mano Ecohostel (p154)

➡ Surfing Turtle Lodge (p153)

➡ Coco Loco Eco Resort (p164)

➡ Hotel El Convento (p148)

➡ Vivir Surf & Fish (p156)

Why Go?

This is Nicaragua at its fieriest and most passionate. The regional capital of León is – and will always be – a hotbed of intellectualism and independence. The city has nourished some of Nicaragua's most important political and artistic moments. Less polished but somehow more authentic than its age-old rival Granada, the city is beloved for its grand cathedral, breathtaking art museum, hopping nightlife and spirited revolutionary air.

Just out of León, more than a dozen volcanic peaks wait to be climbed (some can be surfed). Along the still-crowdless beaches there's the best beach accommodations – and gnarliest surfing – in the country. And the virgin wetlands of the Reserva Natural Isla Juan Venado are not to be missed.

Further afield, you'll find the biggest mangrove forest in Central America, awe-inspiring beauty at Reserva Natural Volcán Cosigüina and unique windows into everyday Nicaraguan life in the little towns along the way.

When to Go

➡ December is good for cooler-than-usual temperatures. This is the hottest part of the country; daytime temperatures are just above 30°C (86°F) almost year-round, spike in sweltering April and dip into the relatively cool mid-20s°C (mid-70s°F) in December.

➡ October and November are the peak months to see nesting turtles at the Reserva Natural Estero Padre Ramos; the whole season lasts between July and December. This is also a good time to think about volunteering as a beach warden or visiting Reserva Natural Isla Juan Venado.

➡ Semana Santa is held in late March to early April – Easter week is a Technicolor dreamscape in León. There are sawdust 'carpets' in colonial suburbs, and a sand-castle competition at a nearby beach.

León & North-western Nicaragua Highlights

1 León (p138)
Mixing with the university crowd and taking in some politically charged street art in this vibrant city.

2 Maribios Chain (p156) Climbing spectacular volcanic peaks then enjoying the thrill of sand-boarding down its slopes.

3 Playa Aserradores (p163) Catching one of Nicaragua's world-class waves, then chilling out in a surf camp.

4 Las Peñitas (p154) Lazing around at a beachfront hostel or boutique hotel in this white-sand paradise and learning to surf.

5 Reserva Natural Estero Padre Ramos (p165) Kayaking through Central America's largest mangrove forest.

6 Playa Jiquilillo (p164) Getting away from it all in a quiet fishing village.

7 Reserva Natural Isla Juan Venado (p155) Going for a peaceful swim and watching nesting turtles in action.

8 Chichigalpa (p162) Learning the secrets of rum production at the Flor de Caña distillery.

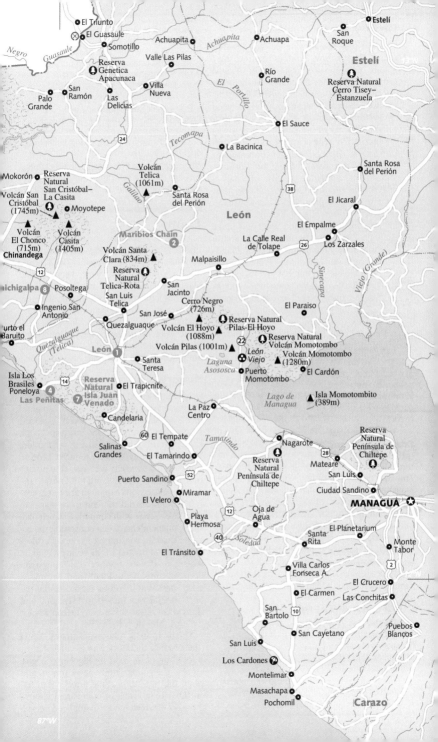

History

The Maribios people were the first inhabitants of what is now León, in the township/suburb of Subtiava. After a series of volcanic eruptions led to the evacuation of the original city of León (now called León Viejo), this site was chosen. It turned out to be a good choice for the Spanish colonisers – Subtiava provided plenty of indigenous labor, it was far enough from the ocean to prevent the pirate attacks that had plagued Granada, and the volcanoes were distant and dormant enough not to threaten the city.

León has produced various heroes, most famously poet Rubén Darío, but also independence fighter Miguel Larreynaga (look for him on the 10-córdoba note) and Luisa Amanda Espinoza, the first female Frente Sandinista de Liberación Nacional (Sandinista National Liberation Front; FSLN) member to die in combat. A Sandinista stronghold, the city saw some of the toughest battles during the revolution, documented in the city's murals, museums and bullet-pocked walls.

Despite León's status as a religious and academic center (and the fact that it had been the nation's capital for 242 years), it was Chinandega, to the north, that was chosen as the meeting place for the ill-fated Confederation of American States in the 19th century. Chinandega's claim to fame as the 'city of oranges' waned in the 20th century, as cotton became the principal crop. This in turn changed as world cotton prices plummeted and farmers turned to sugarcane and peanuts, the region's main crops to this day.

Corinto – these days Nicaragua's busiest commercial port – has entered the history books in a big way twice: firstly when it was the landing site for William Dampier and a band of French and British pirates in the only recorded pirate attack on León, and secondly when US president Ronald Reagan ordered the illegal mining of the bay, which set in motion a series of machinations that would eventually lead to the Iran-Contra affair.

ℹ Getting There & Away

Minivans making the short, sweet run from Managua to León leave regularly from the UCA bus lot (p62). Normal buses and minivans also leave from Mercado Israel Lewites (p61) – frequently for León, less so for Chinandega. The majority of León's lodgings can hook you up with tourist shuttles to Managua Airport, Granada and San Juan del Sur.

There are frequent buses from León to Granada, Las Peñitas and Poneloya, plus several buses daily to Puerto Sandino and to northeastern destinations, such as Estelí and Moyogalpa. Chinandega is another important transportation hub, with several buses daily to Corinto, Playa Asserradores, Playa Jiquilillo and the Cosigüina Peninsula.

You can rent cars in both León and Chinandega; hire a 4WD in the rainy season if you plan to do much exploring. The roads of the Cosigüina Peninsula are improving, but outside dry season you'll need a 4WD.

If you're heading to El Salvador, contact Ruta del Golfo (p152) in León for border crossings across the Gulf of Fonseca via boat and 4WD.

León

POP 169,362 / ELEV 110M

Intensely political, buzzing with energy and, at times, drop-dead gorgeous (in a crumbling, colonial kind of way), León is what Managua should be – a city of awe-inspiring churches, fabulous art collections, stunning streetscapes, cosmopolitan eateries, vibrant student life, fiery intellectualism, and all-week, walk-everywhere, happening nightlife. Many people fall in love with Granada, but most of them leave their heart in León.

History

Originally located on the slopes of Volcán Momotombo, León was the site of some of the Spanish conquest's cruelest excesses; even other conquistadors suggested that León's punishment was divine retribution. When the mighty volcano reduced León to rubble in 1610, the city was moved to its current location, saint by saint, to sit next to the existing indigenous capital of Subtiaba.

The reprisals did not end there. Eager to win the civil war with Granada – which had, since independence, been contesting the colonial capital's continuing leadership role – in 1853 León invited US mercenary William Walker to the fight. After the Tennessean declared himself president (and Nicaragua a US slave state), he was executed; the nation's capital was moved to Managua, and Granada's Conservatives ran the country for the next three decades.

Finally, in 1956, Anastasio Somoza García (the original dictator) was assassinated at a social event in León by Rigoberto López, a poet. The ruling family never forgot, and when the revolution came, their wrath fell on this city in a hail of bullets and bombs, the scars of which have still not been erased.

León has remained proudly Liberal – even a bit aloof – through it all, a Sandinista stronghold and political power player that has never once doubted its grand destiny.

⊙ Sights

⊙ Central León

★ **Museo Histórico de la Revolución**   MUSEUM
(Parque Central; US$2; ⊙ 8am-5pm) León is the heart and soul of liberal Nicaragua. Stop into this museum for an overview of the Nicaraguan revolutionaries who stood up against the Somoza dictatorship, tracing national history from the devastating earthquake of 1972 to the Sandinista overthrow. The true highlight here is being shown around by the former revolutionaries who can tell you all about their role in the conflict.

★ **Museo de Arte Fundación Ortiz-Gurdián**   MUSEUM
(www.fundacionortizgurdian.org; Parque Central, 2c O; US$3; ⊙ 9am-5:30pm Tue-Fri, 9:30am-5:30pm Sat, 9am-4pm Sun) Probably the finest museum of contemporary art in all of Central America, the Ortiz-Gurdián Collection has spilled over from its original home in Casa Don Norberto Ramírez, refurbished in 2000 to its original Creole Civil style, with Arabic tiles and impressive flagstones. The collection, spread across two buildings and surrounding greenery-filled courtyards, includes works by Picasso, Chagall, Miró and a number of noted Nicaraguan artists.

Begin surrounded by the luxurious realism of the Renaissance and spare beauty of the colonial period, then wander through romanticism, modernism, postmodernism and actually modern pieces by Cuban, Peruvian and other Latin American schools. Big names make an appearance, but it's the work by Latin American masters – Diego Rivera, Rufino Tamayo, Fernando Botero, Roberto Matta and more – that defines the collection.

★ **Iglesia de la Recolección**   CHURCH
(Catedral de León, 3c N; ⊙ hours vary) Three blocks north of the cathedral, the 1786 Iglesia de la Recolección is considered the city's most beautiful church, a Mexican-style baroque confection of swirling columns and bas-relief medallions that portray the life of Christ. Dyed a deep yellow, accented with cream and age, the lavishly decorated facade may be what makes the cover of all the tourist brochures, but be sure to stop inside and admire the slender mahogany columns and ceiling decorated with harvest motifs.

Catedral de León   CATHEDRAL
(Basílica de la Asunción; Parque Central; ⊙ 8am-noon & 2-4pm Mon-Sat) **FREE** Officially known as the Basílica de la Asunción, León's cathedral is the largest in Central America, its expansive design famously (and perhaps apocryphally) approved for construction in much more important Lima, Peru. Leonese leaders originally submitted a more modest but bogus set of plans, but architect Diego José de Porres Esquivel, the Capitán General of Guatemala (also responsible for San Juan Bautista de Subtiaba, La Recolección and La Merced churches, among others), pulled the switcheroo and built this beauty instead.

The cathedral is a sort of pantheon of Nicaraguan culture. The **tomb of Rubén Darío**, León's favorite son, is on one side of the altar, guarded by a sorrowful lion and the inscription 'Nicaragua is created of vigor

---

FOLLOWING THE FOOTSTEPS OF RUBÉN DARIO

León is known in Nicaragua as the home of the country's most famous poet, Rubén Darío. Learn about his legacy at the **Museo Rubén Darío** (☑ 8722-1019; cnr Calle Rubén Darío & 4a Av SO; US$2; ⊙ 8am-noon & 2-5pm Tue-Sat, 8am-noon Sun), located at the house where he lived for the first 14 years of his life: indeed, he started writing poetry right here at age 12. His first poem is on display here, as are various personal effects. Of all of Nicaragua's museums and monuments dedicated to the poet, this colonial house seems like the one where you'd be most likely to run into his ghost. Exhibits are displayed throughout the house, ranging from everyday items that provide a window into well-to-do Nicaraguan life in the late 1800s to handwritten manuscripts of Darío's famous works. His Bible, the bed where he died 'an agonizing death,' and the fancy duds he wore as the ambassador to Spain are just highlights among the historic bric-a-brac.

You'll also find a statue of Darío at the aptly named **Parque Rubén Darío** (cnr 2a Av SO & Calle Rubén Darío), and the poet's final resting place inside the Catedral de León.

León

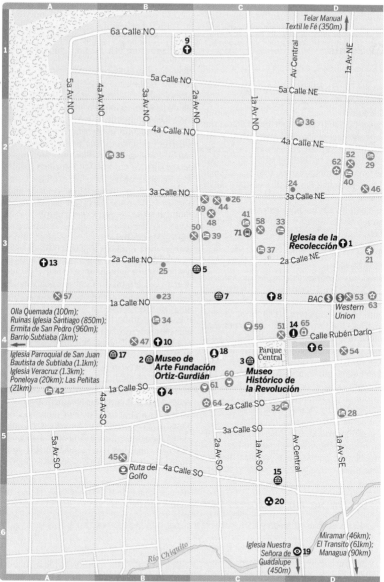

Telar Manual
Textil le Fé (350m)

6a Calle NO

5a Calle NO
5a Calle NE

4a Calle NO
4a Calle NE

3a Calle NO
3a Calle NE

Iglesia de la
Recolección

2a Calle NO
2a Calle NE

1a Calle NO

Olla Quemada (100m);
Ruinas Iglesia Santiago (850m);
Ermita de San Pedro (960m);
Barrio Subtiaba (1km);

Calle Rubén Darío

Iglesia Parroquial de San Juan
Bautista de Subtiaba (1.1km);
Iglesia Veracruz (1.3km);
Poneloya (20km); Las Peñitas
(21km);

Parque
Central

**Museo de
Arte Fundación
Ortiz-Gurdián**

**Museo
Histórico de
la Revolución**

1a Calle SO
2a Calle SO

3a Calle SO

4a Calle SO

Ruta del
Golfo

Miramar (46km);
El Transito (61km);
Managua (90km)

Iglesia Nuestra
Señora de
Guadalupe
(450m)

Río Chiquito

and glory, Nicaragua is made for freedom.'
Nearby rest the tombs of lesser-known Leonese poets Alfonso Cortés and Salomón de la
Selva, as well as Miguel Larreynaga.

Among the magnificent works of art within are the **Stations of the Cross** by Antonio
Sarria, considered masterpieces, and **El Cristo Negro de Pedrarias**, possibly the oldest
Catholic image in the Americas, brought
here in 1528. Marble statues inside are beautifully crafted, most notably the elaborate
Inmaculada Concepción de María.

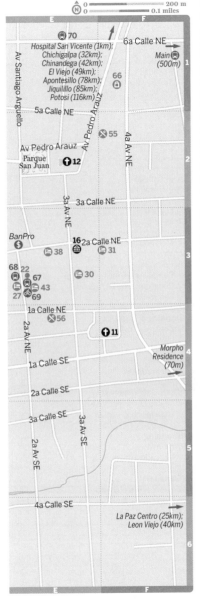

0   200 m
0   0.1 miles

70
Hospital San Vicente (1km);
Chichigalpa (32km);
Chinandega (42km);
El Viejo (49km);
Apontesillo (78km);
Jiquilillo (85km);
Potosí (116km)
6a Calle NE
Main (500m)
66
Av Santiago Argüello
5a Calle NE
Av Pedro Arauz
55
4a Av NE
Av Pedro Arauz
Parque San Juan
12
3a Av NE
3a Calle NE
BanPro
16 2a Calle NE
38   31
68 22
67
43
27 69
30
1a Calle NE
56
2a Av NE
11
Morpho Residence (70m)
1a Calle SE
2a Calle SE
3a Calle SE
3a Av SE
2a Av SE
4a Calle SE
La Paz Centro (25km);
Leon Viejo (40km)

cend through the tower in the cathedral's northwest corner.

Museo de Leyendas y Tradiciones MUSEUM
(2315-4678; 4a Calle SO, frente Ruinas San Sebastián; US$2; 8am-5pm) León's most entertaining and eclectic museum is housed in **La XXI** (the 21st Garrison), decorated with murals graphically depicting methods the Guardia Nacional used to torture prisoners. What makes this museum unmissable is the striking contrast of its main subjects: a quirky collection of life-sized papier-mâché figures from Leonese history and legend (such as Rubén Darío and a musician known as the Divino Leproso), handmade by founder señora Toruña.

If you get the curator to show you around, between each rundown of local legends, your Spanish-speaking guide will cheerfully shift gears to describe the gory human-rights abuses – stretching on racks, beatings, water tortures etc – that took place here regularly until June 13, 1979, when Commander Dora María Téllez successfully breached Somoza's defenses and secured La XXI for the Sandinistas, releasing all prisoners. Signage is in English and Spanish.

Iglesia de San Francisco CONVENT
(Parque Central, 2c O, ½c N; hours vary) The 1639 Iglesia de San Francisco is one of the oldest in the city, a national heritage site with lots of gold, a gorgeous nave, and a rococo interior. It was abandoned between 1830 and 1881, then refurbished with two elaborate altarpieces for San Antonio and Our Lady of Mercy. The convent was badly damaged during the 1979 Battle for León. You can check out what used to be the convent next door at Hotel El Convento (p148).

Iglesia de la Merced CHURCH
(Parque Central, 1c N; hours vary) Home to León's patron saint, la Virgen de la Merced, this is considered the city's second-most-important church. After Volcán Momotombo erupted and forced the city's evacuation, the Leonese built a new church in 1615, replaced with the current baroque building with neoclassical elements in the early 1700s.

Iglesia El Calvario CHURCH
(Parque Central, 4c E; hours vary) A hodgepodge of neoclassical and baroque styles, the richly hued El Calvario dates from the 18th century. It's notable, among other attributes, for the symmetry of its design, and for the

If it's clear, go up on the **roof** (US$3), with a spectacular view of the city and smoking volcanoes beyond. The office selling tickets for roof access is on the eastern side of the cathedral, facing the market, and you as-

León

rather graphic depictions of the crucifixion of Jesus and the two thieves inside.

Galería de Héroes y Mártires MUSEUM
(1a Calle NO, Iglesia de la Merced, ½c O; donation US$1; ☉10am-5pm) A homage to León's more recent history is found at the Galería de Héroes y Mártires, run by mothers of FSLN

veterans and fallen heroes, with murals, photos and biographies of the fallen.

Capilla San Juan de Dios CHURCH
(cnr 1a Calle SO & 3rd Av SO; ☉hours vary) A Victorian-style chapel around the corner from Rubén Darío's one-time home, with a modernist, neoclassical exterior and appealing interior.

Casa del Obrero
HISTORIC BUILDING

(cnr 2a Calle NO & 2a Av NO) An early 20th-century landmark, the Casa del Obrero (House of the Worker) honors Nicaraguan laborers. The building became a historical symbol on September 21, 1956, when the Leonese poet and journalist from León, Rigoberto López Pérez, shot President Somoza at a party inside this building and died immediately in a hail of bullets.

Iglesia San Juan Bautista
CHURCH

(frente Parque San Juan; ⊙ hours vary) This 17th-century neoclassical church was rebuilt more than once and boasts an impressive bell tower.

Ruinas San Sebastián
RUINS

(Parque Central, 3c S) Built on a spiritually significant site for indigenous people, this 1742 church was wrecked during the Somoza's bombardment of León in 1979. You can still see the intact bell tower and outer wall.

Iglesia de San Felipe
CHURCH

(estadio, 2c S; ⊙ hours vary) This 17th-century church occupies a whole block on the northern edge of downtown and was constructed to serve the spiritual needs of working-class worshippers.

Museo Entomológico
MUSEUM

(☑ 2311-6586; www.bio-nica.info; cnr 3a Av NE & 2a Calle NE; US$1; ⊙ 2-4pm Thu-Tue) For a truly comprehensive collection of butterflies, scorpions and other creepy crawlies from all over Central America, drop into this private collection. The specialty is *Lucanidae,* a genus of beetles whose males usually display ferocious-looking pincers. You may have to knock, since it opens according to the owner's whim.

Mausoleo de los Héroes y Mártires
MONUMENT

(frente catedral) A monument to the local heroes, the eternal flame of the Mausoleum of Heroes & Martyrs rests within a small plaza just north of the Parque Central, surrounded by the city's best murals.

Iglesia Zaragoza
CHURCH

(Parque Central, 4c O, 2c N; ⊙ hours vary) For something completely different, swing by the ultra-Gothic 1884 Iglesia Zaragoza. There's an interesting mix of architectural styles here – it looks like a fortress and a fairy-tale castle all at once.

Puente Guadalupe
BRIDGE

(Av Central) An 1850 bridge spanning Rio Chiquito.

⊙ Barrio Subtiaba

A regional capital long before León moved in, the barrio (district) of Subtiaba takes its name from a local tribe who still count themselves apart from León, and Nicaragua, as a whole. After refugees from León Viejo (p146) arrived in 1610, the two separate towns co-existed as equals until 1680. Flexing their rebuilt military muscle, the Spanish forced 12,000 indigenous inhabitants of Subtiaba to become part of León, basically relegating them to slave labor. Tensions simmered for two generations, until a police crackdown in 1725 inspired a revolt. Although the insurrection was violently shut down by the Spaniards, Barrio Subtiaba was able to remain a separate entity until 1902, when it was finally, officially, annexed to the city.

It's a solid 20-minute walk or US$1 taxi ride to Subtiaba from the León cathedral, or else you can take one of the covered trucks (US$0.20) plying the streets. Catch a Subtiaba-bound truck at the southwest corner of the Parque Central (in front of Sandinista headquarters) and yell 'Catedral Subtiaba' as they haul you inside, which might be while the truck is still moving. Hang on!

Iglesia de San Juan Bautista de Sutiaba
CHURCH

(Catedral Subtiaba; cnr 1ra Calle SO & 13va Av SO; ⊙ hours vary) The Subtiaba neighborhood is centered on this church, located about 1km west of the León cathedral. It's better known as 'Catedral Subtiaba,' and is the oldest intact church in the city. Built in the 1530s and reconstructed in 1710, its relatively plain beige facade and precious wood interior are largely unadorned; even the struts are there to stabilize the structure during earthquakes.

There are two exceptions: spirals outside, and an extraordinary sun icon mounted to the typical arched timber roof, pay homage to deities far older than the Spanish conquest.

Museo de Arte Sacre
MUSEUM

(☑ 2311-8288; frente Iglesia de San Juan Bautista de Subtiaba; US$1; ⊙ 8am-noon & 2-5pm Mon-Fri, 8am-noon Sat) Call ahead to make sure this intriguing museum is open. You've probably noticed this neighborhood's churches are in some disrepair, a situation that inspired locals to preserve the region's absolutely beautiful 16th- and 17th-century religious art right here, where it would be safe.

Las Ruinas de Veracruz RUINS

(Iglesia Santiago, 3c O) A few blocks west of the Iglesia Santiago are the ruins of this 16th-century church destroyed by a volcanic eruption in 1835. It remains a spiritual center, and as the indigenous counterpoint to La Gritería, on December 7 people gather here for a pre-Columbian festival involving torches and the sun deity on the roof of San Juan Bautista (p143).

Ermita de San Pedro CHURCH

(Iglesia San Juan Bautista, 2c E, 1c S; ⊙ hours vary) This church, two blocks east and one block south of San Juan Bautista, was constructed between 1706 and 1718. It's considered one of the best examples of primitive baroque style in Nicaragua, meaning that it's almost unadorned – save for three brick crosses inlaid into the adobe.

El Fortín de Acososco FORT

(⊙ 8am-6pm) FREE The Guardia Nacional's last holdout in León can be reached by the 2.5km dirt road from the western side of Guadalupe cemetery, on the southern border of Barrio Subtiaba. The large, squat, gray building was originally constructed in 1889 to take advantage of the great city views. It was abandoned until the 1950s, when the Somozas realized that they needed to keep an eye on León itself. They lost the fort on July 7, 1979.

You may need to ask for permission to enter this grim place; check out the abandoned torture chambers in the basement. Muggings are common on this stretch, so go with other people and take a taxi.

🏃 Activities

Asociación Mary Barreda VOLUNTEERING

(📞 2311-2254; Iglesia de la Recolección, ½c E; ⊙ hours vary) Runs a variety of education programs focusing on women's rights, sex education and STD prevention. Find them on Facebook.

🎓 Courses

La Isla Foundation COURSE

(📞 2315-1261; https://laislanetwork.org; cnr 3a Calle NE & Av Central) Stop by to learn about Spanish, yoga and salsa classes; proceeds go to La Isla Network who work to eradicate chronic kidney disease in rural communities.

León Spanish School LANGUAGE

(📞 8183-7389; www.leonspanishschool.org; La Casa de Cultura, Iglesia de la Merced, 2c O; 20hr

🏃 City Walk
Revolutionary & Cultural León

START PARQUE CENTRAL
END MUSEO-ARCHIVO RUBÉN DARÍO
LENGTH 3–5KM; FOUR TO SIX HOURS

Begin at **①Parque Central**, a fine place for people-watching and enjoying that most Leonese of treats, *raspado* (shaved ice flavored with fruit).

Enjoy your treat in front of the eternal (more or less) flame at **②Mausoleo de los Héroes y Mártires** (p143), on the northern side of the park, where a phenomenal and heartbreaking mural traces Nicaraguan history from the Spanish conquest to the most recent revolution.

Dominating the plaza is **③Basílica de la Asunción** (p139), Central America's largest cathedral; take a rooftop tour early for the clearest views of the Volcanes Maribios.

On the southern side of the cathedral is **④Colegio La Asunción** (1679), the first theological college in Nicaragua. It was partially destroyed by fire in 1935 and rebuilt in its current Gothic style. Next door is **⑤Palacio Episcopal** (Bishop's Palace), designed by Marcelo Targa and one of the first buildings to display Leonese neoclassical architecture. In this group of buildings is also the **⑥Archivo Histórico Diocesano de León**, which holds documents dating back to 1674.

Continuing around the cathedral is the 1680 **⑦Colegio de San Ramón**. Revolutionary hero Miguel Larreynaga, who drafted the first Central American constitution, was educated here. The college was rebuilt in 1752, and housed the Universidad Autónoma, Nicaragua's first university. Though it's been a high school since 1945, paintings of all León's bishops are still on display.

Head south on 1a Av SE, then west on 3a Calle SO one block, then south one block on Av Central to **⑧La XXI** (p141), an old military garrison that's now home to the truly fabulous **⑨Museo de Leyendas y Tradiciones** (p141); check out the mosaic tile work at the entrance. Across the street is the photogenic **⑩Ruinas San Sebastián** (p143) which was bombed almost into oblivion in 1979.

Backtrack up 1a Ave SO and through pleasant Mercado Central, then make a right on Calle Rubén Darío and continue to the early 18th-century ⑪ **Iglesia El Calvario** (p141), famed for its comic book–style facade. Close by, ⑫ **Antiguo Reformatorio de Menores** (Old Reform School) is a rare, almost all-original *casa pinariega*–style building (rustic stone house from the early 1800s). The squat adobe has *tejas* (ceramic half-pipe ceiling tiles), plus classic corner double doors.

Head north on 3a Av NE, stopping in to bug out at ⑬ **Museo Entomológico** (p143). Then it's on to somewhat scruffy 1625 ⑭ **Iglesia San Juan de Dios**, rebuilt in 1860 in the modernist neoclassical style. Close by is ⑮ **Mercado San Juan** (p151) and the ⑯ **old train station**, constructed in 1882 with austere lines and simple, utilitarian design.

Backtrack two blocks along 2a Av NE to 2a Calle NE and make a right to reach the unmissable 1786 ⑰ **Iglesia de la Recolección** (p139). This ornate, ultra-baroque masterpiece was described by one critic as 'the most important monument to passion in Nicaragua.'

Two blocks west on 2a Calle NE is the flagship campus of ⑱ **UNAN,** with several beautiful buildings and a collection of cheap restaurants and festive bars that form the heart of the student scene.

From the UNAN campus, head south on 1a Av NO for the 1615 ⑲ **Iglesia de La Merced** (p141), another of León's signature churches, then head west on 1a Calle NO, stopping at ⑳ **La Casa de Cultura** (p146), with its excellent art collection (including a portrait of former US president Ronald Reagan that you'll want to photograph), then head south on 3a Av NO.

Tired? Fortify yourself at ㉑ **Hotel El Convento** (p148), which has an amazing collection of colonial-era religious art and a good, if pricey, restaurant. Attached ㉒ **Iglesia de San Francisco** (p141) was badly damaged during the revolution but is slowly being restored to its former glory.

Allow at least two hours to appreciate the best art museum in Central America, ㉓ **Museo de Arte Fundación Ortiz-Gurdián** (p139), south of Calle Rubén Darío, then head two blocks further south and one block east to see if anything's on later that night at 1885 ㉔ **Teatro Municipal José de la Cruz Mena** (p151). Finally, backtrack to the corner of Calle Rubén Darío and 4a Av SO for the poet's home and national museum, ㉕ **Museo-Archivo Rubén Darío** (p139).

WORTH A TRIP

LEÓN VIEJO

Buried and lost for over 300 years, **León Viejo** (Puerto Momotombo; US$5; ⊙8am-5pm) was Nicaragua's first capital – a rough-and-ready settlement that some say was doomed from the start. Founded in 1524, the town was governed by unusually cruel and money-hungry tyrants, whose public spectacles included beheadings and setting wild dogs on captured natives in the central plaza.

Tour outfits in León arrange visits to León Viejo (US$45). Buses run hourly between León and La Paz Centro (US$0.80, 45 minutes), meeting Puerto Momotombo buses (US$0.50).

According to local legend, divine intervention played at least a part in the series of earthquakes that shook the town from 1580 to 1609, culminating in the eruption of nearby Volcán Momotombo (1280m) that buried the city under ash in 1610.

The Spanish fled, carrying whatever they could with them (including la Virgen de la Merced), and settled in present-day León, and the old city began to fade from memory.

Fast forward to 1967. After years of searching and theorizing, archaeologists from León's UNAN university finally located the old town, unearthing its chapel and central plaza (and the headless remains of Francisco Fernández de Córdoba, founder of both León and Granada, beneath it).

In 2000 it was declared a Unesco World Heritage site – Nicaragua's first – and excavations have continued (funds allowing). This is not Machu Picchu – most walls are about 1m high and you need a fair bit of imagination to see that there was once a city here – but it makes for an interesting day trip, more than anything for the evocative commentary provided by onsite guides.

León Viejo is a compact grid bisected by the main Calle Real. Those condemned to be beheaded were led along it to the execution spot on the Plaza Mayor, now marked by the Monumento a la Resistencia Indígena. Don't miss the remnants of a fortress on a small hillock, just southwest of the plaza; unobstructed views of the Volcán Momotombo are stupendous.

Admission includes a Spanish-language guided tour, but detailed signs are also in English. The best time to visit is the second Sunday in November, when la Virgen de la Merced leaves her comfortable new church and, leading a procession of the faithful from La Paz Centro, revisits her first home in the New World.

---

course with/without homestay US$250/150) Based in La Casa de Cultura, this is a professional operation with plenty of cultural activities and out-of-town excursions.

La Casa de Cultura COURSE
(☎2311-2116; 1a Calle NO, Iglesia de la Merced, 2c O; ⊙10am-6pm Mon-Fri) Ask here about art, dance and music classes.

👉 Tours

⭐ **Mas Adventures** OUTDOORS
(☎5765-2838; https://masadventures.com; Iglesia Zaragoza, 3c E; ⊙8am-7pm) Operator Anry comes from a rural Nicaraguan community and his passion for the country really comes across in his tours. Apart from city tours of León (US$25) and Nicaraguan cooking tours (US$20) he runs hiking trips up Telica, El Hoyo, Cosigüina and Asososca volcanoes, and can arrange tailor-made tours according to your interests and the time you have.

Volcano Day HIKING
(☎8980-8747; www.volcanodaynicaragua.com; BanPro, 75m S; ⊙9am-6pm) Responsible operator comes highly recommended by travelers for their volcano hikes – from day trips up San Cristóbal (US$70), Cosigüina and El Hoyo, to sunset ascents of Telica (US$40), overnight camping on Telica (US$55) and swims in the Asososca crater (US$35). Sand-boarding and beach shuttles also arranged.

Get Up Stand Up SURFING
(☎5800-2394; www.gsupsurf.com; BanPro, ½c S; ⊙9am-9pm) This cool surf shop – the only one in León – runs daily shuttles to and from Las Peñitas (p154) and arranges lessons and gear rental in conjunction with Bigfoot Beach Hostel. The indie brand also designs and prints its own T-shirts. It's a great stop for information if you're considering a surf excursion.

Quetzaltrekkers ADVENTURE
(☎2311-7388; https//leon.quetzaltrekkers.org; Mercantil, ½c O) 🍃 Outstanding operator running volcano boarding trips on Cerro Negro

(US$30) and hikes up the Telica (US$55), Momotombo (US$55), Cosigüina (US$55), El Hoyo (US$60) and San Cristóbal (US$60) volcanoes. Profits from this outstanding operator go to worthy causes such Las Tias, a charity that helps children from underprivileged areas learn to build their own lives; volunteers are very welcome.

Julio Tours Nicaragua   OUTDOORS
(☑ 8625-4467) A reliable team of bilingual guides runs city tours of León, day trips to the Flor de Caña (p162) rum factory and other day excursions. They can also hook you up with reliable local guides on Ometepe and Solentiname, among other places.

Tierra Tour   ADVENTURE
(☑ 2315-4278; www.tierratour.com; Iglesia de la Merced, 1½c N; volcano boarding US$30) A well-established operator with locations in both León and Granada. Full- and half-day tours go to the volcanoes (including both trekking and sand-boarding excursions) and the likes of León Viejo to Reserva Natural Isla Juan Venado. Also offers daily shuttles to and from Granada, as well as to Antigua and El Salvador. Some tours outsourced to other operators.

✸ Festivals & Events

★ **Semana Santa**   RELIGIOUS
(☺ late Mar or early Apr) The Leonese Semana Santa is something special (and Nicaragua's liveliest!), with Barrio Subtiaba's colorful sawdust 'carpets,' temporary and beautiful images that the funeral procession for Jesus walks over, and a sandcastle competition in Poneloya.

Tertulias Leonesas   CULTURAL
(Parque Central) Every other Saturday, from early afternoon till midnight, the Parque Central comes alive for the Tertulias Leonesas, inviting everyone outside to eat, drink and dance to music played by local combos. Craft and food stalls crowd the square during the day.

Masacre del 23 Julio 1959   CULTURAL
(☺ Jul 23) One afternoon in 1959, local schoolchildren staged a demonstration against Somoza. As they chanted 'Freedom! Freedom!,' the Guardia Nacional fired into the crowd, killing four students and wounding several others. Those wounded, some in wheelchairs, still lead a parade, right after every single marching band from the area has announced that their generation will not forget.

La Gritería Chiquita   RELIGIOUS
(☺ Aug 14) This celebration began in 1947, as an erupting Cerro Negro threatened to bury the city in ashes. The volcano suddenly halted its activity after an innovative priest, Monseñor Isidro Augusto Oviedo, vowed to initiate a preliminary *gritería* (shouting) – similar to December's but changing the response to *¡La asunción de María!* ('The ascension of Mary!').

Día de la Virgen de Merced   RELIGIOUS
(☺ Sep 24) León's saint's day is solemnly observed, but the preceding day is more festive: revelers don a bull-shaped armature lined with fireworks, then charge at panic-stricken onlookers as the rockets fly.

Carnaval Mitos y Leyendas   CULTURAL
(Nov 1) This Halloween-esque fiesta features the papier-mâché crew from the Museo de Leyendas y Tradiciones (p141) on a parade from the cathedral to Barrio Subtiaba.

Día de la Purísima Concepción   RELIGIOUS
(☺ Dec 7) Known simply as 'La Purísima' and observed throughout the country, this lively celebration of Nicaragua's patron saint is the occasion for *La Gritería* (a shouting ritual that honors the Virgin Mary), enjoyed here with unusual vigor.

🛏 Sleeping

★ **Casa Lula León**   HOSTEL $
(☑ 2311-1076; www.casalulaleon.com; esquina SE de la Catedral, 2c S; dm US$10, r with/without bathroom US$30/25; ❋ 🛜) Sociable without being a party hostel, Casa Lula is a budget traveler favorite, largely through the efforts of hosts Eric and Selina and the knowledgeable, helpful staff. There's a strong emphasis on outdoor activities, a large garden to chill out in, a well-equipped kitchen and spotless rooms (with big lockers in the dorm).

Tortuga Booluda   HOSTEL $
(☑ 2311-4653; www.tortugabooluda.com; 1a Calle SO, catedral, 4½c O; dm/r US$9/25; ❋ 🛜) More small hotel than hostel, the revamped 'Lazy Turtle' does, however, offer all the hostel amenities, namely a great kitchen, book exchange, free coffee, pool table, some good chill-out areas and a sociable atmosphere. Rooms are simple but stylish, and dorms are spacious enough. Note that you can't reserve dorm beds – they're first-come, first-served.

Bigfoot Hostel   HOSTEL $
(☑ 2315-3863; www.bigfoothostelleon.com; Ban-Pro, ½c S; dm/d from US$8/26; ❋ 🛜 ☷) With

kitchen access, a miniature swimming pool, freshly made mojitos on offer, and spacious dorms and rooms with ample, secure luggage storage, this place is appealing. It's also well-organised: staff run numerous tours and shuttles daily. There's a good travelers' vibe at this party hostel – staff swear the party shuts down at 10pm – and a sweet little cafe-bar out front.

Vía Vía
HOSTEL **$**

(☑ 2311-6142; www.viaviacafe.com; BanPro, ½c S; dm/r US$9/26; ❋ 🛜) The Vía Vía chain of hostels, which stretches from Kathmandu to Buenos Aires, consistently comes up with the goods. This is no exception, offering beautiful, colonial-style rooms with great bathrooms, and spacious six-bed dorms with their own bathrooms. The patio area is lush and there's a cavernous cafe-bar area out front.

Guesthouse El Nancite
B&B **$$**

(☑ 2315-4323; 3a Av NE btwn 2a Calle NE & 1a Calle NE; r US$35-45; ❋ 🛜) Run by helpful North American John and his lovely wife, this jaunty yellow guesthouse, decorated with Carnival masks and figures, has a handful of fan-cooled economy rooms, a couple of split-level mini-suites facing the leafy courtyard out back, characterful rooms with balconies out front and an upstairs suite with balcony. John's coconut pancakes are ace.

Morpho Residence
B&B **$$**

(☑ 2319-9327; de hielera Celsa, ½c E; s/d from US$23/30; ❋ 🛜) Run by a friendly French-Nicaraguan couple, this three-room guesthouse sits in a quiet location in the southwest corner of downtown. Jean-Michel is an entomologist, happy to share his wildlife expertise, an excellent breakfast is included and there are hammocks in the garden for chilling out. Only one of the rooms has air-con. Find them on Facebook.

Hostal Las Vacaciones
GUESTHOUSE **$$**

(☑ 8552-1568; Iglesia de la Recolección, 200m E; dm/s/d/tr US$8/26/28/30; ❋ 🛜) Quiet dorm and rooms share facilities inside an attractive colonial building, with a sunny upstairs terrace and tranquil courtyard garden. For breakfast, you get eggs or pancakes; staff organize a plethora of local excursions; and amenities include a guest kitchen and bicycle rental.

Lazybones Hostel
HOSTEL **$$**

(☑ 2311-3472; www.lazyboneshostelnicaragua.com; 2a Av NO, Parque Rubén Darío, 2½c N; dm US$9, r with/without bathroom US$30/21;

❋ 🛜 🏊) At this lively hostel, the clean, simple rooms are arranged around the age-old patio and sitting areas that are every bit as lovely as those in some midrange hotels. The bar, good-sized pool and yummy breakfasts make this a good deal. If staying here during a heatwave, bear in mind that the dorm gets uncomfortably hot, even with the fan on.

Hotel El Sueño de Meme
HOTEL **$$**

(☑ 2311-5462; Museo Rubén Darío, 350m N; s/d with fan US$18/28, with air-con US$30/36; ❋ 🛜) With its pastel color scheme and cutesy decorations, this one steps firmly outside the quaint colonial box. Rooms are spacious and comfortable, if a little soulless. It's a bit removed from the action in the city center.

Paz de Luna Bed & Breakfast
B&B **$$**

(☑ 2311-2581; www.pazdelunabb.com; Iglesia de la Recolección, 1½c N; r/q US$45/50, r/q with shared bathroom US$30/40; ❋ 🛜) With rooms laid out around a pretty courtyard, Paz de Luna has old-fashioned charm and lots of potential. Rooms vary; some lack natural light, the upkeep could improve and there are some plumbing and wi-fi issues (it's a colonial house). But the staff are lovely, as are the rooms with own patios, and there's an excellent cafe at the entrance.

Casona Colonial
HISTORIC HOTEL **$$**

(☑ 2311-3178; www.casonacolonialguest.com; 4a Calle NE, Parque San Juan, ½c O; s US$20, d with/without air-con US$45/25; ❋ 🛜) With more character than many in this price range, the medium-sized rooms here are long on colonial atmosphere without all the costly little extras. Beds are big, with lavish bedheads, and the occasional chip in the paintwork or tear in the wallpaper adds to (rather than detracts from) the charm.

★Hotel El Convento
HISTORIC HOTEL **$$$**

(☑ 2311-7053; www.elconventonicaragua.com; Iglesia de San Francisco, 20m N; s/d US$95/140; 🅿 ❋ 🛜) There's atmosphere galore at this historic hotel on the grounds of one of the city's most notable convents and churches. The centerpiece garden is impressive and you're surrounded by precious artwork. Guest rooms, with exposed brick walls, are comparatively simple (as befitting a former place of worship) but comfortable, and there's a good but rather pricey restaurant.

Hotel Azul
BOUTIQUE HOTEL **$$$**

(☑ 2315-4519; www.hotelazulleon.com; catedral, 2½c N; r/tr/q US$74/96/110; ❋ 🛜 🏊) Set in a typical colonial house but decorated with a minimalist twist, petite and slightly upscale Hotel Azul has a courtyard swimming pool – beautifully illuminated at night – and a small patio with a nifty daybed that's suspended, hammock-style, from the ceiling. Guest rooms are simple and compact, with glass French doors.

Hotel Flor de Sarta
BOUTIQUE HOTEL **$$$**

(☑ 2311-1042; www.hotelflordesarta.com; del Parque San Juan, 2c O, ½c N; r/q US$70/100; P ❋ 🛜 🌊) There's a lot to love about this boutique hotel in the heart of León: the central location (yet respite from the heat and noise in the delightful, greenery-filled courtyard); the immaculate, bright rooms, the heavy-beamed common area with splashes of contemporary art, and the wonderfully helpful staff.

Hotel Austria
HOTEL **$$$**

(☑ 2311-1206; www.hotelaustria.com.ni; catedral, 1c S; s/d US$85/95; ❋ 🛜) Tucked away on a side street just south of the cathedral, this well-run hotel has somewhat dark rooms set around a leafy central courtyard with a stone fountain. Several good breakfast options are included in the room rate and the restaurant caters to those hankering for *wienerschnitzel* and *apfelstrudel*.

Hotel La Perla
HISTORIC HOTEL **$$$**

(☑ 2311-3125; www.laperlaleon.com; 1a Av NO, Iglesia de la Merced, 1½c N; r/ste US$127/180; P ❋ 🛜 🌊) A pearl indeed. Set in one of León's most impressive mansions, the Perla has everything you would expect for the price, done with exquisite taste in a great location. There's a classy onsite restaurant and bar, stately rooms with hardwood furnishings and a decent-sized swimming pool. Some of the rooms lack windows.

Hotel Real
HOTEL **$$$**

(☑ 2311-2606; 2a Calle NE, Iglesia de la Recolección, 1½c E; s/d US$48/58; ❋ 🛜) The 'Royal Hotel' has a quaint front sitting area and an old-style *casona* (historic mansion) feel, but with relatively modern rooms bedecked with flatscreen TVs and firm beds surrounding a leafy courtyard. Rooms are big and comfortable, and the rooftop terrace has excellent views of steeple tops and the volcanoes beyond.

Posada Doña Blanca
B&B **$$$**

(☑ 2311-2521; www.posadadonablanca.com; 1a Av NO, Iglesia de la Merced, 1c N; d from US$60; P ❋ 🛜) In a modern Nicaraguan family's home, this downtown oasis is all cool open spaces with colonial flourishes. Rooms are comfortable, and the central courtyard is a lovely place to relax on a hot afternoon. The staff are not likely to be recipients of the Mr/Miss Congeniality prize, however.

🍴 Eating

★ Mercado La Estacíon
NICARAGUAN **$**

(Parque San Juan, 1c E, 1c N; mains US$1.50; ◷ 6pm-late) Head here in the evenings for your fill of the BX, León's famous dish. BX *(bajón extremo)* was coined by local students in the 1990s; it's the local take on the *fritanga*, consisting of *gallo pinto*, slaw, marinated grilled beef, topped with a tortilla and a piece of omelette, and served on *bijagua* leaves. The Mama Tere stall is the best.

Del Norte
NICARAGUAN **$**

(☑ 8716-4365; Iglesia San Francisco, ½c O; mains US$3-5; ◷ 11am-9:30pm Mon-Sat) Run by a friendly family from Matagalpa, Del Norte serves Nicaraguan classics, including heaped portions of *fritanga*, delicious grilled chicken and *tostones* (fried green plantains) to the tune of Nicaraguan country music.

Comedor Lucia
NICARAGUAN **$**

(2a Av NE, Bigfoot Hostel, 10m N; mains US$2.50-4.50; ◷ 7am-3pm Mon-Sat) In 'Backpacker Alley,' this no-frills Nica joint gets a predictable mix of locals and travelers. The typical Nica breakfast involving huevos rancheros and fried plantain (C$85) is a bargain.

Mercado Central
MARKET **$**

(Parque Central, 2c E; ◷ 6am-5pm) León's large produce market is surrounded by simple *comedores* (eateries) and food stands.

Supermercado La Colonia
SUPERMARKET **$**

(La Casa de Cultura, 2c O; ◷ 9am-9pm) A good supermarket for stocking up on supplies; there's also a small cafeteria offering prepared foods, and a juice bar.

La Unión Supermercado
SUPERMARKET **$**

(1a Calle NE; ◷ 8am-10pm Mon-Sat, to 8pm Sun) La Unión is the largest supermarket in town.

★ Pan y Paz
CAFE **$$**

(☑ 8631-2760; www.panypaz.com; esquina de los bancos, 1½c E; mains US$4-10; ◷ 7am-9pm Mon-Sat; 🛜) 🌱 Run by a European couple, this fabulous French bakery specializes in homemade breads. Grab a table on the breezy interior courtyard and choose from a menu of freshly baked pastries and gourmet salads and sandwiches. Later in the day, try the cheese plate; it even has Argentine wines by the glass. There's a second branch just north of the cathedral.

★ Imbir
FUSION $$

(☑ 5728-5887; www.imbirestaurant.com; Iglesia de la Recolección, 150m N; mains US$4-9; ⊙ noon-10pm Mon-Sat; 🛜🍴) A happy marriage of Polish and Sri Lankan dishes, this eclectic restaurant does an equally good job with moreish pierogi (with multiple fillings) and curries ranging from gentle to fruity yet fiery. The shady interior courtyard is also ideal for sipping one of half-dozen local Cerro Negro craft beers, with guest beers chosen from breweries countrywide.

El Desayunazo
NICARAGUAN $$

(☑ 8235-4837; www.facebook.com/leonleonnicaragua; Iglesia de la Merced, 1c O, 2c N; mains US$4-7; ⊙ 6am-2pm Mon, to 9pm Tue-Sun; 🛜🍴) Whether you're being whisked off on an early morning tour or shuttle or are just a fan of all-day breakfasts, this is the place for generous portions of *gallo pinto* (rice and beans) and fried plantain, pancakes with maple syrup, full English breakfasts and waffles.

El Bodegón
LATIN AMERICAN $$

(☑ 8731-5216; Parque Rubén Darío, 3c N; mains US$4-7; ⊙ 4-10pm Tue-Sat, 9:30am-1pm & 4-10pm Sun) Sit inside the greenery-filled courtyard and feast on the likes of pork with boiled yucca, quesadillas, jalapeño chicken, tostadas and more. The food is mostly Cuban, with some international influences, the frozen mojitos hit the spot and there's live music some nights. Find them on Facebook.

Tacubaya
MEXICAN $$

(☑ 8329-6261; Iglesia de la Merced, 1½c N; mains US$5-7; ⊙ 3-11pm Mon-Sat) Quesadillas, burritos and tacos are all on offer at this small Mexican restaurant with a succinct menu. The friendly owner is fluent in English and French and is quick with a joke, and the margaritas really hit the spot.

Cusco Collao
Ceviche Gastrobar
PERUVIAN $$

(☑ 5771-3765; www.facebook.com/cuscocollao; Iglesia de la Recolección, 1c N, ½c E; dishes US$4-10; ⊙ noon-10pm; ✳🛜) This thimble-sized *cevichería* holds such promise! The *tostones con cangrejo* (fried green plantain topped with crab) are a perfect blend of crunchiness and delicate sweetness, the fish *ceviche* has a nice kick to it, but the mixed seafood and fish offerings sometimes let the side down.

Café La Nicaragüita
INTERNATIONAL $$

(☑ 2311-0347; Iglesia de la Merced, 2c N, ½c O; mains US$4-8; ⊙ noon-9pm Thu-Tue) This friendly little restaurant uses fresh and local produce to make a solid range of menu items: sandwiches, salads, burgers, pastas, steaks and fajitas, to name a few, plus a few Nicaraguan small plates (like *tostones*, or fried plantain slices) for good measure. Also on the chalkboard: fresh fruit smoothies and icy rum-based cocktails, from mojitos to daiquiris (US$2).

Paz de Luna Café
CAFE $$

(☑ 2311-2581; www.pazdelunabb.com; Iglesia de la Recolección, 1½c N; mains US$3-6) At this sleek, hipster-friendly coffee shop – think black-and-white tiled floors, a gilded chandelier, fruit crates repurposed as furniture – a wall-sized chalkboard menu spells out the long menu of coffee drinks, breakfasts (both traditionally Nicaraguan and otherwise), crêpes, panini, omelets, salads and pastas.

CocinArte
VEGETARIAN $$

(☑ 8854-6928; 4a Calle SO, frente El Laborío; mains US$5-8; ⊙ noon-10pm Wed-Mon; 🛜🍴) León's vegetarian hot spot. This colorful eatery offers ample portions of vegetable curry, Indonesian noodles and more, in the relaxed surrounds of an old colonial house. There are a few meat dishes (cooked in separate pans and served with separate cutlery) to keep the carnivores happy, and a leafy patio; the most popular tables are on the front porch.

El Sesteo
INTERNATIONAL $$

(☑ 2311-5327; Calle Rubén Darío, frente Parque Central; mains US$6-12; ⊙ 11am-10pm) You can't beat the location of this landmark cafe, positioned right on the plaza with spectacular people-watching and views of the cathedral. The food is hit-or-miss, but you can't go wrong with a fresh fruit smoothie, a cappuccino or a cold beer.

El Mediterraneo
MEDITERRANEAN $$$

(☑ 2311-0756; 2a Av NO, Parque Rubén Darío, 2½c N; dishes US$6-13; ⊙ 6pm-late) Date night? Check out one of the longer-running dining institutions in town. The decor is gorgeous, and carefully prepared seafood, pasta, meats and pizza are generally reliable, but when the place is busy, the serving staff tend to get overwhelmed. The wine list is heavy on Argentinean and Chilean wines.

🍷 Drinking & Nightlife

Given the city's lively student population, there are plenty of places to get your drink on – 1a Calle SO, west of the park is a particularly good area to go bar-hopping. Many hostels have bars for their guests and there are several good dance floors right in the center of town.

Oxygene
CLUB

(☑8321-3743; 1a Calle SE, Parque Central, ½c O; ☺8pm-late Wed-Sat) The hottest dance club in the city center with plenty of sleek, modern styling, bright young things, occasional live bands and 'Techno Saturdays'.

Snake Bar
BAR

(☑2311-5921; Teatro Municipal, 1c N; ☺11am-midnight Tue-Thu, 11am-2am Fri-Sun) Corner bar, popular with students and with live sports on TV. There's usually live music on Tuesdays and Wednesdays.

Bohemios Bar-Disco
CLUB

(☑8810-2039; 1a Av NO, Parque Central, ½c N; ☺8pm-3am Tue-Sat) In the unsigned orange building in front of the basketball court, this is your classic Latin disco – plenty of reggaetón and *bachata* (romantic Dominican dance music), with sweaty bodies packed together on a tiny dance floor.

☆ Entertainment

Olla Quemada
LIVE MUSIC

(☑8817-2723; Calle Rubén Darío, Colegio La Salle, 150m O; ☺4pm-midnight) This hot spot with graffiti-daubed walls features a line-up of live music, indie films and Latin dance nights (from salsa to merengue) all week, and has a good mix of locals and travelers.

Teatro Municipal José de la Cruz Mena
PERFORMING ARTS

(☑8947-7480; 2a Av SO, Parque Central, 1c O, 1c S; ☺hours vary) Check the board in front of this attractive 1885 theater to see what's on here and around town during your visit. It's been impressively restored, and for less than US$3 you may be able to catch anything from Salvadoran rock groups to art films to the national ballet on the very accessible stage. There's also an online schedule.

Alianza Francesa
PERFORMING ARTS

(☑2311-0126; www.alianzafrancesa.org.ni; 1a Av NE, Iglesia de la Recolección, 1½c N; ☺8am-noon & 2-5pm Mon-Fri) Often screens art-house movies in French and Spanish, and sponsors concerts. Drop in for its monthly program.

Cines Siglo Nuevo
CINEMA

(www.psiglonuevo.com; 1a Calle NE, La Unión, 20m E; US$3) León's cinema shows many big-

budget American films, either dubbed or with subtitles.

🛍 Shopping

Telar Manual Textil La Fé
TEXTILES

(☑2315-1728; Iglesia de la Recolección, 6½c N; ☺8am-noon & 1-5pm Mon-Sat) Well worth seeking out for the gorgeous handmade weavings, made by a local family co-op. Find them on Facebook.

Kamañ
ARTS & CRAFTS

(☑8790-4347; www.facebook.com/kmnic; costado norte, catedral; ☺9am-noon & 2-6pm Mon-Sat) Handmade clothes from around Latin America, as well as crafts, toys and artsy postcards.

Mercado San Juan
MARKET

(Av Pedro Aráuz; ☺7am-5pm) A workaday marketplace located on the northeast edge of León's downtown; cheap place to buy fresh fruit and veg.

ℹ Orientation

León actually has a system of clearly signed and logically numbered calles (streets) and avenidas (avenues), allowing anyone to pinpoint any address. Unfortunately, no one actually uses it, preferring the old reliable '2½ blocks east of the Shell station' method instead.

Just for kicks, this is how it works: Av Central and Calle Rubén Darío intersect at the northeast corner of the Parque Central (central park), beside the cathedral, forming the city's northeast, northwest, southeast and southwest quadrants. Calles running parallel to Rubén Darío are numbered NE (Calle 1 NE, Calle 2 NE) north of the cathedral, SE to the south. Av 1 SO (*suroeste;* southwest), one block from Av Central, forms the park's western boundary, paralleling Av 2 SO and so on.

Calle Rubén Darío is the city's backbone, and runs east from the cathedral to striking Iglesia El Calvario, and west almost 1km to Barrio Subtiaba, continuing another 20km to the Pacific. The majority of tourist services are within a few blocks of the cathedral, with another cluster of museums and churches in Barrio Subtiaba.

ℹ Information

DANGERS & ANNOYANCES

Since April 2018, León has been rocked by anti-government protests and deadly police violence. Road blocks and barricades have been put up in some neighborhoods and some government offices have been torched.

INTERNET ACCESS

Nearly every hotel has wi-fi.

MEDICAL SERVICES

Hospital San Vicente (☑ 2311-6990; Av Pedro Aráuz) Out past the main bus terminal, the region's largest hospital is a 1918 neoclassical beauty that attracts architecture buffs as well as sick tourists. A new hospital building was being constructed on the premises at the time of research.

MONEY

Several banks have ATMs that accept Visa/Plus debit cards.

BAC (1a Calle NE, La Unión, 10m O)

BanPro (2a Calle NE, Bigfoot Hostel, 20m N) ATM is open 24 hours and accepts Visa and MasterCard.

Western Union (1 Calle NE; ⊘ 8am-6pm Mon-Sat) International cash transfers.

❶ Getting There & Away

BUS
International Buses

While international bus routes heading north start in Managua, many tend to include a stop in León. Buy your bus tickets at **Tica Bus** (☑ 2311-6153; www.ticabus.com; 6a Calle NE, Palí, 1c O; ⊘ 8am-6pm). Buses headed south stop first in Managua, with an often lengthy wait between connections – it's better to make your own way there and take the bus from Managua.

National Buses

Most buses leave from León's chaotic **main bus terminal** (☑ 2311-3909; 6a Calle NE, Palí, 1.5km E), which has a fun market area nearby (watch your wallet). If you're heading south, you'll invariably pass through Managua.

Shuttle Buses

Popular operators include the following:
Bigfoot Hostel Shuttles (☑ 8852-3279; www.bigfoothostelleon.com/shuttle; BanPro, ½c S) Daily shuttles at 9:30am to San Juan del Sur (US$20) via Managua Airport, Granada (US$12) and Rivas. Daily international shuttles to Anti-

gua, Guatemala (US$37, 2am) via El Tunco, El Salvador (US$25), and to La Ceiba, Honduras (US$65, 1am), via Tegucigalpa (US$45).

Gekko Explorer (☑ 2389-6199; www.gekkotrailsexplorer.com; BanPro, 25m S) Shuttles to Granada (US$12), San Juan del Sur (US$20) and Rivas/San Jorge (US$18). International services to Antigua, Guatemala (US$50), Copán, Honduras (US$70), and El Tunco, El Salvador (US$30).

Tierra Tour (☑ 2315-4278; www.tierratour.com; 1a Av NO, Iglesia de la Merced, 1½c N) Daily shuttles to Granada via Managua Airport (US$15) at 9:30am, and onward from Granada to San Juan del Sur (US$15) at 12:30pm.

Buses to Beaches

Buses to Poneloya and Las Peñitas (US$0.50, 40 minutes) depart hourly, 6am to 6pm, from El Mercadito in Subtiaba. Day-trippers take note: the last bus returns around 6pm, too.

Another option is Bigfoot Hostel (p147) runs a daily shuttle to their hostel in Las Peñitas.

BOAT

A convenient (and beautiful) way to get to El Salvador is the shuttle and boat trip organized by **Ruta del Golfo** (☑ 2315-4099; www.rutadelgolfo.com; Vapues, costado norte, Iglesia de San Nicolás de Laborío; border crossing to El Salvador from US$99; ⊘ 9am-6pm); advance booking required. The trip involves a pickup in León and 4WD transfer to Potosí via Chinandega, then a boat trip across the Gulf of Fonseca to La Unión. Travel time is about five hours, departures were on Tuesdays and Saturdays at research time.

CAR & MOTORCYCLE

Parking in León can be difficult, given the narrow streets and dense traffic in the city center. **Ruedas León** (☑ 2311-6727; www.ruedasleon.com; BanPro, 80m S; ⊘ 8am-6pm Mon-Sat) rents motorcycles and offers motorcycle tours.

❶ Getting Around

The city is strollable, but big enough that you may want to take taxis, particularly at night. Cycling around León is not particularly pleasant, given the heat, the narrow streets and the traffic, but you can rent bikes for around US$5 to US$7 per day from hostels. Ruedas León rents scooters, motorbikes and mountain bikes.

---

❶ SHUTTLE BUSES

The quickest and most comfortable way to get between popular destinations in Nicaragua is by shuttle. Several operators run daily shuttles (book ahead), with private shuttles also an option. If you're headed to less popular destinations, be aware that most shuttles require a minimum of four passengers. Shuttles to San Juan del Sur that stop in Managua and Granada can take longer than direct buses.

Pacific Beaches near León

The most accessible beaches from León are Poneloya and Las Peñitas, both an easy 20-minute bus ride from Mercadito Subtiaba in León. Las Peñitas is a popular backpacker haunt, while Poneloya is much more of a local scene. Next to Las Peñitas, Reserva Natural Isla Juan Venado beckons nature lovers with its vast wetlands.

Some 32km south of León, partially paved NIC-52 branches off towards a trio of beaches: **Miramar**, **Playa Hermosa** and **El Tránsito**, 'discovered' by surfers but off the beaten track for most other travelers.

Poneloya

POP UNDER 1000

This beach has the famous name – it's highly praised in the *Viva León, Jodido* theme song – and this is where affluent Leonese come for the weekend, unlike its sister beach, Las Peñitas, which is popular with foreign surfers and sun seekers. For many travelers, Poneloya is simply the point of departure to the beautiful island of **Isla Los Brasiles**, the location of a popular surfing lodge.

🛏 Sleeping & Eating

Poneloya's best eating is found at the Bocanita – a collection of thatched-roof seafood restaurants at the edge of an estuary, at the north end of Poneloya. They double as bars. No off-site food or drink is allowed at Surfing Turtle Lodge (and the restaurant can be hit or miss).

★ **Surfing Turtle Lodge**　　　　　LODGE **$$**
(📞8640-0644; www.surfingturtlelodge.com; Isla Los Brasiles, Poneloya; dm US$10, r US$35-40, cabin US$60; 🛜) 🏖 The breezy 2nd-story dorm is one of the coolest spots in all of Central America with a giant view to the ocean.

Camping in pre-set-up tents or staying in a bamboo hut will save money, or you can upgrade to a cabin. From El Chepe bar in Poneloya, catch a boat (US$1) to Isla Los Brasiles, then walk 15 minutes.

There's good surf right out front, and bonfires at night. Electricity starts here at 6pm, and there's an onsite restaurant and turtle protection program. The beach break is good for beginners, surf lessons are on offer and the sister hostel in León runs shuttles to Poneloya.

El NicaLibre　　　　　　　　HOTEL **$$$**
(📞2310-7127; www.facebook.com/elnicalibre2017; La Bocanita; r from US$60; 🌀🛜) Overlooking the estuary, this bright blue guesthouse comprises a handful of spotless, colorful rooms, some of them with terraces. Most of the rooms can sleep four people and the attached eatery is excellent.

Bar Margarita　　　　　　　SEAFOOD **$$**
(📞7508-5573; www.facebook.com/bocana505; La Bocanita; mains US$7-10; ⏰10am-9pm) At the very end of the street leading to the estuary, this thatched-roof restaurant and bar serves large platters of grilled catch of the day with rice, beans and plantains, with a side helping of estuary views.

ⓘ Getting There & Away

Buses (US$0.50) run between Poneloya, Las Peñitas, and León (not to the center, but to El Mercadito, a small market on the western edge of town in the neighborhood called Sutiaba) roughly every 45 minutes between 4:30am and 6pm.

NATIONAL BUS SERVICES FROM LEÓN

DESTINATION	COST (US$)	DURATION	FREQUENCY
Chinandega (bus)	0.80-1	1½hr	4:30am-8pm, every 20min
Chinandega (microbus)	1.20	50min	4:30am-8pm, departs when full
Estelí	2.70	2½-3hr	6:20am & 3pm
Granada (microbus)	3	2-3hr	hourly
La Paz Centro	0.75	40min	every 45min
Managua (microbus)	2.75	1¼hr	4:30am-7pm, departs when full
Managua (Carr Nueva, via La Paz Centro) expreso	1.80	1¼hr	5am-4pm, hourly
Managua (Carr Vieja, via Puerto Sandino) ordinario	1.50	1¾hr	5am-6:30pm, every 30min
Masaya	2.90	2½hr	hourly
Matagalpa	3	2½hr	4:20am, 7:30am, 2:45pm
Nagarote	1	1hr	hourly
Rota (Cerro Negro)	0.75	2¼hr	5:50am, 11am, 3:30pm
Salinas Grandes	0.80	2hr	5:15am, 8:30am, 11:40am, 1:40pm

Coming from León, the bus stops in Poneloya first, then goes up the coast to Las Peñitas.

If you're headed to Surfing Turtle Lodge (p153), check the website for information about catching the daily shuttle (US$3 one-way) from León.

Las Peñitas

POP UNDER 2000

A wide, sandy stretch of beachfront paradise fronted by a cluster of surfer hostels and boutique hotels, Las Peñitas offers the easiest access to the turtles and mangroves of Reserva Natural Isla Juan Venado. There's also good, if not spectacular, surfing here, with smallish regular waves that are perfect for beginners. Several hotels and hostels offer tours into the reserve, plus surf lessons and board rentals.

Tours

Barca de Oro   TOUR

(☑2317-0275; www.barcadeoro.com; bayfront, frente parada de buses; ⊙7am-10pm) Barca de Oro is a decent **hotel** (dm/s/d US$8/32/40) with a good seafood **restaurant** (7am to 10pm) that serves traditional Nica breakfasts overlooking the fishing bay – but more importantly, for most travelers, it's one-stop shopping for tours and information about Reserva Natural Isla Juan Venado. Stop in to ask about boat tours, bike rentals, nighttime turtle tours and fishing.

Sleeping

★ Mano a Mano Ecohostel   HOSTEL $

(☑7527-5505; https://somosmanoamano.wixsite.com/hostalmanoamano; La curvita, 50m N; dm/ste US$12/60; ✳🛜) 🏄 Everything a stellar hostel should be, Mano a Mano is all breezy

---

GETTING TO THE BEACHES

There's regular bus service between León, Poneloya and Las Peñitas; hostels and surf outfitters in the city also run private shuttles to Las Peñitas that are convenient for travelers. Miramar is reachable by buses from León to Puerto Sandino, El Tránsito is reachable from Managua's Mercado Israel Lewites, while to reach Playa Hermosa, you need your own wheels. NIC-52B that runs parallel to the beaches is mostly unpaved and bumpy, as is NIC-40, the access road to El Tránsito from NIC-12, the León–Managua highway.

---

bamboo dorms and mezzanine loft suites inside a beautiful, sustainably built structure, with seafront chill-out areas and a bar that overlooks the waves. The multi-ethnic, multi-lingual staff make everyone feel at home, point surfers towards the best waves and organize trips. You'll never want to leave.

Nayal Lodge   BOUTIQUE HOTEL $$

(☑5715-0076; www.nayallodge.com; de la Policía, 300m E; ste US$49; ᴾ✳🛜🏊) Consisting of two thatched-roofed adobe towers, this four-room hotel is run by Spanish owner Catalina and her husband, who are happy to share their extensive local knowledge. Each suite is circular, spacious and with a hammock-strung terrace; a pool and massage room are in the works, and breakfast is an excellent Nica spread.

Simple Beach Lodge   GUESTHOUSE $$

(☑7658-2009; www.simplebeachlodge.com; contiguo a Playa Roca; dm US$10, d US$35-55; 🛜) The name says it all, almost. Simple Beach Lodge has just one breezy dorm with individual reading lights and fans, plus seven simple but comfortable private rooms with bamboo accents, some of which are split-level with loft beds; the priciest one has an ocean-facing balcony. It's right on the beach and has a good restaurant.

Bomalu   GUESTHOUSE $$

(☑7532-5546; www.bomalunicaragua.com; Cruce Peñitas–Poneloya, 900m S; r with/without air-con US$25/34; ✳🛜🏊) This mellow beach-house-style spot, located right on the sand, has seven affordable guest rooms (some of which share a few bathrooms). There's a large shady space beneath the trees and the low-key restaurant does a mix of international meat and seafood dishes. The hotel offers transportation to León for US$5 per person.

Lazy Turtle   HOTEL $$

(☑8546-7403; www.thelazyturtlehotel.com; Parada de buses, 30m S; r US$35; ✳🛜) Facing the calm waters of the tidal bay, this relaxed, Canadian-run *hotelito* (little hotel) has four spartan, rather dark rooms with fans and mosquito nets. The onsite restaurant is well known for its Mexican-inspired cuisine (Tuesday is taco night!) and burgers (including a good veggie burger).

Aáki Hotel   BOUTIQUE HOTEL $$$

(☑8988-1867; www.facebook.com/aakihotel; Entrada a las Penitas, 600m SE; d/q US$90/120; ᴾ✳🛜🏊) Las Peñitas' most stylish little ho-

RESERVA NATURAL ISLA JUAN VENADO

This 20km-long, sandy barrier **island** (US$4.50), in some places only 300m wide, has swimming holes and lots of wildlife, including hundreds of migrating bird species, crocodiles, nesting turtles and mosquitoes galore. On one side of the uninhabited island you'll find long, wild, sandy beaches facing the Pacific; on the other, red and black mangroves reflected in emerald lagoons. Las Peñitas ranger station and various accommodations offer guided boat tours (US$55 for up to four people) and kayaking excursions (US$12 per person).

During the turtle egg-laying season, which runs July through January and peaks in September and October, thousands of olive ridleys, careys and leatherbacks lay their eggs in El Vivero, close to the Las Peñitas entrance. For the best wildlife-watching opportunities, it's best to go at low tide, or at dawn or sunset if you're especially interested in birds. If it's turtles you're here to see, try a nighttime turtle tour (US$25 per person, June to December) with guided camping.

You can also go to the reserve yourself if you can negotiate a ride with a local fisher. Another option is to hire a local guide (US$10) – ask at the Las Peñitas ranger station or stop into the hotel-restaurant-tour outfitter Barca de Oro.

tel overlooks a kidney-shaped pool and its own stretch of beach. There are only nine rooms here – spacious, bright, with bamboo accents, and with either terraces or balconies. Excellent breakfast and imaginative, beautifully presented dishes, and a cool, minimalist interior are part of the draw.

✖ Eating

Restaurant SUA

Grill & Chill   INTERNATIONAL **$$**
(☑ 7823-5320; La curvita, 350m N; mains US$5-8; ☺ 7:30am-10pm Mon-Thu, to midnight Fri-Sun; 🗺 🖉)
Dig your toes in the sand, pop open a Toña, and prepare to feast on the likes of Arabic kofta kebabs, tabbouleh, vegetable curry and gnocchi. Some of the dishes from the chef's international repertoire work better than others, but with the waves lapping at the beach in front of you, you probably won't care.

Dulce Mareas   PIZZA **$$**
(☑ 8827-1161; www.facebook.com/dulcemareas; Barca de Oro, 50m S; mains US$4.50-9; ☺ 8am-9pm Wed-Sun; 🖉) It's known for pizzas baked in a clay-brick oven, but this Italian-owned beachfront eatery also does breakfast and lunch – plus coffee, desserts and cold cocktails, all with a view of the water. You can also rent out rooms (double US$45).

★ La Bombora   FUSION **$$$**
(☑ 8662-9554; www.thebomboragroup.com/relax; Frente Cocteles Las Peñitas; mains US$10-17; ☺ 12:30-8pm; 🖩 🗺) Chef Marc has earned La Bombora its share of local followers with his culinary masterpieces, from slow-cooked ribs and brisket to pulled pork sliders and grilled seafood. Don't leave without trying his jalapeño margarita! There are also four snug

rooms (US$60), brightened up with splashes of tropical art, just steps from the sea.

❶ Getting There & Away

Buses (US$0.50) run between Poneloya, Las Peñitas, and León (El Mercadito de Subtiaba) roughly every 40 minutes between 5:20am and 6.40pm. Coming from León, the bus swings through Poneloya first, then heads north to Las Peñitas. The last stop is at the parking lot outside Barca de Oro, but you can also pick it up at a bus stop outside the hotel Playa Roca.

Another option is the daily shuttle between Bigfoot Hostel (p147) in León and Bigfoot Beach Hostel in Las Peñitas.

In a pinch, you can also hire a taxi from León for about US$15 one-way.

Miramar

POP UNDER 5000

Along the coast from this hard-working port town there are some 'Hawaii-sized waves,' the biggest being **Puerto Sandino** at the river mouth – a world-class monster! About 5km south of Puerto Sandino, at the fishing village of Miramar, there's a left point break called **Punta Miramar**, a beach break called **Pipes**, left and right barrels at **Shacks** (when conditions are right) and **La Derechita**, a right-hander. These are some of the most uncrowded waves on the Pacific Coast, frequented by serious surfers.

🛏 Sleeping & Eating

All surf camps have their own restaurants and there are several low-key local joints along the Miramar beach that serve seafood.

★**Vivir Surf & Fish** LODGE **$$$**

(📞 7648-0354; http://vivirsurf.com; s/d/tr US$101/148/195, 3-night package US$495; 🛜) This Aussie-run surf camp gets rave reviews from surfers for owner Lewis's hospitality, the perfect location for hitting the waves (there are five breaks within a few minutes' walk of the camp, plus three advanced breaks accessible by boat), first-rate accommodations and plenty of camaraderie out of the water, fuelled with soccer, baseball and cricket games. There are brand new surfboards for guest use, as well as SUPs and kayaks.

La Barra Surf Camp LODGE **$$$**

(📞 in US 1-310-424-3530; www.astadventures.com; 4-night package from US$750; 🛜🍴) At this popular and professionally run beachfront surf camp, managed by AST Adventures in California, serious surfers book all-inclusive packages that include everything from airport transportation to all meals, bikes, city tours of León, etc. There are large, breezy rooms, a yoga deck and a pool, as well as excellent surfing instructors, delicious home-cooked meals and a welcoming vibe.

Miramar Surfcamp LODGE **$$$**

(📞 8945-1785; www.miramarsurfcamp.com; s/d US$58/81, surfer package s/d incl meals from US$138/184; 🛜🍴) For surfers of all abilities (including beginners), the location of this surf camp – and the friendly staff – are huge draws. Choose between basic air-con rooms or splurge on the digs in the Ocean View Tower. If you're not playing volleyball on the beach in between catching breaks, you can try your hand at skateboarding the half-pipe next to the surf camp.

ℹ️ Getting There & Away

Surf camps offer pickup and drop-off at Managua Airport. There are several buses daily between Puerto Sandino and León (US$0.85, 30 to 40 minutes), but Miramar is 5km south of the Puerto Sandino turnoff along a partially paved, bumpy road. Commandeer a *tuk-tuk* or drive yourself.

El Tránsito

POP UNDER 2000

This little fishing village on the coast between León and Managua sits on a hill slope around a near-perfect crescent bay. There's a strong undertow, but to the south, near the lava flows, there are protected swimming holes. El Tránsito has gained popularity with surfers, since there's something for all abilities here: four consistent year-round beach breaks. Pistols, Pangas and Main are rights and lefts, while the Corner is a left; there's also a hollow left for advanced surfers 40 minutes up the coast, and the swells are particularly powerful April to June.

🛏️ Sleeping & Eating

Free Spirit Hostel HOSTEL **$$**

(📞 5817-8425; http://thefreespirithostel.com; Escuela, 2c N, 1c O, ½c N; dm/d US$25/70, hippie van US$60; ❄️) Right on the beach, this hostel is a little rough around the edges (rooms not always spotless, bathrooms are small), but you're here for the surfing and the yoga, right? There's a nice communal vibe to the meals (price includes breakfast and dinner), vegetarians are welcome, and there are surf lessons available. Three-night minimum.

Solid Surf & Adventure HOTEL **$$**

(📞 8752-4913; www.solidsurfadventure.com; estadio, 100m al oeste; dm/d incl meals US$15/80, resort per person incl meal US$100; 🛜) Solid Surf runs all-inclusive surf and yoga camps, geared towards beginners, as well as a hostel and B&B. The rooms are pretty basic, but there's a cool beachfront patio with hammocks for hanging out, a decent restaurant and bar, and you're miles away from the crowded waves of the southern beaches. Board rental is US$15 per day.

Olas Clandestinas SEAFOOD **$$**

(📞 8116-1348; www.surfeltransito.com/the-restaurant; Escuela, 2c N, 1c O, ½c N; mains US$6-10; 🕐 7am-10pm Mon-Fri, to 11pm Sat & Sun; 🍴) Next door to the Free Spirit Hostel and attached to a surf camp, this popular beach bar and restaurant serves fresh seafood, and pizza from a wood-fired oven.

ℹ️ Getting There & Away

Buses from Managua's Mercado Israel Lewites (p61) leave for El Tránsito at 11:15am, 12:40pm and 2pm daily (US$1.20, 1½ hours), returning at 5am, 6am and 7am. Many travelers drive themselves here. If driving, the partially paved NIC-40 to El Tránsito is bumpy but passable by regular car in dry season.

Volcanoes near León

The Maribios chain is the epicenter of one of the most active volcanic regions on earth. Trekking up these volatile giants rewards you with tremendous views from the top, whether you go up there for sunset or camp overnight to greet the dawn. The easiest and safest way to visit the volcanoes is on a guided hike or excursion, arranged by many outfitters in León and elsewhere.

If you do decide to go to the volcanoes alone, it's a good idea to consult park management first. Marena León manages Reserva Natural Volcán Momotombo, Reserva Natural Telica-Rota and Reserva Natural Pilas-El Hoyo, which includes Cerro Negro; Marena Chinandega (p161) keeps tabs on Reserva Natural San Cristóbal-La Casita and Reserva Natural Volcán Cosigüina.

◎ Sights

Reserva Natural Volcán
Momotombo VOLCANO
(☑ in León 2311-3776) The perfect cone of Volcán Momotombo, destroyer of León Viejo (p146) and inspiration for its own Rubén Darío poem, rises red and black 1280m above Lago de Managua. It is a symbol of Nicaragua, the country's most beautiful threat, and has furnished at its base itself in miniature – the island of Isla Momotombito (389m), sometimes called 'The Child.' Most people come to climb Momotombo, a serious eight-to-10-hour roundtrip. Guided treks make access easier from the power plant at the trailhead.

There are several other structures worth seeing in the reserve, including the 4km-diameter, 200m-deep Caldera Monte Galán, tiled with five little lagoons (alligators included) that reflect the theoretically extinct Cerro Montoso (500m), but you'd need to arrange a custom tour to see them.

Isla Momotombito is accessible from Puerto Momotombo, just around the corner from the ruins of León Viejo, and Mateare, both on the shores of Lago de Managua. The basaltic cone has long been a ceremonial site, and a few petroglyphs and statues are still visible on it. If you're coming from Puerto Momotombo, ask about private boat transportation. Boat operators hang around the handful of lakeshore restaurants, which all serve beer and traditional Nicaraguan food.

Reserva Natural Pilas-El Hoyo VOLCANO
(☑ in León 2311-3776) Most people come to this reserve to see the volcano Cerro Negro (726m and growing), one of the youngest volcanoes in the world. Almost every guide in León offers a guided hike to the top of El Hoyo, a shadeless, two- to three-hour climb into the eye-watering fumes of the yellow-streaked crater, from where you'll shimmy downhill on a volcano board. Af-

terward, relax in the deliciously cool Laguna de Asososca, a jungle-wrapped crater lake (a popular add-on).

Cerro Negro first erupted from a quiet cornfield in 1850, and its pitch-black, loose-gravel cone has been growing in spurts ever since. Other peaks worth climbing include the dormant Volcán Pilas (1001m), which last had gas in 1954; and El Hoyo (1088m), the park's second-most active peak, which is basically a collapsed crater with fumaroles.

Reserva Natural
San Cristóbal-La Casita VOLCANO
(☑ in Chinandega 2344-2443) Eye-catching Volcán San Cristóbal (1745m), the tallest volcano in Nicaragua, streams gray smoke from its smooth cone. Achieving the summit of this beauty is a serious hike: six to eight hours up, three hours down. A guide is highly recommended, as access is difficult and dangerous and requires crossing private property. The volcano is very active, with two large eruptions at the end of 2012.

There are several other volcanic structures worth seeing here, including El Chonco (715m), an inactive volcanic plug contiguous with San Cristóbal, and nearby Moyotepe, a small crater lake at 917m accessible from the Chinandega–Somotillo road.

Reserva Natural Telica-Rota VOLCANO
(☑ in León 2311-3776) This very active, 90.52-sq-km complex peaks at Volcán Telica (1061m), the twin craters of which are a mere 30km north of León. Also called the 'Volcano of León,' Telica is active in four- to five-year cycles; the last really big eruption was in 1765. Most eruptions these days involve gases and a few pyroclastic belches. It's easy to combine the four-hour hike to the impressively smoking crater with visiting the boiling mud of San Jacinto. Camping overnight is popular, too.

There are several 'extinct' cones around the base, including Cerro Agüero (744m), Loma Los Portillos (721m) and Volcán Rota (832m), which has constant fumaroles.

☝ Activities

This area is ground zero for volcano boarding – also called volcano surfing. With professional outfitters and custom-made boards, you can hurtle downhill at exhilarating speeds. A half-day excursion generally includes transportation, equipment and instruction for around US$35 a person – try Tierra Tour (p147) in León.

ⓘ Getting There & Away

Drive yourself or arrange transportation with one of the many outfitters in León that offer organized excursions into the park.

San Jacinto

POP UNDER 2000

The only town of any size on this stretch of the Ring of Fire, tiny San Jacinto, located 24km northeast of León, is base camp for climbs up Volcán Telica (1061m; six to eight hours), Volcán Rota (832m; three to five hours) – which has great views of Telica – and Volcán Santa Clara (834m; three to five hours).

Organized tours (usually operated out of León) typically stop at Los Hervideros de San Jacinto, an expanse of bubbling mud puddles that are likely connected to Volcán Telica. Boiling hot mud spurts up from the steaming holes, making the field an interesting place to walk around. There are no marked trails, so accept the services of the local teenage guides (US$1) who will invariably approach you – they know their way around.

⦿ Sights

Los Hervideros de San Jacinto SPRING
(US$2; ☺7am-6pm) This series of hot springs and mudholes – likely connected to the Telica volcano and sometimes referred to as 'mud fields,' – is a desolate, sulfur-scented place to wander around. Local kids and teenagers will approach you at the small parking lot (US$1) and offer to show you around (about US$1); it's a really good idea to hire one, as there are no marked trails.

ⓘ Getting There & Away

Most volcano-climbers come here on organized tours with included transportation. To get here by public bus, get on any Estelí-, Malpaisillo- or San Isidro-bound bus from León (US$0.80, 40 minutes) and be sure to catch a return bus by mid-afternoon.

El Sauce

POP 10,350

Once a bustling and important link on the national railway, today scenic El Sauce is just a sleepy mountain town cut straight from an Old West movie. The town bursts to life during the third and fourth weeks in January, when thousands of pilgrims from all over Nicaragua, Guatemala and beyond make their way here to pay their respects to El Señor de Esquipulas (the Black Christ).

The image, to which all manner of miracles have been attributed, arrived in El Sauce in 1723 from Esquipulas, Guatemala, and refused to move another centimeter upon arriving at this lovely spot. The beautiful 1853 Iglesia de Nuestro Señor de Esquípulas was declared a national sanctuary in 1984. Part of it was destroyed in a fire in 1999; the Black Christ, however, was saved.

Religious pilgrimage aside, El Sauce allows you to experience country life and to go hiking in the surrounding mountains.

ⓒ Tours

Sauce Aventuras OUTDOORS
(☑2319-2239, 8691-6870; sauceaventura@gmail.com; Parque Central, 1c E) The local cooperative, founded in 2010, runs tours around El Sauce – from cycling around town to overnight excursions to Los Altos de Ocotal that involve an overnight stay with a host family (US$10), with hiking and horseback riding in the mountains arranged. They also organise friendly homestays in El Sauce – a good way of connecting with the locals.

⨍ Sleeping & Eating

There are simple Nicaraguan eateries and street-food stands scattered around the center of town.

Hotel El Viajero HOTEL $
(☑2319-2325; www.facebook.com/restaurantehotelelviajero; Enitel, 1c N, ½c E; s/d with bathroom & air-con US$25/35, without bathroom US$5/10; ❄) On the northeast outskirts of town, this place will do in a pinch. The rooms are pretty beat down (but clean!) and there's a good restaurant attached, serving Nicaraguan standards.

Hotel Blanco HOTEL $$
(☑2319-2403; alcaldía, 1c S, 1c O; s/d with fan US$22/32, s/d with air-con US$28/38; ☏) Some of the best rooms in town are found at this small and friendly family-run hotel. Twelve rooms are set around a central courtyard; all have cable TV, wi-fi and private bathrooms.

ⓘ Getting There & Away

El Sauce is reachable via partially paved NIC-38 that branches off the east-west main NIC-26 highway between León and Estelí. Buses to León (US$2.75, 2½ hours, six daily) leave from El Sauce's market. There are also daily buses to Managua, Estelí, Achuapa and San Juan de Limay.

Chinandega

POP 111,300

Sultry Chinandega is the regional transport hub with a few decent hotels, a clutch of good restaurants, an excellent archaeological museum and several appealing churches. It's not a bad place to bed down for a night or two (splurge on the air-con, since it's hot as the Sahara); you're likely to acquaint yourself with this busy agricultural town if you happen to be heading towards Nicaragua's northwestern beaches or looking to explore the little-visited Volcán Cosigüina.

◎ Sights

★ Museo Enrique B. Mántica   MUSEUM

(🎫 2341-4291; Farallones Hotel, 2c E, Reparto los Angeles; US$5; ⏱ 8am-5pm Mon-Fri) Anyone with even a passing interest in archaeology should stop in here, one of the finest museums in the country. The beautifully displayed collection focuses on pre-Columbian ceramics and is presented in a logical timeline, from the early inhabitants up until the arrival of the Spanish. It's a little tricky to find, signposted off the NIC-24, near Farallones Hotel, amidst workshops where local youth study various trades.

There are about 1500 pieces in the collection, of which about 400 are on display, from polychrome jaguar jars and ceremonial metates to fine gold jewelry. Of particular interest is the small collection on burial rituals, where the guide will no doubt put forward the theory that the flesh of human sacrifices was sometimes eaten as a religious practice.

Parroquia Santa Ana   CHURCH

(frente Parque Central; ⏱ hours vary) This is Chinandega's most important church, with a splendid Stations of the Cross, lots of gilt and some Russian Orthodox styling that have earned it the reputation of 'Best Interior in Town.' A richer yellow with white trim, it stands watch over the festive Parque Central, crammed full of play equipment, canoodling teenagers and street-food stands. There's sometimes ballet *folklorico* and live music in the central kiosk.

Iglesia Guadalupe   CHURCH

(Santuario de Nuestra Señora de Guadalupe; correo, 3½c S; ⏱ hours vary) Chinandega has some seriously striking churches, including the 1878 Iglesia Guadalupe, which despite the radiant – and rather grandiose – colonial-style facade has a simple, precious wood interior with an exceptionally lovely Virgin.

Iglesia El Calvario   CHURCH

(Mercado, 2c NO; ⏱ hours vary) Features an art deco exterior, a nice bell tower, a simple interior hung with chandeliers and a beautiful blue-and-white tiled ceiling.

Iglesia San Antonio   CHURCH

(Parque Central, 2c S, 1c O; ⏱ hours vary) This dramatic facade is painted pastel-yellow; inside, find delightful Easter egg–blue and yellow columns and arches.

🛏 Sleeping

Hotel Casa Real   HOTEL $$

(🎫 2341-7047; Parque Central, 2c S, ½c E; s/d US$30/40; ❅ 🛜) A couple of blocks south of Parque Central, this is the nicest hotel in this part of town. Think spotless rooms, friendly management, and a belly-filling Nica breakfast thrown in to boot.

Hotel San José   HOTEL $$

(🎫 2341-2723; esquina de los bancos, 2½c N; s/d US$30/41; ❅ 🛜) Heavy, dark-wood furniture and an overload of religious-themed decoration give this place a somewhat somber feel, but the rooms are spacious, with big TVs.

Hotel Los Balcones
de Chinandega   HOTEL $$$

(🎫 2341-8994; www.hotelbalconeschinandega. com; esquina de los bancos, 1c N; s/d US$41/53; 🅿 ❅ 🛜) This colonial-style hotel is one of the nicer places to stay in Chinandega, with colorful splashes of tropical art in the simple, tiled rooms. There are, in fact, balconies, but you may choose to spend your time on the tiny roof terrace instead.

Hotel Plaza Cosigüina   HOTEL $$$

(🎫 2341-3636; www.hotelplazacosiguina.com; esquina de los bancos, ½c S; s/d US$41/53; 🅿 ❅ 🛜) The hodgepodge blend of modern, motel-like styling with hip 1960s accents may not win it any design awards, but the comfort factor is here, along with rather garish bedcovers – and the location is a winner.

🍴 Eating & Drinking

★ Fritanga Las Tejitas   NICARAGUAN $

(Mercado, 2c E; mains US$2-5; ⏱ 8am-9pm) A local institution, this *fritanga* gets packed breakfast, lunch and dinner – and mariachis could show up at any time to play some music. It's a solid buffet with a nationwide reputation and an excellent place to try traditional Nica food.

Chinandega

Chinandega

Palí SUPERMARKET $
(frente Parque Central; ⊗9am-8pm) A supermarket stop for the basics.

La Parrillada NICARAGUAN $$
(Palí, 1c S; set lunch US$3, mains US$4-8; ⊗noon-9pm) This locals' favorite is part steakhouse, part pizzeria, part *fritanga*. Order a slab of meat or help yourself to inexpensive buffet offerings; if you can't find something you want to eat here, chances are you're not hungry.

Hong Kong CHINESE $$
(☑2340-1998; Calle Central, Parque Central, 8½c E; mains US$7-10; ⊗10am-9:30pm; ✳☑) The best of Chinandega's two Chinese restaurants, Hong Kong is a pleasant change from Nica standards. Expect Cantonese-style dishes,

such as shrimp with vegetables and oyster sauce, sweet and sour chicken, braised sea cucumber, and the tasty yet baffling shrimp in 'Chinese' sauce. Cavernous interior, good service, heaped portions.

More Than Coffee COFFEE
(☑2346-8131; Av Rubén Darío, entre Calle Central & Calle S 1; ⊗7:30am-8pm Mon-Fri, 8am-8pm Sat; 🛜) A refreshingly frosty escape from Chinandega heat, this hip coffee shop serves a full range of hot and cold caffeinated beverages, as well as sweet and savoury waffles and burgers.

❶ Information

BAC (Parque Central, 1c E, ½c S)
Banco Lafisse (Parque Central, 2c E)

Intur (☑ 2341-1935; chinandega@intur.gob. ni; Mercado, 1c O, 1½c S; ⊙ 8am-5pm Mon-Fri) Lots of local recommendations in information-packed scrapbooks.

Marena (Ministry of the Environment & Natural Resources; ☑ 2344-2443; www.marena.gob. ni; Iglesia Guadalupe, 1½c O; ⊙ 9am-4:30pm Mon-Fri) Government office with info on Reserva Natural San Cristóbal–La Casita, Reserva Natural Volcán Cosigüina and Reserva Natural Estero Padre Ramos, all with reasonable access; and Reserva Natural Delta del Estero Real, where you're on your own.

❶ Getting There & Away

BUS

Most travelers make their connections through **Mercado Bisne** (Calle Central), on the south side of the city (it's best to take a cab to and from here, as it's not within easy walking distance of downtown), though some buses leave from the smaller station known as **Mercadito** (Parque Central, 1½c N). To take a comfortable Tica Bus to Honduras or El Salvador, you have to double back to Managua, since Tica Bus services don't stop in Chinandega.

Bus Services from Mercadito

El Viejo (bus US$0.80, 20 minutes, 5am to 6pm, every 15 minutes; microbus US$0.60, 10 minutes, 5am to 6pm, departs when full)

Playa Aserradores (US$1, 1½ hours, daily at 12:30pm)

Playa Jiquilillo & Reserva Natural Estero Padre Ramos (US$1-1.20, 1½-two hours, at 6:45am, 9:45am, 11:15am, 2:45pm and 4:15pm)

Potosí (Reserva Natural Volcán Cosigüina) (US$1.50-1.75, 3½ hours, three daily)

TAXI

Taxis also make the runs to El Viejo (US$3 to US$5) and Corinto (US$6 to US$8).

Around Chinandega

We'll be frank with you: there are only two things in Chinandega's immediate environs that warrant attention from travelers. There's a beautiful colonial church in the ancient indigenous capital of El Viejo (of particular interest to pilgrims!), whereas Chichigalpa attracts pilgrimages of a different kind: dedicated imbibers of rum come to the famous Flor de Caña rum factory to learn the tipple's secrets.

North of El Viejo, and totally off the beaten track, you'll find the Reserva Natural Delta del Estero Real, a remote birdwatcher's paradise, while the main highway, NIC-24, snakes northeast from Chinandega, traversing wide open spaces en route to Somotillo, the last town before the border between Nicaragua and Honduras.

❍ Sights

Reserva Natural Delta del Estero Real   NATURE RESERVE
(☑ Asociación Selva 8884-9156) There's no tourist infrastructure at all for this enormous reserve, about 20km – two hours by bus by bumpy road – north of Chinandega in the desperately poor town of Puerto Morazán. But this monumental river delta luxuriating along the Honduran border is beautiful, with alligators lounging alongside the lush, mangrove-lined shores, views to Volcán Cosigüina and natural lagoons all aflutter with migratory birds. Unfortunately, it is also threatened: its inaccessibility has emboldened poachers, loggers and dirty shrimping operations.

To visit, head out early for a day trip to Puerto Morazán; several buses leave daily from the Chinandega Mercadito (US$1, two

BUS SERVICES FROM MERCADO BISNE, CHINANDEGA

DESTINATION	COST (US$)	DURATION (HR)	FREQUENCY
Chichigalpa (microbus)	0.30	15min	5am-6pm, departs when full
Corinto (bus)	0.50-0.60	40min	4:30am-6pm, every 15min
Corinto (microbus)	0.75	25min	4:30am-7pm, departs when full
El Guasaule (Honduran border; bus)	1.70	1¾	4am-5pm, every 25min
El Guasaule (Honduran border; microbus)	2	1	4:30am-7pm, departs when full
León (bus)	0.80	1½	4am-7pm, every 15 min
León (microbus)	1.20	1	4:30am-7pm, departs when full
Managua (bus)	2.70	3	4am-5:20pm, hourly
Managua (microbus)	3	2	4:30am-7pm, departs when full

hours), or else you can arrange a taxi ride. Fishing boats holding four, plus your Spanish-speaking guide, cost about US$25 for a four-hour tour of the reserve.

There are no accommodations here (not that you'd want to stay in Puerto Morazán anyway), so you'll have to sleep in Chinandega and bring your own food and water from town.

ⓘ Getting There & Away

Frequent minibuses run from Chinandega's Mercadito (p161) to Chichigalpa and El Viejo. Also from the Mercadito, there are several daily minibuses to Puerto Morazán (for the Reserva Natural Delta del Estero Real).

While frequent buses connect Chinandega with the Honduran border, to travel to destinations in Honduras proper you need to either have your own wheels (and the right paperwork) or else take a Tica Bus or a tourist shuttle from León.

El Viejo

POP 49,452

Just 5km from Chinandega is the ancient indigenous capital of Tezoatega, today called El Viejo. Its church is home of Nicaragua's patron saint and the venue for the country's biggest national religious event, La Gritería, attended by thousands of pilgrims. If you're not a pilgrim, the church is worth a quick peek if you happen to be passing through.

⊙ Sights

Basílica de Nuestra Señora de la Inmaculada Concepción de la Virgen María   CHURCH

(costado este del Parque Central; ⊙ hours vary) This beautiful church is home to Nicaragua's patron saint and mistress of its biggest national religious event, **La Gritería**, when troupes of *festejeros* shout *¿Quién causa tanta alegría?* ('Who causes so much joy?')

and receive the response, *¡La concepción de María!* ('The conception of Mary!').

Dedicated pilgrims show up a few days early for the **Lavada de la Plata** (Polishing of the Silver) on December 5 and 6. The work is meditative but fun, with mariachis serenading the faithful.

ⓘ Getting There & Away

All buses headed north from Chinandega to Potosí or the Cosigüina beaches stop at the El Viejo *empalme* (junction) about 20 minutes after leaving Chinandega.

To Chinandega, you can get buses and minivans (US$0.60 to US$0.80, 10 to 20 minutes, every 15 minutes) from in front of the basilica. A taxi to Chinandega costs US$3 to US$5.

Drivers: note that this is the last chance for gas on the peninsula if you're heading north.

Chichigalpa

POP 42,000

Chichigalpa, Nicaragua's cutest-named town, is best known as the source of **Flor de Caña rum**, made in seven beloved shades, from crystal clear to deepest amber. It's also home to **Ingenio San Antonio**, the country's largest sugar refinery, fed by the cane fields that carpet the skirts of **Volcán San Cristóbal**, which rises from the lowlands just 15km from the city center. Both the sugar refinery and the Flor de Caña distillery belong to the affluent Pellas family that has been producing rum from 1890 onwards, with a short break during the revolution. The rum factory, hosting several popular tours daily, is Chichigalpa's sole attraction.

⊙ Sights

★**Flor de Caña**   DISTILLERY

(☑ 8966-8200; www.tourflordecana.com; Carretera a Chinadenga Km 120; US$10; ⊙ 9am, 11am & 3pm Tue-Sun) Flor de Caña rum is among

---

TO SOMOTILLO & EL GUASAULE

It's a smooth, paved 80km from Chinandega through mostly empty grazing land to the border town of Somotillo, though you will see signs for **Reserva Genetica Apacunaca** (Apacunaca Genetic Resource Reserve). There's almost no tourist infrastructure, which is sort of the point. It protects one of four known caches of teosinte (wild corn) in the world, only discovered here in the late 1990s.

If you're not deeply interested in corn, then there's little reason to come here, unless you're crossing the border into Honduras. Numerous buses run from Chinandega's Mercado Bisne to the border via Somotillo between 4am and 7pm (US$1.70-2, 1-1¾ hours), but none cross the border. If you're heading into Honduras, you're better off taking a Tica Bus or a cross-border shuttle from León.

CORINTO

Nicaragua's only deep-water port was originally a much older town, Puerto El Realejo; founded in 1522, it was subsequently attacked by such famous pirates as William Dampier and John Davis. As time passed and sand filled in the estuary, the barrier island of Punto Icaco became the port, where Corinto was founded in 1858.

This was where US president Ronald Reagan mined in 1983, after which Congress passed a law specifically forbidding the use of taxpayer dollars for overthrowing the Nicaraguan government. Thus began the Iran-Contra affair.

Corinto's 19th-century wooden row houses, narrow streets and halfway decent beaches score high on the 'adorability potential' scale, although actual adorability ratings are much lower. It's a bit sad: although some 65% of the nation's imports and exports flow through, very little of the money stays here. Cruise ships arrive throughout the year, but passengers are whisked away to more scenic spots. If you happen to pass through around lunchtime, go for seafood and water views at **Restaurante El Espigón** (☑2340-6248; www.facebook.com/elespigonrestaurante; de la Escuela Jose Schendel, 3c O, 1c N, Barrio los Pescadores; mains US$4-9; ☉11am-9pm)—it's *the* place to eat in Corinto.

Buses (US$0.60, 40 minutes) and microbuses (US$0.80, 25 minutes) leave regularly for Chinandega, 19km away, from the bus terminal just outside of town. If you're arriving in Corinto by bus, you can catch a ride from the terminal to the plaza or port in a pedicab (US$0.60 per person).

the world's finest and it has been produced in Chichigalpa since the distillery's founding in 1890. Visitors are initiated into the mysteries of rum production during 1½-hour-long tours, with the guides delving into the distillery's history and showing you every stage of the process that turns raw sugarcane into fine golden liquid. The grand finale? A tasting of two fine aged tipples: Rum Centenario 18 and Gran Reserva 7, of course!

If you are really serious about your rum, you can take the private VIP tour (US$100) that involves tasting every single rum that Flor de Caña produces, plus you get to take home a personalized bottle of Flor de Caña 18.

❶ Getting There & Away

Microbuses to Chinandega (US$0.30, 15 minutes) depart from the market when full, 5am to 6pm.

Cosigüina Peninsula Beaches

The Cosigüina peninsula is well on its way to becoming an island, worn away on two sides by brilliant estuaries and fringed with sandy beaches, ranging from the pearl-grays of Jiquilillo to coal-black at Playa Carbón.

Playa Aserradores and Playa Jiquilillo are both quiet fishing villages that are firmly on the surfing circuit, while the Reserva Natural Estero Padre Ramos is a vast mangrove wetland, ideal for kayaking and birdwatching, and an important breeding ground for sea turtles.

Playa Aserradores

This long, smooth stretch of sand has excellent surfing: the main attraction here is a world-class wave, El Boom – a fast, hollow beach break for experienced wave shredders only. At nearby Aposentillo there are some nice longboard swells, and waves suitable for beginners as well. Aposentillo is a quiet, spread-out village with killer sunsets and a laid-back vibe that's now missing from surfing destinations further south. Surf is best from March to October.

🛏 Sleeping

Las Dunas Surf Resort   GUESTHOUSE **$$**
(☑8476-5211; www.lasdunassurfresort.com; Santa Maria del Mar 11; dm/casita US$15/60; ❄ 🛜) With a clutch of pastel-colored, thatched-roofed *casitas* clustered around the pool, plus a breezy restaurant with attendant playful felines, this is one of the better budget options in Aserradores. You're a 10-minute walk from the waves, too.

★**ThunderBomb Surf Camp**   LODGE **$$$**
(☑8478-0070; https://thunderbombsurf.com; Santa María del Mar; 7-day surf package per person from US$1099; ❄ 🛜) Run by Bostonian Jonathan, this excellent surf camp is all

about hitting the A-frames, pipes and barrels up and down the coast. There are several excellent waves right on your doorstep, and the surf guides whisk guests off in 4x4 and boats in pursuit of the best breaks. Spacious tiled rooms, international food, yoga classes and massages seal the deal.

★ **Coco Loco Eco Resort** RESORT $$$
(☑5797-4244; www.cocolocoecoresort.com; El Manzano 1, Aposentillo; 7-day surf packages per person from US$1245; ☉Mar-Oct; ❈🛜) ⫸ There are only two things to do in this wonderfully tranquil spot: hit the waves and do yoga. Guests are lodged in airy cabins made from sustainable local materials; delicious and nutritious meals are served communal-style to encourage mingling, and surfers are taken daily to the best spots, with post-surfing massages to relax those tired muscles.

Rise Up Surf Tours LODGE $$$
(☑7545-3386; www.riseupsurf.com; Punta Aposentillo; 7-day surf package per person from US$1350; ❈) Steps away from the waves, Rise Up Surf was the brainchild of the former owner of Bigfoot Hostel in León, and he's managed to bring the backpacker institution's popularity to this surf camp. There are surf and yoga packages for rookie surfers and intermediates, terrific food and a great vibe – the instructors take real pleasure in your progress.

Chancletas Beach Resort RESORT $$$
(☑8868-5036; www.hotelchancletas.com; Playa Asseradores; tr with/without bathroom US$110/45, 3-person cottage from US$110; 🅿❈🛜) Perched up on a grassy hillside overlooking Aserradores' famous break, this relaxed spot, run by Miami native Shay, has more to offer than just surfing. You can hit the waves, or hop on an SUP, go kayaking, deep-sea fishing or horseback riding. Bed down in a fan-cooled room with shared facilities, fancier en suite, or rent one of several cottages.

Marina Puesta del Sol RESORT $$$
(☑8880-0019; www.marinapuestadelsol.com; Playa Aserradores; s/d from US$198/225; 🅿❈🛜🌊) A very upmarket yacht club, attracting well-heeled Managuans and offering great views of smoking San Cristóbal from the infinity pool – and even better ones from the enormous, fully equipped rooms and suites. There's a lovely private beach, too, and a nice *restaurant* by the water (open to the public) but the place sometimes feels almost deserted.

✗ Eating

★ **Al Cielo Hotel & Restaurante** FUSION $$$
(☑8993-4840; http://alcielonicaragua.com; El Manzano 2; mains US$8-17; ☉7am-10pm; 🛜) It's well worth making the trek to this excellent French-Italian fusion restaurant on top of a hill, with excellent sea views to complement your rum infusion aperitif. There are *cabañas* too, in case you decide to linger (s/d from US$15/25) and the French owners arrange all manner of excursions.

Pasta La Vista ITALIAN $$$
(☑8275-0035; Azul, Santa María del Mar; mains US$8-17; ☉11am-9pm Mon-Fri, 9am-9pm Sat & Sun; 🛜⫸) A change from surfing resort fare, this Italian restaurant at the entrance to the village serves great pasta dishes and *ceviche* in a green, outdoorsy setting; there's even a pool for guest use. Everything is made from scratch, so settle in and prepare for a leisurely meal.

❶ Getting There & Away

During dry season, the NIC-264 access road is passable in a regular car, but otherwise you'll want a 4WD vehicle for the bumpy ride from the well-signed exit off the Chinandega–Potosí Hwy.

There is only one daily bus from Chinandega to Aserradores, departing from Chinandega's Mercadito (p161) at 12:30pm (US$1, 1½ hours) and returning at 5am. Hotels and surf camps offer private transport for around US$90 for one or two people.

Playa Jiquilillo

POP UNDER 500

This endless pale-gray beach frames what you thought existed only in tales that begin 'You should have seen it back when I was first here...' The spread-out fishing village fronts a dramatic rocky point, where tide pools reflect the reds and golds of a huge setting sun, Cosigüina's ragged bulk rising hazy and post-apocalyptic to the north.

The region remains largely undeveloped, despite its beauty and accessibility, and it's a place to surf, enjoy the tranquility and hang out with locals, to whom non-locals are still a novelty.

🛏 Sleeping & Eating

The guesthouses here all have restaurants, and there are several village eateries both in Jiquilillo and nearby Padre Ramos.

Rancho Tranquilo HOSTEL $

(☎8968-2290; www.ranchotranquilo.wordpress.com; Los Zorros, Playa Jiquilillo; dm/s/d US$7/20/22; 📶) Run by a friendly family, this collection of bungalows and a small dorm on its private stretch of beach is a great budget choice. There's a cool bar and common area, and vegetarian dinners (US$2 to US$4.50) are served family-style. Kayaking in the mangroves and surfing lessons arranged. Check online for information on the area's turtle rescue program.

Rancho Esperanza GUESTHOUSE $$

(☎8680-0270; www.rancho-esperanza.com; Playa Jiquilillo; dm US$8, 2-person cabañas with/without bathroom US$35/25) This quiet and eco-friendly collection of simple, breezy bamboo huts – which are scattered across a grassy field just slightly removed from the beach – offers volunteer opportunities in community projects related to education and environmental issues. There's also a small library of English-language books and a good breakfast (served all day).

Monty's Surf Camp LODGE $$$

(☎8473-3255; www.montysbeachlodge.com; Playa Jiquilillo; dm/d US$35/66; 📶🏊) This midrange surf camp is set right on the waterfront. Rooms are fan-cooled and the beds draped with mosquito nets. Most travelers come here on week-long packages (per person s/d/tr US$700/600/500) that include all meals, but it's entirely possible to just come for a few days, hang by the pool and watch the sunset from a hammock.

Getting There & Away

Buses to Chinandega (US$1, 1½ hours, five daily) come and go roughly between 7am and 4:30pm. Some lodgings can arrange transport if contacted in advance. NIC-58 that runs to Jiquilillo from the main NIC-12 highway is unpaved but in good condition.

Reserva Natural Estero Padre Ramos

POP UNDER 500

Less than 2km north of Playa Jiquilillo is the community of Padre Ramos, a tiny, sleepy fishing village inside the federally protected wetlands of Reserva Natural Estero Padre Ramos. The river delta is part of the largest remaining mangrove forests in Central America, and is key in the proposed **Reserva Biologica Golfo de Fonseca** (Gulf of Fonseca Biological Corridor), a wetlands conservation agreement between Nicaragua, Honduras and El Salvador.

Locals can arrange boat, kayak and birding tours of the mangroves for around US$10 to US$40 per person. Sea turtles lay their eggs here between July and December, peaking in October and November (contact Rancho Tranquilo about the turtle protection program).

WORTH A TRIP

REDWOOD BEACH RESORT

Across the estuary from Padre Ramos, in the fishing village of Mechapa, this cozy little US-owned **resort** (☎8996-0328; www.redwoodbeachresort.com; 100 Beach Way, Las Cabanas, Mechapa; r US$69-139; P❄📶) is shaded by coconut trees right on the beach. Accommodations are in airy cabins and bungalows, each with balcony or terrace overlooking the waves. Come either by three-hour bus ride from Chinandega (one daily), or pre-arranged hotel pickup from Jiquilillo or Padre Ramos.

The restaurant is for guests only, though the Tiki Bar is open to daytime visitors between 10am and 4pm. Activities here include kayak tours of the Mechapa and Padre Ramos estuaries, surfing (beach breaks only), fishing, Cosigüina treks and horseback riding.

Adventurous souls can get here by launch from Playa Jiquilillo; just talk to the local fishers.

Tours

Ibis Exchange KAYAKING

(☎8961-8548; http://ibiskayaking.com; Padre Ramos; day tours per person US$40) Based in Padre Ramos, this excellent operator offers day tours and multiday camping and kayaking tours (2 days, 1 night US$150 per person) of the wetland reserve, as well as multiday tours of the Pacific Coast and Volcán Consigüina climbs. These guys have an organic orchard, composting toilets and solar panels. Contact them in advance.

Sleeping

Finca Ecológica Trinchera FARMSTAY $

(☎8382-8560; www.facebook.com/fincatrinchera; Padre Ramos; hammock US$5, r per person without bathroom US$12) Don't want to be on the beach? This inland option on a 2-hectare fruit farm has plenty of hammocks to spread

🛈 POTOSÍ

This small fishing village is the main base for hiking up Volcán Consigüina and a gateway to El Salvador; regular boat services mean that you can hit El Salvador's beaches while avoiding the lengthy detour overland.

Potosí is 74km northwest of Chinandega. There are up to six buses daily between Chinandega and Potosí (US$1.50 to US$1.75, three hours). If you're driving, it's 59km along the beautifully paved Ruta 12, then 15km from the turnoff to the village, the first 12km unpaved and seriously bumpy, though passable by regular car outside wet season.

out, and helps to arrange kayaking tours in the reserve. It's clean and friendly.

🛈 Getting There & Away

Buses from Chinandega's Mercadito (p161) run to Padre Ramos via Playa Jiquilillo (US$1, 1½-2 hours, 6:45am, 9:45am, 11:15am, 2:45pm and 4:15pm). Some lodgings in nearby Playa Jiquilillo can arrange transport if contacted in advance. NIC-58 to Jiquilillo from the main NIC-12 highway is unpaved; the last 2km to Padre Ramos is sandy. In Padre Ramos, take the estuary road rather than the beach road, or risk getting stuck in sand.

Reserva Natural Volcán Cosigüina

It was once the tallest volcano in Central America, perhaps more than 3000m high, but all that changed on January 20, 1835. In what's considered the Americas' most violent eruption since colonization, this hot-blooded peninsular volcano blew off half its height in a single blast that paved the oceans with pumice, left three countries in stifling darkness for days and scattered ash from Mexico to Colombia. What re-

mains today of Volcán Cosigüina reclines, as if spent, the broad and jagged 872m heart of the peninsula.

Beyond all that lies the Golfo de Fonseca, bordered by the largest mangrove stand left in the Americas. In the other direction, around the volcano's back, Punta Ñata overlooks cliffs that plunge 250m into the sea; beyond lie the Farallones del Consigüina (also known as the Islotes Consigüina), a series of volcanic islets. There are many black-sand beaches around here for DIY exploration.

🏃 Activities

It's a very manageable (if blisteringly hot) climb (five hours roundtrip) up one of two trails to the top: Sendero La Guacamaya, which starts at the ranger's station near El Rosario; and Sendero el Jovo, which descends to more developed Potosí. Trails are difficult to follow, so having a local guide is a good idea. The rare dry tropical forest, home to one of the continent's last sustainable populations of huge red macaws, as well as pumas, spider monkeys and plenty of *pizotes* (coatis), loses its leaves by January. Some León-based operators run organized tours lasting between two and three days, but you can also do a day trip with Ramsar Lodge in La Piscina or with Ibis Exchange (p165) in Padre Ramos.

Sore muscles? Head to the hot springs. In the tiny village of La Piscina, 7km south of Potosí, Ramsar Lodge (☑2344-2381, 8997-8572; www.ecodetur.com; La Piscina; ☺8am-6pm) offers hot springs with shade and food service.

🛈 Getting There & Away

There are up to six buses daily between Chinandega and Potosí via La Piscina (US$1.50 to US$1.75, 3½ hours) that pick up and drop off close to the reserve's entrance. If you're driving, it's 59km along the paved NIC-12 from Chinandega, then 15km from the turnoff to Potosí, the first 12km unpaved and seriously bumpy; 4WD necessary outside dry season.

Northern Highlands

Best Places to Eat

➡ Lunaflor (p196)

➡ Finca a su Mesa (p174)

➡ Libertalia (p189)

➡ Jikao Cafe (p189)

➡ El Pullazo (p196)

Best Places to Stay

➡ La Bastilla Ecolodge (p191)

➡ Montebrisa (p196)

➡ Finca Esperanza Verde (p199)

➡ Maria's B&B (p196)

➡ Hotel Casa Vínculos (p171)

Why Go?

Nicaragua's Northern Highlands are off the typical backpacker route through the country, but nobody with an interest in coffee, cigars and wonderful scenery should miss them. Here colorful quetzals nest in misty cloud forests, and Nicaragua's best coffee and tobacco are cultivated with both capitalist zeal and collective spirit. With a little time and commitment you'll get pounded by waterfalls; explore Somoto's canyon; and pay tribute to the pirates, colonists, revolutionaries, artists and poets who were inspired by these fertile mountains and mingled with the open-hearted people who've lived here for generations.

On either end of the region are its two largest cities: hardworking Estelí buzzes with students, farmers and cigar moguls, while Matagalpa is slightly hipper – and better funded, thanks to nearly a century of successful coffee cultivation. All around and in between are granite peaks and lush valleys dotted with dozens of small towns and their friendly inhabitants.

When to Go

➡ The northern highlands' stunning landscapes are at their best from May to October, when the wet season brings out vibrant shades of green and the many waterfalls are at their best.

➡ If you plan on hiking, consider visiting from November to February, when the weather is fairly dry – yet mild – and the scenery is still lush. This is also the height of the coffee harvest.

➡ The region's other cash crop, tobacco, is harvested from March to April; cigar fans visiting then can follow the leaves from the fields to the rolling tables. However, the countryside is parched at this time of year, with cracked soil and brown leaves.

Northern Highlands Highlights

1 Reserva Natural Cerro Datanlí-El Diablo (p191) Picking coffee beans beneath the towering cloud forest and seeing how locals live and work.

2 Cañon de Somoto (p179) Scrambling, swimming and floating along this magnificent gorge.

3 Área Protegida Miraflor (p175) Riding horses through delightful countryside to secluded swimming holes.

4 Jalapa (p184) Soaking in piping-hot thermal waters surrounded by wonderful mountain scenery.

5 Jinotega (p187) Scrambling up Cerro La Cruz for breathtaking mountain views, then heading back to town for delicious local coffee.

6 Matagalpa (p192) Absorbing the atmosphere in the Northern Highlands' most urbane city.

7 Reserva Natural Macizos de Peñas Blancas (p200) Rappelling down spectacular waterfalls shrouded in old-growth forest.

8 Lago de Apanás (p192) Cruising the high-altitude waters with local fisherfolk and enjoying a good fish lunch.

History

Originally home to Náhuatl refugees from the Aztec empire, the northern highlands were off the radar until gold was discovered here in 1850, attracting an influx of Spanish, mestizos (persons of mixed ancestry; usually Spanish and indigenous people) and the first wave of German immigrants to Matagalpa. The Europeans married local, planted the region's first coffee bushes, and then sold their berries in Berlin.

When the revolution bloomed in 1977, many of the region's impoverished farmers became armed Sandinistas. Some of the heaviest fighting took place in the mountains in and around Jinotega. When the Frente Sandinista de Liberación Nacional (Sandinista National Liberation Front; FSLN) seized power, they made the area a priority, nationalizing and redistributing much of the highlands' arable land into community farming cooperatives. Some have since been divided up among the cooperative members, but the spirit of collective farming remains strong throughout the region, and support for Ortega in the region is steadfast, despite protestors being killed here during the 2018 anti-government protests.

ⓘ Getting There & Away

Bus connections in the region are excellent, and both transportation hubs, Estelí and Matagalpa, are around 2½ hours by bus from Mercado Mayoreo in Managua.

Road conditions can go from bad to worse in the backcountry, especially in the rainy season. Before traversing the dirt roads in a rental car make sure to check road conditions with reliable locals, and consider splurging for the 4WD.

There are two Honduras border crossings: mellow El Espino, close to Somoto; and busy Las Manos, just north of Ocotal.

Estelí

POP 125,000 / ELEV 844M

Estelí has a multifaceted soul: it's both a university town with a large number of progressive students and the main center of commerce for the rural farming communities that surround it. On weekdays you can wake up with sunrise yoga before Spanish class; on Saturday you can mingle with farmers at the massive produce market, then see them again at midnight, dancing like mad in a *ranchero* bar.

Set on the Panamericana close to the Honduran border, Estelí was a strategic gateway that saw heavy fighting and helped turn the revolution and, later, the Contra War. It's no surprise, then, that Estelí has remained one of the Sandinistas' strongest support bases. While it's not a particularly attractive place, its character and easy access to the surrounding mountains make it a popular place for backpackers to base themselves.

◉ Sights

★ Galería de Héroes y Mártires   MUSEUM
(☑8419-3519, 2714-0942; http://galleryofheroesand martyrs.blogspot.com; Av 1a NE & Calle Transversal; by donation; ⊙9:30am-4pm Tue-Fri) Be sure to stop by this moving gallery devoted to fallen revolutionaries, with displays of faded photos, clothes and weaponry. Check out the exhibit (with English signage) on Leonel Rugama, the warrior-poet whose last line was his best. When he and Carlos Fonseca were surrounded by 300 Guardia Nacional troops supported by tanks and planes, they were told to surrender. 'Surrender, your mother!' he famously replied, proving that a 'your mother' retort is always solid. Opening hours are irregular.

Murals   PUBLIC ART
You'll still see some murals around the streets of Estelí, and although many of the original revolutionary pieces have been lost to development, there are also new works that keep the tradition alive. Many of the modern pieces were painted by children through the Funarte program.

Catedral   CHURCH
(Parque Central) The 1823 cathedral has a wonderful facade and is worth a wander. A number of interesting murals can be seen in the surrounding blocks, although most of the original revolutionary works have long disappeared.

Casa de Cultura
Leonel Rugama   NOTABLE BUILDING
(☑2713-3021; cnr Av 1a NE & Calle Transversal; ⊙8am-8pm) In the bullet-hole-marked former home of a high-ranking Somoza official, the Casa de Cultura offers a range of art, dance and music classes to locals (even as the building seemingly falls apart around them).

⮞ Courses

CENAC Spanish School   LANGUAGE
(☑2713-5437; www.spanishschoolcenac.com; Panamericana, btwn Calles 5a SE & 6a SE; per week with/without homestay US$195/120) Professionally run Spanish school with classes for all levels.

Ananda Yoga HEALTH & WELLBEING

(cnr Ave 1a NE & Calle Transversal; per class US$1; ☺6am & 5pm Mon-Fri, 6:40pm Mon-Tue & Thu-Fri) Yoga classes are offered in Spanish here.

Tours

★Tree Huggers CULTURAL

(☑8405-8919, 8496-7449; www.treehuggers.cafe-luzyluna.org; cnr Av 2a NE & Calle 3a NE; ☺8am-9pm) ✐ This friendly and vibrant tour office is the local specialist for trips to Miraflor and Tisey, but also offers other interesting community tourism trips throughout the region, including Cañon de Somoto and a great-value cigar tour (US$10, including a US$2 donation per person). Friendly staff dispense a wealth of impartial information for independent travelers, and profits support excellent local social projects.

★La Gran Fabrica Drew Estate TOURS

(www.cigarsafari.com; Barrio Oscar Gamez 2) Estelí's most innovative cigar company offers all-inclusive, multiday 'Cigar Safari' tours aimed at serious cigar enthusiasts. These are upmarket tours that include superb dining options and a totally immersive cultural experience aimed at the North American cigar aficionado market.

Leo Flores CIGAR TOUR

(☑8754-5959, 5872-2357; leoafl@yahoo.es) Leo Flores of Puro Norte Tours is a specialist cigar guide who can organize access to a variety of factories and also get you out into the tobacco plantations. Contact him for information about his high-quality, expert-led tours, which can be done in English with an interpreter from Leo's team.

Tabacalera Cubanica CIGAR TOUR

(☑2713-2383; cnr Panamericana & Calle 7a SE) This pioneering factory produces Padrón cigars, Nicaragua's most prestigious (and costly) brand.

Festivals & Events

Virgen del Carmen RELIGIOUS

(☺Jul 16) *Fiestas patronales* (patron saint festival) with fireworks, fiestas and Masses.

Virgen de Rosario RELIGIOUS

(☺Oct 7) An annual event since 1521, this was originally celebrated in Villa de San Antonio Pavía de Estelí and moved here with the Virgin in the late 1600s. The festivities involve the image of the virgin, who is prayed to for a week, dressed in a new outfit and then paraded through the streets, visiting various parishes in the city.

Sleeping

Iguana Hostel HOSTEL $

(☑5704-5748; www.facebook.com/jairoaiguanas; Av Central, Calle Transversal, 75m S; s/d US$10/11; ☎) Cheap and cheerful, the Iguana has a central location and everything budget travelers need: spacious rooms, a guest kitchen and hammocks in the courtyard, though sadly there are no dorms. The whole place is charmingly painted and staff are super-friendly.

★Hotel Casa Vínculos HOTEL $$

(☑2713-2044; www.casavinculos.com; Almacén Sony, 1c 1/2 al Oeste; s/d incl breakfast US$31/50; ☎) ✐ This excellent hotel is a real find. It offers eight rooms over two floors surrounding a small tree-filled courtyard, including two rooms for mobility impaired travelers. The fan-cooled rooms positively gleam, and have comfortable mattresses and good bathrooms. Best of all, the profits from your stay go toward supporting educational programs for local children.

★Hotel Los Altos BOUTIQUE HOTEL $$

(☑8998-0675, 2713-5264; www.hotellosaltosesteli.com; Calle Transversal, Av 1NE, 50m E; r incl breakfast US$30-85; ❄☎) In a pleasantly restored colonial house right in the center of town, Los Altos manages to be both stylish and unpretentious. Rooms are all different but each one features bright tile floors, elegant wooden furniture and a desk. Be warned that if you stay here you'll be woken up at 6am by the town alarm siren, right next door!

★Luna International Hostel HOSTEL $$

(☑8441-8466, 8405-8919; www.cafeluzyluna.org; cnr Av 2a NE & Calle 3a NE; dm/r incl breakfast US$10/28; ☎) ✐ With a central location, spotless fan-cooled rooms, a courtyard common area and a wealth of information on Estelí and the surrounding area, this nonprofit hostel is the budget traveler's favorite. There is a small kitchen for guest use and fast wi-fi throughout. Profits are donated to community projects in Miraflor, which also welcome volunteers. All rooms have mosquito nets.

Sonati HOSTEL $$

(☑2713-6043; https://ni.sonati.org/es/hostal-esteli; Catedral, 3½c E; dm US$8-9, s/d/tr from US$15/20/28; ☎) ✐ This chilled hostel feels a lot like a house share, with plenty of

Estelí

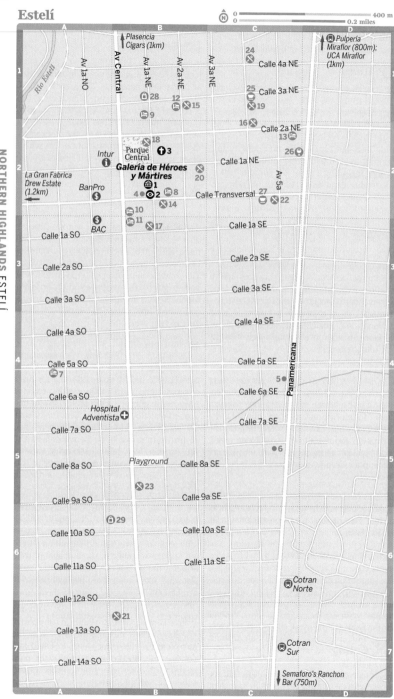

Plasencia
Cigars (1km)

Pulpería
Miraflor (800m);
UCA Miraflor
(1km)

Av 1a NO

Av Central

Av 1a NE

Av 2a NE

Av 3a NE

Calle 4a NE

24

25 Calle 3a NE

28 12

9

15 19

16 Calle 2a NE

13

18

Parque
Central 3

26

Intur

Galería de Héroes
y Mártires

Calle 1a NE

La Gran Fabrica
Drew Estate
(1.2km)

BanPro

20

Av 5a

1

2

4 2 8 Calle Transversal

14 27 22

BAC 10

11

17 Calle 1a SE

Calle 1a SO

Calle 2a SO Calle 2a SE

Calle 3a SO Calle 3a SE

Calle 4a SO Calle 4a SE

Calle 5a SO Calle 5a SE

7

5

Calle 6a SO Calle 6a SE

Panamericana

Hospital
Adventista

Calle 7a SO Calle 7a SE

6

Playground

Calle 8a SO Calle 8a SE

Calle 9a SO 23 Calle 9a SE

29 Calle 10a SE

Calle 10a SO

Calle 11a SO Calle 11a SE

Cotran
Norte

Calle 12a SO

21

Calle 13a SO

Cotran
Sur

Calle 14a SO

Semaforo's Ranchon
Bar (750m)

Estelí

NORTHERN HIGHLANDS ESTELÍ

communal space, a large kitchen and a pleasant rear garden. Rooms are neat and you could get lost in some of the huge bathrooms. The management offers tours and hikes in the area and arranges volunteer placements with local organizations. Profits go toward local environmental education projects.

Hotel Nicarao GUESTHOUSE **$$**
(☏ 2713-2490; hotelnicarao79@yahoo.es; Av Central, Calle Transversal, ½c S; s/d with bathroom from US$13/24, without bathroom US$10/20; 🖨) This charming garden gem doesn't look too inviting from the street, but inside you'll find pleasant rooms at exceptional value set around a spacious courtyard with sofas and rocking chairs.

Hotel Los Arcos HOTEL **$$$**
(☏ 2713-3830; www.hotelosarcosesteli.com; cnr Av 1a NE & Calle 3a NE; s/d/tw US$47/49/53, with air-con US$58/61/65; 🅿❊🖨)
🖉 Run by a nonprofit organization, Los Arcos remains the best value hotel in town, with a dream location, a roof deck with kickass mountain and city views, and spotless rooms with soft sheets, Spanish tiles and high ceilings. The colorfully painted rooms make up for a general lack of light – rooms at the back get the most.

✗ Eating

Burritos Express MEXICAN **$**
(Casa de Cultura, ½c E; mains US$3-6; ⊙ noon-10pm; 🖨) This simple hole-in-the-wall meets

diner place isn't exactly atmospheric (you order on the street before taking your seat in the next-door dining room) but the burritos are filling and great value, with fresh ingredients that come dripping in sauce. There are also good burgers.

El Quesito NICARAGUAN **$**
(cnr Calle 2a NE & Av 4a NE, Del Asoganor, 1c N; breakfast US$1-2.50, mains US$4.50; ⊙6:30am-8pm) Pull up a handmade wooden chair at this rustic corner diner and enjoy homemade yogurt flavored with local fruits, *quesillos* (corn tortillas stuffed with cheese and topped with pickled onions and cream) and *leche agria* (sour milk) – yes, what most of us pour down the sink is a delicacy in Nicaragua! Also prepares excellent, nongreasy Nica breakfasts and good meals.

Koma Rico NICARAGUAN **$**
(☏ 2713-4446; Cinema Estelí, 2c E; mains US$2.50-4; ⊙noon-9:30pm) Stack your plate high at this popular *fritanga* (grill) that's based upon the tried-and-tested marriage of tasty barbecued meats and ice-cold beer. The couple who run it are real charmers and the food is excellent.

Farmers Market MARKET **$**
(Parque Central; items from US$1; ⊙7am-3pm Fri)
🖉 Every Friday morning farmers from the surrounding hills come down to Estelí and set up stalls on the north side of the park to sell fresh organic vegetables, cheeses and other organic specialties.

Repostería Gutiérrez
BAKERY $

(☑2714-1774; Av Central, btwn Calles 8a SE & 9a SE; pastries US$0.30-1.20; ⊙7am-8pm) A local institution that sells delicious cookies, cakes, donuts or local pastries stuffed with fruit and cream.

Mercado Municipal
MARKET $

(cnr Calle 12a SO & Av 1a SO; ⊙6am-6pm) Estelí's municipal market is always stocked with amazingly fresh produce and plenty of street-food stands if you want the cheapest possible meal in town.

★Finca a su Mesa
INTERNATIONAL $$

(☑2713-6458; Hotel Mesón, 3c E; mains US$8-15; ⊙5-10pm Tue-Sat; 🖘) Given the seriously weak dining scene in Estelí, 'Farm to Table' comes as a wonderful surprise. Helmed by American chef Darren, a warm and passionate host who'll make you feel right at home, this is a place to enjoy excellent smoked ribs, an awesome house hamburger, delicious Moropotente craft beer on tap and daily changing specials up on the blackboard.

★Café Luz
INTERNATIONAL $$

(☑8405-8919; www.cafeluzyluna.org; cnr Av 2a NE & Calle 3a NE; snacks US$2-4, mains US$6.50-9; ⊙8am-11pm; 🖘✎) This friendly cafe with comfortable seating and a laid-back atmosphere serves up burritos and fajitas with a kick and organic salads direct from the growers in Miraflor. The diverse menu includes many vegetarian options and this is also one of the best places in town for a social drink in the evening, with frequent live musical performances.

Restaurante Tipiscayán
NICARAGUAN $$

(☑2713-7303; cnr Calle 4a NE & Av 4a NE; mains US$4-10; ⊙noon-10pm Thu-Tue) The family of San Juan de Limay soapstone sculptor Freddy Moreno serves good-quality tradi-tional fare, including great quesadillas and Nica-style tacos in an elegant space full of art. Also serves good coffee and traditional drinks such as *pinolillo* (a chilled beverage of maize and cacao).

El Rincón Pinareño
CUBAN $$

(☑2713-4369; cnr Av 1a SE & Calle 1a SE; mains US$6-11; ⊙noon-10pm) A tasty Cuban diner with a lovely 2nd-floor veranda serving deliciously messy pressed sandwiches, tasty smoked chicken, pork chops and ribs. Also a popular spot for dessert.

Pullaso's Ole
STEAK $$$

(☑2713-4583; cnr Av 5a SE & Calle Transversal; dishes US$10-25; ⊙noon-11pm; 🖘) Named for an Argentine cut of beef (the *pullaso*), this sweet, family-owned grill is the best place in town for a good steak. It serves up certified Angus beef as well as pork, chicken and chorizo dishes on its front porch and in a quaint dining room crowded with racks of South American red.

🍷 Drinking & Nightlife

★Semáforo Ranchón Bar
BAR

(Hospital, 300m S; ⊙6pm-4am Thu-Sun) Get down with the good working people of Estelí, Tisey and Miraflor at a proper *ranchero* bar. This indoor/outdoor club with a *palapa* (thatched) roof and bandstand brings terrific live music to a crowd that's here to dance in their boots and cowboy hats.

Aroma's Ole
CAFE

(cnr Calle 3a NE & Av 4a NE; ⊙10am-10pm Mon-Sat, 7am-10pm Sun; 🖘) Run by the family behind the Pullaso's Ole steakhouse, this street-side cafe serves up great coffee using freshly roasted beans from Dipilto, one of the country's best growing regions. There's

BUSES FROM ESTELÍ (COTRAN NORTE)

DESTINATION	COST (US$)	DURATION (HR)	FREQUENCY (DAILY)
Jalapa	3.20	2¾	4:10am, noon
Jinotega (via Concordia, San Rafael)	1.50	2	5:45am, 8:15am, 9:15am, 2:15pm, 3:45pm, 4:45pm
León (bus)	2.60	2½	3:10pm
León (microbus)	3	2	departs when full around 6am and 1pm
Masaya	3	3	2pm & 3pm
Ocotal	1.80	1½	6am-11am, hourly
San Juan de Limay	1.30	2½	5:30am, 7am, 10am, 12:15pm, 2pm, 3pm
Somoto	1.10	1½	5:30am-6:10pm, hourly
Yalí (via Miraflor)	1.90	2½	6am, 9:15am, 12:30pm, 3:45pm

BUSES FROM ESTELÍ (COTRAN SUR)

DESTINATION	COST (US$)	DURATION (HR)	FREQUENCY
León	2.20	2½	5am, 5:45am & 6:45am Mon-Sat, 6:45am Sun
Managua (expreso)	2.80	2½	hourly from 4:45am-9:45am & 12:15pm-3:15pm (from 6:45am Sun)
Managua (ordinario)	2.50	3½	3:30am-6pm, half-hourly
Matagalpa (ordinario)	1	1¾	5:15am-5:40pm, half-hourly
Tisey	0.65	1½	6:30am, 1:30pm Thu-Tue

also a large cocktail list and a menu of light meals and more hearty, meaty fare.

Hard Bar   BAR
(cnr Panamericana & Calle 1a NE; ⊙8pm-3am) On the highway a few blocks from the park, this 2nd-floor bar is the most popular late-night option in town. It has a wide balcony overlooking the street, which makes it a more laid-back choice than the enclosed discos. On weekends there's a US$2 cover.

Mocha Nana Café   CAFE
(✆2713-3164; Calle Transversal, Av 4a SE, ½c E; ⊙10am-8pm) Where Estelí intellectuals gather to sip caffeine, debate politics and culture, and munch tasty waffles. On Friday evenings there is often live music by local bands (cover US$2.50).

🛍 Shopping

The must-have souvenir of Estelí is a box of cigars, best purchased after a cigar tour. The region is also known for reasonably priced custom leather: saddles, boots and wallets are available at the many workshops located along Av 1a SO.

Calzado Figueroa   SHOES
(✆8946-4341; Av 1a SO, Calle 9a SO, 30m S; ⊙8am-7pm Mon-Sat, to noon Sun) Get in touch with your inner cowboy with some genuine, handcrafted, Cuban-heel riding boots (from US$80 to US$100) at this high-quality leather workshop. Peruse the large selection or order a tailor-made pair and watch the entire boot-making process.

Artesanías La Esquina   ARTS & CRAFTS
(✆2713-3239; cnr Av 1a NE & Calle 3a NE; ⊙8am-noon & 2-6pm Mon-Sat) An artisans cooperative with an extensive inventory that blends tourist kitsch with an array of excellent pottery and sculpted wood bowls.

ℹ Information

MEDICAL SERVICES
Hospital Adventista (✆2713-3827, 8851-5298; Av Central, Calle 6a SO, ½c S; ⊙24hr) Private clinic with a variety of specialists.

MONEY
BAC (Av 1a NO, Calle Transversal, 50m S) MasterCard/Cirrus/Visa/Plus ATM.
BanPro (cnr Calle Transversal & Av 1a NO) Reliable ATM. Also changes euros, as well as dollars.

TOURIST INFORMATION
UCA Miraflor (Unión de Cooperativas Agropecuarias de Miraflor; ✆2713-2971; www.ucamiraflor.org; Gasolinera Uno Norte, 2c E, ½c N; ⊙8am-noon & 1-5:30pm Mon-Fri, 8am-3pm Sat) Arranges tours to Área Protegida Miraflor.
Intur (✆2713-6799; Plaza Plator, Parque Central, ½c O; ⊙8am-4pm) Official tourist office with an abundance of regional brochures, but not a lot of expertise.

ℹ Getting There & Away

Estelí has two bus terminals a short distance from one another: the blue-collar **Cotran Norte** (✆2713-2529; Panamericana, Calle 11a SE) is a bit of a bun fight where you'll have to cram onto provincial buses, while **Cotran Sur** (✆2713-6162; Panamericana, Calle 14a SO) is more refined, with a ticket counter and timetables. Both are located at the southern end of the city on the Panamericana.

Área Protegida Miraflor

Part nature reserve, part rural farming community, Área Protegida Miraflor is a delightful destination for anyone wanting to experience life in a Nicaraguan farming community. Visitors get the chance to immerse themselves and help out warm and welcoming farming families who have an interest in sustainability and the environment.

SUSTAINABLE TOURISM

These days most of the cooperative *colectivos* created after the Contra War have been dissolved, with the lands distributed among their former members. But even though many locals now own their lands, poverty remains widespread.

In 2013, the coffee-rust fungus hit Miraflor's coffee plantations and swaths of local bushes were affected. Losses were greatest among organic farmers. Many farmers have ripped up their affected plantations and planted more hardy varieties and so many farms are still feeling the devastating effects.

With the coffee industry in turmoil, sustainable tourism is more important than ever to local residents seeking to eke out a living.

Its namesake is a small mountain lake around which the Área Protegida Miraflor (declared a reserve in 1999) unfurls with waterfalls, blooming orchids, coffee plantations, swatches of remnant cloud forest home to hold-out monkey troops, hiking trails and dozens of collective-farming communities that welcome tourists. Yes, nature is glorious here, but the chance to participate in rural Nicaraguan life – making fresh tortillas, milking cows, harvesting coffee, riding horses through the hills with local *caballeros* (horsemen) – is unforgettable.

◉ Sights & Activities

Local guides (US$15) are both inexpensive and a great resource. They know all the best hikes and climbs and can share insights into Miraflor's unique history and local daily life. If you're on a day trip here or plan on exploring much beyond your homestay, guides become essential – paths are poorly marked and cross private farms where permission must sometimes be negotiated. Horses are also available (around US$12 to US$15 per day) and are a good choice if you plan on visiting various different communities.

Dedicated coffee tours with tasting sessions (US$70 for up to 10 participants) can be arranged with advanced notice. Other specialized tours include orchid hikes (US$35 for up to 10 participants) and birdwatching trips (US$35 to US$50 for up to six participants).

Some landowners charge admission to visit sights or pass through their property, so bring plenty of change.

UCA Miraflor (p175) in Estelí manages the reserve and can help you plan a visit, hook you up with an English-speaking guide and book family homestays. Alternatively, Tree Huggers (p171) provides detailed, impartial advice on planning a trip and can also make reservations.

Pozo La Pila   WATERFALL
(US$1) A small layered waterfall feeds this lovely, round swimming hole enclosed by rock walls. The water flows from a local spring, so it's clean, and unlike other falls in the area it doesn't dry up. It's accessible from La Pita.

Mirador La Meseta   VIEWPOINT
(US$1) This lookout point near Coyolito is perched at 1100m in the dry zone and offers fine views down the valley.

Los Volcancitos   MOUNTAIN
This destination for wildlife lovers is where you'll find the best remaining patch of virgin cloud forest (although deforestation is a serious issue), home to troops of spider and howler monkeys. It's most easily accessed from Cebollal. Walk 45 minutes to the La Rampla bus stop on the Estelí–Yalí road; it's then a further one-hour walk south to the jungle-covered, volcano-shaped mountain (which, despite the name, isn't actually a volcano).

Coyolito   VILLAGE
The lowest settlement in Miraflor, Coyolito is also the warmest and closest to Estelí. It offers magnificent views, especially from the Mirador La Meseta, and access to several waterfalls that range from trickling to thundering depending upon the season, such as Las Tres Cascadas, a series of cascades and swimming holes. Another is La Chorrera, a 65m-high waterfall once used as an execution site by Somoza's troops; it sometimes dries up completely and is only worth visiting after prolonged rains.

La Perla   VILLAGE
A fine place to immerse yourself in the collective-farming world of Miraflor, this small village is in the high zone, which means there are hundreds of orchid varieties here. It's also home to a women's farming cooperative. Guests are encouraged to wake up to the smacking rhythm of fresh, handmade tortil-

las; milk the cow; collect the eggs and work the farm before hiking into the nearby forests.

Cebollal

VILLAGE

The first settlement to cater to tourists, Cebollal remains the most popular. You can stay with one of many families or in more comfortable *cabañas* and enjoy miles of trails that reach up to 1400m, with pockets of cloud forest that draw colorful quetzals to the canopy in May and June.

🛏 Sleeping

There are several choices of accommodations within the reserve, all of which should be booked through UCA Miraflor (p175) or Tree Huggers (p171) in Estelí. Farmhouse rooms allow the most interaction with local families; *cabañas* have more privacy. Both options are rustic and some accommodations have pit latrines. Expect to pay around US$28 per person, including three meals.

Finca Lindos Ojos

FARMSTAY $$

(☑ 8992-7315, 2713-4041; www.finca-lindos-ojos.com/en; Cebollal; dm US$8, d incl breakfast US$25-45) 🦋 First and foremost a self-sufficient organic farm run by enterprising German transplant Katharina, Finca Lindos Ojos has three charming self-contained *cabañas* that each sleep up to four guests and enjoy wooden porches. There are also cheaper rooms with shared bathrooms and a great-value dorm here as well. The focus for guests is on horseback riding and hiking trips.

Finca Neblina del Bosque

GUESTHOUSE $$

(☑ 7519-5685; www.facebook.com/fincaneblinadelbosque; Cebollal; cabañas per person incl meals US$30-40; 🛜) 🦋 Owned by a Nica-German couple, this pleasant guesthouse on a working farm is the most comfortable option in Miraflor (though it has a decidedly less rural farming flavor than the village homestays). The main cabins are elegantly constructed from bamboo, including one made entirely from recycled material, and each has an ensuite bathroom and a shared solar-heated shower.

ⓘ Getting There & Away

From Estelí there are a number of daily buses heading into Área Protegida Miraflor. For much greater comfort and ease, you can also arrange 4WD transfers and/or a driver for the day via either UCA Miraflor (p175) or Tree Huggers (p171).

For Coyolito (US$0.65, 45 mins) and La Pita (US$0.70, one hour), buses leave Estelí from

Pulpería Miraflor (Panamericana, Calle 14 NE) (near the Uno gas station on the Panamericana north of town) at 5:45am and 1pm daily, returning from La Pita at 8am and 3pm.

There are three daily direct buses (except Wednesday) from Estelí's Cotran Norte (p175) bus station to Cebollal (US$0.65, 45 mins) departing at 6am, 11am and 3:45pm.

To La Perla or El Sontule (US$0.65, one hour), take the Camino Real bus signed Oro Verde/Sontule/Puertas Azules from Cotran Norte (p175) at 2pm Monday to Saturday. The bus returns at 7am Monday to Saturday from La Perla and El Sontule.

Área Protegida Cerro Tisey-Estanzuela

Smaller, drier and less populated but every bit as gorgeous as Área Protegida Miraflor, this *other* protected area, just 10km south of Estelí, has also jumped on the tourism bandwagon. You won't see the same species diversity in Tisey (which is what locals call the region), but those rugged, pine-draped mountains, red-clay bat caves, waterfalls and marvelous vistas that stretch to Lago de Managua – and even El Salvador on clear days – are worth the trip.

It's possible to visit Tisey on a day trip from Estelí; however, the reserve's attractions are spread out all over its 93 sq km and public transportation is limited so you'll see more (and contribute more) if you spend the night.

◉ Sights

The main entrance to Tisey is accessed from the dirt road beside Hospital San Juan de Dios in Estelí. In the park's lower elevations, just 5km from Estelí, is the lovely Salto Estanzuela (p178), a waterfall where it's possible to swim. After the falls, the road begins

---

MIRADOR DE TISEY TRAIL
....

The Mirador de Tisey Trail (2km), found near the **Eco-Posada Tisey** (☑ 8658-4086; r per person US$7, cabañas US$18; **P**), is absolutely spectacular. After meandering up an oak- and pine-draped hillside, you'll reach a peak with 360-degree views that encompass a dozen volcanoes, including mighty San Cristóbal, and the blue outline of a Salvadorian peak. The ASOPASN cooperative (p178) in La Garnacha organizes several interesting activities.

to climb high into the mountains where you'll find the entrance to Alberto Gutiérrez' singular Galería del Arte El Jalacate, where you can see his charming murals carved into the cliff-face.

Galería del Arte El Jalacate
GARDENS, SCULPTURE

(by donation) Artist and naturalist Alberto Gutiérrez is, some might say, a bit of a hermit – but a welcoming one who loves showing off his orchid-studded property, which is carpeted with coffee and accented with a dozen kinds of fruit tree. His pride and joy is a 40m stretch of cliff that he's carved into an ever-evolving mural, with animals from Africa, the Amazon and Nicaragua, an Aztec sun, Jesus on the cross, his vision of downtown USA, Christopher Columbus and Sandino.

Salto Estanzuela
WATERFALL

(US$1) In Tisey's lower elevations, just 5km from Estelí, is the inspiring Salto Estanzuela, a gushing 36m waterfall that careens over a bromeliad-studded cliff and breaks into a half-dozen foaming threads that feed a perfect swimming hole. Locals descend in hordes during Semana Santa, and the entire place suffers from left trash, but it's still a lovely site for a dip.

🖝 Tours

ASOPASN
TOURS

(☑ 8658-1054; garnchaturistica@yahoo.es; Comunidad La Garnacha) This progressive farming cooperative has branched out into tourism and organizes several interesting activities, including organic agriculture tours (US$8 per person) and soapstone-carving classes (US$8 per person). It also rents horses and organizes guides (US$8 per person) for the rugged five-hour trail to the Cuevas de Cerro Apaguaji, three caves at 1580m that are teeming with bats.

ROSQUILLAS

Before the canyon, Somoto was famous for *rosquillas* (crusty cornbread rings), baked with cheese and herbs, and served with black coffee. You can buy a bag anywhere, but the best are found at **Rosquillas Vílchez** (☑ 2722-2002; Enitel, 8c S, 1c E; rosquillas US$0.50-1.50; ☺ 4am-6pm), where you can watch them being baked in massive wood-fired ovens just as they have been since 1954.

🛏 Sleeping

Finca Orgánica El Carrizo
HOMESTAY $$

(☑ 8524-4764; La Garnacha; dm/r per person US$8/20) 🍃 For a full cultural immersion, check out this family homestay, in the house of an energetic local farmer. It's surrounded by lovely gardens and all sorts of livestock roam freely. Accommodations are in a treehouse-style structure, with colorful hammocks and shared bathrooms. Meals are prepared using organic produce fresh from the farm and are very reasonably priced (US$2 to US$4).

Cabañas La Garnacha
LODGE $$

(☑ 8658-1054; garnchaturistica@yahoo.es; La Garnacha; r per person US$10, cabañas US$25-30) 🍃 These cute *cabañas* with hot water are run by the community and overlook a small lake. There are also cheaper, hotel-style rooms with tiled bathrooms by the entrance. Reserve in advance.

🛈 Getting There & Away

Tisey is served by two buses a day (US$1, one hour), which are marked 'La Tejera' and leave from Estelí Cotran Sur (p175) at 6:30am and 1:30pm daily except Wednesday. The buses pass Salto Estanzuela and Eco-Posada Tisey before arriving at the La Garnacha turnoff, a 1.5km walk from the community. Buses return to Estelí from the La Garnacha turnoff at 8am and 3pm daily except Wednesday.

In general, taxis won't do the trip as the road is in fairly poor condition and drivers don't want to rough up their sedans. Tree Huggers (p171) in Estelí offers round-trip transportation in pickups for US$60, which is a good option for day-trippers.

Condega

POP 30,300 / ELEV 560M

Dyed a deep terracotta, scarred proudly by revolution and surrounded by gorgeous, forested hills, Condega translates from the indigenous Náhuatl as 'the place of the potters,' and its ceramics tradition continues to this day. There's not much reason to visit, but if you're passing you might want to see the town's display of its historic wares in the museum and its more contemporary creations at a famed factory shop on the outskirts. If terracotta doesn't get you going, then you can at least check out the Somoza-era bomber shot down here in 1979 and reassembled on a hilltop. Talk about spoils of war.

⊙ Sights

Parque El Avion   PARK
Condega's most unique attraction is the riveted twin-engine bomber used by the FAN (Nicaraguan Air Force) to bomb the region. It was shot down on April 7, 1979. Now it sits, tagged in lovers' graffiti, at Airplane Park, the local make-out point overlooking mountain mesas.

Mirador   VIEWPOINT
(US$0.20) This faux control tower lookout at the Parque El Avion offers fantastic views of the town, its tiled roofs and palm trees jutting out of a canopy of green. To get to the park, climb the steep dirt trail across the street from the museum.

Museo Arqueológico
Julio César Salgado   MUSEUM
(Parque Central; US$0.25; ⊙8am-5pm Mon-Sat) Packed with ceramic bowls, studded incense burners, and stone tools dating back to AD 300. A map in the corner marks some 60 unexcavated or partially excavated archaeological sites in the area.

⊨ Sleeping

Hospedaje Baldovinos   GUESTHOUSE $
(☑2715-2222; Parque Central; per person US$6.50; ℗) Set in a lovely colonial house with a vibrant internal courtyard, this family-run *hospedaje* (guesthouse) offers simple, fan-cooled brick rooms with tiled bathrooms. It's the most comfortable and atmospheric choice in Condega. The hotel also arranges private transport to local attractions, including the workshops (☑2715-2418; Restaurante Guanacaste, 1km O; ⊙9am-4pm) at Ducualí.

❶ Getting There & Away

Buses depart from Condega's modern **bus terminal** (Panamericana) for the following destinations:

Estelí (US$0.50, 45 minutes, 6am to 7pm, every 20 minutes)

Ocotal (US$1, one hour, 7am to 7pm, every 45 minutes)

Somoto (US$0.50, 45 minutes, 4:15am to 5:45pm, every 45 minutes)

Somoto

POP 35,000 / ELEV 705M

One of Nicaragua's most enjoyable natural sites, the magnificent Cañon de Somoto should not be missed by anyone in this part

WORTH A TRIP

RESERVA NATURAL TEPESOMOTO-PATASTE

Somoto's 'other' natural reserve, around 15km to the southwest of town, is rarely visited but has a hiking trail and is a popular spot for horseback-riding tours. The nature at Reserva Natural Tepesomoto-Pataste is unspoiled and you are pretty much guaranteed not to bump into any other hikers during your visit. Private guide Osman Mendoza, who's based in Somoto, runs multiday adventures into the reserve. Alternatively, Somoto Canyon Tours can also organize visits.

of the country. It makes for a super enjoyable and exciting day excursion that combines hiking, swimming, scrambling and boating through a narrow, towering canyon from where the Río Coco, Central America's longest river, begins its epic journey to the Caribbean.

The nearby town of Somoto was until 2003 just another sleepy place in the Honduran shadow, known locally for its donkeys and *rosquillas* (crusty cornbread rings). This was when two Czech scientists 'discovered' what the locals had known about since time immemorial: the dramatic nearby canyon that could have been designed for tourism. Overnight Somoto became a popular backpacker stopover between Honduras and Granada and is today the second most visited attraction in Nicaragua – don't miss it.

⊙ Sights

★Monumento Nacional
Cañon de Somoto   NATIONAL PARK
(Carretera Somoto–El Espino Km 229.5; US$2) The Coco (or Wangki), Central America's longest river, runs all the way to the Caribbean, but its first impression may be its most spectacular. Gushing from underground, it has carved solid rock into this 3km-long gorge that drops 160m, and at times is just a hair under 10m wide. Protected as Monumento Nacional Cañon de Somoto, the canyon is an unmissable experience.

Iglesia Santiago   CHURCH
This wonderfully understated adobe church fronting the shady Parque Central was constructed in 1661, making it one of the oldest places of worship in Nicaragua.

HIKING IN MONUMENTO NACIONAL CAÑON DE SOMOTO

There are three routes to explore the canyon. You won't always have comfortable footing, so reef shoes or sandals help a lot, and you'll have more fun if you're fit. Within the canyon proper there is one deep stretch of about 200m where you'll have to swim (tours will always supply life vests).

The full six-hour, 13km circuit will take you to two bat caves well above the rim before you hike down to the river, boulder-hop, swim through (small) rapids and leap off 8m rocks into deep swimming holes. This version is highly recommended for nature fanatics, as you'll hike through pristine landscapes and get to see the point where the Tapacalí and Comali rivers join at the birthplace of the Río Coco.

The most popular option is the four-hour, 6km classic loop: you head straight to the far entrance of the canyon, from where you'll swim, hike and leap beneath slate-rock faces and jagged peaks until you reach the exit.

For those who are adverse to exercise, there is also a three-hour 'lite' tour where you are paddled up the gorge a short distance in a small boat and then can splash around in the canyon mouth or float around in an inflatable tube.

Following a couple of incidents, local guides (US$15/US$20 half-/full day for up to five people) are now mandatory if you want to venture inside the canyon. In addition to having expert knowledge of river conditions – which can become dangerous during the wet season – guides also blend local insight with adventure and create a richer experience, though very few speak English.

Guides from the local community of Sonis, at the entrance to the reserve, have formed a fantastic community tourism organization called Somoto Canyon Tours and work on a rotation basis. Another option is to visit with one of the guides from local tour operator Namancambre Tours (found in Somoto town).

To visit the canyon take any El Espino–bound bus (US$0.40, 30 minutes) from the bus terminal to the trail head at Km 231 near the community of Sonis (look out for the sign), where you will meet your guide. A taxi will cost around US$8. From here it's a 3km hike to the canyon, including a river crossing that may be over a meter deep. The last bus back to Somoto passes through at around 5:30pm. If you're coming from Honduras via El Espino – the Del Sol bus line has an authorized stop right at the entrance – there's no need to go into Somoto. The canyon often closes in October, when the water is too high. Call the guides to check on conditions.

Tours

Somoto Canyon Tours ADVENTURE
(☎8610-7642; www.somotocanyontours.org; Carretera Somoto–El Espino Km 229.5) A well-run community tourism organization based in the village of Sonis, right by the entrance to the Cañon de Somoto (p179), Somoto Canyon Tours offers a fantastic package, including transportation from Somoto, life vest and water shoes, dry bag, entrance fee, guide, lunch and a boat trip for US$25 per visitor for the standard loop and US$30 for the longer version.

Namancambre Tours ADVENTURE SPORTS
(☎2722-0889; www.facebook.com/somotocanyon; Gasolinera Puma, 1c O, 120m S) A well regarded local tour operator with good equipment offering a range of trips into the Somoto Canyon (p179). The standard four-hour tour costs US$17 per visitor (not including transport) and they will run a trip even with just one client. Also offers overnight canyon trips and other outdoor activities in the region.

Sleeping

Community-run homestays can be found in the settlement of Sonis, right next to the canyon. Sleeping here gives you plenty of time to get out and explore as well as the chance to experience life in a rural community. There are also several decent hotels in the town of Somoto itself.

Casa Huésped Soriano HOMESTAY $
(☎8610-7642; www.somotocanyontours.org; Carretera El Espino Km 229.5, Sonis; dm/r US$8/20) If you are in Somoto only to see the canyon, consider staying at this simple guesthouse in the village of Sonis (right at the canyon entrance), a part of the community tourism project. Accommodations are in simple

rooms with mosquito nets and fans, with meals in the adjacent house costing US$3.50.

Rual's Hotel
HOTEL $$

(☑ 2722-2118; http://ruals-hotel.com; INSS, 2c E; d/tw incl breakfast US$45/55; P❄🛜) This pleasantly renovated colonial building has been transformed into a hotel and has very clean, brightly painted and contemporary rooms with many local design touches. There's also a pleasant alfresco seating area out back, and you're just a short walk from the center of town.

Hotel Colonial
HOTEL $$

(☑ 2722-2040; reloj, 50m S; s/d/tr incl breakfast US$30/40/50; P🛜) Clean, comfortable rooms with tiled floors and thin walls. Some rooms are (much!) bigger than others, so look before you commit. Management is welcoming and go out of their way to assist travelers.

Quinta San Rafael
LODGE $$$

(☑ 8449-1766; info.canondesomoto@gmail.com; entrada Cañon de Somoto; campsite per person US$10, house for up to 12 visitors US$250, cabaña for 6-8 visitors US$120) With a privileged location at the entrance to the canyon, this spacious property offers the most comfortable accommodations for miles around. The main house has two floors, with an open fireplace in the lounge and kitchen area and a wonderful deck with panoramic views of the mountains. There are also several smaller cabañas and camping is possible in the garden.

🍴 Eating & Drinking

Bar y Restaurant El Almendro
NICARAGUAN $$

(☑ 2722-2152; Parque Central, 1c S; mains US$6-10; ⊙ 10am-10pm) This bar-restaurant feels like something from the Wild West, but the food is actually pretty good. Choose from fish, chicken or beef in a variety of sauces served with all the usual extras.

Aroma
CAFE

(Parque Central; drinks US$0.50-2; ⊙ 7:30am-8pm Tue-Sun) Pull up a chair on the deck of this tranquil, open-air cafe within the leafy central park and enjoy a variety of coffees made from quality local beans. Also prepares light meals.

ℹ️ Getting There & Away

The **bus station** (Panamericana) in Somoto itself is on the Panamericana, six blocks from the town center. Buses from Somoto to El Espino pass by the entrance to the canyon – tell the driver where you're headed and they'll drop you off.

Ocotal

POP 42,000 / ELEV 612M

Sunken into a boulder-strewn valley sprinkled with ocote pines and wildflowers and ringed with mountains, Ocotal is the commercial center of the Segovias. These mountains once baited gold-hungry pirates up the Río Coco from the Caribbean Sea. More significantly, in 1927, Sandino and his 'Crazy Little Army' seized control of Ocotal from federal forces in his first big victory. This action won him some extra attention from the US White House, who soon made humble Ocotal the first city in history to be bombed by fighter planes. Today, Ocotal is just a peaceful market town that serves farmers and families who live in the dozens of surrounding *pueblos*. There's little reason to visit, but it's pleasant enough to break up a journey or as a lunch spot.

⊙ Sights

Parque Central
PLAZA

The undisputed star of the town center is Nicaragua's finest Parque Central. Former mayor Fausto Sánchez was a botanist, and he planted hundreds of tropical plants here, including magnolias, roses, orchids and birds of paradise – all set among soaring mature cypress and pine trees.

NORTHERN HIGHLANDS OCOTAL

BUSES TO/FROM SOMOTO

DESTINATION	COST (US$)	DURATION	FREQUENCY
El Espino (Honduran border)	0.40	40min	5:15am-5:15pm, hourly
Estelí	1.10	1¾hr	5:20am-5pm, every 40min
Managua (expreso)	3.40	4hr	5am, 6:15am, 7:30am, 2pm, 3:15pm
Managua (ordinario)	2.50	4½hr	4am-5pm, almost hourly
Ocotal	0.50	1hr	5:15am-4:30pm, every 45min

Templo Parroquial de Ocotal CHURCH

(Parque Central) With mossy columns, twin bell towers (although one was actually built in 2003) and a faded, chipped facade, the baroque-neoclassical Templo Parroquial de Ocotal (1803–69) is a transporting sight, especially in the late-day sun.

🛌 Sleeping

Despite being the closest city to the Honduran border at Las Manos, accommodations options in Ocotal are limited.

Hotel La Frontera HOTEL $$

(☎2732-2668; hofrosa@turbonett.com.ni; Panamericana, contiguo Shell Ramos; s/d with fan US$23/34, with air-con US$50/67; ⏸ ❋ 🛜 ⛱) It's a little removed from the center of town but this place on the highway is easily the most comfortable option in Ocotal. The rooms are spacious and come with creature comforts like hot water, air-con and a great pool, although bathrooms are looking a little tired these days and some rooms need a repaint.

Hotel El Viajero HOTEL $$

(☎2732-2040; Esso, 3½c O; s/d/tr from US$15/20/25; 🛜) The rooms are a little dark but are clean and have big TVs and huge bathrooms. Not all rooms share the same standards, but choose wisely and you'll snag terrific value.

🍴 Eating

Llamarada Cafetín del Bosque NICARAGUAN $

(Parque Central; meals US$2-4; ⏰6am-4pm) This steam-table buffet deluxe is your best breakfast and lunch destination, where trays of fluffy pancakes, *gallo pinto* (rice and beans) and scrambled eggs rotate with great barbecued chicken wings, beef in onion sauce and plantains, all at outstanding value.

★ Casa Vieja NICARAGUAN $$

(Supermercado San Juan, ½c N; mains US$4-8; ⏰11am-11pm Tue-Sun; 🅿) Step through the

DRINKING COFFEE

The only drinking you're likely to find in Dipilto is the caffeinated variety. If you visit some of the local farms you're guaranteed to be invited to try a cup of the local brew.

majestic wooden doors of this lovely old adobe house and enjoy a delicious traditional Nica meal in a wonderfully social atmosphere, accompanied by a *trova* (Latin folk music) soundtrack that complements, rather than dominates, the conversation. It lives up to its name with its ancient implements on the walls, and the welcome is warm and genuine.

Mi Yunta NICARAGUAN $$

(☎2732-2180; Parque Central, 2c O, 1c S; mains US$5-10; ⏰noon-11pm Tue-Thu, to 1am Fri-Sun; 🛜) The smartest restaurant in town, Ocotal's succulent staple serves up big portions of top-quality meals. Being an agricultural town, the menu is focused on the grill and is very meaty. The bar is also a decent place to down a few cold beers – it draws a crowd on weekends.

ℹ Information

MEDICAL SERVICES

Hospital (☎2732-2491; Calle Bosawás) Ocotal has the region's biggest hospital.

ℹ Getting There & Away

Buses depart from the **main bus terminal** (COTRAN; ☎2732-3304; Av Gral Sandino), 1km south of the Parque Central. Border-bound buses stop to pick up passengers by the Shell station at the northern end of town.

Minibus services that get packed go to Ciudad Antigua (US$0.50, 45 minutes, 5am and noon). Alternatively, take any Jalapa- or Jícaro-bound service to the junction and pick up a shared taxi.

Dipilto

POP 200 / ELEV 880M

It would be hard to dream up a sweeter setting than what you'll find in this tiny mountain *pueblo* 20km north of Ocotal, and just a 30-minute drive from Honduras. Think narrow, cobbled streets, surrounded by the pine-studded, coffee-shaded Segovias, carved by a rushing, cascading river.

The majestic mountains around Dipilto are known for producing some of the best coffee in Nicaragua. Staff in the alcaldía (☎8429-3489) can help organize hikes through some of the town's stunning shade-grown plantations with especially trained local guides. It's also possible to arrange guided treks to quetzal nesting grounds in the cloud forest on 1867m El Volcán.

⊙ Sights

Santuario de la Virgen
de la Piedra   RELIGIOUS SITE
The principal sight in town is the lovely Santuario de la Virgen de la Piedra, where a statue of the radiant Virgin of Guadalupe blesses a kneeling pilgrim surrounded by fragrant gardens that attract butterflies. Her faithful arrive on Saturday and Sunday to light candles and voice their prayers.

🛏 Sleeping

Most travelers visit Dipilto as a day trip from Ocotal, where there is a much better range of accommodations.

Finca San Isidro   COFFEE FARM $$
(☑2732-2392; La Laguna; r incl breakfast per person US$20) A charming old coffee hacienda with great views of the surrounding mountains, Finca San Isidro is 10km north of Dipilto and can feed and sleep up to 10 people in rustic rooms with shared bathrooms. Spend the night and enjoy a cup of farm-fresh coffee when you get up. It's best to reserve a couple of days ahead.

ℹ Getting There & Away

Dipilto is divided into two communities, Dipilto Nuevo and Dipilto Viejo, which is a further 3km along the highway toward the Honduran border. The alcaldía and access to the Santuario is from Dipilto Nuevo. Take any bus bound for the Las Manos border crossing and ask the driver to let you out in Dipilto Nuevo ($0.20). Buses run south to Ocotal ($0.60, 30 minutes) and beyond every 30 minutes or so until around 5pm.

Ocotal to Jalapa

North of Ocotal a sinuous, 65km brick road branches into the Segovian pine forests and leads to mountainous Jalapa, Nicaragua's wild north. From ceramic factories to historic towns with ties to British pirate Captain Morgan and the superb scenery of Cerro Mogotón, there are some intriguing sights to see here. It helps to have your own vehicle, though Ocotal buses serve most of these locations several times daily. Remember, when it rains, some of the dirt spur roads get messy, so if you're planning deep off-road adventures make sure to rent a 4WD.

⊙ Sights

Cerro Mogotón   MOUNTAIN
Nicaragua's highest peak, Cerro Mogotón (2107m) towers over the coffee fields of Nueva Segovia, close to the Honduran border. Once off-limits due to land mines, it is now safe to climb with a guide. The easiest access is from the Ocotal–Jalapa road near the village of Achuapa. It's a seven-hour round-trip hike to the peak, which is covered in dense cloud forest. Independent guide Mayerlin Ruiz runs trips to Mogotón (US$70 per person, minimum two people), departing from Ocotal.

Santuario de los Milagros   CHURCH
(Parque Central, Ciudad Antigua) The jewel of Ciudad Antigua is the sensational Santuario de los Milagros, with its gorgeous brick arches and enormous wooden doors. Check out the Christ figure brought from Austria. Local legend has it that any time pirates entered the sanctuary, the sculpture grew to enormous proportions and the pillaging parties could not get it out the doors.

🏃 Activities

Termales Don Alfonso
Nueva Segovia   HOT SPRINGS
(Aranjuez; US$4.50; ⊙7am-5pm Tue-Sun) Around 30km south of Jalapa, these thermal baths are constructed over mineral-rich waters reputed to have medicinal properties. The waters gush out of the ground and are so hot at their source that you can boil an egg (there are even dedicated cooking holes for this). Fortunately the relaxation pools are not quite so hot; there is a large, round pool included in the admission price and three smaller rectangular baths for private soaks, one of which is wheelchair-accessible.

👉 Tours

Mayerlin Ruiz   HIKING
(☑8234-9784; mayerlinruiz89@yahoo.com) An enthusiastic local guide specializing in hikes

DRIVING TOUR: OCOTAL TO JALAPA

The town of **Mozonte**, just 5km from Ocotal, is located on the site of a pre-Hispanic Chorotega community and still retains strong indigenous roots. There are numerous ceramics workshops, where you can watch artisans work a variety of ceramic materials and techniques. It's a fascinating spectacle and you can buy your vases, candleholders, wind chimes and wall ornaments here on the cheap.

Looming above town is **Hermita de la Virgen de Guadalupe**, a rock-top shrine with spectacular views. Take a stroll up the forested hill overlooking town to **Capilla Los Pozos**, where locals gather in the afternoon to play music. Along the way, keep an eye out for the golden warbler, an endangered bird species that migrates between here and Texas.

Back on the main road, continue to the speed bumps of **San Fernando**, which has a great Parque Central and is famous for its *cheles* (individuals with white skin), which many trace to the presence of US marines in the area from 1927 to 1931. Cerro Mogotón (p183), Nicaragua's highest peak, is less than 20km from town.

There's a well-signed turnoff at the beginning of the 4.5km brick road to **Ciudad Antigua**, a cute old Spanish town with a long and colorful history. Founded in 1536 and under almost constant attack from local indigenous groups for the next century, it was sacked in 1654 by the Welsh privateer Sir Henry Morgan – best known to the world as Captain Morgan, yes, he of rum fame – who had come up the nearby Río Coco in a canoe, thirsty for gold. Calling it a 'city' is a bit of a stretch – the main movement around the leafy central park is the slow pace of old donkeys. Also on the town square is gorgeous Santuario de los Milagros (p183), a strikingly beautiful colonial church. Across the road, the small but fun **Museo Segoviano** (frente iglesia, Ciudad Antigua; US$0.30; ☺8am-6pm) has a few curious artefacts worth looking at.

About 10km past San Fernando, you can make a right onto the sketchy dirt road to **El Jícaro (Ciudad Sandino)**, where Sandino's military mined for gold at Las Minas San Albino. It's possible to visit the ruins of the mine and check out what remains of Sandino's rusted old mining gear. The town itself is attractive and friendly, and makes a good base from which to explore the attractions in the surrounding countryside – on foot or on horseback – or just soak up the rural mountain vibe.

If you have a 4WD, stay on this road and you'll eventually come to the community of **Murra**, where the surrounding countryside undulates between 820m and 1300m and hides **Salto El Rosario**, one of the highest – and quite possibly the most spectacular – waterfalls in the country. The water falls for nearly 200m in three sections close to gorgeous Finca Santa Rita, which sits on 200 hectares of land outside Murra.

Returning to the main highway, about 30km south of Jalapa you'll reach Termales Don Alfonso (p183), where mineral-rich waters that locals say have medicinal properties gush out of the ground.

Another 12km further on is the turnoff to **El Limón**, where sulfuric thermal springs seep out of the mountains, forming small caves alongside a river. Somoza once had private thermal baths here, but the pools were destroyed by Hurricane Mitch. To the north of El Limón, there are two sustainable farms around Las Nubarrones, which make for interesting day trips for agriculture and nature lovers.

to the summit of Mogotón (p183), Nicaragua's highest peak.

ℹ Getting There & Away

Buses run on the main highway between Ocotal and Jalapa almost hourly and can drop you anywhere along the route. El Jícaro has services to both Ocotal and Jalapa and you can also use Ocotal–El Murra buses.

For Ciudad Antigua, minibuses leave from Ocotal at 5am and noon, but they can get very crowded. It's often more convenient to take a Jalapa- or Jícaro-bound bus and get off at the junction, from where *colectivo* taxis (US$0.50) run into town.

Jalapa

POP 25,000 / ELEV 687M

In a region freckled with remote mountain towns, Jalapa is one where the emerald hills are so close you can see their dips and grooves, their texture and shadows. While the town itself is not likely to win any beauty contests, the surrounding countryside boasts such dramatic natural beauty and so many adventure opportunities that the utter lack of tourism here is difficult to fathom. That said, you will almost certainly not run into other travelers here, and excursions are very much yours to arrange.

◎ Sights

Cerro de Jesús
MOUNTAIN

Just outside Jalapa you'll find Cerro de Jesús (1885m), the largest mountain in the area. It is dominated by the Jesus Mountain coffee plantation, which boasts 400 hectares of organic coffee. But on the flanks of the mountain you'll also find a small local community, intact primary forest and a gushing 8m waterfall. If you're up to it, you can hike to the peak.

☞ Tours

Hotel El Pantano
TOURS

(☑2737-2031, 8823-8107; www.hotelelpantano.com; Banco Procredit, 8c O) This is by far the area's best resource for tourists. It arranges many guided treks and trips, spanning from one to four days. If you wish to organize your own adventure, the helpful English-, Dutch- and Spanish-speaking owner, Wim Van der Donk, can suggest local guides and offer directions.

⌫ Sleeping

Hotel Yorling E&E
HOTEL $

(☑2737-2139, 8501-4622; Parque Infantil, 1c N; r with/without bathroom US$20/10; ☎) Right in the center of town, this spick-and-span place has spotless rooms arranged in a number of combinations, including a floor of rooms with shared bathrooms.

Hotel El Pantano
HOTEL $$

(☑2737-2031; www.hotelelpantano.com; Banco Procredit, 8c O; s/d/tr incl breakfast US$20/27.50/35; ☎) Easily your best bet in Jalapa, this welcoming hotel is set on lovely, lush grounds by a creek a short walk from town. The comfy though rather aged brick rooms have cable TV and (sometimes) hot water, and you'll be serenaded by birdsong and cockerels in the mornings. Campers are welcome to pitch their tent (per night US$4).

FLOR DE PINO

Members of this small women's co-operative (☑8712-6519; Champigny; ☺9am-6pm) ✐ weave elegant baskets from pine needles. The products are absolutely charming, as are the women who make them. The workshop is in the community of Champigny, 4km north of Jalapa. Look for the signs for the school on your left: the cooperative is in the same building.

✖ Eating

Pizza Giomar
PIZZA $

(☑2737-2607; Mercado, 2½c O; pizza slice US$1, pizzas US$3-8; ☺10am-10pm) Pretty much the only alternative to regional dishes in town, this friendly restaurant serves up surprisingly decent pizza with a smile, albeit with a blaring TV accompaniment. Order it whole or by the slice; delivery is available.

Luz de Luna
NICARAGUAN $$

(Parque Central, 1c S; mains US$5-7.50; ☺11am-10pm) A popular spot that serves plates of *comida típica* (regional specialties) on plastic tables that can be easily jettisoned – which is what happens when this *comedor* morphs into the closest thing to a happening nightclub in Jalapa. There's a public pool in the same building, in case you want to swim off lunch.

❶ Information

There are several banks around town with ATMs.

❶ Getting There & Away

The **bus terminal** is just south of town, near the cemetery. The taxi drivers who hang out here are sharks, so if your bags aren't too heavy, walk a couple of blocks and hail a cab on the road.

Bus services include the following:

El Jícaro (Ciudad Sandino) (US$1.60, 1½ hours, 10:15am and 3pm) Meets buses to Murra.

El Porvenir (US$1.30, 30 minutes, hourly until 6pm)

Estelí (US$3.50, four hours, 4am and 10:50am)

Managua (US$6, 5½ hours, 3am, 4am, 9am, 9:40am,1:45pm and 5:30pm)

Ocotal (US$1.70, 2½ hours, 5am to 4pm, hourly)

Estelí–Jinotega Road

The coffee-country hinterland between Estelí and Jinotega contains tiny farming villages, gorgeous farms clinging to steep mountainsides and tracts of lush forest. It's an accessible yet rarely visited area that offers fascinating insights into authentic rural Nicaraguan culture, many of which can be seen by driving or taking a bus along this scenic road.

❶ Getting There & Away

It's possible to travel these roads on the cheap with public transport. There are half a dozen buses a day from Estelí to Jinotega via Concordia and San Rafael (US$1.50, two hours).

Alternatively there are four buses a day from Estelí to Yalí (US$1.90, 2½ hours) along the rough road through Miraflor. From Yalí there are regular connections to Jinotega (US$1.60, 2½ hours).

San Rafael del Norte

POP 5900 / ELEV 1085M

One of the highest towns in Nicaragua, charming San Rafael del Norte is surrounded by soaring, fissured peaks with coffee *fincas* on their shoulders. Founded in the 1660s, it is rich in culture and a great jump-ing-off point for hikes and outdoor activities high in the mountains. The town also holds an important place in Nicaragua's national consciousness, being the birthplace of the country's first national heroine, Blanca Aráuz, also known as Mrs Augusto César Sandino.

◉ Sights

**Templo Parroquial de
San Rafael Arcángel**　　　　　　CHURCH

(Calle 1a SE) Beginning in 1955, the revered Father Odorico D'Andrea turned this antiquated cathedral into a labor of divine love. It's impeccably restored, with a soaring interior flooded with light streaming through stained-glass skylights that illuminate its altar and a series of murals, which were painted by Austrian artist Juan Fuchs Holl in 1967 and 1968. Controversially, the first mural on the left as you enter the church portrays the temptation of Christ by a devil who looks uncannily like Daniel Ortega.

Santuario Cerro Tepeyac　　　　CHURCH

Climb the steep staircase that disappears into the trees at the northern end of town to find the final resting place of Father Odorico D'Andrea, set at this hillside church modeled after the Shrine of the Virgin of Guadalupe in Mexico. You can pay your respects to the popular priest at his tomb to the left of the main altar.

ⓕ Tours

★ **La Brellera Canopy Tour**　　　ADVENTURE

(☏ 8814-3656; www.canopytourlabrellera.com; per person US$20; ⊗ 8am-5pm Mon-Fri, to 5:30pm Sat & Sun) Tired of coffee? Head just 5km from San Rafael to La Brellera to traverse 1500m through pine forest via nine platforms, eight cables and two hanging bridges. For an extra US$7 you can make the return trip on horseback. There is an onsite restaurant serving barbecue dishes and typical Nica meals.

⨇ Sleeping

San Rafael is very doable as a day trip from either Jinotega or Estelí, but if you want to stick around there are a couple of good hotels in town and two top rural lodges just outside.

Hotel Casita San Payo　　　GUESTHOUSE $

(☏ 2784-2327; casitasanpayo@gmail.com; Parque Central, 2½c N; s/d/tr US$14.50/17.50/19; ☎) This is a terrific budget hotel with sunny

---

❶ FATHER ODORICO D'ANDREA

Father Odorico D'Andrea was born in Italy in 1916, and anointed as a Franciscan friar in 1942. He found his way to San Rafael del Norte 12 years later, where he not only constructed the magnificent temple here, but also got the first roads, running water, schools and clinic into the region. His efforts never sat well with the government – in 1959 he had to flee Somoza's forces, and he later became an outspoken critic of the Sandinistas, though he always worked for peace. And he lived to see it, just barely. On May 3, 1989, in La Naranja, he gave the Eucharist to Sandinistas and Contras together, before dying peacefully a year later. As something of a town hero, his body was exhumed in 2006 in order to rebury it inside the Santuario Cerro Tepeyac and – according to locals – his body was found not to have decayed since dying 15 years earlier.

upstairs rooms with cable TV, and it has a great restaurant, too (mains US$4 to US$7). The fabulous owner, Naraya Zelaya, is beyond helpful – she rents out a pickup and a minibus, complete with driver, to explore the region and can also arrange guides (per half-/full day US$10/20).

Among the destinations the hotel arranges trips to are the Cascadas Verdes and Salto Santa María waterfalls, the Cuevas del Hermitanio caves and pine-blanketed Volcán Yalí (1542m).

Casa Real HOTEL $$
(☑2784-2422; www.facebook.com/hotelcasarealsrn; Del Museo, 1c O, 1c N; s/d/tw US$25/40/50; ☎) This brand-new place opened in late 2017 and is easily the most impressive hotel in town, with a number of artfully designed rooms, many with large balconies or patios, designer bathrooms and good mattresses.

✖ Eating

Coffee Lovers CAFE $
(Del Museo, 1c O, 1c N; mains US$3-5.50; ☎) A very surprising discovery just a couple of blocks from the Parque Central, this gleaming temple to coffee serves up a range of breakfasts as well as quesadillas, panini and crepes. There is, of course, also excellent coffee.

❶ Getting There & Away

Buses (US$0.75, 45 minutes) and minibuses (US$1, 30 minutes) to Jinotega and Estelí (US$1.30, 90 minutes, every two hours) leave at regular intervals from a small **bus station** on the north side of town. Buses for Estelí travel via La Concordia.

San Juan de Limay
POP 4000

San Juan de Limay's cobblestone and brick streets seemingly appear from the dust 44km west of Estelí to form a precious country town, known for its stone carvers and surrounded by soaring peaks.

Look for the enlightened *gorda* (pudgy lady); she's the town's signature symbol. Most often she's carved from *marmolina* (soapstone), a heavy rock that is mined in nearby Cerro Tipiscayán and carved and sanded in home workshops until it shines.

The best gallery, Taller Casco Dablia, is located behind the school and opposite the town square.

⬛ Shopping

Taller Casco Dablia ARTS & CRAFTS
(☑2719-5228, 8842-5162; detras del colegio; ☺8am-6pm) One of the best soapstone workshops in town. Visitors are welcome to come and watch the artisans work (but call first to make sure there is someone around). It also has a room with private bathroom (US$8) available if you want to stay and spend some time learning about the craft.

❶ Getting There & Away

The road to Limay branches off the Panamericana north of Estelí, near the community of La Sirena. Buses leave the Cotran Norte (p175) in Estelí for Limay (US$1.30, 2½ hours) six times daily.

Jinotega
POP 51,800 / ELEV 985M

Hidden at the bottom of a verdant valley, Jinotega, the 'City of Mists,' is enclosed on all sides by mountains dappled in cloud forests, crowned with granite ridges and pocked with deep gorges. Its setting is gorgeous, and even though the city is no colonial beauty, the wide streets and neat public squares are inviting, and the climate is cool and breezy.

Few travelers make it here, but those who do enjoy visiting nearby Lago de Apanás and hiking into the misty mountains, where you can discover the local coffee industry and stroll through primary forest. Just make sure to get to Cerro La Cruz on a clear morning to glimpse Jinotega in all her jade glory.

And that City of Mists moniker is no joke – the average temperature is just 20°C (68°F) and the town can get 2600mm of rain annually – so bring a fleece for the cool evenings.

◉ Sights

★ Cerro La Cruz CHRISTIAN SITE
A steep yet worthwhile hour's hike from the cemetery and embedded in a boulder-crusted ridge is the town cross, originally placed here in 1703 by Franciscan Fray Margíl de Jesús. The view of Jinotega and the layered Cordillera Isabelía from up here is unreal. Take the center path through the cemetery and begin the sweaty climb. When you emerge from the trees and come to a plateau, hug the ridge tightly and keep climbing.

Jinotega

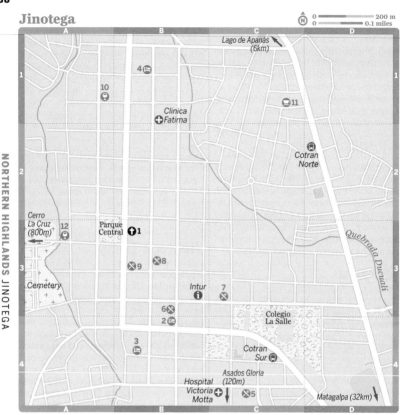

Jinotega

⊙ Sights

🛏 Sleeping

🍴 Eating

🍷 Drinking & Nightlife

Catedral San Juan CHURCH

The beauty of Jinotega's cathedral (c 1805) is in the sanctuary, where you'll marvel at the chestnut and gold-leaf altar, and pristine white arches and rows of heavenly saints, sculpted with so much life and light they make spiritual peace contagious. Outside is the terrific, split-level **Parque Central** shaded by palms and towering laurel trees, full of rides for kids.

🛏 Sleeping

Hotel Primavera GUESTHOUSE **$**

(☎2782-2400; Parque Central, 5c N, 1c E; s/d/tr US$8/12/16; 🛜) The cleanest cheapie in town has tiles in the rooms, cable TV, hot water and decent mattresses, and is owned by a lovely family who hang out in the lobby. The door shuts at 9.30pm sharp, so make arrangements if you intend to stay out late, or request the one room with an independent entrance.

Hotel Neblina
HOTEL **$$**

(☑ 2782-2899; hotelneblinajinotega@gmail.com; Tip Top, 1c S, ½c O; s/d/tw incl breakfast US$30/34/46; ❄☎) In a quiet part of town, this pleasantly painted and secure hotel has comfortable, modern rooms with gas-heated hot water and all the necessary amenities. The upstairs rooms are brighter and accessed by a long balcony with fine mountain views.

★Hotel Café
HOTEL **$$$**

(☑ 2782-2710; Gasolinera Uno, 1c O, ½c N; s/d incl breakfast US$55/65; P❄☎) The most comfy sleep in Jinotega is located at this three-star property. Rooms are a little aged now, with pastel paint jobs and, in some cases, little natural light, but they're decent and have desks and fast wireless. Service is professional and courteous, and breakfast is good. Hyper-speed laundry service and free parking in the garage opposite are bonuses.

✖ Eating

★Libertalia
ITALIAN **$**

(☑ 2782-2548; Casino Atlantic City, 75m O; pizzas US$3-8, pasta US$3-5; ❍noon-11pm Tue-Sun; ☎✍) This friendly Italian restaurant is filled with plants and decorated with maps and local handicrafts. Its menu includes good thin-crust pizza and a range of tasty pastas, salads, meat grills and a range of excellent local craft beer. It might not get particular attention in most cities, but it's definitely a top choice in Jinotega.

La Casa de Don Colocho
BAKERY **$**

(☑ 2782-2584; Parque Central, 3c E, 3c S; pastries US$0.30-1; ❍8am-6pm Mon-Sat) A bakery every town would love. The cinnamon rolls are dense and sugary, the *pan de leche* is crispy on the outside and dense and moist inside, and the pineapple triangles are addictive – and those are just three of the dozens of items this place turns out daily. Either take away from the bakery or sit and enjoy in the cafe.

Asados Gloria
BARBECUE **$**

(Hospital Victoria Motta, 1c E; meals US$2.50-3; ❍9am-9:30pm Thu-Tue) A cheap *fritanga* (grill) with a difference: the stock-standard fluorescent lights and plastic chairs have been replaced with mood lighting and wooden furniture. The grilled meats are tasty and are served with real, lettuce-based salad, rather than cabbage.

★Jikao Cafe
CAFE **$$**

(www.facebook.com/jikaocafe; Hotel Café, ½c N; mains US$3-6; ❍8am-9pm Mon-Sat, noon-9pm Sun; ☎) This lovely new place gets it all just about right: friendly staff, hip decor, excellent coffee (yes, competition is stiff here) and a scrumptious menu that couldn't be further away from *gallo pinto* if it tried – enjoy savoury or sweet crepes, chimichangas, a grilled cheese sandwich or just the heavenly passionfruit mousse.

La Terraza
CAFE **$$**

(Parque Central, 1c E, ½c S; mains US$5-7; ❍noon-10pm; ☎) This cafe-restaurant above Soda El Tico (☑ 2782-2059; buffet meals US$3.50, mains US$5.50; ❍7:30am-10pm) feels just a tad too stylish for hard-working Jinotega with its attractive wrought-iron tables, big sofas, hanging lamps and huge glass windows. It has a full range of caffeinated beverages and a small but diverse menu that includes big salads and meaty sandwiches.

🍷 Drinking & Nightlife

★Bar Jinocuba
BAR

(Alcaldía, 5c N; ❍3-11pm Mon-Thu, to midnight Fri-Sun; ☎) A groovy bohemian bar (and guaranteed *ranchero*-free zone) with occasional, hip live-music performances and cultural events. The young owners are very knowledgeable about tourism in the region and can hook you up with independent English- and German-speaking guides to explore the surrounding mountains. Also serves Cuban and international meals.

★Café Flor de Jinotega
CAFE

(☑ 2782-2617; www.soppexcca.org; Cotran Norte, 1½c N; espresso drinks US$0.50-0.75; ❍8am-6pm; ☎) Quite simply the best cup of coffee in town, and possibly on all of the Ruta de Café (p190), this charming place is run by Soppexcca, a union of local coffee cooperatives. Relax at one of the see-through tables filled with three kinds of coffee beans and enjoy a superlative local roast. Staff also arrange guides to nearby coffee farms.

La Gran Taverna VIP
BAR

(Parque Central, 2c O; ❍noon-midnight; ☎) The coolest dive bar in the northern highlands has timber tables, a dark-wood interior, a lively late-night crowd and tasty beef fajitas (US$5).

WORTH A TRIP

LA RUTA DE CAFÉ

Formed to promote rural tourism in the north, the Ruta de Café is a loose association of coffee *fincas* (farms) that welcome tourists to their fields (which range from *colectivos* of small subsistence growers to grand 100-year-old plantations). While promotion and funding of the project seems to have dried up, most properties involved still welcome visitors.

You can spend the night, hike through neighboring cloud forests, join in harvests (October to March) and sip plenty of local joe. There are four branches to Ruta de Café, which spans the entirety of the northern highlands.

Estelí & Nueva Segovia Near Estelí, the Área Protegida Miraflor (p175) is a tapestry of family coffee fincas that formed in the wake of the Sandinista revolution. Further north, the lush, layered and shady coffee fields of Dipilto (p182) produce some of the most acclaimed beans in Nicaragua, while Finca Cerro de Jesús grows terrific coffee among large tracts of cloud forest in the rocky peaks surrounding Jalapa.

San Rafael del Norte Accessed from San Rafael del Norte, El Jaguar (p192) is a family farm and model of sustainability, with 14 hectares of organic coffee parcels surrounded by 53 hectares of tropical cloud forest. In addition to joining the harvest, you can ride trails to *glorious* miradores (lookout points), plunge into swimming holes and milk the family cows.

Jinotega When German coffee growers and their families first arrived in Nicaragua in the early 20th century, they came to the mountains that soar above Jinotega. It is here that you'll find La Bastilla Ecolodge, a nonprofit initiative within a nature reserve that offers full coffee tours that include tasting sessions. Check in at Café Flor de Jinotega (p189) for information on touring other coffee farms in the nearby cloud forest.

Matagalpa The big draws here are two very different coffee-farm experiences. Selva Negra (p199), an 850-hectare estate, was founded by German immigrants in the 1880s and is still managed by their heirs. It offers sustainable coffee and wildlife tours amid magical scenery. For a more rustic experience, head to the communities surrounding San Ramón (p198), where you can join the locals in the harvest and follow the beans to a community roasting plant.

ℹ Information

MEDICAL SERVICES

For emergencies or serious illness, head for Jinotega's public **Hospital Victoria Motta** (☑ 8524-9722; Parque Otto Casco, 1c S; ☺ 24hr). Appointments with a range of specialists can be had at the private **Clinica Fatima** (☑ 2782-6577; Esso Central, 2½c N; ☺ 8:30am-5pm Mon-Fri, to noon Sat).

MONEY

BanPro and BAC both have several ATMs around town that accept Visa and MasterCard credit and debit cards.

TOURIST INFORMATION

Intur (☑ 2782-4552; Parque Central, 2c S, 3c E; ☺ 8am-4pm) Stop in to pick up the latest brochures.

ℹ Getting There & Away

There are two bus terminals in Jinotega; **Cotran Norte**, on the edge of the market, is little more than a chaotic parking lot, while orderly and clean **Cotran Sur** sits near the town's southern entrance and is the best terminal in the region: it has shops, departure announcements and even a waiting lounge with wi-fi.

Buses departing from Cotran Norte:

Estelí (US$1.60, two hours, 5:15am, 7am, 9am, 1pm, 2:45pm & 3:30pm)

Pantasma (Asturias) (US$1.60, 1½ hours, 4am to 4:30pm, hourly)

Pantasma (San Gabriel) (US$1.60, 1½ hours, 5:30am to 4:30pm, hourly)

San Rafael del Norte (*ordinario* US$0.70, 40 minutes; *expreso* US$1, 30 minutes, both 6am to 6pm, half-hourly)

Yalí (US$1.60, two hours, 6am, 8:30am, 10am, noon, 2:30pm and 4pm)

Buses departing from Cotran Sur:

Managua (US$2.80, 3½ hours, 4am to 4pm, 10 daily) Buy tickets at the office in Cotran Sur.

Matagalpa (US$0.85, 1¼ hours, 5am to 6:15pm, half-hourly)

Reserva Natural Cerro Datanlí-El Diablo

The mountains towering over and buffering the eastern end of Jinotega are part of this stunning 100 sq km reserve, which climbs well into the quetzal zone at 1650m. It's a magical place, with butterflies dancing around coffee bushes that cling to impossibly steep mountainsides in the shade of lush cloud forest. A network of trails connects communities within the reserve and makes for great hiking.

◉ Sights

La Bujona   WATERFALL

(La Esmeralda; US$1) Surrounded by ethereal cloud forest, La Bujona is a wide wall of water that crashes over the rock face in various streams. It feels far from civilization and receives very few visitors. The path begins by two small posts just before the wooden bridge. You can trek the 12km from La Fundadora on your own, but it's more fun with a local guide: the Eco-Albergue will organize one for US$10 per group.

⌂ Sleeping

There are comfortable accommodations options within the reserve both in local communities and on working coffee farms. Sustainable tourism is big here – many accommodations are run either by local cooperatives or as part of development projects.

Eco-Albergue La Fundadora   LODGE $

(☑ 7747-7805, 8855-2573; www.fundadora.org; La Fundadora; d/r per person US$7/10) An incredibly peaceful, community-run rural lodge set in a breathtaking position overlooking mountainside coffee plantations and farmland, La Fundadora is about 5km along a bumpy dirt track off the main Jinotega–Matagalpa highway. The half a dozen cute brick huts with tiled roofs offer clean but rustic accommodations amid utter tranquility, and tasty meals (US$2.30 to US$3.50) are served onsite.

The savvy young management arranges a variety of activities for visitors, including a truly authentic coffee tour (US$10 per visitor) with a local farming family, horseback riding (US$20 for four hours for up to three people), hikes to La Bujona (US$10) and three-hour cycling tours (US$30) through the gorgeous countryside.

★ La Bastilla Ecolodge   LODGE $$$

(☑ 8654-6235, 2782-4335; www.bastillaecolodge. com; Reserva Natural Datanlí-El Diablo; dm/s/d/tr incl breakfast US$20/45/70/100; ℗ 🛜) Set on a dramatic, forested mountainside at 1200m with views all the way down to Lago de Apanás, La Bastilla Ecolodge has easily the most comfortable accommodations in the reserve. The spacious, solar-powered brick *cabañas* have red floor tiles, sparkling bathrooms with solar hot water, and sensational views over coffee plantations full of birds from the wide wooden balconies.

There are also comfy tents (US$15 per guest) set up on wooden platforms with private bathrooms, and panoramic views and a comfortable dormitory. But 1st-class comfort and service is only half the story here. The ecolodge is an entirely nonprofit initiative that funds the nearby technical training center. Many students from the center work as guides and can take you along the 300-hectare farm's three hiking trails. You can even try your hand picking your own coffee.

ℹ Getting There & Away

One daily bus leaves Cotran Norte (p197) in Matagalpa at 1:45pm for Las Nubes, passing through La Fundadora and La Esmeralda, returning at 6am. It gets full, so arrive early or you may be riding on the roof. During the coffee harvest buses also run to the area from Jinotega, but the schedule is irregular and they are usually packed.

If you miss the direct bus, it's also possible to hike into La Fundadora from Las Latas on the old Matagalpa–Jinotega highway; it's a much shorter trek than walking along the main Fundadora road but there's also less traffic, so your chances of hitching a ride are minimal.

For La Bastilla, take any Pantasma bus (via Asturias) from Jinotega and jump out at the

---

ℹ ACCESS TO THE RESERVE

The main southern entrance to the reserve is 12.5km down a lousy dirt road from the signed turnoff 'Km 146' on the Matagalpa–Jinotega road. Continue on straight until you reach the village of La Fundadora, located on the site of an expansive former Somoza hacienda. From La Fundadora, it's another rough 30-minute drive to the impressive La Bujona waterfall in the community of La Esmeralda.

'empalme La Bastilla,' from where it's a tough 5km hike uphill. If you call in advance, staff from La Bastilla Ecolodge (p191) will pick you up at the turnoff (US$5). The same Pantasma bus can drop you at the village of Venencia, a short distance further down the road from La Bastilla, from where it's a 3km, one-hour walk down a rough spur road to El Gobiado. If you phone ahead to La Bastilla Ecolodge, it's possible to organize horses to save you the walk.

Lago de Apanás

The third-largest body of water in Nicaragua came into being in 1964 when the Mancotal dam was built on the Río El Tuma, just 6km north of Jinotega. It's actually two lakes – the much larger Lago de Apanás (54 sq km) to the south, and Lago Asturias (3 sq km) to the north. The scenery here is lovely, with verdant hills running along the lakeshore and thick forest all around. A good sealed road runs along the southern and eastern side of the lake all the way to Pantasma, whereas the road across the northern side of the lake is unsealed and makes for a slow and dusty ride.

◉ Sights & Activities

Try the *guapote* (freshwater bass), on sale at lots of rickety-looking houses lining the lakeshore in the town of Asturias – or if you'd prefer to catch your own, fishers will take you out on the lake for around US$5 per hour in a rowboat, or US$10 per hour with a small outboard.

El Jaguar PARK
(☑ 2279-9219, 8886-1016; www.jaguarreserve. org; costs vary by activity; ⊞) ✿ Both coffee enthusiasts and nature lovers will be enamored with this fantastic private reserve with comfortable *cabañas* (dorm/room per person including three meals US$35/70) and family-friendly trails (read: nothing too long or too steep) as well as strenuous ones through primary cloud forest and past

---

BOATING AROUND THE ISLANDS

On the northern lakeshore in the village of Sisle, local fisherfolk will take you out on boat tours to nearby islands, including Isla Ave (US$2) and Isla Conejo (US$5); departures are from the Malecón Turístico de Sisle (Sisle Tourist Dock) overlooking the water.

---

coffee stands to spectacular viewpoints. Advance reservations are essential.

Yanque VILLAGE
About a 20-minute drive further north from Sisle along the road that hugs the lakeshore, near the community of Yanque, you'll find the Comedor Norita, where you can ride horses, learn about local agriculture and visit a viewpoint with panoramic vistas of the lake and surrounding countryside.

⊨ Sleeping

Most people visit for the day from Jinotega and the surrounding area, where there are plenty of hotels.

Lakum Payaska CABAÑAS $$
(Brisas del Lago; ☑ 2700-2831; cabaña US$30)
This simple restaurant (open 10am to 8pm) has a three-room *cabaña* across the road that it rents out. It's one of the few places to stay by the lake and has some lovely views. The restaurant itself is a rather ramshackle wooden tree house–style place, but serves up decent meals – including fresh fish from the lake – for around US$6.

✕ Eating

Restaurante La Marina NICARAGUAN $
(Asturias; mains US$3-5; ⊗8am-8pm Sun-Thu, to 10pm Fri & Sat) The most scenic spot for lunch on the lake, with a view towards some nearby islands, La Marina has tables right up by the water where they'll serve you gorgeously fresh *guapote* or delicious fish soups at very reasonable prices.

ⓘ Getting There & Away

There are two bus routes to Pantasma from the Cotran Norte (p190) in Jinotega: via Asturias on the eastern shore of the lake and via San Gabriel on the western side. To get to Sisle, take any San Gabriel bus and ask to be let off at the Pulpería Emilio Gomez, from where it's an 800m walk downhill to the dock. For Yanque stay on the bus and ask to be let off at Pulpería Adrian Granados.

Matagalpa

POP 150,600 / ELEV 902M
Matagalpa may be one of Nicaragua's biggest cities, but it remains a fairly provincial and laid-back place, an almost reluctant urban centre for this most bucolic of regions. Here the nearby mountains, which soar in every direction around the city's central neighborhoods, are never far from locals'

minds, not to mention the coffee produced on their hillsides, which accounts for Matagalpa's historic wealth.

The city itself is pleasant enough, with a young and friendly population who seem delighted to see visitors. It is best used, however, as a comfortable urban base for exploring the surrounding countryside, where you can hike through primary forest to gushing waterfalls, explore coffee plantations and disused mine shafts and listen to *ranchero* troubadours jam under a harvest moon.

◉ Sights

★ Casa Museo Comandante Carlos Fonseca   MUSEUM

(Parque Rubén Darío, 1c E; by donation; ⏰9am-5pm Mon-Fri, to noon Sat) Commander Carlos Fonseca, the Sandinista equivalent of Malcolm X (read: bespectacled, goateed, intense, highly charismatic), grew up desperately poor in this humble abode with his single mother and four siblings, despite the fact that his father was a coffee magnate. Now it's a tiny but interesting museum that follows his evolution as a leader from childhood until his death.

Museo Nacional de Café   MUSEUM

(☑2772-0587; Av José Benito Escobar, Parque Morazán, 1c S; ⏰8am-12:30pm & 2-5:30pm Mon-Fri) FREE This absorbing museum features large, glossy, printed displays in Spanish and English on the roots of modern coffee production in the region, as well as antique coffee-processing machinery. Particularly interesting are the panels on the hardy immigrants who set up the first plantations in the region. Well worth a visit before any trip into the surrounding countryside.

Foreigners Cemetery   CEMETERY

Graveyard fans should check out both the Foreigners Cemetery (and nearby National Cemetery) on the eastern edge of town, where you'll find great views and the headstone of Benjamin Linder, an American hydroelectric engineer who was murdered by Contra forces, an event that further polarized US public opinion about the morality of the Contra War.

Iglesia San José   CHURCH

(Parque Rubén Darío) Originally constructed in 1751 and used as a jail for indigenous rebels in the late 1800s, this church was rebuilt in 1917 by Franciscan friars. The baroque gold-leaf altar and arched ceilings are lovely, while its pink facade immeasurably improves the leafy Parque Rubén Darío out front.

Iglesia Catedral San Pedro   CATHEDRAL

(Parque Morazán) Built in 1874, Matagalpa's glorious, whitewashed neoclassical cathedral is flooded with light. Inside the sanctuary are a natural wood altar, gorgeous domes, arches and crown moldings. It fronts Parque Morazán, a reasonably shady hangout with outstanding people-watching.

☆ Activities

Local hiking opportunities abound. The gorgeous boulder fields and red-rock faces of El Ocote are sensational. You can access the trail from behind El Castillo del Cacao and hike two to three hours before rejoining the highway to San Ramón at Finca La Praya. It's just a US$0.50 bus ride back to town.

For more hiking options, pop into nonprofit Cafetín Girasol for detailed leaflets (US$1) explaining a number of self-guided walks in the Matagalpa area that vary in length from four to eight hours.

Cafetín Girasol   HIKING

(☑2772-6030; www.familiasespeciales.org; contiguo Puente Salida Managua; ⏰7am-7:30pm Mon-Sat) 🖉 A charitable setup that accepts volunteers, Cafetín Girasol sells detailed leaflets (US$1) for a number of self-guided walks in the Matagalpa area that vary in length from four to eight hours. While you're here be sure to sample the excellent coffee, pastries and homemade yogurt – the profits support projects for children with disabilities.

Reserva Natural Cerro Apante   OUTDOORS

(US$1.50) Matagalpa's most popular hiking trail leads from Finca San Luis, a 20-minute walk (or US$1 taxi ride) south of Parque Rubén Darío, into this reserve. It's a two-hour round-trip hike to the *mirador* (viewpoint). If you're aiming for the misty, 1442m-high peak, it's best to hire a guide.

⮂ Courses

Escuela de Español Colibrí   LANGUAGE

(www.colibrispanishschool.com; Parque Morazán, 1c S, ½c E; tuition per hour US$11-12) This popular school offers one-on-one Spanish classes, plenty of cultural activities and volunteer placements for students. Packages that include 20 hours of classes per week plus a homestay with a local family and all meals cost US$344.

Matagalpa

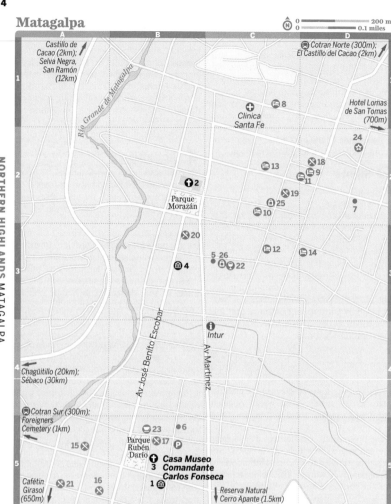

Castillo de Cacao (2km); Selva Negra; San Ramón (12km)

Río Grande de Matagalpa

Cotran Norte (300m); El Castillo del Cacao (2km)

Hotel Lomas de San Tomas (700m)

Clinica Santa Fe

8

24

13

18
9
11

19

2

Parque Morazán

25
10

7

20

12

14

5 26
4

22

Intur

Av. José Benito Escobar

Av. Martínez

Chagüitillo (20km); Sébaco (30km)

Cotran Sur (300m); Foreigners Cemetery (1km)

23

6

15

17

Parque Rubén Darío

Casa Museo Comandante Carlos Fonseca

3

Cafétin Girasol (650m)

21

16

1

Reserva Natural Cerro Apante (1.5km)

🖙 Tours

★ Nativos Tours   TOURS

(📞 2772-7281, 8493-0932; nativotour@hotmail.com; Cancha Brigadista, 4c E) Contact English-speaking Nativo Tours for some of the most imaginative and interesting excursions available in the region. Owner-operator Guillermo is young and hugely passionate about hiking and nature, and his tours include cultural city tours, black pottery workshops, hikes up to the cross above town, horseback riding, herding cattle, visits to waterfalls and even nocturnal hiking.

★ Matagalpa Tours   ADVENTURE

(📞 2772-0108, 2772-5379; www.matagalpatours.com; Parque Rubén Darío, 1c E, 20m N; tours from US$15; 🕐 8am-12:30pm & 2-6pm Mon-Fri, 8am-4pm Sat) Matagalpa Tours offers nearly a dozen interesting and enriching ways to get into this city and the surrounding country-side. In Matagalpa proper it offers urban walking tours and rents out bicycles, but its best work is done around the local mountains, where it offers both day trips and multiday excursions, including a fascinating tour of local coffee farms.

Matagalpa

El Castillo del Cacao   FOOD & DRINK
(☑ 2772-2002; Carretera La Dalia; US$6; ⊘ 9am-noon Tue-Sat) On the road to San Ramón is Matagalpa's sweetest site. You've seen the chocolate bars by now, and if you know what's good(-tasting) for you, you've also tasted Castillo de Cacao. Now tour the 'castle' where they mix the cacao with sugar, cashews and coffee beans. Call first to make sure they're working.

🛌 Sleeping

★ **Buongiorno Principessa**   GUESTHOUSE $$
(☑ 2772-2721; buongiornoprincipessa35@gmail.com; Cancha Brigadista, 2c E ½c N; dm/r incl breakfast US$12/30; 🛜) This laid-back guesthouse is an excellent base for exploring town. Dorms feature good mattresses and are not overcrowded, while private rooms are bright and welcoming. All boast fans, hot water and are spotless. The included breakfast is top quality, but the highlight is the hammock-slung and plant-strewn rooftop terrace offering 360-degree views of Matagalpa.

★ **La Buena Onda**   HOSTEL $$
(☑ 2772-2135; www.labuenaonda.com.ni; Cancha Brigadista, 2½c E; dm/s/d US$9/25/30; 🛜) Clean, centrally located and with a chilled vibe, this popular hostel in a cozy, converted house with well-furnished rooms offers spacious dorms (with private bathrooms and big lockers) and an upstairs balcony overlooking the street. There is a communal kitchen, a small garden and laundry service available. The helpful management provides plenty of information on attractions in town and beyond.

Martina's Place   HOSTEL $$
(☑ 2772-3918; www.martinasplace-hostal.com; Cancha Brigadista, 1½c E; dm/s/d/tr/q without bathroom US$9/20/25/40/50, s/d/tr/q with bathroom US$25/30/45/55; 🛜) An excellent hostel in a convenient location offering neat and comfortable private rooms and a massive 20-bed dorm. The mattresses are good and the owners are extremely helpful and can help organise tours. There's also a spacious courtyard area complete with BBQ and outdoor kitchen, and scooter rental is available (US$20 per day).

Brisas Hotel   HOTEL $$
(☑ 2772-6061; brisashotel2015@gmail.com; Clinica Santa Fe, 75m E; s/d incl breakfast from US$25/40; ❄🛜) This modern place offers spotless, pastel-colored rooms with good mattresses, desks and good bathrooms. The accommodations are not particularly spacious but are good value. Add US$10 for air-con.

Hostal Don Guillermo   HOTEL $$
(☑ 2772-3182; hostaldonguillermomatagalpa@gmail.com; Enitel, ½c E; s/d/tw/tr US$28/35/45/60; ❄🛜) With a great location, elegant if rather dated furnishings and a relaxed atmosphere, this small hotel offers some of the best-value accommodations in town. The rooms are bright and spacious and the ample bathrooms have piping-hot water and good

GÜIRÍILAS

Matagalpa has a few good restaurants, but you'll need to look to the smoky booths that set up at sunset just north of Palí supermarket and the cathedral for the regional specialty, *güiríilas*. Made with a fresh corn *masa*, they are sweeter and thicker than your average tortilla; a *servicio* includes a hunk of crumbly, salty *cuajada* cheese and *crema*.

pressure. Breakfast is served in the small, plant-filled courtyard. Air-con is an extra US$10 per room per night.

★ **Maria's B&B** B&B $$$
(☎2772-3097; www.mariasbnb.com; BanPro, 1c E, ½c N; s/d/tr incl breakfast US$46/51/66; P❋✿) This intimate place right in the center of town has just half a dozen bright, spotless and comfortable rooms surrounding inviting common areas and feels like staying with a rather fancy friend. Guests can use the open-plan kitchen and dining room, while service is warm and welcoming, particularly from doña Chepa, who will cook your breakfast to order each morning.

Montebrisa BOUTIQUE HOTEL $$$
(☎2772-4392; https://montebrisa.com; Parque Morazán, 3c E; r US$90-120; P❋✿) This beautifully renovated art deco house is a modern classic set in lush gardens on a hill just three blocks from Parque Morazán. The eight rooms are spacious and light-filled, with elegant cedar furniture; some boast small private balconies that offer glimpses of Cerro Apante through the trees. Reservations are essential – walk-ins are not accepted.

Hotel Lomas de San Tomas HOTEL $$$
(☎2772-4189; snthomas2006@yahoo.com; Escuela Guanuca, 350m E; s/d US$59/70; P❋✿) For a total change of pace to the bustle of town, try this impressive hilltop hacienda property which boasts huge rooms with ceramic-tiled floors, walk-out balconies and lovely gardens. It's a US$1.50 taxi ride from downtown, and while it's often creepily empty, staying here is a way to enjoy Matagalpa in some style.

Eating

★ **Kiss Me** ICE CREAM $
(Parque Rubén Darío; ice cream from US$2; ⊙1-9pm; ✿) This fabulous little ice-cream par-

lor sets the tone with its pink screen doors, checkerboard floor and hipstery hanging lights. It may be serving a rather retro vibe, but the ice cream is all innovation, with flavors including salted caramel, passionfruit and 'fruit punch in the face.' Easily the best of the lot though is the off-menu Miel Mi Amor.

Guakmole MEXICAN $
(www.facebook.com/guakmolematagalpa; Parque Rubén Darío, 1c S; mains US$3-5; ⊙noon-9pm Mon-Fri, 11am-9pm Sat & Sun; ✉) This quasi-hipster joint serves up a delicious selection of simple Mexican dishes, including a damn fine burrito. The eponymous guacamole is also worth checking out.

Taquero NICARAGUAN, MEXICAN $
(Parque Rubén Darío, 1c S, 1½c O; meals US$3-8; ⊙5:30pm-midnight) Part *fritanga* (grill), part Mexican diner, this hugely popular hybrid serves up impossibly tender BBQ beef, tangy chicken and ribs from the grill, as well as quality tacos, burritos and quesadillas.

Repostería Gutiérrez BAKERY $
(☎2772-2502; Parque Morazán, ½c S; pastries US$0.50-2; ⊙7am-8pm) This excellent bakery serves tasty fresh pastries and excellent local coffee to a dedicated clientele.

★ **Lunaflor** INTERNATIONAL $$
(☎8617-8600; contiguo a tienda la Piñata; mains US$4-8; ⊙4-10pm Mon-Sat; ✿✉) 🍴 This fantastic arrival on Matagalpa's dining scene will be a godsend to travellers bored of typical Nica cuisine, with curry and teriyaki-based dishes, bruschetta, bagels and artisanal beer topping the list of things you won't find elsewhere in the northern highlands. The whole place is gorgeous, with tables scattered under a fairy light-strewn tree on a breezy terrace.

Gato Blanco MEDITERRANEAN $$
(☎2772-3868; frente a Sinsa; mains US$4-12; ⊙noon-10:30pm Tue-Sun; ✿✉) The White Cat has a rather dark and unappealing interior, but the tables in the little courtyard out front are far more inviting. The food here is varied and you can choose between daily specials, paella, pizza, ceviche and several vegetarian options.

El Pullazo STEAK $$
(Carretera Managua; dishes US$6-18; ⊙10am-10pm; ✿) Matagalpinos love beef and it's no surprise that their steakhouse of choice is El Pullazo, which serves big portions of tender cuts of meat at bargain prices. It's so popu-

lar they've constructed a second floor. Come with an appetite. It's a US$1.50 to US$2 taxi ride from town.

La Vita é Bella
ITALIAN **$$**

(☑2772-5476; Parque Morazán, 2½c E, 1½c N; mains US$4-8.50; ⊙noon-10pm Wed-Mon; 🛜🎍) This local institution serves up flavorful authentic Italian dishes at low prices in a relaxed bistro atmosphere. The thin-crust pizza is some of the best in town and the pasta dishes are also full of flavor. Vegetarians can take their pick from a wide selection of menu items. Come early to get a table.

🍸 Drinking & Nightlife

Selección Nicaragüense
CAFE

(☑2772-7415; Parque Rubén Darío; ⊙11am-8pm Sat-Thu, 8am-10pm Fri) Pretty slick for the northern highlands, this modern cafe serves up good hot and cold coffee-based drinks using single-origin beans from around the region. Enjoy a cup in the fancy air-con lounge space or on the large patio out the back. It also sells bags of coffee to go – whole or ground – as well as light meals.

Artesanos
BAR

(☑2772-2444; Parque Morazán, 1c S, ½c E; ⊙4:30pm-midnight Tue-Thu, to 2am Fri-Sun) Hands down the coolest bar in town and a fiercely popular meeting point for Matagalpa's students and in crowd. There's an all-dark-wood dining room, a large patio, great coffee and even better cocktails. The hipster crowd grooves to electronic and Latin rhythms until late.

☆ Entertainment

Centro Cultural Guanuca
CULTURAL CENTER

(☑2772-3562; Guadalupe, 1½c S; ⊙7am-8pm) 🎍 Run by a nonprofit women's organization, this great venue shows art-house movies and hosts concerts and live events ranging from theater to dance competitions.

🛍 Shopping

Telares de Nicaragua
ARTS & CRAFTS

(☑8950-2791; www.telaresnicaragua.com; Biblioteca del Banco Central, 25m S; ⊙8am-5pm Mon-Fri, to 2pm Sat) 🎍 This fair-trade association sells brightly colored fiber arts from indigenous artisans in El Chile, corn-husk dolls, beaded jewelry, baskets and a selection of the smooth, black local pottery, which is mixed with volcanic ash and fired at extreme temperatures.

Cerámica Negra Tradicional
ARTS & CRAFTS

(☑2772-2464; Centro Cultural Héroes y Martires, 2c O; ⊙9am-5:30pm Mon-Sat) Mrs Rosa Ernestina Rodriguez has been crafting traditional indigenous black pottery sculptures for over 30 years and is a well-known local artist and expert on *cerámica negra*. You're welcome to come by and see her simple one-room showroom where you can purchase her work and hear the stories behind the pieces from Rosa herself.

ℹ Information

MEDICAL SERVICES
Clinica Santa Fe (☑2772-2690, emergency 8419-6283; Catedral, 3c N, ½c E; ⊙24hr)

MONEY
Most banks are located on Av Martínez, a block south of Parque Morazán.

TOURIST INFORMATION
Intur (☑2772-7060; inturmatagalpa@gmail.com; Av Martínez, Parque Morazán, 3c S; ⊙8am-noon & 1-5pm Mon-Fri) Friendly office with good information on attractions around town.

ℹ Getting There & Away

There are two main bus terminals in Matagalpa. Fairly well-organized **Cotran Sur** (☑2772-4659), about 800m west of Parque Rubén Darío, generally serves Managua, Jinotega and most points south.

Disorienting by comparison, **Cotran Norte** (Cotramusun) is next to the northern market and goes to mostly rural destinations in the north.

BUSES FROM MATAGALPA (COTRAN NORTE)

DESTINATION	COST (US$)	DURATION	FREQUENCY (DAILY)
Cerro Colorado (via Yucul)	2	2hr	5:30am-4pm, hourly
El Cuá	2.50	4hr	6am, 7am, 9am, 10:30am, noon, 1:30pm
Esquipulas	1.30	1½hr	5:40am, 7am, 8am, 9am, noon, 1:30pm, 3pm, 4:30pm, 5:30pm
San Ramón	0.50	30min	5am-7pm, half-hourly

BUSES FROM MATAGALPA (COTRAN SUR)

DESTINATION	COST (US$)	DURATION (HR)	FREQUENCY
Chinandega	3.10	3½	5am & 2pm
Ciudad Darío	0.90	1	5:30am-3pm half-hourly
Estelí	1.15	2¼	5:20am-5:40pm, half-hourly
Jinotega	0.80	1	5am-6pm, half-hourly
León	2.80	2½	6am, 3pm, 4pm
Managua (expreso)	2.60	2¼	5:20am-5:20pm, hourly
Managua (ordinario)	2	2¾	3:35am-6:05pm, half-hourly
Masaya	2.40	3	2pm & 3:30pm

San Ramón

POP 2400 / ELEV 641M

Only 12km from Matagalpa, the small highland town of San Ramón feels a world away, with a rural sensibility and a relaxed vibe. While the town itself isn't of particular interest to travelers, the real reason to come here is to get an authentic taste for rural life among the hardworking farmers in the surrounding hills, and there are half a dozen working coffee farms nearby that offer tours and sometimes accommodations. Like many coffee *fincas* in northern Nicaragua, San Ramón's were hit hard by the outbreak of coffee rust disease in 2013 and some local farmers lost up to 80% of their crops. But growing new, hardier varieties has seen a return to almost full production at most farms in the area and the future looks bright.

🏃 Activities

Local agricultural cooperative **UCA San Ramón** (📋 8927-9066, 2772-5247; www.tourism.ucasanramon.com; frente Parque Municipal; ⊗ 8am-5pm Mon-Fri) has developed a tempting menu of activities in seven nearby villages and farms. All of the communities offer hikes through the countryside and classes in preparing traditional foods, and during the harvest (November to February) visitors can try their hand picking and sorting organic coffee.

It's possible to visit the attractions on a day trip from Matagalpa (US$15 per person) but it's highly recommended to spend the night in one of the villages for the full cultural experience. Make reservations in advance by email with the UCA. If you want to stay longer, you can also organize a volunteer placement with them.

Reserva Natural La Hermandad FARM

📍 Located 6km north of San Ramón, this ecologically focused working coffee plantation also functions as a nature reserve and has some great birdwatching opportunities. It has rustic wooden cabins and serves up delicious Nicaraguan food three times a day to its visitors. Hiking, birdwatching and coffee tours are all laid on. You'll need a 4WD to get here.

Finca Esperanza Verde HIKING, VOLUNTEERING

(www.fincaesperanzaverde.com; Yucul) Hikers will love the five well-marked nature trails weaving through coffee plantations and forest from this plantation lodge. Birdwatching is fantastic, with more than 250 species recorded here, but you might also spot sloths and monkeys near the paths. Other activities include a butterfly enclosure, Nicaraguan cooking workshops and specialized coffee tours.

Day trippers can come and enjoy the trails or just relax at the restaurant (meals US$10 to $12), though in both cases advanced reservations are essential. Volunteer opportunities are also available. The *finca* is located 3.5km up a rough dirt road from the village of Yucul, 15km from San Ramón. You'll need a 4WD vehicle if you plan on driving. If you don't have heavy luggage it's possible to walk, otherwise the lodge can arrange transportation from the Yucul junction or from Matagalpa.

👉 Tours

La Reina CULTURAL

📍 La Reina, 3km east of San Ramón, was once one of Nicaragua's main mining communities; local guides can take you deep into an abandoned mine. Other activities include spotting howler monkeys, sloths and toucans in the forest, cooking classes and learning to make handicrafts. Hiking, horseback riding and coffee harvesting and roasting are also possible, and volunteers are accepted.

El Trentino Obrero   CULTURAL
📍 This small community 4km south of San Ramón differs from others in the region as it's in the dry zone and is mainly dedicated to the harvesting of basic grains; there's also an organic orchard. Visitors can learn to prepare traditional Nicaraguan dishes, discover indigenous customs and find out how the farmers defended their land during the civil war.

El Roblar   CULTURAL
(Cooperative El Privilegio) 📍 Located 35km from San Ramón, this community has great hiking and horseback-riding opportunities, including a trek up into the mountains to three spectacular *miradores* (viewpoints). It is also home to Cooperativa El Privilegio, a women's farming cooperative that grows and roasts its own coffee. There are six buses a day from Cotran Norte (p197) in Matagalpa to El Roblar.

La Corona   CULTURAL
(Yasica Sur) 📍 This community is located near the Yasica Sur waterfall, which is surrounded by forest and has a deep swimming hole. It is also home to a large coffee cooperative where visitors can learn about the entire coffee cultivation process. There are four buses a day from Cotran Norte (p197) in Matagalpa to Yasica Sur.

🛏 Sleeping

⭐ Finca Esperanza Verde   LODGE $$
(www.fincaesperanzaverde.com; Yucul; dm from US$17.50, budget/luxury cabaña US$30/111; 🅿 🛜)
📍 With lush gardens full of hummingbirds, spectacular mountain views and enchanting nature trails, this large organic farm is a fantastic place to stay whether you want to get active or just relax with a good book. The various types of accommodations are simple in design but well constructed and very comfortable, offering top vistas right from your bed.

ℹ Getting There & Away

Buses between Matagalpa and San Ramón (US$0.50, 30 minutes) run every half-hour between 5am and 7pm, leaving from Cotran Norte (p197) in Matagalpa and the park in San Ramón.

Colectivo taxis (US$0.80, 20 minutes) run on the same route from 5am to 7pm, leaving from the Parada San Ramón in Matagalpa.

Reserva Natural Cerro El Arenal

A short drive from Matagalpa along the old highway north to Jinotega, this 14 sq km nature reserve is home to cloud forest interspersed with shade-grown coffee plantations. Despite being one of the smallest nature reserves in the country, it boasts varied landscapes and a wide variety of flora and fauna. It has a pleasant, cool climate – making it an attractive destination for great hikes through ethereal forest landscapes sprinkled with orchids.

◉ Sights

Selva Negra   NATURE RESERVE
(☑ 8100-9100, 2770-1963; www.selvanegra.com; Carretera Jinotega–Matagalpa Km 140; ⊙ 7am-9pm) If you're looking for comfort with your virgin cloud forest experience, then Selva Negra – part family resort, part coffee farm and part rainforest preserve – could be for you. The 850-hectare estate blooms with bromeliads and rare orchids year-round and is home to nesting quetzals in April and May. Founded in the 1880s by German immigrants – who were a part of the original German coffee invasion that created the industry – it's named after Germany's Black Forest.

Their descendants still manage the reserve, which is webbed with several kilometers of lush jungle trails. Visitors can go on nature tours (US$15 per hour, at 7:30am), coffee tours (US$22 per person, at 9:30am and 2pm), sustainable agriculture tours (US$15 per person, at 10am and 1:30pm) and night walks (US$10 per person, at 6pm), and enjoy horseback riding (US$5 per hour). Alternatively, you can simply hike the 20km of trails at your leisure or relax at the restaurant, which overlooks a lake backed by cloud

---

HOMESTAYS IN THE VILLAGES

Many of the villages around San Ramon offer homestays (US$35 to US$45 per visitor), which include three meals and activities. There is also a hotel in San Ramón itself.

NORTHERN HIGHLANDS RESERVA NATURAL CERRO EL ARENAL

forest. Given the setting and abundance of activities, it's no surprise that North American families and package tourists flock here, which means that it doesn't always have the most authentic flavor.

🛌 Sleeping

A number of coffee farms within the reserve have taken the plunge into tourism and offer tours, meals and *cabañas* for overnight guests. The most popular, Selva Negra Ecolodge, has the air of a holiday camp, while the less visited and more remote Aguas del Arenal offers a far more tranquil and secluded experience.

★**Aguas del Arenal**   LODGE **$$**
(📞8160-8431, 8886-3234; aguasdelarenal@gmail. com; Carretera Matagalpa–Jinotega Km 142.5; rooms s/d incl breakfast US$30/40, cabañas s/d/ tr/q incl breakfast US$50/60/70/80; 🎇) 🍴 In the heart of the Reserva Natural Cerro El Arenal, this secluded and intimate family-run lodge is perfect for those looking for a more laid-back coffee country experience. The 7-hectare coffee farm has five spacious and comfortable *cabañas* as well as four rooms in the main house, where you'll also find the cozy common area, complete with a fireplace.

Selva Negra Ecolodge   LODGE **$$$**
(📞2770-1963; www.selvanegra.com; Carretera Jinotega–Matagalpa Km 140; dm US$15, r US$55-120; 🎇) As well as being an impressive nature reserve with numerous tours on offer through its gorgeous grounds, Selva Negra runs a popular ecolodge. The cheaper superior rooms are actually some of the most charming, as they are right on the lake, while the cute brick *cabañas* boast fireplaces, roofs sprouting bromeliads and plenty of privacy.

ℹ️ Getting There & Away

The reserve can be accessed via a number of dirt spur roads leading off the old Matagalpa–Jinotega highway. The most used entrance is the road to Aranjuez.

One bus a day leaves from Cotran Sur (p197) in Matagalpa (US$0.70, one hour, 12pm) to Aranjuez, traveling into the reserve. You can also take any Matagalpa–Jinotega bus to the Aranjuez junction and hike in.

For Selva Negra, take the Matagalpa–Jinotega bus and get off 12km north of town at the signed turnoff, which is marked by an old tank from the revolution. From there it's a pleasant 1.5km walk to the lodge.

It's also possible to access the reserve from the Matagalpa–La Dalia highway, near San Antonio de Upas.

La Dalia & Peñas Blancas

Easily accessible from both Matagalpa and Jinotega, the area around the hardworking rural town of La Dalia is dotted with thundering waterfalls, working coffee farms and the north's most impressive tracts of virgin forest. The undoubted star of the show is the Reserva Natural Macizos de Peñas Blancas, a series of spectacular stone bluffs topped by cloud forest that is inhabited by scores of monkeys as well as jaguars and other pockets of rarely seen creatures.

🔘 Sights

**Reserva Natural Macizos
de Peñas Blancas**   NATURE RESERVE
What is possibly the most enchanting nature reserve in northern Nicaragua has the mossy, misty, life-altering cloud-forest scenery you've been waiting for. Besides massive cathedral trees draped in orchids and bromeliads, there are about four dozen waterfalls, some of which pour into crystalline swimming holes; at least one of them is over 120m tall. In addition, the 116 sq km reserve is home to an incredible array of wildlife, including pumas, jaguars, large troops of monkeys and many rare bird species.

Cascada La Luna   WATERFALL
(La Empresa) The unassuming community of La Empresa, just off the main road, is the surprising home of the Cascada La Luna, a towering 40m-high waterfall that splits into twin streams. There's a high-adrenaline, three-stage zipline that crosses the falls, giving incredible views.

Cascada Blanca   WATERFALL
(Salto Santa Emilia; Carretera La Dalia Km 147; US$2; ⏰8am-5pm) Surrounded by forest, this impressive 15m waterfall a short walk from the highway fills a large deep swimming hole. When it's quiet it's absolutely lovely but it loses its appeal when it gets rammed with sightseers; come early. A path leads behind the falls to the cave on the other side. There are also around 2km of trails through coffee, banana and cacao plantations along the river that pass several other swimming holes.

🏃 Activities

Parque Aventura
Cascada La Luna　　　ADVENTURE SPORTS
(☑8825-5653; Comunidad La Empresa; US$6; ☺8am-5pm) Runs a three-segment zipline high above La Luna waterfall, an incredibly exhilarating run that gives you wonderful views of the falls, the gorge and the river below.

☞ Tours

Guardianes del Bosque　　　ECOTOUR
(☑8471-8380; empalme la Manzana, 400m E, Peñas Blancas) 🖉 This environmentally focused farming cooperative offers a variety of activities around the reserve, including treks with local Spanish-speaking guides (US$15 to US$20) to many waterfalls and lookouts. It also offers coffee tours (US$10) and can organize accommodations in its own basic lodge or in homestays nearby.

Centro Entendimiento
con la Naturaleza　　　ECOTOUR
(CEN; ☑7671-9186; cenbosawas@gmail.com; empalme la Manzana, 800m E, Peñas Blancas) 🖉 To delve deep into the reserve, pay a visit to this grassroots environmental education and conservation project. Besides reforesting and managing vast swaths of the protected area, it also serves as a research post and even produces its own honey. It organizes guides for the trek to the magnificent Arco Iris waterfall (US$10) and wildlife zones high in the mountains.

🛏 Sleeping

Eco-Albergue Guardianes
del Bosque　　　LODGE $
(☑8471-8380; empalme la Manzana, 400m E, Peñas Blancas; dm US$10, r per person US$20) It's possible to stay in the village of Peñas Blancas at this interesting but basic place run by the Guardianes del Bosque cooperative. Rooms are simple wooden boxes, the water is cold and some mattresses are way too thin, but the staff are super-friendly. Meals are available (US$3 to US$5) onsite.

Centro Entendimiento
con la Naturaleza　　　LODGE $$
(CEN; ☑Matagalpa 8940-0891, Peñas Blancas 7671-9186; cenbosawas@gmail.com; empalme la Manzana, 800m E, Peñas Blancas; dm full board US$15-25, s/d full board US$40/80) On the grounds of this environmental education center you'll find one lovely wooden *cabaña*

split into two private rooms. The upstairs room is open to the elements – a wire wall at the far side lets in the sounds of the jungle – while downstairs has a small porch and more conventional walls with windows (for those who fear creepy-crawlies).

La Sombra Ecolodge　　　LODGE $$$
(☑8468-6281; www.lasombraecolodge.com; Carretera Waslal, La Dalia; r per person incl full board & activities US$50-60; 🅿🌂) This vast coffee *finca* set among tracts of cloud forest has wonderful views and plenty of activities for guests run by the warm and welcoming staff. Accommodations are in wood-crafted, fan-cooled rooms that come with mosquito nets, hot water and solar-generated electricity. Best of all, there are three pools fed by cold mountain water, perfect for cooling down post-hike.

ℹ Getting There & Away

If traveling in a private vehicle note that the road north from La Dalia is paved until the turnoff to El Cuá, after which it is dirt and often features muddy puddles. A 4WD vehicle is highly recommended if visiting Peñas Blancas.

Buses leave Matagalpa for La Dalia (US$1.30, 1½ hours) almost hourly from 6am to 6pm. To get to Peñas Blancas, take any bus leaving Matagalpa for El Cuá and get off at 'Empalme la Manzana' – the Peñas Blancas turnoff (US$2.20, three hours). There are also two buses a day from Jinotega to Peñas Blancas. The village is 600m off the main road.

South of Matagalpa

The smooth, paved road from Matagalpa to Managua slithers down the shoulders of stunning peaks into prairies framed by distant volcanoes. Most travelers zip right through on their way to or from Managua, but the road passes an enjoyable museum and some other interesting diversions including the petroglyphs of Chagüitillo and the birthplace of Nicaragua's most famous writer, Rubén Darío.

Chagüitillo

You may miss the right turn into dusty Chagüitillo, just 20km south of Matagalpa and 4km north of Sébaco. There's no Spanish grid or *parque central*, just a single brick road where all *pueblo* life blooms, surrounded by unpaved backstreets. The only reason to visit is to check out the

HACIENDA SAN JACINTO

It will take a history buff to appreciate this **national monument** (US$0.50; ☺ 8am-4pm Tue-Sun), which is a shadeless 3km walk from the closest bus stop. The early-1800s Spanish hacienda is famed for the Battle of San Jacinto, where William Walker's filibusters and León Liberals were met by stiff resistance from the southern Conservatives. Walker lost the battle and, ultimately, the war. Inside the renovated building are a couple of murals and a few busts depicting the event.

It's about 25km south of Ciudad Darío. Managua-bound *ordinario* buses can drop you off at the spur that leads to the hacienda.

pre-Columbian museum and the two petroglyph sites around town.

◉ Sights

Santuario de los Venados   ARCHAEOLOGICAL SITE
This archaeological site up on a hill outside town features more than 60 zoomorphic petroglyphs, including many depicting deer. The path is not at all marked and so a local guide, arranged at the town museum (US$5 to US$7), is highly recommended.

Museo Precolombino de Chagüitillo   MUSEUM
(☎ 5755-9148, 8731-8604; puente, 1c N, 2c O, 1c S; US$1; ☺ 8am-noon & 1-5pm Mon-Fri) This worthwhile little museum has two rooms of Chorotegan pottery and an exhibit on local hero Domingo Sánchez Salgado (aka Chagüitillo), one of the leaders of the early resistance against the Somozas. Museum staff can arrange guides (US$5 to US$7) to visit the petroglyph sites at Salto Apa Mico and Los Venados, though it pays to call ahead, as staff are often absent.

Santuario Salto Apa Mico   ARCHAEOLOGICAL SITE
This petroglyph site alongside a stream just outside town features a swirl of moons, snakes and dancers 3m long and 2m high carved into rocks. The site is just about signposted, but it's well worth hiring a guide at the museum to learn more about the site. Do take care at this isolated spot though and ideally don't go alone.

❶ Getting There & Away
Any *ordinario* bus between Matagalpa and Managua can drop you at the entrance to town, from where you can walk in to the museum.

Ciudad Darío
POP 21,000 / ELEV 433M
About 5km down a paved turnoff from the highway, and tucked back into the chaparral-speckled Cordillera Dariense, is hilly Ciudad Darío, an otherwise unremarkable Nicaraguan town that was the birthplace of its most famous poet, for whom it's now named. The house museum here is worth a stop for lovers of Spanish literature.

◉ Sights

Casa Natal Rubén Darío   MUSEUM
(☎ 2776-3846; Parque Central, 2c E; US$4; ☺ 8am-4:30pm Tue-Fri, 9am-4pm Sat & Sun) Two blocks east of the Parque Central you'll find the town's primary roadside attraction, where Nicaragua's most famous writer Rubén Darío was born. Although the young poet didn't spend more than a few weeks in this sweet 19th-century adobe (this was his aunt's house), the museum is quite cool, with a mid-1880s kitchen, a Rubén Darío timeline and a wonderful amphitheater on the grounds, where the museum hosts the rare poetry reading or theater production.

❶ Getting There & Away
Buses leave for Managua (US$1.50, two hours) and Matagalpa (US$0.90, one hour) every half-hour.

Caribbean Coast

Best Places to Eat

➡ Darinia's Kitchen (p237)

➡ Desideri (p237)

➡ Pizzeria Italia (p232)

➡ Restaurante Faramhi (p208)

➡ Casa Ulrich (p225)

Best Places to Stay

➡ Yemaya Island Hideaway & Spa (p236)

➡ Queen Lobster (p224)

➡ Hotel Casa Royale (p222)

➡ Hostal Garífuna (p227)

Why Go?

Nicaragua's remote Caribbean coast often feels like an entirely separate country to 'mainland' Nicaragua; barely connected to the rest of the nation and looking out towards the Caribbean rather than inwards to Managua. Here you'll find English-speaking Creole people living side-by-side with indigenous Miskito, Mayangna, Rama and Garifuna populations; some of the country's best beaches on the Corn Islands and Pearl Keys; and various slices of wilderness bisected by wide muddy rivers, lined with thick jungle, and connected by mangrove-shrouded black-water creeks and lagoons.

Travel in the Nicaraguan Caribbean is challenging and exciting, and the rewards – including superb scuba diving, epic treks through dense rainforest, wildlife watching and fishing in the mangroves – are huge. The area is officially made up of two vast and sparsely populated autonomous regions known by their official names, Región Autónoma Atlántico Norte (North Atlantic Autonomous Region; RAAN) and Región Autónoma Atlántico Sur (South Atlantic Autonomous Region; RAAS).

When to Go

➡ From February to April visitors are greeted by clear skies and perfect beach weather, although in the Corn Islands you'll find bigger crowds and pricier accommodations.

➡ The region's strong winds drop off significantly from March to April, bringing the best conditions for diving around the Corn Islands and snorkeling in the Pearl Keys.

➡ While technically in the middle of the wet season, during September and October the heavy rains ease off, prices are low and beaches are empty.

➡ For a high-energy full-color carnival experience, head to Palo de Mayo (Maypole Festival) in Bluefields in May for a full month of partying, culminating in the colorful Carnival and Tulululu.

Caribbean Coast Highlights

1 **Little Corn Island** (p233)
Diving, swimming and sunbathing on this wonderful, carfree slice of the old Caribbean.

2 **Pearl Lagoon** (p224) Experiencing true Caribbean food and culture in this laid-back Creole town surrounded by thick jungle and mangrove forests.

3 **Pearl Keys** (p227) Chartering a speedboat to visit these tiny snow-white islands and snorkeling with magnificent sea turtles in their cerulean waters.

4 **Great Corn Island** (p228) Grooving to classic reggae while sipping a drink by the water's edge, or striking

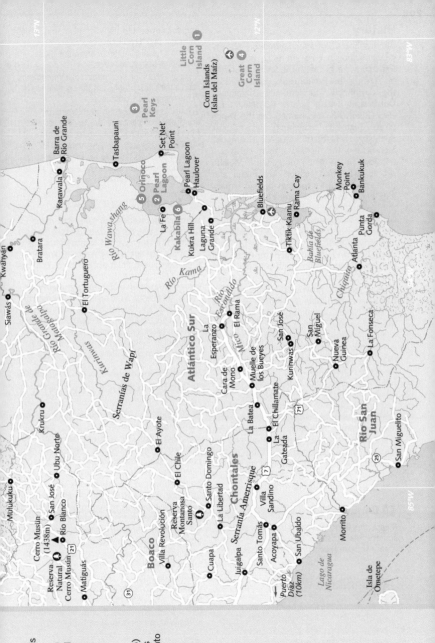

out to explore the beaches and hike this gorgeous island.

⑤ **Orinoco** (p226) Eating fresh fish and listening to talented Garifuna drummers, especially during National Garifuna Week.

⑥ **Kakabila** (p226) Hiring an indigenous guide to trek deep into the dense jungle.

History

Christopher Columbus landed on Nicaragua's Caribbean coast in 1502, during his fourth voyage, but with the Spanish focused on settling the Pacific coast, their hold on the Caribbean was tenuous. Portuguese, Dutch and British pirates patrolled these seas (Bluefields was named for the Dutch pirate Blauvelt), attacking and robbing Spanish vessels full of South American gold. Meanwhile, the British crown cultivated relations with the indigenous Miskito people, who had battled Mayangna and Rama communities for regional supremacy long before Columbus came calling. In 1687 they created the puppet kingdom of Mosquitia, which ruled until the mid-19th century.

During this period, British colonists moved with their African slaves from Jamaica to the Corn Islands, which until then had belonged to the Kukra and Sumu people. They also arrived in Bluefields, where slaves worked banana groves and mingled with free West Indian laborers of mixed ethnicity to form English-speaking Creole communities that are still thriving today.

English-speaking Nicaraguans have never fully bought into Spanish-speaking rule. During the Contra war, many took up arms against the Frente Sandinista de Liberación Nacional (Sandinista National Liberation Front; FSLN) while many more fled to neighboring Costa Rica to avoid the conflict, emptying villages that have still not recovered. Although the region was eventually granted special autonomy by the government in Managua, with the rights to have a say in the exploitation of its natural resources, it remains the poorest and least developed part of the country.

ℹ Dangers & Annoyances

Nicaragua's Caribbean coast is as poor as the country gets. Outside Bluefields and the Corn Islands you can expect dodgy infrastructure,

---

ℹ DRINKING WATER

Tap water on the Caribbean coast generally comes from wells or rainwater collection tanks and is usually untreated. Often it is potable, but it may also contain bacteria; bring water purification tablets if you don't want to take the risk. Bottled water is widely available and some hotels offer filtered water refills.

---

frequent power cuts, nonexistent internet or cell coverage, and terrible roads.

➡ Bring a flashlight (torch) and enjoy those occasional bucket showers.

➡ Local agents for Colombian coke impresarios keep a fairly low profile, but the cocaine traffic in the region isn't bloodless.

➡ Tourists won't have any problems with drug-related violence as long as they refrain from purchasing and consuming cocaine.

➡ Given the poverty, even in seemingly innocuous small towns, stick to big-city rules: stay alert, don't wander far alone, take taxis at night and watch your valuables.

ℹ Getting There & Away

You can travel overland from Managua to the Caribbean coast, but most visitors take the frequent and inexpensive La Costeña flights. There are active airstrips in Bilwi, Waspám, Bluefields, Great Corn Island and two of the three Las Minas towns. Still, if you have more time than cash and enjoy the (really) slow lane, there are two main overland routes into the region. A new road from Nueva Guinea to Bluefields was nearing completion in 2018, the first sealed road connecting the region to the rest of Nicaragua, which will result in far shorter journey times and much more comfortable overland travel.

Bilwi (Puerto Cabezas)

POP 48,500

This impoverished Caribbean port town and ethnic melting pot sprawls along the coast and back into the scrubby pines on wide brick streets and red-earth roads, full of people and music, smiles and sideways glances. Old wooden churches, antique craftsman homes and ramshackle slums are knitted together with rusted sheet-metal fencing, coconut palms and mango trees. In a single stroll you'll eavesdrop on loud jagged Miskito banter, rapid-fire Spanish and lovely, lilting Caribbean English. Sure, this city has systemic problems (poverty, decay, crime), and its ramshackle infrastructure lags years behind the rest of the country. But with tasty seafood, great-value historic lodging options, and seaside indigenous communities a boat ride away, it can be as alluring as a sweet, yet slightly sketchy, new friend.

◎ Sights

There is next to no tourism in Bilwi; missionaries and aid workers still far outnumber travelers, and this is hardly a surprise when you consider the beaches here are nobody's idea of a Caribbean fantasy. La Bocana, an old pirate hangout at the river mouth north of town, has a stretch of decent beach, but it's not safe to visit alone.

Muelle Viejo PORT

Take a stroll along the wooden boards of the historic Muelle Viejo (Old Pier), where both Sandino and the Contras received arms smuggled in from abroad, the former with the assistance of the town's prostitutes. But the 420m-long pier's biggest moment in the spotlight was in 1961, when Somoza lent the facility to US-funded Cuban exiles to launch the disastrous Bay of Pigs invasion.

Casa Museo Judith Kain MUSEUM

(2792-2225; Parque Central, 4c N, 1c O; 8am-5pm Mon-Fri) FREE Set in the former home of a prolific local painter, this museum provides a window into what it was like to live in Bilwi in the good old days. There are black-and-white photos, old dugout canoes, terrific local handicrafts and an antique collection (the sewing machines are especially cool); dozens of Kain's paintings are also on display.

Mercado Municipal MARKET

(7am-3pm) This ramshackle collection of stalls selling ripe produce, traditional fried-fish breakfasts and sweet, savory *rundown* (seasoned fish or meat cooked in coconut milk with root vegetables) is a popular place to pass the morning.

🎏 Festivals & Events

Dance of King Pulanka CULTURAL

(Jan 6–mid-Feb) First performed in the late 1800s, the dance of El Rey and La Reina is still performed throughout the Mosquitia. Two groups of dancers wearing 18th-century costumes, representing the king's allies and enemies, stage a mock battle using arrows, machetes and *triki trakas* (firearms). The good guys win and there's traditional food and drink to keep the party going.

🛏 Sleeping

Lodging in Bilwi is generally full of charm and great value, even if somewhat rustic and aged in style. Even with the town's dearth of tourism, it helps to reserve ahead, as those doing business and the NGO brigade often snap up the best rooms.

★ Casa Museo Judith Kain HOTEL $

(2792-2225; Parque Central, 4c N, 1c O; r/tw with fan US$14/16, r/tw/tr with air-con US$25/30/35; ❋🐱) In a town with an abundance of atmospheric lodging, this may be the best of

the bunch. The 19 rooms occupy various buildings, set back from the house-museum of a local artist. Sadly, the rooms themselves aren't all in good condition, but they do have high ceilings, the odd antique and shared access to the lovely gardens.

El Cortijo GUESTHOUSE $

(2792-2340; cortijoarguello@yahoo.com; Parque Central, 1½c N; s/d with air-con US$18/20, with fan

CARIBBEAN COAST BILWI (PUERTO CABEZAS)

LOBSTER FEAST

Most local lobster is exported, but when it's in season you'll find it at around US$7.50 a plate – often the same price as chicken or fish. If you're pinching pennies, head to the Mercado Municipal (p207), where you'll find some stalls selling tasty fried fish.

US$14/17; 🌢 🛜) This beautiful wooden home is so nice the Sandinistas once used it as their east-coast base. Grab one of the more attractively furnished rooms upstairs in the original house; they have wooden fixtures and high ceilings. Downstairs rooms are less charming, but cheaper. Fabulous breakfasts (US$3) with terrific coffee are served on the wide deck overlooking a rambling garden.

Hospedaje Rivera   GUESTHOUSE $
(☑ 2792-2471; Parque Central, 1½c S; r with/without bathroom US$11/9.50; 🛜) The best budget option in town, Hospedaje Rivera has great-value rooms on the upper floor of this fine, centrally located family home. Each one comes with cable TV and giant fake flowers balanced on artistically arranged towels.

Lori's Place   GUESTHOUSE $$
(☑ 8725-0633, 2792-1035; Barrio Nueva Jerusalem; r/tr US$25/40; 🌢 🛜) Despite being located somewhat out of town, Lori's Place is an excellent choice, managing to be both secure and quiet *and* just a block from the bus terminal. The two-story yellow house has no sign, but it has a large garden, lots of comfortable public areas and seven super-clean rooms, all with air-con, TV and bathroom.

Hotel Liwa Mairin   HOTEL $$
(☑ 2792-2315; hotelliwamairin@gmail.com; Parque Central, 2c E, 1c S; s/d US$15/20, with air-con US$25/30; 🌢 🛜) This centrally located hotel right by the Caribbean offers spacious air-con rooms with firm mattresses, wooden furnishings and high ceilings. It's a fantastic deal, even if the rooms are equipped with temperamental electric-shock showers. The hotel even has its own small beach, though it's unlikely you'll want to swim here.

✖ Eating

Comedor Alka   NICARAGUAN $
(frente Parque Central; meals US$3; ⊙ 11am-9pm)
Stop at this simple *comedor* (basic eatery) for savory and cheap eats such as fantastic

barbecued beef and chicken, served with a bit of attitude. It's all in good fun and the food is as good, if not better, than many more upmarket restaurants.

★ Restaurante Faramhi   SEAFOOD $$
(☑ 2792-1611; frente Aeropuerto; mains US$5-10; ⊙ 11am-10pm; 🛜) Close to the airport, this popular restaurant serves easily the best food in town. It's a very Bilwi kind of place: the open-air dining area features seashell light shades, a random disco light and a country music soundtrack. The menu reflects the town's multiethnic roots, with typical seafood plates starring alongside an ensemble of good Chinese dishes.

Wachi's Pizza   PIZZA $$
(Parque Central, 2c E; pizzas US$5-12; ⊙ noon-10pm; 🛜) Probably the most atmospheric dining option in town, the only real pizzeria within a 200km radius runs a brisk trade, serving generously sized pizzas with thick crusts and tasty toppings on a pleasant porch complete with fairy lights and its own little beach.

Kabu Payaska   SEAFOOD $$
(Parque Central, 1.5km N; mains US$7-12; ⊙ 11am-10pm; 🛜) Bilwi's best-loved seafood house is set on a large concrete patio overlooking the swirling Caribbean. The food is very tasty and the view and fresh breeze make it worth a visit. The coconut-based mixed seafood soup (US$10), featuring fish, shrimp and a whole lobster, is the one you want to go for.

This neighborhood is considered unsafe, so take a taxi (US$0.70).

🍷 Drinking & Nightlife

Kabu Yula   BAR
(Parque Central, 5c S; ⊙ 2pm-2am) A two-story open-air bar with unbroken sea views, the 'Sea Dog' is the perfect place for an afternoon tipple.

Bar-Restaurant El Malecón   CLUB
(Parque Central, 2c E, 1c S; ⊙ 6pm-2am Thu-Sat) This large air-con disco space by the water plays a mix of dancehall, reggae and Latin pop to keep the young crowd moving.

ℹ Information

DANGERS & ANNOYANCES
➡ Be cautious when wandering alone even during daylight, and avoid carrying nonessential items with you.

➡ Take taxis after dark, as the streets are not safe to walk after sunset.

➡ Avoid empty side streets and the seafront if you're alone at any time of day.

MEDICAL SERVICES
Hospital (📞 2792-2243, 2792-2259)

MONEY
BanPro Changes dollars and has a Visa/MasterCard ATM.

TOURIST INFORMATION
Intur (📞 2792-1564; puertocabezas@intur.gob.ni; Parque Central, 2c N; ☺8am-4pm Mon-Fri) Staff know the area in detail and can facilitate trips to local communities.
Migración (Immigration Office; 📞 2792-2258; contiguo la Policía; ☺8am-4pm Mon-Fri) Visa extensions and entry/exit stamps for the Honduran border.

Getting There & Away
AIR
Most visitors arrive in Bilwi by plane. **La Costeña** (📞 2792-2282; Aeropuerto) offers three daily flights from **Puerto Cabezas Airport** (📞 2792-2282) to Managua (one way/round trip US$97/149, 1½ hours) and thrice-weekly services to Bluefields (one way/round trip US$96/148, 50 minutes).

BOAT
The boat connecting Bilwi to Bluefields and Corn Island sank in 2017 after a collision with another vessel. There is currently no replacement boat service connecting Bilwi to the southern Caribbean coast. For nearly all villages to the south of Bilwi, collective boats leave from the dock at Lamlaya, 2km south of town.

BUS
Uncomfortable, overcrowded and slow buses depart from the chaotic bus terminal, 2km west of town. A taxi colectivo from the center will cost C$20 (US$0.60).

Managua (US$16.50, 16 to 20 hours, 10am, 1pm & 4pm)
Rosita (US$6.50, six to 10 hours, 7am & 11:45am)
Siuna (US$9.50, 10 to 12 hours, 11:30am)
Waspám (US$6.50, six hours, 6am & 6:30am)

Getting Around
Bilwi is not the safest place to be strolling off the main streets at any time. Colectivo taxis around town cost US$0.30; use them for all journeys after dark, and even during the day if you're unsure of where you're going – neighborhoods can change from fine to sketchy very quickly.

Around Bilwi
The shores of the Caribbean to the north and south of Bilwi are dotted with ultra-laid-back Miskito villages rich in culture and surrounded by nature. Exploring here is a true adventure, as the locals are fascinated to see foreigners and will give you a warm welcome wherever you go.

Haulover
POP 1750
The first Moravian missionaries reached Haulover, 30km south of Bilwi, in 1860, and named it in honor of the sandbar that boats had to cross to enter the lagoon. Protected by the surrounding wilderness of Reserva Natural Laguna Kukalaya and Reserva Natural Layasiksa, Haulover is only accessible by water. It's a peaceful town of colorful wooden houses, where horses roam free on soft grass studded with coconut palms. There is no electricity here – the only sounds are the crashing of the sea and the occasional Miskito hit emanating from small, battery-powered radios.

TRAVEL LOGISTICS
Traveling from Siuna to Bilwi (Puerto Cabezas) onto Waspám & Río Coco? We won't sugarcoat this: you're in for a grueling ride on a beat-up old school bus packed to the gills. It begins with a 10- to 12-hour bus ride from Managua to Siuna in Las Minas, where you can access the Reserva de Biosfera Bosawás (Bosawás Biosphere Reserve). From Siuna, it's another 10 to 12 hours on a horrendous road to Bilwi. Waspám and the Río Coco are a smoothish six hours north from there.

The (much!) preferred trip to the crystalline Caribbean Sea (Juigalpa–El Rama–Bluefields–Corn Islands) unfurls on the smooth, paved road to El Rama, with rejuvenating side trips to the mountain towns of Boaco and Juigalpa. From El Rama, you can hop on a testing five-hour bus journey along the rutted dirt road to Pearl Lagoon, or take a convenient two-hour fast boat ride down the Río Escondido to Bluefields, from where there are twice-weekly boat services to the Corn Islands and daily speedboats to Pearl Lagoon.

Unfortunately the town's comfortable *cabañas* (cabins) have fallen into disrepair and are no longer in operation, but it's possible to organize homestays (US$6.50 per visitor) in the village. Excellent seafood meals are available at simple shacks, starting from US$3.

ⓘ Getting There & Away

Collective *pangas* leave from the dock at Lamlaya (p209) around noon (US$9), and return at 5am daily. A private charter will set you back around US$150.

Wawa & Karatá

POP 650

Wawa is a scenic Miskito village 17km south of Bilwi, at the mouth of the Río Wawa. There's a beautiful lagoon packed with migratory birds and alligators, plus a sandy oceanfront beach. Further upriver is Karatá, which is perched on the edge of the lagoon and surrounded by mangrove forests. Hiking, fishing and canoeing options abound in both villages.

It's possible to spend the night in both Wawa and Karatá in simple homestays (US$6.50 per visitor).

ⓘ Getting There & Away

Transportation is by collective *panga* (Wawa/Karatá US$2.20/3.30), which leave from Lamlaya, 2km south of Bilwi.

Krukira

POP 1500

About 20km north of Bilwi, this is the gateway to the Reserva Natural Laguna Pahara, with lots of wildlife, including huge tarpon.

SPENDING THE NIGHT

There are no hotels in the Miskito Keys, but having spent a fortune to get out here you are going to want to spend the night. Fortunately it's possible to arrange a bed or hammock in the stilted homes of locals on arrival.

The closest restaurants to the keys are in Bilwi and the fisherfolk have a very monotonous diet. It's highly recommended to bring your own rations and water from Bilwi and cook for yourself, or hire a local to prepare meals. You obviously don't need to bring any fish and lobster though.

It's a tranquil yet well developed town with a Moravian church and a neat central park. You can organize canoe tours and fishing trips in the lagoon, as well as visits to Trakislandia, a freshwater swimming hole.

ⓘ Getting There & Away

Buses leave Bilwi for Krukira daily at 1pm (US$1.50, one hour), returning early in the morning.

Miskito Keys

Sitting 50km offshore, the Miskito Keys are a group of rocky Caribbean isles rimmed with stilted Miskito fishing villages. Their thatched over-water bungalows loom above crystalline turquoise coves that double as an ideal lobster habitat. The historic first meeting between the British pirate, Captain Sussex Camock, and his future Miskito allies took place here in 1633. Today, the keys are still a haven for seafaring bad guys, so if you see any boats with Colombian plates, look the other way.

Unlike the Pearl Keys further south, this is a cultural rather than beach destination – very few of the islands have any sand at all. Most are pure rock with the odd bit of scrubby vegetation. Nevertheless, a visit to this isolated community sticking out of the ocean is a fascinating experience, although it doesn't come cheap. Bring plenty of insect repellent, too!

ⓘ Getting There & Away

All access to the Miskito Keys is from Bilwi. From there you can arrange overnight visits for US$600 for up to six visitors, a large chunk of which goes toward transportation costs. Transport in a larger, faster *panga* for up to 12 will cost you around US$800 round-trip; Intur (p209) in Bilwi is able to recommend responsible captains. To make the journey on the cheap, you'll need to make arrangements with a lobster fisher who is already going: doable, but your return could take days. It's two hours to the keys on a fast boat, up to five on a lobster vessel, and the ride is often rough.

Waspám & the Río Coco

POP 7000

Waspám, the end of the line in Nicaragua and as about as remote as you can get here, is a poor and developmentally challenged place that nevertheless still enjoys a simple beauty: children at play, twittering flocks of parakeets in the trees, and dugout canoes plying the edges of Waspám's biggest attraction, the lazy brown waters of the Río Coco.

Known as Wangki in Miskito, the Río Coco is the longest river in Central America and links some 116 Miskito communities that run from the rainforested interior to the Caribbean coastal marshlands. This makes Waspám, its epicenter, the cultural, geographic and economic heart of the Mosquitia. The river also forms a natural border with Honduras, a fact most Miskitos prefer to ignore. You shouldn't. If you plan on crossing into Honduras, get your passport stamped at Bilwi Migración (p209).

◉ Sights

The town is worth a wander. You'll see the oddly constructed Iglesia San Rafael, you can dangle your legs over the cinder-block outfield walls of the baseball stadium with the locals on weekends, and you can stroll parque central. Its war monument is erected for fallen Contras overrun by the Sandinistas, who then torched and occupied Waspám until the war was over.

★ **Museo Auka Tangki**　　　　MUSEUM
(☑ 8417-8128; brownmelgara@hotmail.com; Planta Electrica, 150m E; donations accepted; ⊙ by appointment) Don't miss Dr Dionisio Melgara Brown's museum, a 10-minute walk along dirt roads curving away from the river. Brown, a retired teacher, built this museum on the ground floor of his home with his own savings in order to preserve Miskito language, history and tradition.

⊨ Sleeping

Hotel Casa de la Rose　　　　HOTEL $
(☑ 5729-9380; frente la pista; s/d with fan US$11/15, with air-con US$18/22; 🕸🛜) One of Waspám's two really good hotels. Rooms are clean with fresh tiles, cable TV and a lovely wooden porch nestled in the banana palms of the gorgeous garden. It also has a terrific restaurant set in a sweet wooden *cabaña* patrolled by parrots.

★ **Hotelito El Piloto**　　　　HOTEL $$
(☑ 8331-1312, 8642-4405; hotelitoelpiloto@live.com; Muelle, 20m S; r/tw US$25/35; 🕸🛜) Waspám's best all-round choice. Rooms have fresh paint and bathroom tiles, and a terrific location steps from the river. The friendly owners are a wealth of information and will happily arrange all manner of local excursions, as well as serve up quality meals.

MISKITO CUISINE

Although authentic Miskito cuisine is hard to find, keep an eye out for delicacies such as *wabul*, *pihtu talla laya* (fermented pineapple-rind drink), *twalbí* (corn liquor), *takrú* (fish and yucca baked together in banana leaves) and *auhbi piakan* (Miskito for 'mixed together'), a stew of plantains, meat and coconut.

❶ Information

DANGERS & ANNOYANCES

Mosquitoes are the big drawback, particularly during rainy season (June to October). Wear long sleeves and pants at dusk, and be liberal with your repellent of choice.

MONEY

There are no banks in Waspám, so bring sufficient funds. If you run short, it's possible to receive transfers at Western Union (☑ 8416-9999; Muelle, 20m S; ⊙ 9am-5pm).

❶ Getting There & Away

AIR

La Costeña (☑ 8415-8210; Aeropuerto) planes only seat 12, so it's best to book in advance. Flights depart on Tuesday, Thursday and Saturday from Managua to Waspám (one way/round trip US$104/160, 1½ hours) at noon, and return to Managua at 1:40pm.

BUS

Buses leave for Bilwi (US$6.50, six hours) at 6am and 7am daily. Come early if you want a seat. There are also several direct buses a week to Managua (US$25, 25 hours), usually departing on Monday, Wednesday, Thursday and Saturday at around 8am.

Río Coco

Waspám's prime attractions are out of town and accessible by the Río Coco, which upriver from town forms the northern boundary of the Bosawás reserve and downriver flows to Cabo Gracias a Dios and into the Caribbean. Access is pricey but easily organized with local captains who hang around at Waspám's dock.

◉ Sights & Activities

The Río Coco, while spectacular and full of wildlife, is also hellishly buggy, particularly the further downriver you go towards the Caribbean. The two main places visited are Cabo Gracias a Dios and Cabo Viejo.

DISPUTED LANDS

The Río Coco is no stranger to bloodshed and unfortunately it has once again become a hotbed of violence, with land disputes between indigenous communities and mestizo farmers spawning armed conflict between the two sides. There have been deaths on both sides with heavily armed mestizo groups taking on villagers, who are often equipped with just homemade weapons. The troubles have even made it to the center of Waspám, where in 2015 a shoot-out left one Miskito leader dead and many wounded.

Indigenous leaders say that the local communities have been abandoned by the government, which is letting the armed mestizo farmers run them off their ancestral land. Many Miskito villagers have left the region and fled across the river to Honduras or to Bilwi (Puerto Cabezas), while the Inter-American Commission on Human Rights has ordered the Nicaraguan government to take measures to protect the Miskito communities.

For its part, the government claims the dispute stems from the illegal sale of land by members of the indigenous communities and needs to be resolved between the two parties, without the intervention of the military.

With no solution in sight, it's important to check the latest before planning a trip to the Río Coco. While foreign visitors are unlikely to be targets, there is always the chance of getting caught in the cross fire, and at present tourism is the last thing on the mind of locals in many communities.

A similarly exciting trip, but one where you're not quite as ravaged by biting insects, is the 135km journey upriver and then up the Río Waspuk to Salto Yaho, a spectacular waterfall (US$450 per boat). After swimming in the falls, you'll spend the night in the small village downriver before returning home in the morning. It's also possible to continue up the Waspuk and onto Bonanza, where you can jump onto a flight or bus to Managua – but this requires travel in a long wooden boat rather than a *panga*.

If you're short on time or money, consider a day trip from Waspám to the local riverside Miskito communities of Ulwas, Sowpuka, Bilwas Karma, Kisalia or Kum, where the former Miskito royal family still resides. You can organize a private *panga* (US$40, two hours) at the main dock.

❶ Getting There & Away

Expect to pay US$60 per day for boat hire plus fuel, which will make up most of the cost. You can also arrange trips through Hotelito El Piloto (p211) in Waspám, where owner Barry Watson speaks English.

Managua–El Rama Road

If you plan on heading to or from the Costa Atlantica overland (and don't fancy the grueling 24-hour journey from Managua to Bilwi), then you will most likely take the smooth paved roads from the capital to El Rama, a river-port town that is just a two-hour boat ride from Bluefields.

You can make the trip in six hours on a reasonably comfortable (but usually overcrowded) bus, but then you'll miss the rugged Serranía Amerrisque. In and around these muscular granite peaks are a number of cute ranching *pueblos* (villages) and the worthwhile city of Juigalpa, linked by twisting, rutted back roads that also connect to Matagalpa and the northern highlands. So, embrace that whole 'journey is the destination' cliché, take the slow road and enjoy a welcome blast of earthy Nicaraguan culture before or after diving into the Caribbean.

❶ Getting There & Away

Buses run frequently along the length of Hwy 7 between Managua and the terminus at El Rama. If you're just passing through, make sure to hop on an *expreso* service, which are considerably faster than the *ordinarios*. Both options get packed to the rafters.

Old beat-up school buses serve the spur roads off the highway, but service is irregular at best. To truly explore the back roads of the region, a rental vehicle is the best way to go.

Boaco

POP 57,000 / ELEV 1020M

'The City with Two Floors' was once two ranching communities separated by a steep 400m slope. They've grown together over the years, and now this *ranchero* market town, a couple of hours' drive from Managua, is a bustling agricultural hub. Being off the main highway, Boaco receives few visitors, but its charming central square and good hotels and restaurants make it a decent overnight stop for those looking to explore the region's petroglyph-studded mountain hinterland.

◉ Sights & Activities

Sitio Arqueologico
La Laguna
ARCHAEOLOGICAL SITE

(Comarca La Laguna) FREE Around 10km from Boaco, this archaeological site is only just beginning to be investigated and features a number of petroglyphs in stones scattered around local farms. The site is off the Boaco–Camoapa road, near the settlement of Boaco Viejo. Contact Gerardo Polanco (8924-7392) in Boaco to arrange a visit, or ask Intur (p215) to organize a guide.

Parroquia de Nuestra Señora
del Perpetuo Socorro
CHURCH

(salida, 1c N, 2c E) This intriguing church on the lower level of town has brightly painted onion domes that hint at a Russian heritage, but it's Catholic and always has been.

Parque El Cerrito del Faro
PARK

(Parque Central, 2c N, 1½c O; ⊙10am-9pm) A small park on the upper level of town offering fantastic views over the surrounding mountains.

Aguas Claras
THERMAL BATHS

(☑2244-2916; admission US$1.50; ⊙Tue-Sun) On Hwy 9, 15 minutes west of town, you'll find this ageing mid-level hot-springs resort. Water is mineral rich, if not steaming, and funneled into concrete pools. Midweek it's mostly deserted, but it pulls a big local crowd on weekends. Any Managua-bound bus from Boaco (or Juigalpa) will drop you here. A taxi from Boaco runs about US$8.

🛏 Sleeping

Hotel Sobalvarro
HOTEL $

(☑2542-2515; hotelsobalvarro@gmail.com; frente al Parque Central; r with/without bathroom US$16/11; ⊛) You'll sacrifice some comfort here, but the clean, wooden-floored budget rooms have a fresh coat of paint and come with access to the deck, offering fine mountain views. The shared bathrooms are downstairs, next to the more expensive rooms with tiled floors and private bathrooms. The family who runs the place is friendly, and you're right on the square.

★ Tijerino's Hotel
HOTEL $$

(☑2542-2798; hoteltijerinos@gmail.com; frente al Parque Central; r with/without air-con US$30/40;

⊛ 🛜) This fancy hotel on the park seems a little too smart for rural Boaco. Yes, the decor is on the garish side, but the bright, modern rooms boast ultra-comfortable bedding and are the finest for miles around. The biggest draw, however, are the two ample terraces with majestic mountain panoramas. Outstanding value.

Hotel Farolitos
HOTEL $$

(☑2542-1938; Abajo, salida, 4c E; s/d US$40/45; ⊛ 🛜) On the main road through the lower town, Hotel Farolitos boasts large, clean rooms with Spanish tiles, mosaic baths and cable TV. It's great value considering the amenities, and the upstairs terrace is a cozy spot to hang and peer down over the bustling main road. Breakfast is available for an additional US$3.50.

✕ Eating & Drinking

Being a farming town, most restaurants here serve several cuts of steak alongside loads of poultry dishes. There are several good semi-formal restaurants and cafes on the upper level of town.

Kónoha Café
INTERNATIONAL $

(Alcaldía Municipal, ½c O; mains US$3-6; ⊙8am-10pm Mon-Sat, from 2pm Sun; 🛜) There's a jazz soundtrack, good coffee and a friendly owner at this great little spot just off the Parque Central. The menu is simple rather than anything particularly exciting, but features

---

BACK ROAD TO MATAGALPA

If you're heading north from Boaco and are not in any hurry, consider taking the scenic backcountry route to Matagalpa through peaceful, pastoral lands at the foot of rugged and rarely visited mountains. This is a route you're guaranteed to be virtually the only traveler on, and its rustic villages and rolling scenery make for a thoroughly relaxing drive.

Public transport on this route is very limited and it's best explored in a private 4WD vehicle. There are buses from Teustepe (US$1, one hour) to San José de los Remates at 7am and 5pm, the latter of which continues to Esquipulas. Alternatively once in San José, try to track down the town's only taxi driver to arrange a private transfer for the 8km trip. From Esquipulas, there are frequent onward bus services to Matagalpa.

RESERVA DE BIOSFERA BOSAWÁS

Buffered to the north by three neighboring reserves in Honduras, Reserva de Biosfera Bosawás makes up part of the largest protected expanse of rainforest north of the Amazon, itself clocking in at some 20,000 sq km. A vast wilderness crisscrossed by rivers and shrouded in dense jungle, it's a vital part of the Mesoamerican biological corridor, the land route between North and South America that is used by many migratory species of animal, and is home to some of the region's last giant anteaters, spider monkeys, jaguars, harpy eagles, tapirs and crocodiles.

Named for three geographical features that delineate the reserve – the Río Bocay, Cerro Saslaya and Río Waspuk – Bosawás is a destination for seriously intrepid adventurers and wildlife enthusiasts. Come here to explore a true wilderness, canoe down giant rivers, birdwatch and see an extraordinary array of creatures in their natural habitat.

It's a challenging place, covered in thick, steamy rainforest bisected by brown rivers, that isn't remotely set up for tourism. With some careful planning, not insignificant expense and no attachment to creature comforts, it is possible to visit, however.

Come prepared: someone in your group (don't do this alone) should speak a fair amount of Spanish, and you should consider taking malaria pills for longer adventures. Water-purification technology is necessary for most of the reserve. But the real key to access is persistence – you can get in, just don't count on it happening on your timetable, and expect to be following leads like: 'find Jaguar José at the *pulpería* near the *empalme* of (something unpronounceable); he's got a truck that can get through.'

During the reserve's February-to-April dry season, rivers (read: the freeway system) may be too low to travel, unless you help carry the canoe around the rapids. Luckily, it's usually raining, and some spots (for instance, the Río Waspuk region) get 3200mm of rain per year – regular roads may be impassable most of the year. Temperatures average a sweaty 26.5°C (80°F), but bring a fleece for Cerro Kilambé (1750m).

The easiest access to the Reserve de Biosfera Bosawás is from Siuna via the Parque Nacional Saslaya. Head to the ranger station, 3.5km from the community of Rosa Grande, where you'll register and contract a guide for the trek to Piedra Colorada. You'll overnight by a pine-shaded lagoon and in the morning begin the three-day climb to Cerro El Toro (1652m), or an overnight trip up El Revenido. A rolling trail circumnavigates both peaks, and can be done in one day.

Hormiguero is another national-park gateway. From the ranger station at the trailhead, it's a five-hour hike to Camp Salto Labú, with a stunning swimming hole that has a cave, canyons and petroglyphs. From here, you can also begin a four-day trek to the top of Cerro Saslaya (1651m). Bring a sleeping bag, tent and water purification for both treks.

Getting There & Away

You can begin inquiries at the Bosawás office at Marena Central (p60) in Managua, or any of the satellite offices located in most large towns bordering the reserve, where they can arrange guides and transportation, or at least point you in the right direction. It's often easiest to access the reserve through lodges on the periphery or private organizations, however, so ask around. Following are some points of entry:

Peñas Blancas (p200) Take guided trips to waterfalls and the stunning cliff-top mesa.

Siuna (p239) Park rangers guide you to campsites in Parque Nacional Saslaya.

Waspám and the Río Coco (p210) Take a riverboat ride into the waterfall-strewn wilderness, spending the night in a jungle paradise.

Musuwas Head from Bonanza into the heart of the Mayangna nation.

Reserva Natural Cerro Cola Blanca (p239) These waterfall-strewn highlands were named for the white-tailed deer teeming on its forested slopes. The Bonanza Intur (☑ 8665-9534; adentro alcaldía, Bonanza; ⊙ 8am-4pm) office can get you there.

atypical treats such as burgers, fajitas, quesadillas and crepes, as well as nachos for two people to share.

Restaurante Alpino NICARAGUAN $$
(Banpro, 40m N; mains US$6-10; ☺9am-9pm Mon-Thu, to 10pm Fri-Sun) This spotless tiled-floor restaurant with pressed yellow tablecloths serves up tasty Nica cuisine. The menu is pretty much the same as every other restaurant around here, but the plates are well prepared with fresh ingredients and service is prompt.

Restaurante Maraita BAR
(Parque Central, 1c N, 1c O; ☺9am-midnight) Locals descend on this sociable watering hole after work to knock back cold beers to a classic rock soundtrack. Also serves up fairly decent meals (US$4-7).

ⓘ Information

Banpro (Iglesia Santiago, 1c N)
Hospital (☑2542-2301)
Intur (☑2542-4760; Alcaldía, 20m E; ☺8am-5pm Mon-Fri)

ⓘ Getting There & Away

Boaco is 12km from the Empalme de Boaco junction, on the main Managua–El Rama Hwy. Local buses leave from the market. Managua-bound buses leave from the station, another 200m uphill. Matagalpa-bound folks need to take the bus to San Benito, from where there are frequent departures for Matagalpa. Bus services include:
Managua (US$1.50, two hours, 3:45am to 5:25pm, half-hourly) Express minivans (US$1.90, 1½ hours) depart when full from the market area until around noon.
San José de los Remates (US$1.25, 1½ hours, noon)
Santa Lucia (US$0.75, 30 minutes, noon and 3pm)

Santa Lucia

POP 3000

Just 12km north of Boaco, the picturesque, crumbling Spanish-colonial town of Santa Lucia is nestled in the heart of a 1000-year-old volcanic crater, surrounded by forested peaks that are part of Reserva Natural Cerro Cumaica-Cerro Alegre. It's a quiet spot that sees almost no visitors, but is a pleasant place to wander.

⊙ Sights

There's not much to do in town but stroll the crumbling colonial streets. The intrepid might want to undertake the challenging 4km hike to **Cueva Santo Domingo**, though it's a good idea to take a guide, such as **Helman Rene Luna** (☑5813-9908). There are petroglyphs at **Piedra de Sapo** on the top of the volcanic rim, from where you can see Masaya, Managua and the country's two biggest lakes on a clear day.

ⓘ Getting There & Away

Irregular buses connect Santa Lucia with Boaco (US$0.70, 30 minutes). If you're in a hurry, consider taking a taxi (US$3.50).

Juigalpa

POP 71,300 / ELEV 117M

Blessed with a wonderful setting, Juigalpa is nestled on a high plateau peering into a golden valley quilted with rangeland carved by a crystalline river. It's enclosed on all sides by the looming Serranía Amerrisque, the sheer granite faces and layered peaks of which are ripe for contemplation and adventure. To the west is a series of smaller hills and dry valleys that crumble into marsh, which then melts into Lago de Nicaragua.

The town itself, sprinkled with well-preserved colonial buildings and peopled by ranchers, rambles along both sides of the Managua Hwy. Apart from a fascinating archaeological museum, there are not a lot of attractions here and the pulse of tourism is quite faint, but it's a good place to break a journey for lunch or overnight if you're passing through.

⊙ Sights

★**Museo Arqueológico**
Gregorio Aguilar Barea MUSEUM
(☑2512-0784; Parque Central, 2½c E; US$0.40; ☺8am-noon & 1-5pm Tue-Fri, 8am-noon & 1-4pm Sat, 9am-noon & 1-3pm Sun) Mystical stone statues rise like ancient totems in the courtyard entrance here. It houses the most important collection of stelae in the country, with more than 120 basalt statues carved between AD 800 and 1500, including *La Chinita,* known as 'The Mona Lisa of Chontales.' She too has appeared at the Louvre.

Parque Palo Solo PARK
(Parque Central, 5c E) This rather lovely, beautifully tended and shady park is where couples come to whisper, cuddle and kiss beneath palm and ficus trees, and absorb a truly magnificent view of the distant Serranía Amerrisque.

Parque Central PLAZA
The central plaza is constantly buzzing with man gossip thanks to the steady stream of ranchers, who come to get their boots shined next to *El Lustrador,* the beloved statue of a shoe-shine boy. El Templo de Cultura, the large gazebo in the center, occasionally hosts live music, poetry readings and other cultural events.

⭐ Festivals & Events

Fiestas Patronales CULTURAL
(⊙ Aug 11-18) Internationally known for its *hípicas* (horse parades and rodeos), the party's beating heart is Juigalpa's Plaza Taurina Chontales, a rodeo venue that hosts events and shows throughout the year.

🛏 Sleeping

Hotel Casa Country HOTEL $
(☑ 2512-2546; casacountryhotel@yahoo.es; frente Parque Palo Solo; r with fan/air-con US$15/20; ❋) In front of Palo Solo park, this small hotel has a variety of accommodations set around a compact internal courtyard. While they're not big on space, rooms are quiet and comfortable.

Hotel Nuevo Milenio GUESTHOUSE $
(☑ 2512-0646; Iglesia, 1c E; s/d US$8/12, r with air-con US$12-20; ❋ 🤖) The best of the cheapies, this homey place has a sweet family atmosphere and clean and basic rooms.

★**Hotel Los Arcangeles** HOTEL $$
(☑ 2512-0847; detras Iglesia; r US$40; ❋ 🤖) This highly atmospheric ranch-style hotel, decorated with dozens of folk-art archangels, has a variety of spotless rooms set around plant-filled corridors in a top location directly behind the cathedral. Some are too enclosed while others are spacious with high ceilings, so ask to see a few – they're all the same price. Breakfast is an extra US$5.

🍴 Eating

Mercado MARKET $
(Parque Central, 1c E, ½c N; meals US$2; ⊙ 6am-6pm) For super-cheap eats, hit the market, where local mothers bring home cooking to the masses. Come for full chicken meals (grilled and fried) served with *gallo pinto* (rice and beans) or refried beans and freshly made tortillas.

Palo Solo NICARAGUAN $$
(☑ 2512-2735; Parque Palo Solo; dishes US$6-12.50; ⊙ 11am-11pm Thu-Tue; 🤖) Set on a shady patio at the western edge of Palo Solo park,

this restaurant serves up tasty Nicaraguan mixed grill plates. It's not exactly fine dining, but it's lively, the food is good and the view is fantastic.

Coffee Break INTERNARIONAL $$
(frente Petronic; mains US$8-12.50; ⊙ 6am-10pm; 🤖) This friendly diner-style place with comfy booths on the main highway through town serves up soups, salads, panini, quesadillas and grilled meats. It also has a baked goods selection and does good coffee, making it perfect for a pit stop.

ℹ Information

BanPro (frente Parque Central) Reliable Visa/MasterCard ATM.

Hospital (Barrio Hector Ugarte)

ℹ Getting There & Away

Buses to Managua, El Rama and San Carlos all leave from the **Cotran** (Hwy 7) bus terminal, across Hwy 7 from downtown (taxis there cost around US$0.60). Minivans for Managua (US$3.50) leave the Cotran when full. Passing *expreso* buses between Managua and San Carlos or El Rama do not enter the Cotran – hail them on the highway. Buses to Cuapa, La Libertad and Puerto Díaz leave from the Mercado.

El Rama (US$3.50, five hours, almost hourly from 4:30am to 2:45pm)

Managua (*expreso* US$2.70, two hours, 5:45am & 1:15pm; *ordinario* US$2.20, three hours, 4am to 6pm, half-hourly)

Puerto Díaz (US$1, one hour, 5:30am, 9:30am, 11:30am and 1pm) The later buses do not always run – check at the market.

San Carlos (US$3.50, four hours, 3am to 1:30pm, every two hours)

Puerto Díaz

On the shores of beautiful Lago de Nicaragua, the rustic village of Puerto Díaz defines the term *tranquilo.* Aside from enjoying some of the least-visited islets in the lake, eating fresh fish and contemplating the vast expanse of water before you, there's not a whole lot to do here, and that's part of its charm.

🏃 Activities

Mirador Vista Linda SWIMMING
(☑ 8360-5508; adult/child US$1/0.50; ⊙ 8am-7pm Sat & Sun) Up on the hillside, this swimming pool has panoramic views. Even if you don't plan to jump in, it's worth walking up here for the view, which is magnificent. It takes in the three islands, with a stunning

TERRITORIO RAMA-KRIOL

Jointly administered by the indigenous Rama and Creole peoples of the region, the little-visited Territorio Rama-Kriol stretches from the southern half of Bahía de Bluefields all the way to the Costa Rican border. It includes stunning solitary beaches, mysterious ruins cloaked in virgin rainforest and lazy mocha-colored rivers teeming with wildlife. It's possible to visit the territory on a loop from Bluefields or continue all the way down to San Juan de Nicaragua, near the mouth of the Río San Juan.

Begin with a visit to **Rama Cay**, the tiny and rocky barbell-shaped island 15km south-east of Bluefields, is the de facto capital of the Rama nation. Dotted with coconut and banana palms and mango and breadfruit trees, the island is laced with earthen trails that link clusters of stilted thatched bungalows, home to more than 1000 people – over half of all remaining Rama. A trip here is a cultural experience rather than an island excursion. Check out the Moravian Church or head up to the breezy point on the north side of the island to chill out under coconut trees. The population here still speaks its own language, which you'll hear wherever you go. If you're feeling active, learn to sail a traditional dory (dugout canoe) on the bay and head across to wild Mission Cay for a picnic. Visits to Rama Cay can be organized through the Gobierno Territorial Rama-Kriol (p223) office in Bluefields, which can arrange transportation and lodging. the tiny and unofficial island capital of the Rama people. Across the bay and up the Kukra River you'll find Tiktik Kaanu, a remote Rama community that's a great place to spend the night surrounded by the sounds of the jungle.

Heading out of Bahía de Bluefields through the Hone Sound passage (a turbulent gathering of breaking waves that is a true test of your captain's skills) you'll come to **Monkey Point**, a Rasta-influenced Creole community spread out on hillsides by the sea and surrounded by thick jungle. Here you'll find some of the best beaches on the Caribbean mainland and a fascinating yet unexplored indigenous burial site shrouded in thick foliage, which is said to be one of the country's oldest archaeological sites.

A short boat ride further south is Bankukuk, a small Rama community with fine beaches and jungle-covered headlands jutting out into the calm Caribbean Sea.

Continuing south past Punta Gorda, you'll arrive at **Corn River**, one of the most important waterways of the magnificent Reserva Biológica Indio-Maíz. At the river mouth you'll find a tiny Creole community, but the real attraction here is upriver, where you'll be treated to some of the best wildlife viewing in the country. The towering trees are awash with birds and monkeys and you may spot sloths or even a tapir.

Getting There & Away

There are irregular *pangas* from Bluefields to the communities of the Territorio Rama-Kriol. Normally, you'll either have to charter a boat or hitch a ride with a traveling local – you'll be expected to contribute to fuel costs.

It may also be possible to get to some of the communities using the regular Bluefields–San Juan de Nicaragua express *panga*, but you'll have to negotiate with the driver as most villages require a deviation from the normal journey.

backdrop of Isla de Ometepe's smoldering crater. Order a cold beer and let the view work on you a while.

✖ Eating

El Pescadito SEAFOOD **$**
(☑ 8732-6774; meals US$3-5; ⊗ 6am-10pm) In a breezy ranch by the water, El Pescadito serves a terrific fried fish with panoramic lake views. The owner also arranges boat trips on the lake.

Bar y Restaurant Lizayel SEAFOOD **$**
(☑ 8840-3629; meals US$3.50-5; ⊗ 6am-10pm) Serves big plates of fried fish and typical dishes in an open-air dining area. Many sailing boat captains hang out here between voyages, and so it's a good place to organize boat trips to the islands too.

❶ Getting There & Away

Buses and trucks (US$1, one hour) run to Juigalpa at 4am, 5:30am, 7am, 3:40pm and 4:30pm. These schedules change often and the return buses

BOAT TRIPS FROM PUERTO DÍAZ

It's possible to arrange boat trips with local fishers (per day US$50, six to seven passengers) to the archipelago in front of Puerto Díaz, where you can visit each of the three rocky islands with their array of birdlife and beaches, where you can swim. There's a house on Isla Redonda where you may be able to sling your hammock for the night, but you'll need to bring food and water with you from the mainland. Isla Grande is home to a tiny farming community and Isla El Muerte is owned by an absent foreigner, but the guard will probably let you poke around.

don't always run – so check in Juigalpa before setting out. Taxis from Juigalpa cost around US$25.

If you're feeling adventurous, it's also possible to travel from here to Isla de Ometepe (US$4, six hours) on one of the sailing boats that bring plantains to the mainland. Departures depend on cargo, but they leave around four times a week, usually setting sail around 7pm.

Cuapa

POP 7950

This small, picturesque mountain town became a famous pilgrimage destination thanks to the Virgin of Cuapa, the porcelain statue holding flowers in her angelic hands at the entrance to town. There's little reason to come here, but the small, rural town is pleasant enough and pretty in parts.

◎ Sights

El Monolito de Cuapa   NATURAL FEATURE
A massive stone monolith that rises from a hillside savanna outside Cuapa. If you walk from town, it will take about two hours to reach the peak. Alternatively, you could drive to the base and scramble up the back until you reach the top (10 to 20 minutes). According to local legend, the rock is home to goblins.

Virgen de Cuapa Santuario   CHRISTIAN SITE
(☉8am-5:30pm) Most visitors to Cuapa come with the purpose of making a pilgrimage to this porcelain statue holding flowers in her hands, located at the entrance to town. On April 15, 1980, when tailor Bernardo Martínez was walking home, the statue began to glow. The Virgin then appeared to him five

times, three times as apparitions and twice in his dreams, over the next five months. Her message was that all Nicaragua would suffer without peace.

❶ Getting There & Away

Buses run regularly during the day between Juigalpa's market terminal and Cuapa (US$0.50, 30 minutes).

Villa Sandino

POP 13,100

It doesn't get many visitors, but the tiny rural town of Villa Sandino on the Juigalpa–El Rama Hwy is the gateway to one of Nicaragua's most important archaeological sites: the impressive petroglyphs at Parque Arqueológico Piedras Pintadas, 8km north of town.

If you are feeling particularly Dr Jonesish, ask at the *alcaldía* about the three-hour horseback ride to some pre-Columbian pyramids, the largest ruins of their kind in Nicaragua. What you see are the partially buried bases of larger pyramids that once stood on the site. It's no Tikal, but it's interesting to sit and contemplate how the area looked when the pyramids were complete and the area was full of indigenous worshippers.

◎ Sights

Parque Arqueológico
Piedras Pintadas   ARCHAEOLOGICAL SITE
(US$1; ☉8am-4pm) Here you'll find hundreds of petroglyphs carved into the mossy boulders, including deer, snakes, turtles, crocodiles and spirals, set among rolling green hills. There are also large stones with carved channels, which are said to have been used for ritual sacrifice, and an impressive bathing pool carved out of a single massive boulder. Buy your entrance ticket and organize guides (US$12 per group) at the **Alcaldía** (☎2516-0058; Iglesia Catolica, 1c O; ☉8am-4pm) before leaving Villa Sandino. The park is overgrown with thick scrub and high grass – bring sturdy footwear. It's 8km north of town on a firm dirt road. A round-trip taxi from town is around US$10.

⏠ Sleeping

Hotel Santa Clara   HOTEL $
(☎2516-0055; maisalar@hotmail.com; frente Alcaldía; r with/without air-con US$20/15; ❄🛜) The best option in town, Santa Clara has comfortable air-con rooms and serves meals.

❶ Getting There & Away

Any Juigalpa–El Rama bus will drop you here. The town center is just a couple of blocks from the highway.

El Rama

POP 14,000

The Río Rama and Río Escondido converge at El Rama, turning an otherwise lazy tropical river into an international thoroughfare that empties into Bahía de Bluefields. Roads between El Rama and Managua are some of the best in the country thanks to the commerce of Rama International Port, Nicaragua's only heavyweight Atlantic harbor.

While you are still 60km from the Caribbean sea, take a walk around town and you'll notice plenty of Creole influence, with booming reggae, braided hair and a plethora of Bob Marley T-shirts. Despite this, Rama remains a scruffy port town that does not generally inspire travelers to stop for long on their way between Managua and Bluefields.

⊨ Sleeping

Hotel Río Escondido   HOTEL $

(☑ 2517-0287; rioescondidohotel@yahoo.es; Enitel, 1c E, 30m S; r with/without air-con US$16/12.50, tr with fan US$16.50; ❉ ☏) This reliable hotel has spacious rooms with high ceilings, spotless tiled bathrooms, small flat-screen TVs and wooden beds with firm sprung mattresses. It's not in good shape anymore but is about as good as it gets in Rama.

Hotel Doña Luisa   HOTEL $

(☑ 2517-0073; frente Muelle; r with/without TV US$10/8) If you've got an early boat (or express bus) this is where you want to be. It's right by the dock and offers clean rooms with fans and cable TV. Don't worry about missing your connection – the hustle outside should get you out of bed.

✕ Eating

If you're after a quick bite between bus and boat, there are several tasty buffet-style restaurants in the blocks around the dock.

Casa Blanca   NICARAGUAN $$

(☑ 2517-0320; Bancentro, 1c S, 1c E; mains US$4-9; ❂ 8am-midnight) A popular open-air restaurant perched on the banks of the Río Escondido on the south side of town that serves solid portions of Nicaraguan favorites. It's also a fine place to kick back with a drink

and watch the comings and goings on the river, complete with a *ranchero* soundtrack.

El Expresso   NICARAGUAN $$

(Muelle, 4c E; meals US$6-12; ❂ noon-10pm) This modern, spacious dining room is known for its generous cuts of export-quality beef and seafood dishes, including lobster prepared in nine different ways.

❶ Information

BanPro Has an ATM and changes US dollars.

❶ Getting There & Away

El Rama is walkable, but you may choose to take a pedicab (US$0.30) the 1.5km to **Rama International Port** (☑ 2517-0315) for large, slow boats to Bluefields. The *Río Escondido* (US$9, five hours), the most punctual service, leaves at 9pm on Tuesday and spends the night in Bluefields before continuing to Corn Island.

At the Muelle Municipal, close to the *expreso* buses, **Transporte Vargas** (☑ 2517-0073; ❂ 24hr) and **Transporte Jipe** (☑ 8937-2913, 8622-2937; ❂ 24hr) have a faster, more convenient collective *panga* service to Bluefields (US$8, two hours). Boats leave at first light in the morning and then 'when full' throughout the

---

SAN JOSÉ DE LOS REMATES

Impossibly scenic and peacefully pastoral, San José de los Remates has relatively easy access to the Reserva Natural Cerro Cumaica-Cerro Alegre, and boasts an impressive municipal tourism program launched to help preserve its own clean water supply. Several years ago, a Boaco-based cattle-ranching operation had polluted the watershed to the point that municipal groundwater was threatened. The townspeople mobilized, convinced the rancher to grow sustainable organic coffee instead, and reforested much of the property themselves. The land is now protected as a municipal park, **Reserva Hídrica Municipal La Chorrera**, adjacent to the national reserve. Local tourism helps foot the bill, making San José an exemplary case of successful ecotourism. Visiting will please anyone with an interest in the subject.

There are buses from Teustepe (US$1, one hour) to San José de los Remates at 7am and 5pm, the latter of which continues onto Esquipulas.

day. There is usually always service around noon and another around 3pm if there is demand.

Transporte Vargas also runs private *expreso* buses to Managua that are timed to leave once the morning *pangas* arrive from Bluefields, with a further service leaving around noon.

Other *expreso* buses, which actually stop along the way, depart from outside the Muelle Municipal throughout the day. Even slower *ordinarios* park at the small square one block east and one block south.

Bus services include:

Juigalpa (US$3.50, four hours, 4:40am to 2:55pm, hourly)

Managua (*expreso* US$7, six hours, 2am, 3am, 9am, 10:30am, noon, 5pm and 7pm; *ordinario* US$5.50, eight hours, 4:40am to 9:40am, hourly)

Pearl Lagoon (US$4.75, five hours, 4:20pm)

Bluefields

POP 45,500

Named after the Dutch pirate Abraham Blauvelt, who made his base here in the 1700s, Bluefields is the beating heart of Creole culture, famed for its distinctive music, colorful dances and delicious cuisine – considered by many as the best in the country. And while it is not your typical Caribbean dream destination, if you give it a chance and get to know some of the town's ebullient locals, Bluefields will definitely grow on you. Still, you probably won't linger too long. After all, you are just a boat ride away from the intriguing Pearl Lagoon basin, the spectacular Pearl Keys and those luscious Corn Islands.

Bluefields is the capital of the RAAS (Región Autónoma Atlántico Sur; South Atlantic Autonomous Region), also known as the Región Autónoma de la Costa Caribe Sur.

◉ Sights

★ **Waiku Centro de Arte**   CULTURAL CENTER
(www.waikuart.wordpress.com; Movistar, 15m S; ◷9am-7pm Mon-Sat) This excellent social project is run by two English-speaking activists, Greta and Yesi, whose small arts center displays painting, handicrafts, clothing and jewellery for sale, made by members of all six ethnic groups present in the RAAS. Above all, the center encourages reading, and it provides chairs, coffee (US$0.05 per cup!) and a book exchange.

★ **Museo Histórico Cultural de la Costa Caribe**   MUSEUM
(CIDCA; Iglesia Morava, 2c S; admission US$2; ◷8am-noon & 2-4:30pm Mon-Fri) Learn about the Caribbean region's diverse cultures with a visit to this fascinating museum, which contains an interesting mix of historical items from the pre-Columbian era and British rule, including a sword belonging to the last Miskito king and artifacts left by the Kukra indigenous group.

Moravian Church   CHURCH
(Iglesia Morava) This large concrete church is Bluefield's most iconic building, constructed to the exact specifications of the 1849 wooden original, which was destroyed by Hurricane Juana in 1985. Like all churches of the order, it has a red tin roof and all-white exterior.

Malecón de Santa Rosa   WATERFRONT
(Barrio Santa Rosa) This waterfront area on the way to the airport offers views across Bluefields Bay and is a popular gathering place for families. It also pulls a crowd for social drinks in the evening.

El Bluff   PORT
Across the bay, the port of El Bluff is nestled at the point of a long sliver of land where the Caribbean Sea rushes into Bahía de Bluefields. There is not much to see in the town, but the enormous oil tanks and shipping tankers are cool if you like a certain industrialized tropical setting.

Mercado   MARKET
(◷7am-3pm) Spilling out from a dank warehouse perched on a public pier, the local market is packed with small stands displaying pineapple, banana, citrus and casaba. Other stalls sell fresh fish, shrimp, prawns and crab. Fishing boats dock and unload right at the market's back doors. It's an especially interesting scene early in the morning.

Reserva Silvestre Greenfields   NATURE RESERVE
(◷2779-0589; www.greenfields.com.ni; Kukra Hill; day admission 1-2 visitors US$30; ◷by appointment) ◢ This privately managed, 284-hectare wildlife reserve near the village of Kukra Hill has tracts of both mangroves and jungle, and offers a variety of activities including canoeing, swimming and hiking. Advanced reservations are essential. Kukra Hill is a 30-minute boat ride from the Muelle Municipal (p223) in Bluefields. Return transport from the village to the reserve, if you're not staying overnight, costs US$10 per visitor.

◷ Tours

Rumble in the Jungle   FISHING
(◷8832-4269; www.rumbleinthejungle.net; Casa Rosa, Loma Fresca; packages per day from US$400) The only sportfishing outfitter in the area,

Bluefields

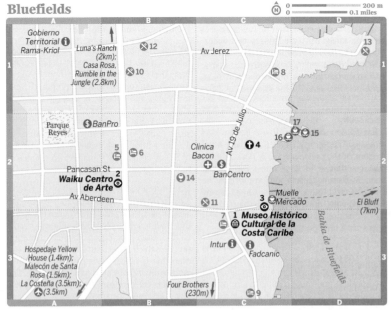

Bluefields

◉ Top Sights

◉ Sights

⊜ Sleeping

⊗ Eating

⊝ Drinking & Nightlife

ⓘ Transport

Rumble in the Jungle is run by owner Randy Poteet, who knows all the best fishing spots and offers lagoon, river and blue-water options around Bluefields, Pearl Lagoon and beyond.

🎊 Festivals & Events

★ Palo de Mayo
CULTURAL

(Maypole Festival) Nicaragua's best street party simmers along throughout May with a series of neighborhood fiestas and cultural events. The highlights are the energetic Carnival on the last Saturday of the month and the closing Tululu march on May 31st.

🛏 Sleeping

Hostal Doña Vero
GUESTHOUSE $

(☏ 2572-2166; hostaldvero@yahoo.com; Galileo, ½c N; s/d US$12.50/14.50, with air-con US$20/21.50, without bathroom US$9.50/11; ❀ ᐟ ᙇ) A great centrally located budget option with clean, comfortable rooms including private bathroom, unlimited coffee and filtered water. There is a small pool area out the back, which feels far removed from the downtown bustle.

Hospedaje Yellow House
HOSTEL $

(☏ 8212-5575; www.facebook.com/Hospedaje YellowHouse; El Malecón, Santa Rosa; dm/s/d/tr

US$5/7/13/18; ☎) ⏱ The closest thing Blue-fields has to a hostel, the Yellow House is a brightly painted collection of buildings set in some fairly wild gardens by the water-front in the *barrio* of Santa Rosa, a short cab ride from downtown. Rooms are ultra-basic and share bathrooms, but come with mos-quito nets and use of a big kitchen.

Hotel Jackani GUESTHOUSE $$

(☎2572-0440; hoteljackani@gmail.com; frente Policia, Barrio Punta Fria; s/d/tw/tr incl breakfast US$30/40/50/60; ❄☎) This family-run hotel in front of the police station is popular with travelers thanks to its spotless rooms and warm welcome. Guests also appreciate the hot water, fast internet and the large balcony out front with views over to the bay, even if the furnishing choices in the rooms them-selves are a little on the garish side.

Central Hotel Quinto HOTEL $$

(☎2572-0035; Galileo, ½c N; s/d/tw US$13/24/27; ❄☎) Rooms in this centrally located hotel are spotless and very competitively priced considering the amenities – just don't ex-pect a lot of atmosphere. What little there is can be summed up by the aquariums in the lobby and the wagon-wheel rocking chairs on the porch. However, the welcome is cer-tainly warm.

Hotel Caribbean Dream HOTEL $$

(☎2572-0107; londa66@hotmail.com; Mercado, 1c O, ½c S; r with fan US$18-28, with air-con US$22-32; ❄☎) A reliable downtown hotel that strikes a good balance between price and amenities. Rooms are not particularly inspiring but feature air-con and hot water, and there is a great balcony with rockers overlooking the street – perfect for getting to know some of Bluefields' colorful characters.

★ Hotel Casa Royale HOTEL $$$

(☎2572-0668, 2572-0675; www.hotelcasaroyale.com; Calle Neysi Rios, Barrio Pointeen; r from US$70; P❄☎🏊) This excellent hotel is easily the best choice in town, with mod-ern, sleek and spotless rooms, an excellent location with a great view over the bay, help-ful staff and an impressively good top-floor restaurant. Add to the mix a good pool and a delicious *desayuno típico* each morning, and you're onto a winner.

✗ Eating

Bluefields' favourite snack is the *paty* – a sa-vory spiced meat pastry sold for US$0.30 by roaming vendors all over town. Elsewhere, you'll eat decently, but there's definitely some flair lacking in the town, which is a shame, as the region is known for its excellent seafood.

★ Cevicheria El Chino SEAFOOD $

(frente Colegio Bautista; ceviche US$2; ⏱7am-9pm) Don't leave Bluefields without trying El Chino's marvelous *ceviche,* prepared fresh every day and served in small polystyrene cups, alongside an array of auto parts at this unremarkable grocery shop. Choose from shrimp, fish, oyster or mixed and watch out for the outrageously spicy homemade 'Ass in Space' chili sauce – made with pounds of habanero chilies.

Maranatha Vineyard Bakery BAKERY $

(Colegio Dinamarca; items US$0.25-1; ⏱8am-7pm Mon-Sat; ☎) Totally unmarked from the street, this traditional Creole bakery of local preach-er and career politician Rayfield Hodgson prepares the best coconut bread in town – but even that is nothing compared to the delec-table cinnamon-infused pineapple roll. The soda cakes (ginger cookies) ain't bad either.

★ Galeria Aberdeen CAFE $$

(☎2572-2605; Mercado, 1½c O; light meals US$4-7; ⏱8am-9pm; ☎) Feeling just a tad too chic for grimy Bluefields, this light-filled, split-level cafe serves real coffee in addition to panini, pasta dishes, salads and other meals you won't find anywhere else. There's also a great selection of desserts and a fridge full of imported beers. The walls are covered with works by local artists and it hosts regular cultural events.

Pelican Bay NICARAGUAN $$

(☎2572-2089; Barrio Pointeen; mains US$7-12.50; ⏱11am-11pm) At the end of the Pointeen peninsula, this well-situated restaurant has an elevated, breezy balcony with fantastic views across the bay to El Bluff. The house specialty is seafood, and the mixed plate (US$12.50), featuring shrimp, fish and lob-ster sautéed with herbs, is outstanding.

Bay View Bar & Restaurant CARIBBEAN $$$

(Calle Neysi Rios, Barrio Pointeen; mains US$10-20; ⏱6am-10pm; ☎) On the top floor of the Ho-tel Casa Royale, the Bay View offers exactly that – great vistas over the enormous lagoon and a perfect vantage point for watching the *pangas* come and go. Service is formal, on white linen tablecloths, and the large menu specializes in seafood, including *ceviches* (marinated seafood) and steak. Breakfast here is also the best in town.

🍷 Drinking & Nightlife

★ Four Brothers   CLUB
(Parque Reyes, 6c S, 3c E; ⊘8pm-4am Thu-Sun)
Dance up a storm to dancehall, country and
reggae on the wooden dance floor at this
legendary disco ranch, comfortable in the
knowledge that your dignity is protected by
the extremely low-wattage lighting. It doesn't
get going until after midnight. Go in a group:
it sometimes gets a little rough later on.

Cima Club   CLUB
(✆2572-1410; Mercado, 2c O, 1c N; ⊘8pm-late)
This popular, massive late-night venue has
two distinct zones. The open terrace bar
downstairs is favored by hard-drinking sea-
farers and prostitutes, while upstairs is one of
the more upmarket clubs in town, playing an
eclectic mix of Latin pop, rock and dancehall.

ℹ️ Information

DANGERS & ANNOYANCES
➡ Take care in Bluefields, even during daytime,
if you're alone: do not walk down empty streets
or stray into areas without a good number of
people in them.

➡ At night always take a taxi.

➡ Beware of pickpockets in the downtown area.

➡ Do not visit local bars and clubs alone, and if
possible, go with locals.

MEDICAL SERVICES
Clinica Bacon (✆2572-2384; Iglesia Morava,
1c S, ½c O) Private clinic with a range of specialists and a laboratory.

MONEY
BanCentro (Iglesia Morava, ½c S) Visa/Plus
ATM.

BanPro (frente Iglesia) Reliable Visa/Master-
Card ATM.

TOURIST INFORMATION
The following organizations can help with infor-
mation:
Fadcanic (✆2270-0536; www.fadcanic.org.ni;
Barrio Punta Fria, oficinas del PNUD; ⊘9am-
5pm Mon-Fri, to noon Sat)
Gobierno Territorial Rama-Kriol (GTRK;
✆8622-8407, 2572-1765; ramagob@gmail.
com; Parque Reyes, 2c N; ⊘8am-5pm)
Intur (✆2572-0221; Iglesia Morava, 2c S,
Punta Fria; ⊘8am-5pm Mon-Fri)

ℹ️ Getting There & Away

AIR
Take a taxi (US$0.50) to **Bluefields Airport**,
where **La Costeña** (✆2572-2500, 2572-2750;

Aeropuerto; ⊘6am-5pm) has three daily flights
to Managua (one way/round trip US$83/127, 45
minutes) and Great Corn Island (one way/round
trip US$65/99, 25 minutes) and flies to Bilwi (one
way/round trip US$96/148, 50 minutes) three
days a week when there's enough demand. If there
aren't enough passengers for the direct Bilwi
flight, you'll fly through Managua at no extra cost.

BOAT
Bluefields is the heart of the *panga* and shipping
network connecting the various towns and settlements along the Caribbean coast. Just bear
in mind that you'll often need to make journeys
that don't feel particularly safe and are nearly
always far from comfortable. There are three
main piers from where *pangas* leave, the **Muelle
Municipal** (Municipal Dock), the **Terminal Costa Atlántica** and the **Muelle Mercado**.

Following an accident in 2017, which saw the
Captain D ferry overturn and sink, the only con-
nection between Bluefields and Corn Island is
now the government-run *Río Escondido* (US$8,
five hours), which departs from the Muelle Municipal at 9am on Wednesday and Saturday, with
return runs on Thursday and Sunday. There are
also a number of cargo boats making the trip on
irregular schedules; enquire at the docks.

For Pearl Lagoon (US$5.25, one hour), *pan-
gas* leave when full from the Muelle Municipal
throughout the day, with the last ones leaving by
4pm. There's also a weekly *panga* to San Juan de
Nicaragua (US$32, three hours) that leaves the
Muelle Municipal at 8.30am on Friday, returning
on Wednesday. Bring bin bags for your luggage
and prepare yourself for a tough journey if the
water is anything other than dead calm.

Those heading to El Rama (US$8, two hours)
can take a *panga* from the far more orderly and
cleaner Terminal Costa Atlántica, where *pangas*
are run by **Transporte Vargas** (✆2572-0724,
2572-1510; contiguo Muelle Municipal; ⊘5am-
4pm) and **Transporte Jipe** (✆2572-1879; Calle
Municipal; ⊘5am-4pm). These leave when full
throughout the day, with the first departures
between 6am and 7am and a final one at around
3pm. Transporte Vargas also runs boats to
Tasbapauni and Orinoco in the greater Pearl
Lagoon area.

Pangas crossing the bay to El Bluff (US$1.30,
30 minutes) leave throughout the day from
Muelle Mercado when full.

BUS
There are now bus services that link Bluefields
to Managua via the town of Nueva Guinea. At the
time of writing, the road to Nueva Guinea was
still rough in places, but passable unless there's
been heavy rain, and was due to be completely
sealed soon. Buses run by Transporte Vargas
and Transporte Jipe leave from the area outside
the Muelle Municipal every day at 6.30am
(US$12.75, seven hours).

Pearl Lagoon

POP 4900

In charming Pearl Lagoon you'll find dirt roads, palm trees, reggae music and mangrove forests, all brought to life by a friendly English-speaking Creole community that lives of the sea and still refers to Nicaraguans elsewhere in the country as 'Spaniards.' You can feel the stress roll off your shoulders as soon as you get off the boat, after a gorgeous journey down wide rivers and across glass-still lagoons. Best of all, Pearl Lagoon still sees very few tourists – which means you may well be the only foreigner buzzing through the mangroves and jungle.

Pearl Lagoon is a perfect base from which to visit the nearby Pearl Keys, where you'll find sugar-white beaches that double as turtle hatcheries, and swaying coconut palms that invite inner peace. You'll be glad to return here afterwards, though, to enjoy cold beers and stellar local seafood on the waterfront.

◉ Sights

Awas & Raiti Pura   VILLAGE

Take the path opposite the church due west along the paved road through the savanna and, after 30 minutes, you will reach the humble Miskito fishing communities of Raiti Pura and Awas. The grassy shore here is perfect for a picnic, and a lovely sunset can be seen. The water is perfect for swimming too. You can also make the journey by bike; Queen Lobster Tours rents bikes for US$1 per hour.

⌗ Tours

★Captain Sodlan McCoy   BOATING

(☑8368-6766, 8410-5197; Sunrise Hotel, Up Point) Anyone can take you to the Pearl Keys, but few know the area even half as well as Captain Sodlan McCoy, a colorful, no-nonsense fisherman who has been visiting the islands since he was a boy. A trip with Sodlan is much more than sightseeing – it's a cultural experience. He also offers birdwatching, fishing and community trips.

Kabu Tours   ECOTOUR

(☑8714-5196) 🖉 A community-run venture set up by the Wildlife Conservation Society to offer an alternative source of income to turtle fishers from the community of Kakabila. It offers overnight and multiday trips to the Pearl Keys, including turtle spotting and snorkeling. It also runs fascinating cultural tours to communities in the Pearl Lagoon basin. See the website for a list of packages.

Queen Lobster Tours   BOATING

(☑2572-5028, 8662-3393; Muelle, 200m N) Professionally run ecotourism outfit specializing in overnight trips to the Pearl Keys, as well as inventive activities around town such as traditional cooking classes, bike riding, visits to indigenous communities, farm trips, jungle adventures and fishing expeditions.

⌸ Sleeping

Pearl Lagoon has a good range of accommodations for a town its size. If you really want to get a feel for the place, try to get a room near the water, where you can watch canoes and fishing boats bringing in their catch.

Slilma Guesthouse   GUESTHOUSE $

(☑2572-0523; slilma_gh1@yahoo.com; Enitel, 1c S, 1c E; r with air-con US$30-35, with fan US$15-20, without bathroom US$10; ❈⊗) The only indigenous-owned guesthouse in Pearl Lagoon, Slilma is a spacious and sprawling place, with a wide range of rooms running from small and simple shared accommodations to larger rooms with air-con and private bathrooms upstairs. To get here take the first left after the cell tower.

★Queen Lobster   BUNGALOW $$

(☑8662-3393; Front Rd, Muelle, 200m N; s/d/tr/q US$30/40/50/60; ❈⊗) Easily the best and most charming choice in Pearl Lagoon, Queen Lobster offers seven rooms on stilts over the water, with private bathrooms and hammocks on the porch. The two original rooms are made of bamboo and thatch, and are a rustic, somewhat darker affair, while the newer rooms have more modern design, air-con and enjoy more light.

Casa Ulrich   HOTEL $$

(☑8907-1483, 8603-5173; casaulrich@hotmail.com; Up Point; s/d with air-con US$30/35, dm/s/d without bathroom US$6/10/12; ❈⊗) Overlooking the water, this large hotel and restaurant up near the point is one of the few places in town that caters to backpackers. It has a variety of rooms, including budget options with shared bathrooms and a dormitory, while the private rooms are spacious. The welcome is warm and, when the restaurant is busy, it feels like the center of town.

Best View Hotel   HOTEL $$

(☑8824-3962, 2572-5099; Up Point, Barrio Ivan Dixon; s/d/tr US$30/40/50; ❈⊗) Jutting out into the water at the end of the sidewalk, this modern hotel catches plenty of breeze and is a good place to observe Miskito sailing canoes and local fishing boats out on the lagoon. Rooms are small but modern and come with cable TV, air-con and reliable wi-fi. There's also a good restaurant here.

Casa Blanca   HOTEL **$$**
(☑ 2572-0508, 8362-6946; casa_blancalp@yahoo.com; Enitel, 250m O; r with air-con US$30, s/d/tr without bathroom US$10/20/30; ❋ ⏾) A great local experience, this lovely white house has wooden floors and furnishings made in the attached workshop. Miss Dell makes her guests feel right at home, and you'll almost certainly find yourself sitting down with the family to shoot the breeze during your stay. The rooms out the back are the best; spacious and full of natural light.

✖ Eating

Pearl Lagoon is a great place to try traditional Creole cuisine, either in one of the town's restaurants or with a freshly cooked meal out in the open during a boat trip.

Warner's Place   FAST FOOD **$**
(Centro de Salud, 1c Sur; mains US$2-4; ⏲ erratic) Now the president of the territory, Mr Warner isn't always around to open his restaurant, but when he is, this is *the* place to go for *frito* – the Caribbean coast's favorite cheap meal. It consists of a pile of thin green plantain chips topped with fried chicken and salad. It ain't healthy but it sure is tasty.

Coconut Delight   BAKERY **$**
(Miss Betty's; Muelle, 30m S; items US$0.25-US$1; ⏲ 8am-8pm Mon-Sat) Follow the sweet smells to this wooden hut to discover Caribbean baking at its finest. Tear into hot coconut bread, *toto* (sticky gingerbread), journey cakes, fluffy soda cakes and even vegetarian *paty,* all served with a smile by jolly giant and all-round nice guy Mr Byron.

★ Casa Ulrich   INTERNATIONAL **$$**
(☑ 8603-5173; Up Point, Muelle, 350m N; mains US$4.50-12.75; ⏲ 7am-10pm; ⏾) Local boy and Swiss-trained chef Fred Ulrich returned to Pearl Lagoon after a long absence working in resorts all over the Americas, and has invested in his own impressive two-floor restaurant right by the water. Everything on the menu is top-notch, but the delicate shrimp pasta and the grilled fish in garlic are outstanding.

BOAT TOURS

Fuel costs make up the lion's share of any boat charter on Pearl Lagoon. Plan on paying around US$60 to US$80 per day for the boat and captain plus fuel. If you're on a budget, look for a boat with a small engine: it will take longer but you'll save plenty. Note that small engines are only an option when the weather is calm.

While fluctuations in fuel costs affect prices dramatically, a ballpark price for one-day trips to the keys is around US$180 to US$200 for a small group. For larger groups, budget around US$45 per visitor. All tours include transportation and lunch on one of the islands.

ℹ Information

MONEY

There are no banks in Pearl Lagoon, so come with ample cash and plan on staying longer than anticipated. You can receive emergency cash transfers at **Western Union** (frente Muelle, Tienda Miss Isabel; ⏲ 9am-5pm Mon-Fri). The nearest ATM is in the village of Kukra Hill, 22km away.

TOURIST INFORMATION

Wildlife Conservation Society (WCS; ☑ 2572-0506; www.wcs.org; Muelle, 20m S, Pearl Lagoon; ⏲ 9am-5pm Mon-Fri)

ℹ Getting There & Away

Timetabled boats run to Bluefields (US5.25, one hour) at 6am and 1pm from Pearl Lagoon's busy **wharf** (Muelle). Sign up the day before for the early boat. Throughout the day, other *pangas* coming from other communities around the lagoon stop here too.

Every Monday, Thursday and Saturday, a *panga* makes the run to Orinoco and nearby Marshall Point from Bluefields via Pearl Lagoon (US$10.50, two hours, 9am); it returns to Pearl Lagoon and Bluefields the following day. This boat can also drop travelers at the communities of Kakabila, Brown Bank and La Fe. There are *pangas* from Bluefields to Tasbapauni (US$10.50, 2½ hours) that pass Pearl Lagoon every day at 11am. Times are liable to shift depending upon the season, so you'll need to ask about departure times at the dock.

One bus (US$6.30, five hours) a day leaves Pearl Lagoon at 5.30am for El Rama, where you can connect to services to Managua and elsewhere in the country. There is also a weekly bus service to Managua (US$10.50, nine hours). The same bus returns overnight Friday to Pearl Lagoon. All bus services leave from outside the basketball court.

Around Pearl Lagoon

With a dozen villages belonging to three distinct ethnic groups clinging to its shores and a similar number of jungle-lined rivers feeding it, a boat trip on Pearl Lagoon can make you feel like an 18th-century explorer venturing into an intriguing new world. This is authentic, off-the-beaten-track cultural tourism at its best, and there is nothing like it anywhere else in the country.

ℹ Getting There & Away

Infrequent public transport schedules mean that most travelers visit the communities on an organized boat tour from Pearl Lagoon.

Kakabila

POP 350

Crossing the lagoon to the northwest from Pearl Lagoon town, you'll come to Kakabila, a welcoming Miskito village carpeted with soft grass and studded with mango, pear and breadfruit trees and coconut palms. There's definitely some tropical country romance happening here. To the south of town is Tuba Creek, a narrow, jungle-lined river that is great for wildlife spotting.

🛏 Sleeping

Lakiya Tara   GUESTHOUSE $
(dm US$10) This small community lodge is located just north of the village on the beach and has simple accommodations in thatched huts. The night sky here is spectacular and the lodge organizes interpretive treks through the thick jungle behind the village, where you'll learn about bush food and natural medicines. Simple meals can be ordered in advance.

ℹ Getting There & Away

A private transfer from Pearl Lagoon to Kakabila will cost around US$50 for a large boat or US$20 to US$30 in a motorized canoe. Alternatively, the 9am daily public *panga* from Bluefields to Orinoco (US$11) will drop you here on request.

Río Wawashang

This lazy, wide, mocha-colored river surrounded by jungle flows into Pearl Lagoon just west of Orinoco. Its banks are home to two fascinating projects, a reforestation scheme and a sustainable agriculture training school for locals. Both can be visited by anyone who makes it out here – call or visit Fadcanic (p223) in Bluefields to arrange a trip. The main settlement here is the unremarkable Pueblo Nuevo, where buses from Bluefields arrive.

◎ Sights

Reserva Natural
Kahka Creek   NATURE RESERVE
(☑ 2570-0962, 8725-0766; Pueblo Nuevo) 🐾 This reforestation and ecotourism project near Pueblo Nuevo is set in lush gardens surrounded by jungle. There are a number of hiking trails and a lookout tower above the forest canopy. Visitors can also get involved in the reforestation process by planting trees. It's a 2km walk from Pueblo Nuevo.

☞ Tours

Wawashang Education Center   ECOTOUR
(☑ 8930-0248; Río Wawashang) 🐾 A vocational training school where youth from all over the RAAS region learn about sustainable agriculture. You can tour the greenhouses, check out the cool coconut farm or sample artisanal chocolate made from locally grown cacao.

🛏 Sleeping

Kahka Creek Lodge   LODGE $
(☑ 2570-0962; Pueblo Nuevo; dm/r US$8/15) Simple rooms are available for guests in this solar-powered wooden lodge in the Reserva Natural Kahka Creek. Cheap meals are served too.

ℹ Getting There & Away

Pangas depart Bluefields for Pueblo Nuevo (US$9, 2½ hours) at 7:30am on Sunday and Wednesday and 2pm on Thursday, via Pearl Lagoon and the Río Wawashang. They can drop visitors directly at the Wawashang Education Center.

Reserva Natural Kahka Creek is a 2km walk from Pueblo Nuevo. It's possible to make the journey on horseback – ask around.

Orinoco

POP 2000

When you hear the evocative call of the *djimbe* (wood and animal-skin drum) spilling out across the rippling water from the red-earth streets of Orinoco, you know you're approaching Garifuna country.

Orinoco is home to 2000 of Nicaragua's approximately 5000 Garifuna people. Here you can learn to paddle a dugout canoe, try your hand at fishing or take the 30-minute stroll northeast along the water to Marshall Point, a neighboring Creole village.

Festivals & Events

National Garifuna Week CULTURAL
(⊙Nov) Events at this celebration of Garifuna culture include live music and dance performances, and historical and cultural symposiums that climax on November 19.

Sleeping

★**Hostal Garífuna** GUESTHOUSE $
(☑8648-4985; www.hostalgarifuna.net; per person US$15) Owned by local anthropologist, activist and entrepreneur Kensy Sambola, this very comfortable budget hotel has spotless fan-cooled rooms, all but one of which share bathrooms. The restaurant serves tremendous seafood meals (US$6-9) and Kensy and her staff can organize a range of cultural activities, including boat transport to La Fe, a Garifuna village famous for its acoustic troubadours.

ℹ Information

DANGERS & ANNOYANCES

Note that a number of robberies targeting tourists, including serious assault, have been reported in and around Orinoco. All visitors, but particularly female travelers, should exercise caution and not walk through remote areas without a trusted local guide. Ask at your hotel for a recommendation.

ℹ Getting There & Away

Daily public boats run from Bluefields to Orinoco (US$11, two hours) via Pearl Lagoon, leaving from next to the municipal dock in Bluefields between 9am and 10am and passing Pearl Lagoon one hour later. A private round-trip boat transfer from Pearl Lagoon to Orinoco costs around US$120.

Pearl Keys

The snow-white, palm-shaded, turquoise-fringed Pearl Keys are home to Nicaragua's best Caribbean beaches. Located 30km out to sea from the village of Pearl Lagoon, there were once 18 pearls, but rising tides and beach erosion have trimmed the number to just 10, with more threatened by disappearance in the future.

Once communally owned by Miskito and Creole villagers on the mainland, some of the keys have been bought by foreign inves-

---

ℹ **CATCH A BOAT TO LA FE**

From Orinoco it's possible to travel across the bay to La Fe, a charming Garifuna village on a grassy peninsula surrounded by bush and famous for its troubadours.

---

tors – much to the anger of locals, frustrated at lack of promised jobs and the apparent indifference of developers to the existential crisis the keys face.

Unless you're lucky enough to be visiting the exclusive hotel here, you'll either be coming on a day trip from Pearl Lagoon, or spending a night on the beach as part of a tour. Either way, do not miss this dazzling string of tiny Caribbean islands, the closest thing to paradise that Nicaragua has.

◉ Sights

Grape Key ISLAND
Home to an abandoned hotel, this lovely round island has probably the best swimming in the archipelago, with pure white sand beaches sloping down to deep crystal-line water. The caretaker may charge visitors to land on the island, which is why many local operators don't dock here.

Wild Cane Key ISLAND
This large island with a long and spectacular beach once hosted the family paradise of a young New Zealand millionaire. However, following a series of disputes with the local community, this is now an eerie ruin – all that's left is the pool (now a fearsome mosquito breeding ground) and the stilts the hotel was built on. It's assigned to the local community, who bring tourists here.

Crawl Key ISLAND
Pronounced 'Claw Key' by locals, this slender crescent of white sand is covered with soaring coconut palms. It's also home to an unfinished three-story concrete building that was destined to be a private pad for a wealthy American until the community called in the authorities, because the beach is a prime hawksbill-nesting ground. The island is now set aside for community tourism use and is usually visited by day-trippers from Pearl Lagoon.

Sleeping

Calala Island LUXURY HOTEL $$$
(www.calala-island.com; Lime Key; r incl full board from US$1450; ❄🛜🌊) This is Nicaragua's

PRIVATIZING PARADISE

For the fishers of the Pearl Lagoon basin, the Pearl Keys are like a second home, a place to rest and gather fresh water while out at sea for days. So when in 1997 a foreigner purchased some old deeds to the islands – the legality of which are disputed – and proceeded to sell them off to wealthy expat dreamers, things took a turn for the worse.

Soon the new 'owners' began raising foreign flags, constructing large houses and hotels and ordering the locals to keep off the islands, despite Nicaraguan laws guaranteeing public access to beaches.

In response, the local community hired a lawyer to take up the case. In addition to claiming to be the legitimate owners of the keys, the community expressed concerns that the unregulated construction was destroying the sensitive ecosystem.

A combination of community pressure, the harsh realities of life on a remote island, and the failure of an expected tourism boom to materialize has seen many of the original buyers abandon their island dream and move out. The Nicaraguan government has overseen the return of Crawl Key and Wild Cane Key to local communities for use in tourism activities, but several foreign owners remain and there has yet to be a definitive resolution of the ownership dispute. Locals, while not interested in wealthy foreigners simply taking over the islands to build private residences on, are keen for genuine investors to help develop tourism and bring much needed jobs to the area.

most exclusive and expensive hotel, which is frequently booked out for private family vacations. When it's not exclusively reserved, you can book one of the six suites here, which are exactly what you'd expect for the price: gorgeous rooms with all-inclusive food and drink, great snorkeling, shimmering white beaches and wonderful sunsets.

🛈 Getting There & Away

The only way to visit the keys is on a private boat tour. Arrange trips in Pearl Lagoon town. A day trip will typically set you back US$200 to US$300, depending on the size of your group and how many islands you want to visit.

In calm weather, it's just another hour (and another US$200) by *panga* from the keys to the Corn Islands. Considering the adventure quotient, the price and the time involved, it actually makes good sense to travel to the Corn Islands from Pearl Lagoon via the Pearl Keys, rather than doubling back to Bluefields and flying to Great Corn from there.

Corn Islands

The Caribbean coast's biggest tourist draw is actually 70km offshore, on a pair of enchanting English-speaking islands with crystalline coves, horseshoe bays and underwater caves. Great Corn is larger and peopled by a Creole population that lives in colorful wooden houses, many of which are sprinkled along the main road around the island. And though tourism is the second-largest industry, behind lobster

fishing, you won't see mega-developments here.

Little Corn, a tiny, jungled jewel, actually attracts more tourists, with visitors suitably seduced by myriad dining options, creatively realized beachside *cabañas,* plenty of cheap hostels and even a luxury resort. The dive sites are also more diverse on Little Corn, which explains why so many transit the larger island and head directly to this car-free utopia. During high season there can be more foreigners than locals, but the charms of *Likkle Corn,* as locals call it, cannot be overstated.

🛈 Getting There & Away

By far the fastest and easiest way to reach the islands is by air. La Costeña links Great Corn Island with Bluefields and Managua with three daily flights.

Alternatively, there are also at least a couple of boats a week carrying passengers between Bluefields and Great Corn. While these journeys might be good fodder for your memoirs, they're generally extremely uncomfortable, involve sitting on top of banana crates or being surrounded by livestock, can be unbearably hot, not to mention unsafe, and involve a fair measure of throwing up. If you have the choice, take the plane.

Great Corn Island

POP 7100

The bigger of Nicaragua's two most lovely islands, Great Corn (called Big Corn by locals) is a wonderfully manageable and authentic slice of the Caribbean that combines some cracking stretches of golden sand beach with a rich and independently minded English-speaking culture. Here you'll find barefoot bars, commercial fishing wharfs, baseball games on the beach and smiling young lobster divers, catch in hand, wherever you go. An ever-present armada of elders sitting in rocking chairs on creaky front porches, and several jungle-swathed headlands to explore, complete the picture. It's a place where reggae and country music can coexist without irony, where fresh lobster is a staple ingredient rather than a luxury, and where the longer you stay, the less you'll want to leave.

◉ Sights

Great Corn is looped by one main road, with several spur roads leading to various beaches and neighborhoods. Long Bay is where you'll find the island's best stretch of golden sand. Southwest Bay beckons with another outstanding wide beach. For the best views, hike up to Mount Pleasant or make your way to **Quinn Hill**, where you'll also find some interesting public art.

★ Long Bay   BEACH
This stunner of a beach arcs from a pile-up of local fishing *pangas* and lobster traps to a wild, jungle-covered headland at its far end. If you're looking for a place to snooze and swim in absolute tranquility, this is your destination, although be careful in the water, as the riptide can be strong and the waves very rough.

Southwest Bay   BEACH
The most popular beach on Great Corn, Southwest Bay has calmer, more sheltered water than at most other beaches on the island, though the area is more developed, with several hotels, guesthouses and restaurants lining the roadside behind it. It's a good spot to watch the sunset, too.

Mount Pleasant   HILL
Walk up the dirt trail behind the Sunrise Hotel in South End past the banana groves and you will be rewarded with panoramic views from Mt Pleasant, preferably enjoyed as the sun plunges beneath the Caribbean Sea.

🏃 Activities

The **tourist office** (🖉ext 29 2575-5091; contiguo Estadio; ⊙8:30am-noon & 1:30-5pm Mon-Fri) is able to organize guides (US$15 to US$30 per person) for hikes all over the island, including to the wild **Bluff Point**.

There's terrific snorkeling along the reef off the Sally Peachie coast. Among the other highlights for snorkelers are the remains of a Spanish galleon off Waula Point, and a more complete wreck of a steamship full of fish in shallow water off Sally Peachie. Paraíso Club rents snorkel gear and also arranges chartered snorkeling tours (US$25 per person) and fishing trips (US$40 per person).

There are two dive shops on the island and new dive sites are being discovered all the time, leading to an ever-expanding list of attractions for divers of all skill levels.

Dos Tiburones   DIVING
(🖉2575-5167; www.divecornisland.com; Sally Peachie; ⊙7am-5pm) On the north side of the island, this well-run dive shop is very popular among visitors for its friendly staff, professional approach and quality equipment. In addition to local dive sites, it offers one-day dive trips to Little Corn and snorkeling. The onsite cafe, overlooking the water, is a great place to chill between dive sessions.

Corn Island Dive Center   DIVING
(🖉8851-5704, 8735-0667; www.cornisland-divecenter.com; Brig Bay Front Road; ⊙7am-5pm) An excellent dive center with good quality equipment and professional instructors offering dives around the local reefs and beyond, with a maximum ratio of six divers per guide. Also offers snorkeling trips and diving courses.

🎉 Festivals & Events

Fiesta del Cangrejo   CULTURAL
(⊙Aug) Great Corn Island's big party celebrates the emancipation of the island's slave population on August 27 with parades, concerts, beauty contests and lots of delicious

---

ISLAND HISTORY

Christopher Columbus breezed through the Corn Islands in 1502, but it wasn't until 1660, when a French pirate by the name of Jean-David Nau arrived, that relations with the indigenous Kukras were cultivated. In the 1700s, European pirates patrolled these waters and British residents of the island brought in African slaves to work the fields. Both groups mingled with the Kukras. Although the British were asked to leave the islands in 1786, as part of their treaty with the Spanish, they returned in 1841 after Nicaragua's independence from Spain, and English culture continues to dominate the islands.

Great Corn Island

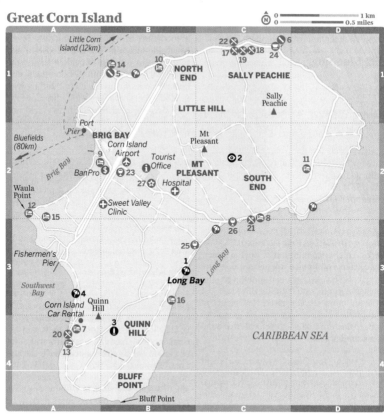

CARIBBEAN COAST CORN ISLANDS

Great Corn Island

crab soup. Most events are focused around the baseball field in South End. If you're in the region, make sure you're there.

🛏 Sleeping

★ Island Roots Hostel
HOSTEL $

(☑ 8366-6795, 8694-7355; www.islandrootsnicaragua.com; South End; dm US$10-14, r with/without bathroom US$30/28; ✻) This superbly friendly and laid-back place opened in 2018 and feels more like staying in a private home than a hostel. There's an eight-bed dorm and three private rooms, one of which shares a bathroom with the dorm. Breakfast is an extra US$4, but all guests are free to use the communal kitchen at any time.

Mi Mundo
HOSTEL $

(☑ 8225-5934; www.mimundocornislandhostel.com; Brig Bay; dm US$10-14, r with fan/air-con US$30/48; ✻ 🛜) This welcoming hostel on the waterfront offers comfortable rooms and dormitories. It also boasts a breezy common area and kitchen upstairs, with fantastic views over the brilliant turquoise Caribbean and plenty of hammocks to laze in. Management specializes in deep boarding, offers great local advice and rents snorkel gear.

Hotel Morgan
HOTEL $$

(☑ 2575-5502; kerrygean.morgan@gmail.com; North End; r with/without air-con US$25/15, cabañas US$40-50; ✻ 🛜) An efficient and good-value hotel offering a range of accommodations, the best of which are found in split-level duplexes. Downstairs are pink concrete apartments with two full-sized beds, air-con, cable TV, hot water and a minibar. The same amenities and layout are found upstairs in the wooden bungalow-style rooms, which also have ample deck and ocean views.

Hotel G&G
HOTEL $$

(☑ 2575-5017; martinez-downs69@hotmail.com; contiguo Pasenic, Brig Bay; r with fan US$15-25, with air-con US$25-45; ✻ 🛜) If you don't need to be right by the water's edge, save your cash for lobster and beers and check into this friendly and laid-back hotel in town. Offering outstanding value on clean, brightly painted and spacious rooms, it's within walking distance of a fairly inviting stretch of beach and the main dock.

★ Arenas Beach Resort
HOTEL $$$

(☑ 2575-5145, 8851-8046; www.arenasbeachhotel.com; Southwest Bay; s/d/tr bungalow incl breakfast US$117/146/175, s/d/tr incl breakfast US$146/187/229; ✻ 🛜) Following a full renovation in 2017, Great Corn Island's most professionally managed resort has added a modicum of style to its already lovely beachside location. You can choose to stay in a colorful wooden bungalow room with sea views from the hammocks on the porch, or modern rooms in the main building with fantastic bathrooms boasting rain showers.

The white-sand beach comes raked and dotted with cushy lounge chairs surrounding a bar in a wooden boat.

La Princesa de la Isla
HOTEL $$$

(☑ 8854-2403; www.laprincesadelaisla.com; Waula Point; r incl breakfast US$60; 🛜) Set behind thick coral walls overlooking a picturesque beach is this handful of wooden bungalows and attractive rustic rooms. All come with indoor-outdoor bathrooms, hammocks and sea views. There is a large communal lounge area with a great sundeck up top, and the whole place is run by a smiley Italian couple who love Corn Island.

Casa Canada
HOTEL $$$

(☑ 8644-0925, 8666-2825; www.casa-canada.com; South End; s/d US$95/106, cabaña s/d/tr US$128/139/145, all incl breakfast; ✻ 🛜 ✻) Casa Canada resort unfurls amid tropical flower gardens on the rocks just above the sea. Long Bay glows to the south, palms sway above and waves crash endlessly against the small beach. The standard rooms are comfortable and clean, but the large, dark-wood *cabañas* with soaring ceilings, Spanish-tiled floors, ceiling fan, leather sofa and queen-sized bed are fabulous.

Paraíso Club
HOTEL $$$

(☑ 2575-5111; www.paraisoclub.com; Waula Point; s/d cabaña US$59/75, bungalow US$69/89, all incl breakfast; ✻ 🛜) With a lively bar-restaurant and half a dozen attractive red-painted thatched duplexes, where hammocks are strung on mosaic and stone verandas scattered beneath the coconut palms, this is a popular choice. There's a great little beach at the end of the garden and the hotel organizes many activities for guests, including yoga and snorkeling excursions.

Sea Star Spa
RESORT $$$

(☑ 8901-2410; Long Bay; ste US$125; ✻ 🛜 ✻) Right on the beach at the far end of gorgeous Long Bay, Sea Star has easily the best location of any hotel on the island. Sadly though, it's rather overpriced and its rooms and furnishings aren't nearly as lovely as they could be, with some baffling design choices and an air of incompletion about the place.

That said, if you want comfortable seclusion with friendly staff and a stunning beach on your doorstep, this is an ideal choice.

Martha's Bed & Breakfast
HOTEL $$$

(☑8835-5884, 8835-5930; Southwest Bay; s/d incl breakfast US$55/59; ❄☎) Tucked among the coconut palms at the end of Southwest Bay beach, this family-owned B&B offers well-maintained rooms with tiled baths and cable TV. Sadly, the rectangular concrete structure does not really take advantage of the prime location.

Eating

There are more than a dozen restaurants around the island serving seafood and other local dishes, with the highest concentration around Brig Bay and Sally Peachie. Most hotels also have their own restaurants.

Chillin Cafe
CAFE $

(☑8212-1570; Brig Bay; mains US$3-6; ❤7am-10pm; ☎♨) Above one the island's most popular diving schools, Chillin Cafe is a top place to have a meal or a drink before, during or after a long day on the water. It serves up breakfast all day, offers a selection of light lunch dishes and does a nacho night every Saturday. After dark the place takes on a bar vibe.

Island Bakery & Sweets
BAKERY $

(Sally Peachie; ❤8am-7pm Mon-Sat) Head to this good old-style Caribbean bakery to indulge in all kinds of delicious sweet snacks, including fantastic cinnamon rolls, coconut pies and cakes. There's also a good variety of natural drinks – try the ginger and pineapple. Also hires bikes (US$10 per day).

★Big Fish
SEAFOOD $$

(☑8383-8442; North End; mains US$10-14; ❤7am-9pm; ☎) This fantastic place is run by a friendly team of locals, who give a consistently warm welcome. The menu is one of the most interesting on the island, and specialties include Jamaican jerk lobster, shrimp in jalapeño sauce and a giant seafood soup. There's a good stretch of beach outside and they also offer three comfortable rooms (US$30-40).

Relax
BREAKFAST $$

(☑2575-5885; South End; mains US$4-15; ❤7am-10pm; ☎) Between South End and Sally Peachie, halfway around the island from the dock, Relax is a reliable bar-restaurant serving good home-cooked Caribbean breakfasts, as well as more substantial meals. The

2nd-floor open-air dining area and bar is a fine place to break your island circuit.

Comedor Mari
SEAFOOD $$

(☑2575-5135; Sally Peachie; mains US$7-11; ❤8am-9pm) Eat under the palms with a cricket serenade at your Great Corn mom's house. You'll have the chance to taste dishes such as kingfish braised in tomato sauce, shrimp sautéed in garlic and lobster *al gusto* (to your liking). Mari also makes *rundown* (fish and seafood cooked in coconut milk) upon request – order it a day in advance.

★Pizzeria Italia
PIZZA $$$

(☑8232-9103; South End; pizzas US$10-15; ❤6-10pm Tue-Sat) While the restaurant doesn't look like much, these are certainly some of the best pizzas available along Nicaragua's Caribbean coast. We love the fact that there's a whole section for 'Pizzas with Garlic,' which may be the biggest understatement of all time, not to mention the lobster pizza, in case you can't stand an evening without a crustacean on your plate.

Sea Side Grill
SEAFOOD $$$

(North End; mains US$9-18; ❤7am-9pm) A friendly waterside restaurant that serves up consistently excellent seafood dishes with a choice of three sides, as well as lobster burgers and other light meals. The open-air dining area catches a good breeze and is inviting enough to keep you there for a few beers after you've finished your meal.

Picnic Center
NICARAGUAN $$$

(Southwest Bay; dishes US$8-16; ❤8am-10pm) The first resort on the island boasts thatched pagodas set on a magnificent stretch of sand and makes a great spot to eat shrimp and lobster in coconut sauce, or order drinks from the well-stocked bar and bob your head to reggae tunes.

Drinking & Nightlife

★Darrien's
BAR

(Aeropuerto, 50m S; ❤11am-late) This all-wood open-air bar, right by the road just south of the airport, pulls a crowd when everywhere else is empty and is generally held by locals to be the best place to party on the island. It's big and the music is not always too loud for conversation. It also serves fairly good local meals.

Spekito's Place
BAR

(South End; ❤11am-midnight) At the far side of South End, this laid-back local watering hole has several tables out the back overlooking rock pools full of fish and across the sea to windswept Long Bay. Also does good seafood dishes.

Island Style
BAR

(Arturito's; Long Bay; ⊙10am-10pm) The only bar and restaurant on Long Bay is of the barefoot, palm-thatched variety. It's not as popular as it once was, but draws its biggest crowds on Sunday afternoons for a soulful reggae jam after the baseball games. During the week you'll probably have the place to yourself. Good seafood is served here too, but be prepared to wait.

Dive Cafe
CAFE

(☑2575-5167; inside Dos Tiburones; ⊙7am-10pm) Sit on stools overlooking the multihued sea out on the grass foreshore and enjoy quality coffee prepared on the island's only espresso machine. Also serves a variety of breakfasts (US$4-9) and light meals (dishes US$7-14).

☆ Entertainment

Estadio Municipal Karen Tucker
BASEBALL

(Mt Pleasant; admission US$1-2) This large, well-manicured ballpark with cinder-block walls hosts regular games on Saturday and Sunday, weather permitting.

❶ Information

INTERNET ACCESS
Wireless, while theoretically present in almost all hotels, is extremely unreliable and patchy on Great Corn Island. Your best bet is to come armed with a local SIM card – Movistar reception is the best here.

MEDICAL SERVICES
Hospital (☑2575-5236; Alcaldía, 500m E)
Sweet Valley Clinic (Doctor Somarriba; ☑8355-3140, 2575-5852; Costado Derecho Estadio; ⊙8am-noon & 3-6pm Mon-Fri)

MONEY
There is only one **ATM** (Brig Bay) on Great Corn Island and it does run out of money occasionally, so you should still plan ahead and carry ample cash. Only a few businesses on the island accept credit cards.

❶ Getting There & Away

Great Corn's small airport is served by La Costeña, which runs flights to Bluefields (one way/round trip US$65/99, 20 minutes), with continuing service to Managua (one way/round trip US$107/164, 1¼ hours) three times a day.

The island's port is where boats leave for Bluefields and Little Corn. The government-run *Río Escondido* (US$8, five hours) leaves Great Corn

on Thursday and Sunday at 9:30am, and travels back from Bluefields on Wednesday and Saturday at the same time. The service is extremely uncomfortable and the sea can be rough, so we don't recommend it.

There are a number of other even less comfortable fishing and cargo boats that make the Bluefields run and there is usually at least one departure on Sunday nights. Bring a hammock or you will be trying to get comfortable on the cold steel deck.

❶ Getting Around

Taxis cost US$0.70 per person (US$1 at night) to anywhere on the island. During the day, there is one bus (US$0.35) that continuously runs a clockwise circuit, but you might wait a while until it passes.

Rentals are a great way to explore the island. **Corn Island Car Rental** (☑8543-9881, 2575-5222; cornislandcarrentals@hotmail.com; Southwest Bay; golf cart per 2hr US$25-40, per day US$50-100, scooter or motorcycle per day US$25-46) offers scooter and golf-cart rentals, while **Lulu Scooter Rental** (☑5773-8424, 8844-9611; scooter per day US$30) offers scooters. Both will deliver your vehicle to you by arrangement.

Little Corn Island
POP 800

Little Corn is the stuff of fantasy, a dreamy Caribbean escape where arty characters from all over the world have created private refuges on virgin beaches, and where ambitious chefs compete quietly to be the most sought after on the island. With no cars allowed, there's a certain old-world magic to any walk beneath the mango, coconut and breadfruit trees and on into the thick forest that buffers the northern and eastern coasts.

Backpackers love this tiny place, and make up the bulk of its visitors, though there's also plenty for midrange travelers and even a couple of top-end resorts. Whether you want to spend the day snorkeling, swimming and sunbathing at one of a dozen golden coves, or prefer to spend your time getting to know the charismatic locals in the Village, it's hard to imagine anywhere better in Nicaragua to relax and recharge.

◉ Sights

The two best beaches on the island are Cocal Beach (p235) and Otto Beach (p235), which are both great for swimming and have just a few non-intrusive beachside guesthouses hidden away on them.

Little Corn Island

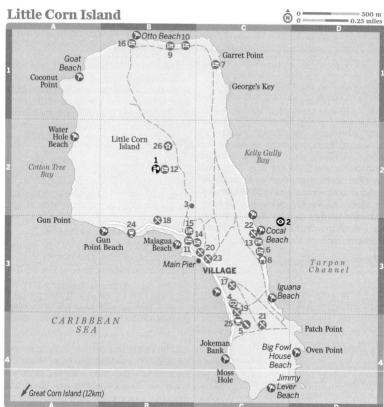

CARIBBEAN COAST CORN ISLANDS

Little Corn Island

Adventurers can also walk to the windward shore, which involves a scramble over the rocks to get to Big Fowl House Beach, then Jimmy Lever Beach, both totally wild coves where it's possible to swim. Alternatively, ramble the rugged northern shore from the Village until you find the spectacular Goat Beach, framed by two headlands.

Don't forget to head up to the lighthouse, a steel tower jutting 6m above the mango trees, where you can glimpse the island's curves and coves, and catch an outrageous sunset. Finally, if you're on Little Corn on Saturday morning, do not miss the amazing sight of the supply boat from Bluefields arriving at the main pier (p239) around 9 or 10am. This weekly event sees hundreds of people heading to the Village with their carts to collect their groceries, and it's an incredible sight.

Tarpon Channel   DIVE SITE

One of the best places to see hammerhead sharks in the Caribbean, this excellent intermediate dive site off the eastern side of Little Corn is a long channel between massive coral walls that bottoms out at 22m. Even if you don't see hammers, you'll be able to see lots of fish, eagle rays and sting rays.

Cocal Beach   BEACH

A long stretch of white sand fronted by brilliant turquoise waters. Cocal has lost a lot of its mass through erosion but is still a fine place for a stroll and swim, although between April and July it can be piled high with seaweed.

Otto Beach   BEACH

The island's most popular beach, Otto boasts multicolored waters perfect for swimming and a fun young crowd. Here you'll find the island's fanciest address, Yemaya Island Hideaway & Spa (p236), as well as a recently opened beach bar.

Iguana Beach   BEACH

Really just the southern extension of Cocal Beach, Iguana boasts a solid stretch of sand as it is protected by the headland.

Big Fowl House Beach   BEACH

An easy but unmarked walk through the bush leads to this fine secluded cove. Pass the former Casa Iguana and turn left where you see a small blue hut, then follow the sound of the ocean to get here.

Goat Beach   BEACH

A gorgeous, secluded bay surrounded by jungle on the north side of the island that gets very few visitors.

Lighthouse   LIGHTHOUSE

Little Corn's lighthouse is actually a metal tower that doesn't emit any light these days, but it does offer fine panoramas of the island and is a dreamy spot to watch the sunset. You'll need to climb the somewhat terrifying ladder for the view, though – definitely not for the fainthearted.

Jimmy Lever Beach   BEACH

On the southern side of the island, this remote beach faces the open water, which has quite a few rocks. Scenic rather than idyllic.

🏃 Activities

There is great snorkeling on the island's east and north sides. Many hotels in these areas rent snorkeling gear, as do the dive shops. If you want a guide, ask in the Village for Aqua Boy. Up the hill from the school, **Alfonso** (☑ 8732-6398; Escuela, 300m N; fishing per person US$60) organizes fishing trips in his boat.

Kite Little Corn   KITESURFING

(☑ 8498-5381; www.kitelittlecorn.com; Steadman's Place; ⊘ 8am-6pm) Soar over the turquoise waters of Little Corn with this kitesurfing school run by Nacho, an affable Spaniard who is passionate about the sport. Located on the windy side of the island, it offers two-day intensive courses (US$300) and group tuition (US$50 per hour).

Aqua Boy   SNORKELING

(☑ 8422-4500; Front Rd, Village; snorkeling US$20) The best organized of the many local guides offering snorkeling adventures, Aqua Boy has two daily departures at 9am and 1pm, as well as a night snorkeling tour, and offers fishing trips, tubing, wakeboarding, water-skiing and trips to Pearl Keys.

Dolphin Dive   DIVING

(☑ 8917-9717; www.dolphindivelittlecorn.com; Village; 1/10 dives US$35/300; ⊘ 8am-6pm) Professional yet laid-back, this locally owned dive shop has good equipment and experienced instructors who really know these reefs. They visit over 20 different sites and offer open-water (US$330) and advanced open-water (US$260) courses.

Dive Little Corn
DIVING

(☎ 8856-5888; www.facebook.com/divelittlecorn; Village; 1/10 dives US$35/280; ⊕ 8am-6pm) Little Corn's original dive shop provides a high level of service. It offers open-water (US$330) and advanced open-water (US$270) courses, and goes out for single dives three times a day.

🛌 Sleeping

You can stay either in the Village, which is convenient and offers the most restaurant and nightlife options, or in one of the more secluded slices of paradise by the beach. Most businesses have signs in the Village telling you which path to take. High season here is from mid-November until late April. Outside those times, hotel rates can drop considerably.

★Green House Hostel
HOSTEL $

(☎ 5877-5642; Village; dm US$10-17; 🕾) The best budget option on the island, Green House is located very conveniently for the arrival jetty in the heart of the Village. It has three fan-cooled dorms, each of which has several handcrafted pine bunks with their own lockers. Each dorm has its own bathroom and access to a good kitchen and a large garden.

★Lighthouse Hotel
HOSTEL $$

(☎ 8403-6189; www.thelighthouseci.com; dm/d/tw US$18/65/75; ⊕ closed Oct 1-Nov 15; 🕾) On the island's highest point, this welcoming backpacker place has cute wooden *cabañas* with fantastic views over the waters of Little Corn's windward side. Both the private *cabañas* and dorm are simple but comfortable, and the onsite bar-restaurant serves great food and has become a local hot spot for drinks. It's an easy walk uphill from both sides of the island.

Ensueños
BUNGALOW $$

(www.ensuenos-littlecornisland.com; Otto Beach; cabañas/casas from US$25/100) 🏖 Surrounded by forest and fruit orchards, and perched on a golden crescent of sand in a gorgeous sheltered turquoise cove lined by coconut palms, this enchanting place features a variety of (very!) rustic *cabañas* on stilts. There are also three idiosyncratically designed solar-powered *casas* (houses) with small kitchens a bit further back.

Carlito's Sunrise Paradise
CABAÑAS $$

(☎ 8219-4091; www.carlitosplacelittlecorn.com; Cocal Beach; huts US$30-45, apt US$50-99) A little quieter than its neighbors, Carlito's features spartan cabins right on the beach with firm beds and little porches that are kept

cool by ocean-facing windows. The beach is cleaned regularly and the fine restaurant prepares some great juicy fried chicken, but the rooms are a little pricey for what you get.

Elsa's Place
HUT $$

(☎ 8848-8136; elsasplace@yahoo.com; cabañas US$30-60, r without bathroom US$15-25) Miss Elsa sticks to a winning formula: cheap, comfortable fan-cooled rooms right by the water. Choose from a variety of simple but neat yellow-painted wooden bungalows with private bathrooms and some basic cheapies out the back. Probably the best deal on this stretch.

Three Brothers
GUESTHOUSE $$

(☎ 8658-8736; Escuela, 50m S; d/tr US$25/35, dm/r without bathroom US$10/15; 🕾) A favorite among budget travelers, this guesthouse in the middle of the Village is run by the extremely laid-back Randy and has a communal, hostel-like vibe. It offers bright, simple rooms with big screened windows, and self-caterers will dig the spacious kitchen. The attached store means guests will never want for Tupperware.

★Yemaya Island Hideaway & Spa
HOTEL $$$

(☎ 8741-0122; 8329-5330; www.yemayalittlecorn. com; Otto Beach; r incl breakfast from US$279; ❄🕾) Yemaya offers the most luxurious accommodations on the island and boasts professional service to match. The 17 fan-cooled rooms are stylish, bright and comfortable and offer fantastic sea views through their large glass sliding doors, which open onto porches with comfy bamboo chairs. Five of the rooms even have their own infinity plunge pools, and the beach below is sumptuous.

The restaurant, set on a wide deck with waves crashing on the rocks below, offers ambitious cuisine that makes use of ingredients grown in the hotel's own organic gardens. Yoga classes are offered in a fan-cooled pavilion surrounded by trees and on a seaside platform, and there are three massage studios in the banana groves. Another perk is the very comfortable transfer from Great Corn (US$40 per person) on the resort's own boat, which sure beats the hot and crowded *panga*. All in all, if you can afford it, this place is a wonderful treat.

★Sunshine Hotel
HOTEL $$$

(☎ 8544-4165; www.sunshinehotellittlecorn.com; Village; dm/r incl breakfast US$20/59; ❄🕾) Just moments from the arrival jetty, the lovely Sunshine takes up a large yellow house and has spacious and clean rooms downstairs sharing a large garden area, while upstairs it has a fun bar-cafe that offers good food, a pool table and table tennis. The hotel suspended operations in 2018, but will hopefully reopen.

Little Corn Beach & Bungalow
BUNGALOW $$$

(☑8923-2517; www.littlecornbb.com; Cocal Beach; r U$109-209; ☎) The most upmarket place on Cocal Beach has elegantly furnished, spotless timber and bamboo bungalows with big doors opening onto a hammock-strewn beach with plenty of coconut palms. The downside: it's pricey for what you get and the rooms are fairly close together, detracting from any castaway fantasies. There's an excellent bar and restaurant on the beach here, too.

Farm Peace & Love
FARMSTAY $$$

(www.farmpeacelove.com; Otto Beach; apt US$85-100) Set back from a gorgeous sheltered cove and nestled in the palms is this farm with just two accommodations options. The smaller cabin is joined to the main farmhouse and has one bedroom and a kitchenette, while the larger one is a traditional white house with a kitchen and rockers on the front porch. No children under 12 are accepted.

Derek's Place
BUNGALOW $$$

(www.dereksplacelittlecorn.com; Garret Point; cabañas US$60-125) 🖉 The island's most charming beach bungalows are found spread out over a lovely grassy promontory covered with coconut palms that feels far from the crowds. The *cabañas* are thatched, geometrically inspired and artfully fashioned from bamboo, wood, recycled bottles and other natural materials. There's dedicated hammock space, snorkel gear for rent and a small, friendly dive shop onsite.

✖ Eating

Rosa's
NICARAGUAN $

(Village; breakfast US$3.50, meals US$4-7; ☺6:30am-9:30pm; 🖉) This humble *comedor* on the trail between the Village and Iguana Beach is a fine spot for breakfast and has vegetarian pastas and coconut curries, as well as other typical local dishes.

★ Comedor Bridget
NICARAGUAN $$

(☑8437-7295; Village; meals US$7-10; ☺7am-10pm) Pull up a chair on the porch of this converted family home and order the superb salt-dusted, lightly fried fish and a cold beer. Alternatively, try its mind-bogglingly good shrimp coconut

---

DECIDING WHERE TO STAY

Garret Point The northeastern corner of Little Corn island has a cluster of mid-range accommodations, some of Little Corn's most beautiful beaches and great snorkeling just offshore. It's a solid 2km, 25-minute hike from the Village, which is a bit of a mission in the dark. All of these accommodations serve meals.

Cocal & Iguana Beaches This side of the island gets a constant breeze, which keeps the mosquitoes at bay. Budget travelers should head to Cocal Beach, where there are several similar places side by side. Take a walk and see which of them appeals. Accommodations here are more basic, but with a beach like this on your doorstep, you won't be spending much time inside.

---

curry or the great-value lobster. Bridget pioneered tourism on the island and her homely place is still your number one choice for no-nonsense authentic local dining.

Zen Den
INTERNATIONAL $$

(www.funkyogaandsup.com; Village; wraps & burritos US$5.50-7; ☺5:30am-1:30pm Mon-Fri; 🖉🖉) This cool little spot near Little Corn's wharf is a great place to get breakfast before setting off on the 6am-daily *panga* to Great Corn. It does excellent smoothies, easily the best wraps on the island, and its breakfast burrito is fast becoming famous. Don't miss the sublime tropical lollipops, either. There's a popular yoga studio upstairs.

★ Darinia's Kitchen
INTERNATIONAL $$$

(☑8744-3419; dariniabonilla@gmail.com; Village; per person US$25; ☺by reservation only; 🖉) For a truly local experience in the Village, reserve an evening meal at this ambitious and eclectic supper club. Self-taught Managua transplant Darinia cooks up a four-course feast that can easily accommodate vegetarians and vegans at her simple alfresco dining table. Food is superb, featuring fresh vegetable, fish and seafood dishes with a Thai bent and superb desserts.

★ Desideri
INTERNATIONAL $$$

(☑8412-6341; Front Rd, Village; mains US$9-15; ☺7am-10:30pm Wed-Mon; 🖉🖉) Boasting the most interesting menu in the Village, this popular restaurant overlooking the water tempts hungry travelers with authentic

Italian pastas, tasty burritos and the house specialty, lobster Thermidor. There's also a good selection of desserts and excellent coffee. The spacious deck is a fine place for a drink after the plates have been cleared away.

★ **Habana Libre**   CUBAN $$$

(☑ 2572-9086; Village; mains US$8-14; ☺ 11am-8pm Tue-Sun; 🛜) Long considered the Corn Islands' best restaurant, this Cuban-run kitchen serves up outstanding plates of fish, shrimp, roast pork and *ropa vieja* (a Cuban shredded-beef delicacy) on a smart dining patio. But the absolute star of the show is the lobster in jalapeño sauce – don't leave the island without trying it.

Turned Turtle   CARIBBEAN $$$

(www.littlecornbb.com; Little Corn Beach & Bungalow, Cocal Beach; mains US$9-18; ☺ 7:30am-8:30pm Sun-Fri, 8am-2:30pm Sat; 🛜) Escape to the far side of the island and enjoy a meal on the sand with the waves crashing at your feet. Here it's all about Caribbean hospitality, and you can't go wrong with dishes including pork sliders, parmesan-crusted fish and cashew pesto chicken. Their signature cocktail is the piña colada, and it's without doubt the finest in Nicaragua.

🍷 Drinking & Nightlife

Despite the island's tiny size, there's plenty going on after sunset. Highlights include Wednesday night at Tranquilo Cafe for impressive drumming performances, after which the night continues at Reggae Bar. Popular 'Sunday Funday' at Lighthouse Hotel (p236) features a barbecue, drinks specials and music from the early afternoon onwards. Do not miss the island's best piña colada at the Turned Turtle.

Tranquilo Cafe   CAFE

(www.tranquilocafe.com; Village; ☺ 8am-late; 🛜) Head to this hip open-air cafe for great burgers, buffalo wings and bruschetta with an indie-rock soundtrack. It's the most popular haunt among travelers for evening drinks, and it does a wide range of cocktails. Happy hour is from 5pm to 7pm, and there's usually a beach bonfire and live music on Saturday, while Wednesday sees superb performances of Garifuna drumming.

Reggae Bar   BAR

(Las Aguilas; Village; ☺ 11am-1am) Little Corn Island's most popular after-hours hangout. Full of local flavor, the sweaty pool hall is a hotbed of hustling and competition, and the music thumps in the open-air dance hall just above the beach. You'll almost certainly end up here at some point during your stay.

☆ Entertainment

Baseball Field   BASEBALL

Head up the hill in the center of the island on weekends to catch local baseball games. You'll know when they're on because there will be no one around in town. Sunday is the big day – take a seat in the bleachers with the locals and enjoy the drama.

ℹ Information

ELECTRICITY

Little Corn only has power between 1pm and 6am, with its generator resting for several hours each morning. Some hotels have solar- or wind-power backups, meaning they're never without electricity, but in most cases expect to wake up sweaty when the fans stop running at dawn.

INTERNET ACCESS

Some hotels around the island have wi-fi, but it's generally unpredictable and slow. The most

---

ALAMIKANGBAN & PRINZAPOLKA

Nature lovers might want to consider making the trip to the isolated towns of Alamikangban, about 70km southeast of Rosita, and Prinzapolka, another two hours by boat along the Río Prinzapolka river to the Caribbean coast. The main reason to go is the Río Prinzapolka, which marks the southern boundary of natural pine forest that phases into tropical rainforest, with wetlands that are a haven for all sorts of birds. The fishing is also top-notch.

The towns themselves are traditional Miskito settlements, typically comprising board houses with rusted tin roofs and no fences between neighbors. Both towns, as well as the smaller communities lining the river, have indigenous government structures, so ask for the *wihta* (judge) or *síndico* (resource manager) when trying to find guides or lodging. The entire region is susceptible to flooding; during rains, check on conditions before heading out.

Buses leave Rosita (US$4, four hours) twice daily for Alamikangban, where you can hire a private boat to Prinzapolka.

reliable way to be online is to get a local SIM card at Managua airport before you come – Claro gets the best 3G on the island – but you cannot buy SIM cards here or on Great Corn.

MEDICAL SERVICES

Sol's Drug Store (Sunshine Hotel) is open 8am to 2pm, Monday to Friday.

MONEY

There are no banks and certainly no ATMs on Little Corn, so bring all the cash you'll need with you. Some hotels do accept credit cards, but be sure to check before you travel.

❶ Getting There & Away

Collective *pangas* to Little Corn (US$5, 40 minutes) leave from the pier on Great Corn at 10am and 4:30pm daily. In the other direction, boats leave Little Corn at 7am and 1:30pm from the **main pier**. Be sure to come in good time to get a ticket, as you are unable to book ahead and boats sometimes sell out during high season.

If you're taking the morning flight to Managua from Great Corn, it's best to travel back the day before. Bear in mind that the journey can get very rough and you may get soaked. Bringing garbage bags to cover your luggage is a good idea. For a smoother ride, it's possible to ride on the large cargo ships (US$2 to US$3, 1¼ hours) that supply the *islita*, but there are only a handful of departures per week – ask at the main pier in the Village.

❶ Getting Around

Little Corn is only about 1.5km across. You can walk end to end in under an hour – which is just as well, because the only wheels on the island's jungle trails belong to wheelbarrows.

Las Minas

During their heyday early last century, the gold-mining towns of Las Minas bustled with immigrants from China, Europe, North America and the Caribbean looking to strike the mother lode. These days very few outsiders visit this wild and remote part of the country and its main towns, Siuna, Rosita and Bonanza, are most notable for their shocking lack of infrastructure and their abundance of armed, inebriated men.

While gold panning is still popular among villagers, the gold rush is well and truly over and the only real money being made here is in Bonanza, where a large foreign-owned mine continues to operate despite criticism from environmentalists.

◉ Sights & Activities

Siuna has a number of worthwhile attractions. Locals love the nearby, crystalline aguas calientes (hot springs). Take a taxi to La Bomba, then follow the trail for about an hour across private Finca Dorado to the springs. Also popular are the rocky beaches of the lazy Río Wani, a slow-motion, sinuous beast carving rocky sandbars and encroaching jungle with lazy grace about 11km from town.

Bonanza is the jumping-off point for Reserva Natural Cerro Cola Blanca and the Mayangna indigenous communities downriver on the Río Waspuk and Río Pispis. There are also a couple of great swimming holes and waterfalls around town.

If you plan to visit the mines, local tour operator Wiwi Tours (☎2794-2097, 8495-9820; laposadadonachella@gmail.com; Barrio Gilberto Romero) in Siuna is a good first port of call. It offers a number of overnight packages to local attractions, as well as a rugged six-day adventure into Parque Nacional Saslaya.

❶ Getting There & Away

All three towns have airstrips, but only Bonanza and Siuna have daily flights to and from Managua. Make reservations in advance, as the 12-seat planes fill up. Flights leave Managua daily at 8am for Bonanza (one way/round trip US$96/148, 1½ hours) and at 9am for Siuna (one way/round trip US$82/127, one hour). Return flights to Managua leave daily from both destinations at 10am.

The road here from Managua is scenic but terrible. It's a long, hard slog in a bus from Managua to Siuna (12 hours, US$18) and an even more challenging journey to Bonanza (14 to 17 hours, US$21). The Río Blanco–Siuna stretch of the 12-hour hump from Managua is considered one of the country's worst. Rosita is a slightly more manageable eight-hour ride from Bilwi (US$6.50). It involves a river crossing by cable barge and lots of ceiba trees.

❶ Getting Around

Although roads are 4WD-accessible in dry season, self-driving through this sparsely populated region is not recommended. Most local cars and even the beat-up old school buses boast modified suspensions.

The Las Minas towns are linked by frequent – though horrendously overcrowded and slow – bus services. You can also charter taxis locally, which cuts your road time in half and quadruples your comfort level.

San Carlos, Islas Solentiname & the Río San Juan

Best Places to Eat

➡ Lara's Planet (p256)

➡ Restaurante Kaoma (p245)

➡ Casa de Huésped Chinandegano (p256)

Best Places to Stay

➡ Sábalos Lodge (p253)

➡ Hospedaje La Comunidad (p247)

➡ Lara's Planet (p255)

➡ Hotel Cocibolca (p245)

➡ Grand River Lodge (p251)

Why Go?

Perhaps Nicaragua's best kept secret and certainly one of its most unfairly overlooked regions, the steamy Río San Juan runs from Lago de Nicaragua into the Caribbean, forming the border with Costa Rica for much of its journey through the wilderness. The thick jungle here is a haven for migratory birds and dozens of animal species including jaguars, howler monkeys, alligators, sloths and fluorescent fingernail-sized tree frogs.

It's also a place thousands of travelers simply pass through on their way to Costa Rica, ignoring the sweet Archipiélago de Solentiname, a remote group of islands with an artistically minded population, as well as the towns and villages along Río San Juan and the spectacular Reserva Biológica Indio-Maíz. This is a mistake, but as long as it continues, you'll find you have much of Nicaragua's far south to yourself: do not miss it.

When to Go

➡ Dry season in the Río San Juan runs from February to April with more sunshine and shrinking pools of water concentrating migratory waterfowl in Los Guatuzos.

➡ In June, you'll find the best birdwatching in the jungles around Boca de Sábalos.

➡ Around mid-September, top anglers descend on the Río San Juan for the Torneo Internacional de Pesca (in September) and it's possible to hook huge tarpon in the Caribbean Sea at the mouth of the Río Indio.

➡ October offers the best birdwatching in San Miguelito and dancers and artists from all over the country descend on San Carlos for the Río San Juan's biggest party – the Carnival Acuático (p244).

History

Almost as soon as Columbus happened upon Nicaragua in 1502, the search was on for a passage that would link the Atlantic to the Pacific Ocean. In 1529, the Spanish finally navigated the rapids and reached the mouth of the river at the Caribbean Sea, where they established San Juan de las Perlas in 1539, later known as San Juan del Norte and nowadays San Juan de Nicaragua.

In the 17th and 18th centuries, Granada was growing wealthier by the year. This attracted unwanted attention from English, French and Dutch pirates, who sacked the city three times in five years. A series of forts, including one in San Carlos and another in El Castillo, were built along the river and lake to ward them off.

When the gold fever took hold in North America in the 1800s, the Río San Juan became part of the fastest route between New York and San Francisco. American Cornelius Vanderbilt's ships sailed from New York to New Orleans and then steamed down to Greytown (yet another name for San Juan de Nicaragua) before continuing upriver to Lago de Nicaragua, where voyagers traveled overland to an awaiting steamship on the Pacific.

After the Panama Canal was built in 1914, dashing hopes for a local version, Greytown reverted to a sleepy outpost at the end of a rarely transited jungle river. The region was in the news in 2018 for all the wrong reasons, sadly, when a massive forest fire consumed a vast swathe of the Reserva Biológica Indio-Maíz, Nicaragua's greatest environmental disaster to date and something the region will take decades to recover from.

✆ Getting There & Away

The Río San Juan is an international entry point to Nicaragua with buses linking San Carlos with Los Chiles in Costa Rica across a new bridge that spans the Río San Juan.

La Costeña operates twice-weekly flights between San Carlos and Managua via Ometepe. The flight continues to San Juan de Nicaragua. You can also arrive in San Carlos and San Miguelito by bus from Managua, Juigalpa and El Rama.

All other destinations in this region are only accessible by boat from San Carlos.

San Carlos

POP 12,200

Located where Central America's biggest lake meets one of its largest rivers, the capital of the isolated Río San Juan department is the gateway to some of Nicaragua's most compelling countryside. San Carlos itself enjoys a lovely natural position surrounded by water, the silhouettes of the Islas Solentiname in one direction and distant volcanic peaks framed by rainforest in the other.

During the day the town sees plenty of travelers, which explains the bustling waterfront lined with restaurants. But when night falls, the magnificent views disappear with the setting sun and San Carlos quickly falls quiet.

◉ Sights

San Carlos is less a tourist destination and more a place to wait for your ship, or *panga* (small motorboat), to come in, but there is beauty here – particularly on the grounds of Centro Cultural Jose Coronel Urtecho, which is set within the crumbling walls of Fortaleza de San Carlos. It's no El Castillo, but it was built in 1724 and has amazing lake and Río San Juan views. There's another old Spanish observation post, with cannons, at the end of the *malecón*.

Fortaleza de San Carlos   FORT
(⊙9am-5pm) FREE There's not much left of the town's fortress, which dates from 1724, but it enjoys some impressive Lake Nicaragua and Río San Juan views from several lookout points linked by garden trails. The cultural center inside has some interesting displays on local culture, biology and history. It even has a map (c 1791) of the Nicaraguan canal that never was.

Mirador   VIEWPOINT
(contiguo Restaurante Mirador) A charming old Spanish observation post complete with cannons and panoramic views. To reach it, head up the staircase at the far end of the *malecón*.

Malecón   WATERFRONT
The social heart of the town, this waterfront promenade overlooks both the lake and river and is always busy with children playing and couples taking a stroll. It's also where you'll find most of the town's restaurants and bars.

🏃 Activities

Fundación del Río   ECOTOUR
(☏2583-0035; www.fundaciondelrio.org; El Proyecto) 🖉 A nonprofit organization staffed by an enthusiastic crew that arranges visits to Isla Mancarroncito (p249) in the Archipiélago de Solentiname and Reserva Privada El Quebracho (p252) near Boca de Sábalos.

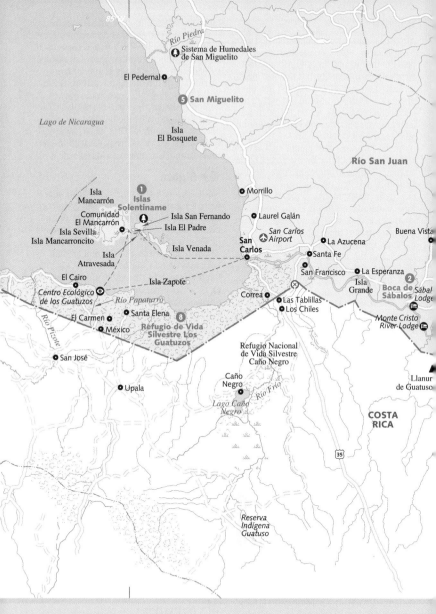

San Carlos, Islas Solentiname & the Río San Juan Highlights

1 Islas Solentiname (p246) Hiking, swimming and stargazing on this peacefully artistic group of remote islands.

2 Boca de Sábalos (p251) Catching up with your reading while swinging in a hammock on a riverside balcony.

3 El Castillo (p254) Scaling an imposing Spanish fortress with delectable river views and exploring the surrounding jungle.

4 Reserva Biológica Indio-Maíz (p256) Trekking beneath the canopy of 500-year-old orchid-jeweled giants.

5 San Miguelito (p245)
Spotting migratory birds on a tour through humid forests.

6 San Juan de Nicaragua (p257) Taking a boat ride through hidden, jungled lagoons inhabited by manatees.

7 Río San Juan (p251)
Trolling for tarpon along isolated stretches of a mighty river.

8 Refugio de Vida Silvestre Los Guatuzos (p250)
Spotting alligators at night on cruise through the wetlands.

San Carlos

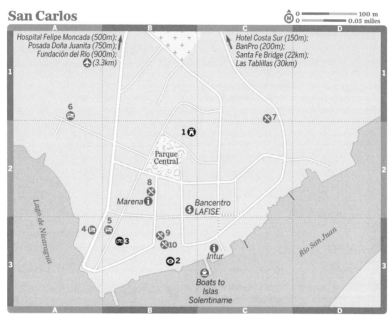

In dry weather it also organizes an excellent multiday trip for bird enthusiasts into the forests around Boca de Sábalos (p251) to spot the rare *lapa verde* when it is nesting.

✦✦ Festivals & Events

Carnival Acuático   DANCE, FOOD
(⊙Oct) The Río San Juan's biggest party features a colorful river parade, concerts and a food festival on the *malecón*.

🛏 Sleeping

Hotel Costa Sur   HOTEL $
(⌨2583-0224,8853-6728; hotel.costasur@hotmail. com; Terminal de Buses, 20m N; r US$9.50; 🛜) The best cheapie in town, the Costa Sur has rather small, windowless rooms painted in lurid green, each with its own bathroom (though no sink!). It is however clean and absolutely fine for the night, as well as handy to the bus station.

Hotel Gran Lago   HOTEL $$
(⌨8823-3488, 2583-0075; www.grandhotelsnica ragua.com; Parque Central, 1c O, 1c S; s/d/tr incl breakfast from US$37/41/60; ❄🛜) Right on the edge of the lake with views over to the Archipiélago de Solentiname, this small hotel is the best San Carlos has to offer, with a variety of rooms split over two levels. Those downstairs are a bit closed in and dark but the bigger upstairs rooms are spacious, get plenty of light and enjoy lake views.

Hotel Ocaso   HOTEL $$
(⌨2583-0340; moacruf@hotmail.com; Iglesia Católica, 1½c S; s/d incl breakfast US$35/40; ❄🛜) This seven-room hotel has small but tidy rooms with good amenities and an open-air restaurant upstairs with fine views. The interior rooms are a little dark, but rooms 4 and 5 on the end of the corridor overlooking the street are a good deal.

Posada Doña Juanita   GUESTHOUSE $$
(⌨2583-0024, 8423-7085; posada_juanita@hot mail.com; del Hospital 2c N, 1c O, ½c N; s/d incl breakfast US$30/45; ❄🛜) It's a bit of a hike from the center but the five rooms in this cute guesthouse on the 2nd floor of a family home are luminous, spacious and comfortable. The place is decked out with brightly painted handicrafts and the breakfasts are good quality.

Hotel-Cabinas Leyko   HOTEL $$
(⌨8699-6841, 2583-0354; leykou7@yahoo.es; Parque Central, 2c O; d with/without air-con, incl breakfast US$50/30, d with fan, without bathroom US$24; 🅿❄🛜) The rooms overlooking the wetlands at the rear of the hotel are a little pricey but are the most peaceful accommodations in San Carlos. Avoid the dingy cheaper rooms above reception, which are

San Carlos

all a bit cramped and dark. The friendly owners speak English and arrange tours.

✗ Eating

Soda La Fortaleza   CAFE $
(Malecón; dishes US$2-5; ⊘6am-10pm Mon-Sat) This lively spot on the lakefront serves up filling breakfasts and cheap, tasty Nica dishes. In the evening it's a fantastic place from which to observe the frenetic football games, canoodling couples and dedicated drinkers on the *malecón* against a background of improbably loud reggaeton.

Comedor Alondra   NICARAGUAN $
(Terminal de buses; meals incl beverage US$3; ⊘6am-10pm) The most popular of the row of restaurants at the bus terminal serves filling lunches to travelers and locals alike.

★**Restaurante Kaoma**   NICARAGUAN $$
(📞2583-0293; Parque Central, 1½c S; mains US$6.50-11.50; ⊘11:30am-10pm; 🐾) Just about the only full-service restaurant in town, this attractively set place has old wooden floors, beamed ceilings and pleasant lake views. The extensive menu includes some excellent tender beef dishes and fish, which comes sautéed in a buttery garlic sauce or stuffed with shrimp. The fish and crab soup is also delicious.

Pizza House   PIZZA $$
(Parque Central, 1c S; pizza US$6-10; ⊘10am-10pm) This small pizzeria in the center of town does passable pizzas, which you can design yourself.

⊙ Information

MEDICAL SERVICES
Hospital Felipe Moncada (📞2583-0244)

MONEY
There are two ATMs in town, **BanPro** (frente alcaldía) on the main road through town and **Bancentro LAFISE** (Parque Central, 1c S) just off the *malecón*.

TOURIST INFORMATION
Intur (📞2583-0301; riosanjuan@intur.gob. ni; contiguo a Migración; ⊘8am-4pm Mon-Fri) Right next to the Migración office on the *malecón*, this place is staffed by friendly and knowledgeable people.

Marena (📞2583-0296; Parque Central, 1c S; ⊘8am-4pm) Processes fishing licenses.

⊙ Getting There & Away

San Carlos is no longer the isolated corner of Nicaragua it once was thanks to the construction of a good road to Juigalpa and the opening of a modern bridge over the Río San Juan at Santa Fe, which links the region by road with Las Tablillas in Costa Rica.

San Miguelito

POP 2800
Most travelers miss this mellow lakeside fishing community and gateway to the region's least-visited reserve, the Sistema de Humedales de San Miguelito or San Miguelito Wetlands. A handful of rivers meander through the reserve, including the Río Tepenaguazapa, the Río Camastro, the Río Tule and the gorgeous Río Piedra. Occasionally the grasslands and lotus fields teeming with birds and butterflies intervene. If you're lucky, you may even see some alligators. This is your chance to easily get onto the path less beaten.

⊙ Sights

Sistema de Humedales de San Miguelito   NATURE RESERVE
The San Miguelito wetlands contain a handful of rivers, including the gorgeous Río Piedra, a glassy slice of black water framed by a dense tangle of jungle. Trees, hip-deep in water and sprouting with orchids and bromeliads in the canopy, stretch back as far as you can see, while birds and butterflies proliferate in the grasslands. The best time for birdwatching is at daybreak or dusk in September and October, when the migration peaks.

⊟ Sleeping

★**Hotel Cocibolca**   HOTEL $
(📞8845-5029; hotelcocibolca@yahoo.com; frente muelle; s/d/tr without bathroom US$6/12/16; 🐾)

A fantastic budget choice with wooden rooms boasting high-beamed ceilings and French doors that open onto private balconies overlooking the lake. The owners can arrange fishing and birdwatching trips to the San Miguelito wetlands (US$20 for a two-hour tour).

ℹ Getting There & Away

Never particularly well connected to the main tourist trail, San Miguelito was further isolated when the boat link with Ometepe and San Carlos, which called here, was cancelled in 2015.

These days the only practical way in is by road. Direct buses to San Miguelito (US$1.60, two hours) leave the San Carlos bus station at 12:20pm and 1pm each day, and there are also minivan services (US$2, two hours) from the *malecón* that leave at 10:30am and 5pm daily. Any San Carlos–Managua or San Carlos–Juigalpa bus can also drop you off at the Empalme de San Miguelito, from where *colectivos* (shared taxis; US$1) make the 8km trip into town.

Islas Solentiname

POP 800 / ELEV 40M TO 250M

If you're the type who likes islands draped in jungle, surrounded by crystalline waters that reflect the forest, sun and sky, and populated by farmers and fishers who share their wealth and also happen to be terrific artists and craftspeople, you do not want to miss this oft-overlooked archipelago. And we haven't even mentioned the gators, monkeys, orchids and migratory waterfowl, the sensational offshore fishing, the mind-blowing sunsets and the spectacular starlight. Almost forgotten for 500 years, and nearly destroyed in a single day, the Archipiélago de Solentiname does not seem entirely of this world.

ℹ Getting There & Away

Transol (p248) runs a daily fast boat service (US$10, 90 minutes) between San Carlos and the islands, leaving from the dock next to Migración in San Carlos at 3pm and returning at 9am the following day. This is by far the fastest and most comfortable way to get to the archipelago.

If you're on a tight budget and have a flexible itinerary, slow public boats (US$4, two to three hours) run on Tuesday and Friday leaving Mancarrón at 5am and stopping about 30 minutes later at San Fernando before continuing on to San Carlos. They return to Solentiname from the dock next to Migración in San Carlos at 1pm.

If that doesn't work with your schedule, you can hire a private boat (seating at least six)

between San Carlos and the islands for US$120 to US$150.

Isla Mancarrón

This island feels small because residents, guests and commerce converge on a rather slender slice of land that includes the harbor and the village. But hike the muddy trails, which traverse these jungled hills, and you'll quickly notice that the island is deceptively large, sprawling into the azure lake and forming a succession of sheltered coves. The extreme western end seeps into an 800m-long stretch of wetlands that nurture fish and turtle hatcheries and are teeming with migratory waterfowl.

◉ Sights

★ **Nuestra Señora de Solentiname**   CHURCH

(US$1) Mancarrón's greatest human-made gift is Nuestra Señora de Solentiname, where populist priest Ernesto Cardenal ran a rather enlightened parish. Constructed by the community in 1979, it features a beautiful whitewashed nave from within which you can still hear the lake and feel the trees. The altar spares the usual golden idolatry and instead is graced with a colorful yet humble mural depicting life in the archipelago. If there's no one around, ask up the hill at the museum.

El Refugio   VILLAGE

(Comunidad El Mancarrón) The highest concentration of craft workshops on the islands are just inland from the dock in Comunidad El Mancarrón (also called El Refugio). Feel free to wander and watch as families carve balsa-wood figures in their homes and front yards. Children sand the pieces smooth, and the most talented adult paints. Wooden animals cost US$1.20 to US$50; prices rise with size and quality.

Museo Arqueológico   MUSEUM

(US$1; ☉8am-noon & 1-5pm) This fine museum up the hill from the church houses a small but intriguing collection of pre-Columbian metates, pottery and idols unearthed in the archipelago.

🏃 Activities

Familia Pedro Rivas   KAYAKING

(☑8983-7289; detras museo; ☉8am-5pm) ⭐ Local family that rents out kayaks and canoes for US$11 per day. To find the house,

SAN CARLOS, ISLAS SOLENTINAME & THE RÍO SAN JUAN ISLAS SOLENTINAME walk past the museum and take the path to the left that passes through the jungle and down to the waterside.

👉 Tours

Conoce Solentiname
TOURS

(☑8963-2845, 8869-6619; hostalbuenamigo@gmail.com; Hospedaje Buen Amigo; tours US$20-100; ⊙6am-8pm) Energetic tour operator that offers a great variety of natural and cultural activities including fishing, birdwatching in the wetlands, hikes to petroglyphs and trips to Los Guatuzos. Proprietor Evert spends a lot of time in San Carlos, so call ahead to make sure he will be around.

🛏 Sleeping & Eating

Hotel Sueño Feliz
GUESTHOUSE $

(☑8478-5243, 8582-9024; El Refugio; r per person with/without breakfast US$10/8) A simple guesthouse set in the home of a friendly local artisan family. It offers three simple rooms with peach paint jobs in the main house as well as a log-and-concrete *cabaña* out the back that sleeps up to six. Affordable meals are available and it offers a full range of tours around the archipelago.

Guests can sign up for the 'artisan for a day' tour (US$10) where you'll try your hand at carving and painting your own Solentiname-style animals (and you get to take home your masterpiece).

Hostal Buen Amigo
GUESTHOUSE $

(☑8869-6619; hostalbuenamigo@gmail.com; El Refugio; r per person with/without bathroom US$12/8) This popular cheapie has several neat, freshly painted rooms with good mattresses set in a pleasant garden; those with private bathrooms are brighter and more spacious and are worth the upgrade. You can order cheap meals at the *comedor/tienda* (basic eatery/small shop), which doubles as a popular local watering hole.

★Hospedaje
La Comunidad
GUESTHOUSE $$

(☑8966-7056; www.hospedajelacomunidad.com; contiguo muelle; r per person with/without meals US$40/20) 🛶 Easily the best deal on Mancarrón, these three charming solar-powered wooden houses overlooking the bay have breezy hammock-strung balconies, spacious rooms and huge bathrooms with outdoor showers. Guests can use the wi-fi at the library, and hotel profits support the local school. If there is no one around, ask for Ernesto at the library.

Good meals can be enjoyed up by the museum or in the private dining area of each house. Management also organize very reasonably priced tours around the archipelago.

Hotel Mancarrón
HOTEL $$$

(☑8852-3380, 2270-9981; www.hotelmancarron.com; r per person incl meals US$55) This rambling whitewashed hotel surrounded by tropical gardens on a hillside above the southern shore was the archipelago's first. The rooms are large and comfortable but fairly spare. The restaurant, however, is exceptional, serving tasty, inventive meals in a large, screened dining room.

ℹ Information

Internet access is available for a small fee in the **Biblioteca Ernesto Cardenal** (internet per hr US$0.60; ⊙8am-noon & 1-5pm Mon-Sat). This is the only public internet access in the archipelago.

ℹ Getting There & Away

Both the Transol (p248) express service and the slow local boat call at Mancarrón as their final stop on arrival from San Carlos. Morning boat services to San Carlos originate from here. You can use these services to travel between Isla Mancarrón and Isla San Fernando (US$1.60).

Isla San Fernando

With even fewer people than Isla Mancarrón, tranquil Isla San Fernando has comfortable accommodations, delicious meals, and the islands' only art gallery. But the biggest attraction is the San Fernando sunset. First

GETTING AROUND THE ISLANDS

Most visitors hire private *pangas* (small motorboats) between the Islas Solentiname; it's at least US$20 round-trip between San Fernando and Mancarrón. Alternatively, if you are heading from Mancarrón to San Fernando you can take the morning Transol (p248) service between the islands for US$1.60 and return when the afternoon boat passes from San Carlos.

A cheaper and more adventurous way to explore the archipelago is to paddle. Kayaks and canoes are available for rent on both Mancarrón and San Fernando.

the lake loses its color before reflecting the deep jungle green of the surrounding forests. Then the sky pales, streaks pink and burns gold behind the neighboring islands. Even better, once it gets dark, expect a black dome sky full of stars.

◉ Sights & Activities

The **Sendero El Trogón** is a 45-minute walking trail that passes some impressive petroglyphs and a lookout point. It costs US$5 to pay for path maintenance. Pay at your hotel or the tourist office. Albergue Celentiname rents two-person canoes (US$4 per hour) to explore the surroundings, while Hostal Vanessa organizes sportfishing trips (US$100 per day for up to three participants).

Unión de Pintores y Artesanos de Solentiname 'Elvis Chavarría'   GALLERY
(☑7250-8882; upassolentiname@yahoo.com; ⊙8am-noon & 1-4pm) Set in an old mahogany house uphill from the sheltered dock, this cooperative features the work of about 50 of the islands' top artists and artisans. Affordable balsa sculptures are in one room, and higher-end paintings (US$40 to US$1200) are in the other. The view from here is incredible. If it's closed, ask for the key at the **tourist office** (☑7250-8882; solentinamecantur@yahoo.com; ⊙9am-5pm).

Museo Archipiélago Solentiname   MUSEUM
(Musas; US$2; ⊙8am-noon & 1-5pm) Follow the trail to the right of the dock uphill through the avocado grove to this museum. The view and surrounding gardens alone are worth the hike. Inside you'll find terrific natural-history and cultural exhibits, including a collection of pre-Columbian pots and pestles.

🛏 Sleeping

All hotels are located to the west of the dock along the path that runs along the southern edge of the island. Most larger hotels offer rates with and without meals.

Hostal Vanessa   GUESTHOUSE $
(☑5872-9731; hostalfamiliarvanessa07@gmail.com; muelle, 10m 0; r per person with/without bathroom US$12/10) The wooden rooms with shared bathrooms by the path are a little cramped and noisy but the spacious new rooms with private bathrooms up on the hill

offer fantastic views and are a great deal. Sportfishing trips can be arranged.

Hospedaje Mire Estrella   GUESTHOUSE $
(☑7255-6293; https://mireestrella.weebly.com; r per person with/without bathroom US$10/8) With tidy wooden rooms right by the water's edge, this simple *hospedaje* is a fine budget choice. The laid-back owner offers cheap tours around the islands in his small boat, including archeological tours, fishing tours and artist tours.

Albergue Celentiname   GUESTHOUSE $$
(☑8465-2426; www.hotelcelentiname.blogspot.com; r per person incl full board US$40) Tucked into a flowering garden that feels like something out of a tropical utopia is this secluded guesthouse, a gorgeous 10-minute walk from the main dock on the extreme northern end of the west-coast trail. Very basic but neat wooden *cabañas* come with two beds and a terrace with lake and garden views.

Some rooms are better than others, so ask to look around – the larger *cabaña familiar* is the one you want. Guests get free access to kayaks and canoes. It also offers budget packages for backpackers including accommodations and two simple Nica-style meals for US$30. It rents canoes to nonguests.

Hotel Cabañas Paraíso   HOTEL $$
(☑2278-3998, 8904-6778; s/d/tr US$30/45/60) These modern, concrete rooms have wooden shutters and new shower tiles but are fairly basic and don't really take full advantage of the magnificent setting. Meals (US$6 to US$8.50) are served in a lovely dining area with 180-degree lake views.

✗ Eating

Pulpería Doña Juanita   NICARAGUAN $
(muelle, 200m 0; mains US$3-6; ⊙7am-7pm) With just one table on the porch outside the family shop, this is the only eating option not attached to a hotel. The menu is limited to simple Nica *comida corriente* (a mixed plate of typical regional foods) but it's cheap and filling. Swing by to order in advance.

❶ Getting There & Away

Both the **Transol** (☑8828-3243, 8555-4739) express service and the slow local boat call at San Fernando as their final stop on arrival from San Carlos. Morning boat services to San Carlos originate from Isla Mancarrón, but call at San Fernando on the way to the mainland.

Isla Mancarroncito

Across a narrow strait from Isla Mancarrón's western shore is this small, rocky jewel thick with the last stands of primary forest in the archipelago. **Loma San Antonio**, a 15m boulder, protrudes from a hill on the eastern shore. Local legend has it that *brujas* (witches – not the good kind) once lived in the caves at the top of the cliff, which may explain why the island is still so wild. There are exploratory trails on the island (admission US$5) which are maintained by the local biological station and guides can be arranged for US$18 per group.

🛏 Sleeping

Estación Biológica   LODGE **$**
(r per person US$12) This biological research station offers basic lodging in its wooden cabin. Call Fundación del Río (p241) in San Carlos in advance to arrange your stay. Meals cost US$6.

ℹ Getting There & Away

Full-day motorboat tours around the archipelago will make a stop at Mancarroncito on request. Kayakers can reach the island by paddling across the narrow channel on the west side of Mancarrón. Overnight guests should arrange transportation directly with the Fundación del Río (p241) in San Carlos, which costs US$25 round-trip per boat from Isla Mancarrón or US$180 to US$200 from San Carlos.

Isla Venada

Meet the Aurellanos. Three generations of the archipelago's most renowned artists come from the jumble of wooden homes overlooking a gorgeous, glassy strait on the northwestern shore of this wooded island.

Rodolfo Aurellano was the trailblazer. His works are dreamy, colorful reflections of Isla Venada and the surrounding islands, Rosita, Carolina and El Padre. Take some time to talk with the elderly, barefoot artist and he might tell you about how he used to have to hide deep in the bush to paint to avoid being identified as a revolutionary by Somoza's forces. Despite being in his late 70s, Rodolfo still paints regularly and maintains a small collection of works for sale (US$30 to US$1000).

Rodolfo's daughter and granddaughter, Clarissa and Jeyselle Aurellano, have followed his example and also have works on display in the family home.

EXPLORING THE CAVES

A system of caves at the waterline honeycombs Isla Venada's northern shore and are only visible in the dry season. You'll need a boat to explore them and see the many petroglyphs carved into their walls. Guides are available (US$7 per day) at the Aurellano residence. Guides can also be arranged to explore the island on foot.

🛏 Sleeping

Familia Aurellano   GUESTHOUSE **$**
(☑ 8815-1761; r per person US$10) The Aurellano homestead functions as a homestay and is the only accommodations option on the island.

ℹ Getting There & Away

Both the express and regular boats from San Carlos will drop you on Isla Venada on request. From other islands, private round-trip transport costs around US$35.

Isla Atravesada

Named because it's the only island oriented north–south, rather than east–west like the rest of the archipelago, Atravesada (meaning 'to cross') is famed for its enormous 5m alligators and rich birdlife. Flocks of ives, with their crab-cracking beaks, congregate in the north-shore canopy alongside trees full of the dangling nests of the resident black cormorants.

ℹ Getting There & Away

Most visitors get to Isla Atravesada on a package tour of various islands in the archipelago. It's also close enough to paddle a kayak or canoe from either Mancarrón or San Fernando.

Other Islands

There are at least 36 further Solentiname Islands in the archipelago, many privately owned and most without much to interest the casual visitor. There are several exceptions to the rule, mainly offering excellent wildlife-watching opportunities.

⊙ Sights

Islas Zapote & Zapotillo   ISLAND
Avid birders won't want to miss tiny Islas Zapote and Zapotillo, which feature Nicaragua's highest concentration of birds,

> ## ℹ NO MAN'S LAND
>
> There are no buildings on Isla Atravesada and staying overnight is not permitted. There's nowhere to eat on Isla Atravesada, either, so bring a packed lunch if you plan on hanging around a while to observe the wildlife.

most famously flocks of roseate spoonbills that nest in February and March. Migratory birds of all kinds converge here between December and April – more than 30,000 nests have been counted by visiting biologists.

Isla El Padre   ISLAND
You will hear the residents of Isla El Padre before you see them. Set between Mancarrón and San Fernando and named for yet another priest who long ago sought solitude in these tranquil waters, it's inhabited by a troupe of howler monkeys.

Isla Sevilla   ISLAND
Isla Sevilla, just west of Mancarroncito, is a haven for birdwatchers, with thousands of cormorants, tiger herons and pelicans here to enjoy some excellent fishing.

ℹ Getting There & Away

The closer islands can easily be explored by kayak or canoe. Islas Zapote and Zapotillo are in a remote location, 12km from the rest of the archipelago, but can be visited on a chartered motorboat trip from the main islands or San Carlos. They also make an interesting stop on the way to or from Los Guatuzos.

Refugio de Vida Silvestre Los Guatuzos

Like so many national treasures, Los Guatuzos wildlife reserve, a 440 sq km band of rich, river-streaked wilderness wedged between the Costa Rican border and Lago de Nicaragua, was conserved by accident. The earliest inhabitants, the Guatuzos, were sold into slavery and their lands co-opted by farmers whose crops (rubber and cacao) demanded shade. Just as foreign timber companies were poised to buy out the subsistence farmers, revolution and war hit hard along the border, and the various minefields left the region inaccessible and pristine. Declared mine-free in 2001, the area is now a wonderful side trip from San Carlos.

⊙ Sights

Reserva Esperanza Verde   NATURE RESERVE
(⌨ 2583-0459; www.fundeverde.org; Río Frío) Nestled on the Río Frío, roughly halfway between San Carlos and Los Chiles, is this private 50 sq km humid tropical forest reserve. Expect to see hundreds of bird species, three kinds of monkeys, fingernail-sized tree frogs and an array of rare orchids. You can do it in a day trip from San Carlos (US$30 per person, two-person minimum), including local transport, guide and trail access, which can be arranged through Hotel-Cabinas Leyko (p244) in San Carlos.

Alternatively, you can spend the night in one of its simple, solar-powered rooms (per person full board US$50).

🛌 Sleeping

★ Cabañas Caiman   GUESTHOUSE $
(⌨ 506-8704-3880, 8676-2958; aillenm@hotmail.com; Río Papaturro; per person incl breakfast US$18) Papaturro's original crocodile man and former Centro Ecológico manager Armando Gomez runs this guesthouse on the opposite bank of the river. The two wooden rooms are charming and comfortable and tasty meals are served, but where this place really excels is in the fantastic tours with one of the region's most energetic and knowledgeable ecologists.

It also rents bicycles (US$5 per day) to explore the village and surrounding area.

Centro Ecológico de Los Guatuzos   LODGE $
(⌨ 2270-3561, 8772-9630; www.losguatuzos.com; Río Papaturro; r per person US$15) 🅿 This professionally run research station in the Río Papaturro community is primarily geared to scientists and students. However, tourists are welcome to bunk down in the basic but comfortable wooden cabañas. Typical Nica meals (US$5) are available at local homes.

The center offers several tours, including a two-hour guided hike (US$10 per person) with visits to an alligator hatchery and a short detour through the jungle canopy on a hanging bridge, and a moonlight alligator tour (US$45 for one to three visitors). Kayaks are also available to rent.

ℹ Getting There & Away

The best way to get to Río Papaturro is on the 10am Saturday morning fast boat (US$4.75, two hours) from San Carlos. The rest of the time, you'll need to make the journey in a painfully slow colectivo boat (US$3.30, five hours) which leaves San Carlos on Monday, Tuesday, Wednesday and Friday at 9am. These return at 8am on Monday, Tuesday, Thursday and Sunday, with a fast service at 9am on Friday from the Papaturro dock. All boats leave from the westernmost pier on the San Carlos waterfront.

It costs around US$130/240 one way/round-trip from San Carlos for a transfer in a private *panga*. Note that it's normally cheaper to rent a boat (round-trip boat/*panga* US$70/100) in Solentiname, so it makes sense to combine trips to both places.

Río San Juan

Surging purposefully through rolling green hills, thick jungle and dense wetlands on its irrepressible march to the Caribbean, the Río San Juan forms much of Nicaragua's natural border with Costa Rica and is today a slowly developing traveler destination popular with those who enjoy wildlife-watching, hiking and kayaking. Once the domain of indigenous traders, Spanish conquistadors, British pirates, gold-hunting travelers and even Mark Twain, this river has history in bucketloads. Follow their example and penetrate the vine-hung wilderness of jaguars and macaws that is the Reserva Biológica Indio-Maíz, troll for tarpon, search for alligators in the moonlight and then make a toast to your adventures while overlooking the remains of a 16th-century Spanish fort. All of which will cost you. But it's worth it to fully experience this spectacular and unforgettable waterway.

ⓘ Getting There & Away

You can access both the start of the river, San Carlos, or its end, San Juan de Nicaragua, by air twice a week on La Costeña's flight from Managua, which stops in both towns. The flight is quite spectacular and highly recommended, though it's also possible to connect to San Carlos by bus from all over Western Nicaragua, as well as to reach San Juan de Nicaragua by *panga* once a week from Bluefields.

La Esperanza

The first major settlement after passing under the Santa Fe bridge, La Esperanza is a typical Río San Juan rural community surrounded mostly by pasture but with some pockets of jungle and plenty of birdlife. It's mainly visited for the popular rustic lodge here that's one of the few places to experience Nicaraguan rural life.

🛏 Sleeping

Grand River Lodge HOSTEL $

(☎ 8375-7248, 7892-8374; grandriverlodgehotel@gmail.com; tents or hammock US$3, dm/s/d US$7/10/20) On a hill overlooking the Río San Juan you'll find Grand River Lodge, one of the few backpacker-orientated places on the river and a great place to experience Nicaraguan rural life. It is run by affable local and veteran cruise-ship employee, Marvin, who has converted his family farm into a rural lodge with 11 simple thatched-roof huts with private bathrooms.

Prices include free use of kayaks and canoes and the friendly staff organize plenty of activities to keep clients occupied, including treks to see resident monkeys, horseback riding and artisanal cheese-making workshops. It also runs a cacao tour (US$5) beginning in the plantation beside the lodge and a massive swimming pool is in the works. Tasty and filling meals (including a beverage US$4.50 to US$6.50) are served in the rustic bar-restaurant.

It also offers cheap secure parking for those heading down river by boat. The lodge is 2km from the village and can be reached by boat or bus; just let the driver know where to drop you off.

ⓘ Getting There & Away

Any San Carlos–El Castillo (US$3, one hour) boat will drop you off at the Grand River dock from where it's a five-minute walk along a boardwalk through the swamp and up to the hotel. It's also possible to arrive by bus – take any Sábalos-bound bus from San Carlos (US$2.20, 1½ hours) and ask to be let off at the entrance from where it's a short walk down to the lodge.

Boca de Sábalos

POP 800

It sometimes feels that the thick jungle looming on the edges of Boca de Sábalos is about to reclaim this muddy, dusty town set at the confluence of the Ríos San Juan and Sábalos (Tarpon River). And therein lies its appeal. When you lounge on the terrace of your hotel, lodge or guesthouse at sunset, you'll watch birds fish and ride end-of-the-day thermals as you hear that familiar, primordial roar of the howler monkeys in the distance.

Río Sábalos effectively splits the town in half, with the inexpensive *hospedajes* and main road on one side, and a smaller community, threaded by a slender footpath past

CONFLICT ON THE BORDER

The Río San Juan is no stranger to conflict. Ever since Spanish colonizers and pillaging pirates began battling it out at El Castillo, these strategic waters have been the source of many a battle.

Well before the inauguration of the Panama Canal, the river had been identified as the key piece in any interoceanic route through Nicaragua. After countless border disputes, in 1858 the US facilitated a treaty between Nicaragua and Costa Rica that defined the border along the southern bank of the river but awarded the river in its entirety to Nicaragua, making it clear that any future canal project would only have to negotiate with one government. Thus the Río San Juan became one of the few border rivers on the planet that belongs exclusively to one country, a fact that has been a constant source of friction between the two nations, especially over the extent of Costa Rica's navigation rights.

The long-running dispute hit the headlines in 2010 when the government of Daniel Ortega began dredging the lower stretches of the Río San Juan in what they claimed was an attempt to restore the river's natural course that had been diverted by Costa Rican dredging in the Río Colorado in the 1960s.

Costa Rica immediately expressed concerns about the environmental impact of the dredging and soon afterward alleged Nicaragua was hacking a new channel through one of its islands, Isla Calero, in order to annex part of the territory. Dredging boss, and former Contra leader, Edén Pastora rejected those claims, even famously pulling up Google Maps to make the point that the island, which Nicaragua refers to as Harbour Head, had always been part of that country.

Tensions escalated and Costa Rica sent heavily armed police to the area. Amid fears of a military confrontation, Costa Rica took the issue to the International Court of Justice (ICJ). Fed up with not being able to navigate the river freely, Costa Rica constructed a 160km highway along the edge of the San Juan to facilitate movement to and from the delta.This saw Nicaragua taking its turn to don the environmentalist hat, denouncing deforestation and erosion along the length of the new road.

In late 2015, the ICJ handed down its ruling, backing the Costa Rican position that Nicaragua had violated their territory at Isla Calero and ordering the Ortega government to pay compensation. But it wasn't a total win for the Ticos: the court also ruled that they had violated their international obligations by not conducting an environmental impact study of their riverside road.

While the ruling brings a definitive close to one particular source of friction between the belligerent neighbors, it is highly unlikely to mark an end to the bickering over the strategic waterway.

rustic homes and gardens, on the other. It costs two córdobas (US$0.06) to cross the canal in the dugout canoe that goes back and forth.

◉ Sights

**Reserva Privada
El Quebracho**   NATURE RESERVE
(☎2583-0035; www.fundaciondelrio.org; US$5) ⚐ Administered by the Fundación del Río in San Carlos, this 90-hectare property borders Reserva Biológica Indio-Maíz, and offers a peek at the region's very big trees, very small frogs, beautiful rivers and wealth of wildlife. Take a bus or taxi to Buena Vista and walk the last hour to the reserve, where you can hike and horseback ride along two trails through primary forest dangling with

orchids. If you stick around, accommodations are available in simple rooms with shared bathrooms.

If you are visiting for the day, take the *colectivo* from the dock in Sábalos to Buenavista at 7am (US$2.50, one hour) and make sure you are back in Buena Vista by 1pm for the bus back to town.

☞ Tours

Asociación de Guías Jacamar   ADVENTURE
(☎8441-5958, 8970-0007; asociacionguiasjacamar @yahoo.com; frente muelle; ⊙8am-5pm) ⚐ This association of young nature guides offers a variety of kayaking trips along jungle-clad rivers, in addition to treks through nature reserves and night alligator-spotting boat trips. It's also possible to hire a guide to

follow your own itinerary. The office in the kiosk by the dock is rarely attended, though, so try calling or ask around.

🛏 Sleeping

Basic budget lodging is located in town while two comfortable midrange hotels are just across the Río Sábalos from the dock. A fine pair of more comfortable ecolodges are further downstream on the Río San Juan; tell the riverboat driver where you're staying and you'll be dropped in the right spot when you arrive.

Hospedaje Kateana GUESTHOUSE $
(☑ 2583-3838; muelle, ½c N; s/d with bathroom US$11/16, without bathroom US$9/14; ▣) The best of the cheapies, Kateana is far from luxurious but is a decent choice in town with small but clean wooden rooms, a nice porch overlooking the main street and, absolutely essential for vegetarians in Sábalos, kitchen access. They'll also lend you the washing machine to clean that bag of stinking clothes you've been hauling through the jungle.

Hotel Sábalos HOTEL $$
(☑ 8659-0252; www.hotelsabalos.com.ni; frente muelle; s/d/tr incl breakfast US$27/45/55; 🛜) Perched on stilts over the water at the mouth of the Río Sábalos, this charming hotel has comfortable wooden rooms with hot water, and rocking chairs on the wide veranda, which is a gorgeous place to sit. It also has the only real restaurant in Sábalos. Staff will pick you up from the dock in their boat if you call them.

Tarpon River Lodge HOTEL $$
(☑ 8629-0940, 8944-1898; alojamientoriosabalo @hotmail.com; muelle, 100m N; s/d/tr US$20/30/45) A decent choice a little upstream from the dock on the quieter side of the Río Sabalos, Tarpon River is housed in a cute wooden house with spacious polished rooms and sparkling tile floors. The best reason to stay here is the onsite thermal water, which you can enjoy in your bathroom or in the Jacuzzi out the back.

There is a breezy riverside restaurant area across the street too.

★ Sábalos Lodge LODGE $$$
(☑ 8823-5514, 8823-5555; www.sabaloslodge. com; muelle, 1km E; s/d inc breakfast US$39/65, f incl breakfast US$80-95; 🛜) 🌿 These rustic stilted bungalows set on the riverside a short distance from town are surrounded by flowering trees and thick jungle. Each one has an indoor-outdoor living room with hammocks, a bed swathed in mosquito netting, and an outdoor shower. The best part: each bungalow has its own view of the river, which is alive with birds at sunset.

Montecristo River Eco Lodge LODGE $$$
(☑ 8649-9012; www.montecristoriverlodge.com; muelle, 2km E; per person incl meals US$50) This riverside reserve attracts tarpon fishing expeditions but the 120-*manzana* (block) property also boasts 60 *manzanas* of primary forest with 300-plus cathedral ceiba and almond trees, hiking trails, free kayaks, a coffee plantation and a cacao grove. The rooms are rather run-down and the place feels a bit neglected, sadly, but if you're here for fishing it's a top choice.

A full-day boat hire for snook and tarpon expeditions or touring the region cost around US$300 per day. Non-fishing guests should note that the location is remote and on the far side of the Río San Juan, so any trip into town requires a boat shuttle.

ℹ Getting There & Away

Boca de Sábalos is pretty much the last town on the river accessible by road and has fairly frequent bus services, which makes it a convenient place to spend the night if you miss the last boat downstream from San Carlos.

BOAT

Boat services from Boca de Sábalos:
El Castillo (*colectivo* US$0.65, one hour, 2pm Monday to Saturday and 4:30pm Monday, Tuesday, Friday and Saturday; express US$1, 20 minutes, 6:30am, 9:30am, noon, 4:30pm and 5:30pm)
San Carlos (*colectivo* US$3, 2½ hours, 6am, 7am, 8am and 3pm Monday to Saturday, 6am and 3pm Sunday; express US$3.80, 1½ hours, 6am, 11am and noon)

BUS

Buses from San Carlos can be picked up at the top of the pathway on either side of the the Río Sábalos. Buses cross the river on a sketchy-looking barge and continue right on into town.
Bus departures from Sábalos:
Buena Vista (US$1.50, one hour, 11am and 4pm) Returning at 6am and 1pm.
San Carlos (US$2.50, two hours, 4am, 6am, 7am, 1pm and 3pm)

ℹ Getting Around

Public transportation by road to communities surrounding Boca de Sábalos consists of 'taxis' – beat-up old 4WD vehicles that are filled to bursting point and make collective runs (US$2.50) to local communities. They have no fixed schedule, departing from the dock when full, usually coinciding with the arrival of river transport to the port.

It's also possible to hire a vehicle (up to eight passengers) for an express trip – expect to pay around US$50 to US$60 to Buena Vista.

El Castillo

POP 1000

Lined with brightly painted timber houses and crowned by a wonderfully evocative 17th-century Spanish fortress, it's no surprise that El Castillo is the Río San Juan's showpiece destination. It's laced with pebbled-concrete walking paths that wind up, down and around the hill, shaded by mango, coconut, orange and almond trees, and fronted by a fast-flowing bend in the massive Río San Juan with two sets of rapids on it. A town this civilized means that the jungle has been tamed here, so don't expect the howlers to sing you to sleep, though you're also just 15 minutes by boat from Nicaragua's best-preserved lowland rainforest, the Reserva Biológica Indio-Maíz, making El Castillo an ideal base for numerous jungle adventures.

◉ Sights

La Fortaleza   FORT
(US$2, camera fee US$1; ⊙ 8am-5pm Mon-Fri, to 4pm Sat & Sun) Properly known as La Fortaleza de la Limpia Pura e Inmaculada Concepción, this photogenic fortress was constructed between 1673 and 1675, commissioned after Granada was sacked five times in five years. The Raudal El Diablo rapids were key – they slowed the pirates down just long enough to aim enormous cannons their way. Still, the fortress was attacked, rebuilt and fortified every other decade for 200 years.

🏃 Activities

Fábrica de Cacao   FOOD & DRINK
(Coodeprosa; frente colegio; US$5; ⊙ 8am-noon & 1-4pm) 🍫 This cooperative on a path behind the baseball field organizes a fascinating tour of its cacao factory explaining the chocolate-making process. It sells a variety of locally made chocolate in the small shop. Taking the tour and selflessly buying the products on sale is a great way to support an important local cooperative. Ask around to find it, as there are no signs.

🖝 Tours

★ Nena Tour   ADVENTURE
(☑ 2583-3010; www.nenalodge.com; muelle, 110m E) A fantastic tour operator based at Nena Lodge offering the full range of hikes in the Reserva Indio-Maíz plus canoe tours on the nearby Río Juana (US$15 per person, three hours) and a night alligator tour (US$45, up to four passengers). Also rents an inflatable raft to run the rapids in front of town (US$20, up to three participants).

Basiliscus Tour   RIVER TOUR
(☑ 5798-9313; darwing86@gmail.com; muelle, 110m E) Specialists in canoe trips down the river, including a four-day, 160km trip all the way to San Juan de Nicaragua (US$350 per person, minimum two people). You'll sleep in tents on the river bank. The same trip in kayaks costs US$550, while a five-day kayak version is US$600. Prices include all meals.

Alfonso Tapia   HORSEBACK RIDING
(☑ 8431-2389; Pulpería Tropical) Offers excellent half-day horseback-riding tours (US$15 per person) through lush countryside with fantastic birdwatching. Unlike those of some operators in the region, don Alfonso's horses are in good condition. Book at Pulpería Tropical on the main path through town just before Hotel Victoria (p256).

🛏 Sleeping

There are a number of lovely small hotels and guesthouses in El Castillo, all of which are a short walk from the arrivals dock.

Nena Lodge   GUESTHOUSE $
(☑ 2583-3010, 8821-2135; www.nenalodge. com; muelle, 110m E; s/d/tw without bathroom US$12/16/22, s/d/tr/q with bathroom US$16/26/33/44; 🛜) New rooms upstairs at this long-running tour agency are spotless, with wooden floors and walls, crisp sheets and decent shared bathrooms. Three rooms have their own bathrooms, and all rooms boast mosquito nets and fans. The gorgeous light-filled family room, with two double beds and a single, is the best of the lot.

Casa de Huesped Chinandegano   GUESTHOUSE $
(☑ 2583-3011; muelle, 240m E; s/d with bathroom US$12/18, without bathroom US$8/15; 🛜) This creaky wooden house done up with potted tropical plants and a shabby-chic dining area is built right over the river and is the best cheapie in town. The wood and bam-

GUIDED TOURS

Conveniently located at the dock, El Castillo's **tourist office** (☑8526-9267; frente muelle; ⊙8am-6pm) sources local guides for a variety of tours. It helps to make reservations a day in advance. Guided hikes and *panga* trip itineraries include:

Reserva Biológica Indio-Maíz, Río Bartola (US$75 for up to five people, four hours) Take a private *panga* to the Río Bartola entrance of the Indio-Maíz reserve, then hike 3km through primary forest, where you'll be dwarfed by 500-year-old giants, taste medicinal plants, and spot tree frogs, green iguanas and three types of monkey (spider, white-faced and howler). After the hike you'll motor up Río Bartola, where you'll swim in a crystal-clear river surrounded by jungle.

Reserva Biológica Indio-Maíz, Aguas Frescas (US$85 for up to five people, five hours) Virtually identical to the Bartola trip in terms of scenery but the Aguas Frescas trail is a slightly longer and more challenging hike.

Reserva Biológica Indio-Maíz, Caño Sarnoso (US$120 for up to five people, five hours) This boat trip travels further down the Río San Juan to observe the ruins of the old steamboats and abundant wildlife around El Diamante rapids, including crocodiles and birdlife. It can also be combined with one of the trails within the reserve.

The tourist office also organizes a night caiman-watching tour (US$45 for up to four visitors).

You don't have to go through the tourist office, which can seem less than helpful at times, though. There are several private operators with signs up around town offering similar tour rosters.

boo rooms are breezy and have high ceilings, with brightly painted bathrooms in some. Get the corner room if you can, or just come for a meal.

Hostal Fortaleza　　　　　　HOTEL **$$**
(☑8431-2389; hostalfortaleza1@yahoo.com; muelle, 180m E; s/d incl breakfast US$15/30; ☞) A good value hotel on the main path offering rooms on two levels. Those downstairs are a bit noisy but grab one of those up the tight spiral staircase and you'll enjoy high ceilings, wooden floors, a large shared balcony and plenty of natural light.

Hotel Tropical　　　　　　HOTEL **$$**
(☑8820-1347, 8275-3035; pxiniadelsocorro@yahoo.com; muelle, 130m E; r/f incl breakfast US$25/50; ❄☞) Lie back in a gorgeous setting and listen to the rushing water of El Castillo's rapids outside your window. The traditional wooden home at the foot of the hillside has flowers and plants all around it, while rooms enjoy air-con, cable TV and tiled bathrooms. The best thing is the breezy wooden porch perched right above the rapids.

Posada del Rio　　　　　GUESTHOUSE **$$**
(☑2583-3014, 8405-9998; muelle, 300m E; s/d/tr incl breakfast US$30/40/60, r without bathroom, with fan US$10; ❄☞) Friendly family-run

place at the end of the path with neat wooden rooms and a generous breakfast. Good value, especially the cheaper fan-cooled downstairs rooms that share bathrooms. The restaurant here is one of the best in town too.

★**Luna del Rio**　　　　　HOTEL **$$$**
(☑8624-6263; riosanjuannicaragua@yahoo.es; frente raudal; s/d/tr incl breakfast US$45/60/70; ❄☞) A stylish hotel in a beautifully painted small house right by the rapids, Luna del Rio offers just five charming and well appointed wooden rooms, complete with gorgeous hot-water bathrooms that open onto private balconies with swinging chairs. There is not a lot of space but the place exudes a welcoming, homely vibe and a boutique sensibility.

★**Lara's Planet**　　　　　HOTEL **$$$**
(☑8637-1440; muelle, 200m O, 80m N; r incl breakfast US$75-90; ☞) Beautifully crafted from polished wood and bamboo and with fabulous views over the river, Lara's Planet is a gorgeous spot at the far end of the village. Rooms are huge, with high ceilings, quality fittings, bar fridges and private balconies high over the river, while the welcome from owner and world traveler Natasha is warm.

Hotel Victoria HOTEL $$$
(☎ 8381-6589, 8697-2509; hotelvictoria01@
yahoo.es; muelle, 250m E; s/d/tr incl breakfast
US$45/60/75; ❉🔊) On the eastern edge of
town, the rooms in this professionally run
hotel are spread over two buildings. Some
single rooms are a little small, but the spa-
cious doubles are easily the best in town and
look like luxury yacht cabins, with air-con,
hot water, shiny wooden floors, stylish mod-
ern bathrooms and private balconies.

🍴 Eating

Lara's Planet INTERNATIONAL $$
(☎ 8637-1440; muelle, 200m O, 80m N; mains
US$6-10; ⊙ 7am-10pm; 🔊🍴) Nonguests are
very welcome to come for a meal at Lara's
Planet, where there's a gorgeous bamboo
terrace overlooking the river. Owner Nata-
sha will cook from an international menu
that includes burgers and several vegetarian
options (try the Lara's Planet special penne
with spinach, peanuts, white cheese and
fresh tomatoes from the garden).

**Casa de Huésped
Chinandegano** NICARAGUAN $$
(☎ 2583-3011; muelle, 240m E; meals US$5-7.50;
⊙ 7am-10pm) The fish here is served perfectly
grilled and glazed with garlic butter, gar-
nished with a tomato salad dressed in vin-
egar and plated with golden *tostones* (fried
green plantains). Tasty chicken dishes are
also served and the service is just as good
as the food.

Comedor Vanessa NICARAGUAN, SEAFOOD $$
(☎ 5772-5283; muelle, 2c E; meals US$6-8;
⊙ 11am-9pm) Perched over the roaring rapids is one of the river's better restaurants.
It serves a variety of fish, chicken, beef and
pork dishes and also pours a damn fine *mi-
chelada* (beer with Bloody Mary and margarita fixings) if you're in the mood.

❶ Getting There & Away

From El Castillo, *colectivo* boats leave for San
Carlos (US$3, three hours) via Boca de Sábalos
(US$0.50, 30 minutes) at 5am Monday to Friday,
with an additional sailing at 6am on Monday,
Tuesday, Friday and Saturday. Fast *pangas* to
San Carlos (US$5, two hours) via Boca de Sába-
los (US$1, 20 minutes) leave at 5:15am, 7am,
9am, 11am and 2pm daily.

Slow boats to San Juan de Nicaragua (US$10,
seven to eight hours) pass El Castillo around
9am on Tuesday, Thursday and Friday. Express

services (US$20, four to five hours) pull into the
dock at around 8am on Tuesday and Friday.

Reserva Biológica Indio-Maíz & the River Eastward

Nicaragua's second-largest tract of intact
primary forest, the 2606-sq-km Reserva
Biológica Indio-Maíz, lies about 15 minutes downriver from El Castillo. Thanks
to a combination of geographic isolation
and inaccessibility, the reserve was spared
the chainsaw under Somoza, and once the
Sandinistas took power it was legislated
as a reserve and has remained off-limits to
tourists.

Tragically a devastating forest fire in April
2018 destroyed over 50 sq km of forest, in
what has been termed Nicaragua's worst-
ever environmental disaster. To add insult to
injury, Costa Rica's attempt to send backup
firefighters and equipment was rejected by
the Nicaraguan government, the cause of
great anger locally.

Today the vast majority of the reserve
remains restricted, but it's possible to visit
some small designated sections where you
can hike among 50m-tall, 500-year-old cathedral trees, search for brightly colored
tree frogs and watch monkeys leap through
the canopy.

◉ Sights

**Reserva Biológica
Indio-Maíz** WILDLIFE RESERVE
The second-largest tract of intact primary
forest in the country, the Reserva Biológica
Indio-Maíz is a vast wilderness and a hugely
important rainforest ecosystem with incredible biodiversity. While much of the reserve
is restricted, it is possible to visit certain
parts of it. In 2018 horrific fires caused by
outsiders, who were clearing forest illegally
to use as farmland, destroyed huge areas of
ancient forest and it will take decades for
the reserve to recover.

🛏 Sleeping

⭐ **Basecamp Bartola** TENTED CAMP $$$
(☎ 8919-6320, 8433-4664; indio.maiz@gmail.com;
Comunidad Bartola; per person incl meals, transport
& activities US$60-175) 🌿 Run by the tiny com-
munity of Bartola, 6km up the Río Bartola,
this groundbreaking project run as a co-
operative by 26 local families is the future
of sustainable tourism in the region. Visitors
sleep in tents (complete with mattresses and

towels folded into swans) on wooden platforms overlooking the thick canopy of the Indio-Maíz across the river.

Refugio Bartola LODGE **$$$**
(☑8873-8586, 8376-6979; www.facebook.com/ref ugiobartola; s/d/tr incl meals US$70/110/156) 🖉
Set at the confluence of Ríos San Juan and Bartola, opposite the ranger post, this rustic wooden lodge and private reserve is the superlative option in the region for true nature lovers. Accommodations are in simple, breezy wooden rooms with high ceilings set around a lovely garden overlooking the river where agoutis rummage around oblivious to your presence.

❶ Getting There & Away

Most visitors to the Indio-Maíz explore its eastern reaches on a day trip form El Castillo. While riverboats heading to San Juan de Nicaragua from San Carlos and El Castillo can drop you at either Bartola or Aguas Frescas, you'll need to bring a local guide with you if you want to enter the reserve.

The hotels on the far bank of the Río Bartola offer transport from El Castillo.

San Juan de Nicaragua

POP 1100

Dripping wet and laid-back, one of the Americas' oldest European towns feels like it's on the edge of the world. There are wide streets but no cars to fill them, and life is slow, even though the fishers and boatbuilders work hard and want for little. How could they, in a town surrounded by rivers teeming with fish, virgin rainforest and jungle-fringed lagoons? They are cash poor, however, which leads to spotty electricity (carry a flashlight) and water service (shower when you can), and the locals dream of a tourism gold rush that, while theoretically possible, is unlikely to ever happen in this far-flung corner of Nicaragua. For now, however, it remains a dream destination for those comfortable on the edge.

◎ Sights & Activities

More and more visitors are using San Juan de Nicaragua as a base to explore the nearby Reserva Biológica Indio-Maíz. There are few hiking trails – you will spend most of your time exploring the spectacular jungle by boat.

WORTH A TRIP

GREYTOWN

San Juan de Nicaragua's traditional tourist attraction is the swampy remains of Greytown, a short boat ride (up to four people US$80 to US$100, three to four hours) across the bay. Here you'll find a few solid building foundations and four very interesting cemeteries: one for the British (including those members of Horatio Nelson's doomed campaign who were not fed to the sharks), another for Catholics, a third for North Americans and the last for Freemasons from St John's Lodge.

You can spend a glorious six hours cruising between enormous yet hidden **Laguna Silica**, **Laguna de San Juanillo** and **Laguna La Barca** (US$200 for up to four people), which are surrounded by primary rainforest. You will occasionally hack through humid forests with machetes just to get from place to place; you may spot manatees.

Dedicate a day or two to the jungle and its original Rama inhabitants along the Río Indio, which runs parallel to the Caribbean Sea before turning inland and winding deep into the heart of the reserve.

On a typical one-day trip (US$200 for up to six people) you'll cruise upriver through **Laguna Manatee** to **El Encanto**, where there is a hiking trail in the forest. On the way back you'll stop on the beach at El Cocal, where you'll sip fresh coconut water on the sand.

The two-day version (US$400 per group) continues upriver to **Makenge**, a Rama community where you'll spend the night in the solar-powered communal house or in a homestay with a Rama family. The next morning hike four hours through primary forest to **Canta Gallo (Piedras Basálticas)**, a basalt outcrop that local Rama say is the foundation of an ancient pyramid. Others say the formation is geological in nature. Either way, it's stunning and the hike is tremendous. It's also possible to extend this trip to three or four days in the jungle in order to fully explore the area.

Prices listed here are those charged by experienced professional tour guides with well equipped boats and include transport, guides, meals, accommodations and refreshments. It's possible to find cheaper deals if you're prepared to go in a smaller boat with a less powerful engine and bring your own food.

In addition to being top jungle guides, the Gutiérrez family at **Hotelito Evo** (☑8350-5145, 8624-6401; vohotel@yahoo.es; muelle, 150m O, 20m S; s/d incl breakfast US$15/30) offer kayaking trips (US$25 per person, minimum two people) and nocturnal alligator-spotting tours (US$25 per person, minimum two people) in the waters around town. They also offer half-day sportfishing trips (US$180 per boat).

🛏 Sleeping

★**Hostal Familiar**   GUESTHOUSE $$
(☑8660-6377, 8446-2096; muelle, 300m S; r with river view US$25, s/d US$15/20) A fantastic choice offering two big, breezy wooden rooms right on the river and a couple of cheaper options upstairs. The attached restaurant serves outstanding fresh seafood (imagine shrimp and snook steaks braised in coconut-tomato sauce).

Río Indio Lodge   LUXURY HOTEL $$$
(☑in Costa Rica 506-2231-4299, in the US 866-593-3168; www.therioindiolodge.com; s/d incl all meals & drinks US$231/370, sportfishing packages US$2650; ❄☞) This enormous, and at times deserted, sportfishing lodge has an epic perch on the Río Indio, surrounded by rainforest with views of Vanderbilt's dredge ruins. It offers opulence in the middle of the jungle with fine wooden rooms linked by elevated walkways through the jungle. Prices include some local tours. Don't expect to drop in; you'll need to reserve well in advance.

✗ Eating

There are just a couple of places to eat in town. There's usually fish on the menu alongside standard Nica fare of *gallo pinto* with pork, chicken or beef.

Soda El Tucán   NICARAGUAN $
(muelle, 100m S; mains US$4.50; ⊘6:30am-9:30pm) Centrally located and easy to find, this cheery wooden diner will do just fine. The menu is simple: chicken or fish, grilled or fried, but it's one of the few places you

can always find a meal in town. It also rents cheap rooms out the back.

ℹ Information

There are no banks or ATMs in San Juan and no businesses in town accept cards – bring enough funds from San Carlos. Free wi-fi is available 24 hours in the small kiosk outside the telecommunications center.

ℹ Getting There & Away

AIR

San Juan de Nicaragua's airport is located across the bay, next to the Greytown ruins. La Costeña flies from Managua via Ometepe and San Carlos to San Juan (one way/round trip US$110/165) at noon on Thursday and Sunday, returning at 1:35pm the same days. The airline has no office in San Juan town, so you'll need to purchase your round-trip ticket online or before you arrive. There is also no public transport from the airport to San Juan, but Hotelito Evo offers a water taxi service for US$10 per person (minimum two people) – call before you arrive to arrange a pick up.

BOATS

Slow boats leave from San Carlos for San Juan de Nicaragua (US$10.50, nine to 12 hours) at 6am on Tuesday, Thursday and Friday stopping in Boca de Sábalos at 8:15am and El Castillo around 9am. Fast boats leave San Carlos for San Juan de Nicaragua (US$20, seven to eight hours) at 6am Tuesday and Friday stopping in Boca de Sábalos and El Castillo one hour or 90 minutes later respectively.

Slow boats return from San Juan de Nicaragua at 5am Thursday, Saturday and Sunday. Fast boats return at 5am Thursday and Sunday.

There is a fairly regular *panga* service between San Juan and Bluefields (US$32, three hours) leaving on Wednesday mornings and returning on Fridays. Note that this is a long trip in a small boat on the open ocean that oscillates between uncomfortable and spine shattering depending on the swell. You'll probably also get soaked; bring plastic bags for your luggage. When the sea gets high, the boat is sometimes unable to depart, so don't count on this service if you have a tight schedule.

Otherwise, it is occasionally possible to pay for a ride on a local boat that is making the trip, but these journeys often involve delayed departures, breakdowns, fuel shortages and a really rough ride.

Understand Nicaragua

Nicaragua Today

As of April 2018, Nicaragua has been descending into chaos. A series of clashes between protesters and pro-government supporters over president Daniel Ortega has led to hundreds of deaths. Ortega ignited a firestorm when he attempted to reform social security and welfare benefits. Though the reforms were eventually rescinded, protesters called for the divisive leader to step down. Ortega refused and has approved the use of deadly force against anyone deemed a threat to political stability.

Best on Film

La Yuma (2009) Portrays the challenges facing a female boxer from Managua.

Palabras Magicas (2012) The making of modern Nicaragua through the lens of a young filmmaker.

Walker (1987) Biopic of a megalomaniac, with music by the late, great Joe Strummer.

Carla's Song (1996) British bus driver falls for Nicaraguan dancer in exile, in a romantic drama with a political edge.

Pictures from a Revolution (1991) The story behind the famous war images of Susan Meiselas.

Best in Print

Blood of Brothers (Stephen Kinzer; 1991) Fascinating account of revolution and war.

The Country Beneath My Skin (Gioconda Belli; 2002) Autobiography by revolutionary poet.

Selected Poems of Rubén Darío (translated by Lysander Kemp; 2001) Bilingual anthology of the master poet's best work.

The Jaguar Smile (Salman Rushdie; 1987) Accessible insider's look at the Sandinistas during the revolution.

Tycoon's War (Stephen Dando-Collins; 2008) Documents the epic battle between imperialists Vanderbilt and Walker.

2018 Descent into Chaos

Traditionally, Nicaraguan presidents have only been permitted to serve two five-year terms. But 2014 saw the decision to abolish term limits. The implications for Daniel Ortega were significant – in November 2016, he won the presidential election, securing a third term, and his wife, Rosario Murillo, was made vice-president.

Since then Ortega has been busy dismantling Nicaragua's institutional democracy by assuming full control of the military, the police, and all branches of government. Opposition parties have been hobbled and rumors abounded that Ortega expected his wife to succeed him as president.

Ortega's hostile takeover of Nicaragua's political system was made possible by an alliance between the government and COSEP, Nicaragua's council of business chambers. However, matters came to a head on April 18, 2018, when Ortega decided to overhaul the social security system without consulting either COSEP or the workers due to be adversely affected.

On April 12, hundreds of university students took to the streets to protest the government's slow response in tackling a massive wildfire that destroyed 50 sq km of forest in Nicaragua's top biodiversity hotspot, Indio Maíz Biological Reserve. On April 18, students joined thousands of other protesters who pushed back against Ortega's attempt to increase social security taxes and reduce pension benefits for the elderly.

Police used live bullets against the crowd and Nicaragua has been descending into chaos ever since. At the time of writing, 325 people had been killed and over 2000 injured by riot police and government-funded Sandinista paramilitaries. There has been looting of businesses, and Ortega has blamed everything on foreign agitators and organized crime.

Violent clashes have taken place in Masaya, Managua, Granada and León, among other places, with citizens digging up their streets, setting up road blocks, barricading their neighborhoods against the riot police and fending them off with rocks and homemade mortars. On May 30, police and snipers opened fire on a peaceful Mother's Day demonstration, leaving 16 people dead and 88 people injured.

Talks between the government, COSEP, student representatives and the Catholic Church have broken down and are unlikely to resume. More than 600 anti-government supporters have been imprisoned and thousands of Nicaraguans have fled the country.

The economy is crumbling and Ortega's power seems to only be growing despite worldwide pressure. In February 2019, the government announced it would put into effect the same reforms that sparked the protests in the spring of 2018.

The Economy

Since the Frente Sandinista de Liberación Nacional's (Sandinista National Liberation Front; FSLN) return to power in 2006, the government's economic and social programs had been bankrolled through aid, loans and subsidized fuel from its partner in the Alianza Bolivariano por Las Americas (ALBA), Venezuela.

And while the hunger eradication programs, new houses and other initiatives have been well received by FSLN supporters, the lack of transparency of their funding has caused controversy.

Furthermore, since the death of Venezuelan president Hugo Chavez in 2013, Venezuela's economy has descended into chaos due to falling oil prices. Consequently, aid to Nicaragua has dried up, which has been one of the main catalysts for the anti-government protests and deadly violence that has gripped Nicaragua since April 2018.

At the time of writing, there was a great deal of uncertainty about the economy, with tourists fleeing the country, businesses shutting down, people withdrawing their savings, and a 24-hour national strike looming, following the negotiations breakdown between Ortega and the Catholic Church.

The Nicaragua Canal

The Hong Kong Nicaragua Development (HKND) Group put up the original investment for the 286km interoceanic canal but initial excitement, mostly about job creation and an expected uptick in the economy, has been tempered by practical concerns. Though work commenced in late 2014, progress has halted several times, hinging on the fluctuating fortunes of HKND frontman, the Chinese billionaire Wang Jing. At the time of writing, construction had stalled altogether, partly because the project is projected to cost US$50 billion and the money has dried up, and partly because there is strong opposition to the project on the part of the *campesino* (farmer) movement which, incidentally, has been very active since April 2018 in putting up road blocks to deter police and government forces.

POPULATION: **6.3 MILLION**

AREA: **130,375 SQ KM**

GDP: **US$13.81 BILLION**

GDP GROWTH: **4.9%**

INFLATION: **3.89%**

UNEMPLOYMENT: **4.44%**

if Nicaragua were 100 people

69 would identify as Mestizo
17 would identify as White
9 would identify as Black
5 would identify as Indigenous

belief systems
(% of population)

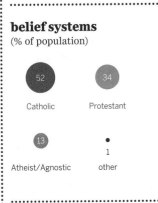

52 Catholic

34 Protestant

13 Atheist/Agnostic

1 other

population per sq km

USA   MEXICO   NICARAGUA

≈ 1 person

History

For such a small country, Nicaragua has played a disproportionate role in modern history. In the midst of cold-war tensions, the young Sandinista revolutionaries' reforms captured the attention of the most powerful governments on earth and unleashed scandals in the corridors of power. But when the bullets stopped flying, the world lost interest, leaving the clean-up, reconstruction and return to power of the Sandinistas like a captivating sequel that never made it to the big screen. Until now.

Indigenous Nicaragua

Pre-Hispanic Nicaragua was home to several indigenous groups, including the ancestors of today's Rama, who live on the Caribbean coast, and the Chorotegas and Nicaraos, on the Pacific side. The latter spoke a form of Náhuatl, the language of the Aztecs. Many Nicaraguan places retain their Náhuatl names.

By 1500 BC Nicaragua was broadly settled, and though much of this history has been lost, at least one ancient treaty between the Nicarao capital of Jinotepe and its rival Chorotegan neighbor, Diriamba, is still celebrated as the Toro Guaco.

European Arrival

In Situ Petro-glyphs

....

Isla Ometepe

....

Chagüitillo

....

Islas Solentiname

....

Villa Sandino

Although Columbus stopped briefly on the Caribbean coast in 1502, it was Gil González de Ávila, sailing north from Panama in 1522, who would really make his mark here. He found a chieftain, Cacique Nicarao, governing the southern shores of Lago de Nicaragua and the tribe of the same name. The Spaniards thus named the region Nicaragua.

Nicarao subjected González to hours of inquiry about science, technology and history. González famously gave Nicarao an ultimatum: convert to Christianity, or else. Nicarao's people complied, a move that in the end only delayed their massacre at the hands of the Spanish; other native groups were thus warned.

Six months later González made Cacique Diriangén the same offer; Diriangén went with 'or else.' His troops were outgunned and eventually destroyed but inspired further resistance. After conquering four Pacific

TIMELINE	6000 BC	450 BC	AD 800
	Indigenous groups construct elaborate burial sites out of clam shells at Monkey Point on the Caribbean coast.	The agricultural revolution arrives in the region, with the introduction of domesticated corn, yucca and beans. Soon after, trade links with modern-day Colombia and the USA are established.	Petroglyph and statue fever sweeps across Nicaragua. Many designs, including an Aztec calendar and representations of the deity Quetzalcóatl, herald the arrival of one of Nicaragua's most important migrations.

tribes – 700,000 Chorotega, Nicarao, Maribios and Chontal were reduced to 35,000 in 25 years – the nations of the central highlands halted Spanish expansion at the mountains, with grim losses.

Colonial Settlement

The main Spanish colonizing force arrived in 1524, founding the cities of León and Granada. Both were established near indigenous settlements, whose inhabitants were put to work.

The gold that had attracted the Spaniards soon gave out, but Granada and León remained. Granada became a comparatively rich colonial city, with wealth due to surrounding agriculture and its importance as a trading center. It was also a center for the Conservative Party, favoring traditional values of monarchy and ecclesiastical authority. Originally founded on Lago de Managua, León was destroyed by volcanic eruptions in 1610 and a new city established some 30km northwest. León in time became the center for radical clerics and intellectuals, who formed the Liberal Party and supported the unification of Central America and reforms based on the French and American Revolutions.

The difference in wealth between the two cities, and the political supremacy of León, led to conflicts that raged into the 1850s, at times erupting into civil war. The animosity stopped only when the capital was moved to the neutral location of Managua.

Enter the USA

In 1893 a Liberal general named José Santos Zelaya deposed the Conservative president and became dictator. Zelaya soon antagonized the US by seeking a canal deal with Germany and Japan. Encouraged by Washington, which sought to monopolize a transisthmian canal in Panama, the Conservatives rebelled in 1909.

After Zelaya ordered the execution of two US mercenaries accused of aiding the Conservatives, the American government forced his resignation, sending marines as a coercive measure. Thus began a period of two decades of US political intervention in Nicaragua. In 1925 a new cycle of violence began with a Conservative coup.

The Conservative regime was opposed by a group of Liberal rebels including Augusto C Sandino, who recruited local peasants in the north of the country and eventually became leader of a long-term rebel campaign resisting US involvement.

Somoza Era

When the US marines headed home in 1933, the enemy became the new US-trained Guardia Nacional, whose aim was to put down resistance by Sandino's guerrillas, as is documented in Richard Millett's

There were forgers even before coins were invented and the currency was cacao – they'd scoop the cacao out of the seed and replace it with mud.

HISTORY COLONIAL SETTLEMENT

1502	1523	1635	1821
Christopher Columbus sails down the Caribbean coastline looking for a sailing route to the Pacific Ocean, landing briefly in the north. First recorded contact between indigenous inhabitants and Europeans.	The main colonizing force arrives, led by Francisco Fernández de Córdoba. Cities of León (later moved after being buried by Volcán Momotombo) and Granada are founded soon after.	The first European settlement on the Atlantic coast is founded near Cabo Gracias a Dios by the grandly named British Providence Company.	Nicaragua, along with the rest of Central America, becomes independent from Spain and briefly joins the Mexican Empire and then the United Provinces of Central America.

comprehensive study *Guardians of the Dynasty: A History of the US-Created Guardia Nacional de Nicaragua and the Somoza Family*. This military force was led by Anastasio Somoza García.

Somoza engineered the assassination of Sandino after the rebel leader was invited to Managua for a peace conference. National guardsmen gunned Sandino down on his way home. Somoza, with his main enemy out of the way, set his sights on supreme power.

WILLIAM WALKER: SCOUNDREL, VAGABOND, PRESIDENT

In a country long accustomed to land grabs, none has managed to shine quite like Tennessee-born William Walker, an infamous figure in Nicaragua.

A quiet, poetry-reading youth who had mastered several languages and earned various degrees by early adulthood, Walker first worked as a newspaper editor, publishing outspoken pieces condemning slavery and the interventionist policies of the US at the time.

A different type of opportunity presented itself in 1848 when the Treaty of Guadalupe was signed, ceding half of Mexico to the US and leaving the other half dangling temptingly. Walker quickly jettisoned his liberal ideals, got a posse of thugs together, and embarked on a career in filibustering.

Taken from a Dutch word meaning pirate, filibustering came to mean invading a country as a private citizen with unofficial aid from your home government.

Walker's foray into Mexico was as successful (he managed to take the Mexicans completely by surprise, raise his flag and name himself president before getting chased back over the border) as it was short-lived.

Word of Walker's derring-do spread, though, and it wasn't long before the city of León offered him the job of taking care of their pesky rivals in Granada.

With another rag-tag group of mercenaries at his command, Walker arrived in San Juan del Sur in September of 1855 and, aided by the element of surprise and the latest in US weaponry, easily took Granada.

Walker's Liberal Leónese employers must have felt a bit put out when he decided not to hand over Granada after all, but instead stayed around, got himself elected president, reinstituted slavery, confiscated huge tracts of land and led an ill-fated invasion attempt on Costa Rica.

These audacious actions, supported by then US president Franklin Pierce, inspired something that has been sadly lacking ever since – Central American unity. But even getting chased back to the US by every Central American army in existence didn't dampen Walker's imperial ambitions. He returned to Nicaragua once more (and was sent briskly packing) before trying his luck in Honduras, where the locals put him before a firing squad in September 1860.

1838	1853	1857	1912
In abandoning the regional union, Nicaragua becomes the first modern Central American nation to declare independence.	Filibuster William Walker arrives in San Juan del Sur, taking Granada quickly and installing himself as president soon after.	In an effort to quell continued fighting between León and Granada, the small fishing village of Managua is named capital. The fighting stops, but the rivalry continues to this day.	The USA, in response to a rebellion against the corrupt Conservative administration, sends 2500 marines to Nicaragua, thus beginning two decades of US-dominated politics in Nicaragua.

Overthrowing Liberal president Sacasa a couple of years later, he established himself as president, founding a family dynasty that would rule for four decades.

After creating a new constitution to grant himself more power, Somoza García ruled Nicaragua for the next 20 years, sometimes as president, at other times as a puppet president, amassing huge personal wealth in the process (the Somoza landholdings attained were the size of El Salvador).

After his assassination in León, Somoza was succeeded by his elder son, Luis Somoza Debayle. In 1967 Luis died, and his younger brother, Anastasio Somoza Debayle, assumed control, following in his father's footsteps by expanding economic interests throughout Nicaragua.

Rising Opposition

In 1961 Carlos Fonseca Amador, a prominent figure in the student movement that had opposed the Somoza regime in the 1950s, joined forces with Colonel Santos López (an old fighting partner of Sandino) and other activists to form the Frente Sandinista de Liberación Nacional (Sandinista National Liberation Front; FSLN). The FSLN's early guerrilla efforts against Somoza's forces ended in disaster for the fledgling group, but over the years it gained support and experience, turning it into a formidable opponent.

On December 23, 1972, at around midnight, an earthquake devastated Managua, leveling more than 250 city blocks. The *Guardian* newspaper reported that, as international aid poured in, the money was diverted to Anastasio Somoza and his associates, while the people who needed it suffered and died. This dramatically increased opposition to Somoza among all classes of society.

By 1974 opposition was widespread. Two groups were widely recognized – the FSLN (Sandinistas) and the Unión Democrática de Liberación, led by Pedro Joaquín Chamorro, popular owner and editor of the Managua newspaper *La Prensa,* which had long printed articles critical of the Somozas.

In December 1974, the FSLN kidnapped several leading members of the Somoza regime. The government responded with a brutal crackdown in which Carlos Fonseca was killed in 1976.

Revolution & the FSLN

For a Nicaraguan public tired of constant violence, the last straw was the assassination of Chamorro. As street violence erupted and a general strike was called, business interests and moderate factions in the Frente Amplio Opositor (Broad Opposition Front; FAO) unsuccessfully attempted to negotiate an end to the Somoza dictatorship.

Hyperinflation played havoc with Nicaragua's currency during the war. Immediately prior to Somoza's fall, one US dollar would buy you 10 córdobas but it eventually peaked at 3.2 million to the dollar. The Sandinistas were unable to print money fast enough and resorted to stamping existing bills with new values.

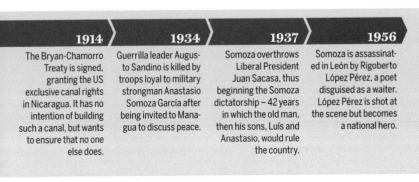

1914	1934	1937	1956
The Bryan-Chamorro Treaty is signed, granting the US exclusive canal rights in Nicaragua. It has no intention of building such a canal, but wants to ensure that no one else does.	Guerrilla leader Augusto Sandino is killed by troops loyal to military strongman Anastasio Somoza García after being invited to Managua to discuss peace.	Somoza overthrows Liberal President Juan Sacasa, thus beginning the Somoza dictatorship – 42 years in which the old man, then his sons, Luís and Anastasio, would rule the country.	Somoza is assassinated in León by Rigoberto López Pérez, a poet disguised as a waiter. López Pérez is shot at the scene but becomes a national hero.

By mid-1978 many major towns were rising up against government forces. The Guardia Nacional's violent reprisals garnered further support for the Sandinistas.

The FAO threw in its lot with the Sandinistas, whom they now perceived as the only viable means with which to oust the dictatorship. This broad alliance formed a revolutionary government provisionally based in San José, Costa Rica, which gained recognition and arms from some Latin American and European governments.

Thus the FSLN was well prepared to launch its final offensive in June 1979. The revolutionary forces took city after city, supported by thousands of civilians. On July 17, as the Sandinistas were preparing to enter Managua, Somoza fled the country. He was assassinated by Sandinista agents a year later in Asunción, Paraguay. The Sandinistas marched victorious into Managua on July 19, 1979.

They inherited a shambles. Poverty, homelessness, illiteracy and inadequate health care were just some of the problems. An estimated 50,000 people had been killed in the revolutionary struggle, and perhaps 150,000 more were left homeless.

Trying to salvage what it could of its influence over the country, the USA (under President Jimmy Carter) authorized US$75 million in emergency aid to the Sandinista-led government.

However, by late 1980 it was becoming concerned about the increasing numbers of Soviet and Cuban advisers in Nicaragua and allegations that the Sandinistas were supplying arms to leftist rebels in El Salvador.

Contra War

After Ronald Reagan became US president in January 1981, relations between Nicaragua and the US began to sour. Reagan suspended all aid to Nicaragua and, according to the Report of the Congressional Committees Investigating the Iran-Contra Affair, by the end of the year had begun funding the counterrevolutionary military groups known as Contras, operating out of Honduras and Costa Rica, despite the US maintaining formal diplomatic relations with Managua.

Oliver North, coarchitect of the Iran-Contra scheme and the man whom Ronald Reagan called 'an American hero,' is now a TV host and video-game consultant.

Most of the original Contras were ex-soldiers of Somoza's Guardia Nacional, but as time passed, their ranks filled with disaffected local people. Honduras was heavily militarized, with large-scale US-Honduran maneuvers threatening an invasion of Nicaragua. The Sandinistas responded by instituting conscription and building an army that eventually numbered 95,000. Soviet and Cuban military and economic aid poured in, reaching US$700 million in 1987.

A CIA scheme to mine Nicaragua's harbors in 1984 resulted in a judgment against the US by the International Court of Justice. The court found that the US was in breach of its obligation under customary inter-

1961	1967	1972	1974
Diverse guerrilla groups, inspired by the Cuban revolution and united by their opposition to the Somozas, combine to become the Frente Sandinista de Liberación Nacional (FSLN).	Luis Somoza Debayle dies, and his younger brother, Anastasio Somoza Debayle, assumes control of the country.	A devastating earthquake hits Managua, killing more than 6000 people and leaving 300,000 homeless. Somoza embezzles international relief funds, fomenting support for the FSLN.	The FSLN kidnaps several members of the Somoza regime, exchanging the hostages for ransoms and the freeing of political prisoners.

national law not to use force against another State and ordered it to pay repatriations to the Nicaraguan government; the Reagan administration rejected the findings and no payments were ever made.

Shortly afterward, the *New York Times* and *Washington Post* reported the existence of a CIA-drafted Contra training manual promoting the assassination of Nicaraguan officials and other strategies illegal under US law, causing further embarrassment for the Reagan administration.

Nicaraguan elections in November 1984 were boycotted by leading non-Sandinistas, who complained of sweeping FSLN control of the nation's media. The Sandinistas rejected the claims, announcing that the media was being manipulated by Contra supporters (*La Prensa*

TEN WHO SHAPED NICARAGUA

President Violeta Barrios de Chamorro (president 1990–96) The first female president in the hemisphere pulled together a fractured nation.

Cacique Nicarao Along with Cacique Nagrandano (for whom the Llanura Nagrandano, or northwestern plains, are named) and Cacique Diriangén (still remembered on La Meseta), wise Nicarao gave the nation his name.

President Daniel Ortega (president 1984–90, 2007–present) Sandinista-turned-authoritarian who waited 17 years for another bite at the presidential apple and whose present presidential term has brought deadly violence back to the streets of Nicaragua.

Rubén Darío Began busting rhymes at age 12 and went on to become the favorite poet of a poetry-obsessed nation.

Carlos Fonseca Cofounder of the Frente Sandinista de Liberación Nacional (Sandinista National Liberation Front; FSLN). The martyred, intellectual hero of the Sandinista revolution, felt by many to represent its true ideals.

US President Ronald Reagan (president 1981–89) Together with political philosopher Jeanne Kirkpatrick, Secretary of State Alexander Haig Jr and Colonel Oliver North, Reagan masterminded the Iran-Contra debacle.

Augusto C Sandino His somber silhouette still dominates the Managua skyline, and his refusal to back down dominates the Nicaraguan collective consciousness.

Costa Rican President Oscar Arías Sánchez (president 1986–90, 2006–10) Architect of the 1987 peace accords that finally brought peace to Central America. Picked up a Nobel Prize for his efforts.

The Somozas A dynasty of Nicaraguan dictators, the first installed by the US military, and the last deposed more than four decades later by popular revolution.

William Walker The Tennessean who thought he could take on Central America but ended up in front of a Honduran firing squad.

1976	Jan 1978	Aug 1978	1979
The government responds to FSLN kidnappings and attacks with a brutal crackdown in which FSLN co-founder Carlos Fonseca is killed.	A general strike is declared following the assassination of newspaper editor and Somoza critic Pedro Joaquín Chamorro. Moderates unsuccessfully attempt to negotiate an end to the Somoza dictatorship.	FSLN occupies the Palacio Nacional, taking more than 2000 hostages and securing release for 60 imprisoned Sandinistas. There are uprisings in many towns. Guardia Nacional responds by shelling cities.	At the end of seven years of guerrilla warfare and 52 days of all-out battles, Sandinistas march on Managua. Anastasio Somoza flees the country on July 17 – the revolution is victorious.

eventually acknowledged receiving CIA funding for publishing anti-Sandinista views). Daniel Ortega was elected president with 63% of the vote, and the FSLN controlled the National Assembly by a similar margin.

In May 1985 the USA initiated a trade embargo of Nicaragua and pressured other countries to do the same. The embargo lasted for five years, helping to strangle Nicaragua's economy.

With public opinion in the US growing wary of the war, the US Congress rejected further military aid for the Contras in 1985. According to the congressional report into the affair, the Reagan administration responded by continuing to fund the war through a scheme in which the CIA illegally sold weapons to Iran and diverted the proceeds to the Contras. When the details were leaked, the infamous Iran-Contra affair blew up.

After many failed peace initiatives, the Costa Rican president, Oscar Arías Sánchez, finally came up with an accord aimed at ending the war. It was signed in Guatemala City in August 1987 by the leaders of Costa Rica, El Salvador, Nicaragua, Guatemala and Honduras. Less than a year later, the first ceasefire of the war was signed by representatives of the Contras and the Nicaraguan government at Sapoa, near the Costa Rican border.

Polls & Peace

By the late 1980s the Nicaraguan economy was again desperate. Civil war, the US trade embargo and the inefficiencies of a centralized economy had produced hyperinflation, falling production and rising unemployment. As it became clear that the US Congress was preparing to grant the Contras further aid, Daniel Ortega called elections that he expected would give the Sandinistas a popular mandate to govern.

The FSLN, however, underestimated the disillusionment and fatigue of the Nicaraguan people. Economic problems had eclipsed the dramatic accomplishments of the Sandinistas' early years: redistributing Somoza lands to small farming cooperatives, reducing illiteracy from 50% to 13%, eliminating polio through a massive immunization program and reducing the rate of infant mortality by a third.

The Death of Ben Linder by Joan Kruckewitt is a painstaking investigation (incorporating declassified CIA documents) into the assassination of Linder, the first US citizen to die at the hands of the Contras.

The Unión Nacional Opositora (UNO), a broad coalition of 14 political parties opposing the Sandinistas, was formed in 1989. UNO presidential candidate Violeta Barrios de Chamorro had the backing and financing of the USA, which had promised to lift the embargo and give hundreds of millions of dollars in economic aid to Nicaragua if UNO won. The UNO took the elections of February 25, 1990, gaining 55% of the presidential votes and 51 of the 110 seats in the National Assembly, compared with the FSLN's 39. Ortega had plenty of grounds for complaint, but in the end he went quietly, avoiding further conflict.

1980s	1984	1985	1990
Opposition fighters known as the Contras carry out nationwide attacks. With US funding, the Contras grow in number to 15,000; the FSLN responds by implementing compulsory military service.	Daniel Ortega is elected president with 63% of the vote. The FSLN controls the National Assembly by a similar margin.	Daniel Ortega takes power in his first five-year term – a term that Nicaragua's Supreme Court will later rule doesn't count toward his term limits.	Violeta Barrios de Chamorro beats Daniel Ortega in presidential elections. Ortega cedes power graciously. The process of national reconciliation begins as the Contra War and US-led economic embargo end.

Politics in the 1990s

Chamorro took office in April 1990. The Contras called a heavily publicized ceasefire at the end of June. The US trade embargo was lifted, and foreign aid began to pour in.

Chamorro faced a tricky balancing act in trying to reunify the country and satisfy all interests. Economic recovery was slow; growth was sluggish and unemployment remained stubbornly high. Nevertheless, in 1996, when Nicaragua went to the polls again, the people rejected the FSLN's Ortega and opted for former Managua mayor Arnoldo Alemán of the PLC, a center-right liberal alliance.

Alemán invested heavily in infrastructure and reduced the size of the army by a factor of 10, but his administration was plagued by scandal, as corruption soared and Alemán amassed a personal fortune from the state's coffers, earning himself a place on Transparency International's list of the top 10 corrupt public officials of all time. Meanwhile, however, the Sandinistas had their own image problems, as the ever-present Ortega was accused by his stepdaughter of sexual abuse. In a gesture of mutual self-preservation, Ortega and Alemán struck a sordid little deal, popularly known as *el pacto* (the pact), which *Time* magazine reported was designed to nullify the threat of the opposition, pull the teeth of anti-corruption watchdogs and guarantee Alemán immunity from further investigation.

Sandinista diehards felt betrayed by Ortega's underhanded dealings, but many still believed in their party, and Ortega remained an important figure.

Daniel Ortega's 2006 presidential comeback featured its very own theme song – a Sandinista version of the John Lennon classic 'Give Peace a Chance'. Oh, the irony.

Sandinista 2.0

After losing three successive elections, FSLN leader Ortega returned to power in the November 2006 elections, capitalizing on disillusionment with neoliberal policies that had failed to jump-start the country's economy and an *el pacto*–sponsored law that lowered the threshold for a first-round victory to 35% of the votes (Ortega received 38%).

Taking office in January 2007, Ortega proclaimed a new era of leftist Latin American unity, leaving the USA and some international investors a little jumpy. The early days of Ortega's presidency were a flurry of activity, with Nicaragua's energy crisis seemingly solved via a deal with Venezuela's Hugo Chávez, and Ortega pledging to maintain good relations with the USA while at the same time courting closer ties with US archrival Iran.

But as the Ortega government found its feet, there was no sign of radical land reforms or wave of nationalizations that the business sector had dreaded and some die-hard FSLN supporters had hoped for.

1996	2001	2006	2008
Voters go to the polls again, once more rejecting the FSLN's Ortega, opting instead for former Managua mayor Arnoldo Alemán of the PLC, a center-right liberal alliance.	Enrique Bolaños is elected president by a small margin. After 11 years of trying to make a comeback, it is Ortega's third defeat.	After three failed bids, Ortega regains the presidency with 38% of the vote. He seeks closer ties with left-wing governments in Venezuela, Bolivia and Cuba.	The Electoral Council bans two opposition parties. The FSLN sweeps countrywide municipal elections, which are widely denounced as fraudulent resulting in a reduction in foreign aid.

Ortega for the most part followed the economic course set by the previous government and continued to honor Nicaragua's international financial obligations.

The first test for Nicaraguan democracy under the new Ortega government surfaced in 2008, with countrywide municipal elections. The FSLN claimed victory in over 70% of municipalities, when it had come to power with only 38% of the vote. Opposition forces claimed widespread voter fraud and *La Prensa* labeled the election 'the most fraudulent elections in Nicaraguan history.'

Nevertheless Ortega weathered the storm and by the end of his return term was able to point to solid economic growth alongside the reintroduction of free health care and education among the achievements of his government.

FSLN Nicaragua

Between 2008 and 2018 Ortega and the FSLN worked hard to cement their power in the country, establishing an increasingly autocratic state maintained by generous social welfare programs in the Venezuelan style. Despite Ortega's age and poor health (he was at this time first reported to be suffering from lupus, preventing many public appearances), the activities of government became more and more focused on him and his wife, Rosario Murillo, who many increasingly saw with unease as Ortega's preferred successor.

Unlike the austere Ortega, his wife enjoyed a reputation for her lavish tastes, which became the stuff of legend to the Nicaraguan public, who marvelled at her never repeated outfits and imperious personal style. Increasingly Murillo became the public face of the government, making announcements, chairing cabinet meetings and heading the Citizen Power Councils (Consejos de Poder Ciudadano), the all-important network of local organizations channeling food and other government assistance to the local population. The Ortega's extended family rose to positions of power throughout the government and came to dominate many Nicaraguan businesses too, prompting many local observers to compare the family rule of the Ortegas to that of the hated Somozas.

In 2014, Ortega managed to remove term limits to the presidency, thanks to a court system now full of his own appointees. This cleared the way for his third term following the presidential elections of 2016, in which he faced limited opposition as the most popular candidates from other parties were disqualified from running. Ortega received a landslide victory with some 72% of the votes, although the election was described as 'flawed' by the US government. Most significantly of all, Murillo became his vice president, cementing her succession should Ortega die in office.

2011	2014	2016	2018
After the FSLN-dominated Supreme Court overturns a constitutional ban on successive terms, Ortega wins reelection with an increased majority.	Nicaragua's Congress abolishes presidential term limits and a long-held rule that victorious presidential candidates must win 35% of the vote, sparking public protests.	Current president Daniel Ortega wins reelection again, this time by a landslide margin, securing 72% of the vote.	Nicaragua is brought to a standstill by outbreaks of deadly violence when President Daniel Ortega unleashes riot police and Sandinista thugs on largely unarmed protesters.

Nicaraguan Way of Life

Nicaraguans strike a wonderful balance of pride and humility. While many live in poverty and even the middle classes struggle to make ends meet, when asked about their country, most prefer to highlight its rich culture and natural beauty than dwell on the difficulties. And while the nation's distinct ethnic groups have their own cultures, all Nicaraguans are united by their laid-back style, great sense of humor and an openness that manifests itself in their love of socializing.

The National Psyche

Nicaragua has a fierce cultural streak and prides itself on homegrown literature, dance, art, music and cuisine. This spiritual independence is a holdover not only from the revolution and Contra War, but back to Spanish colonization, when indigenous nations won limited autonomy at enormous personal cost.

Though ideological divisions between former Contras and Sandinistas recently seemed to have been addressed and worked through, it seems that the ongoing political unrest of 2018 will lead to yet another generation of Nicaraguans to suffer the trauma of violence. Opinions differ about the original Sandinista years and, no doubt, in time to come, they will differ about the events that are unfolding today, but resilience and the ability to deal with adversity with humor is very much a part of who Nicaraguans are.

Attitudes differ from place to place. Residents of the English- and Miskito-speaking Atlantic coast rarely consider themselves part of Nicaragua proper, and many would prefer to be returned to the British Empire than suffer further oppression by the 'Spaniards' on the other side of the country. The cattle ranchers of the central highlands resist interference from the federal government, while coffee pickers in Matagalpa and students in León are willing to walk to Managua to complain to the government if they perceive that an injustice has been done.

Many of Managua's retired old school buses have been converted into buses *pelones* (bald buses) – open-air party buses that give residents without vehicles the chance to cruise the streets of the city in the evening.

Lifestyle

Nicaragua is a country in motion. One in five Nicas live outside the country, most in the USA, Costa Rica and Honduras. Waves of migration to the cities, which began in the 1950s, have created a population that is 59% urban. Most internal immigrants are young women, and most go to Managua; men tend to follow the harvest into rural areas and the surrounding countries. Regular jobs are difficult to find, and more than half of employed Nicaraguans are in the 'informal sector' – street vendors, cleaners, artisans – without benefits or job security.

While a strong sense of community permeates all strata of Nicaraguan society, there's a marked difference in mindsets between urban and rural dwellers. The young and the educated in big cities such as Managua, León and Granada have more disposable income, much greater exposure

Stunning Pearl Lagoon's handful of ethnic fishing villages are home to Miskito, Creole and Garifuna people who have lived and traded with one another for more than 300 years.

to social media and global trends and a keen interest in what's happening in the world. Life in smaller towns is more laid back and steeped in tradition, with a strong culture of hospitality (you will be fed until you burst!), with everyone taking a keen interest in everyone they know in lieu of soap operas. The *campesino* lifestyle is simpler still, and means long hours and hard physical labor. Visiting extended family is pretty much the only respite from the constant work, but there's also a strong sense of self-sufficiency from the living you make from farming.

Despite the country's Catholic background, couples often live together and have children without being married, especially in larger cities. Nicaraguans are generally fairly accepting of the LGBT community, although the community is still fighting for full legal recognition.

Wealth is distributed unequally, with the moneyed elite living much as they would in Miami or elsewhere. For the vast majority of Nicaraguans, however, just putting food on the table is a daily struggle, with over 50% living below the poverty line in rural areas and perhaps a third of the country subsisting on two meals or fewer per day; almost one-fifth of children are at risk of problems relating to malnutrition, while in the Atlantic regions that figure is around 30%.

However, when hitting the streets, even the poorest Nicaraguans will generally always appear in clean, freshly pressed clothes, which is why they find 'wealthy' backpackers in smelly rags so amusing.

Economy

Nicaragua's solid grounding as an agricultural nation is a blessing and a curse. While the average *campesino* (farmer) will generally have something to eat, the sector as a whole is vulnerable to a range of threats. Plunging world commodity prices, natural disasters and environmental factors such as soil degradation and water shortages are all problems that Nicaraguan farmers face regularly. Coffee remains Nicaragua's main agricultural export, followed by beef, shrimp, dairy products and tobacco. Industrial production, encouraged under the last of the Somozas, was all but destroyed by the war and is only now beginning to slowly pick up again. By far the biggest industry is textile and apparel production, but the cigar industry is growing rapidly and Nicaragua is the largest producer of premium cigars in the world (mostly for export rather than

FREE TRADE VS FAIR TRADE

In March 2006 Nicaragua ratified the Dominican Republic-Central America Free Trade Agreement (DR-CAFTA). An agreement between an economic superpower like the US and various struggling nations is always going to be controversial, and plenty of political mileage was made, but it's worth remembering that, in the end, the agreement was approved by liberals and Sandinistas alike.

The central question to any such agreement is this: who benefits? The US stood to gain from cheaper imports, wider markets, investment opportunities and access to cheap foreign labor, but what was in it for Nicaragua?

The short answer was exports, foreign investment and jobs. What *kinds* of exports, investment and jobs? Well, there's been a little spike in the export of primary products such as beef and sugar, but the biggest change to Nicaragua's economic landscape has been the spread of the *maquilladoras* (clothing assembly factories) across the country. These factories provide much-needed work (Nicaragua's underemployment rate runs at around 43%), but critics say the *maquilladoras* are no real solution – they set up in Free Trade Zones (Nicaragua has four), which aren't bound by Nicaraguan law, so they don't pay minimum wage or respect workers' rights. When exported, goods don't incur export duty, so Nicaragua ends up earning very little.

local consumption). Gold mining is another important industry. Tourism plays an increasingly important role in the economy, and it is here more than anywhere else that many see a bright future for Nicaragua.

By the end of the war, Nicaragua was a heavily indebted nation. In 1979 the departing dictator Somoza emptied the country's coffers. The incoming Sandinista government engaged in some shaky economic policies (including massive public spending financed by foreign lending), while the economy was being slowly strangled by the US trade embargo. In 2000 Nicaragua was included on the Heavily Indebted Poor Countries list, meaning that a large chunk of its massive foreign debt was canceled after it complied with a series of conditions set down by the World Bank and IMF. These measures – which included privatizing public assets and opening the economy to foreign markets – are highly controversial and it still remains to be seen whether Nicaragua's participation in the program will produce long-term gains for its citizens.

Before the crisis of 2018, things were looking promising. Nicaragua had the fastest-growing economy in the region after Panama, though at the time of writing, how much of a hit the country's various industries will take remains to be seen. One bright spot for urban, educated Nicaraguans is the increased outsourcing of jobs in the USA and Canada to Nicaragua in the fields of customer service, research, marketing, software development and call centers. Unlike other sectors of the economy, these white-collar jobs are less impacted by political unrest.

Population

With 6.3 million people spread across 130,375 sq km, Nicaragua is the second-least densely populated country in Central America after Belize. The CIA World Factbook estimates that 69% of the population is *mestizo* (of mixed ancestry, usually Spanish and indigenous people), 17% white, 9% black and 5% indigenous. The most recent census reports that just over 440,000 people describe themselves as indigenous: the Miskito (121,000), Mayangna/Sumo (9800) and Garifuna (3300), all with some African heritage, occupy the Caribbean coast alongside the Rama (4200). In the central and northern highlands, the Cacaopoeras and Matagalpas (15,200) may be Maya in origin, while the Chorotegas (46,000), the Subtiavas (20,000) and the Nahoas (11,100) have similarities to the Aztecs.

European heritage is just as diverse. The Spanish settled the Pacific coast, while a wave of German immigrants in the 1800s has left the northern highlands surprisingly *chele* (white, from *leche,* or milk). And many of those blue eyes you see on the Atlantic coast can be traced back to British, French and Dutch pirates.

The original African immigrants were shipwrecked, escaped or freed slaves who began arriving soon after the Spanish. Another wave of Creoles and West Indians arrived in the late 1800s to work on banana and cacao plantations in the east.

Sports

It's just not a weekend in Nicaragua without the crack of a baseball bat, but there really are other sports in the country. Football (soccer) is growing in popularity and is especially big in the north of the country. Boxing is also extremely popular and Nicaragua produces some champion pugilists, especially in the lower weight divisions.

Many towns have pickup soccer, baseball, volleyball and basketball games, and foreigners are usually more than welcome to join in. It's a fine opportunity to interact with the locals without worrying about the subjunctive tenses.

In Caribbean Nicaragua, domino tournaments are serious events with neighborhood clubs decked out in team T-shirts slamming down tiles in front of noisy spectators.

Cockfighting and bullfights, while considered controversial by many people, are still some of Nicaragua's most popular spectator sports, especially in rural areas. Alpha roosters with knives strapped to their feet slash each other apart in miniature bullrings while the spectators place bets and drinks copious amounts of moonshine.

Rodeos and bullfights generally take place during *fiestas patronales* (saints days). Though considerably less gory than their Spanish counterparts – it's illegal to use any weapons or kill the bull – if you're even moderately concerned about animal welfare, you might be unsettled by either event.

Most Nicaraguan TV stations have two types of news: a sensationalist ambulance-chasing edition featuring graphic portrayals of fights and accidents – usually displayed on the big screen at dinner time – followed by a far less popular political edition.

Media

International media-monitoring bodies have reported that freedom of the press in Nicaragua has deteriorated significantly under the Frente Sandinista de Liberación Nacional (Sandinista National Liberation Front; FSLN) government, although an independent media still operates in the country.

The current FSLN leadership are particularly media savvy and have made controlling the airwaves a priority. According to the *New York Times,* since returning to power, Daniel Ortega has invested heavily in media operations, while at the same time cutting government advertising in non-Sandinista outlets. The newspaper goes on to report that Ortega's children run television networks Multinoticias, Channel 6, Channel 8 and Channel 13, and that the FSLN leader now controls nearly half of Nicaragua's television outlets.

According to the Committee to Protect Journalists (CPJ), Ortega uses these media outlets to launch character attacks against his critics as part of an effort to marginalize independent media.

CPJ stated that one such example was directed at television journalist Carlos Fernando Chamorro, son of former *La Prensa* editor Pedro Joaquín Chamorro whose assassination by Somoza was one of the sparks of the revolution. Following the airing of reports on an extortion scheme involving the Sandinista party, Chamorro was formally investigated for money laundering. After a wave of domestic and international criticism,

TAKE ME OUT TO THE BÉISBOL GAME

Every Sunday, all over the country, from abandoned lots to the national stadium, there's one game that's got Nicaraguans obsessed.

Despite popular belief, baseball was big here even before the marines arrived in 1909 – their presence just gave the sport a shot in the arm. The first recorded series was played in 1887, when two Bluefields teams – Four Roses and Southern – battled it out over seven games. Four years later, baseball fever hit the Pacific coast and by 1915 there was a national championship.

While major-league Nica players are generally treated like royalty here, the majority dream of going to the US to join a long list of their countrymen, including Tony Chevez, Albert Williams, David Green, Porfirio Altamirano, Vincent Padilla, Marvin Bernard and, of course, Hall of Famer Dennis 'El Presidente' Martínez, who pitched more winning major-league games than any Latino and who had Nicaragua's national stadium, Estadio Dennis Martínez, named after him.

Games are played on Sunday in villages, towns and cities all over the country, but if you'd like to catch some major-league action, log on to http://lbpn.com.ni (in Spanish) for schedules. For even better atmosphere, check out the biennial Atlantic Series, which features teams from all over the Caribbean region playing off for a cup.

the charges were later dropped, however a police raid in January 2019 led him to exile in Costa Rica.

Despite Nicaraguan law stating that officials must supply accurate information to the media upon request, local journalists have reported restrictions in accessing government press conferences and officials, while those working for government-linked news outlets are given free reign. According to the CPJ, First Lady Rosario Murillo is like a virtual prime minister, managing all government communications; officials in the executive branch are permitted to talk to the press only with her authorization.

While the government controls many of the radio and TV stations, Nicaragua's two national daily newspapers – *La Prensa* and *El Nuevo Diario* – remain critical of the Ortega government (a fact the FSLN repeatedly alludes to when confronted with claims of censorship and media control). The former is your classic conservative rag – understandably railing against all things Sandinista. The latter (more classically a blue-collar publication) seems to draw a distinction between the old-school Sandinistas (whom it still vaguely supports) and the new-breed Danielistas (for whom it has very little patience).

As it consolidates its power and media empire, the Ortega government seems increasingly less inclined to tolerate independent opinion.

Religion

Although Nicaragua's majority religion is Catholic, Nicaraguan Catholicism retains many indigenous elements, as the decor and ceremonies of churches such as San Juan Bautista de Subtiava and Masaya's María Magdalena make clear. Liberation theology also made its mark on Nicaraguan Catholicism, influencing priest and poet Ernesto Cardenal to advocate armed resistance to the Somoza dictatorship. Publicly chastised and later defrocked by Pope John Paul II, Cardenal remains a beloved religious leader. Nicaragua's incredible selection of Catholic churches and fascinating *fiestas patronales* (saints days) remain highlights of the country.

On the Atlantic coast, Moravian missionaries from Germany began arriving in the early 1800s, and today their red-and-white wooden churches are the centerpieces of many Creole and Miskito towns. More recently, in the 1990s, more than 100 Protestant sects, most US-based and collectively referred to as *evangelistas,* have converted around 34% of the population; in fact, many of the foreigners you'll meet in rural Nicaragua are missionaries, who may try to convert you too.

Interestingly, around 13% of Nicaraguans say they are atheist or agnostic, which is unusual in Latin America.

Women in Nicaragua

Women, especially in rural sectors, are likely to work outside the home and do half of all agricultural labor. This stems in part from ideals espoused by the (original) Sandinistas, who considered women equal players in the remolding of the country, but also from necessity, as many men died or were maimed during the wars, or later emigrated to find work; after the Contra War, the country was more than 55% female. The strong women's movement is fascinating; check out *Boletina* at www.puntosdeencuentro.org to learn more.

Despite loud protests by many organizations, in 2006 Nicaragua passed a controversial law declaring abortion illegal even when the life of the mother is at risk. Women's groups say the law has led to the deaths of dozens of women and mostly affects the poor as the wealthy (including the daughters of politicians) are able to travel to other countries for medical attention without restrictions.

In traditional Miskito societies – mostly concentrated on Nicaragua's Caribbean coast – women own the farmland and plant crops.

Arts & Architecture

Nicaragua, as any book will tell you, celebrates literature, and particularly poetry, with appropriate passion, revering its writers with a fervor reserved for Hollywood stars in more developed countries. But it's not all about printed prose, Nicaragua also boasts a variety of homegrown musical genres, energetic dances and renowned painters all shaped by the nation's dominant themes of romance and rebellion.

Nation of Poets

Selected Poems by Rubén Darío (translated by Lysander Kemp) has verses from Nicaragua's most famous poet in the original on one page and in English translation on the facing page.

Poetry lies at the very heart of Nicaragua's cultural identity. Both major daily newspapers run a literary supplement in their Friday editions, high-school kids form poetry clubs, and any *campesino* (farmer) picking coffee in the isolated mountains can tell you who the greatest poet in history is: Rubén Darío, voice of the nation. They will then recite a poem by Darío, quite possibly followed by a few of their own.

Nicaragua is also home to the peculiar cultural archetype of 'warrior poets,' folks who choose to fight with both the pen and the sword. Among the most famous are Leonel Rugama, who held off the Guardia Nacional while hero Carlos Fonseca escaped; Rigoberto López Pérez, who assassinated the original Somoza in León; liberation theologian Ernesto Cardenal; and former Sandinista undercover agent, Gioconda Belli.

The nation's original epic composition, the Nica equivalent to *Beowulf* or *Chanson de Roland,* is *El Güegüense,* a burlesque dating from the 1600s. A morality play of sorts, it pits an indigenous Nicaraguan businessman against corrupt and inept Spanish authorities; using only his sly wit and a few multilingual double entendres, the Nica ends up on top.

León has been home to the nation's greatest poets, including Darío, Azarías H Pallais, Salomón de la Selva and Alfonso Cortés, the last of whom did his best work while going insane in Darío's childhood home. The most important modern writers include Pablo Antonio Cuadra, a former editor of *La Prensa,* and Ernesto Cardenal.

One of the few Nicaraguan writers and poets regularly translated into English is Gioconda Belli (www.giocondabelli.org), who was working undercover with the Sandinistas when she won the prestigious Casa de las Americas international poetry prize. Her internationally acclaimed work is both sexual and revolutionary, and is the best way to get a woman's-eye view of Nicaragua in the 1970s.

Music

Folkloric music and dance received a huge boost from the revolution, which sought to mine Nicaraguan culture for cultural resources rather than import more popular options, quite possibly at great cost. As a result, you'll probably be able to see a musical or dance performance during even a short visit, the most convenient being *Noches Verbenas,* held every Thursday evening at the Mercado Artesanías (National Artisans

RUBÉN DARÍO

To say that Rubén Darío is a famous poet is an outrageous understatement. The man is a national hero – his birthplace (Ciudad Darío), the national theater and the entire Cordillera Dariense mountain range are named after him.

Something of a child prodigy, Darío could read by age four (he'd polished off *Don Quixote* and various other classics by age 10) and had his first poetry published in León newspapers at age 12.

Deemed too 'antireligious' to be awarded a scholarship to Europe, Darío was sent to El Salvador at the age of 15. There he met and befriended Salvadorian poet Francisco Gavidia, whose work and teachings would have a profound influence on Darío's style.

Darío traveled extensively – to Chile, where he worked as a journalist and wrote his breakthrough piece, *Azul;* Argentina, where he became a leading member of the Modernist literary movement; and, last, to Europe, where he continued to write what Chilean poet Pablo Neruda called some of the most creative poetry in the Spanish language.

Darío was appointed Nicaragua's ambassador to France, then Spain, but such officialdom never slowed him down. His hard-drinking, womanizing lifestyle was by now legendary (and somewhat requisite for poets of the era), but it took its toll in 1914 when Darío contracted pneumonia. He recovered, but was left weak and bankrupt. Friends banded together and raised the money for him to return to Nicaragua. He died in León two years later, at the age of 49.

Market) in Masaya. Also check out cultural centers, close to the Parque Central in most larger towns, or at the municipal theaters in Granada, León and Managua, to see what's on. *Fiestas patronales* (saints days) are a good time to catch a performance, which in the northern highlands will likely have a polka component.

Perhaps the most important musical form is marimba, usually played on xylophones made of precious wood with names such as 'The Lovers,' 'Dance of the Black Woman,' and 'Fat Honey,' which you'll enjoy over a cold glass of chicha (mildly alcoholic corn beverage) at some shady parque central. The guardians of this and other traditional forms of Nicaraguan music are the Mejía Godoy brothers, whom you can (and should) catch live in Managua. Luis Mejía (the prince of salsa) is internationally renowned. Manifesto Urbano is another Nicaraguan music collective well worth checking out.

Marimba music was given a new sense of cool with the arrival on the scene of La Cuneta Son Machín (www.lacunetasonmachin.com), a cumbia-rock fusion group heavily influenced by traditional Nicaraguan sounds. If you get the chance, check out their energetic live performances.

On the Atlantic coast reggae and country are king but there are also homegrown sounds including upbeat Maypole music, which is often accompanied by spicy dance moves, and Miskito pop, heavily influenced by the electronic-keyboard music of rural churches, where many of the musicians learned to play.

Considering how few venues there are available for them to play, new talents are plentiful in Nicaragua. If you're looking for laid-back electronica, try Momotobo. Into alternative rock? Check out Nemi Pipali. Quirky bossa-pop fans should hunt down anything by Belén, while Division Urbana is probably the best of many groups doing the hard-rock thing. Manu Chao fans will probably like Perrozompopo, and for sheer lyrical beauty, floating melodies and electro-pop crossover, keep an eye out for discs by Clara Grun.

Famous Nicaraguan musician Carlos Mejía Godoy, who wrote theme songs for the Sandinista revolution, went on to sue the FSLN for improper use of those very songs.

Painting & Sculpture

The oldest artistic tradition in Nicaragua is ceramics, dating from about 2000 BC with simple, functional vessels, developing into more sculptural representations by around AD 300. By the time the Spanish arrived, Nicaraguan ceramics were complex, artistic and often ceremonial, and indicate a pronounced Aztec influence in both design and decoration. Remember that it's illegal (and lame) to remove pre-Columbian ceramics from Nicaragua.

Today, top-quality ceramics are most famously produced in San Juan de Oriente, which is known both for its precise replicas of pre-Columbian museum pieces and exquisite contemporary pieces that blend several ceramic styles; in Mozonte, near Ocotal; and at Matagalpa and Jinotega, which are renowned for their black ceramics.

Almost as ancient an art, stone carving probably became popular around AD 800, when someone realized that the soft volcanic basalt could be shaped with obsidian tools imported from Mexico and Guatemala. Petroglyphs, usually fairly simple, linear drawings carved into the surface of a stone, are all over the country, and it's easy to arrange tours from Isla de Ometepe, Granada and Matagalpa.

Stone statues, expressive and figurative, not to mention tall (one tops 5m) are rarer but also worth seeing; the best museums are in Granada and Juigalpa. Much finer stone statues are being produced today, using polished, translucent soapstone worked in the backyard workshops of San Juan de Limay, near Estelí.

Painting apparently arrived with the Spanish (though there's evidence that both statues and petroglyphs were once more vividly colored), the earliest works being mostly religious in nature; the best places to see paintings are in León, at the Museo de Arte Sacre and the Museo de Arte Fundación Ortiz-Guardián. The latter also traces Nicaraguan painting through to the present, including the Romantic and Impressionistic work of Rodrigo Peñalba, who founded the School of Beaux Arts, and the Praxis Group of the 1960s, led by Alejandro Arostegui and possessed of a heavy-handed social realism, depicting hunger, poverty and torture.

In the 1970s Ernesto Cardenal founded an art colony on the Islas Solentiname, an isolated group of islands in the southeast corner of Lago de Nicaragua, today internationally renowned for the gem-toned

> Gioconda Belli's *The Inhabited Woman* is well worth tracking down. It's a loosely political tale based partly on true events, but the magic here is in Belli's sensual, poetic prose.

THE PAINTING ON THE WALL

Nothing quite captures Nicaraguans' spirit, creativity and political sentiment like their love for murals. Often strikingly beautiful pieces of art in their own right, murals served a practical and political purpose in the days before the Sandinistas' Literacy Crusade, of broadcasting a message to an audience that was largely illiterate.

There are murals in all major cities, but the Sandinista strongholds of León and Estelí are standouts, where at one stage nearly every blank wall in the downtown was covered with colorful revolutionary messages. The area around the UCA university in Managua has some fine examples, too.

However, with the modernization of the cities, some of the best examples have been painted over, often with propaganda from multinational cell-phone networks.

Estelí has its own NGO teaching mural painting to children and teenagers, and is also home to a new movement of *muralistas*, who use more recognizable graffiti techniques but continue to paint the walls of the city with images of a social slant.

For a look at murals from around the country, check out the gorgeous coffee-table book *The Murals of Revolutionary Nicaragua* by David Kunzle.

CHURCHES OF NICARAGUA

Nicaragua hasn't always been this poor – in the 1960s Costa Ricans were sneaking across the border to work here. From the first days of the Spanish conquest through to the late 1800s, when Nicaragua controlled the only warm-water route between the world's two great oceans, this little country was a major power broker.

With cash to spare and a Catholic population to impress, the authorities constructed churches even devout atheists will enjoy. León may be the nation's pinnacle of religious architecture, but here are a few other must-sees.

Cathedrals of Managua The interior of the poignant, burnt-out husk of Managua's original cathedral is off-limits, but you're welcome to ponder the new cathedral's ultramodern domes: cooling towers for a divine nuclear reactor? Homage to Islam? Eggs hatching into a peaceful tomorrow?

Basílica de Nuestra Señora de la Inmaculada Concepción de la Virgen María Even Pope John Paul II visited the beautiful Virgen del Trono, patron saint of Nicaragua and mistress of La Gritería, the nation's most important religious event.

Templo de El Sauce Quite literally a pilgrimage-worthy destination; every January thousands come to see El Señor de Esquipulas, the Black Christ.

Moravian Church in Bluefields Faithfully rebuilt to its Victorian-era specs after Bluefields' utter destruction during Hurricane Juana; it's not just lovely, it's a symbol of hope and perseverance.

Iglesia Catedral San Pedro This baroque 1874 beauty, known for its twin bell towers, remains one of the country's most elegant churches despite its desperate need for renovation.

Templo Parroquial de San Rafael Arcángel This is religion as sensory overload, with beautiful architecture and truly amazing murals.

Nuestra Señora de Solentiname Ernesto Cardenal and the Solentiname community built this heartfelt and humble adobe church, its murals designed by children.

paintings and balsa-wood sculptures that so colorfully (and accurately) capture the tropical landscape. If you can't get to the islands yourself, try the Masaya markets, or any of the art galleries in Managua or Granada.

A more venerable form of the art is on display every Semana Santa in the Subtiava neighborhood of León, when 'sawdust carpets,' scenes painstakingly rendered in colored sawdust, are created throughout the neighborhood, and then swirled together as religious processions go by.

Theater & Dance

Traditional music, dance and theater are difficult to separate; all are mixed together with wild costumes to create spectacles that generally also have a religious component, plus plenty of fireworks. Pieces you'll see performed by street-side beggars and professional troupes include *La Gigantona,* with an enormous Spanish woman and teeny tiny Nicaraguan guy. Another common piece is *The Dance of the Old People,* in which an older gentleman woos a sexy grandma, but once she gives in, he starts chasing younger women in the audience.

Modern theater is not well developed in Nicaragua, and only major towns have performance spaces. There's a growing independent film scene, and you can catch very low-budget, usually documentary films, often with overtly feminist or progressive themes, at cultural centers – but never movie theaters, which show mostly Hollywood blockbusters.

To Bury Our Fathers by Sergio Ramírez – one of Nicaragua's most respected writers (and former Sandinista vice president) – is possibly the best fiction-based portrait of the Somoza years in print.

Architecture

The success of the Spanish conquest let the motherland finally break free of French architectural forms, such as Gothic architecture, and experiment with homegrown styles both at home and in the Americas.

Some of the earliest New World churches are a Moorish-Spanish hybrid called *mudéjar*, with squat silhouettes, wooden roofs and geometric configurations. Influenced by Islam as well as the Italian Renaissance are *plateresque* (elaborate silver filigree) on altars such as in El Viejo.

Baroque hit big in the mid-1600s, and was the most popular choice for major buildings over the next century. Primitivist baroque, featuring graceful but unadorned adobe and wood columns, and common in smaller colonial towns, was followed by full Spanish baroque style, with extravagant design (stone grapevines wending up massive pillars, for example), sometimes called *churriguera*.

The most famous examples of Spanish colonial architecture can be found in Granada and León, but colonial gems are scattered throughout the country.

Land & Wildlife

With more than 10,000 sq km of virgin forest, 19 active volcanoes, vibrant coral reefs, thriving populations of birds and butterflies, tropical fish, and various species of turtles, Nicaragua has been endowed with more than its share of natural beauty. Combine that with a low population density and very little industrialization and you'll discover that in Nicaragua, wilderness is never far away – and you'll have it mostly to yourself when you get there.

The Land

The formation of the Central American isthmus began about 60 million years ago, connecting the two massive American continents for the first time three million years ago. Marking the volcanic crush of the Cocos and Caribbean tectonic plates, the Maribios Volcanic Chain is one of the most volcanic places in the world.

There are 40 major volcanic formations, including 28 volcanoes and eight crater lakes, among them Reserva Natural Laguna de Apoyo, with hotels and private homes, Laguna Tiscapa in downtown Managua, and Laguna Asososca, with no development at all.

The region's appeal to early colonists increased as they realized that the soil was further enriched by this striking geological feature. Earthquakes and volcanoes are a part of life along the borders of the Caribbean and Cocos plates, and you'll find very few authentic colonial buildings that haven't been touched up since the 1500s.

Nicaragua's highest mountains, however, are metamorphic, not volcanic. Running down the center of Nicaragua like an opening zipper, they rise to their greatest heights as a granite chain contiguous with the Rocky Mountains and the Andes. They go by several names, including Cordillera Dariense (after Rubén Darío). Topped with cool cloud forests above 1200m, these refreshing regions are home to some of the best national parks and protected areas. Two of the most accessible reserves up north are Área Protegida Miraflor, close to Estelí, and Reserva Natural Cerro Apante, a hike from Matagalpa. Or go deeper, to Reserva Natural Macizos de Peñas Blancas, actually part of Bosawás, the largest protected swath of rainforest north of the Amazon. It's 7300 sq km of humid tropical and subtropical forest, also accessible by the largest river in Central America, the Río Coco (560km).

Nicaragua also has the two largest lakes in Central America, Lago de Managua (1064 sq km) and Lago de Nicaragua (8264 sq km), with more than 500 islands, some protected, as well as wonderful wetlands, such as Refugio de Vida Silvestre los Guatuzos.

The Caribbean coast is worlds apart, geologically as well as culturally, from the drier, more developed Pacific side. A vast eroding plain of rolling hills and ancient volcanic plugs, here's where around 90% of the country's rainfall ends up. This is the region with the wildest protected reserves and worst access – with very few exceptions, it's difficult and relatively expensive to travel here, as most transportation is by boat. The lowlands are remarkable for their dry pine savannas and countless wet-

Wildlife-watchers migrating to Central America should read L Irby Davis' *Field Guide to the Birds of Mexico & Central America* or Adrian Forsyth's *Tropical Nature: Life & Death in the Rainforests of Central & South America*.

lands and have four major river systems. The easiest way in is along the Río San Juan, a Unesco biosphere reserve.

Flora & Fauna

You can learn all you ever wanted to know (and probably a fair bit more) about Nicaragua's stunning biodiversity at www.bio-nica.info.

Nicaragua is home to about 1800 vertebrate species, including around 250 mammals, and 30,000 species in total, including 764 bird species (551 resident and 213 migratory).

Animals are slowly working their way northward, a migration of densities that will one day be facilitated by the Mesoamerican Corridor, a proposed aisle of shady protected rainforest stretching from Panama to Mexico. Other countries in on the agreement are just getting started on the project, but Nicaragua's two enormous Unesco biosphere reserves, Bosawás and southeast Nicaragua (Río San Juan), make up a significant chunk.

Animals

Most people are looking for monkeys, and there are three natives: big howler monkeys, smaller spider monkeys and sneaky capuchins. *Pizotes,* elsewhere called coatis, are the long-tailed, toothy-smiled rodents that are particularly bold on the Rivas peninsula. Several cats (pumas, jaguars and others) survive, but you probably won't see them. Baird's tapirs, 250kg herbivores, are another rare treat. At night you'll see hundreds of bats, including, maybe, vampire bats – which usually stick to livestock.

Birders are discovering Nicaragua, in particular the estuaries of the wild east coast, where migratory birds flock, starting in August and packing places like the Río San Juan and Islas Solentiname by September and October.

While Nicaragua has no endemic bird species of its own, 19 of Central America's 21 endemics are represented here, including the Nicaraguan grackle, endemic only to Nicaragua and northern Costa Rica. Nicaragua's spectacular national bird, the turquoise-browed motmot (*guardabarranco* in Spanish), has a distinctive notched tail.

Kingfishers, swallows, scarlet tanagers and Tennessee warblers are just a few of the birds that make their winter homes here. Local birds

---

DID THE EARTH MOVE FOR YOU?

Straddling two tectonic plates has had mixed results for Nicaragua. On the one hand, it's produced the spectacular Maribios chain and the rest of the 40 volcanic formations that make up western Nicaragua's dramatic skyline, providing geothermal energy, poetic inspiration and hiking opportunities galore.

On the down side, over the years volcanoes have blackened skies, changed landscapes and buried entire villages, not to mention the entire original city of León.

Nicaragua's position between the stationary Caribbean plate and the eastward-moving Cocos plate (the two are colliding at a rate of about 10cm per year) has produced some other geologic excitement as well – most of it spelling bad news for the locals.

Tension builds between colliding plates and is released in the form of earthquakes. Nicaragua gets rocked on a regular basis – the 1972 quake all but flattened Managua, which had already been hit hard in 1931. In 2000, two major quakes in two days leveled villages in the southwest.

When earthquakes happen at sea they cause tsunamis. Tsunamis were registered in 1854 and 1902, but the biggest one in recent history was in 1992, when waves of up to 10m pummeled the Pacific coastline, killing 170 people and leaving 130,000 homeless.

Slower (but no less dramatic) plate movement produced the Lago de Nicaragua – the theory being that the Pacific and Atlantic were once joined, but the upward thrust of earth caused by plate collision cut them off. Volcanic sedimentation and erosion then created the Pacific and Caribbean coastlines.

PARKS & RESERVES

About 17.3% of Nicaragua's land is federally protected as part of 78 wildlife areas. The system isn't even close to perfect, and problems with poaching and deforestation are rife. But the government has deemed it worth fighting for and is stepping up patrols in and around parks.

Nicaragua's national parks and reserves are unlike those in many other countries in that the majority have next to no facilities for visitors. Accommodations within park boundaries are rare; dedicated zones to pitch a tent even more so. There are very few marked trails, which makes hiring local guides even more important, and reliable maps of the reserves are also hard to come by.

The Ministry of the Environment and Natural Resources (Marena) administers most wildlife areas, often through other public and private organizations. There's a Marena office in most major towns, and while tourism is not its main job, staff may be able to find guides, transportation and lodging for more-difficult-to-access parks. They can at least point you toward folks who can help; it could be, for example, a women's organic coffee collective. Have fun!

Following are Nicaragua's main parks and reserves.

MAJOR PARK OR NATURAL AREA	FEATURES	ACTIVITIES
Parque Nacional Volcán Masaya	most heavily venting volcano in Central America, possible gateway to hell; lava tunnels; parakeets	driving to the edge of an active crater, birdwatching, hiking
Reserva Natural Volcán Concepción & Parque Nacional Volcán Maderas	1 island, 2 volcanoes: gently smoking Concepción & dormant Maderas, crowned in cloud forest	hiking, petroglyph hunting, swimming, kayaking
Reserva Biológica Indio-Maíz	epic riverboat rides, macaws, walking trees, frogs	canoeing, kayaking, hiking
Reserva de Biosfera Bosawás	largest reserve in Central America, indigenous villages	testing your limits, trail-free hikes
Reserva Natural Cerro Musún	quetzals, cloud forests, huge waterfalls, real trails	hiking, birdwatching, swimming
Área Protegida Miraflor	cloud forest reserve innovatively managed by agricultural cooperative: it's nature & culture!	milking cows, hiking, swimming in waterfalls, admiring orchids
Reserva Natural Cerro Tisey-Estanzuela	cloud forests, views across the Maribios Volcanic Chain, goat's cheese	hiking, swimming, eating cheese
Monumento Nacional Cañón de Somoto	the Río Coco is born – in the 'Grand Canyon' of Nicaragua	hiking, scrambling swimming
Reserva Natural Isla Juan Venado	sandy Pacific barrier island; mangroves, sea turtles, lagoons	boating, surfing, camping, swimming
Parque Nacional Archipiélago Zapatera	isolated islands covered with petroglyphs, ancient statues, small volcano, rustic accommodations	climbing, hiking, boating, amateur archaeology
Refugio de Vida Silvestre La Flor	leatherback & olive ridley turtles, primary dry tropical forest, beaches	surfing, camping, sea-turtle ogling
Reserva Natural Volcán Mombacho	volcanic views of Granada & Cocibolca, dwarf cloud forest, 100 species of orchid, fumaroles, butterfly garden	hiking, camping, riding in military transport
Reserva Natural Volcán Cosigüina	volcanoes, hot springs, crater lakes, macaws, archaeological sites	hiking, camping, swimming, thermal baths

are even more spectacular, including the red macaw, the yellow-chested oropendola (which hangs its ball-shaped nests from trees), the three-wattled bellbird of the cloud forests, with its distinctive call, and of course the resplendent quetzal.

The tiny strawberry poison dart frog *(Dendrobates pumilio)* is famous for its color morphs, with around 30 different color combinations identified.

Other winged attractions are the uracas, (huge blue jays) of Isla de Ometepe, the canaries living inside the fuming crater of Volcán Masaya and the waterfall of Reserva Natural Chocoyero–El Brujo, and the beautiful waterfowl of the Río San Juan.

Other visitors are more interested in the undersea wildlife, which on the Pacific side includes tuna, rooster fish and snook. Lago de Nicaragua and the Río San Juan have their own scaly menagerie, including sawfish, the toothy gaspar, mojarra, guapote and, most importantly, tarpon, as well as the extraordinary freshwater bull shark.

There are lots of reptiles, including five kinds of sea turtle, two kinds of iguana and several snakes. When walking in rainforests, keep your eyes peeled for the feared tercipelo (fer-de-lance, *Bothrops asper*), the most dangerous snake in Central America. Unlike many snakes found in the region, it is aggressive and often chooses to attack rather than flee danger. It's common in the jungles of the Río San Juan. Other poisonous snakes to look out for include the coral snake and the cascabel, a danger mostly to cattle.

Nicaragua also has plenty of scorpions, you'll find them living in dark corners (they love those atmospheric old houses), under rocks, in wood piles and on the beach. But while they look mean, their sting is not lethal and is more like a hardcore bee sting.

Insects, of course, make up the vast majority of species, including more than 1000 species of butterflies. Tarantulas are common, and be on the lookout for leaf-cutter ants, which raise fungus for snacks beneath massive anthills the size of VW Beetles. Acacia ants are hidden inside the hollow thorns of acacia trees – and the weird-looking woody balls in the trees? Termites.

Endangered Species

Nicaragua has numerous animal species on the endangered list – 200 mammals, 179 reptiles and 61 amphibians – including sea turtles and iguanas, both traditional food sources, as well as boa constrictors and alligators. Golden frogs and blood frogs, like amphibians across the globe, are also dwindling. Endangered birds include quetzals, peregrine falcons and macaws, with two of Central America's last viable populations in Reserva Natural Volcán Cosigüina and Reserva Bíologica Indio-Maíz. Several endangered or threatened mammals also make their homes here, including howler, white-face and spider monkeys; several kinds of cats, including jaguars and mountain lions; as well as aquatic species such as manatees and dolphins. Offshore fisheries are being, or have been, depleted of oysters, lobsters, green turtles and all manner of fish.

The Reserva Biologica Indio-Maíz, arguably Nicaragua's best-preserved rainforest, is home to more than 400 bird species, 200 reptile species and four species of wildcats (including puma and jaguar). It's a biodiversity hotspot with a greater number of animal species than the whole of Europe.

Plants

Nicaragua has four major environment zones, each with very different ecosystems and at least 12,000 species of plants spread across the four. Dry tropical forests are the rarest, as their location – below 500m, often right by the beach – and seven-month dry season make them perfect places to plant crops and build resort hotels. These forests are home to more than 30 species of hardwood, including precious mahogany.

Some dramatic species found in the ecosystem include strangler figs, which start out as slender vines and end up entombing the host tree in a dramatically buttressed encasement; the wide-spreading guanacaste of the endless savannas; and the pithaya, a branch-dwelling cactus with delicious edible fruit. Most plants lose their leaves by January, except in the largest remaining mangrove stand in Central America, partially preserved as Reserva Natural Isla Juan Venado and Reserva Natural Estero Padre Ramos, and crossing borders into El Salvador and Honduras.

Subtropical dry forests have sandy acidic soils and four species of pine tree (this is their southernmost natural border); they can be seen in the Región Autónoma Atlántico Norte (Northern Atlantic Autonomous Region; RAAN) and the Segovias.

Humid tropical forests are home to the multistory green canopies most people think of as classic rainforest. Conditions here are perfect for all plant life; almost no nutrients are stored in the soil, but there is a vast web just beneath the fallen leaves of enormous ceibas, formed of

SEE SEA TURTLES

At least five of the world's sea-turtle species nest on the shores of Nicaragua, all (theoretically) protected except for green turtles, present only on the Caribbean coast and legal to catch July to April.

The most common Pacific turtles, the *paslama* (olive ridley), are only 45kg and at their most impressive when invading a nesting beach (July to December, peaking in August and September) in flotillas of 3000 or more that storm ashore at the same time to lay. Often using the same beaches from November to February, *tora* or *baula* (leatherbacks) are the largest (450kg) and rarest of the turtles; because they eat jellyfish they often accidentally consume plastic bags and bottles, which kill them. Both species have edible, illegal and widely available eggs, considered by locals to be an aphrodisiac. In this book we do not list establishments that serve them, but if you see them on the menu, make your distaste known to the proprietors.

Carey (hawksbill) turtles – which nest May to November, peaking in September and October – are inedible and have lousy-tasting eggs; they're generally caught only for their shells, which are made into graceful, beautiful jewelry that we hope you won't buy. *Caguama* (loggerhead) turtles are also inedible, but their 160kg bulk often gets caught in the green-turtle nets.

Most tours only take you to see the eggs being laid, usually between 9pm and 2am, except during olive ridley arribadas (arrivals), when the beaches are packed day and night. Babies usually hatch about 60 days later, just before sunrise, then make their run to the sea; it's worth camping to see this. It's important never to touch the hatchlings. If you want to get more involved, you can hook up with grassroots turtle-conservation initiatives once you arrive, or contact the Cocibolca Foundation (www.mombacho.org) or the Wildlife Conservation Society (p225).

Places to see the turtles:

Refugio de Vida Silvestre La Flor (p134) Easily accessible from San Juan del Sur, La Flor's wildlife reserve has the best infrastructure, access and protection for its collection of olive ridley and leatherback turtles – plus camping!

Refugio de Vida Silvestre Río Escalante-Chacocente (p123) Access to this wildlife reserve is limited, but it's within walking distance of rapidly developing Playa El Astillero, so guided tours are just a matter of time.

Reserva Natural Isla Juan Venado (p155) Conveniently close to León, and olive ridleys show up right on time.

Reserva Natural Estero Padre Ramos (p165) Not much infrastructure, but there's a grassroots turtle-conservation program where you can volunteer.

Pearl Keys (p227) This group of expensive-to-access Caribbean islands hosts hawksbill turtles, while green turtles feed on the seagrass just offshore.

Other nesting sites on the Caribbean coast include the Miskito Keys, even more difficult to get to, and Río San Juan Wildlife Preserve, where green, hawksbill and leatherback turtles nest, and which can only be reached via San Juan de Nicaragua, a challenge in itself.

tiny roots, fungus and other assorted symbiotes that devour every stray nutrient as soon as it hits the ground.

Cloud forests are found above 1200m and are easily the most impressive (and rarest) biome, with epiphytes, bromeliads (a variety of high-humidity plant that grows in the branches of other trees), mosses, lichens and lots of orchids, which you can see at Reserva Natural Datanlí–El Diablo, among many other places.

The central subtropical forests of Boaco and Chontales have been largely devoured by cattle ranches, and while there are a few reserves, including Reserva Natural Sierra Amerisque, access to these areas is limited. Just to the east are the Caribbean lowlands, where there are swamps and thick, dense foliage that you can see on the riverboat ride from El Rama.

The Naturalist in Nicaragua by Thomas Belt was published in 1874 but is still available in reprints. As much about human life as the insects it studies, Charles Darwin called it 'the best of all natural history journals.'

Environmental Issues

With a developing economy, poor infrastructure and limited resources, Nicaragua faces a tough task in protecting the environment at the same time as lifting its citizens out of poverty.

While there has certainly been progress in recent times, the country still faces a variety of pressing environmental issues.

Deforestation

One of the biggest environmental issues facing Nicaragua is deforestation – the country has lost about 85% of its virgin forest cover since the colonial period. Since the end of the war, overall forest cover has fallen from 63% to 25%, although the rate of deforestation has slowed somewhat since 2000.

Deforestation is a major issue because it affects the entire biosystem. Root systems prevent erosion, thus keeping water supplies clean of soil runoff. Foliage supplies habitat for wildlife. Trees also help maintain climatic conditions. With climate change, scientists are noticing that pollinating insects are migrating to more favorable environments, leaving plants unpollinated.

Part of the problem is commercial logging. With the national economy struggling after the war, environmental issues took a back seat and liberal governments granted a number of forest concessions that contributed significantly to deforestation.

Illegal logging is another contributing factor, particularly on the Caribbean coast, where the environment ministry has limited resources to patrol and manage vast reserves with difficult access. Farmers illegally

NICARAGUA'S ECO-WARRIORS

If you see a large bunch of heavily armed men making their way through the canopy while you are in one of the country's nature reserves don't be alarmed, it's probably just the national army's Batallón Ecológico (BECO; Ecological Batallion).

And if you think Nicaragua is not serious about environmental protection, try telling these guys. Made up of some 700 soldiers, the battalion was created in late 2011 to combat deforestation and the illegal lumber trade, and has an annual budget of US$6.2 million. It sounds like a reality TV show, but these guys take their job very seriously.

And they've already had some success. Only months after their inception, they seized 112,000 cubic meters of illegally felled lumber in the Wawashang reserve on the Caribbean coast.

But the soldiers don't just carry guns, they also carry shovels so they are able to plant trees in their downtime. Together with the national forestry institute, they have created a network of 28 tree nurseries that will supply saplings for an ambitious reforestation plan in natural reserves affected by illegal logging.

NOT FOR SALE: NICARAGUA'S NATURAL RESOURCES

It's not ecologists or politicians but Nicaragua's indigenous communities that are the most fundamental players in the conservation of the disappearing forests of the Caribbean lowlands.

In 2001 the indigenous Mayangna of Awas-Tingni won a landmark battle when the Inter-American court ruled that the Nicaraguan government had violated the rights of the community by signing a deal with an Asian company for lumber extraction on 620 sq km of the community's land.

Shortly afterward, the national government passed a new autonomy law giving the indigenous communities of the Atlantic autonomous regions free determination of the use of their territories and the management of all natural resources found on their land. Nicaragua has since issued land titles to Awas-Tingni and many other indigenous groups in both the Región Autónoma Atlántico Sur (South Atlantic Autonomous Region; RAAS) and Región Autónoma Atlántico Norte (North Atlantic Autonomous Region; RAAN).

However, the issuing of titles without providing support to reclaim the lands has created problems for some of the communities. Many indigenous groups don't have the resources to patrol and protect their lands, which are subject to land invasions by mestizo farmers. Particularly affected are the indigenous Rama, who number less than 5000, but administer a large territory stretching from the Río San Juan to Bluefields Bay. Many Rama have been displaced by armed farmers who refuse to respect the titles.

Sustainable tourism is one way these communities are able to exercise ownership and derive profits from their lands without destroying precious natural resources.

clearing land for cultivation are thought to have been responsible for the 2018 fire that destroyed 50 sq km of Nicaragua's prime biodiversity hotspot, Reserva Biológica Indio-Maíz, believed to be Nicaragua's biggest environmental disaster to date.

Another major concern is the advance of the 'agricultural frontier' – the eastward migration by small farmers slashing and burning forest in the hope of carving out a subsistence livelihood. As the land often occupied is usually humid tropical forest, the soil generally only has enough oomph for two or three harvests, when the would-be farmer has to carve another farm from the jungle. Even more alarming are the wealthy land speculators who illegally clear large tracts of forest, then sell the land and move on.

The traditional dependence on firewood as a means of cooking and heating is another contributor to deforestation, especially affecting the dry tropical forests that surround densely populated regions.

The pine forests of Nueva Segovia took a huge hit from their natural enemy the pine bark beetle in late 1999, with an estimated 60 sq km of forest destroyed by the time it had finished its rampage. Recent hurricanes, particularly Hurricane Felix in 2007, have felled large numbers of trees in the Caribbean region and caused erosion and landslides in areas that have been deforested.

Agricultural Chemicals

Another pressing issue is the use of agricultural chemicals, which is widespread in Nicaragua, although nowhere near the levels of its famously 'green' neighbour Costa Rica. Any time you travel in rural areas you'll see farmers decked out with their pump backpacks ready to spray herbicides, fungicides, pesticides or fertilizers on their crops. Chemical use is poorly regulated and many of these products end up in the local river systems.

In 2010 there was a major fish kill in Pearl Lagoon that was unlike any that even older members of the community had seen. Many locals blamed agricultural run-off, either from the local palm oil plantations

The Mesoamerican Biological Corridor, the world's third-largest biodiversity hotspot, was established in 2008 to protect 106 critically endangered species. It stretches from Panama to Mexico.

or farmlands up the Río Grande de Matagalpa, although a government-sponsored investigation found no evidence of this.

Whether or not it was connected to the fish kill, environmentalists maintain that large-scale African palm plantations destroy critical habitat for endangered species and contribute to soil erosion.

Mining

While mining companies provide well-paid employment (even if profits do go straight out of the country), conservation groups maintain that cyanide, mercury and other industrial pollutants flow into the water table. The mines in Las Minas are of particular concern to environmentalists because they are located on the edge of the Reserva de Biosfera Bosawás, the largest nature reserve on the Central American isthmus. Small-scale mining in rural Chontales has led to mercury contamination in local water supplies around La Libertad.

Climate Change

Global warming is taking its toll in Nicaragua. Of the 18 original Pearl Keys, six have been swallowed by rising sea levels. A few are visible seasonally, but they are no longer the full islands they used to be. The smaller keys remain at risk.

Nicaragua is also particularly at risk to both flooding and drought. The extended dry period is often followed by heavy downpours. Flooding is made worse by deforestation in catchment areas.

Erratic rains have severely affected small-scale farmers, many of whom have no access to irrigation systems. However, a water-harvesting project in the north of the country is dramatically increasing yields among farmers in that region.

Positive Developments & More Information

It's not all ecological doom and gloom in Nicaragua. Environmental consciousness is growing within Nicaragua and there has been a variety of victories, on small and large scales.

The government has declared the environment a national priority and has made a measurable commitment to fighting deforestation and other pressing environmental issues. (Of course, with the violence gripping the country since summer 2018, environmental protection has once again taken a back seat).

Each municipality now has a department devoted to natural resources and, in general, respect for conservation laws has grown, while practices such as wildlife hunting and trafficking are on the downturn.

The government has also mobilized the army to protect endangered sea turtles and created a special ecological battalion to fight the illegal lumber trade.

Nicaraguans are starting to organize on a community level. Restaurant owners in San Juan del Sur have agreed not to offer menu items made from turtle eggs, and the communities in the Cordillera Volcanica act as volunteer firefighters when wildfires threaten the endangered dry tropical forest. There has also been a significant move toward growing organic coffee and vegetables in the north of the country, with many farming cooperatives adopting chemical-free methods.

For an overview of Nicaragua's protected areas, the issues they are facing and some of the efforts being made to save them, start with the official Ministry of Natural Resources website, www.marena.gob.ni. For general activism (some of it related to the environment), check www.nicanet.org.

Sustainable Harvest International works with indigenous communities to help them move away from slash-and-burn agriculture and toward more sustainable methods. For more info go to www.sustainable-harvest.org.

Survival Guide

Political Unrest & Traveler Safety

GOVERNMENT TRAVEL ADVICE

Australian Department of Foreign Affairs (www.smartraveller.gov.au)

British Foreign Office (www.gov.uk/foreign-travel-advice)

Canadian Department of Foreign Affairs (https://travel.gc.ca)

US State Department (http://travel.state.gov)

Since April 2018, when political unrest led to violent clashes between pro-government supporters and protesters, potential tourists to Nicaragua have been left asking the question: 'Should I travel?'

As of January 2019, while the use of deadly force by the paramilitaries and the police against anti-government protesters is at a minimum, the situation on the ground is still unpredictable. The general population is living with the consequences of the failed protests, with the police rounding up those suspected of having taken part in demonstrations. In December 2018, Ortega's government expelled international observers documenting alleged human rights abuses and shut down prominent NGOs and news outlets.

Notwithstanding all this, events on the ground do not pose a direct threat to visitors, who are unlikely to be exposed to political violence. Indeed, Ortega's government is keen to entice travelers back to help perpetuate the illusion of normality, which poses a dilemma for travelers: visit and indirectly aid the government or stay away and negatively impact the locals and an already fragile economy.

On the Ground

The security situation varies, depending on what part of the country you're in:

Managua Large police presence and harassment of locals suspected of anti-Ortega sympathies, with a greater chance of political demonstrations and deadly violence. The capital is not dangerous for visitors (unless you happen to be in the wrong place at the wrong time), but unsafe for local journalists and activists.

Masaya & Los Pueblos Blancos There has been an increase in visitor numbers to some of the Pueblos Blancos, but travelers should exercise full caution if visiting Masaya.

Granada Around 60% of hotels, restaurants and tour operators have closed down following the weeks of clashes between paramilitaries and anti-government protesters, but tourists are back in small numbers.

Isla de Ometepe Heavy police persecution during the peak of the crisis; multiple businesses have closed down. Few tourists now.

Pacific Beaches & San Juan Del Sur Escaped violent events. Some businesses have closed down, but surfers are coming back to the Pacific coast and tourism in San Juan del Sur is almost back to pre-April 2018 levels.

León Was the site of numerous clashes between students and riot police and has also suffered closures of many businesses, though visitors are beginning to trickle back.

Northern Highlands There have been two recent fatalities in Jinotega (paramilitaries killed in retaliation following violence against civilians).

Caribbean Coast & Corn Islands Avoided violence altogether.

Dos & Don'ts

➡ Don't take photos of police.

➡ Do be conscious of where you spend your money and try to support small local businesses.

➡ Don't get involved in demonstrations.

➡ Don't mistakenly look like a journalist by toting a large camera.

Directory A–Z

Accessible Travel

While Nicaraguans are generally accommodating toward people with mobility issues, and will gladly give you a hand getting around, the combination of cobbled streets, cracked sidewalks and stairs in pretty much every building can make life tough.

There are few regular services for disabled travelers and because of difficulties in finding suitable transport, it's easiest to go through a tour company. Vapues Tours (www.vapues.com) is an experienced local operator, specializing in accessible travel.

There are very few wheelchair-accessible toilets and bathrooms in Nicaragua, so bringing toilet-seat extensions, and wall-mountable mobility aids are highly recommended.

Download Lonely Planet's free Accessible Travel guides from http://lptravel.to/AccessibleTravel.

Accommodations

Ranging from five-star resorts to windowless shacks with shared latrines, you really have your choice of accommodations in developed A-list destinations such as Managua, Granada, León, San Juan del Sur and the Corn Islands. Top-end places start to thin out a bit as you head for the interior.

We divide hotels into categories according to price, then order by writer preference. The majority of hotel rooms in Nicaragua have their own bathroom, and in our listings we stipulate when the bathroom is shared, except of course in dorms where the bathroom is always shared.

Absolute peak season in Nicaragua is really only two weeks or so – Christmas and Easter, when entire towns book out and prices skyrocket. Outside that time, many hotels maintain prices year-round. If there is a high season, it's somewhere between November and March – outside the rainy months. We list prices for normal high season, not absolute peak.

Budget

Budget hotels, sometimes called *hospedajes,* are inexpensive compared to the rest of Central America. You can almost always get your own clean wooden room, with a window and a shared bathroom, for under US$6 per person per night. Double that and you get a bigger room

and a private bathroom. Prices are higher in A-list destinations, where there are always cheap dorm beds (US$8 to US$12) if you're traveling on a shoestring. In less-developed regions, you may be using bucket-flush toilets and bucket showers in this price range. Budget travelers should always bring candles and a flashlight (torch), just in case. If there's no mosquito net, just ask.

Midrange

In every major town there's a good midrange option, with clean, modern rooms, private bathroom, 24-hour electricity, running water and a nice setting or neighborhood. It tends to cost US$20 to US$35 for a double; tack on US$10 to US$15 for an A-list destination. Solo travelers usually get, at most, a 20% discount in this category. Also note that hotels in the midrange and top-end categories have a 15% tax added to the rate. In Granada and León there are a few characterful midrange hotels and B&Bs inside historic houses and mansions.

BOOK YOUR STAY ONLINE

For more accommodation reviews by Lonely Planet authors, check out http://lonelyplanet.com/hotels/. You'll find independent reviews, as well as recommendations on the best places to stay. Best of all, you can book online.

Top End

Luxury accommodations, where they exist, can be a good deal – the most expensive resort in the country clocks in at around US$280 per person, which certainly isn't for everyone, but is a steal compared to Costa Rica. Boutique hotels (with doubles going for US$70 to US$150), concentrated in Managua and Granada, generally have fewer than 10 rooms, and are creatively decorated with lots of little luxuries.

Other Accommodations

In rural areas, there may not be signed guesthouses, but almost all small towns have families who rent rooms. Ask at the *alcaldía* (mayor's office) for leads on weekdays, or any open business on weekends. Some communities have formalized homestays through Spanish schools (you don't need to be a student – just ask at the school) or as part of community-based alternative tourism, such as at Área Protegida Miraflor. Camping is available in a few private and natural reserves, and is also allowed for free on most less-developed beaches.

House- and room-sharing services have become popular in the most-visited destinations, such as Granada, León and Managua.

Along Nicaragua's Pacific coast there are numerous surfing lodges that offer

SLEEPING PRICE RANGES

Price indicators for sleeping options in our listings denote the cost of a standard double room with private bathroom.

$ less than US$20

$$ US$20–50

$$$ more than US$50

Climate

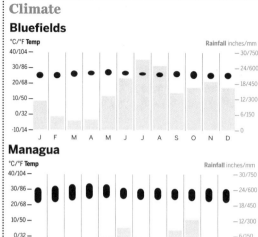

Bluefields

Managua

all-inclusive week-long surfing packages for around US$1200 to US$1400 per person. Expect breezy, comfortable digs and excellent food, though you may have to share your room if you're a solo traveler.

Activities

Nicaragua has almost unlimited opportunities for outdoor activities but few places to rent or buy equipment, so come prepared. Well-established sports include canoeing and kayaking, diving and snorkeling, hiking, fishing and surfing. Sports with particular promise for development (once there's money invested) include windsurfing, parasailing and kitesurfing.

Children

Nicaragua, like all Latin American countries, is relatively easy to travel around with children, despite the lack of infrastructure. Parents rarely pay extra for hotels, transportation or other services for youngsters small enough to fit comfortably on your lap, and even complete strangers will make an effort to entertain children.

Practicalities

➡ Some top-end (and very few midrange) hotels will be able to arrange a cot if you ask ahead. Otherwise the assumption is that the child will share your bed or use a single.

➡ Major car-rental companies can organize car seats if given enough notice, but don't count on it or expect one at the last minute. Car seats for Nicaraguan toddlers tend to be mom's lap.

➡ Breastfeeding in public is very common and should only really be avoided in places of worship.

➡ Baby formula is widely available, while disposable diapers are available in every *pulpería* (corner store) around the country.

➡ Baby changing tables are almost nonexistent.

Customs Regulations

When you leave Nicaragua, among the regular list of things that shouldn't be in your backpack are pre-Columbian or early colonial artifacts – you could end up in prison for trying to take these out of the country. On arrival, you can bring pretty much anything legal as long as it's obviously for personal use and not for resale within the country.

Electricity

**Type A
120V/60Hz**

Embassies & Consulates

Most embassies and consulates are located in Managua.

Canadian Embassy (Map p46; ☑2268-0433; http://travel. gc.ca/assistance/embassies-consulates/nicaragua; Calle Nogal 25, Los Pipitos, 2c E, Barrio Bolonia; ☺8am-noon & 12:30-4pm Mon-Thu, 7:30am-1pm Fri)

Costa Rican Consulate (Map p50;☑2276-1352; www.rree. go.cr; 28 Calle Sureste, del Seminole Plaza, 2c N, ½c O; ☺8am-4pm Mon-Fri)

Dutch Honorary Consul (☑8787-9067; Carretera a Los Nubes, del Club Terraza, ½c N; ☺7:30am-4:15pm Mon-Thu, 9am-1pm Fri)

French Embassy (Map p46; ☑2228-1056; www.amba-france-ni.org; 7 Calle Suroeste, Iglesia del Carmen, 1½c O; ☺7:30am-12:30pm & 1:30-4:30pm Mon-Thu, 7:30am-12:30pm Fri)

German Embassy (Map p50; ☑2255-6920; www.managua. diplo.de; Carretera a Masaya Km 5, Calle Erasmus de Rotterdam, del Colegio Teresiano, 1c S, 1c O; ☺8am-5pm Mon-Fri)

Guatemalan Embassy (☑2279-9606; Carretera a Masaya Km 11.5; ☺8am-noon & 1-4pm Mon-Fri)

Honduran Embassy (Map p50; ☑2270-2347; Edificio OPUS II, Modulo 103, semáforos Enitel Villa Fontana, 1c E, 50m N, Planes de Altamira No 3; ☺9am-5pm Mon-Fri)

Mexican Embassy (Map p50; ☑2278-4919; http://embamex. sre.gob.mx/nicaragua; Carretera a Masaya Km 4.5, Optica Matamoros, 25m E; ☺9am-5pm Mon-Fri)

Panamanian Embassy (☑2277-0501; https://panama.visahq. com/embassy/nicaragua; Reparto Villa Fontana, del Club Terraza, 1c E, ½c N; ☺9am-5pm Mon-Fri)

Salvadoran Embassy (☑2276-0712; https://el-salvador.visahq. com/embassy/nicaragua; Carretera a Masaya Km 9.5, Pasaje Los Cerros 142, Las Colinas)

US Embassy (☑2252-7100; https://ni.usembassy.gov; Carretera Panamericana; ☺9am-5pm)

Food

Many Nicaraguans eat lunch on the go, but the majority eat dinner at home, so outside tourist areas you may find eating options are reduced in the evening. Budget eateries including *comedores* (basic eateries), where you choose from a variety of ready-prepared dishes, and market stalls serve a limited range of filling dishes and set meals from US$2 to US$5. Also in this price range are *fritangas* (grills), which serve grilled meats and fried sides. Midrange eateries will have a decent-sized menu charging US$5 to US$10 per plate. Top-end establishments (mostly found in Granada, León, Managua and San Juan del Sur) will have an even better range, including dishes from around the world, costing more than US$10.

While both breakfast and dinner are often served with a big scoop of *gallo pinto* (a common meal of blended rice and beans), at lunch the rice and beans are usually separate – it's said to be more filling that way. Be sure to keep an eye out for local specialties including *nacatamales* (banana-leaf-wrapped bundles of cornmeal, meat, vegetables and herbs), *baho* (plantain and beef stew) and *rundown* (seasoned fish or

---

THE BASICS OF NICARAGUAN FOOD

Eating in Nicaragua is generally a casual affair, but in popular destinations there are restaurants where you should reserve ahead. In more remote locations you'll dine at your hotel or hostel.

Fritangas Often your best bet. Around dusk, locals light up simple grills – usually on or near the main plaza of town – and serve up steak, chicken, fried plantains and *gallo pinto* to hungry passersby.

Comedores Nearly every town in Nicaragua has one or two of these basic eateries, often featuring a set lunch plate.

Restaurants Some specialize in gourmet breakfasts, others double as bars in the evening.

EATING PRICE RANGES

Price indicators for eating options in our listings denote the cost of a typical main course.

$ less than US$5

$$ US$5–10

$$$ more than US$10

meat cooked in coconut milk with root vegetables).

Nicaragua has a wonderful array of fresh fruits, which are often sold cut up in small bags on the side of the road or as *refrescos naturales* (juices in water with sugar).

Health

Most visitors to Nicaragua travel without incident. However, it is a developing nation with poor infrastructure and a tropical climate, and so there are certain things you should be aware of to avoid an unnecessary visit to the doctor.

Stomach problems and diarrhea are the result of bacteria, viruses and parasites which may be present in contaminated food and water. Many other illnesses affecting travelers, such as infected bug bites, rashes and heat exhaustion, are the result of Nicaragua's tropical climate.

Other more serious diseases are carried by infected mosquitoes; bring clothes that provide protection against bites and repellent.

Particular attention should be paid to the Zika virus, which poses serious risks for pregnant women. Travelers who are pregnant should seek medical advice before making plans.

Medical checklist

Travelers should consider packing the following items:

➡ antidiarrheal drugs (eg loperamide)

➡ acetaminophen/ paracetamol (Tylenol) or aspirin

➡ anti-inflammatory drugs (eg ibuprofen)

➡ antihistamines (for hay fever and allergic reactions)

➡ antibacterial ointment (eg Bactroban) for cuts and abrasions

➡ steroid cream or cortisone (for poison ivy and other allergic rashes)

➡ bandages, gauze, gauze rolls

➡ adhesive or paper tape

➡ scissors, safety pins, tweezers

➡ thermometer

➡ pocket knife

➡ DEET-containing insect repellent for the skin

➡ permethrin-containing insect spray for clothing, tents and bed nets

➡ sunblock

➡ oral rehydration salts

➡ iodine tablets or a Steripen (for water purification)

➡ syringes and sterile needles

➡ tampons

➡ contraceptive pills

Insurance

Nicaragua is an unpredictable kind of place and infrastructure is poor, so travel insurance is always a good idea. Health care is generally cheap but in many places well below acceptable standards. Insurance is essential in the case of a big emergency, so that you can get transport to and treatment at the best private hospitals in Managua.

Make sure your policy covers emergency helicopter evacuation, full coverage for lost luggage and, if you're into it, extreme sports.

Worldwide travel insurance is available at www.lonelyplanet.com/travel-insurance. You can buy, extend and claim online any time, even if you're already on the road.

For long-term visitors, the **Hospital Metropolitano Vivian Pellas** (☎2255-6900; www.hospitalvivianpellas.com; Carretera a Masaya Km 9.75) in Managua offers a variety of monthly packages that include emergency coverage and discounts on appointments with specialists.

Internet Access

Internet cafes have pretty much disappeared with the proliferation of free wi-fi in most accommodations and a growing number of restaurants, bars and cafes. Some hostels have free computers for guest use. Top-end hotels mostly have 'business centers' and often connections for laptops and wi-fi in rooms. The internet icon used in our hotel listings signifies that the hotel has a computer with internet access available to guests free of charge.

Public wi-fi is still rare outside big cities and tourist hot spots. If you're staying for a while, consider purchasing a USB modem, which works well in larger cities but is often very slow in rural areas.

RECOMMENDED VACCINATIONS

There are no obligatory vaccinations for Nicaragua, with the exception of Yellow Fever for travelers arriving from affected areas. However, you may consider getting rabies, tetanus, typhoid and hepatitis shots before you set out. If planning on extended travel in the remote northwest corner of the Caribbean coast, it's worth considering taking anti-malaria medications.

Nicaragua's mobile data network is continually improving and works well in big cities but can be painfully slow in rural towns where everyone is trying to get online through one tower. SIM cards are cheap, and prepaid internet plans are also very affordable.

Language Courses

The northern highlands are a fine place to take Spanish classes due to the abundance of professional schools, pleasant climate and great immersion opportunities.

Escuela de Español Colibri (Map p194; www.colibrispanish-school.com; Parque Morazán, 1c S, ½c E; tuition per hour US$11-12), Matagalpa

CENAC Spanish School (Map p172; ☑2713-5437; www.spanishschoolcenac.com; Panamericana, btwn Calles 5a SE & 6a SE; per week with/without homestay US$195/120), Estelí

Legal Matters

Nicaragua's police force is notoriously corrupt and underpaid, and renowned for stopping foreign motorists, in particular, on minor or made-up charges.

For minor traffic violations or made-up offences your driver's license will normally be confiscated and you will need to go to the bank to pay your fine and then to the nearest police station to retrieve your document. This can be a pain if you are only driving through. Trying to bribe a traffic cop is a really bad idea and they're unlikely to let you off with just a warning. However, sometimes they'll 'do you a favor': instead of an official fine of US$100, they may refrain from holding onto your license if you pay them US$50. Another alternative for foreign visitors is this: if you are certain that it's a

shakedown (and it will be quite obvious if it is), you have the option of surrendering your license, not paying the fine, and simply replacing your license when you get home.

If you get caught with drugs or committing a more serious crime, it won't be that easy to get away from the law.

At the time of writing, the police were involved in a violent crackdown on Nicaragua's unarmed student protestors, using live bullets and a disproportionate amount of force.

LGBT Travelers

While consensual gay sex was decriminalized in Nicaragua in 2008, attitudes have taken a bit longer to change. As in most of Latin America, gay and lesbian travelers will run into fewer problems if they avoid public displays of affection, and ask for twin beds. That said, lots of Nicaraguan gays and lesbians flaunt their sexuality, so you probably won't have much difficulty figuring out the scene.

There is a small selection of gay and lesbian bars and clubs in Managua, an underground gay scene in Masaya and a vaguely tolerant scene in Granada, but apart from that, it's a pretty straight (acting) country.

Maps

Detailed maps are hard to find inside Nicaragua, so consider purchasing one before you arrive if you plan to get off the beaten track.

Intur (www.intur.gob.ni) Offices have a tourist-oriented regional and city map.

Ineter (Nicaragua Institute for Territorial Studies; ☑2249-3890; www.ineter.gob.ni; Av Xolotán, frente Dirección de Migración y Extranjería; ⊙8am-5pm Mon-Fri) Has the best selection of detailed maps in the country. Many are out of print, but bring a flash drive and they'll upload the files.

International Travel Maps & Books (www.itmb.ca) Publishes a detailed road map (US$12.95), but don't trust it completely for secondary roads.

Reise Maps (www.reise-know-how.de) Has a detailed road map (US$12) that's waterproof and tear-proof and reasonably accurate when it comes to rural roads.

Maps.me Extremely useful app for smartphones, with super-detailed GPS maps of the whole country. Reasonably accurate mapping of minor rural roads and hiking trails.

Money

Nicaragua's currency is the córdoba (C$), sometimes called a 'peso' or 'real' by locals. Córdobas come in coins of C$0.50, C$1 and C$5, and plastic bills of C$10, C$20, C$50, C$100, C$200 and C$500. Older plastic bills are flimsy and tear easily and some paper bills remain in circulation. Bills of C$200 and larger can be difficult to change; try the gas station.

US dollars are accepted almost everywhere, but they will be rejected if they are even slightly marked, ripped or damaged. Córdobas are usually easier to use, particularly at smaller businesses and anywhere off the beaten track – always keep at least 200 córdobas on you, preferably in smaller bills.

The córdoba is valued according to a fixed plan against the US dollar. Our listings give prices in US dollars (US$), as the costs in córdoba are more likely to fluctuate with the exchange rate.

ATMs & Banks

Cajeros automatícos (ATMs) are the easiest way to access cash in Nicaragua. They are available in most major towns and tourist regions.

Visa is the most widely accepted card followed by MasterCard. Amex is not generally accepted. Most Nicaraguan ATMs charge a fee (around US$3) on top of what your bank charges.

It's possible to organize a cash advance over the counter in many banks.

Branches of the following banks have reliable ATMs:

BAC Visa/Plus and MasterCard/Cirrus

Bancentro/La Fise Visa/Plus and MasterCard/Cirrus

Banco ProCredit Visa/Plus

BanPro Visa/Plus and MasterCard/Cirrus

Credit Cards

Visa and MasterCard are accepted throughout Nicaragua, and you can almost always count on midrange hotels and restaurants to accept them. In places where electricity is unreliable – for instance, most of the Caribbean coast – credit cards may not be widely accepted, so be prepared.

Tipping

Tipping is not widespread in Nicaragua except with guides and at restaurants.

Guides Tipping guides is recommended as this often makes up the lion's share of their salary.

Restaurants A tip of around 10% is expected for table service. Some high-end restaurants automatically add this to the bill. Small and/or rural eateries may not include the tip, so leave behind a few coins.

Opening Hours

Opening hours vary wildly in Nicaragua as there are many informal and family-run establishments. General office hours are from 9am to 5pm.

Comedores (cheap eateries) usually open for breakfast and lunch while more formal restaurants serve lunch and dinner.

Banks 8:30am to 4:30pm Monday to Friday, to noon Saturday

Comedores 6am to 4pm

Government Offices 8am to noon and 1 to 4pm Monday to Friday, 8am to noon Saturday

Museums 9am to noon and 2 to 5pm

Restaurants noon to 10pm

Bars noon to midnight

Clubs 9pm to 3am

Shops 9am to 6pm Monday to Saturday

Photography

Drones are banned in Nicaragua. Should you try to bring one in, if you're lucky, the border guards will confiscate it and let you collect it upon leaving the country (you'll have to pay an export fee). If you're unlucky, they'll just confiscate it. It is possible to obtain permission to bring a drone into the country for professional purposes, but it's a difficult and costly process.

Post

Nicaragua's postal service is slow, but reasonably reliable. It costs about US$0.80 to send a standard letter or postcard to the US, about US$1 to Europe. If you send a package home via the postal service, it'll take four to eight weeks to reach its destination. For posting anything really valuable, consider using FedEx or similar.

Palacio de Correos (Map p44; Plaza de la Revolución, 2c O; ☺9am-5pm Mon-Fri, to 2pm Sat) is Managua's main post office; there's also a handy post office at **Managua International Airport** (MGA; www.eaai.com.ni; Carretera Norte Km 11).

Public Holidays

New Year's Day (January 1) Shops and offices start closing at noon on December 31.

Semana Santa (Holy Week; Thursday, Friday and Saturday before Easter Sunday) Beaches are packed, hotel rates skyrocket and everything is closed – make sure you have a place to be.

Labor Day (May 1)

Mother's Day (May 30) No one gets away with just a card – more places close than at Christmas.

Anniversary of the Revolution (July 19) No longer an official holiday, but many shops and government offices close anyway.

Battle of San Jacinto
(September 14)

Independence Day (September 15)

Indigenous Resistance Day (October 12)

Día de los Difuntos (November 2) All Souls' Day.

La Purísima (December 8) Immaculate Conception.

Navidad (December 25) Christmas.

Safe Travel

At the time of writing, political unrest in Nicaragua has led to street protests, road blocks and outbreaks of violence. For more information see p290.

Note that as a 'wealthy' foreigner traveling in Nicaragua you may be considered a potential target by scam artists and thieves.

➡ Pay extra attention to personal safety in Managua, the Caribbean region, around remote southern beaches and in undeveloped nature reserves.

➡ In larger cities, ask your hotel to call a trusted taxi.

➡ Backcountry hikers should note there may be unexploded ordnance in very remote areas, especially around the Honduran border. If in doubt, take a local guide.

Telephone

➡ Nicaragua's calling code is 505.

➡ There are no area codes within Nicaragua.

➡ All numbers are made up of eight digits; fixed line numbers begin with 2, while cell phone numbers begin with 8, 7 or 5.

➡ To call abroad from Nicaragua, dial 00 + country code + area code + phone number.

Time

Local Time in Nicaragua is GMT-6, equivalent to CST in the US.

Toilets

➡ In cities and towns, toilets are your regular sit-down flush variety.

➡ Public toilets are not common but most businesses will let you use their facilities.

➡ As you venture into rural areas you will come across dry latrines, which are little more than a hole in the ground covered by a wooden box.

➡ There is often no toilet paper in public bathrooms. Always carry a spare roll. And when you've finished, throw it in the trash basket, don't flush it – the pipes get blocked easily.

Tourist Information

Intur (☑2263-3174; www.intur.gob.ni; Managua Airport; ⊗8am-10pm), the government tourism office has branches in most major cities. It can always recommend hotels and activities (but not make reservations) and point you toward guides, though branches of Intur are usually sparsely stocked and their staff are not hugely knowledgeable.

In destinations popular with travelers, hostels are a good source of local info, as well as traveler message boards.

The *alcaldía* (mayor's office) is your best bet in small towns without a real tourist office. Although tourism is not the mayor's primary function, most will help you find food, lodging, guides and whatever else you might need. In indigenous communities, there may not be a mayor, as many still have

councils of elders. Instead, ask for the president (or *wihta* in Miskito communities), who probably speaks Spanish and can help you out.

Visas

Visitors from most countries can stay in Nicaragua for up to 90 days without a visa, as long as they have a passport valid for six months, proof of sufficient funds (US$200 cash or a credit card) and an onward ticket (rarely checked).

Citizens of some parts of Eastern Europe and Latin America, and many African and Asian nations, need visas to enter Nicaragua, while others can apply for a visa on arrival. Check the Nicaraguan Foreign Ministry website (www.migob.gob.ni) for the full lists.

Nicaragua is part of the CA-4, a regional agreement covering Nicaragua, Honduras, El Salvador and Guatemala. Officially, you can only stay for 90 days maximum in the entire CA-4, at which point you can get one extension of 90 days at the **Migración (Immigration) office** (☑2251-2271; www.migob.gob.ni/migracion/sertramis; Av Xolotán, semáforos de la Tenderí, 300m N; ⊗8am-5pm Mon-Fri) in Managua for around US$10 per month. After those 90 days, you must leave the region (this means going to Costa Rica, basically) for 72 hours, which automatically renews your visa.

Don't bet on it, but flying between CA-4 countries may get you another 90 days on landing, especially if you transit a nation outside the agreement. Land border officials are stricter in adhering to the regulations.

Volunteering

Nicaragua has a very developed volunteer culture, traceable to the influx of

ADDRESSES IN NICARAGUA

As few streets are named and fewer houses are numbered, Nicaraguans use a unique system for addresses. They take a landmark, then give the distance from it in blocks, using cardinal points for directions.

N	norte	north
E	este	east
S	sur	south
O	oeste	west
C	cuadra	block

For example, 'de la universidad, 2c S, 1c E' would be two blocks south, then one block east from the university. Some locals use arriba (up) and abajo (down) to refer to east and west respectively, terminology derived from the rising and setting of the sun.

We sometimes provide other landmark-based addresses such as 'frente catedral' (in front of the cathedral) in Spanish, so that locals can point you in the right direction.

'Sandalistas' (young foreign volunteers) during the revolution. Many hostels and Spanish schools maintain lists of organizations. Also check out Volunteer South America (www.volunteersouthamerica.net) and Go Abroad (www.goabroad.com).

Local Organizations

Fundacion del Río (www.fundaciondelrio.org) Runs environmental and social projects in the Río San Juan.

UCA San Ramon (www.ucasanramon.com) Works with rural coffee-growing communities near Matagalpa.

Luna International Hostel, Estelí (https://cafeluzyluna.org/volunteer) Welcomes volunteers who can promote local development projects.

Colibri Spanish School, Matagalpa (http://colibrispanish-school.com/en/volunteer-work) Works with children and in the area of agro-ecological farming techniques.

Neblina del Bosque, Area Protegida Miraflor Free board and lodging to guests who volunteer to teach English at the local school.

International Organizations

Habitat for Humanity (www.habitatnicaragua.org) Construction brigades work on new housing in impoverished communities.

Seeds of Learning (www.seedsoflearning.org) Sends work brigades with an educational focus to Nicaragua.

Techo (www.techo.org) Operates poverty-reduction projects in impoverished urban areas.

Women Travelers

The biggest problems that many solo female travelers encounter in Nicaragua are the piropos (catcalls) and general unwanted attention. Nicaragua is not particularly dangerous for women, but, like always, stay alert. Dress conservatively when not on beaches (knees should be covered, though shoulders are OK), especially when in transit; avoid drinking alone at night; and – this is the hard one – reconsider telling off the catcalling guy so the situation does not escalate. Sigh.

Work

Nicaragua is one of the poorest countries in the hemisphere, with almost 50% of its adults unemployed or underemployed. Thus, finding a job in Nicaragua is difficult and taking one that a Nicaraguan could be doing is probably just plain wrong. Backpacker-oriented businesses may offer you under-the-table employment, usually in exchange for room and board, but this is mostly about extending your vacation. If you're a serious, qualified English teacher, you may be able to find a job in an international school or private-language center.

To legally work in Nicaragua you are required to apply for a work permit through the immigration office.

Transportation

GETTING THERE & AWAY

Nicaragua is accessible by air via the international airport in Managua, by road using four major border crossings with Honduras and Costa Rica (plus another crossing to Costa Rica at San Pancho – Las Tabillas, which sees few visitors), and by boat between El Salvador and Potosí, and Costa Rica and San Carlos.

Flights, cars and tours can be booked online at lonely planet.com/bookings.

Entering the Country

All visitors entering Nicaragua are required to purchase a Tourist Card for US$10, make sure you have US currency handy.

Those entering by land also pay a US$2 migration processing fee. Upon departure by land or boat there is another US$2 migration fee, while a small municipal charge – usually around US$1 – may also be levied by the local government depending on the border crossing.

Air

Nicaragua's main international hub is Managua International Airport (www.eaai.com.ni). Nicaragua has no national airline, but is served by several major American carriers, as well as Copa and Avianca. It's worth checking fares to neighboring Costa Rica, which is an air-conditioned bus ride away and may be significantly cheaper.

Land

Visitors entering Nicaragua by land must purchase a tourist card for US$10 and pay a US$2 immigration fee. Land departures are also subject to the immigration fee.

DEPARTURE TAX

Departure tax is included in the price of tickets.

Border Crossings

Nicaragua shares borders with Costa Rica and Honduras. Generally, Nicaraguan border crossings are chaotic (there are no signs anywhere), but the procedure is fairly straightforward provided you have your documents in order. Two of the busiest border crossings – with Honduras and Costa Rica – are open around the clock, while the rest have limited opening hours.

OCOTAL TO TEGUCIGALPA, HONDURAS

See the sunny Segovias and the Honduran capital at this major, business-like border. The Las Manos crossing point is efficient, although sometimes crowded.

CLIMATE CHANGE & TRAVEL

Every form of transport that relies on carbon-based fuel generates CO_2, the main cause of human-induced climate change. Modern travel is dependent on aeroplanes, which might use less fuel per kilometre per person than most cars but travel much greater distances. The altitude at which aircraft emit gases (including CO_2) and particles also contributes to their climate change impact. Many websites offer 'carbon calculators' that allow people to estimate the carbon emissions generated by their journey and, for those who wish to do so, to offset the impact of the greenhouse gases emitted with contributions to portfolios of climate-friendly initiatives throughout the world. Lonely Planet offsets the carbon footprint of all staff and author travel.

SOMOTO TO CHOLUTECA, HONDURAS

A high-altitude crossing that comes with an amazing granite canyon. Crossing point El Espino is laid-back and easy.

EL GUASAULE TO CHOLUTECA, HONDURAS

The fastest route from Nicaragua, an easy cruise north from León. The El Guasaule 24-hour crossing is hectic and somewhat disorganized.

SAPOÁ TO PEÑAS BLANCAS, COSTA RICA

The main, 24-hour border crossing is generally easy unless your arrival coincides with an international bus or two, in which case it could take hours. The local municipality charges an additional US$1 fee at this crossing.

SAN PANCHO TO LAS TABLILLAS, COSTA RICA

Uncrowded border crossing (open 8am to 4pm daily) that uses a bridge and beautifully paved road.

Bus

International buses have reclining seats, TVs, air-conditioning, bathrooms and sometimes even food service, and are definitely safer for travelers with luggage. Crossing borders on international buses is generally hassle-free. At many borders the helper will take your passport, collect your border fees, get your stamp and return your passport to you as you get back on the bus. At the Costa Rican border post at Peñas Blancas you must complete the formalities in person.

There are direct bus services (without changing buses) to Costa Rica, Honduras, El Salvador and Guatemala, and connecting services to Panama and Mexico.

Nica Expreso (https://nicaexpreso.online.com.ni) Runs from Chinandega (via Managua) to San José, Costa Rica.

Tica Bus (Map p46; ☑8739-5505; www.ticabus.com; 9

Calle Suroeste, Barrio Bolonia) Travels to Costa Rica, Honduras and El Salvador with connecting services to Guatemala, Panama and Mexico.

Transnica (Map p50; ☑2270-3133; www.transnica.com; Metrocentro, 300m N, 50m E) Serves Costa Rica, Honduras and El Salvador.

Transporte del Sol (Map p46; ☑2422-5000; frente Tica Bus, Barrio Bolonia) Same-day service to Guatemala and El Salvador.

COSTA RICA

There are several bus companies running direct services between San José and Managua. The journey usually takes around nine to 10 hours and costs around US$30.

EL SALVADOR

Although there is no common border, there are several direct buses a day to San Salvador passing through Choluteca in Honduras. The journey costs US$40 to US$52 and takes around 11 hours, but may be significantly longer if there are delays at any of the two border crossings.

HONDURAS

There are two main bus routes between Honduras and Nicaragua. From Tegucigalpa it's around seven hours and costs US$30, while from San Pedro Sula it's 12 hours and costs US$46.

GUATEMALA

There is a direct service from Managua to Guatemala City that takes around six hours and costs US$70.

Car & Motorcycle

To bring a vehicle into Nicaragua, you'll need the originals and several copies of the ownership papers (in your name), your passport and a driver's license.

You'll get a free 30-day permit (lose it and you'll be fined) and you will need to purchase obligatory accident

insurance for US$12. You may also be required to pay US$3 to US$4 for the fumigation of your vehicle. Your passport will be stamped saying you brought a vehicle into the country; if you try to leave without it, you'll have to pay import duty. It's possible to extend the vehicle permit twice at the DGA office in Managua before you have to leave the country.

You can drive across two border crossings to Costa Rica. The most popular is at Sapoá–Peñas Blancas near Rivas; the crossing at San Pancho-Las Tablillas in the Río San Juan sees few vehicles.

It's possible to drive across the Nicaragua–Honduras border at El Guasaule, Somoto–El Espino and Ocotal–Las Manos.

River

The river crossing between San Carlos and Los Chiles, Costa Rica is a breeze, but only if you hire a boat to take you down an egret-lined river. Due to the San Pancho bridge, the ferry to Los Chiles no longer exists. From Los Chiles there are regular bus services onto Ciudad Quesada and San José.

You can also cross into Honduras from Waspám to Puerto Lempira, but it's a serious jungle adventure.

Sea

It's now possible to travel directly between Nicaragua and El Salvador by boat through the Golfo de Fonseca. Ruta del Golfo (www.rutadelgolfo.com) runs at least one boat per week to La Union, El Salvador (US$65, 2½ hours) across the picturesque Golfo de Fonseca, typically departing at 12:30pm, with optional 4WD pickup from León at 8:30am (US$99 total). Prices do not include *migración* (immigration) fees.

GETTING AROUND

Air

The hub for domestic flights is **Managua International Airport** (MGA; www.eaai.com.ni; Carretera Norte Km 11). Other airports are little more than dirt strips outside town (or in Siuna and Waspám, in the middle of town). The airport in San Juan de Nicaragua is located across the bay in Greytown and is one of the few airports in the Americas where you need to take a boat to get on your flight.

La Costeña (www.lacostena.com.ni) is the domestic carrier with a good safety record. It services Bluefields, Bonanza, the Corn Islands, Las Minas, Ometepe, Rosita, San Carlos (via Ometepe), San Juan de Nicaragua, Puerto Cabezas, Siuna and Waspám. Many domestic flights use tiny single-prop planes where weight is important and bags necessarily get left behind, so keep all necessities in your carry-on luggage.

Flights on all routes are grounded in bad weather, but this is actually fairly rare. Normally the worst that happens is delays. The Bluefields–Bilwi flight is typically cancelled unless there is enough demand.

Bicycle

Nicaragua gets praise from long-distance cyclists for its smooth, paved roads and wide shoulders. Apart from in the mountainous northern region, the main highways through the country are fairly flat, which gives cyclists plenty of opportunities to enjoy the spectacular scenery.

Bicycles are the most common form of private transport in the country and most drivers are used to seeing them everywhere from main highways to country roads. However, while the infrastructure is designed to accommodate bicycles, the extremely limited enforcement of speed limits and drink-driving legislation is an issue, and the hazards of riding on Nicaraguan roads are not negligible.

Rental

Renting bicycles is difficult outside Granada, San Juan del Sur, Ometepe and León, but your hotel can probably arrange it for you. Bikes rent for around US$5 to US$7 per day – weekly discounts are easily arranged. Bike-rental places may require a few hundred córdobas or your passport as deposit.

Purchase

Buying a bike is easily done; even the smallest towns will have somewhere selling them. The price-to-quality ratio is not great – expect to pay a little under US$100 for a bottom-of-the-line model. Something fancy will probably cost more than it would back home. Selling your bike when you leave is a matter of luck; places such as Granada, León and San Juan del Sur all have notice boards in travelers' cafes, which would be your best bet. As a last shot, try selling it to a bike-rental place, but don't expect to recoup much of your investment.

Boat

Many destinations are accessible only, or most easily, by boat. Public *pangas* (small open motorboats) with outboard motors are much more expensive than road transport – in general it costs around US$6 to US$8 per hour of travel. In places without regular service, you will need to hire your own private *panga*. Prices vary widely, but you'll spend about US$50 to US$100 per hour for four to six people;

tour operators can usually find a better deal. It's easy, if not cheap, to hire boat transport up and down the Pacific coast. On the Atlantic side, it's much more difficult. While it's not common, boats do sink here and tourists have drowned – wear your life jacket.

River boats on the Río San Juan tend to be slow and fairly cheap. There are often express and regular services – it's worth paying a bit extra for the quicker version.

Following are the major departure points with regular boat service.

Bluefields To Pearl Lagoon, El Rama and Corn Island.

Corn Islands Regular boats run between Great Corn and Little Corn Islands.

El Rama To Bluefields.

San Carlos To the Islas Solentiname, the Río San Juan, the scenic border crossing to Costa Rica and several natural reserves.

Waspám The gateway to the Río Coco.

Bus

Bus coverage in Nicaragua is extensive although services are often uncomfortable and overcrowded. Public transport is usually on old Bluebird school buses, which means no luggage compartments. Try to avoid putting your backpack on top of the bus, and instead sit toward the back and put it with the sacks of rice and beans.

Pay your fare after the bus starts moving. You may

NICARAGUA'S TRAVELING TRADERS

Who said traveling by bus is boring? In Nicaragua not only are there awe-inspiring volcanic landscapes to gaze at through the windows, inside the bus is a whole world of entertainment.

And we're not talking about the soft-rock soundtrack or classic Steven Seagal marathon on the tiny TV. The real entertainment on Nicaragua's battle-scarred school buses comes from the traveling salesmen, particularly those hawking cut-priced medicines and ointments.

Need to get smarter before arriving in Rivas? No problem. Hair loss issues? There's an elixir to cure both of these. And you probably didn't even know that in addition to your backpack, you were carrying around all those parasites on the unnecessarily graphic images on the salesman's full-color poster.

While they are not doctors, nor even pharmacists, these 'medicine men' always seem to do a brisk trade. Although they haven't yet cracked the traveler market. Perhaps the lack of a hangover cure has something to do with it.

be issued a paper 'ticket' on long-distance buses – don't lose it, or you may be charged again. Some bus terminals allow you to purchase tickets ahead of time, which should in theory guarantee you a seat. While buses sometimes cruise around town before hitting the highway, you're more likely to get a seat by boarding the bus at the station or terminal.

Bus terminals, which are often huge, chaotic lots next to markets, may seem difficult to navigate, particularly if you don't speak much Spanish. Fear not! If you can pronounce your destination, the guys yelling will help you find your bus – just make sure they put you on an *expreso* (express) and not an *ordinario* (ordinary bus) or you'll be spending more time on the road than you planned.

Car & Motorcycle

Driving is a wonderful way to see Pacific and central Nicaragua, but it's best to use public transportation on the Caribbean side as roads are, for the most part, terrible.

Driver's License

Your home driver's license is valid for driving in Nicaragua for the duration of the entry stamp in your passport.

Rental

To hire a car, you'll need a driver's license and major credit card. Most rental companies want you to be at least 25 years old. Renting a car at Managua International Airport costs 15% extra, so consider taking a taxi to an off-site office. If you rent a car outside Managua, drop-off fees at Managua Airport are very reasonable.

Following are some of the better car-rental agencies:

Budget (www.budget.com.ni)

Dollar (www.dollar.com.ni) Also rents vehicles with drivers in the Managua area.

Hertz (☏2233-1237; www.hertz.com.ni; Managua Airport; ◷6am-9pm)

Lugo (Map p46;☏2266-4477; www.lugorentacar.com.ni; de la Estatua Montoya, 300m S; ◷8am-7pm)

Road Conditions

Road conditions vary wildly throughout the country,

although there has been some progress with continuing projects to improve them.

The Panamericana (Pan-American Hwy) is paved all the way from Honduras to Costa Rica while the roads from Managua to both El Rama and San Carlos are also wide, paved highways. There is now a paved highway from Managua to Nueva Guinea, with the last section between Nueva Guinea and Bluefields being sealed at the time of writing, making it considerably easier to access the Caribbean coast.

Some secondary roads are very good, particularly in the north, while others are suspension breakers. Access to Pacific beaches is generally poor and requires a 4WD outside dry season, as is the majority of the road network on the Atlantic side. If you can afford it, rent a 4WD instead of a city car.

There are no up-to-date maps showing real road conditions, which change every rainy season. Ask locals if you're not sure. Older paved roads are often horribly pockmarked with axle-cracking potholes.

During rainy season, roads flood, wash away and close. Some roads are never recommended for casual drivers, including the Río Blanco–Bilwi road, easily the worst in the country.

Road Rules

Nicaragua's traffic laws are pretty standard. Driving on the right, giving way to anything bigger than you, wearing a seat belt at all times and keeping speeds below 45km/h in cities should keep you out of trouble. Speed limits tend to be 60km/h on rural roads and 80 or 100km/h on motorways.

Many towns are mazes of unsigned one-way streets that prove a boon to traffic cops.

Nicaragua's traffic cops are notorious for targeting foreigners, looking for a quick shakedown. Officers may wave drivers over and accuse them of something as vague as 'poor driving.' Drivers should never initiate a bribe – it may be an honest officer who just wants to give a warning. If a bribe is requested, prudent drivers pay it.

If a ticket is issued (the police get a cut of the fine you pay to banks), you'll need to surrender your license and then pay the fine at the bank, before picking up your documents at the departmental police station closest to the infraction (which may be a fair distance from your final destination). The procedure may take several days and is more than a little inconvenient, so if you're certain that you have been shaken down, one option for foreign visitors is to not pay the fine, abandon the license and get a new license when you get home.

Hitchhiking

Hitchhiking is never entirely safe, and we don't recommend it. Travelers who hitchhike should understand that they are taking a small but potentially serious risk.

Nevertheless hitchhiking is very common in rural Nicaragua, even by solo women – to find a ride, just stick out your thumb. Foreign women, particularly those carrying all their bags, should think twice before hitchhiking solo. Never hitchhike into or out of Managua.

In rural areas where bus service is rare, anyone driving a pickup truck will almost certainly stop for you. Climb into the back tray (unless specifically invited up front) and when you want to get off, tap on the cabin roof a couple of times.

You should always offer to pay the driver, which will almost always be refused.

Local Transportation

Bus

The only city really big enough to warrant catching local buses is Managua, where the bus routes are really convoluted, the bus stops are often not marked and the service is only worth using if you've been living in the city for some time and know exactly where you're going. Given how inexpensive Managua's taxis are, it's not really worth spending time figuring out the bus routes for the sake of saving a few coins, particularly if you're only in the city for a day or two.

Dirt Bikes, Quad Bikes & Beach Buggies

In popular destinations with notoriously rough roads, such as Isla Ometepe, San Juan del Sur and several of the Pacific beaches, you'll often get outlets renting rugged sets of wheels that make tackling those roads a piece

of cake. Expect to pay around US$25 per day for a dirt bike, up to US$65 per day for a quad and up to US$80 for a serious dune buggy.

Rickshaw & Tuk-Tuk

In smaller towns there are fewer taxis and more tuk-tuks (motorized three wheelers) and *triciclos* (bicycle rickshaws). They're inexpensive – around US$0.50 per person to go anywhere in town – and kind of fun. Tuk-tuks are also the easiest and quickest way to get between the Pueblos Blancos near Masaya.

Taxi

Almost all taxis in Nicaragua are *colectivos* (shared taxi or minibus), which stop and pick up other clients en route to your destination; however, it is always possible to pay a bit extra for an express service.

Managua taxis are unmetered and notorious for ripping off tourists. Always negotiate the fare before getting in. Taxis at major border crossings may also overcharge, given the chance.

Most other city taxis have set in-town fares, usually around US$0.50 to US$0.70, rising slightly at night. Ask a local how much a fare should cost before getting into the cab.

Hiring taxis between cities is a comfortable and reasonable option for midrange travelers. Prices vary widely, but expect to pay around US$10 for every 20km.

Language

Spanish is the national language of Nicaragua. Latin American Spanish pronunciation is easy, as there's a clear and consistent relationship between what you see written and how it's pronounced. Also, most sounds have equivalents in English.

Note that kh is a throaty sound (like the 'ch' in the Scottish *loch*), v and b are like a soft English 'v' (between a 'v' and a 'b'), and r is strongly rolled. There are some variations in spoken Spanish across Latin America, the most notable being the pronunciation of the letters *ll* and *y*. In our pronunciation guides they are represented with y because they are pronounced as the 'y' in 'yes' in most of Latin America. Note, however, that in some parts of the continent they sound like the 'lli' in 'million'. Read our colored pronunciation guides as if they were English, and you'll be understood. The stressed syllables are indicated with italics in our pronunciation guides.

The polite form is used in this chapter; where both polite and informal options are given, they are indicated by the abbreviations 'pol' and 'inf'. Where necessary, both masculine and feminine forms of words are included, separated by a slash and with the masculine form first, eg *perdido/a* (m/f).

BASICS

Hello.	Hola.	o·la
Goodbye.	Adiós.	a·dyos
How are you?	¿Qué tal?	ke tal

WANT MORE?

For in-depth language information and handy phrases, check out Lonely Planet's *Latin American Spanish Phrasebook*. You'll find it at **shop.lonelyplanet.com**, or you can buy Lonely Planet's iPhone phrasebooks at the Apple App Store.

Fine, thanks.	Bien, gracias.	byen gra·syas
Excuse me.	Perdón.	per·don
Sorry.	Lo siento.	lo syen·to
Please.	Por favor.	por fa·vor
Thank you.	Gracias.	gra·syas
You are welcome.	De nada.	de na·da
Yes./No.	Sí./No.	see/no

My name is ...
Me llamo ... — me ya·mo ...

What's your name?
¿Cómo se llama Usted? ko·mo se ya·ma oo·ste (pol)
¿Cómo te llamas? ko·mo te ya·mas (inf)

Do you speak English?
¿Habla inglés? a·bla een·gles (pol)
¿Hablas inglés? a·blas een·gles (inf)

I don't understand.
Yo no entiendo. yo no en·tyen·do

ACCOMMODATIONS

I'd like a single/double room.
Quisiera una habitación individual/doble. kee·sye·ra oo·na a·bee·ta·syon een·dee·vee·dwal/do·ble

How much is it per night/person?
¿Cuánto cuesta por noche/persona? kwan·to kwes·ta por no·che/per·so·na

Does it include breakfast?
¿Incluye el desayuno? een·kloo·ye el de·sa·yoo·no

campsite	terreno de cámping	te·re·no de kam·peeng
guesthouse	pensión	pen·syon
hotel	hotel	o·tel
youth hostel	albergue juvenil	al·ber·ge khoo·ve·neel
air-con	aire acondicionado	ai·re a·kon·dee·syo·na·do

EL VOSEO

Nicaragua differs from much of Latin America in its use of the informal 'you' form. Instead of *tuteo* (the use of *tú*), Nicaraguans commonly speak with *voseo* (the use of *vos*).

This chapter uses the *tú* form in relevant phrases, as it's more useful throughout Latin America – Nicaraguans will have no trouble understanding if you only use the *tú* form. Examples of *-ar*, *-er* and *-ir* verbs are given below – the pronoun *tú* is only given for contrast.

Verb	Tuteo	Voseo
hablar (to speak): You speak./Speak!	*Tú hablas./¡Habla!*	*Vos hablás./¡Hablá!*
soñar (to dream): You dream./Dream!	*Tú sueñas./¡Sueña!*	*Vos soñás./¡Soñá!*
comer (to eat): You eat./Eat!	*Tú comes./¡Come!*	*Vos comés./¡Comé!*
poner (to put): You put./Put!	*Tú pones./¡Pon!*	*Vos ponés./¡Poné!*
admitir (to admit): You admit./Admit!	*Tú admites./¡Admite!*	*Vos admitís./¡Admití!*
venir (to come): You come./Come!	*Tú vienes./¡Ven!*	*Vos venís./¡Vení!*

bathroom	*baño*	ba·nyo
bed	*cama*	ka·ma
window	*ventana*	ven·ta·na

DIRECTIONS

Where's ...?
¿Dónde está ...?   don·de es·ta ...

What's the address?
¿Cuál es la dirección?   kwal es la dee·rek·syon

Could you please write it down?
¿Puede escribirlo,   pwe·de es·kree·beer·lo
por favor?   por fa·vor

Can you show me (on the map)?
¿Me lo puede indicar   me lo pwe·de een·dee·kar
(en el mapa)?   (en el ma·pa)

at the corner	*en la esquina*	en la es·kee·na
at the traffic lights	*en el semáforo*	en el se·ma·fo·ro
behind ...	*detrás de ...*	de·tras de ...
in front of ...	*enfrente de ...*	en·fren·te de ...
left	*izquierda*	ees·kyer·da
next to ...	*al lado de ...*	al la·do de ...
opposite ...	*frente a ...*	fren·te a ...
right	*derecha*	de·re·cha
straight ahead	*todo recto*	to·do rek·to

EATING & DRINKING

Can I see the menu, please?
¿Puedo ver el menú,   pwe·do ver el me·noo
por favor?   por fa·vor

What would you recommend?
¿Qué recomienda?   ke re·ko·myen·da

Do you have vegetarian food?
¿Tienen comida   tye·nen ko·mee·da
vegetariana?   ve·khe·ta·rya·na

I don't eat (red meat).
No como (carne roja).   no ko·mo (kar·ne ro·kha)

That was delicious!
¡Estaba buenísimo!   es·ta·ba bwe·nee·see·mo

Cheers!
¡Salud!   sa·loo

The bill, please.
La cuenta, por favor.   la kwen·ta por fa·vor

I'd like a	*Quisiera una*	kee·sye·ra oo·na
table for ...	*mesa para ...*	me·sa pa·ra ...
(eight) o'clock	*las (ocho)*	las (o·cho)
(two) people	*(dos) personas*	(dos) per·so·nas

Key Words

bottle	*botella*	bo·te·ya
breakfast	*desayuno*	de·sa·yoo·no
(too) cold	*(muy) frío*	(mooy) free·o
dinner	*cena*	se·na

ADDRESSES

Following are some terms and abbreviations commonly used in Nicaraguan addresses.

abajo	down
arriba	up
costado	beside
entre	between
esq (esquina)	at the corner of
frente	in front of
int	inside
salida	exit
semaf semáforo	traffic lights

SIGNS

Abierto	Open
Cerrado	Closed
Entrada	Entrance
Hombres/Varones	Men
Mujeres/Damas	Women
Prohibido	Prohibited
Salida	Exit
Servicios/Baños	Toilets

fork	tenedor	te·ne·dor
glass	vaso	va·so
hot (warm)	caliente	kal·yen·te
knife	cuchillo	koo·chee·yo
lunch	comida	ko·mee·da
plate	plato	pla·to
restaurant	restaurante	res·tow·ran·te
spoon	cuchara	koo·cha·ra
appetisers	aperitivos	a·pe·ree·tee·vos
main course	segundo plato	se·goon·do pla·to
salad	ensalada	en·sa·la·da
soup	sopa	so·pa
fish	pescado	pes·ka·do
with/without	con/sin	kon/seen
fruit	fruta	froo·ta
vegetable	verdura	ver·doo·ra

Meat & Fish

beef	carne de vaca	kar·ne de va·ka
chicken	pollo	po·yo
duck	pato	pa·to
lamb	cordero	kor·de·ro
pork	cerdo	ser·do
prawn	langostino	lan·gos·tee·no
salmon	salmón	sal·mon
tuna	atún	a·toon

QUESTION WORDS

How?	¿Cómo?	ko·mo
What?	¿Qué?	ke
When?	¿Cuándo?	kwan·do
Where?	¿Dónde?	don·de
Who?	¿Quién?	kyen
Why?	¿Por qué?	por ke

turkey	pavo	pa·vo
veal	ternera	ter·ne·ra

Fruit & Vegetables

apple	manzana	man·sa·na
apricot	albaricoque	al·ba·ree·ko·ke
banana	plátano	pla·ta·no
beans	judías	khoo·dee·as
cabbage	col	kol
capsicum	pimiento	pee·myen·to
carrot	zanahoria	sa·na·o·rya
cherry	cereza	se·re·sa
corn	maíz	ma·ees
cucumber	pepino	pe·pee·no
grape	uvas	oo·vas
lemon	limón	lee·mon
lettuce	lechuga	le·choo·ga
mushroom	champiñón	cham·pee·nyon
nuts	nueces	nwe·ses
onion	cebolla	se·bo·ya
orange	naranja	na·ran·kha
peach	melocotón	me·lo·ko·ton
peas	guisantes	gee·san·tes
pineapple	piña	pee·nya
plum	ciruela	seer·we·la
potato	patata	pa·ta·ta
spinach	espinacas	es·pee·na·kas
strawberry	fresa	fre·sa
tomato	tomate	to·ma·te
watermelon	sandía	san·dee·a

Other

bread	pan	pan
cheese	queso	ke·so
egg	huevo	we·vo
honey	miel	myel
jam	mermelada	mer·me·la·da
oil	aceite	a·sey·te
pepper	pimienta	pee·myen·ta
rice	arroz	a·ros
salt	sal	sal
sugar	azúcar	a·soo·kar

Drinks

beer	cerveza	ser·ve·sa
coffee	café	ka·fe

(orange) juice	zumo (de naranja)	soo·mo (de na·ran·kha)
milk	leche	le·che
red wine	vino tinto	vee·no teen·to
tea	té	te
(mineral) water	agua (mineral)	a·gwa (mee·ne·ral)
white wine	vino blanco	vee·no blan·ko

EMERGENCIES

| Help! | ¡Socorro! | so·ko·ro |
| Go away! | ¡Vete! | ve·te |

Call ...!	¡Llame a ...!	ya·me a ...
a doctor	un médico	oon me·dee·ko
the police	la policía	la po·lee·see·a

I'm lost.
Estoy perdido/a.   es·toy per·dee·do/a (m/f)

I'm ill.
Estoy enfermo/a.   es·toy en·fer·mo/a (m/f)

I'm allergic to (antibiotics).
Soy alérgico/a a   soy a·ler·khee·ko/a a
(los antibióticos).   (los an·tee·byo·tee·kos) (m/f)

Where are the toilets?
¿Dónde están los   don·de es·tan los
baños?   ba·nyos t

SHOPPING & SERVICES

I'd like to buy ...
Quisiera comprar ...   kee·sye·ra kom·prar ...

I'm just looking.
Sólo estoy mirando.   so·lo es·toy mee·ran·do

Can I look at it?
¿Puedo verlo?   pwe·do ver·lo

I don't like it.
No me gusta.   no me goos·ta

How much is it?
¿Cuánto cuesta?   kwan·to kwes·ta

That's too expensive.
Es muy caro.   es mooy ka·ro

There's a mistake in the bill.
Hay un error   ai oon e·ror
en la cuenta.   en la kwen·ta

ATM	cajero automático	ka·khe·ro ow·to·ma·tee·ko
internet cafe	cibercafé	see·ber·ka·fe
post office	correos	ko·re·os
tourist office	oficina de turismo	o·fee·see·na de too·rees·mo

TIME & DATES

What time is it?	¿Qué hora es?	ke o·ra es
It's (10) o'clock.	Son (las diez).	son (las dyes)
It's half past (one).	Es (la una) y media.	es (la oo·na) ee me·dya

morning	mañana	ma·nya·na
afternoon	tarde	tar·de
evening	noche	no·che
yesterday	ayer	a·yer
today	hoy	oy
tomorrow	mañana	ma·nya·na

Monday	lunes	loo·nes
Tuesday	martes	mar·tes
Wednesday	miércoles	myer·ko·les
Thursday	jueves	khwe·ves
Friday	viernes	vyer·nes
Saturday	sábado	sa·ba·do
Sunday	domingo	do·meen·go

January	enero	e·ne·ro
February	febrero	fe·bre·ro
March	marzo	mar·so
April	abril	a·breel
May	mayo	ma·yo
June	junio	khoon·yo
July	julio	khool·yo
August	agosto	a·gos·to
September	septiembre	sep·tyem·bre
October	octubre	ok·too·bre
November	noviembre	no·vyem·bre
December	diciembre	dee·syem·bre

NICA SLANG

Here's a small selection of the huge array of Nicaraguan slang.

¡Chocho!	Wow!
¡Tuani!	Good!/Relaxed!/Cool!
bochinche	an all-in brawl
chele	white person
chunche	a small object
dominguear	to dress up
estar hasta el tronco	to be very drunk
palmado	broke, penniless
pateperro	aimless wanderer

TRANSPORT

Public Transport

boat	barco	bar·ko
bus	autobús	ow·to·boos
plane	avión	a·vyon
taxi	taxi	tak·see
train	tren	tren
first	primero	pree·me·ro
last	último	ool·tee·mo
next	próximo	prok·see·mo
A ... ticket, please.	Un billete de ..., por favor.	oon bee·ye·te de ... por fa·vor
1st-class	primera clase	pree·me·ra kla·se
2nd-class	segunda clase	se·goon·da kla·se
one-way	ida	ee·da
return	ida y vuelta	ee·da ee vwel·ta
bus stop	parada de autobuses	pa·ra·da de ow·to·boo·ses
ticket office	taquilla	ta·kee·ya
timetable	horario	o·ra·ryo
train station	estación de trenes	es·ta·syon de tre·nes

Does it stop at ...?
¿Para en ...?   pa·ra en ...

What stop is this?
¿Cuál es esta parada?   kwal es es·ta pa·ra·da

What time does it arrive/leave?
¿A qué hora llega/sale?   a ke o·ra ye·ga/sa·le

Please tell me when we get to ...
¿Puede avisarme   pwe·de a·vee·sar·me
cuando lleguemos a ...?   kwan·do ye·ge·mos a ...

I want to get off here.
Quiero bajarme aquí.   kye·ro ba·khar·me a·kee

Driving & Cycling

I'd like to hire a ...	Quisiera alquilar ...	kee·sye·ra al·kee·lar ...
bicycle	una bicicleta	oo·na bee·see·kle·ta
car	un coche	oon ko·che
motorcycle	una moto	oo·na mo·to
helmet	casco	kas·ko
mechanic	mecánico	me·ka·nee·ko
petrol/gas	gasolina	ga·so·lee·na
service station	gasolinera	ga·so·lee·ne·ra

MISKITO PHRASES

There are more than 150,000 native speakers of Miskito scattered along the Caribbean coast. Here are a few phrases to get you started.

Hello./Goodbye.	Naksa./Aisabi.
Yes./No.	Ow./Apia.
Please./Thank you.	Plees./Dingki pali.
How are you?	Nakisma?
Good, fine.	Pain.
Bad, lousy.	Saura.
friend	pana
Does anyone here speak Spanish?	Nu apo ya Ispel aisee sapa?
My name is ...	Yan nini ...
What's your name?	An maninam dia?
Excuse me, could you help me?	Escyus, man sipsma ilpeimonaya?
How do I get to ...?	Napkei sipsna gwaiya ...?
Is it far/near?	Nawina lihurasa/lamarasa?
Could you tell me where a hotel is?	Man ailwis hotel ansara barsa?
Do you have a bathroom?	Baño brisma?
Where is the bus station?	Ansarasa buskaba takaskisa?
What time does the bus/boat leave?	Man nu apo dia teim bustaki/duritaki sapa?
May I cross your property?	Sipsna man prizcamku nueewaiya?
Are there landmines?	Danomite barsakei?
Where can I change dollars?	Ansara dalas sismonaya sipsna?
How much is it?	Naki preis?
I'm a vegetarian.	Yan wal wina kalila pias.
I feel sick.	Yan síknes.

Is this the road to ...?
¿Se va a ... por   se va a ... por
esta carretera?   es·ta ka·re·te·ra

(How long) Can I park here?
¿(Cuánto tiempo)   (kwan·to tyem·po)
Puedo aparcar aquí?   pwe·do a·par·kar a·kee

The car has broken down.
El coche se ha averiado.   el ko·che se a a·ve·rya·do

I have a flat tyre.
Tengo un pinchazo.   ten·go oon peen·cha·so

I've run out of petrol.
Me he quedado sin   me e ke·da·do seen
gasolina.   ga·so·lee·na

GLOSSARY

See p310 for more useful words and phrases dealing with food and dining.

alcaldía – mayor's office
arroyo – stream or gully
ave – bird

banco – bank
baño – bathroom
barco – boat
barrio – district, neighborhood
bicicleta – bicycle
bomba – gas station; short funny verse; bomb
bosque – forest

caballo – horse
cabinas – cabins
cacique – chief
calle – street
cama – bed
campesino/a – peasant; person who works in agriculture
campo – field or countryside
carretas – wooden ox carts
carretera – road or highway
cascada – waterfall
catedral – cathedral
caverna – cave
cerro – hill or mountain
chele/a – White/European, from *leche* (milk)
ciudad – city
cocina – kitchen; cooking
colectivo – buses, minivans or cars operating as shared taxis; see also *normal* and *directo*
colibrí – hummingbird
colina – hill
cooperativa – cooperative
cordillera – mountain range
córdoba – Nicaraguan unit of currency
correo – mail service
coyote – moneychanger; people smuggler
cruce – crossing
cueva – cave

dios – god
directo – direct; long-distance bus that has only a few stops

emergencia – emergency
empalme – three-way intersection
estación – station (as in ranger station or bus station); season
estero – estuary

farmacia – pharmacy
fiesta – party or festival
finca – farm or plantation
flor – flower
frontera – border

gringo/a – male/female North American or European visitor (can be affectionate or insulting, depending on the tone used)
guapote – large fish caught for sport, equivalent to rainbow bass
hacienda – a rural estate

iglesia – church
Ineter – Nicaragua Institute for Territorial Studies
Interamericana – Pan-American Hwy
Intur – Nicaraguan Institute of Tourism
isla – island

jardín – garden

laguna – lagoon
lancha – boat (usually small); see also *panga*
lapa – parrot
lavandería – laundry facility, usually offering dry-cleaning services

malecón – pier; sea wall; waterfront promenade
Marena – Nicaragua's Ministry of the Environment & Natural Resources
marimba – xylophone
mercado – market
mesa – table
mestizo – person of mixed descent, usually Spanish and Indian
migración – immigration
mirador – lookout point
mono – monkey
moto – motorcycle
muelle – dock

museo – museum

Nica – Nicaraguan, male or female
normal – long-distance bus with many stops

panga – light boat; see also *lancha*
pántano – swamp or wetland
parque – park
parque central – central town square or plaza
parque nacional – national park
piropos – catcalls
piso – floor (as in 2nd floor)
pista – airstrip
playa – beach
posada – guesthouse
pueblo – village
puerto – port
pulpería – corner grocery store

rancho – thatched-roof hut
refresco – soda or bottled refreshment
refugio nacional de vida silvestre – national wildlife refuge
río – river

salto – waterfall (literally, jump)
sendero – trail; path
sierra – mountain range
soda – very Costa Rican term for a simple cafe; they're all over southern Nicaragua
supermercado – supermarket

tienda – store
típica/o – typical; particularly used to describe food (*comida típica* means 'typical cooking')
tope – dead end or T-intersection
tortuga – turtle
tucán – toucan

Unesco – UN Educational, Scientific and Cultural Organization

viajero – traveler
vivero – plant nursery
volcán – volcano

zona – zone

FOOD GLOSSARY

arroz – rice

baho – dry plantain, yucca and beef stew

camarones – shrimp
chicharrón – fried pork rinds
chile – vinegar with chilli peppers
cuajada – fresh, salty, crumbly cheese

ensalada – salad

frijoles – beans

gallo pinto – rice and beans

hamburguesa – hamburger
huevos del toro – bull testicles
huevos de paslama – turtle eggs
huevos fritos/revueltos – fried/ scrambled eggs

maduros – ripe plantains served boiled or fried
mondongo – tripe soup

nacatamales – cornmeal with spices and meat

postre – dessert

raspados – shaved ice flavored with fruit juice

rundown – also *rondon;* thick Caribbean soup with coconut

quesillo – soft cheese with cream wrapped in a *tortilla*
queso – cheese

salchicha – sausage
salsa de ajillo – garlic sauce

tajadas – thin sliced green plantain fries
tortilla – cornmeal pancake
tostones – green plantains cut thick, mashed then fried

Behind the Scenes

SEND US YOUR FEEDBACK

We love to hear from travelers – your comments keep us on our toes and help make our books better. Our well-traveled team reads every word on what you loved or loathed about this book. Although we cannot reply individually to your submissions, we always guarantee that your feedback goes straight to the appropriate authors, in time for the next edition. Each person who sends us information is thanked in the next edition – the most useful submissions are rewarded with a selection of digital PDF chapters.

Visit **lonelyplanet.com/contact** to submit your updates and suggestions or to ask for help. Our award-winning website also features inspirational travel stories, news and discussions.

Note: We may edit, reproduce and incorporate your comments in Lonely Planet products such as guidebooks, websites and digital products, so let us know if you don't want your comments reproduced or your name acknowledged. For a copy of our privacy policy visit lonelyplanet.com/privacy.

OUR READERS

Many thanks to the travellers who used the last edition and wrote to us with helpful hints, useful advice and interesting anecdotes:

A Alexandre Voirol, Alison Berry, Alyssa Kreikemeier, Anne-Marie Summerhays, Annet Derks, Arturo Llorente **B** Bernd Johann, Bonnie Douglas, Brenna Klassen-Glanzer, Bruce Vangroenigen **C** Carme Galindo, Celine Kooiker, Charles Lambert, Claudia Wouters **D** Daan Vossers, David Melero, Douglas Dockey **E** Emilie Vermeiren, Erik van Hirtum, Esther de Boer **F** Felix Bestle, Fiona Fry **G** George Nicola **J** Jon Telletxea Aragon **K** Kai Gogolin, Karine Berneche, Karl Pineault, Kerstin Schneider **L** Laura Jeffords, Laura Waz, Liesbeth Vringer, Linda Osterwalder, Lyndsay Cutler **M** Mark Williams, Maurice Stewart, Michaela Fasching, Miranda Smit, Monika Schindlerova **N** Niels Jaetzold **O** Olaf Piers **P** Patrick Condon, Paul van de Sande, Pauline & Rob Stannard, Penny Gage, Pim Dings **R** Renate Raff, Rick Akerboom **S** Sabrina Prioletta, Sabrina Svidt, Samuel Jacques, Saphira Laaraj, Sarah Noël, Sébastien Audet, Silke Langkitsch, Sjoerdje Smedinga **T** Theodore Polites **W** Wolfgang Jaetzold.

WRITER THANKS

Anna Kaminski

Huge thanks to Alicia for entrusting me with half of this beguiling country, and to everyone who's helped me along the way. In particular: Claudio in Managua, Brian on Ometepe, Jorge and Kristin in Granada, Helio in San Juan de Oriente, Catalina in Las Peñitas, John in León, plus Brett and Carol in San Juan del Sur and Granada for the company and research input.

Tom Masters

I was accompanied on a big chunk of my travels through Nicaragua by the imperturbable Rosemary Masters, who didn't allow civil strife to keep her away. Huge thanks also to Claudio Perez Cruz, Juana Boyd, Henry Soriano, Alex Egerton, Anna Kaminski, Salvador & Mina Acosta, Guillermo González Prado, Darling Rayo, Romain at Lighthouse, Teresa Mariscal, Leopoldo Flores Lovo and the various staff at ¡Hola Nicaragua!, Hotel Los Arcos in Estelí, Maria's B&B in Matagalpa and Hotel Casa Royale in Bluefields.

ACKNOWLEDGMENTS

Climate map data adapted from Peel MC, Finlayson BL & McMahon TA (2007) 'Updated World Map of the Köppen-Geiger Climate Classification', Hydrology and Earth System Sciences, 11, 1633–44.
Cover photograph: Toucan, Ondrej Prosicky/Shutterstock©

THIS BOOK

This 5th edition of *Nicaragua* was curated by Bridget Gleeson, and researched and written by Anna Kaminski and Tom Masters. The previous edition was written by Bridget and Alex Egerton and the 3rd edition was written by Alex and Greg Benchwick. This guidebook was produced by the following:

Destination Editor Alicia Johnson

Regional Senior Cartographer Corey Hutchison

Senior Product Editor Saralinda Turner

Product Editor Kate Kiely

Senior Cartographer Valentina Kremenchutskaya

Book Designer Fergal Condon

Assisting Editors James Bainbridge, Carolyn Boicos, Heather Champion, Emma Gibbs, Victoria Harrison, Lou McGregor, Lauren O'Connell, Maja Vatrić

Cover Researcher Naomi Parker

Thanks to Sasha Drew, Bailey Freeman, Martine Power, Amanda Williamson

Index

Map Legend

Sights
- 🏖 Beach
- 🐦 Bird Sanctuary
- ⛪ Buddhist
- 🏰 Castle/Palace
- ✝ Christian
- ☯ Confucian
- 🕉 Hindu
- ☪ Islamic
- Jain
- ✡ Jewish
- ❗ Monument
- 🏛 Museum/Gallery/Historic Building
- ✖ Ruin
- ⛩ Shinto
- ☬ Sikh
- ☯ Taoist
- 🍷 Winery/Vineyard
- 🐾 Zoo/Wildlife Sanctuary
- ⊙ Other Sight

Activities, Courses & Tours
- Bodysurfing
- Diving
- Canoeing/Kayaking
- Course/Tour
- Sento Hot Baths/Onsen
- Skiing
- Snorkeling
- Surfing
- Swimming/Pool
- Walking
- Windsurfing
- Other Activity

Sleeping
- Sleeping
- Camping
- Hut/Shelter

Eating
- Eating

Drinking & Nightlife
- Drinking & Nightlife
- Cafe

Entertainment
- Entertainment

Shopping
- Shopping

Information
- 💲 Bank
- Embassy/Consulate
- ➕ Hospital/Medical
- @ Internet
- Police
- ✉ Post Office
- Telephone
- Toilet
- Tourist Information
- ● Other Information

Geographic
- Beach
- ⊢ Gate
- Hut/Shelter
- Lighthouse
- Lookout
- ▲ Mountain/Volcano
- Oasis
- Park
-)(Pass
- Picnic Area
- Waterfall

Population
- Capital (National)
- Capital (State/Province)
- City/Large Town
- Town/Village

Transport
- ✈ Airport
- ⊗ Border crossing
- Bus
- Cable car/Funicular
- Cycling
- Ferry
- Ⓜ Metro station
- Monorail
- Ⓟ Parking
- Petrol station
- Subway/Subte station
- Taxi
- Train station/Railway
- Tram
- Underground station
- ● Other Transport

Routes
- Tollway
- Freeway
- Primary
- Secondary
- Tertiary
- Lane
- Unsealed road
- Road under construction
- Plaza/Mall
- Steps
-)=(Tunnel
- Pedestrian overpass
- Walking Tour
- Walking Tour detour
- Path/Walking Trail

Boundaries
- International
- State/Province
- Disputed
- Regional/Suburb
- Marine Park
- Cliff
- Wall

Hydrography
- River, Creek
- Intermittent River
- Canal
- Water
- Dry/Salt/Intermittent Lake
- Reef

Areas
- Airport/Runway
- Beach/Desert
- + + Cemetery (Christian)
- × × Cemetery (Other)
- Glacier
- Mudflat
- Park/Forest
- Sight (Building)
- Sportsground
- Swamp/Mangrove

Note: Not all symbols displayed above appear on the maps in this book

OUR STORY

A beat-up old car, a few dollars in the pocket and a sense of adventure. In 1972 that's all Tony and Maureen Wheeler needed for the trip of a lifetime – across Europe and Asia overland to Australia. It took several months, and at the end – broke but inspired – they sat at their kitchen table writing and stapling together their first travel guide, *Across Asia on the Cheap*. Within a week they'd sold 1500 copies. Lonely Planet was born.

Today, Lonely Planet has offices in Franklin, London, Melbourne, Oakland, Beijing and Delhi, with more than 600 staff and writers. We share Tony's belief that 'a great guidebook should do three things: inform, educate and amuse'.

OUR WRITERS

Bridget Gleeson

Bridget has written and taken photos for a variety of web and print publications including Lonely Planet, BBC Travel, BBC Culture, the *Guardian*, Budget Travel, *Afar*, *Wine Enthusiast*, Mr & Mrs Smith, Jetsetter, Tablet Hotels, the *Independent*, Delta Sky, Continental, LAN Airlines and Korean Air. She's lived in Italy, the Czech Republic, Nicaragua and Argentina.

Anna Kaminski

Managua; Masaya & Los Pueblos Blancos; Granada; Southwestern Nicaragua; León & Northwestern Nicaragua Originally from the Soviet Union, Anna grew up in Cambridge, UK. She graduated from the University of Warwick with a degree in Comparative American Studies, a background in the history, culture and literature of the Americas and the Caribbean, and an enduring love of Latin America. Her restless wanderings led her to settle briefly in Oaxaca and Bangkok and her flirtation with criminal law saw her volunteering as a lawyer's assistant in the courts, ghettos and prisons of Kingston, Jamaica. Anna has contributed to numerous Lonely Planet titles. When not on the road, Anna calls London home. Anna also researched and wrote the Plan Your Trip, Understand and Survival Guide chapters.

Tom Masters

Northern Highlands; Caribbean Coast; San Carlos, Islas Solentiname & the Río San Juan Dreaming since he could walk of going to the most obscure places on earth, Tom has always had a taste for the unknown. This has led to a writing career that has taken him all over the world, including North Korea, the Arctic, Congo and Siberia. Despite a childhood spent in the English countryside, as an adult Tom has always called London, Paris and Berlin home. He currently lives in Berlin and can be found online at www.tommasters.net. Tom also contributed to the History chapter.

Published by Lonely Planet Global Limited
CRN 554153
5th edition – July 2019
ISBN 978 1 78657 489 3
© Lonely Planet 2019   Photographs © as indicated 2019
10 9 8 7 6 5 4 3 2 1
Printed in China